Debugging C++

Troubleshooting for Programmers

About the Authors

Chris H. Pappas and William H. Murray, III are professors of computer science at the B.C.C. campus of the S.U.N.Y. system in Binghamton, NY. They have co-authored over four dozen books on such programming topics as assembly language, Visual Basic®, C and C++, HTML, Visual J++™, Java™, JavaScript, Microsoft Foundation Class Library, OS/2, Standard Template Library, Windows® 95, Windows® 98, Windows NT™, and more. Their books have been translated into more than twenty-five foreign languages.

Debugging C++

Troubleshooting for Programmers

Chris H. Pappas and William H. Murray, III

Osborne/**McGraw-Hill**

Berkeley / New York / St. Louis / San Francisco / Auckland / Bogotá
Hamburg / London / Madrid / Mexico City / Milan / Montreal / New Delhi
Panama City / Paris / São Paulo / Singapore / Sydney / Tokyo / Toronto

Osborne/**McGraw-Hill**
2600 Tenth Street
Berkeley, California 94710
U.S.A.

For information on translations or book distributors outside the U.S.A., or to arrange bulk purchase discounts for sales promotions, premiums, or fund-raisers, please contact Osborne/**McGraw-Hill** at the above address.

Debugging C++: Troubleshooting for Programmers

234567890 CUS/CUS 019876543210

ISBN 0-07-212519-5

Publisher	Brandon A. Nordin
Associate Publisher and Editor-in-Chief	Scott Rogers
Acquisitions Editor	Wendy Rinaldi
Project Editor	Patty Mon
Acquisitions Coordinator	Monika Faltiss
Technical Editor	Greg Guntle
Copy Editor	Nancy Crumpton
Proofreader	Stefany Otis
Indexers	Chris H. Pappas
	William H. Murray, III
Computer Designers	Elizabeth Jang
	Roberta Steele
Illustrator	Michael Mueller
Series Design	Peter Hancik
Cover Design	Dodie Shoemaker

This book was composed with Corel VENTURA™ Publisher.

Dedicated to our brother,
Benny Hinn

Contents at a Glance

Contents

Introduction

In the fall of 1999, we approached Osborne/McGraw-Hill acquisition editors with a book proposal that radically stood out from their usual programming books. The idea was to produce a book that explained the use of the Visual C++ Debugger across a wide range of programming solutions, while focusing on real-world programming problems.

This is not a programming book, although an awful lot of programming is between the two covers. This book takes you beyond the normal one- or two-chapter introduction to the C++ Debugger found in most complete reference books (ours included) and into the mind of the programmer.

First, you'll learn how to develop good code writing skills. In Chapters 1–5, you'll see how the optimizing compiler works to help you, the programmer, produce robust code that is free of both logical and syntactical errors. You'll also learn debugging fundamentals.

In Chapters 6–8, you'll learn how command-line code can be developed and debugged. In-line assembly language code is introduced as a means of achieving programming results that are hard to code in C++. Finally, you'll get a glimpse of programming problems that occur in procedure-oriented Windows programming.

In Chapters 9–11, you'll enter the exciting world of object-oriented programming with the debugger. This part of the book thoroughly examines command-line code and MFC Windows code. In Chapter 11, you'll see some interesting real-world coding problems solved with the Debugger and other software tools.

Chapters 12 and 13 examine the Standard Template Library (STL). We discuss various STL coding practices and then look at locating, analyzing, and repairing programming errors.

Chapters 14–17 are devoted to those special debugging situations encountered when working with DLLs, ActiveX, COM, and programs developed with both the STL and MFC.

Join us now as we investigate all of the tools available to help a programmer in the Visual C++ environment. Join us as we enter the mind of the C++ programmer.

Conventions Used in This Book

We have included three special elements in almost every chapter:

This text is used to indicate programming practices that should be adopted to ensure that your code will be robust, stable, and capable of keeping your application up 24 hours a day, 7 days a week.

This indicates areas of programming likely to contain logical or syntactical errors.

 This guides you toward better programming practices and helps you avoid developing bad coding habits. Design Tips usually guide you around poorly designed, but working, code.

Note: All of the code used in this book is available for download from www.osborne.com.

PART I

Code Development Skills

CHAPTER 1

Writing Good Code

How does the saying go? "We can do this the easy way, or we can do this the hard way!" The bottom line is this: you want to get your programs up and running, reliably, as quickly as possible. With the complex demands of today's programs, combined with the complexity of the languages used to develop these solutions, you need to be a better programmer, out of the gate, than ever before.

If you have been programming for 15 years or more, you know the preceding statement is true. No longer does a compiler (for example, Borland International's Turbo Pascal) fit on one 5 1/4-inch floppy diskette. Instead, a typical compiler installation gobbles up a whopping 350+ megabytes of your hard disk. And while we can praise Dennis Ritchie, the inventor of the C language, and Bjarne Stroustrup, the inventor of the C++ language, for their undeniably powerful new programming tools, we are left with the task of mastering their potentials.

The need to navigate through the plethora of options presented by today's development environments, whether they are Microsoft's Visual Studio components, Borland International's IDE (Integrated Development Environment), or any Unix-based design tools, can be added to the programming burden of mastering C/C++.

There's also the target environment or, should it be said, environments. Today's applications, in order to be truly marketable, must run on diverse architectures and, in many cases, multiple human language formats (welcome to Unicode, the 16-bit counterpart to the ANSI ASCII code). Oh, and did anyone mention that this must all be accomplished on a multitasking GUI operating system?

Oh, and one more point, did anyone mention the ANSI/ISO STL (Standard Template Library), and how this library of routines *standardizes* common programming solutions such as vectors, stacks, queues, binary trees, and so on? Oh, and what about the new C/C++ cast operators, and, and, and.... You see, even as you are reading this, both the C and C++ languages are growing and evolving.

Who Needs This Book?

Whether you are taking your first C or C++ course or have been programming in these new languages for years, this book is for you! Why? Because many programmers are unaware of the powerful debugging tools available to help them get their programs working quickly and accurately.

The authors have a combined fifty years' worth of teaching students how to program. These students have been anywhere from beginners to experienced local major corporation programmers, involved in many of our nation's most top-secret military development environments.

24x7

The single key factor that all programmers have in common is scarcity of time. There never seems to be enough time to master all of the components involved in developing programs for today's environments.

Pedagogy

The layout of the book is simple. The first few chapters begin with a review of all of the code design fundamentals a beginning student is taught in an introductory Language Independent Design course. This chapter could be titled, "All the Things I Was Never Taught by a Programming Instructor Who Used to Teach English (or Math, or Science, or Geology, or any other area of study having nothing to do with formal programming skills).

Chapters 2 through 5 explain how to set up the Microsoft Visual C/C++ Debugger, describing the options available. Finally, you are taught with code examples how to use these various tools to debug algorithms of increasing complexity. First, you are taught how to meaningfully debug procedure-oriented programs, then on to object-based technology, and on up to algorithms incorporating the new ANSI/ISO STL templates.

Chapters 14 through 17 complete the coded example debug sessions by examining applications using Dynamic Link Libraries (DLLs), ActiveX controls, COM files, and finally STL and MFC (Microsoft Foundation Class) libraries together!

Where Should I Start Reading?

Unless you feel that you are one of the lucky few that has had a superb "formal" education in programming, you should read every page of this book as if your professional career depended on it! Whoever said, "What you don't know can't hurt you," wasn't a programmer.

Here are ten questions that prove why you need to read every page of this book. Ask yourself the following questions; if you can honestly say that you understand every concept involved, then maybe you can move on to Chapter 2 immediately. Be honest.

- **Question 1**   As a C/C++ programmer, all of your subroutine code is encapsulated within function bodies. Do you know that there are other types of subroutines? (Many languages, other than C/C++, have an additional category of subroutine called a *procedure*.)

- **Question 2**   Do you know all of the differences between a procedure subroutine and a function subroutine?

- **Question 3**   Were you taught how to parse an expression, taking into consideration operator precedence levels?

- **Question 4**   Do you know what the terms *look-ahead EOF* and *non-look-ahead EOF* mean?

- **Question 5**   Do you know what a *priming read* statement is?

- **Question 6**   Do you know what a sentinel loop is?

- **Question 7**   Do you know what the **static** keyword does at the internal level, external level, on a (data or method) class member?

- **Question 8**   Do you know the compiler translation difference between a method body formally defined within the owning class versus a method body defined outside the owning class?

- **Question 9**   Do you know when the operator **sizeof()** function reports back (apparent) incorrect values and why?

- **Question 10**   Do you know what a recursive algorithm is? (For the definition of recursion: see recursion <grin>.)

If you answered no to any one of these questions, you need to read the remainder of this chapter.

WARNING! Not All C/C++ Compilers Are the Same

Before proceeding any further, there is one concept you need to get straight. This book will teach you how to correctly design, implement, and efficiently debug C and C++ programs as viewed through *Microsoft's eyes!* The warnings and error diagnostics used throughout the text will give you a biased view of the C and C++ languages. As both Dennis Ritchie and Bjarne Stroustrup left "gray areas" in their formal language descriptions, compiler manufacturers have gone off on their own and filled in any missing details. For this reason, it would be unwise to take many of the concepts presented throughout the remaining chapters and attempt to apply them to some other manufacturer's C/C++ compiler.

Error Watch   *Remember, the debugging examples in this book, and their related analysis and discussions, all relate to the Microsoft Visual C++ Debugger. How Visual C++ warns, diagnoses, and flags errors is product specific.*

Language-Independent Design Tools 101

Experienced programmers have what we call a "programmer's tool kit." Inside this kit are language-independent design courses, multiple languages (assembler, COBOL, Fortran, Pascal, PL/I, Visual Basic, and so on), hardware courses like Digital Logic, Small Systems Design, and of course, hands-on course and job experiences.

Oddly enough, one of *the* most important tools in their kit is their first course—Language-Independent Design Tools. Why? Because this course lays down the foundations upon which all of the past and today's languages are based. Yes, even object-oriented design technology has its roots in this initial procedure-oriented course.

Ask yourself this question: Does an executable file (.exe) whose origins came from *any* object-oriented language source need execution on a specially designed microprocessor? Of course the answer is no. In other words, no matter how sophisticated object-oriented code looks, it must still be compiled and/or translated down to machine code. So whether an executable's source file is procedural or object oriented, it executes on the same chip!

What is the object-oriented syntax difference? Packaging! Objects automate what could have been done procedurally, but they do *not* give your program any additional raw horsepower. Typically, if an object-oriented program misbehaves, it is because some procedural underpinning was poorly designed. For this reason, the beginning of a good code solution *must* begin with an understanding of the building blocks or individual components.

The following LIDT 101 (Language-Independent Design Tools) discussion quickly takes you through the meat (if you are a vegetarian, the protein) of a good LIDT 101 course. Should *you* read it? Well, *not* reading this section is like saying you want to learn how to fly a plane and simply knowing how to turn the auto-pilot on and off will do.

The following section uses the normal pedagogy for an LIDT 101 course, from a discussion of logic flow diagrams, simple data types, logic control statements, iteration, subroutines, and finally to object-oriented considerations.

Setting the Stage

The following hypothetical situation is chosen because of its surprise factor. You are given a programming problem that most programmers will never encounter in order to prove a point.

One day you walk into class or work and your fearless leader gives you the following task: Jamie, I want you to write a program that will efficiently operate an airport with seven runways. Your solution must be able to handle all emergency conditions from passengers' having heart attacks, to stranded refuelers in the middle of a runway, to wind shear, and so on. Your primary objective is to safely land and launch as many planes as possible per hour.

Your response is to:

- Quit
- Start biting your nails, grab a cigarette, look for another Nicoderm patch, or start chewing five pieces of Nicorette gum
- Move from the coffee machine over to the espresso machine
- Sit down immediately and begin writing code
- Confidently and skillfully apply all sound design principles to a robust solution

This hypothetical programming problem, by design, is not something any programmer could solve *in his or her head!* Now the question becomes, what mixture of shotgun programming will the programmer combine with a smattering of Post-It notes containing to-dos? Any approach other than a thoroughly developed, good initial design can potentially lead to a life-threatening situation.

Model!

The simplest, most obvious, yet frequently ignored starting point for a good design solution is modeling. Simply taking the *time* to play what-if scenarios. For some programming problems, writing down the logical steps you would use if solving the problem without a computer, will do. For other programming problems, modeling is best.

Although it may initially seem trite, the beginning of a good solution to the airport application could be a trip to Toys "R" Us to purchase seven toy airports, complete with refuelers, hangers, planes, and crew, then off to Lowe's for a fan, glue, and thumbtacks, and finally, a trip to the local sporting goods store for some clear fishing line.

Returning from your shopping spree, you cordon off the most strategically used room (remember, you want to impress your superiors with your diligence) and begin building the model airport. You place planes on runways, equipment around the airport and hangers, maintenance crew, passengers, luggage, and so on. Since this is a model for a busy airport, you glue the fishing line to the tops of a few planes and thumbtack them from the ceiling, mimicking planes in holding patterns.

Taking a break for lunch, you decide to turn the fan on to check the effects of wind shear—OK, picking the entire airport up off the floor, you realize that a variable-speed fan would have been a better idea. The point? What may initially appear to be a mental breakdown, "playing airport" can actually lead to insights not previously considered. Even the initially unexpected destruction of the entire airport, brought on by the over-powered fan, causes you to consider the effects of a tornado or hurricane on the safe operation of the airport. And had you not "played airport," maybe you would (or wouldn't) have considered writing the code necessary to make your application weather condition friendly!

24x7

Professional software engineers all know that the roots of a robust, bulletproof program solution begin with a good design and that good designs begin with a real-world model.

Structure Charts, Pseudo-Code, and IPO Diagrams

After modeling, the next phase to a knock-my-socks-off program solution continues with a computer language–independent representation of the logical steps the application will take. Historically, this visual program solution was represented using flowchart symbols. However, flowcharting is best for either assembly language solutions (now rarely used to write an entire application) or very high-level hierarchy charts.

Hierarchy charts at this stage typically represent all of the subroutines, or algorithms (black-box concept), needed in the application and their priorities (who owns whom). Moving in for a more granular look, the visual program solution now concentrates on the individual subroutine code. For this phase, structure charting, which is visual and language independent, is best mixed in with pseudo-code (syntax-independent logic statements). A quick review of structure chart symbols follows. Each structure chart symbol is preceded by a coded example.

Design Tip   *Use Hungarian Notation (invented by Charles Simonyi) to give program identifiers a more meaningful name. Hungarian notation simply places a mnemonic, or data type abbreviation, in front of an identifier's name. For example, integer variables like NumberOfElements become iNumberOfElements using Hungarian style. More information on Hungarian Notation is provided later in this chapter.*

Inline Statements

Inline statements are simply represented by rectangular boxes, as in the following:

```
int iNumberOfElements;
```

Translating this statement into structure chart pseudo-code looks like Figure 1.1.

Conditional Statements

Conditional structure chart symbols represent a program's **if** or **if...else** constructs, as in the following:

```
if ( argc = 2 )
  ofstream outputFile( argv[1] );
else
  ofstream outputFile( "lpt1" );
```

Translating this statement into structure chart pseudo-code looks like Figure 1.2.

Selection Statements

C and C++ use the **switch...case** syntax for representing selection, as in the following:

```
switch( cValueToCategorize )
{
  case 'a':
  case 'e':
  case 'i':
  case 'o':
  case 'u':
  case 'y': cVowelCount++;
            break;
  case '.':
  case '!':
  case '?': cSentenceCount++;
            break;
  default : cConsonantCount++;
}
```

which looks like Figure 1.3 when translated into structure chart form.

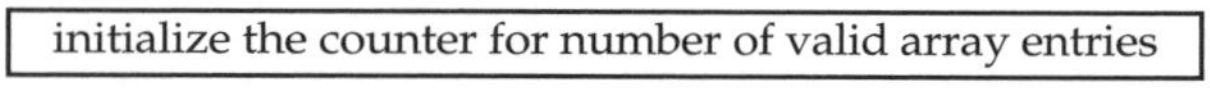

| initialize the counter for number of valid array entries |

Figure 1.1 Inline structure chart symbol

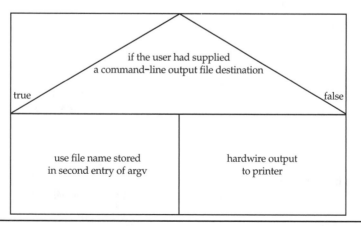

Figure 1.2 Conditional structure chart symbol

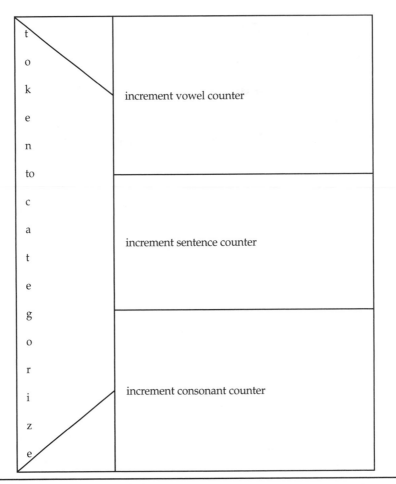

Figure 1.3 Selection structure chart symbol

Iteration Statements

There are two types of iteration in most programming languages: pre-test (**for** and **while**) and post-test (**do...while**) loops, as in the following:

```
for( int rowOffset = 0; rowOffset < MAXELEMENTS; rowOffset++)
{
   someArray[ rowOffset ]...
}
```

which in structure chart form looks like Figure 1.4.

while loop structure chart symbols are the same as for pre-test **for** loops, as in the following:

```
while( ( cValue = cin.get()) != EOF )
{
  process data...
}
```

while loop structure chart symbols when translated into structure chart form look like Figure 1.5.

Post-test **do...while** loop structure chart symbols are simply the inverse of pre-test, as in the following:

```
do
{
  cout << "Company Name\n";
  cout << "\t\tProgram options include:\n";
  cout << "\t\tPress 1 for Online Consultant";
  . . .
} while (   (toupper(cMenuSelection = cin.get()))   != 'Q' )
```

Post-test **do...while** loops represented in a structure chart look like Figure 1.6.

Subroutine Call Statement

Structure chart symbols are the same for both function and method (member function) calls, using a slight modification of the line statement symbol, as in the following:

```
myFunctionCall( myArg1, myArg2, myArg3);
myMethodCall(myArgA, myArgB, myArgC);
```

which looks like Figure 1.7 in structure chart form.

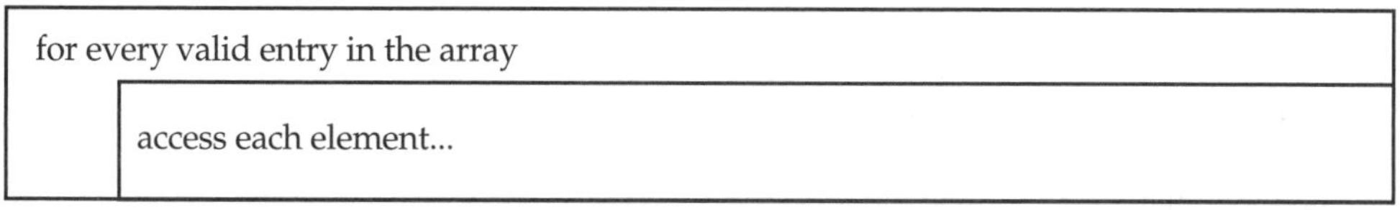

Figure 1.4   Pre-test **for** loop structure chart symbol

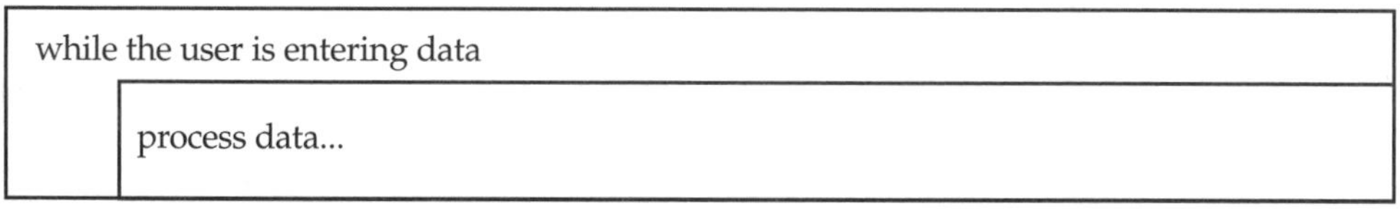

Figure 1.5   Pre-test **while** loop structure chart symbol

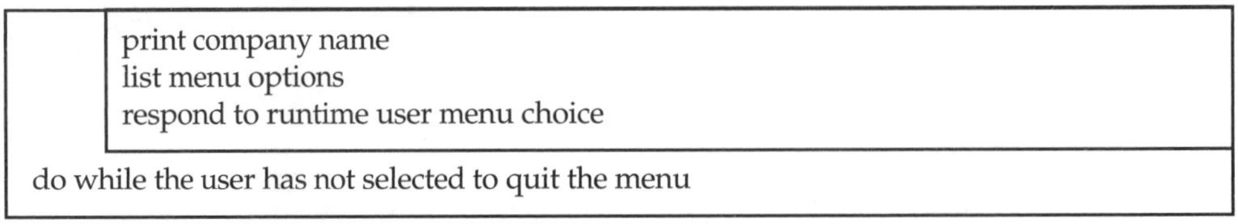

print company name list menu options respond to runtime user menu choice
do while the user has not selected to quit the menu

Figure 1.6   Post-test **do...while** structure chart symbol

Design Tip   *The "one-page" rule yardstick is a great and useful quick check for any subroutine body. The rule simply implies that an algorithm exceeding one written code page is doing too much! Consider rewriting the algorithm—streamlining its purpose. Leaving the code as is can potentially lead to a design that is breaking the rules for modularity and upgrade ability with an overly complicated logic sequence.*

Structure charting, combined with good pseudo-code, allows you to easily walk through an algorithm's completeness, without the burden of debugging the equivalent syntax.

Object-Oriented Statements

As object-oriented programs syntactically repackage procedural underpinnings, their structure chart symbols are combinations of their procedural language counterparts.

Five Elements of a Good Program Design

You may be familiar with a problem-solution format called an *IPO diagram*. IPO diagrams are a stylized approach to the age-old programming problem of input/process/output. The following list elaborates on these three fundamentals and encapsulates the entire application development cycle. All programs must address the following five components:

- Obtain information from some input source.

- Decide how this input is to be arranged and stored.

- Use a set of instructions to manipulate the input. These instructions can be broken down into four major categories: single statements, conditional statements, loops, and subroutines.

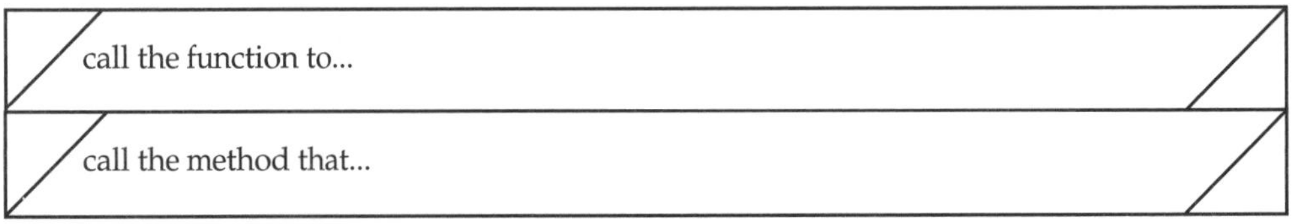

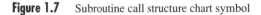

Figure 1.7   Subroutine call structure chart symbol

- Report the results of the data manipulation.

- Incorporate all of the preceding fundamentals, expressed by using good modular design, self-documenting code (meaningful variable names, and so on), and a sound indentation scheme.

Rules Are Meant to be Broken

The following sections detail professional DOs and DON'Ts when physically representing a robust algorithm in code. However, all programmers understand that every programming solution involves unique application-specific goals.

Besides getting the job done, an application may need to be streamlined for minimum code size. Some applications will have to exist for years and years, with a design goal of ease in modification. Still other application solutions will need tweaking for lightning-fast executions. Finally, a coded solution may exist as an instructional example for some product-specific or architecture-specific feature. While all four scenarios use the same basic raw horsepower, each naturally presents a slightly modified algorithm. The tweaked solution may even break the rules for good code design in order to meet a specific goal. For this reason, one set of DOs and DON'Ts that uniformly apply themselves to all situations does not exist. Professional programmers earn their tremendous salaries not only because of their good design capabilities, but also for skillfully applying or ignoring code practices in order to meet the specified goal.

Ansel Adams or Picasso

Experienced software engineers not only invest tremendous man-hours in developing their program solutions, but equal amounts of time visually representing their solutions in code. True professionals bring to focus all of their formal training and experiential skills to every keystroke entered.

The idea is quite simple really: viewing the code page as a painting, or road map. Realizing that proper selection of UPPERcase and lowerCASE (similar to a painter's selection of colors) and an indentation scheme (similar to an artist's horizon line) can dramatically affect the understanding or tone of the underlying algorithm. Improper use of the preceding generates source code resembling a Picasso painting, while proper use of these style tools allows another programmer to quickly diagnose and/or get onboard with just how a code segment operates.

Comment Blocks

Professionally written code always incorporates good comments. A good comment is defined as one that neither insults the intelligence of a programmer, as in the following:

```
float fManagersSalary;   // fManagersSalary holds the manager's salary
```

nor does it bypass explaining any code intricacies.

There is a simple test for whether or not a code statement or segment needs a comment. Imagine that you, the author of the code, were called away on another project and did not see your program for several weeks. Now, when you return to the application, you quickly bring yourself back onboard where you left off, and all of a sudden, you find yourself looking at a statement or code segment that causes you to start scratching your head. In other words, the intricacies of the syntax or algorithm at this point immediately elude you. That's the time to comment!

Design Tip *A good comment neither insults the intelligence of another programmer, nor does it assume too much.*

identifiers, IDENTIFIERS, Identifiers

Older high-level programming languages never had the overall file structure of today's C/C++ applications. In addition, most were *not* case-sensitive, so identifier names like *mytype*, *MYTYPE*, and *MyType* were all viewed as the same name.

With today's typical Windows application including tens of files and, in many cases, hundreds of identifiers, professional code generation and placement almost require the skills of a top-notch interior decorator! Beyond proper comments lies the world of expert use for UPPERcase and lowercase.

24x7

Imagine that a programmer looking at your code is non-case-sensitive, meaning that to them, identifiers using the same symbols but only mixing their case are all the *same* variable. You, however, covertly make use of C/C++'s sensitivity to UPPERcase and lowercase to limit the number of uniquely spelled identifiers (since we are pretending case is *not* important here) a programmer must keep track of. In the end, you both win since you have created an algorithm that is much easier to read, trace, and debug.

A simple example will make the point. First, a nonprofessional approach:

```
typedef struct employees {
  ....
  ....
  employees *pToAWorker;
} personnelRecord;

void main ( void )
{
  personnellRecord employees;
...
}
```

Let's begin the analysis with a simple identifier count: `employees`, `pToAWorker`, `personnelRecord`, and generate a total of four unique identifiers. Take a moment to think about some of the confusing choices. For example, **typedef** uses the tag name *employees* implying plurality, and yet the structure will only hold a single employee's record.

Next, while the structure member `pToAWorker` does logically indicate just *how* the member will be used, in readability, it seems to imply a pointer to some other logical concept, that is, `AWorker`. The final code insult comes from the variable declaration for `employees`, which is a plural noun, possibly implying an array of structures, which this obviously is not.

Now examine a professional rewrite of the same statements using C/C++'s sensitivity to mixed case to keep the compiler happy (by supplying each syntax a unique mixture of uppercase and lowercase letters), while using the readability of each identifier to minimize programmer confusion.

```
typedef struct An_Employee {
  . . . .
  . . . .
  An_Employee *pAn_Employee;
} AN_EMPLOYEE;

void main ( void )
{
  AN_EMPLOYEE An_employee;
. . .
}
```

The total for uniquely spelled identifiers in the preceding code section: one! (When reading Hungarian Notation, professional programmers skim the mnemonic, as in *p...An_Employee*, viewing the main portion of the identifier—*An_Employee*.) This code represents a huge improvement in number of unique identifiers (from a human standpoint) and, more importantly, eases a programmer's burden of tracking all of a program's identifiers.

The rewritten section uses the same spelling for the structure's tag_field and typedef name. The pointer member matches, except for the preceding *p*. Finally, the variable *An_employee*'s type *AN_EMPLOYEE* logically connects the **typedef** statement to the variable's name. With the rewritten code segment, all any programmer has to do is understand the members in the structure `An_Employee` (spelled in any combination of UPPERcase and lowercase) to use the application-specific definition, type, or variable properly!

24x7

C/C++ software engineers use all UPPERcase for header file definitions and reserve MiXeD case for source file (.c/.cpp) declarations. The only exceptions are for function prototypes, class definitions, and STL syntax.

Spacing and Indentation

The extra effort needed to generate readable source code is absolutely mandatory at times. Under certain circumstances, standard spacing and indentation schemes fail to visually discriminate important code details.

Take, for instance, the following code segment. There is absolutely nothing wrong with the syntax, and in the coding style is, well, typical. The code segment does not use UPPERcase and lowercase or Hungarian Notation, nor does it space or indent meaningfully:

```
#include <iostream>
#define m1 50
#define m2 4
typedef enum cars{ yugo, ford, buick, pontiac } carmakes;
typedef struct one_carsale {
    carmakes CarMake;
    char CustomerName[m1],CarModel[m1];
    float Cost;
    one_carsale *NextCarSalePtr;
} acar;
typedef struct salesperson {
    char SalesPersonsName[m1];
    float CommissionRate,BaseSalary,WeeklyPaycheck;
    acar **NextNode;
} aperson;
acar *NextNodePtr[m2];
aperson Sale[m2];
```

Now, imagine this code segment sitting, nested within thousands of lines of code, within a company's application that will evolve over the next two decades. Imagine also, some programmer, not the author of the code, having to get onboard with the data types, constructs, and user-defined definitions.

A rewrite of the same syntax, designed to separate the data types from the identifier names, to application-specific enumerated types, and their interrelationships, might look like this:

```
#include <iostream>

#define  MAX_NAMELENGTH    50
#define  MAX_SALESPEOPLE    4


/* ........................ makes of cars being sold */

typedef enum car_makes{ yugo, ford, buick, pontiac } CAR_MAKES;


/* ............. structure to represent each car sale */

typedef struct one_carsale {

    CAR_MAKES         enCarMake;
    char              pszCustomerName [ MAX_NAMELENGTH ];
    char              pszCarModel     [ MAX_NAMELENGTH ];
    float             fCost;
    one_carsale       *pstNextCarSalePtr;
```

```
} ONE_CARSALE;


/* structure to represent each individual sales person */

typedef struct salesperson {

    char           pszSalesPersonsName[ MAX_NAMELENGTH ];
    float          fCommissionRate,
                   fBaseSalary,
                   fWeeklyPaycheck;
    ONE_CARSALE    **ppstHeaderNode;

} ONE_SALESPERSON;


/* .... declaration for non-standard array-of-pointers */

ONE_CARSALE *apstHeaderNodePtr[ MAX_SALESPEOPLE ];


/* ........................... array of salespeople */

ONE_SALESPERSON astSalesTeam[ MAX_SALESPEOPLE ];
```

Here, the programmer can easily ask several important questions, with the style of the code enhancing a quick access to the answer. For example, looking at this code section, a programmer could easily answer the following questions:

- *Which* header files are needed in this code segment?
- What are the *names* for the *symbolic constants?*
- What are the *substitution values* for the symbolic constants?
- What are the *standard* data types used in this application?
- What, if any, are the *user-defined* types?
- What are the member *names?*
- What are the *dimensions* of the *arrays*, if any?
- Does the code section say anything about the underlying *logical assumptions?*
- *How* are the variables used in the program?

From the more meaningful identifier names—for example, *m1* to MAX_NAMELENGTH—to the Hungarian Notation *ppstHeaderNodePtr* (both implying the hidden double-pointer ** and the logical use of the member—dummy header node ptr, as opposed to data node ptr), to the spacing, this example is much clearer in meaning.

The symbolic constant substitution values *50* and *4* are columnized. Structure definitions visually separate member data types from member names and ease in viewing scalar size descriptions:

```
typedef struct one_carsale {

        CAR_MAKES           enCarMake;
        char                pszCustomerName [ MAX_NAMELENGTH ];
        char                pszCarModel     [ MAX_NAMELENGTH ];
        float               fCost;
        one_carsale         *pstNextCarSalePtr;

} ONE_CARSALE;
```

ONE_CARSALE uses one option when defining variables of the same data type—in this case, **char**. Here, each string member receives its own line with **char** as the type. To a professional programmer, this style implies a need for the programmer to pay particular attention to the member *names*.

However, the next structure definition uses an alternative approach. Notice the **float** members defined in the following section:

```
typedef struct salesperson {

        char                pszSalesPersonsName[ MAX_NAMELENGTH ];
        float               fCommissionRate,
                            fBaseSalary,
                            fWeeklyPaycheck;
        ONE_CARSALE         **ppstHeaderNode;

} ONE_SALESPERSON;
```

In this example, placing only one data type for all like-type members (**float**) subtly indicates a logical relationship between the three members.

Now granted, an .exe is an .exe is an .exe, and if all you are shipping is a final product, well maybe you do not want to take the extensive time necessary to reprocess source code in such a readable format. However, if an application will have a reasonable development life cycle, a code-style rewrite could have significant payback in ease of modularity for the years that follow. By way of a contrasting example, the following program styles an algorithm's contents for the purposes of generating an instructional overhead. Nested within the style are many professional coding practices. The example code teaches how to use Borland International's dos.h and conio.h header files to output simple text mode graphics and turn on the mouse via interrupt 33h (anathema to a Windows operating system–controlled application). First, here's the algorithm:

```
/**************************************************/
/* program to use interrupt 33h for mouse control */
/**************************************************/

#include <stdio.h>               /*        standard C I/O definitions */
#include <dos.h>                 /*  containing intr() function prototype */
#include <conio.h>               /*    simple text mode graphics routines */

#define FILE_MENU_Y_COORD      1  /*   symbolic constants used to delimit */
#define FILE_MENU_LOW_X_COORD  1  /*   the FILE menu item row and starting */
#define FILE_MENU_HIGH_X_COORD 4  /*  starting and ending column positions */

void main( void )
{

  struct REGPACK all_gp_registers;            /* REGPACK defined in dos.h */
  int iButton = 0, iRow, iColumn;

  clrsc          (             );
  _setcursortype ( _NOCURSOR );                /* conio.h, turn cursor off */

  textbackground ( BLUE      );
  textcolor      ( LIGHTGRAY );
  gotoxy         ( 1,1       );
  cprintf        ("FILE"     );                 /* cprintf for color output */

  all_gp_registers.r_ax = 1;            /*              show pointer */
  intr ( 0x33,&all_gp_registers );      /*         call-by-reference */

  while ( iButton == 0 )      {

    iButton = all_gp_registers.r_bx;    /*         get button status */
    gotoxy ( 30, 10 );
    cprintf ( "%2d Button (0-none,1-left,2-right)",iButton);

    iColumn  = all_gp_registers.r_cx/8+1;   /*   divisions by 8 convert */
    gotoxy ( 30, 11 );                      /*  pixels to rows, columns */
    cprintf ( "%2d x coordinate", iColumn );

    iRow     = all_gp_registers.r_dx/8+1;
    gotoxy ( 30, 12 );
    cprintf ( "%2d,y coordinate", iRow     );

    if ( ( iRow    == FILE_MENU_Y_COORD      ) &&    /*  if mouse row and */
         ( iColumn >= FILE_MENU_LOW_X_COORD  ) &&    /* column coordinates */
         ( iColumn <= FILE_MENU_HIGH_X_COORD ) )     /*     over FILE menu */
           printf( ( "\a" );                         /*        ring bell */

  }                                                  /* end while */

}                                                    /* end  main */
```

This instructional algorithm uses intra-line spacing to logically collect statements performing specific tasks. Intra-line spacing allows a programmer to ask the following questions (viewing the algorithm from top to bottom):

- What does this algorithm do? (Answered by the first comment block.)
- What header files does the algorithm need?
- What, if any, symbolic constants are required?
- What variables are needed?
- What code is necessary to initialize the screen?
- What code is necessary to set screen output preferences?
- What menu item(s) is/are output?
- What code is necessary to initialize the mouse interrupt?
- What code detects and reports a mouse button press?
- What code deals with mouse-reported column coordinates?
- What code deals with mouse-reported row coordinates?
- What code acknowledges the mouse's presence over a menu item?

The comprehension-enhancing code style continues with columnized comment segments, allowing a programmer to easily view comments versus executable code. The three **#define** symbolic constants:

```
#define FILE_MENU_Y_COORD       1   /*    symbolic constants used to delimit */
#define FILE_MENU_LOW_X_COORD   1   /*   the FILE menu item row and starting */
#define FILE_MENU_HIGH_X_COORD  4   /*  starting and ending column positions */
```

set up a precedence for the algorithm. The program is written to use three symbolic constants for each (in this example only "FILE") menu-item program may choose to display and mouse-detect.

Should the programmer decide to display more menu-items, they could uniformly define three more symbolic constants for each new menu-item. Each new trilogy would mark the new menu-item's row (Y_COORD), starting column (LOW_X_COORD) and ending column (HIGH_X_COORD) screen coordinates. A matching **if...** statement could then detect when the reported mouse coordinates were over the new menu-item.

Notice that this relationship between symbolic constant definitions and a matching **if...** statement were designed into the algorithm from the beginning, allowing further menu-item displays and detections to be inserted later on with a uniform code style.

Columnized actual arguments, as in the following, allow a programmer to easily view *which* functions are needed by the algorithm versus the current argument values:

```
textbackground ( BLUE      );
textcolor      ( LIGHTGRAY );
gotoxy         ( 1,1       );
cprintf        ("FILE"     );              /* cprintf for color output */
```

Finally, because of the three symbolic constant definitions, the following code segment:

```
if ( ( iRow    == FILE_MENU_Y_COORD      ) &&    /*   if mouse row and */
       ( iColumn >= FILE_MENU_LOW_X_COORD  ) &&    /* column coordinates */
       ( iColumn <= FILE_MENU_HIGH_X_COORD ) )     /*     over FILE menu */
          printf( ( "\a" );                        /*         ring bell */
```

combines the three symbolic constant definitions, with a stylized conditional **if...** statement that allows a programmer to know which menu-item's (in this example "FILE") row/column coordinates are being compared to the current mouse location. Notice how this style allows you to easily:

- View the owning control statement (**if...**)
- Check which menu item is being examined (FILE_)
- Count the number of conditions (three)
- Detect which logical operators are used in the combination
- View the generated, if *true*, results

Debates over the meaningfulness, style details, and time requirements needed to visually enhance an algorithm's page presentation go both ways. However, the professional rule of thumb is quite simple: use a code style that makes it easy for someone else, *not* the author of the code, to understand!

Data Types

One of the simplest sources of program calculation errors begins with the improper selection of the storage variable's data type. In the case of C/C++ with multi-platform support, it may be as simple as a programmer not realizing that a 32-bit C/C++ compiler allocates four bytes to the **int** data type, while a 16-bit C/C++ compiler allocates only two! Naturally, if you were using the maximum legal integer value available to a 4-byte integer, but running the program on a 16-bit environment, you will generate calculation errors.

Three main approaches guarantee that your program does *not* introduce these types of runtime errors. First, you can print the compiler's Help screen, detailing the value ranges for your current implementation. Table 1.1, which lists the C/C++ data types, is included here as a reference tool for Microsoft Visual Studio C/C++ programmers.

The long double data type (80-bit, 10-byte precision) is mapped directly to double (64-bit, 8-byte precision) in Windows NT and Windows 95.

Signed and unsigned are modifiers that can be used with any integral type. The char type is signed by default, but you can specify /J to make it unsigned by default.

The int and unsigned int types have the size of the system word. This is two bytes (the same as short and unsigned short) in MS-DOS and 16-bit versions of Windows, and four bytes in 32-bit operating systems. However, portable code should not depend on the size of int.

The second approach to guaranteeing that your program does *not* introduce runtime errors involves the simple use of the C/C++ **sizeof**() operator. **sizeof**() is an operator (not a function) that

Type Name	Byte	Other Name	Range of Value
int	*	signed, signed int	System dependent
unsigned int	*	unsigned	System dependent
__int8	1	char, signed char	−128 to 127
__int16	2	short, short int, signed short int	−32,768 to 32,767
__int32	4	signed, signed int	−2,147,483,648 to 2,147,483,647
__int64	8	None	−9,223,372,036,854,775,808 to 9,223,372,036,854,775,807
char	1	signed char	−128 to 127
unsigned char	1	None	0 to 255
short	2	short int, signed short int	−32,768 to 32,767
unsigned short	2	unsigned short int	0 to 65,535
long	4	long int, signed long int	−2,147,483,648 to 2,147,483,647
unsigned long	4	unsigned long int	0 to 4,294,967,295
enum	*	None	Same as int
float	4	None	3.4E +/- 38 (7 digits)
Double	8	None	1.7E +/- 308 (15 digits)
long double	10	None	1.2E +/- 4932 (19 digits)

Table 1.1   Microsoft C/C++ Standard Data Types

returns the number of bytes an object requires in memory. This object can be either a blueprint for something, like the data type **int** (sizeof(int)) or an actual variable or object instance, as in *int_number_of_scores* (sizeof(int_number_of_scores)). A simple test condition could switch-hit a code solution for the appropriate architecture, as in the following:

```
int ivalue;
float fvalue;
if(sizeof(ivalue) == 4)
  ivalue = user_response;
else
  fvalue = user_response;
```

The final approach involves the awareness of a specific standard C/C++ header file, called **limits.h**, designed specifically for this purpose. A portion of limits.h is reproduced here for illustration purposes:

```
#define CHAR_BIT      8            /* number of bits in a char */
#define SCHAR_MIN    (-128)        /* minimum signed char value */
#define SCHAR_MAX     127          /* maximum signed char value */
#define UCHAR_MAX     0xff         /* maximum unsigned char value */

#ifndef _CHAR_UNSIGNED
#define CHAR_MIN     SCHAR_MIN     /* mimimum char value */
#define CHAR_MAX     SCHAR_MAX     /* maximum char value */
#else
#define CHAR_MIN      0
#define CHAR_MAX     UCHAR_MAX
#endif  /* _CHAR_UNSIGNED */

#define MB_LEN_MAX    2                  /* max. # bytes in multibyte char */
#define SHRT_MIN     (-32768)            /* minimum (signed) short value */
#define SHRT_MAX      32767              /* maximum (signed) short value */
#define USHRT_MAX     0xffff             /* maximum unsigned short value */
#define INT_MIN      (-2147483647 - 1)   /* minimum (signed) int value */
#define INT_MAX       2147483647         /* maximum (signed) int value */
#define UINT_MAX      0xffffffff         /* maximum unsigned int value */
#define LONG_MIN     (-2147483647L - 1)  /* minimum (signed) long value */
#define LONG_MAX      2147483647L        /* maximum (signed) long value */
#define ULONG_MAX     0xffffffffUL       /* maximum unsigned long value */

#if      _INTEGRAL_MAX_BITS >= 8
#define _I8_MIN      (-127i8 - 1)   /* minimum signed 8 bit value */
#define _I8_MAX       127i8         /* maximum signed 8 bit value */
#define _UI8_MAX      0xffui8       /* maximum unsigned 8 bit value */
#endif
```

```
#if      _INTEGRAL_MAX_BITS >= 16
#define _I16_MIN    (-32767i16 - 1) /* minimum signed 16 bit value */
#define _I16_MAX     32767i16       /* maximum signed 16 bit value */
#define _UI16_MAX    0xffffui16     /* maximum unsigned 16 bit value */
#endif

#if      _INTEGRAL_MAX_BITS >= 32
#define _I32_MIN    (-2147483647i32 - 1) /* minimum signed 32 bit value */
#define _I32_MAX     2147483647i32 /* maximum signed 32 bit value */
#define _UI32_MAX    0xffffffffui32 /* maximum unsigned 32 bit value */
#endif
```

Hungarian Notation

Originated by Microsoft's Charles Symonyi, Hungarian Notation provides a programmer with instant access to an identifier's type by placing a data type mnemonic in front of each identifier's name. This inline declaration greatly enhances the efficiency of deciphering a code statement without having to backtrack to each identifier's definition.

First, look at the following typical identifier syntax:

```
Value1 = 1;
Value2 = 2;
Result = Value1 / Value2; // Result assigned 0
```

This example relays absolutely no information about the variable's types or any potentially underlying logical error. Now, look at this simple equation rewritten using Hungarian Notation:

```
iValue1 = 1;
iValue2 = 2;
fResult = iValue1 / iValue2; // fResult assigned 0 not 0.5
```

Here the preceding mnemonics *f* for float variables and *i* for integer variables flag a potential truncation error for any programmer examining the code statement. Potentially imbedded in this calculation is the lost precision, as the C/C++ divide operator /, when passed two integral values, returns an integral result.

The name of the variable *fResult* implies that the author of the code was anticipating a floating-point result. When Hungarian Notation is uniformly applied throughout an entire application, many such potential code errors are visually diagnosed instantaneously on the offending line.

With a typical C++ Windows application employing tens of data types, constants (using the **const** keyword), symbolic constants (using the **#define** syntax), structures, classes, message types, and so forth, Hungarian Notation saves a programmer the burden of always searching through nested header file **#include**s for source code definitions.

Tables 1.2 through 1.10, which are well worth your time to peruse, detail just how Microsoft standardizes Windows definitions.

Naming Conventions for MFC, Handles, Controls, and Structures

Microsoft uses the naming conventions listed here for relationships between MFC and Windows handles, controls, and structures.

Windows Type	Sample Variable	MFC Class	Sample Object
HWND	hWnd;	CWnd*	pWnd;
HDLG	hDlg;	CDialog*	pDlg;
HDC	hDC;	CDC*	pDC;
HGDIOBJ	hGdiObj;	CGdiObject*	pGdiObj;
HPEN	hPen;	CPen*	pPen;
HBRUSH	hBrush;	CBrush*	pBrush;
HFONT	hFont;	CFont*	pFont;
HBITMAP	hBitmap;	CBitmap*	pBitmap;
HPALETTE	hPalette;	CPalette*	pPalette;
HRGN	hRgn;	CRgn*	pRgn;
HMENU	hMenu;	CMenu*	pMenu;
HWND	hCtl;	CStatic*	pStatic;
HWND	hCtl;	CButton*	pBtn;
HWND	hCtl;	CEdit*	pEdit;
HWND	hCtl;	CListBox*	pListBox;
HWND	hCtl;	CComboBox*	pComboBox;
HWND	hCtl;	CScrollBar*	pScrollbar;
HSZ	hszStr;	CString	pStr;
POINT	pt;	CPoint	pt;
SIZE	size;	CSize	size;
RECT	rect;	CRect	rect;

Naming Conventions for General Prefixes

Microsoft uses the general prefix naming conventions listed in Table 1.2.

Prefix	Type	Example
C	Class or structure	CDocument, CPrintInfo
m_	Member variable	m_pDoc, m_nCustomers

Table 1.2   General Prefix Naming Conventions

Naming Conventions for Variables

Table 1.3 lists the Microsoft naming conventions used for Windows-specific variables.

Naming Conventions for Application Symbols

Microsoft uses the symbolic constant prefixes listed in Table 1.4 in their Windows applications.

Naming Conventions for Microsoft MFC Macros

Table 1.5 lists the MFC macro prefixes that help a programmer immediately understand a macro's category.

Naming Conventions for Library Identifiers

The Microsoft libraries use the naming conventions listed in Table 1.6.

Naming Conventions for Static Library Versions

Table 1.7 lists Microsoft-specific library naming conventions.

Prefix	Type	Description	Sample
ch	char	8-bit character	*chGrade*
ch	TCHAR	16-bit character if **_UNICODE** is defined	*chName*
b	BOOL	Boolean value	*bEnabled*
n	int	Integer (size dependent on operating system)	*nLength*
n	UINT	Unsigned value (size dependent on operating system)	*nLength*
w	WORD	16-bit unsigned value	*wPos*
l	LONG	32-bit signed integer	*lOffset*
dw	DWORD	32-bit unsigned integer	*dwRange*
p	*	Pointer	*pDoc*
lp	FAR*	Far pointer	*lpDoc*
lpsz	LPSTR	32-bit pointer to character string	*lpszName*
lpsz	LPCSTR	32-bit pointer to constant character string	*lpszName*
lpsz	LPCTSTR	32-bit pointer to constant character string if **_UNICODE** is defined	*lpszName*
h	handle	Handle to Windows object	*hWnd*
lpfn	callback	Far pointer to **CALLBACK** function	*lpfnAbort*

Table 1.3   Variable Prefix Naming Conventions

Prefix	Type of Symbol	Example	Range
IDR_	Identification shared by multiple resources of different types	IDR_MAINFRAME	1 to 0x6FFF
IDD_	Dialog resource	IDD_SPELL_CHECK	1 to 0x6FFF
HIDD_	Dialog-resource Help context	HIDD_SPELL_CHECK	0x20001 to 0x26FF
IDB_	Bitmap resource	IDB_COMPANY_LOGO	1 to 0x6FFF
IDC_	Cursor resource	IDC_PENCIL	1 to 0x6FFF
IDI_	Icon resource	IDI_NOTEPAD	1 to 0x6FFF
ID__	Command from menu item or toolbar	ID_TOOLS_SPELLING	0x8000 to 0xDFFF
HID_	Command Help context	HID_TOOLS_SPELLING	0x18000 to 0x1DFFF
IDP_	Message box prompt	IDP_INVALID_PARTNO	8 to 0xDFFF
HIDP_	Message box Help context	HIDP_INVALID_PARTNO	0x30008 to 0x3DFFF
IDS_	String resource	IDS_COPYRIGHT	1 to 0x7FFF
IDC_	Control within dialog box	IDC_RECALC	8 to 0xDFFF

Table 1.4 Naming Conventions for Symbols Used by Windows Applications

Name	Type
_AFXDLL	Standalone Dynamic Link Library (DLL) version
_ALPHA	Compilation for the DEC Alpha processor only
_DEBUG	Debug version including diagnostics
_MBCS	Compilation for multibyte character sets
_UNICODE	Enables Unicode in an application
AFXAPI	Function provided by MFC
CALLBACK	Function called back via pointer

Table 1.5 Naming Conventions for Microsoft MFC Macros

Specifier	Value and Meaning
u	ANSI (N) or Unicode (U)
d	Debug or Release: D=Debug; omit specifier for Release

Table 1.6 Library Naming Conventions

Library	Description
NAFXCWD.LIB	Debug version: MFC Static Link Library
NAFXCW.LIB	Release version: MFC Static Link Library
UAFXCWD.LIB	Debug version: MFC Static Link Library with Unicode support
UAFXCW.LIB	Release version: MFC Static Link Library with Unicode support

Table 1.7   Static Library Versions

Naming Conventions for Dynamic Link Libraries

Table 1.8 lists the naming conventions used by Microsoft Dynamic Link Libraries, or DLLs.

Naming Conventions for windows.h

Table 1.9 details Microsoft's new standard types used by windows.h. These polymorphic types for any given application may contain different kinds of data. For a more detailed list, use the Visual C++ Help utility and do an index search for "Win32 Simple Data Types."

Operator Precedence

Another source for program errors comes from the improper selection and/or placement of C/C++ operators. Table 1.10 lists the standard C/C++ operator precedence levels for easy code verification, and their precedence and associativity, from highest precedence to lowest precedence.

There's a popular television commercial that asks the question: "Would you rather buy car insurance or have a root canal?" Well, writing good code may be compared to flossing: you *know* you should do it, it takes extra time, you probably *don't* want to take the extra time, but the paybacks are priceless. A clean, robust, well-designed algorithm shines and sparkles with an efficiency of execution, visual interface, and data integrity that puts a smile on everyone's face, from bosses, to coworkers, to end users!

Name	Type
_AFXDLL	Standalone Dynamic Link Library (DLL) version
WINAPI	Function provided by Windows

Table 1.8   Naming Conventions for DLL Macros

Typedef	Description
WINAPI	Use in place of **FAR PASCAL** in API declarations. If you are writing a DLL with exported API entry points, you can use this for your own APIs.
CALLBACK	Use in place of **FAR PASCAL** in application callback routines such as window and dialog procedures.
LPCSTR	Same as **LPSTR**, except used for read-only string pointers. Defined as (**const char FAR***).
UINT	Portable unsigned integer type whose size is determined by host environment (32 bits for Windows NT and Windows 95). Synonym for **unsigned int**. Used in place of **WORD** except in the rare cases where a 16-bit unsigned quantity is desired even on 32-bit platforms.
LRESULT	Type used for return value of window procedures.
LPARAM	Type used for declaration of lParam, the fourth parameter of a windows procedure.
WPARAM	Type used for declaration of wParam, the third parameter of a windows procedure (a polymorphic data type).
LPVOID	Generic pointer type, equivalent to (**void ***). Should be used instead of **LPSTR**.

Table 1.9   Naming Conventions Used by windows.h

Symbol	Operator	Associates from...
	Highest Precedence	
++	Post-increment	Left to right
--	Post-decrement	
( )	Function call	
[ ]	Array element	
->	Pointer to structure member	
.	Structure or union member	
++	Pre-increment	Right to left
--	Pre-decrement	
!	Logical NOT	
~	Bitwise NOT	
-	Unary minus	
+	Unary plus	
&	Address	
*	Indirection	

Table 1.10   C/C++ Operator Precedence Levels

Symbol	Operator	Associates from...
sizeof	Size in bytes	
new	Allocate program memory	
delete	Deallocate program memory	
(type)	Type cast [for example, (float) i]	
.*	Pointer to member (objects)	Left to right
->*	Pointer to member (pointers)	
*	Multiply	Left to right
/	Divide	
%	Remainder	
+	Add	Left to right
-	Subtract	
<<	LEFT-SHIFT	Left to right
>>	RIGHT-SHIFT	
<	Less than	Left to right
<=	Less than or equal to	
>	Greater than	
>=	Greater than or equal to	
==	Equal	Left to right
!=	Not equal	
&	Bitwise AND	Left to right
^	Bitwise exclusive OR	Left to right
|	Bitwise OR	Left to right
&&	Logical AND	Left to right
||	Logical OR	Left to right
? :	Conditional	Right to left
=	Assignment	Right to left
*=, /=, %=, +=, -=, <<=, >>=, &=, ^=, |=	Compound assignment	
,	Comma	Left to right
	Lowest Precedence	

Table 1.10   C/C++ Operator Precedence Levels *(continued)*

Conclusion

With the complexity of today's programming environment, a programmer *must* employ every design tool, technique, and bell'n whistle in order to generate *the* most robust algorithm and one that is easily read and modified by *other* programmers. That task is not easy!

In this chapter, you learned about all the design tools available to an application developer. Whether it be a good language-independent design, using structure charts for "desk checks," meticulous code-page spacing, or Hungarian Notation, C/C++ provide ample syntax variations enabling concise *visual* enhancements to source code presentation.

In the next chapter, you will learn about various C++ Debugger settings. This next chapter is important because you can turn on or off various meaningful Debugger options at the Debugger settings stage. A slip-up at this stage can leave you without important Debugger options or with confusing and meaningless application-specific display formats.

CHAPTER 2

Optimizing with the Compiler

In the last chapter, you looked at the language-independent components of a good program solution and those concerns specific to the C/C++ languages. In this chapter, you will come one step closer to understanding how to generate the most efficient executables possible with the Microsoft Visual C++ compiler.

Many programmers are unaware of the help a compiler can lend when trying to maximize the performance of an algorithm, whether it be from a minimal use of memory viewpoint or creating an executable with lightning-fast performance.

All language compilers, assemblers, and interpreters do the same thing: they translate their respective source file syntax down to the only language the microprocessor understands—machine code. The Microsoft C++ compiler is no exception. By default, Microsoft Visual Studio generates a debug version of your program. This is a literal translation, producing a series of low-level machine instructions in the finished executable program that exactly represent the high-level instruction of the source file.

In contrast, Microsoft Visual Studio can output a release version (debug and release candidates are discussed in detail in Chapter 5). This option gives the compiler much more latitude in which to work because a literal translation of the source is not necessarily desirable. The goal of a release build is to generate the smallest or the fastest object code possible without introducing any new or unintended behaviors to the algorithm.

This chapter first introduces the available compiler switches and their uses. The chapter then moves on to illustrate how minor code rewrites can work in a symbiotic relationship with the compiler options to produce the cleanest executables possible.

Indirectly, the chapter addresses the issue of code size versus code speed. These two factors do not necessarily go together. For example, an aerospace engineer may inform you that your entire space-shuttle program *must* run in only 5K of memory. Under these circumstances, where minimum code size is the goal, liberties may be taken in code design that would, on the surface, look like some hacker had thrown together a solution. On the other hand, to generate the most lightning-fast performance, a programmer may break other design fundamentals, like excessive use of global variables, in order to minimize call stack usage. In general, it is true that faster algorithms usually require more code than simpler, more straightforward methods.

Your Coding Responsibilities Versus the Optimizing Compiler's

Creating the fastest executables possible requires that you, the software engineer, have an accurate understanding of the optimizing compiler's capabilities.

Let's take a quick look at what your task entails. First, look at the following code segment:

```
for( int iOffset=0; iOffset < MAX_ELEMENTS; iOffset++ )
  iArrayOne[iOffset] = iOffset;
for( int iOffset=0; iOffset < MAX_ELEMENTS; iOffset++ )
  iArrayTwo[iOffset] = iOffset;
```

While there is nothing inherently wrong with the syntax from a code efficiency point of view, the segment could be rewritten as follows:

```
for( int iOffset=0; iOffset < MAX_ELEMENTS; iOffset++ ) {
  iArrayOne = iOffset;
  iArrayTwo = iOffset;
}
```

The rewrite combines the two loops into a single loop that does the logical equivalent tasks, without the overhead of the second **for** loop. Technically speaking, a code rewrite of this nature is called *jamming*. Microsoft Visual C++ is not capable of identifying these types of code optimizations. They are left to your implementation.

However, the optimizing compiler *is* capable of machine-specific tricks to save a byte or clock cycle here and there, savings that become more significant when accumulated over an entire program. For example, the statement

```
and    dword ptr mytable[si],0
```

is three bytes smaller from a memory-use point of view but executes three times slower than the following equivalent statement:

```
mov    dword ptr mytable[si],0
```

Unfortunately, with microprocessors executing millions, and soon billions, of instructions (or clock ticks) per second, a program needs to massively accumulate these types of timesaving tricks to effect a noticeable performance shift. The best design approach is to worry first about efficient algorithm design techniques, then tweak performance with compiler optimizations.

In practice, only algorithmic optimizations result in the appreciable improvement over execution speed. Lower levels of optimization usually do not save the millions of clock cycles required for human detection. One exception would be optimization tricks applied to specific loops or functions that execute many hundreds of times. Microsoft Windows especially encourages the use of small executables by not generating page faults for a program maximizing shared memory. Page faults force Windows to reload memory from disk, an expensive operation.

Microsoft Visual C++ Optimizations

Table 2.1 lists the most frequently used Microsoft Visual C++ optimizations. The table breaks these options down into two categories: those that generate the smallest executable possible and those that optimize for speed of execution.

Optimization Technique	Used to Generate Efficient Executables	Used to Generate Minimum Code Size
Scheduling instructions	✓	
Function-level linking		✓
String pooling		✓

Table 2.1   Microsoft Visual C++ Compiler Optimizations

Optimization Technique	Used to Generate Efficient Executables	Used to Generate Minimum Code Size
Use of **register** keyword	✓	✓
Propagation of constants and copies	✓	✓
Removing dead code and dead stores	✓	✓
Removing redundant sub expressions	✓	✓
Optimizing loops	✓	✓
Strength reduction	✓	✓
Use of **inline** keyword	✓	✓
Frame pointer omission	✓	✓
Disabling stack checking	✓	✓
Stack overlays	✓	✓
Allowing aliasing across function calls	✓	✓

Table 2.1   Microsoft Visual C++ Compiler Optimizations *(continued)*

The following discussions explain the use of each Microsoft Visual C++ optimization technique.

Scheduling Instructions

Today's programmers, using the latest Intel Pentium *super scalar* processors, can take advantage of these new chips' inherent hardware ability to simultaneously execute two instructions, each in their own pipeline. Of course, this assumes that the outcome from one instruction is independent from the concurrently executing one. Unfortunately, inexperienced programmers can inadvertently generate such collisions, generating what is called *pipeline stall.* By using *instruction ordering*, the compiler is instructed to prevent such dependencies by rearranging the order of the machine code instructions.

The following example illustrates an inevitable pipeline stall:

```
add       ax,shortInteger     ;statement One
mov       bx,ax               ;statement Two
sub       dx,dx               ;statement Three
```

Were the microprocessor to simultaneously execute statement One and statement Two, unpredictable results could occur since ax would not have a copy of shortInteger. On the other hand, the execution of statement Three is independent of either statement One or statement Two. A simple reordering of the preceding three statements eliminates the problem as follows:

```
add       ax,shortInteger     ;statement One
sub       dx,dx               ;statement Three
mov       bx,ax               ;statement Two
```

While it is true that instruction scheduling can improve runtime performance, this is true only for Pentium-class microprocessors, and the statement rearrangement has no affect on code size.

Function-Level Linking

There may be occasions when your excellent code design, combined with just the right set of optimization switches, optimizes a function right out of existence. This is possible with function inlining or when the compiler recognizes that it can compile the program in such a way that the function itself is never called. However, the function itself must still be compiled and included in the object file. Unfortunately, the compiler has no way of determining whether other source modules access the function. Only the linker can recognize when a function is never invoked.

Function-level linking guarantees that all functions in a source module are encrypted into the object code by a COMDAT record in a Common Object File Format (COFF). This information allows the linker to identify noninvoked functions so they can be removed from the executable file. This process is impossible without the inclusion of the COMDAT record.

String Pooling

This relatively straightforward optimization instructs the compiler to recognize any duplicate string definitions. When this situation occurs, the compiler simply substitutes a reference address to the unique version of the string.

Using the *register* Keyword

Using the **register** keyword is the first example of an optimization technique that can simultaneously reduce code size while improving runtime performance. The **register** keyword, similar to a local variable, is legal only at the *internal level*—in other words, inside a function. In principle, the keyword instructs the compiler to give the associated variable *register storage* instead of stack allocation.

Actually, the **register** keyword is a *request* of the compiler to give the associated variable register storage. This approach not only saves stack space, but by keeping the variable in a register, assures the fastest possible access to it because the processor reads and writes its own registers much faster than it reads and writes memory. There is also a slight decrease in code size for register-encoded local variables.

The Microsoft Visual C++ compiler does *not* recognize the **register** keyword. Instead, the compiler automatically scrutinizes each internal and external variable's usage, juggling data between registers and memory. Nearly any data object is a candidate for register storage, including constant values, structure members, function arguments, and even pointers to arguments passed by reference!

The decision is based on a sophisticated overview, by the compiler, determining just how the data is used. A weighted score is assigned to each data object relating to the benefit gained from storing the variable in a register. As the compiler generates the object code, it places the highest-scoring variables in registers whenever possible.

One last technical note: if you are using some other C++ compiler, beware of writing function statements that apply the address operator, **&**, to any register variable, as in the following:

```
void somefunc( void )
{
  register int iregValue;
  int *piregValue;
```

```
    piregValue = &iregValue;
    ...
}
```

You are treading on thin ice here because it is up to the C++ compiler manufacturer to decide if this combination of ideas generates a warning or error message, or simply assumes that the need to have the address of a memory location is more important than register storage and defaults to standard memory allocation.

> **Note** *The compiler does not accept user requests for register variables; instead, it makes its own register choices when global register-allocation optimization (/Oe option) is on. However, all other semantics associated with the **register** keyword are honored. ANSI C does not allow for taking the address of a register object; this restriction does not apply to C++. However, if the address operator (**&**) is used on an object, the compiler must put the object in a location for which an address can be represented—in practice, this means in memory instead of in a register.*

Propagation of Constants and Copies

From a code optimization viewpoint, accessing values stored in registers is quicker than accessing a constant, which in turn is more efficient than accessing a value stored in memory. All things being equal, if a code section runs out of available register storage, consider replacing an expression with a constant. This approach allows the compiler to take advantage of forward constant propagation by reusing the constants throughout the code segment. The compiler is able to optimize statements by replacing any expression that evaluates to a constant value, with the value itself, as in the following:

```
iValueOne = 10;
iResult = iValueOne;
```

With constant propagation, the compiler encodes the two statements as if they had been entered as follows:

```
iValueOne = 10;
iResult = 10;
```

In a similar manner, copy propagation involves the compiler's recognition of a single value being forwarded from one variable to another in a series of assignments in which the intermediate assignments do *not* use the value in a calculation, but merely pass it on to the next variable. In the following statements:

```
iValue = iSomeValue;
iValue = myFunctionCall( iValue );
```

`iValue` being assigned `iSomeValue` really serves no useful purpose. The optimizing compiler recognizes this sequence and instead rewrites and encrypts the following logical equivalent:

```
iValue = myFunctionCall( isomeValue );
```

Here the compiler makes a harmless substitution of the parameter `iValue` with `iSomeValue`. Because of this optimization, the first statement becomes superfluous, generating what is known in the industry as *dead store*.

Eliminating Dead Code and Dead Stores

In the preceding section, you learned how the optimizing compiler can kind of skip over code statements when they are recognized as meaningless, generating a condition known as dead store. Naturally, by being aware that these conditions may occur in the foreground while you are generating program statements, you can avoid these situations manually. Simply use caution when generating your original algorithm.

Dead code, sometimes referred to as *unreachable code*, represents those code blocks that, for one reason or another, based on the logic of your algorithm, are truly unreachable, useless, or "dead." The following example illustrates this concept with a simple **if...else** statement:

```
bFlag = true;
if( bFlag )
   cout << "This statement always executes the true statement.";
else
   cout << "This is an unreachable statement.";
```

Based on the initialization of the variable `bFlag` to **true**, the **else** portion of this **if...else** statement can never be reached.

Sometimes, however, as a by-product of a previous compiler optimization, the compiler generates no object instructions for dead code or dead store, automatically eliminating these conditions from the final optimized executable!

Removing Redundant Sub Expressions

Similar to constant propagation, when the compiler detects a series of sub expressions all accessing the same value, it calculates the intermediate result of the sub expression once and then replaces all sub expressions with the calculated value. So for example, the following two statements:

```
iResultOne = iValueOne / iValueTwo;
iResultTwo = iValueOne / iValueTwo;
```

could be rewritten as follows:

```
iIntermediateResult = iValueOne / iValueTwo;
iResultOne = iIntermediateResult;
iResultTwo = iIntermediateResult;
```

While this simple rewrite eliminates a duplicate divide operation, if the intermediate calculation is complex, the resulting optimization is significant. Performance increases are directly proportional to the number of times the intermediate result is reused. Under such conditions, the simple substitution can significantly reduce code size while increasing runtime efficiency.

Optimizing Loops

Naturally, combining any of the previously discussed optimization techniques to loop bodies produces dramatic effects directly proportional to the number of times the loop iterates. However, there are other design approaches to tweaking loop performance. Take a look at the following example code segment:

```
for( int iOffset = 0; iOffset < MAX_ELEMENTS; iOffset++ )
  iArray[iOffset] = iValueOne * iValueTwo;
```

The invariant portion of the loop-body statement is the multiplication of `iValueOne` and `iValueTwo`. With the following simple code rewrite:

```
iTempResult = iValueOne * iValueTwo;
for( int iOffset = 0; iOffset < MAX_ELEMENTS; iOffset++ )
  iArray[iOffset] = iTempResult;
```

moving the multiplication operation out of the loop reduces by (`MAX_ELEMENTS` * expression) the number of times the algorithm must redundantly calculate the product! The term *hoisting* describes this process of moving a loop-body statement above the loop iteration statement.

Strength Reduction

Strength reduction or optimization involves the compiler's recognition of complicated expressions that can be rewritten in a simpler form, without changing any calculated results. Most processors add or subtract two values in less machine cycles than when multiplying or dividing. Likewise, certain multiplication and divide operations can be substituted with the much more efficient shift operator. Take, for example, any value multiplied or divided by some power of two, as in the following:

```
fResult *= 2;
```

The preceding is substituted with the more efficient shift left operator as follows:

```
fResult << 1; // left by one bit effectively multiplies by two
```

This simple substitution can eliminate the more clock-tick intensive multiply operation with a savings of over 30 machine cycles. Mind you, this savings in itself is humanly unobservable at runtime, but it is the total accumulation of each optimization that generates an obvious performance boost.

Use of the *inline* Keyword

Many programmers are unaware of the large number of machine code statements generated each time a function call is compiled. All they see is a single statement

```
myFunctionCall(arg1, arg2, arg3,…);
```

Function calls require tracking addresses for the next instruction to be executed when the called routine terminates, pushing copies of the actual arguments, updating the instruction pointer to point to the first called subroutine statement, code to pop the passed parameters, storage allocation statements for any calculated and returned results, and so on. When function calls occur within loop bodies, the performance hit can be significant due to this behind-the-scenes execution sequence.

> **Note** *Stack checking under 16-bit versions of Windows invokes a call to a C runtime function called a* stack probe. *Under 32-bit versions of Windows, Windows itself responds by allocating more stack memory when an access is attempted near the bottom of the application's stack.*

C++ allows a programmer to eliminate this bottleneck by declaring a function to be **inline**. Inline functions are similar to macros in C++ but go one better in that they require function prototypes. This allows the compiler to perform compile-time checks between a function's actual arguments versus the formal argument list. True C++ macros fly blind if invoked with improper values.

Inline functions do *not* use the call stack, do *not* update the instruction pointer to the beginning of some other memory segment, and when used properly, can significantly improve runtime performance.

Frame Pointer Omission

Frame pointer optimization is available only on the Microsoft Visual C++ Professional and Enterprise editions. The /Oy option suppresses creation of frame pointers on the call stack. This option speeds function calls because no frame pointers need to be set up and removed. It also frees one more register, EBP on the Intel 386 or later, for storing frequently-used variables and sub expressions.

Using EBP as the frame pointer is an unnecessary legacy of older versions of Windows designed to run on the Intel 80286 processor. When frame pointer omission is in effect, the compiler references stack data relative to the ESP register instead of the EBP register. A function's prologue becomes a single instruction that adjusts the ESP stack pointer to create the stack frame. Without this option, the compiler generates prologue code for each function that requires a stack frame and points the processor's EBP register to the top of the frame. The disadvantage of frame pointer omission is that encoding a memory reference relative to ESP takes one byte more than the same EBP reference.

To find this option in the development environment, click Settings on the Project menu. Then click the C/C++ tab and click Optimizations in the Category box. Under Optimizations, choose Customize.

Disabling Stack Checking

Before discussing the disabling stack checking optimization, it is necessary to examine just how Windows adds memory to the stack. Windows allocates space on the stack in pages. The size of the page is architecture dependent, with Intel microprocessors allocating 4K per page. The trigger for allocating this additional space occurs when an access falls off the end of the stack into an area called the *guard page*. The guard page is the last page allocated to the stack. When the application reaches this page, Windows commits another page to increase stack size, which is called *growing* the stack.

Programs requesting more stack space than is available on the guard page attempt to dip into reserved memory, as in the following:

```
void myFunction( void )
{
  char cArray[2 * 4096]; // allocates 2 pages or 8 Kb
  cArray[8000] = 'a';
  ...
}
```

Problems do not immediately surface because the compiler allocates space for the automatic data by decrementing the processor's stack pointer ESP by the requested 8K. However, this does not cause Windows to allocate more stack space. If the space allocated for the array begins near the bottom of the stack, accessing an element near the end of the sequence may reach over the stack's guard page into reserved memory. Windows immediately grabs your attention at this point by terminating the application with an illegal access violation.

When stack checking is turned on, the C++ compiler computes the total size of each function's local variables. When an offending definition generates an object that may overreach the guard page, the compiler generates a call to the C runtime library's stack check routine. This C function simply accesses sequential pages of the stack at 4,096-byte increments.

Unfortunately, while stack checking builds a more robust application, it adds overhead to a program, unnecessarily slowing down runtime efficiency. The alternative, once again, is accomplished by a careful rewrite of the subroutine. In the previous example, the statement triggering the access violation is as follows:

```
cArray[8000] = 'a';
```

not

```
char cArray[2 * 40966];
```

Remember that the access violation does not occur until the code statement causes an actual memory access. However, were the subroutine to sequentially access array elements within 4,096-byte increments, the program would execute properly, as follows:

```
cArray[4090] = 'a';  // page one access
cArray[5100] = 'a';  // page two access
```

Stack Overlays

For this optimization to be of any benefit, an application must employ short-lived internal, or local, variable declarations. When the optimization is turned *off*, every internal variable is given unique address space, with Windows quietly responding by growing the stack—a time-consuming activity. When stack overlay optimization is turned *on*, the compiler reuses stack space to store internal variables whose lives do not overlap. This reduces the potential for a stack overrun while the program is executing.

With stack overlay optimization turned on, a program may gain a two-fold performance boost by also minimizing the distance between a local variable on the stack and the top of the stack frame. For example, when local variables are within 128 bytes from the frame pointer, each variable's address is shorter by 3 bytes.

Allowing Aliasing Across Function Calls

Sometimes referred to as *overlay defining*, *aliasing* means that an algorithm is using more than one name to access the same memory location. The most common sources for this type of coding involve the use of a **union** or pointer variable, as in the following:

```
char cValue, *pcValue = &cValue;
```

where both variables, cValue and pcValue access the same byte. This type of code style may cripple certain types of compiler optimizations—for example, preventing a variable from receiving register storage (pcValue) because a code statement requires the address of a variable's memory allocation (pcValue = &cValue).

When a programmer activates the Assume No Aliasing optimization switch, the programmer is, in effect, promising the compiler that variables have no hidden associations or aliases. This gives the compiler the go-ahead to aggressively optimize code involving pointers. Microsoft Visual C++ goes this optimization switch one better by providing a middle-ground switch called Assume Aliasing Across Function Calls. Here the programmer is promising the compiler that no aliasing exists in the code except across a function call, as in the following:

```
int iExternalArray[MAX_ELEMENTS];
void main( void )
{
  int *piExternalArrayOne = iExternalArray,
      *piExternalArrayTwo = myFunctionReturningArrayAddress();
}
int * myFunctionReturningArrayAddress( void )
{
  return( iExternalArray );
}
```

In this example the alias exists between **main()** and myFunctionReturningArrayAddress(), which both request the starting address of the iExternalArray. With Assume Aliasing Across Function Calls activated, the compiler *is allowed* to optimize any code involving pointers, as in the previous example.

```
char cValue, *pcValue = &cValue;
```

where the compiler can now go ahead and decide if register storage is advantageous for both variables cValue and pcValue.

Global Optimizations

This broad scope option bundles several optimization techniques, including peephole optimizations, enregistering (similar to the **register** keyword request), loop optimizations, and elimination of dead code and dead store.

Generate Intrinsic Functions Inline

Table 2.2 lists the intrinsic functions. When Maximize Speed optimization is selected, the compiler uses the intrinsic form of these functions, effectively replacing each function call with the *intrinsic* inline counterpart. As with all inline substitutions, this can significantly increase program speed, with the potential downside of increasing program size. For size-critical applications, intrinsic equivalents may actually be worse than the standard function call. Take, for example, **strcpy()**, which, in its intrinsic form, requires approximately 41 code bytes instead of the 18 bytes used for the function call version.

_disable	_enable	_inp
_inpw	_lrotl	_lrotr
_outp	_outpw	_rotl
_rotr	_strset	abs
fabs	labs	memcmp
memcpy	memset	strcat
strcmp	strcpy	strlen

Table 2.2   Microsoft Visual C++ Intrinsic Functions

Optimizing *math.h*

Although the functions prototyped in math.h do not have true intrinsic equivalents, when choosing Generate intrinsic functions inline optimization, any program using math.h gets an additional execution-speed boost. Though these functions have no intrinsic counterpart, the compiler will optimize their performance by placing the function arguments directly into the coprocessor instead of pushing them onto the stack. Yes, this requires more coding, but the tradeoff is a faster-executing function.

Microsoft C++ Optimization Switches

Remember, code optimization is supported only in Visual C++ Professional and Enterprise editions. Table 2.3 describes the available switches. All of the options are also available through various Visual Studio menus and dialog boxes and are discussed throughout the book.

Professional/Enterprise Optimization Switch	Description
/G5	Code optimized for Pentium processors.
/G6	Code optimized for Pentium Pro processors.
/GB	Combines the optimizations for the 80386 (/G3), 80486 (/G4), Pentium (/G5), and Pentium Pro (/G6) options.
/G3	Code optimized for the 80386 processor.
/G4	Code optimized for the 80486 processor.
/Gd	Defines function-calling conventions.
/Ge	Enables stack checking for function calls that require storage for local variables.
/Gf	String spooling of identical strings into one location in the executable file.
/GF	Same as /Gf except string copies are placed into read-only memory.
/Gh	Calls a user-defined function at the beginning of every function call. Executable file is larger and slower.
/Gi	Enables incremental compiles of only those functions that have changed since the last build. Executable files are larger.
/Gm	Streamlines build process for workspaces with many files that have not changed since last build.
/Gr	Defines function-calling conventions.
/GR	Adds runtime code to check object types. Executable files are larger.
/Gs	Enables stack checking.
/GX	Specifies when destructors are called for automatic objects during a stack unwind triggered by a Windows NT structured exception or a C++ exception.
/Gy	Enables compiler packaging of individual functions in COMDAT form.
/Gz	Defines function-calling conventions.
/O1	Code optimized for minimum size. Uses /Os as well as other switches.
/O2	Code optimized for maximum speed. Uses /Ot as well as other switches.
/Oa	Used for source files that do not use aliasing.
/Ob	Enables inline expansion of functions.
/Od	Disables optimizations.
/Og	Eliminates local and global common sub expressions, allows automatic register allocation, and allows loop optimization.
/Oi	Substitutes optimizable function calls with inline function expansion.
/Op	Guarantees the precision of floating-point operations.
/Os	Generates smaller executable files.
/Ot	Generates faster executable files.
/Ox	Code optimized to use the fastest possible code. Microsoft recommends the use of /O2.
/Oy	Disables frame pointer creation on the call stack.
/Ow	Alerts the compiler that your application does not use aliasing.

Table 2.3   Microsoft Visual C++ Optimization Switches

Using Microsoft Visual Studio to Set Compiler Options

Microsoft Visual C++ has predefined its own set of default optimization settings depending on the build target. For example, when building a debug version, the Developer Studio switches off all optimizations, guaranteeing that the executable file is a literal translation of the source. The default for a release build is to optimize the code for speed of execution, at the expense of possibly bursting final code size. These two commonly used build targets can suffice for the majority of project developments. However, at times, you may want to manually fine-tune a project's compiler optimizations.

You access compiler optimization switches by first selecting Project and then Settings, as shown in Figure 2.1.

The actual switches are contained within the Project Settings dialog box shown in Figure 2.2.

This section concentrates on the Project Settings dialog box's C/C++ tab, containing all of the switches that govern how the compiler optimizes a project's source files.

Before setting any optimization switches, you need to first decide *which* files you want to optimize. You do this by clicking inside the left pane of the Project Settings dialog box (shown in Figure 2.2). The project's source file list is similar to the FileView pane of the Workspace window. In this example, all of the files within the project were selected by clicking on main, the highest-level reference.

If you wanted to optimize only selected files within the project, you would, instead, hold down the CTRL key and click on the individual files. This approach allows you to fine-tune file optimizations to match specific requirements. One group of project files may need optimization for speed, while another group might need to be optimized for minimal use of space.

The initial build target shown in the upper-left corner of the Project Settings dialog box depends on the current active configuration for the project. The target should be Win32 Release when setting compiler optimizations. Note, however, that the project's active configuration is not changed even when selecting alternate settings.

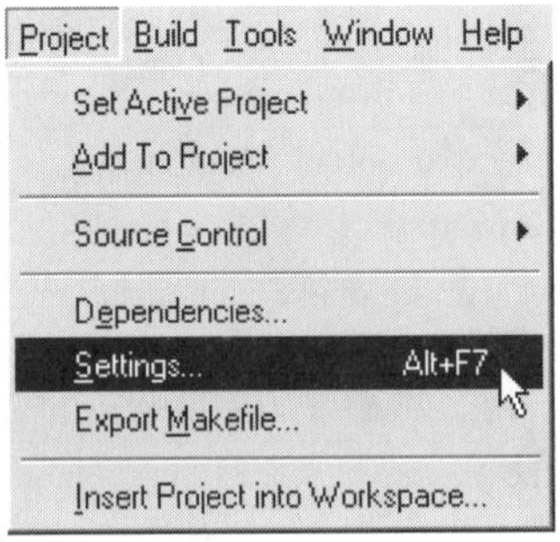

Figure 2.1   Project | Settings option

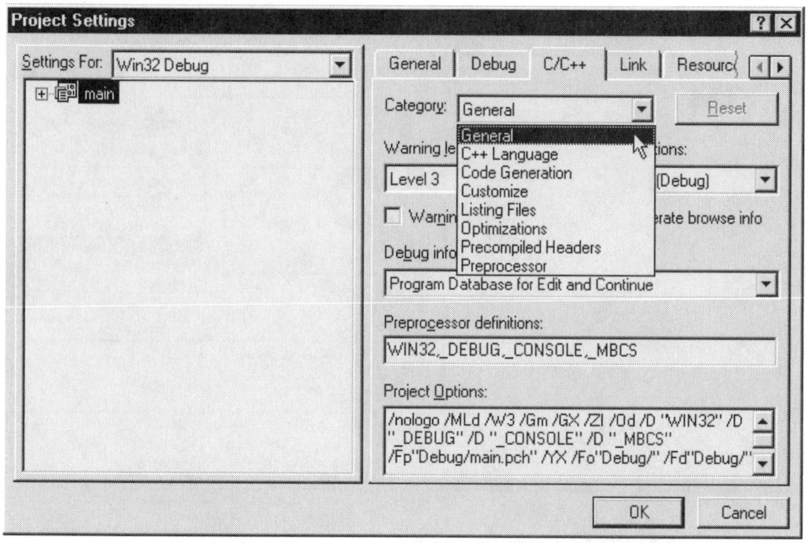

Figure 2.2   Project Settings dialog box

Referring back to Figure 2.2, the list of optimizations is dependent on the selection in the Category drop-down list. Of the eight possible categories for compiler settings listed, four specifically contain all the switches relating to compiler optimizations. These include:

- **General** (selected in Figure 2.2)   Providing the most efficient approach to selecting a general optimization goal, but not permitting fine control over individual optimization techniques.
- **Code Generation**   Selecting a processor-specific optimization along with a project's default calling conventions.
- **Customize**   Automatically selecting function-level linking and string pooling.
- **Optimizations**   Allowing you to fine-tune a project's optimizations.

The grayed-out Reset button is activated anytime you make a selection in the Category drop-down list and change one of the defaults. This is a convenient way to restore the complete set of initial settings for the next project.

The General Category in the Project Settings Dialog

With the General category selected (see Figure 2.3), you can choose one of five selections in the Optimizations drop-down list: Default, Disable (Debug), Maximize Speed, Minimize Size, and Customize. Disable turns off all optimizations, producing an executable with a one-on-one literal

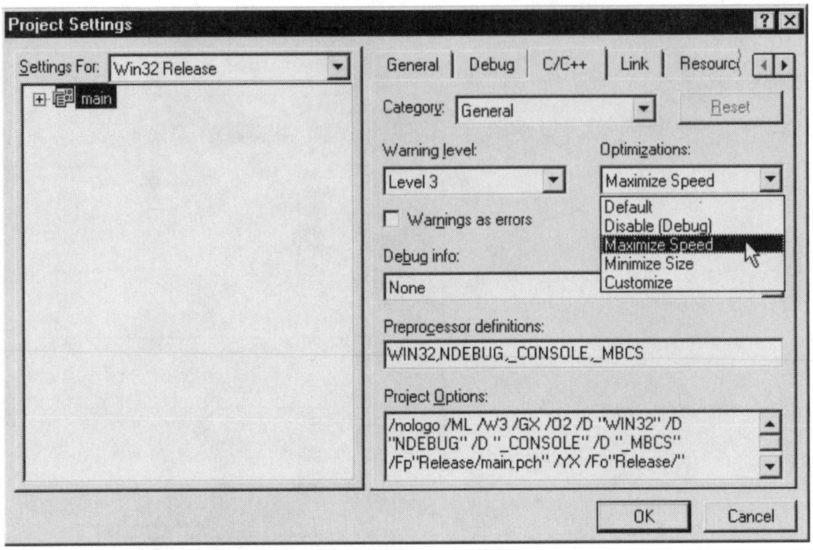

Figure 2.3   Choosing compiler optimizations

source code translation. You use Default optimization whenever you want the compiler to perform some optimizations that favor faster code, while clearing all other optimizations, including the Disable switch. Customize optimization provides manual control over optimizations switches for function-level linking and string pooling.

Of particular interest are the Maximize Speed and Minimum Size selections, which select the best combination of optimization options. Table 2.4 details which optimizations are active for Maximize Speed and Minimum Size.

Optimization	Maximize Speed	Minimum Size
Generate intrinsic functions inline	✓	no
Optimize for fast code	✓	no
Optimize for small code	no	✓
Global optimizations enabled	✓	✓
Omit frame pointer	✓	✓
Stack checking disabled	✓	✓
String pooling enabled	✓	✓
Function-level linking enabled	✓	✓

Table 2.4   General Category's Maximize Speed and Minimum Size Settings

The favor fast code and favor small code optimizations tell the compiler which priority you have chosen when a code sequence can be optimized one of two ways.

The Code Generation Category in the Project Settings Dialog

Figure 2.4 displays the Code Generation category options. These include user-selection of optimizations for specific processors, the default calling convention, the type of runtime library used by the application, and structure member alignment.

Selecting the Processor

The Processor options direct the compiler to optimize code generation for the 80386, 80486, or Pentium processors. The default setting, Blend, represents a compromise that favors the Pentium class but adds selected optimizations for ancestor-generations.

Selecting the Calling Convention

Visual C++ acknowledges three calling conventions: __cdecl, __fastcall, and __stdcall. (See Table 2.5—note the table defines conventions for C code or C++ algorithms employing the **extern** "C" keywords. C++ uses a slightly different calling convention.) Calling conventions determine left-to-right or right-to-left parameter passing, who cleans up the stack, and function name *mangling* (sometimes called a *signature* or *decoration*).

The __**fastcall** convention improves the __**cdecl** default only when the called C function has at least one parameter. With this option selected, the compiler will pass the first two actual arguments in registers (ECX and EDX), rather than using the stack. All other arguments default to the normal __**cdecl** stack order.

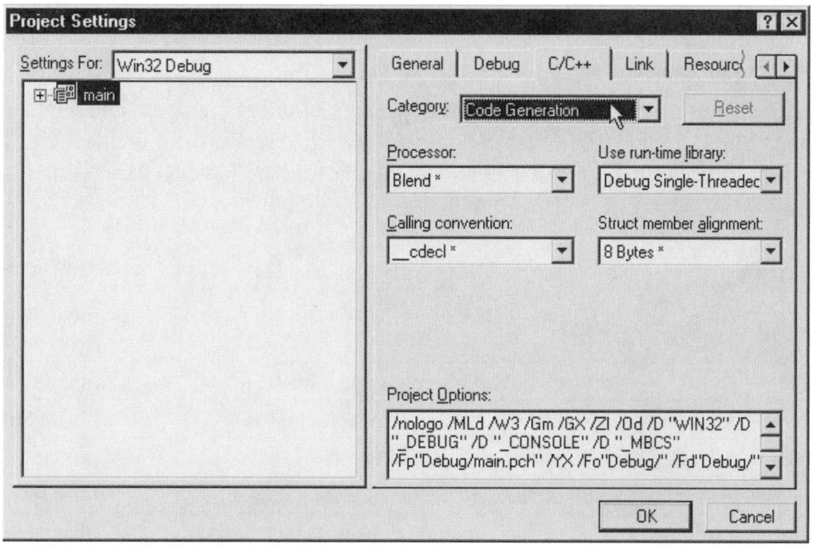

Figure 2.4   Code Generation category optimizations

Calling Convention	Passing Order	Who Cleans Up the Stack	Mangling Style
__cdecl	Right-to-left	Calling routine	_functionName
__fastcall	Right-to-left	Called routine	@functionName@*nnn*
__stdcall	Right-to-left	Called routine	_functionName@*nnn*

nnn—represents the number of bytes in the parameter list.

Table 2.5 Visual C++ Recognized Calling Conventions

> **Note** *The __fastcall calling convention does not allow functions to have varying argument lengths and is currently tied to the ECX and EDX registers by default. Microsoft does not guarantee this relationship in future releases of Visual C++.*

The __stdcall calling convention is used by the Windows API. While reducing overall code size, this convention also allows for functions with variable argument lists. However, under these circumstances, the call is implemented using the __cdecl calling convention.

Selecting the Runtime Library

Correctly selecting the appropriate runtime library can help reduce an application's code size, although the defaults are usually best. Table 2.6 lists the options available in the Use runtime library list.

Linking statically or dynamically to a runtime library involves the same considerations as linking statically or dynamically to the MFC library. While static linking makes the size of the executable file larger, dynamic linking makes the code smaller but dependent on the prior existence of the file Msvcrt.dll.

Selecting the Structure Alignment

This last setting defines the boundary on which a structure or union member is aligned. Applications should generally align structure members at addresses that are "natural" for the data type and the processor involved. For example, a 4-byte data member should have an address that is a multiple of 4.

Library Setting	Use	Runtime Library Accessed
Single-Threaded	Static link to library, single thread	libc.lib
Multithreaded	Static link to library, multiple threads	libcmt.lib
Multithreaded DLL	Import library for Msvcrt.dll	msvcrt.lib
Debug Single-Threaded	Static link, single thread (debug release)	libcd.lib
Debug Multithreaded	Static link, multiple threads (debug release)	libcmtd.lib

Table 2.6 Visual C++ Runtime Library Options

While you can select an alignment as granular as 1 byte, definitely reducing the amount of memory used, beware: the Pentium class processors can access 4-byte integers in one clock tick. Accessing within these alignment boundaries requires a processor stall of three additional cycles. Accumulated over time, this can degrade execution performance significantly.

Selecting a "natural" alignment boundary is especially important when you write code for porting to multiple processors. A misaligned 4-byte data member, which is on an address that is not a multiple of 4, causes a performance penalty with an 80386 processor and a hardware exception with a MIPS RISC processor. In the latter case, although the system handles the exception, the performance penalty is significantly greater.

The Customize Category in the Project Settings Dialog

Figure 2.5 lists the optimizations available when Customize is selected in the Category drop-down list. You will notice that some of the options are grayed-out by default. This is because the default optimization is set to Speed. To enable the two grayed-out options (Enable function-level linking and Eliminate duplicate strings), you need to select either Minimum Size or Customize, which are available when General is selected in the Category list.

Remember from previous discussions that, by default, function-level linking applies only to packaged functions identified through the linker via a COMDAT record or C++ class inline member functions. Enabling function-level linking packages all functions.

The Optimizations Category in the Project Settings Dialog

The last selection we will look at in the Category list is Optimizations. Figure 2.6 shows the initial window defaults.

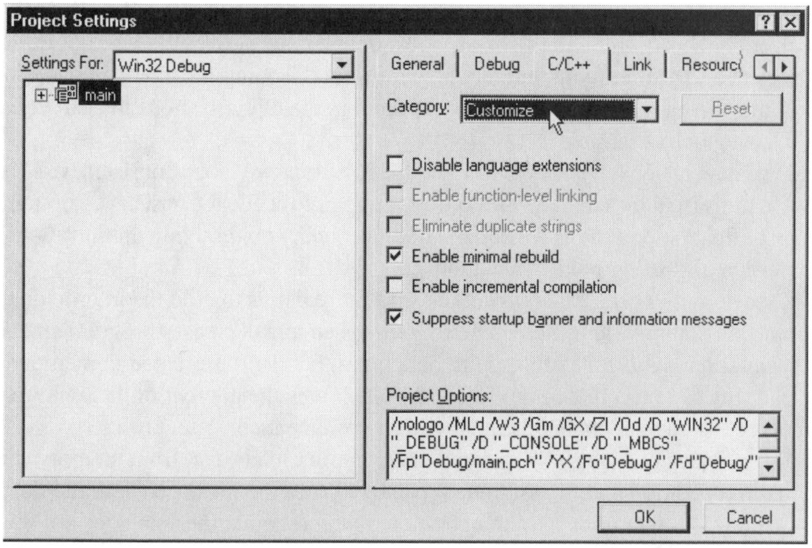

Figure 2.5   Customize category optimizations

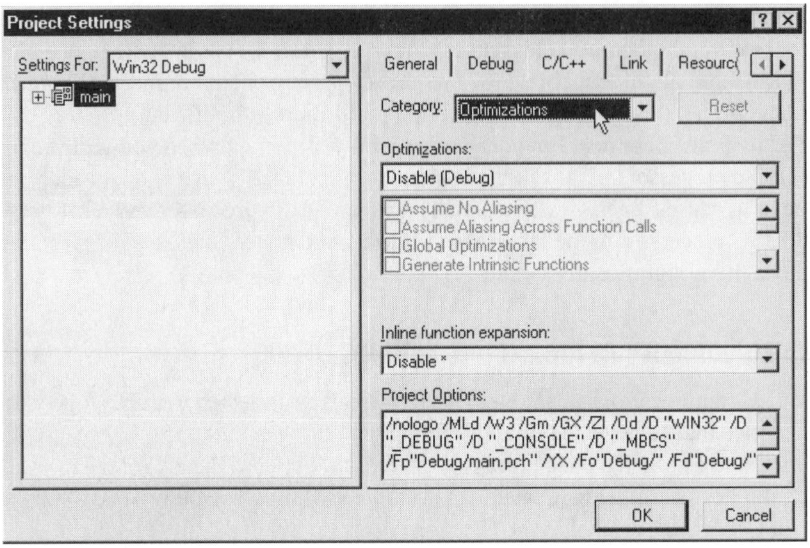

Figure 2.6   Optimizations category options

The Optimizations drop-down list, expanded in Figure 2.7, displays the same optimization setting that can be selected when General is selected in the Category list—in this case, Disable (Debug). Changing this selection, either in the Optimizations list (as in Figure 2.7) or when General is selected in the Category list causes the other Category drop-down list to synchronize the optimization selected.

Unlike the General Category: Optimizations selection, the Optimizations Category: Optimizations: Customize selection (shown in Figure 2.7) provides greater control over the types of optimizations applied to a project and also lets you define whether or not the compiler should expand functions inline. Only in this dialog box, with Customize selected in the Optimizations list can you enable the Assume No Aliasing optimization!

One of the two new options, not visible in Figure 2.7, is Improve Float Consistency. This feature is available only in the Visual C++ Enterprise Edition. The Improve Float Consistency option improves the consistency of floating-point tests for equality and inequality by disabling optimizations that could change the precision of floating-point calculations.

By default, the compiler uses the coprocessor's 80-bit registers to hold the intermediate results of floating-point calculations. This increases program speed and decreases program size. However, because the calculation involves floating-point data types that are represented in memory by less than 80 bits, carrying the extra bits of precision (80 bits minus the number of bits in a smaller floating-point type) through a lengthy calculation can produce inconsistent results.

When Improve Float Consistency is *enabled*, the compiler loads data from memory prior to each floating-point operation and, if assignment occurs, writes the results back to memory upon completion. Loading the data prior to each operation guarantees that the data does not retain any

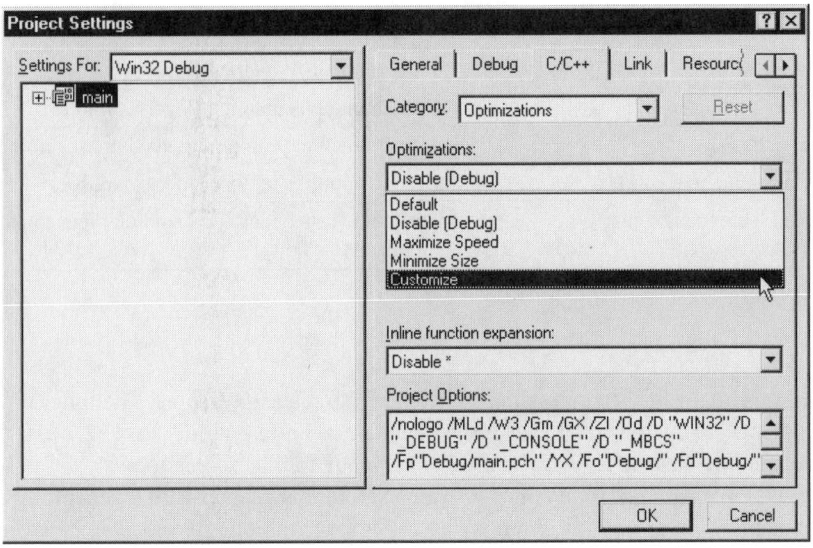

Figure 2.7   Changing the mode in the Optimizations list

significance greater than the capacity of its type. However, as anticipated, a program compiled with optimization enabled may be slower and larger than one compiled without it.

The second option, not visible in Figure 2.7, that requires some explanation is Full Optimization. This option enables all optimizations for inline expansions and intrinsic functions, favors fast code, disables stack checking, and enables global optimizations.

Build Recommendations

For obvious reasons, there is no advantage in selecting a release build version until an application is thoroughly debugged and robustly tested. However, given that assumption, a few surprises may still be in store in this final stage.

One relatively simple cause for a release version to fail is an unrecognized alias. To locate the offending code, simply rebuild the release version with Assume No Aliasing turned off. If the build succeeds, locate the hidden alias.

Under certain circumstances, disabling stack checking for a function that requires more than a page of stack space for its local variables may cause a release build crash, while the debug version, which inserts a stack check, runs fine. The solution requires rewriting the function to touch each new stack memory page or inserting a check_stack pragma.

In addition, the C++ keyword **new**, compiles differently under debug and release modes. The debug version adds extra guard bytes to memory, while the release version omits this code. Any code segment assuming the existence of the guard bytes would need to be rewritten.

Optimization	Cause of Release Build Error
Global optimization	Failure to initialize internal (local) variables.
Inline expansion	Failure to initialize internal (local) variables.
Frame pointer omission	Incorrect function prototyping leading to corrupted stack.
Generate intrinsic functions inline	Failure to initialize internal (local) variables.
Improve floating-point consistency	Algorithm is dependent upon explicit precision in value comparisons.

Table 2.7 Optimization Breaks by Category and Possible Cause

One other surprise awaits your transition from debug to release versions. The order in which your function arguments are evaluated can vary between the two build options. Table 2.7 lists the optimizations and likely cause as you change from a debug to release version.

Undoubtedly, the most important concept to glean from this chapter is that generating the most efficient executable form of your program is the result of a symbiotic relationship between code design and compiler optimizations.

Chapters 1 ("Writing Good Code") and 3 ("Logical Versus Syntactical Errors") will help you with your code development skills, while this chapter, along with Chapter 4 ("Debugger Essentials"), details the Visual Studio C++ compiler tools available for code optimization.

Conclusion

In this chapter, you have undoubtedly learned more about Visual C++'s Debugger capabilities than you ever knew existed! The good news is that you do not need all of them, all the time. The bad news is that you may cripple the Debugger's abilities to efficiently detect and diagnose code bugs if you forget *what* Debugger options are available to you or *where* their settings/switches are located.

In the next chapter, you will take a look at the types of bugs an algorithm can generate. Time is spent in forewarning you of design-time changes you can make to help prevent compile-time or runtime bugs.

CHAPTER 3

Logical Versus Syntactical Errors

It is often difficult for beginning programmers to appreciate the importance of learning good programming habits that lead to the design of readable and robust algorithms. The reason is that programs written in an academic environment are often quite different from those developed in real-world situations, in which program style and form are critical. Student programs are usually quite small (usually less than a few hundred lines of code). They are executed and modified only a few times (almost never after they have been handed in), are rarely examined in detail by anyone other than the student and the instructor, and are not developed within the context of budget constraints.

On the other hand, real-world applications may be very large (several thousand lines of code), developed by teams of programmers, commonly used for long periods of time and therefore require maintenance if they are to be kept current and correct, and are often maintained by someone other than the original programmer.

In today's programming environment, hardware costs continue to decrease while programmer costs steadily increase. Now more than ever, the importance of reducing programming and maintenance costs, with the corresponding importance of writing programs that can be easily read and understood by others, continues to grow. Certainly, the most important characteristic of any program is that it be correct.

No matter how well structured a program is, how well it is documented, or how nice it looks, if it does not produce correct results, it is worthless. But as we all know, the fact that a program executes without producing any error messages is no guarantee that it is correct. The results produced may be wrong because of logical errors that the computer system cannot detect.

The detection and correction of errors is an important part of software development and is known as *validation and verification.* Validation is concerned with checking that the algorithms and the program meet the problem's specification. Verification refers to checking that the algorithms and the program are correct and complete. Validation is sometimes described as answering the question: Is the program solving the correct problem? And verification is answering the question: Is the program solving the problem correctly? Figure 3.1 represents a good program development strategy.

In this chapter, you will examine each of the four types of errors that can occur in developing software systems. You will also learn good program development, design philosophies, and review strategies for preventing errors. The chapter closes with an explanation of how to use Visual C++'s online Help utility to track warning- or error-specific debug messages.

24x7

The Visual C++ Debugger automatically synchronizes watch window variables with the scope of the statement being executed. To continually view a variable's contents, click and drag it from the auto-tracking watch window (left side of display) to the right half of the window.

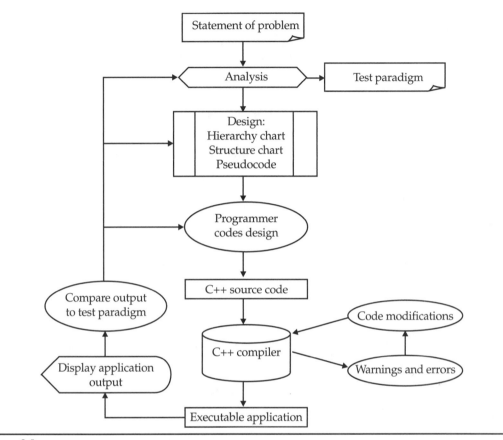

Figure 3.1   Good program development strategy

A Good Debug Strategy

Experienced programmers have long since learned the need to debug a program using a systematic and commonsense approach. They do not change something just because they hope it will work and do not know what else to do. Instead, they skillfully use their resources to isolate and correct the problem. Such resources include the algorithm, a program listing, the integrated Visual C++ Debugger, reference manuals, this book, and the rich on-line Help files.

Logic and runtime errors are usually the result of a serious flaw in your program. They will not go away and cannot be corrected by blindly making changes to your program. One good way to locate errors is to have your program print out preliminary results as well as messages that tell when a particular part of the process begins and ends execution.

Four Program Error Categories

There are basically four categories of errors an application may encounter:

- **Syntax or compile-time**   Errors that occur during compilation.
- **Linker**   Errors that occur during the linking process used to create the executable file.
- **Runtime**   Errors that occur while the program is executing.
- **Logical or Intent**   When an application runs without any errors, yet produces incorrect results.

Many of these errors occur during the transformation of the C++ programs you write into their executable form. Additionally, as you will see throughout this book, different combinations of errors may occur depending on if you are building a debug or release executable version.

Figure 3.2 represents the compiling and linking phases. First, the compiler translates your source code into object code format (an object file format is *almost* an executable file with only a few references missing). For a typical Windows application, many object code files need to be linked together. Of course, all of this is taken care of by your workspace or project file.

Syntax Errors

For first-time or seasoned 3:00 A.M. programmers, the most common type of error is the syntax error, in which a program contains a coded statement that violates one of the grammar or syntax rules of C/C++. These types of errors are automatically detected when the program is compiled.

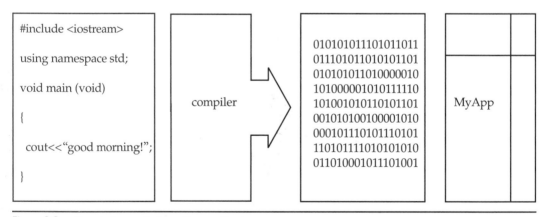

Figure 3.2   Translation cycle for a C++ application

For example, the following output statement was incorrectly entered as the following:

```
cout << "String-literal output
     << "that exceeds one line";
```

with the following associated fatal error:

```
-------------------Configuration: syntax - Win32 Debug-------------------
Compiling...
syntax.cpp
c:\debuggingbook\chp03\syntax.cpp(7) : error C2001: newline in constant
Error executing cl.exe.

syntax.obj - 1 error(s), 0 warning(s)
```

Beginners and rushed pros share errors of this nature. Of course, the fix is to close the string literal in the first line with a double quotation mark:

```
cout << "String-literal output"
     << "that exceeds one line";
```

Although most programmers, beginning or otherwise, are upset by syntax errors, they are actually the easiest errors to deal with. Correcting a syntax error is simply a matter of finding the point at which the program violates a C/C++ grammar rule and correcting the mistake. With experience, programmers gain familiarity with the grammar rules of the programming language, decreasing the frequency of this type of error. Even when syntax errors do occur, they are more easily corrected.

As the C/C++ compilers translate your source code into an executable program that can be run on the computer, the compiler attempts to locate and report as many syntax errors as possible and also warns of potential problems that are legal but might cause errors later. The Visual C++ compiler is capable of reporting declared variables that are never used and the use of a variable before it has been initialized, and the compiler is even capable of telling you when you have generated a logic flow that would prohibit code segments from ever executing—these are flagged as "unreachable code."

Linker Errors

Another source for program errors occurs when a compiled program is linked to the libraries it uses. A common example occurs in programs on Unix systems that use the square root function sqrt(), whose definition is stored in the math library. This function is declared in the file <math.h> (for nonstandard applications) or <cmath> (for using namespace standard applications) and requires the #include <[math.h|cmath]> preprocessor statement for the program to compile correctly.

However, such a program will still not link correctly because the standard Unix linker does not automatically search the math library, but instead must be instructed to do so using the –lm switch. Correcting linking errors often requires more knowledge about the computing system than most beginning programmers have.

More often than not, with your source code attempting to interface with hundreds of Microsoft-supplied object definitions, the compiler will simply pick up on your mIsScAsing a given identifier's name or generating a message that looks like the following linker error message:

```
-------------------Configuration: syntax - Win32 Debug-------------------
Compiling...
syntax.cpp
Linking...
LIBCD.lib(crt0.obj) : error LNK2001: unresolved external symbol _main
Debug/syntax.exe : fatal error LNK1120: 1 unresolved externals
Error executing link.exe.

syntax.exe - 2 error(s), 0 warning(s)
```

when you embarrassingly omit the function **main**()! Notice that the identifier *main* in the debug message has a prepended underscore _, as in _*main*. That underscore actually tells you something about when the error occurred. A careful examination of the preceding debug message shows that the program *did* actually compile; it just did *not* link.

Beginning programmers seeing an error message of this nature typically respond with a statement like: "Gee, I've searched all through my code, and nowhere do I use the identifier _*main*!" What they fail to understand is what experienced programmers know to be the linker is reporting its inability to find a match with a mangled function name (sometimes called its *signature*) and a correspondingly defined library routine.

Of course, in this example, the debug-diagnosed problem of omitting main() altogether is trite. However, in a program with thousands of lines of code and hundreds of user-defined identifiers, along with the use of compiler-defined macros and labels, linker messages of this type can initially throw any programmer for a curve.

Runtime Errors

Program execution may begin after all compile-time errors have been removed and the linker has created an executable program. But errors may still occur while the program is executing. Such runtime errors may cause the program to terminate abnormally (before it should have) because an event occurs that the computer cannot handle.

Of course, even a syntax and linker error-free build does not catch an incorrect arithmetic expression that performs a divide-by-zero, takes a square root of a negative number, or attempts to input invalid numeric data. Runtime errors are not detected until execution of the program begins, which is where the error category gets its namesake. So, for example, the following program executes properly until the user enters a value of 0 for *iNumberOfStudents*, generating a runtime zero-divide exception:

```
#include <iostream>

using namespace std;

void main ( void )
{
  int    iNumberOfStudents;
  float  fClassTestTotal;

  cout >>
          "Enter the class test total: ";
  cin  >>  iNumberOfStudents;

  cout << "The Test Average is: "
       <<  (fClassTestTotal \ iNumberOfStudents) << endl;
```

Runtime errors include the following:

- Hardware-detected errors such as division by zero, arithmetic overflow, memory violations, and device errors
- System errors such as failure of a file operation or a full message queue
- Logical errors such as an out-of-bounds array index or removing an element from an empty queue
- Exceptions or application-specific errors such as an invalid input format

Exceptions occur infrequently during execution, but a robust system must be prepared to deal with them. The worst response is to simply continue execution with no notification that the results produced are invalid. However, immediate termination of an application under such circumstances complicates implementation of the language and is not a proper response for a production system that may need to deallocate system resources or restore the state of files.

In addition, some indication of the nature of the error should be provided. In many cases, such as application-specific exceptions, it may be possible to limit the effect of the problem and proceed with execution—that is, the program can recover from the error and continue.

Finding such errors is easiest using a symbolic debugger. The Visual C++ Debugger allows you to trace through the execution of the program one statement at a time until the statement generating the error is encountered. Once the errors have been identified, they must be corrected by replacing the incorrect statements with correct ones, and the modified program must be recompiled, relinked, and executed again.

Oftentimes, the subprogram that detects an exception is not the one that has the information necessary to deal with it. For example, if a stack function signals a stack underflow because the caller popped an empty stack, then it is more appropriate for the user of the object, than the designer of the stack module, to specify the action to be taken. Similarly, the module that detects an invalid input may not be the same module that communicates with the user. In addition, the subprogram that can detect the error condition might be called by many other subprograms in the system (like the stack pop function) and may have been written and compiled separately.

Fortunately, many of C/C++'s operations return error codes upon failure. Each invocation of such an operation becomes a conditional statement that tests for a potential error condition and specifies the action to be taken if an error occurs. To propagate the error notification, each subprogram must pass that information back to its caller and, ultimately, to the subprogram that can handle the error condition.

Note, however, that this approach tightly binds those subprograms and is inconvenient if subprograms must detect, propagate, or handle more than one exception. It also clutters the logic of all the intervening subprograms, especially since the error information and its propagation is irrelevant to the purpose of those subprograms. In addition, there is no guarantee that the caller of a function that may signal an error will check for the error condition.

Logical Errors

Of the four error categories, logical errors are the most difficult to find because they stem from mistakes in reasoning about the solution to the problem. Matters are made worse by the fact that compilers do not produce error messages for logical errors; they simply produce incorrect results or even break the application. This necessitates testing the execution of the program with various sets of test data. It is only by thoroughly testing a program with a wide variety of data values that you can have any confidence that the program does not contain a logical error.

Once again, the easiest way to locate a logical error is with a symbolic debugger tracing the execution of each program statement. Debuggers allow you to display the value of a given variable or expression at any point during the execution. The correct values can be compared with the computed values, and when a mismatch is found, the source of the logical error has been located.

Another approach to dealing with logical errors involves the insertion of output statements at key points throughout the program to display the values of the variables involved in the computation of the incorrect results. By tracing through the execution by hand, a mismatch between the output values and the predicted values can be used to find the source of the error.

Locating logical errors takes a great deal of patience. They are most easily avoided by devoting careful attention to the first three stages of the software life cycle: problem analysis and specification, design, and coding.

Even when a process has been automated and delivered to the customer in working order as per the perceptions of the developers, there may still be errors. There have been many instances of software working, but not doing what it was supposed to do. This is a failure to meet the problem specifications.

A related error occurs when the requester of a program specifies the problem incorrectly. This could be the case when the requester isn't sure what he or she wants. A trivial or critical omission in the specification may occur, the request may not be written clearly, or—as is often the case—the requester may change his or her mind after program development has begun.

Error Watch *If you think of a C/C++ statement as being equivalent to an English language sentence, then data objects are the nouns in a sentence, and data processing statements are the verbs. When attempting to debug an application, look for the nouns and verbs within a problem statement: they often provide clues to the required output, input, and processing. The nouns suggest output and input, while the verbs relate to processing steps.*

Looking Up Error Messages

When you compile and link your program in Visual C++, the build process automatically opens the Output window, displaying specific information about the build success, including any warning and error messages. The Output window has two ways of helping you find and fix the causes of error and warning messages by auto-tracking to the line of code where the message is generated and hot-linking you to a context-sensitive help topic providing additional information about the message.

To see the code statement that generated a specific diagnostic message, you simply double-click the associated diagnostic message in the Output window. The appropriate source file opens, and a pointer shows the line that generates the diagnostic message.

To get help on an error message, you first click the mouse pointer on the error message number (for example, C2001; see Figure 3.3) in the Output window, followed by pressing the F1 key. The topic corresponding to the selected error number is opened in the Help window.

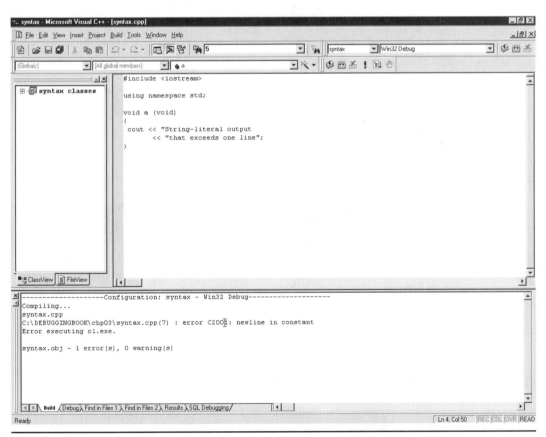

Figure 3.3   Setting up the Debugger to auto-track an error number (C2001)

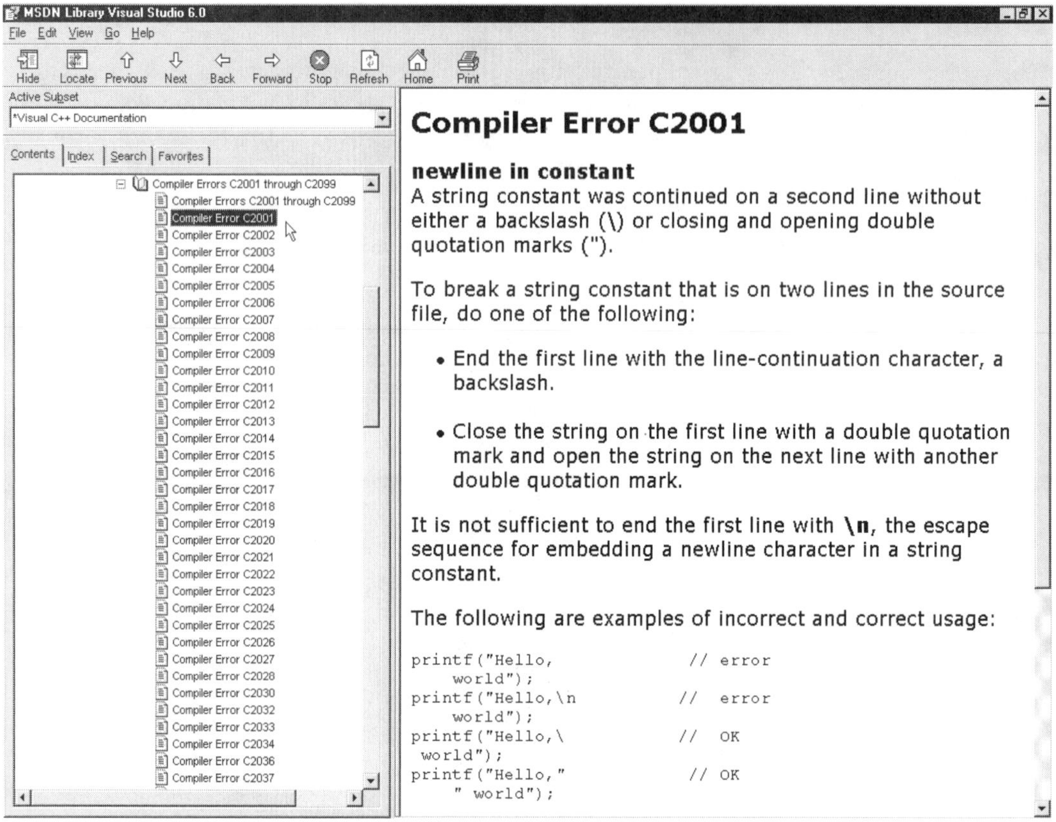

Figure 3.4   Results of pressing F1 after selecting the C2001 error

Figure 3.3 demonstrates how this is done with error C2001. Figure 3.4 displays the corresponding help file. Oftentimes, these help files explain either the missing syntax or logical statement error that enables you to repair the offending statement.

As Visual C++ has evolved, these help files have grown to frequently include coded example statements demonstrating how the error may be generated.

Preventative Maintenance

Most software engineers are aware that it is a rare and joyous occasion when a coded program actually runs the first time without any errors. Of course, good problem definition and planning will avoid many program mistakes, or bugs. However, a few bugs always manage to go undetected, regardless of how much planning you do. Getting rid of the program bugs is often the most time-consuming job in the whole programming process. Industrial statistics show that over 50 percent of a programmer's time is often spent on program debugging!

Desk-Checks! What Are They?

Depending on your years of programming experience, you may remember back to the time when all programs were written for and debugged on multimillion-dollar mainframe computers. These brontosaurus multi-building behemoths typically performed so many corporate-wide vital tasks that a programmer was allowed one compile/run cycle a day!

Now if, as you read this, you stressfully remember the "good" old days, you greatly appreciate today's development environments. However, if the thought of one compile/run cycle a day scares the living daylights out of you because you could never imagine such a nightmare, you need to seriously stop and ponder this scenario. Why? It's because that archaic compile/run restriction *made* many a programmer today a much better programmer.

If a software engineer's goal is to produce a correct, efficient, modular, maintainable, robust algorithm, *on time*, there is only one approach. That approach uses all of the design principles taught in a good Language-Independent Design course. When a programmer has had only one shot at the machine a day, you better believe he or she didn't attempt a compile/run without being firmly convinced the algorithm would fly. Desk-checks and walks through the code were *mandatory*, or else the programmer didn't keep his or her job.

The rule of thumb, then, and one that should still exist, is to do a desk-check of an algorithm. Desk-checking a program is similar to proofreading a letter or manuscript. The idea is to trace through the program mentally to make sure that the program logic is workable. You must consider various input possibilities and write down any results generated during program execution. In particular, try to determine what the program will do with unusual data by considering input possibilities that *shouldn't* happen. Always keep Murphy's Law in mind when desk-checking a program: If a given condition can't or shouldn't happen, it will!

One simple example involves a program requiring the user to enter a value whose square root must be found. Of course, the user shouldn't enter a negative value because the square root of a negative number is imaginary. However, what will the program do if this situation occurs? Another possibility that should always be considered is an input of zero, especially when used as part of an arithmetic operation, particularly division.

Human nature seems to propel a programmer to the keyboard when solving a problem, tempting the programmer to skip the desk-checking phase. Somehow, this physical action soothes the mind into thinking real progress is being made. However, as you gain experience, you soon will realize the time-saving advantage of desk-checking.

Designed in Exception Handling

Error handling is an essential part of programming, so it is appropriate that it is reflected by a language construct. The ANSI C++ Committee recognized that exceptions are semantically different from loop exits and other control structures, so they recommended a special mechanism for handling these situations in the language. C++ provides the following exception-handling constructs for:

- Defining exceptions
- Flagging the occurrence of an exception
- Defining handlers for each exception category

In actual use, a subprogram or code block can specify an exception handler that will be invoked when a particular error condition occurs in any subprograms it calls, or subprograms indirectly called. It can also specify different handlers for different types of exceptions. The C++ translator must implement the mechanism for transferring control from a signaler to a handler.

Unlike the use of error return codes, the programmer does not have to specify error handling separately for each operation, or for each subprogram in a sequence of invocations. In addition, if no subprogram in the sequence of invocations defines a handler for an exception that occurs, the program is terminated.

Exception handlers are intended to perform any cleanup of the program state necessary before processing or terminating the program. This feature allows the programmer to separate application logic from error-handling code, making the design and implementation of each logical code segment clearer.

"Give 'em a Hand"

You've seen the signs "Give 'em a Hand" every time you approach a road construction site. What's the idea behind the message? Slow down; watch out for the maintenance crew; they're out here trying to make your life better. Documentation to a programmer who is not the author of the code is similar to this simple message.

This chapter has attempted to categorize errors and recommend how to detect them, and it has also suggested ways to avoid them altogether. However, real-world programmers frequently *maintain existing* algorithms. This means their first task is to "get onboard" with the logic behind the code they are to update, port, and/or repair. Oftentimes, good documentation is the difference between a programmer being able to understand an application quickly or not.

This final step in the programmer's algorithm is frequently overlooked, but it is probably one of *the* more important steps, especially in commercial programming. Documentation is easy if you have done a good job of defining the problem, planning the solution, coding, testing, and debugging the program. The final program documentation is simply the recorded result of these individual steps. At a minimum, good documentation should include the following:

- A narrative description of the problem definition, which includes the type of input, output, and processing employed by the program.
- Any design restrictions and assumptions about the target architecture, memory restrictions, data source(s), precision(s), and output formats and devices.

- The algorithm.

- A source code listing that includes a clear commenting scheme (see Chapter 1). Commenting within the program is an important part of the overall documentation process. Each program should include comments at the beginning to explain what it does, any special algorithms that are employed, and a summary of the problem definition. In addition, the name of the programmer and the date the program was written and last modified should be included.

- Examples of both the expected input and output generated.

- Information on testing and debugging results.

- User's manual.

Once again, it is the problem statement (see Figure 3.1) that determines an algorithm's design goals, defining a program's data structures, efficiency, modularity, code style, and need for no, minor, or detailed documentation.

Microsoft Visual C++ Help

A quick trip to your local Barnes and Nobel bookstore under the Programming Languages reference section for Microsoft Visual C++ will quickly prove the following point: today's compiler documentation can fill an entire bookshelf. From a weight, cost-of-duplication, and portability viewpoint, the good news is that Microsoft has bundled all of this information into the MSDN CD Library (Microsoft Developer Network).

Figure 3.5 shows the MSDN Library's Contents tab set to track Visual C++'s definitions for C++ keywords, operators, and standard data types. This can be your first stop for figuring out the solution to a compiler syntax warning or error message.

Figure 3.6 shows the MSDN Library's Index tab set at the beginning of several nested topics detailing the C++ language's syntax. Unlike Figure 3.5, which shows you how to learn the fundamentals of C++'s keywords and operators, Figure 3.6 shows you how to obtain syntax help for expressions, statements, classes, and Microsoft-specific C++ language extensions.

They say, "Wisdom comes at the school of hard knocks." Experienced programmers know that coding is the least important phase of a problem solution. It is correct problem definition, analysis, and logic design combined with extensive desk-checks and walk-throughs that produce *on-time* robust applications.

If you imagine that you had only three tries at the compiler to get your application up and running—the first, to catch simple syntax errors; the second, to test the logic; and the third, run your perfected product—how would you approach your design phase? Fortunately, none of us has to face this scenario; yet it does switch the focus from quick-coding to robust precoding analysis and design! You can do it the hard way or the easy way.

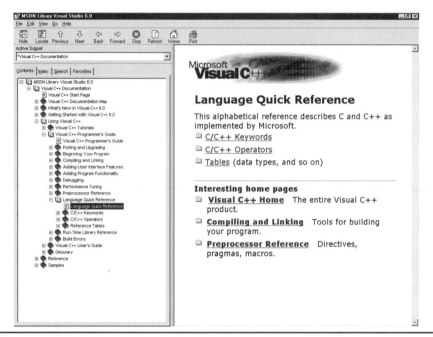

Figure 3.5 Using the Contents tab to locate the Language Quick Reference

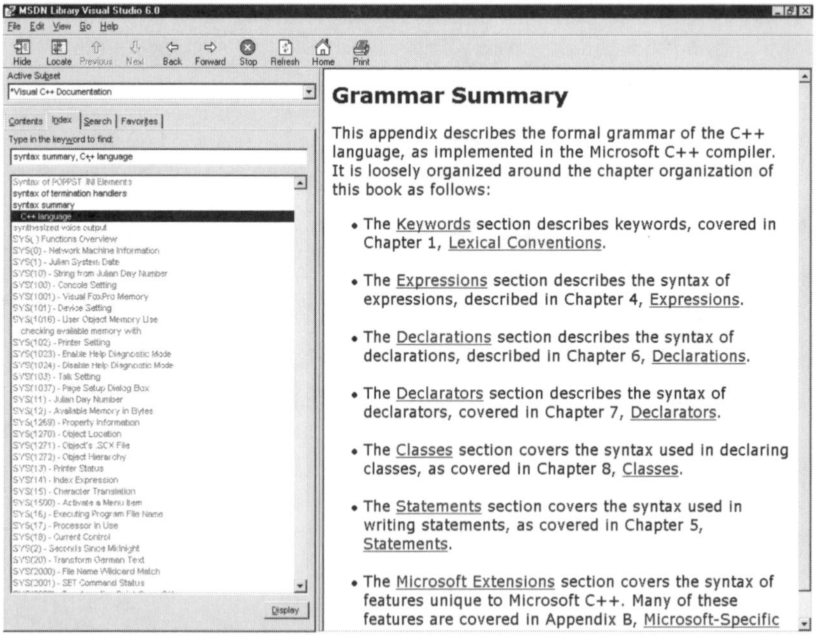

Figure 3.6 Using the MSDN Index tab to locate C++ language Grammar Summary

Conclusion

In this chapter, you learned about the four major categories involved in generating program bugs. You also learned that Visual C++ can detail any specific error message by tracking its error number into the help files. You also learned, or were reminded, that there is no shortcut around a good design followed by a "desk-check!"

In the next chapter, you are introduced to the most fundamental Debugger features, ones that you will use daily. The information presented in Chapter 3 alone can easily save you from 25 to 50 percent in time-savings while debugging an application.

CHAPTER 4

Debugger Essentials

The Microsoft Visual Studio C++ development environment provides a variety of tools that enable you to quickly and efficiently track down errors in your source code and program components. The Debugger's visual interface includes unique menus, windows, dialog boxes, and spreadsheet fields. You can even access Window's useful drag-and-drop functionality for transferring debug information with other Debugger components.

This chapter describes the most frequently used menus, windows, dialog boxes, and spreadsheet fields available from within the Visual C++ Debugger. The chapter also describes customization options available to the programmer for fine-tuning the Debugger's tools.

Error Watch   *Make certain you configure the Debugger's options before starting any debug cycles. In many cases, overlooking this most critical setup phase leads to unnecessary frustration when debugging because the Debugger has not been customized to provide application-specific debug output.*

While most programmers initially prefer to interact with an application via mouse clicks, on many occasions, just knowing a few "hot-key" combinations will save you the time of having to reactivate an inactive window, along with having to reposition the cursor within a window *before* a specific Debugger option is accessible.

In this chapter, you are first shown how to select a Debugger option with drop-down menu/mouse interaction, immediately followed by any available hot-key combinations. For ease of reference, the chapter closes with a brief hot-key summary table that you can quickly refer back to. Many of the techniques discussed in this chapter, plus several others, are used in examples throughout the remaining chapters.

Making Certain the Debugger Is Available

Before you can run the Visual C++ Debugger, you need to build a debug version of your program. This version causes the compiler to insert additional symbolic debugging information into the object files. Debug builds are the default mode in Visual C++, but if you have previously performed a release build, you will need to select the debug target.

Before you select the target build type, you need to make certain that you have set the active project (only necessary if there is more than one project open). To do so, you click on the Visual C++ Project menu and choose the Set Active Project option (see Figure 4.1). If you have more than one

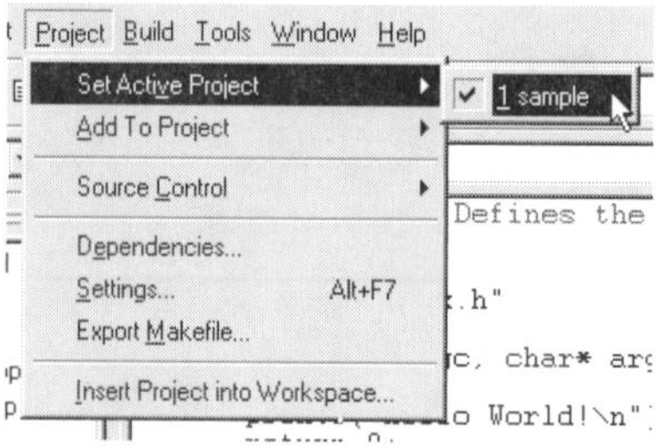

Figure 4.1   Setting the active project

project open, make certain you click on the one you want to build. In this example, there is only one "sample."

Figure 4.2 shows the Build toolbar with the two target types available in the drop-down list. Single-click on the Win32 Debug option. From left to right on the Build toolbar, your options include the Active Project drop-down list (in Figure 4.2, sample is selected), the build version drop-down-list (Win32 Debug is selected in Figure 4.2), followed by the Compile, Build, Stop Build, Execute, Go, and Insert/Remove Breakpoint icons. The Build toolbar buttons are described in the sections that follow.

Note | *If you do not see the Build toolbar, simply place the mouse anywhere on the Visual C++ menus (at the top of the screen), right-click the mouse once, and select the Build checkbox.*

Design Tip | *Visual C++ allows a workspace to encapsulate multiple projects. Make certain you have selected the appropriate active project in order to generate all necessary debug information.*

Starting the Debugger

The Debugger's options are not available until you have a Visual C++ workspace, project, or application opened.

24x7

You cannot use the Debugger on C/C++ support files alone—for example, in a project containing only initial header files. There must be an executable source file (for example, somesource.c or somesource.cpp) that has been compiled and built with zero errors.

Assuming you have a zero-error compile of a C/C++ program, you start the Debugger by selecting an option from the main Visual C++ Build menu, shown in Figure 4.3. (Note that you *can* run the Debugger with warning messages, just *not* error messages.)

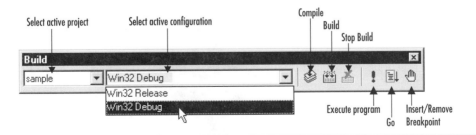

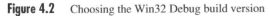

Figure 4.2 Choosing the Win32 Debug build version

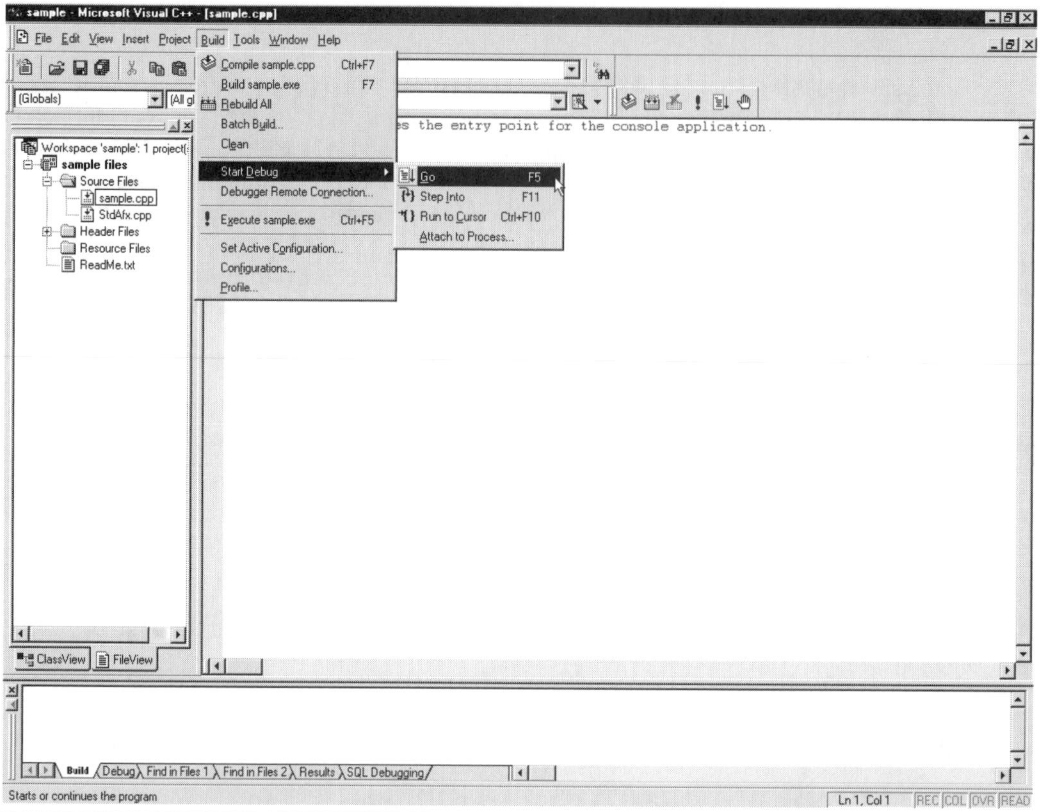

Figure 4.3   Starting the Debugger from the Build menu option

By clicking on the Build | Start Debug option, you open up a list of four options, shown in Figure 4.4.

Selecting any one of the options causes Visual C++ to change the main Build menu option to the Debug menu, which appears in the menu bar while the Debugger is running (even if it is stopped at a breakpoint).

From the main Debug menu, you can control program execution and access the QuickWatch window. When the Debugger is not running, the Debug menu is replaced by the Build menu. Table 4.1 describes each Start Debug option along with its associated hot-key combination.

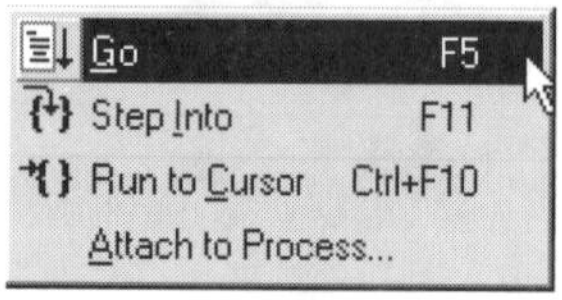

Figure 4.4   Build | Start Debug options menu

Start Debug Option	Action	Hot-Key
Go	Starts the Debugger and/or executes your program, full-speed, until a breakpoint or the end of the program is reached, or until the application pauses for user input. Similar to the Go button on the toolbar.	F5
Step Into	Starts the Debugger and/or single-steps through your source file line by line. When the statement being traced involves a function or method call, Step Into enters the called subroutine.	F11
Run to Cursor	Starts the Debugger and/or executes your program as far as the line that contains the insertion point. This option may be used as an alternative to setting a regular breakpoint at the insertion point.	CTRL+F10
Attach to Process	Attaches the Debugger to a process that is running. Then you can break into the process and perform debugging operations as usual. (This option is for advanced users and is discussed in later chapters.)	

Table 4.1   Start Debug Options

One other hot-key combination, F10, is not listed in this initial menu. F10 represents Step Over. By pressing F10, you can start the Debugger and/or execute your program line by line.

The Difference Between Step Into and Step Over

The difference between F10 and F11 is apparent only when the statement about to be executed, on the *next* press of F10 or F11, is a subroutine call (function or method). As the name *Step Over* implies, pressing F10 on a call statement instructs the Debugger to full-speed execute the *called* subroutine and stop on the code statement, below the call, in the calling routine.

On the other hand, when the *next* press of F10 or F11 will call a subroutine, F11 or Step Into, traces *into* the called subroutine (function or method), stopping the Debugger inside the called subroutine.

24x7

You should use F10, not F11 (Step Into), to Step Over standard C/C++ subroutines to avoid triggering the Debugger to debug compiler-supplied code.

Go

At times, selecting either F10 (Step Over) or F11 (Step Into) is too time consuming. For example, with many well-written programs reusing previously written and debugged algorithms, single-stepping through old news wastes your time. Under these circumstances, select the Go (F5) option.

Go executes your program *full-speed* up to the first breakpoint (discussed later in this chapter) or the next breakpoint encountered when repeatedly pressing F5, or to the end of your program.

> **Design Tip**   *One of the best uses for the Go option involves efficiently debugging loops. Setting a breakpoint within the loop-body and repeatedly pressing F5 instructs the Debugger to full-speed execute the loop-body. Use this approach when testing for correct loop iterations.*

Run to Cursor

The Run to Cursor option (CTRL+F10) is similar to the Go command, except that Run to Cursor does not require you to have previously defined a breakpoint (discussed later in this chapter). To use Run to Cursor, you simply move the I-beam cursor onto the source file statement where you want to begin debugging the algorithm and press CTRL+F10.

Understanding the Debugger Toolbar Icons

Once you start debugging your program, using any of the methods described in the previous section, you will see the Debugger toolbar by default. The Debugger toolbar is shown in Figure 4.5.

Figure 4.5 shows the Debugger toolbar over the Workspace pane. If you do not like its default location, simply click on the toolbar and drag it to any preferred position. Of course, you can drag the toolbar into the main menu location and dock the icons.

Figure 4.6 shows an exploded view of the Toolbar icons. The following discussion explains each icon, starting from the top-left icon in the first row and continuing from the lower-left icon on the second row to the right-most icon.

Restart

The Restart icon (CTRL+SHIFT+F5) tells Visual C++ that you want to begin debugging your program from the beginning, instead of from the current trace location.

Stop Debugging

If at any point during your debug phase, you realize that your project or workspace need updates, you cannot get back to the Build menu options until you first use Stop Debugging (SHIFT+F5) to terminate the Debugger.

Break Execution

You use the Break Execution button to halt the program's execution at the current point.

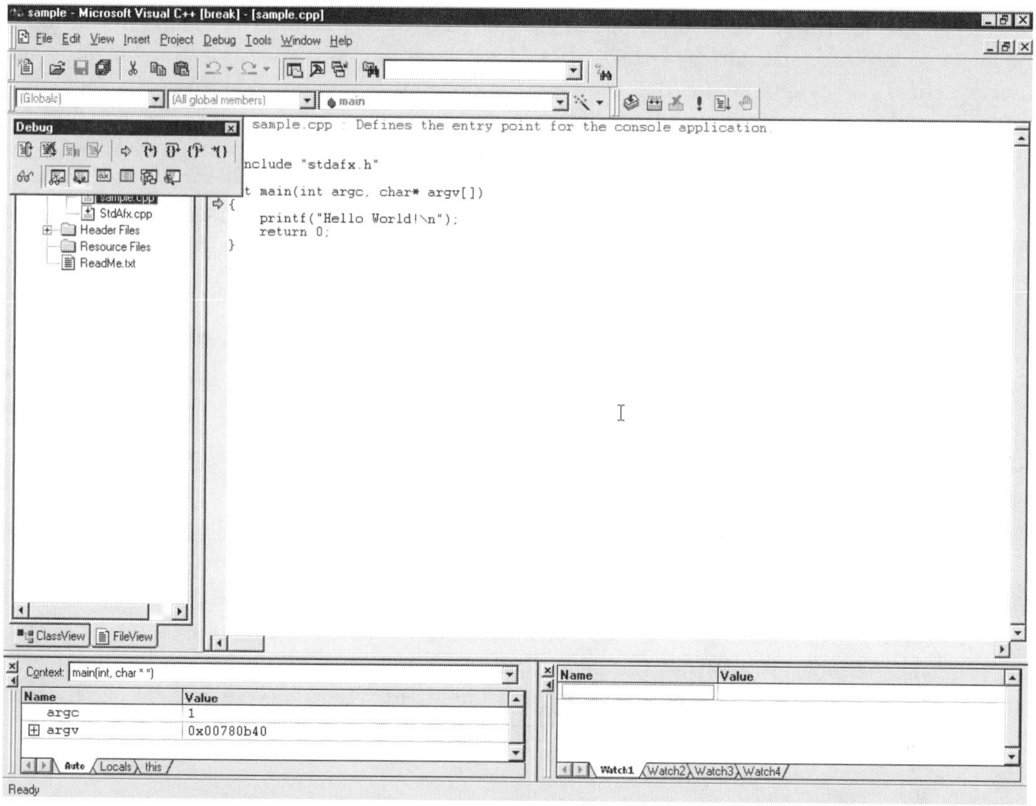

Figure 4.5 Initial Debugger toolbar

Apply Code Changes, Edit, and Continue

With Apply Code Changes (ALT+F10), which is a new feature in Visual C++ 6.0, you can make changes to your source code while the program is being debugged. You can apply code changes while the program is running or halted under the Debugger. To apply code changes to a program you are debugging, click Apply Code Changes on the Debug menu.

With Edit and Continue, you can also apply changes *automatically* when you select a Go or Step command for a program that is halted. You can turn off this automatic Edit and Continue, if you prefer. (If you turn the automatic feature off, you can still apply code changes manually using Apply Code Changes.)

Figure 4.6 Debug toolbar

You can enable/disable Automatic Edit and Continue by clicking on the Tools | Options menu and selecting the Debug tab. On the Debug tab, select or clear the Debug commands invoke Edit and Continue checkbox, as appropriate. Because Debug commands invoke Edit and Continue is a tools option rather than a project option, altering this setting affects all projects you work on. You do not need to rebuild your application after changing this setting. You can change the setting even while debugging.

The Program Database stores the information needed for the Edit and Continue code changes. When you create a new project, Visual C++ chooses the appropriate option (Program Database for Edit and Continue) in the Project Settings dialog box. If you change this option (in order to use C7 compatible debug information, for example), Edit and Continue is disabled.

If you want to turn Edit and Continue off for a specific project, you can. Select the Project | Settings menu option, followed by selecting the C/C++ tab and the General category. Next, select the Debug Info drop-down list and choose Program Database for Edit and Continue to enable or disable this option. Click on OK and rebuild the application.

Design Tip   *Do not enable Edit and Continue if you are debugging optimized code. Edit and Continue is incompatible with optimizations. The result is a compiler error.*

Types of Statements You Cannot Edit and Continue

Because of the internal mechanism used for Edit and Continue, there is a limit of 64 bytes on the total size of the new variables you can add to an active function. An active function is any function that is currently on the call stack. On the other hand, there is no limit for functions not currently on the call stack. The following list enumerates the types of code changes Edit and Continue cannot handle:

- Updating resource files
- Changing code in read-only files
- Changing optimized code using the optimizations /O1, /O2, /Og, /Ox, /Ob1, or /Ob2
- Modifying exception-handling blocks
- Changing data types, including class, structure, union, or enumeration definitions
- Adding new data types
- Eliminating of functions or changes to function prototypes
- Changing global or static code
- Updating executables that are copied from another machine and not built locally

If you make one of these changes and then try to apply code changes, an error message appears in the Output window.

Show Next Statement

This option (ALT+NUM*) shows the next statement in your program code. If your source code is not available, Show Next Statement displays the statement within the Disassembly window.

Step Into

When you choose Step Into (F11) and the statement being traced is a subroutine call (function or method), this option single-steps *into* the called subroutine.

Step Over

When you choose Step Over (F10) and the statement being traced is a subroutine call (function or method), this option single-steps *over* the called subroutine by executing the called subroutine full-speed. The Debugger stops on the next statement after the subroutine call.

Step Out

Step Out (SHIFT+F11) causes the Debugger to switch back to full-speed execution to the end of the called subroutine and stop on the instruction immediately following the call to the subroutine. You can use this command to quickly finish executing the current subroutine after determining that a bug is not present in the subroutine.

Run to Cursor

The Run to Cursor option (CTRL+F10) is similar to the Go command, except that Run to Cursor does not require you to have previously defined a breakpoint (discussed later in this chapter). To use Run to Cursor, you simply move the I-beam cursor onto the source file statement where you want to begin debugging the algorithm and press CTRL+F10!

QuickWatch

QuickWatch (SHIFT+F9) displays the QuickWatch window, where you can evaluate expressions.

Design Tip *You can now display MMX registers in the Watch and QuickWatch windows using the symbols MM0–MM7. MMX registers are 64-bit integer registers and will be displayed on all x86 machines, whether or not they support the MMX instructions.*

Watch

The Watch icon opens up the Watch window containing the application's variables by name and current value, along with any selected expressions.

Variables

The Variables button opens up the Variables window containing information about the variables used in the current and previous statements and function return values (in the Auto tab), the variables local to the current function (in the Locals tab), and the object pointed to by this (in the This tab).

Registers

The Registers button opens up the Debugger's Register window showing the microprocessor's general purpose and CPU status registers.

Memory

You use the Memory button to open up the Memory window displaying the application's current memory contents.

Call Stack

When you click on the Call Stack button, the Debugger opens up the Call Stack window listing the names of all called subroutines that have not yet returned.

Disassembly

The Disassembly icon opens up a window containing the assembly language code derived from disassembly of the compiled program.

Debugger Toolbar Menu Equivalents

Of course, should you choose to close the Debugger toolbar, all of the same Debugger options are available through the main Debug menu (see Figure 4.7). Remember that the Visual C++ main Build menu option changes its title to Debug when the Debugger is active.

Additional Debug Menu Options

Actually, if you look closely at Figure 4.7, you'll notice a few additional debug options not immediately available on the Debug toolbar. These are Step Into Specific Function (which is grayed-out in Figure 4.7), Exceptions, Threads, and Modules.

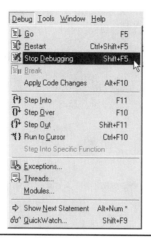

Figure 4.7   Debug menu equivalents to Debug toolbar icons

Step Into Specific Function

The Step Into Specific Function option single-steps through instructions in the program and enters the specified function call. This works for any number of nesting levels of functions.

Exceptions

The Exceptions option opens the Exceptions dialog box, displaying the list of exceptions you want to handle. You can modify, delete, or add exceptions as needed. The list is saved in a file with a .dsw file extension and persists with the project.

Threads

The Threads menu option displays the Threads dialog boxes. The Threads dialog box lets you suspend, resume, or set focus to program threads.

Modules

The Modules window lists all the Dynamic Link Libraries (DLLs) loaded by your application. The list is sorted by the order in which they are loaded. By clicking on the buttons at the top of the list, you can order the list by name, memory address, path, or order loaded.

Local Menu Debugger Options

Figure 4.8 displays the list of available Debugger options you can get to from within the Edit window while the Debugger is active. You activate the pop-up menu by right-clicking the mouse button once within the Visual Studio C++ Edit window. The following discussion covers only those menu selections not previously discussed in this chapter.

List Members

The List Members option displays a drop-down listbox containing the properties and methods available for a selected object. As you type an object name using the *object.member* syntax, the list will appear after you type the period member operator. You can select a member by typing the first letter or letters of the member name until the desired member is highlighted. You can also navigate through the list using the UP-ARROW, DOWN-ARROW, PAGEUP, PAGEDOWN, CTRL+PAGEUP, or CTRL+PAGEDOWN keys.

Type Info

The Type Info option, when selected, causes the Visual Studio to display the syntax for a variable, function, or method selected in the Edit window.

Figure 4.8   Debugger options available from the Edit window

Parameter Information

You can quickly access information about the parameters of a function or statement by clicking on the Parameter Info option. If you have a function or statement that contains function calls as its parameters, choosing Parameter Info provides information about the first function. Quick Info provides information about each embedded function. While the Parameter Info window is visible, typing a comma (,) causes the next parameter to be displayed in bold. To cancel Parameter Info, you need to do the following:

- Click anywhere in the Edit window
- Enter all of the required parameters
- End the function without using all of the optional parameters
- Press ESC

Complete Word

The Complete Word option fills in the rest of the word you are typing once you have entered enough characters for the editor to identify the word you want.

Go To Definition/Reference

Go To Definition or Go To Reference quickly displays the definition or reference of a symbol. The development environment opens the source file containing the first definition or reference and highlights the symbol. To see the next definition or reference, click the Next Definition/Reference button on the toolbar.

Go To Disassembly

See the section "Disassembly," earlier in this chapter.

Insert/Remove Breakpoint

In this chapter's previous discussion of the Go (F5) Debugger command, you learned that Go full-speed executes your program to a breakpoint or to the end of your application, if no breakpoint exists. The Insert/Remove Breakpoint option is a toggle menu item that can turn a breakpoint on or off. To set a breakpoint, you simply place the cursor on the line of code in the Edit window where you want the Debugger to stop and select this option.

Debugger Windows

Depending on the type of Windows application you are debugging and your personal preferences, Visual C++ provides a Debugger window specifically for the task at hand. When you are debugging, you can access these windows using the View menu. Table 4.2 lists the Debugger windows and describes the information they display.

When a window is in floating mode, you can resize or minimize the window to increase the visibility of other windows. You can copy information from any Debugger window.

Design Tip *You can print information only from the Output window.*

By using the Debug tab in the Options dialog box, you can customize the formatting and other options for these windows (accessed from the Tools menu).

Trace Window

The Edit window changes into the Trace window whenever you activate the Debugger. The Trace window allows you to see your lines of code as they are being executed.

Tracing Object Code

When debugging object-oriented source code, the Trace window is associated with the object displayed in the Object list. The Object list contains all objects contained in the highest-level parent container of the object whose code is currently executing.

Debugger Window	Display
Output	The Output window displays information about the build process, including any compiler, linker, or build-tool errors, as well as output from the OutputDebugString function or the afxDump class library, thread termination codes, loading symbols notifications, and first-chance exception notifications.
Watch	The Watch window outputs the names and values of variables and expressions.
Variables	The Variables window outputs information about variables used in the current and previous statements and function return values (in the Auto tab), the variables local to the current function (in the Locals tab), and the object pointed to by this (in the This tab).
Registers	The Registers window displays the current contents of the general purpose and CPU status registers.
Memory	The Memory window displays the current memory contents.
Call Stack	The Call Stack window shows a stack of all function calls that have not returned.
Disassembly	The Disassembly window shows the assembly-language code derived from disassembly of the compiled program.

Table 4.2 Standard Visual C++ Debugger Windows

Tracing Procedure-Oriented Code

When tracing functions or methods, the code in the Trace window is associated with the method or event displayed in the Procedure list. The Procedure list contains all methods of the object in the Object list that have code associated with them.

Watch Window

The Watch window displays expressions and their current values, and sets breakpoints on an expression. Within the Watch window, you can type expressions to add them to the grid of active watch expressions, which is situated below the Watch window.

The Name category displays the names of the current watch expressions, followed by the Value column showing the values of the current watch expressions. You can use the Type category to view the characters that represent the data types of the current watch expressions. In addition, the Watch window allows you to select expressions, delete them, or add breakpoints to them.

View Menu, Debugger Window

You can activate a hidden or collapsed Visual C++ Debugger window by first clicking on the main View, or the View | Debug Windows menu option, followed by one of the window categories discussed in the sections that follow.

Workspace

The Workspace pane, or window, shows the current project's source files, class objects, and resources.

Error Watch *If you have collapsed this pane by placing your mouse on the right edge of the pane and moving it against the left-most edge, this menu command will not redisplay the window. You will have to locate the collapsed pane dividing line manually and re-expand the window.*

Output

This option activates the Debug Output window. Note that if the windows are docked, there is no visual indication that they have been activated, although associated menu items are enabled or disabled.

Clear Output Window

This window deletes all text displayed in the Debug Output window (which is only active in the Output window shortcut menu—activated with a right-mouse click within the Output window).

Viewing Watch Variables as Different Data Types

In the following chapters, you will begin to use the Debugger options described in the preceding sections. However, before looking at the output from the various Debugger windows, you should familiarize yourself with the formatting symbols listed in Table 4.3.

These symbols also allow you to change the display format of variables in the QuickWatch and Watch windows.

The Watch window allows you to change the interpretation of a variable's data type. To use a formatting symbol, you simply type the name of a variable, followed by a comma and the appropriate symbol. For example, if the hexNumber has a value of *0x0041*, and you want to see the value in character form, type hexNumber,c in the Name column on the tab of the Watch window. When you press ENTER, the character-format value appears:

```
hexNumber,c = 'A'
```

Table 4.4 lists the formatting symbols you can use in the Watch window to format the contents of memory locations.

You can also use the memory location formatting symbols on any statement you type that evaluates to a location (memory address). To display the value of a character array as a string, precede the array name with an ampersand (&) as in *&ArrayName*. You can also follow an expression with a formatting character as in *&ArrayName,x*.

Symbol	Format	Value	Representation
d,I	**signed** decimal integer	0xF000F061	-268373911
U	**unsigned** decimal integer	0x006	102
O	**unsigned** octal integer	0xF064	0170144
x,X	Hexadecimal integer	70148 (decimal)	0x000011204
l,h	**long** or **short** prefix for: d, i, u, o, x, X	00406040,hx	0x0c20
F	**signed** floating-point	5./2.	2.500000
E	**signed** scientific notation	5./2.	2.500000e+000
G	**signed** floating-point or **signed** scientific notation, whichever is shorter	5./2.	2.5
C	Single character	0x0066	'f'
S	String	0x0012fde8	"The String"
su	Unicode string		"The String"
St	Unicode string or ANSI string, depending on Unicode Strings setting		
Hr	**HRESULT** or Win32 error code	0x00000000L	S_OK
wc	Window class flag	0x00000040	WC_DEFAULTCHAR
wm	Windows message numbers	0x0010	WM_CLOSE

Table 4.3   Debugger Display Formatting Symbols

Symbol	Format
Ma	64 ASCII characters
M	16 bytes in hexadecimal, followed by 16 ASCII characters
Mb	16 bytes in hexadecimal, followed by 16 ASCII characters
Mw	8 words
Md	4 doublewords
Mq	4 quadwords
Mu	2-byte characters (Unicode)

Table 4.4   Memory Formatting Symbols

Finally, to monitor the value at a specific memory location or the value pointed to by a register, use the **BY**, **WO**, or **DW** operators described in the following list:

- **BY** returns the contents of the byte pointed to.
- **DW** returns the contents of the dword or doubleword pointed to.
- **WO** returns the contents of the word pointed to.

To use these operators, you simply follow the operator with the name of a variable, register, or constant as in *BY Achar*. When you do this, the Watch window displays the byte, word, or doubleword (dword) at the address contained in the variable.

You can also use the context operator { } to display the contents of any location. To display a Unicode string in the QuickWatch or Watch windows, use the **su** format specifier. To display data bytes with Unicode characters in the QuickWatch or Watch windows, use the **mu** format specifier.

Design Tip   *Formatting symbols work with arrays, structures, pointers, and objects as unexpanded variables only. If you expand the variable, the specified formatting affects all members. However, you cannot apply formatting symbols to individual members.*

Enabling Just-in-Time Debugging

One option available to you is Microsoft's Just-in-time debugging. With Just-in-time debugging, your application runs outside the Visual C++ development environment until an error occurs. When a program error is encountered, Just-in-time debugging automatically launches the Visual C++ Debugger. To enable Just-in-time debugging, follow these steps:

1. From the Tools menu, click Options.
2. Select the Debug tab.
3. Select the Just-in-time debugging checkbox.
4. Click OK.
5. From the Build menu, choose Build *myApp*.exe.

Note  *Windows NT programmers must have administrator privileges to enable Just-in-time debugging.*

The Debug Tab in the Options Window

The Debugger is very flexible in its output display formatting. While many options can be changed on the fly, sometimes a consistent output format is preferable. Figure 4.9 displays the Debug tab options available for predefining these formats. You can access the Debug tab by clicking the Tools menu and choosing Options. The options available on the Debug tab are discussed in the sections that follow.

Hexadecimal Display

This option displays all values in hexadecimal format and parses all user and dialog input in hexadecimal. When this option is checked, you can enter decimal values using the *0n* prefix, as in *0n123456789*.

Source Annotation

This option simultaneously displays your source code along with the assembly language translation.

Code Bytes

This option displays bytes associated with each assembly language instruction.

Symbols

The Symbols option displays symbolic names for addresses in the Disassembly window.

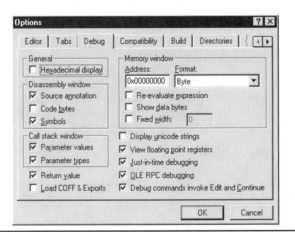

Figure 4.9   Debug tab

Parameter Values

The Parameter values option displays each value passed to each parameter in a subroutine call on the call stack.

Parameter Types

This option displays the type information for each parameter passed to a subroutine call on the call stack.

Return Value

This option displays subroutine return values in the Variables window.

Load COFF & Exports

This option enables the Debugger to load COFF-format debugging information or DLL exports when debugging information is not available.

Address

The Address option allows you to select the default starting address for the Memory Dump window.

Format

This option allows you to select from over 13 data type mappings, such as ASCII, Byte, Long, Real, and Int64, to the displayed Memory Dump window contents.

Re-evaluate Expression

This option dynamically relocates the Memory Dump window's contents. When this option is active and you have entered the name of a pointer variable into the Memory Dump window, the contents of the window will update every time the pointer variable's address-contents change. With this option disabled, the contents of the Memory Dump window will *not* change, even if the pointer variable's address-content *does* change.

Show Data Bytes

This option displays data in raw bytes along with the chosen format.

Fixed Width

The Fixed width option displays the Memory Dump window contents in a fixed-width format. The value you enter here works in conjunction with the format type selected.

Display Unicode Strings

This option displays Unicode-format strings. It's useful when debugging applications that input and output text data in multi-language formats.

View Floating Point Registers

This option displays floating-point registers in the Registers window.

Just-in-Time Debugging

This option enables the automatic invocation of the Visual C++ Debugger when encountering a runtime failure of an application not currently loaded into the Visual Studio development environment.

OLE RPC Debugging

The OLE (Object Linking and Embedding) RPC (Remote Procedure Calls) debugging option enables the debugging of remote procedure calls.

Debug Commands Invoke Edit and Continue

With this option enabled, many, but not all, code changes are automatically applied to your source code the next time you use a Debugger command, such as Go, Step Into, Step Over, or Run.

Keyboard Map

You can display the current keyboard shortcuts, including custom key settings and editor emulations by choosing the Visual C++ Help | Keyboard Map option shown in Figure 4.10.

The keyboard mappings for the Debugger options are shown in Figure 4.11.

The Keyboard Map option can come in handy, particularly when you want to use a Debugger capability that you cannot remember how to activate. With today's development environments having so many options and menus, it is easy to forget which menu, button, or dialog box has what you need. By bringing up the Help Keyboard window, you can quickly read the list of options. This alone is often enough to jog your memory as to where a Debugger option is located. Even better is finding a hot-key combination that does the same thing, short-circuiting the equivalent nested menu, dialog box, or calling sequence.

Figure 4.10 Selecting the Visual C++ Help | Keyboard Map option

Catego	Command	Keys	Description
Debug	ApplyCodeChanges	Alt+F10	Applies code changes made to C/C++ source files while debugging
Debug	DebugBreak		Stops program execution; breaks into the debugger
Debug	DebugDisableAllBreakpoints		Disables all breakpoints
Debug	DebugEnableBreakpoint	Ctrl+F9	Enables or disables a breakpoint
Debug	DebugExceptions		Edits debug actions taken when an exception occurs
Debug	DebugGo	F5	Starts or continues the program
Debug	DebugHexadecimalDisplay		Toggles between decimal and hexadecimal format
Debug	DebugMemoryNextFormat	Alt+F11	Switches the memory window to the next display format
Debug	DebugMemoryPrevFormat	Alt+Shift+F11	Switches the memory window to the previous display format
Debug	DebugModules		Shows modules currently loaded
Debug	DebugQuickWatch	Shift+F9	Performs immediate evaluation of variables and expressions
Debug	DebugRemoveAllBreakpoints	Ctrl+Shift+F9	Removes all breakpoints
Debug	DebugRestart	Ctrl+Shift+F5	Restarts the program
Debug	DebugRunToCursor	Ctrl+F10	Runs the program to the line containing the cursor
Debug	DebugSetNextStatement	Ctrl+Shift+F10	Sets the instruction pointer to the line containing the cursor
Debug	DebugShowNextStatement	Alt+Num *	Displays the source line for the instruction pointer
Debug	DebugStepInto	F11	Steps into the next statement
Debug	DebugStepIntoSpecificFunction		Steps into the selected function
Debug	DebugStepOut	Shift+F11	Steps out of the current function
Debug	DebugStepOver	F10	Steps over the next statement
Debug	DebugStepOverSource		Steps over the next source level statement
Debug	DebugStopDebugging	Shift+F5	Stops debugging the program
Debug	DebugThreads		Sets the debuggee's thread attributes
Debug	DebugToggleBreakpoint	F9	Inserts or removes a breakpoint
Debug	DebugToggleMixedMode	Ctrl+F11	Switches between the source view and the disassembly view for this instruction
Debug	UpdateImageToggle		Applies code changes made to C/C++ source files while debugging

Figure 4.11 Keyboard mappings for the Debugger options

Debugger Keyboard Shortcuts

Table 4.5 summarizes the most frequently used Debugger options along with their associated hot-key combinations.

Taking the time to familiarize yourself with this list of hot-key combinations will make using the Debugger a more efficient and enjoyable experience.

Conclusion

This chapter presents *the* most frequently used Debugger options. Watching a variable's contents while you execute an algorithm line-by-line is invaluable in instantaneously detecting any misbehaving code statement.

In the next chapter, you will learn about new bugs that can suddenly appear when a build version changes from debug to release. Ultimately, the chapter teaches you how to avoid such scenarios by explaining *how* the different build versions view your source code and *why* bugs suddenly appear as you switch build candidates.

Action	Keyboard
Resume	F5
Cancel	ESC
Step Into	F11
Step Over	F10
Step Out	SHIFT+F11
Run To Cursor	CTRL+F10
Trace Window	ALT+8
Watch Window	ALT+3
Locals Window	ALT+4
Call Stack Window	ALT+7
Debug Output Window	ALT+2
Toggle Breakpoint	F9
Clear Breakpoints	CTRL+SHIFT+F9
Breakpoints	CTRL+B
Open File	CTRL+O
Save Configuration	ALT+S
Exit Debugger	ALT+F4

Table 4.5   Debugger Hot-Key Combinations

CHAPTER 5

Debug Versus Release Candidates

This chapter finalizes your formal introduction to the Microsoft Visual Studio C++ Debugger. Chapters 2 ("Optimizing with the Compiler") and 4 ("Debugger Essentials") provide a high-level discussion of the various Debugger capabilities and how to access these options within the Visual Studio development environment. In this chapter, you will learn about additional code considerations for debug and release builds, along with the Visual C++ libraries that make it all happen. Some of these libraries become very important as you move on to dual-system, remote debugging. The chapter also explains the various intermediate files created by a debug version build.

Officially, Microsoft defines the debug version of an application as a version of a program built with symbolic debugging information, or with a debug library. A library version (for example, of the Microsoft Foundation Class library) includes diagnostic aids and performs various integrity checks to aid in debugging a program. Microsoft defines the release version as a compiled version of a program that does not include the debugging and diagnostic features included in a build compiled in debug mode. For example, a release version does not include the source code contained in ASSERT macros.

Default Debug Build Versus Release Build Settings

Whenever you begin a new Visual C++ project, both Win32 Debug and Win32 Release versions are automatically created with default options. Table 5.1 lists the initial default settings for each version.

When building a debug version, you can select several options without hindering the debug phase. For example you can change the default Debug Build options, such as outputting line numbers only, redirecting output, or generating a mapfile.

Changing Project Settings for a Debug Build

While you can override many of the default Debug Build settings, only certain options are considered safe. Table 5.2 lists the Debug Build options you can select without dramatically affecting the order or type of statement translation performed by the optimizer. You can change the project settings in the C/C++ tab of the Project Settings dialog (from the Settings command on the Project menu).

Changing the Debug Options

The following four steps describe how to change the Debugger's options:

1. Select the main Project menu and then click on Settings. You will see the Project Settings dialog box displayed.

Build Version	Default Compiler Settings
Win32 Debug	This option inserts complete symbolic debugging information in Microsoft format, without any optimizations. Enabling any optimization switches at this stage makes debugging more difficult.
Win32 Release	Does not include any symbolic debugging information. Source code is optimized for maximum speed.

Table 5.1   Default Debug and Release Versions Compiler Settings

Safe Debug Build Options	Causes Debug Build to...
Program Database for Edit and Continue (default)	Generates an additional output file called the program database (.pdb). This file contains your program's type information and symbolic debugging information.
Line Numbers Only	Modifies the translation of the .obj file or executable (.exe) file so that it contains only global and external symbol and line number information (does not contain any symbolic debugging information).
C7 Compatible	Produces an .obj file and an .exe file with both line numbers and full symbolic debugging information for use with the debugger.
None	No debugging information is generated.

Table 5.2   Safe Debug Build Options

2. Click on the C/C++ tab.

3. Select an option from the Debug info drop-down list.

4. Click on the OK button to accept the choices and close the Project Settings dialog box.

Changing the Format of Generated Debug Information

The following five steps detail how to configure Link for Microsoft Format (default), or COFF Format, or both:

1. From the Project menu, click Settings. You will see the Project Settings dialog box displayed.

2. Click on the Link tab.

3. Select the Debug option from within the Category drop-down list.

4. Choose Microsoft Format (default), COFF Format, or Both Formats.

5. Click on the OK button to accept the settings and close the Project Settings dialog box.

Generating a Mapfile

When you are debugging an application, especially when you need to do specific memory dumps, a mapfile may be helpful at times. A mapfile is simply a text file that contains the following information about the program being linked:

• The module name, or the base name, of the file

• A timestamp for the program header file

• A list of program groups, with each group's start address in the form **segment:offset**, along with the length, group name, and class

- A listing of public symbols, with each address in **segment:offset** form, including the symbol name, flat address, and .obj file where the symbol is defined
- The module entry point in **segment:offset** form

To turn on the mapfile Debug option, follow these steps:

1. From the Project menu, click Settings. You will see the Project Settings dialog box displayed.
2. Select the Link tab.
3. Choose the Debug option from the Category drop-down list.
4. Check the Generate mapfile checkbox.
5. Choose a name in the Mapfile name text box for the output file generated, or accept the default.
6. Click on the OK button to activate the settings and close the Project Settings dialog box.

Redirecting Debug Input and Output

Microsoft Visual C++ allows you to redirect any Win32 console application's file input or output locations. You select these options by completing the following steps:

1. Click on the Project menu and select the Settings option. You will see the Project Settings dialog box displayed.
2. Click on the Debug tab.
3. From the Program Arguments text box, specify one or more of the I/O redirection commands listed in Table 5.3. You can use any combination of I/O redirection commands.
4. Click on the OK button to activate the redirection and close the Project Settings dialog box.

What Is a .pdb File?

When the Debugger is enabled with the Use Program Database option, an additional file is generated at build time. The .pdb, or Program Database file, contains debugging and project state information. This file enables Visual Studio to perform incremental linking of debug program versions.

Command	Action
< *filename*	**stdin** input from *filename*
> *filename*	**stdout** output to *filename*
>> *filename*	Appends **stdout** to *filename*
2 > *filename*	**stderr** outputs to *filename*
2 >> *filename*	Appends **stderr** to *filename*
2 > &1	Sends **stderr** (2) output to same location as **stdout** (1)
1 >&2	Sends **stdout** (1) output to same location as **stderr** (2)

Table 5.3   Debug I/O Redirection Commands for Win32 Console Applications

Historically, the linker on 16-bit versions of Visual C++ placed the debugging information at the end of the .exe or .dll. Today's newer 32-bit Visual C++ allows both the linker and the integrated debugger to use the .pdb files directly.

Normally, Visual C++ will generate only one output .pdb file. However, if you run a makefile that is not created using Microsoft Visual C++, you will discover two .pdb files. The first, VCx0.pdb (the x is substituted with the current version of Visual C++), contains all of the debugging information for the separate .obj files. The second file created is named under your *projectname*.pdb. It contains all of the debugging information for the *projectname*.exe file and is found in the \WINDEBUG subdirectory.

The VCx0.pdb file is created because the compiler does not know the name of the executable file being generated. Which .obj files are needed isn't a settled issue until the linker is invoked, so the information is temporarily stored in the VCx0.pdb file. The compiler merges the debugging information into the VCx0.pdb file each time you compile an .obj file.

The VCx0.pdb and *projectname*.pdb files contain different types of information. The VCx0.pdb file has all of the information for your program's types but does not contain any symbol information. There is an efficiency advantage to this approach when an application includes standard header files such as windows.h. Because the VCx0.pdb file does not contain symbol information, each .obj file doesn't carry the redundant overhead of duplicate windows.h symbolic information.

The *projectname*.pdb file is generated at the link phase. This file contains the debugging information for the project's .exe file. All debugging information, including function prototypes and everything else, is placed into *projectname*.pdb. The two kinds of .pdb files share the same extension because they are architecturally similar and they both allow incremental updates. The Debugger inserts the location of the .pdb file in the .exe or .dll file. The Debugger can locate the .pdb file at an alternate location if the path has changed. Under these circumstances, the Debugger will use the current default directory for the .pdb file.

What Is a .dbg File?

The latest release of Visual C++ allows the disassembly and call stack windows to undecorate C++ names, which was not the case in earlier releases, such as when displaying system call stacks from Windows NT .dbg (debug) files. You can now view the C++ names with the correct argument list. The .dbg files created with the 32-bit NT toolset contain sections with COFF and Codeview information. The Debugger can read both types of .dbg files; however, it ignores the COFF symbol sections and looks only for Codeview information.

When the source code is not available, the Debugger can still use the .dbg files as long as they are made from a binary containing Codeview format debugging output. Without the source code, you can still use .dbg files to set breakpoints, watch variables, and view the call stack.

Design Tip *Because the information in the optimized code has been rearranged, the Debugger cannot always identify the source code that corresponds to a set of instructions. For this reason, it is advisable to debug your code before optimizing it whenever possible.*

Debugging Optimized Code

In Chapter 2 ("Optimizing with the Compiler"), you learned that optimizations can cause the compiler to restructure and/or reorder source code instructions for the purposes of minimizing the use of memory, or to optimize execution performance. You can enable optimization after you finish debugging.

You also learned in Chapter 2 that some bugs appear only in optimized code and do not affect unoptimized code. The following discussion provides several suggestions for those situations where you must debug optimized code. First, enable the Program Database (you can use the /Zi compiler option to get maximum symbolic information for the application). Second, use the Disassembly and Registers windows to track logic flow and data precisions. Appropriate breakpoints in the Disassembly window can be very useful at this phase.

To see why the Disassembly window can be so useful, consider the following **for** loop example (bolded code statements highlight some of the differences between the two build candidates):

```
for ( int i = 0; i < 5; i++ )
    cout << i;
```

This first listing shows the debug version of the translation as it appears in the Disassembly window:

```
5:        for ( int i = 0; i < 5; i++ )
00401778    mov         dword ptr [ebp-4],0
0040177F    jmp         main+2Ah (0040178a)
00401781    mov         eax,dword ptr [ebp-4]
00401784    add         eax,1
00401787    mov         dword ptr [ebp-4],eax
0040178A    cmp         dword ptr [ebp-4],5
0040178E    jge         main+40h (004017a0) // or OUT of loop
6:            std::cout << i;
00401790    mov         ecx,dword ptr [ebp-4]
00401793    push        ecx
00401794    mov         ecx,offset std::cout (004767e0)
00401799    call        @ILT+245 (std::basic_ostream
                        <char,std::char_traits<char> >::operator<<)
                        (004010fa)
0040179E    jmp         main+21h (00401781)
7:        }
```

This second listing shows the optimized release version as it would appear in the Disassembly window:

```
00401080    push        esi
00401081    xor         esi,esi
5:        for ( int i = 0; i < 5; i++ )
6:            std::cout << i;
00401083    push        esi
00401084    mov         ecx,offset std::cout (00427318)
00401089    call        std::basic_ostream<char,std::char_traits<char>
                        >::operator<< (004010a0)
```

```
0040108E    inc         esi
0040108F    cmp         esi,5
00401092    jl          main+3 (00401083) // back INTO loop!
00401094    pop         esi
7:    }
```

While the two listings contain several interesting variations, this discussion will concentrate simply on the initialization of the variable *i*. First, the C++ program uses this statement in the **for** loop:

```
i = 0;
```

The debug version translates this source code statement into one assembly language equivalent:

```
00401778    mov         dword ptr [ebp-4],0
```

However, the release version uses a logically equivalent set of statements but opts for a more efficient coding (from a machine cycles viewpoint):

```
00401080    push        esi
00401081    xor         esi,esi
```

You can also compare the ways the last two **for** loop statements, *i < 5;* and *i++;* are uniquely interpreted. The easier of the two is the increment of the LCV (loop control variable) *i*, which in the debug version looks like the following:

```
add         eax,1
```

The release version uses the more efficient **inc** instruction and looks like the following:

```
inc    esi
```

Finally, the **for** loop test condition, *i < 5;*, seems to have almost been logically inverted when comparing the two translations. First, the debug version is as follows:

```
0040178A    cmp         dword ptr [ebp-4],5
0040178E    jge         main+40h (004017a0) // or OUT of loop
    .
    .
    .
0040179E    jmp         main+21h (00401781)
```

Notice that what logically appears to be a *pretest* loop encoding in the release version resembles a *posttest* loop!:

```
    .
    .
    .
0040108F    cmp         esi,5
00401092    jl          main+3 (00401083) // back INTO loop!
```

24x7

Using the _DEBUG label along with conditional preprocessor statements (directives) allows you to selectively debug code segments. Consider this approach when the majority of your application contains previously debugged algorithms.

The point is that a debug version (with a total of 12 statements) and a release version (with a total of 9 functionally equivalent statements) are not identical twins. Translation units that work under one build candidate can easily break under the other.

Another Way to Enable the Debugger

An alternative approach to activating the Debugger, without using the Project | Settings options, is to use the _DEBUG label. This approach allows you to selectively switch the Debugger on and off.

The following header file syntax demonstrates the use of the **_DEBUG** symbolic constant with the **#ifdef** preprocessor directive (remember that for every conditional **#if...** preprocessor directive, you must have a closing **#endif** as highlighted in the code segment):

```
// Macros for setting or clearing bits in the CRT debug flag
#ifdef _DEBUG
#define   SET_CRT_DEBUG_FIELD(a)    _CrtSetDbgFlag((a) |
_CrtSetDbgFlag(_CRTDBG_REPORT_FLAG))
#define   CLEAR_CRT_DEBUG_FIELD(a) _CrtSetDbgFlag(~(a) &
_CrtSetDbgFlag(_CRTDBG_REPORT_FLAG))
#else
#define   SET_CRT_DEBUG_FIELD(a)    ((void) 0)
#define   CLEAR_CRT_DEBUG_FIELD(a) ((void) 0)
#endif
```

You also must link with the debug versions of Microsoft Foundation Class (MFC) libraries. Setting the Win32 Debug option in Visual C++ ensures linking with the debug libraries. All debug versions of the library routines have the letter D at the end of the library name. The static debug version of MFC is NAFXCWD.LIB, and the static release version (nondebug) is NAFXCW.LIB. The DLL debug version of MFC is MFCvvD.LIB, and the DLL release version (nondebug) is MFCvv.LIB (where vv is the version number).

Using the Base or Debug Version

The Microsoft Visual C++ runtime library now contains special debug versions of the heap allocation functions that use the same names as the base versions and add the _dbg ending. This section describes the differences in behavior between the debug version and the base version in a debug build of an application. The information in this section is presented using malloc and _malloc_dbg as an example but is applicable to all of the heap allocation functions.

Applications that contain existing calls to malloc do not need to convert their calls to _malloc_dbg to obtain the debugging features. When _DEBUG is defined, all calls to malloc are resolved to _malloc_dbg. However, explicitly calling _malloc_dbg allows a program to perform additional debugging tasks: it can separately track _CLIENT_BLOCK type allocations, and it can include the source file and line number where the allocation request occurred in the bookkeeping information stored in the debug header.

Because the base versions of the allocation functions are implemented as wrappers, the source filename and line number of each heap allocation request are not available by explicitly calling the base version. Applications that do not want to convert their malloc calls to _malloc_dbg can obtain the source file information by defining _CRTDBG_MAP_ALLOC. Defining _CRTDBG_MAP_ALLOC causes the preprocessor to directly map all calls to malloc to _malloc_dbg, thereby providing the additional information. To track particular types of allocations separately in client blocks, _malloc_dbg must be called directly, and the *blockType* parameter must be set to _CLIENT_BLOCK.

When _DEBUG is *not* defined:

- calls to malloc are not disturbed
- calls to _malloc_dbg are resolved to malloc; the definition of _CRTDBG_MAP_ALLOC is ignored
- source file information pertaining to the allocation request is not provided

Because malloc does not have a block type parameter, requests for _CLIENT_BLOCK types are treated as standard allocations.

C/C++ Runtime Debug Libraries

Tables 5.4, 5.5, and 5.6 list the debug versions of the Microsoft Visual C, C++, and iostream runtime debug library files, along with their associated compiler options and environment variables. Prior to Visual C++ 4.2, the C runtime libraries contained the iostream library functions. In Visual C++ 4.2, the old iostream library functions were removed from LIBCD.LIB, LIBCMTD.LIB, and MSVCRTD.LIB. This change was made because the standard C++ library was added to Visual C++, and it contains a new set of iostream libraries.

Error Watch *Mixing the old style iostream.h with the Standard Template Library (STL) and its associated **using namespace std;** statement can lead to data loss! Instead, make certain you use iostream (without the .h).*

Confusion Between the Old iostream.h and New iostream

It's slightly confusing that *two* sets of iostream functions are now included in Visual C++. In a way, you can view the C/C++ languages as moving targets; "moving" in the sense that both languages are, via the ANSI C/C++ (American National Standards Committee) committee, keeping pace with today's programming development needs.

The old iostream functions now exist in their own libraries: LIBCID.LIB, LIBCIMTD.LIB, and MSVCIRTD.LIB. The new iostream functions, as well as many other new functions, exist in the standard C++ libraries: LIBCPD.LIB, LIBCPMTD.LIB, and MSVCPRTD.LIB.

The standard C++ library and the old iostream library are incompatible, and only one of them can be linked with your project. When you build a debug version of your project, one of the basic C runtime debug libraries (LIBCD.LIB, LIBCMTD.LIB, or MSVCRTD.LIB) is linked by default, depending on the compiler option you choose (single-threaded, multithreaded, or DLL). Depending on the headers you use in your code, a debug library from the standard C++ libraries or one from the old iostream libraries may also be linked.

If you include a standard C++ library header in your code, a standard C++ library will be linked in automatically by Visual C++ at compile time. For example:

```
#include <iostream>
```

If you include an old iostream library header, an old iostream library will be linked in automatically by Visual C++ at compile time. For example:

```
#include <iostream.h>
```

Note that headers from the standard C++ library and the old iostream library cannot be mixed. Headers determine whether a standard C++ library, an old iostream library, or neither will be linked. Compiler options determine which of the libraries to be linked is the default (single-threaded, multithreaded, or DLL). When a specific library compiler option is defined, that library is considered to be the default, and its environment variables are automatically defined.

The C Runtime Debug Library (does not include iostream)	Description	Setting	Use
LIBCD.LIB	Used with statically linked single-threaded applications	/MLd	_DEBUG
LIBCMTD.LIB	Used with statically linked multithreaded applications	/MTd	_DEBUG, _MT
MSVCRTD.LIB (import library for MSVCRTD.DLL)	Used with dynamically linked multithreaded applications	MDd	_DEBUG, _MT, _DLL
Allows you to find out which version of a DLL your application is using; look for the Visual C++ version number in the filename. For example, if you are using Visual C++ version 6.0, then the library name would be MSVCR60D.DLL.			

Table 5.4   C Runtime Debug Libraries

The Standard C++ Debug Library	Description	Setting	Use
LIBCPD.LIB	For statically linked single-threaded applications	/MLd	_DEBUG
LIBCPMTD.LIB	For statically linked multithreaded applications	/MTd	_DEBUG, _MT
MSVCPRTD.LIB	For dynamically linked multithreaded applications	/MDd	_DEBUG, _MT, _DLL

Table 5.5   Standard C++ Debug Library

Remember that the debug versions of the C/C++ library functions differ from the release versions. Specifically, the debug information is included when you compile the C/C++ Library functions using the /Z7 or /Zi compiler option, optimization is turned off, and source code is available. A few of the debug library functions also contain asserts that verify parameter validity. Using one of these debug libraries is as simple as linking it to your application with the /DEBUG:FULL linker option set. You can then step directly into almost any runtime function call.

Linker Reference

The Microsoft Visual C++ linker is a 32-bit tool that links Common Object File Format (COFF) object files and libraries to create a 32-bit executable (.exe) file or dynamic link library (dll) file. Table 5.7 lists many of the more frequently used options for LINK.EXE.

Detecting Release Version Errors in a Debug Build

Some bugs normally arise only when you switch to a release build (/O1, /O2, /Ox, or /Og). You can use the /GZ option to enable runtime checks to catch these bugs in a debug (/Od) build. /GZ is not compatible with /O1, /O2, /Ox, or /Og builds (the /GZ option will disable any #pragma optimize statements in your code). When you use the /GZ option, Visual C++ will automatically initialize all local variables, validate function pointers on the call stack, and validate the call stack (many of the examples discussed here are used as examples in later chapters).

The iostream Debug Library	Description	Setting	Use
LIBCID.LIB	For statically linked single threaded applications	/MLd	_DEBUG
LIBCIMTD.LIB	For statically linked multithreaded applications	/MTd	_DEBUG, _MT
MSVCIRTD.LIB	For dynamically linked multithreaded applications	/MDd	_DEBUG, _MT, _DLL

Table 5.6   iostream Debug Libraries

Linker Option	Description
/ALIGN:*number*	Selects the alignment of each code segment
/BASE:{*address* | @*filename,key*}	Defines the base address for your program
/COMMENT:["]*comment*["]	Adds a comment block in header
/DEBUG	Inserts debugging information
/DEBUGTYPE:CV	Selects CV debug type
/DEBUGTYPE:COFF	Selects COFF debug type
/DEBUGTYPE:BOTH	Includes both types of debug formatting
/DEF:*filename*	Sends a module-definition or .def file to the linker
/DEFAULTLIB:*library*	Uses defined file in search path for external library references
/DELAY [NOBIND or UNLOAD]	Delays the loading of dlls
/DELAYLOAD	Defines which file uses delayed loading
/DLL	Creates a DLL
/DRIVER[:UPONLY]	Builds a Windows NT kernel mode driver
/ENTRY:*function*	Sets the starting address
/EXETYPE:DYNAMIC	Creates a virtual device driver
/EXPORT	Exports a function
/FIXED[:NO]	Builds a program that can be loaded only at the specified base address
/FORCE[:{MULTIPLE|UNRESOLVED}]	Causes the linker to ignore unresolved or duplicate defined identifiers
/GPSIZE:#	Sets the size of communal variables for MIPS and Alpha architectures
/HEAP:*reserve*[,*commit*]	Delimits the size of the heap in bytes
/IMPLIB:*filename*	Allows for the selection of an alternate import library
/INCLUDE:*symbol*	Enforces symbol references
/INCREMENTAL:{YES|NO}	Determines incremental linking
/LARGEADDRESSAWARE	Permits an application to have addresses larger than two gigabytes
/LIBPATH:*path*	Selects alternate environmental library path
/LINK50COMPAT	Creates import libraries in Visual C++ version 5.0 format
/MACHINE:{IX86|ALPHA|ARM|MIPS|MIPS16|MIPSR41XX|PPC|SH3|SH4}	Selects the target architecture
/MAP	Generates a mapfile
/MAPINFO:{EXPORTS|FIXUPS|LINES}	Adds the selected information into the mapfile
/MERGE:*from=to*	Merges specified sections

Table 5.7   Microsoft Visual C++ Linker Options

Linker Option	Description
/NODEFAULTLIB[:*library*]	Ignores selected default libraries when resolving external references
/NOENTRY	Generates a resource-only DLL
/NOLOGO	Eliminates the startup banner
/OPT:{REF|NOREF|NOWIN98|WIN98ICF [,*iterations*]|NOICF}	Selects the linker optimizations
/ORDER:@*filename*	Inserts COMDATs into the image in a predetermined format
/OUT:*filename*	Selects an output filename
/PDB:*filename*	Generates the Program Database, .pdb file
/PDBTYPE:{con[solidate]|sept[ypes]}	Selects the location for the Program Database debug type information
/PROFILE	Turns profiling on
/RELEASE	Determines the checksum in the .exe header
/SECTION:*name*, [E][R][W][S][D][K][L][P][X]	Overrides the attributes of a section
/STACK:*reserve*[,*commit*]	Defines stack size in bytes
/STUB:*filename*	Attaches an MS-DOS application to a Win32 program
/SUBSYSTEM:{CONSOLE|WINDOWS|NATIVE| POSIX|WINDOWSCE} [,*major*[.*minor*]]	Instructs the operating system how to run the .exe file
/SWAPRUN:{NET|CD|TSAWARE[:NO]}	Instructs the operating system to copy the linker output to a swap file before execution
/VERBOSE[:LIB]	Outputs linker progress messages
/VERSION:*major*[.*minor*]	Inserts a version number
/VXD	Generates a virtual device driver VxD
/WARN[:*level*]	Selects the warning level
/WS:AGGRESSIVE	Optimizes memory usage

Table 5.7   Microsoft Visual C++ Linker Options *(continued)*

Auto-Initialization of Local Variables

Assuming the stack is zero, code with uninitialized variables may fail with /GZ. Consider the following example. When compiled with /Od or /Ox without /GZ, this code may produce an access-violation exception, or it may appear to run correctly. When compiled with /Gz /Od, it always produces the exception. You can catch the exception in the Debugger and get some hints about the exact location of failure.

```
#include <stdio.h>

void myFuncA(char **ppszString)
{
```

```
      /* output uninitialized ppszString address in hex        */
      printf("*ppszString = 0x%X\n", *ppszString);
      if(*ppszString == NULL)
         *ppszString = "/GZ option ACTIVE";
}
void myFuncB()
{
   int memBuff[25];          /* uninitialized internal variable */
   char * pszString;         /* uninitialized memBuff pointer   */

   myFuncA(&pszString);
   puts(pszString);          /* dangerous - attempts to print   */
}                            /* myFuncA allocated string!!!     */

void main( void )
{
   int memBuff[ 1000 ];   /* stack page - cleared              */
   myFuncB( );
}
```

By debugging this application, you can see how the uninitialized pszString pointer behaves with or without the /GZ switch active. When active, the pointer is automatically initialized to NULL. In either case, the last statement in *myFuncB()* attempts to output a dangerous condition—accessing a called subroutine's internal variables.

Validating the Function Pointer Call Stack

Function pointer call stack validation makes certain the stack pointer is checked before and after the call through the function pointer to make certain both are the same. This can catch any mismatch between the calling function's cleanup **__cdecl** calling convention and called function's cleanup calling conventions **__fastcall** and **__stdcall**, when calling through a function pointer.

This example works with /Od, fails with /Ox, and raises an exception with /GZ. You get an exception breakpoint pop-up if compiled with a release version of the runtime library and a more meaningful message when compiled with the debug version of the runtime library.

```
void __stdcall myFuncA(char *p)
{
   puts(p);
}

typedef void (*function_pointer)(char *);

void main( void )
{
   function_pointer pmyFuncA = (function_pointer)myFuncA;

   pmyFuncA("This is just a test.");
}
```

This example demonstrates the kinds of trouble you can run into when using calling convention modifiers and how the Debugger flags the mismatch differently, depending on whether you are generating a debug or release version.

Validating the Call Stack

When active, Microsoft Visual C++ checks the stack pointer at the end of the function to see that the stack pointer has not been changed. This can catch cases where the stack pointer has been corrupted in inline assembly or a nonpointer function's calling convention is set improperly.

The TRACE Macro

The Debugger TRACE macro displays debugging messages from a program. The messages are output to your Debugger.

Note | *With 32-bit MFC, the only way to get debug output is via the Debugger.*

Similar to the printf() function, the TRACE macro can handle a variable number of arguments. Following are examples of different ways to use TRACE macros:

```
char a = 'a';
char b = 'b';
TRACE( "TRACE statement." );
TRACE( "\na = %c", a );
TRACE( "\nb = %c", b );
```

The TRACE macro is active only in the debug version of the class library. After a program has been debugged, you can build a release version to deactivate all TRACE calls in the program.

 Tip | *When debugging Unicode, the TRACE0, TRACE1, TRACE2, and TRACE3 macros are easier to use because the _T macro is not needed.*

The VERIFY Macro

When building an MFC debug version, you can use the VERIFY macro to evaluate arguments. When VERIFY returns a zero, the macro prints a diagnostic message and halts the program. If the condition is nonzero, it does nothing. The syntax for the diagnostic message looks like the following:

```
assertion failed in file <identifier> in line <ln>
```

where *identifier* is the name of the source file and *ln* is the line number of the assertion that failed in the source file.

When building an MFC release version, you can use VERIFY to evaluate expressions without printing or interrupting the program; for example, if the expression is a function call, the call will be made.

Porting Older 32-Bit Versions of Visual C++

The good news is that all your old application workspaces or projects, built in previous 32-bit versions of Microsoft Visual C++, can be automatically ported to the newer Visual C++ environment. However, if you have built a 32-bit Visual C++ project from the command line with your own makefile, the Visual C++ development environment does not recognize project data in your file. Instead, the development environment offers to wrap your makefile. If you choose this option, a project is created with one file, your makefile, in it, but the project will still build and run within the development environment.

| Note | *However, if you want to take advantage of the newer Microsoft Visual C++ wizards and integrated debugging features, you should create a new project in the development environment, add your existing files to it, and then build and save it as an up-to-date project.* |

Converting Older 32-Bit Workspaces and Projects

You need to follow only four easy steps when converting your older Visual C++ 32-bit projects. First, click on the File | Open Workspace menu option; when the Open Project Workspace dialog box appears, follow these steps:

1. In the Files of Type drop-down list, select All Files (*.*).

2. Route yourself over to the drive and directory containing the previous makefile or project file.

3. Double-click on the makefile or project file from the list.

4. Click on Yes when you see the message asking if you want to convert to the new project format.

Microsoft Visual C++ creates a new project workspace file (.dsw), and a new project options file (.opt) is created with your old project workspace name. In addition, a project build file (.dsp) will be created in each project directory for each project in the workspace. For example, suppose you're converting a single-project workspace called oldapptoconvert.mdp, then oldapptoconvert.dsw, oldapptoconvert.dsp, and oldapptoconvert.opt are created and saved to the same directory. In the more complicated example of a two-project workspace called oldapptoconvert2.mdp, which also includes a subproject myOwndll2, then oldapptoconvert2.dsw, oldapptoconvert2.dsp, and oldapptoconvert2.opt are created and saved to the same directory, and myOwndll2.dsp is created in the myOwndll2 directory.

Affected CRT Files	MSVCRTd.dll, MSVCRTd.pdb, MSVCIRTd.dll, MSVCIRTd.pdb
Affected MFC Files	MFC42d.dll, MFC42d.pdb, MFC42u.pdb, MFC42ud.dll, MFC42ud.pdb, MFCd42d.dll, MFCd42d.pdb, MFCd42ud.dll, MFCd42ud.pdb, MFCn42d.dll, MFCn42d.pdb, MFCn42ud.dll, MFCn42ud.pdb, MFCo42d.dll, MFCo42d.pdb, MFCo42ud.dll, MFCo42ud.pdb

Table 5.8   Affected Files When Mixing Microsoft Visual C++ Versions

Coexisting with Previous Versions of Visual C++

With each new version of Microsoft's Visual C++ development environment, each new install program overwrites the older library DLLs and PDBs used by previous Visual C++ versions. Visual C++ 4.2 and 5.0 cannot read the new format debugging information in these DLLs. (Table 5.8 lists the affected files for version 6.0 versus versions 4.2 and 5.0.) When you need to use Visual C++ version 6.0 with either version 4.2 or 5.0, you can do the following:

- Use separate machines for each environment.
- Use the different Visual C++ versions with separate installations of the operating system on the same machine.
- Use the Visual C++ 6.0 Debugger for debugging in the new DLLs.
- Copy the old versions of the affected files into your Visual C++ 5.0 or 4.2 project Debug directory. (Do this before you install Visual C++ 6.0, or get the old versions from the \MSDEV\DEBUG directory of the Visual C++ 4.2 or 5.0 CD.)

Microsoft recommends that you do not replace the new versions of MFC42.dll, MFC42u.dll, and MSVCRT.dll with the older versions. If you do, you may break other applications dependent on the new versions of these DLLs. The Visual C++ 6.0 development environment, for example, requires the current version of MFC42.dll. If you need to use Visual C++ 6.0 to generate import libraries in Visual C++ 5.0 format, you can use the /LINK50COMPAT option.

Conclusion

Even if you were already familiar with standard Debugger essentials such as Watch windows and Step Into, Step Over, you may have been unaware of the Debugger's ability to perform sophisticated tasks such as debugging from the current location with a *new* value. This chapter also presented advanced topics such as the call stack and the *efficient* use of standard Debugger essentials by clever breakpoint insertions. With practice, you will evolve into more and more efficient debug cycles and spend less time debugging "old news."

In the next chapter, you will examine the Debugger's capabilities relating to assembly language code. This is an exciting addition to your programmer's toolkit because C/C++, from day one, had a close, symbiotic relationship with assembly language code.

PART II

The Procedure-Oriented Environment

Locating, Analyzing, and Repairing Errors in Command-Line Code

ecause many types of C/C++ development environments and architectures are available to
today's programmers, Chapter 6 has two main objectives. First, to give someone unfamiliar with
Microsoft's Visual C++ Debugger an introduction to a meaningful subset of Debugger commands
that he or she can begin using today. Second, to apply those commands to what Microsoft calls their
"Win32 Console Application."

The second half of Chapter 6, "Advanced Debugger Tricks," begins the introduction to debugging
philosophies. These philosophies combine a logical component added to one or more Debugger
commands, designed to efficiently locate and diagnose program bugs.

Quick, Get Me Started Debugging

This step-by-step introduction to the Visual C++ Debugger assumes that you have never used the
product before. Each successive figure highlights, in detail, exactly what you should see on your
monitor screen. Because the Debugger is a programmer/product, interactive experience, it is
suggested that you enter, compile, build, and try each Debugger command option.

Additionally, you may want to jot down Debugger command sequences on a small notepad. The
chapter's discussions frequently detail more than one mouse/menu, key/hot-key combination for
accessing a Debugger feature, and you will probably prefer one approach over another. While it is
true that Microsoft's Visual C++ Debugger is capable of surgical diagnosis, you will not be using
hundreds of Debugger commands on a day-to-day basis; instead, you will be using a small subset.
Writing down these commands by name and programmer/product interaction sequence won't take
that much time and will have immediate paybacks in time saved while debugging.

24x7

The ANSI C++ Committee has changed the syntax, scope, and internal representations for
C/C++ header file use. All of the programs in this book use the new standard. You can always
recognize an up-to-date algorithm by examining the #include statements. Any program using a
standard C/C++ header filename ending with a .h, is *not* up-to-date. (There is more to the ANSI
C++ standard but a discussion would be inappropriate at this point.) In addition, this latest ANSI
C++ evolution requires not only the use of header files without the .h extension, but a symbiotic
use of a "using namespace std;" statement in order for the application to compile and run.

At this point, if you are going to try the chapter's examples, you need to enter and save the
VarsYourCode.cpp program:

```
//
//VarsYourCode.cpp
//Debugging YOUR code versus Stroustrup's
//
```

```
#include <iostream>
#include <string>

using namespace std;

void main ( void )
{
   //sample variables of common data types

   char cValue  = 'A';
   int  iValue  = 10;

   float fValue  = 3.19143;
   string szString = "Oh NO - not another Hello World!";

   cin  >> szString;
   cout << szString << endl;

}
```

Figure 6.1 shows a sample program, *VarsYourCode.cpp*, that has simply been edited and saved. At this point, no build or compile instructions have been executed.

> **Note** *Any action you need to take to follow the examples in this chapter are italicized, bolded, and underlined for clarity. Some parts of the discussion are introductory and explain all of your options, but only those actions in **italics, boldface,** and/or **underline** are executed by you.*

Fast Ways to Start the Debugger

Once you have saved your source file, the simplest way to begin a debug session is to simply ***press the F10 key***. This initiates a series of automated phases.

Step One—Press F10

Figure 6.2 illustrates the first phase initiated by Visual C++.

The new message window is prompting you to create the executable version, *VarsYourCode.exe*, of your program. Notice that saying Yes (or pressing ENTER) not only begins the creation of the .exe version but also, in the process, automatically executes a compile/build.

Step Two—Click Yes

Simply ***click on the Yes button*** (or better yet, just press the ENTER key, as the Yes button is the default action). Figure 6.3 may look slightly different on your monitor screen due to default toolbar locations; however, the "meat" of the windows' contents should be the same.

Figure 6.3 shows the updated Visual C++ window content. First, you'll notice the Debug toolbar. If you are trying this example on your own system, your Debug toolbar may be in a different location

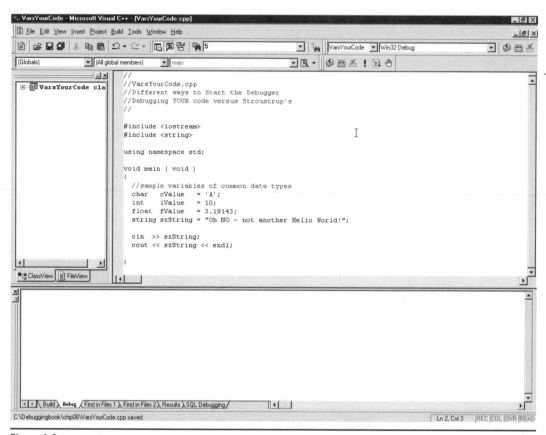

Figure 6.1   Sample program *VarsYourCode.cpp* prior to build, compile, or debug

and/or shape; also, your screen may show the Workspace View pane to the left of the source code. The Workspace View pane was collapsed for this example in order to minimize screen clutter and allow you to concentrate on the topic at hand (you can right-click the mouse within this pane and choose Hide).

Figure 6.4 displays a close-up view of the Debug toolbar. The sixteen icons are listed here from left-to-right and top row to second row with any associated hot-key combinations (Chapter 4 describes each Debug toolbar button's action in detail):

- Restart (CTRL+SHIFT+F5)
- Stop Debugging (SHIFT+F5)
- Break Execution (grayed here)
- Apply Code Changes (ALT+F10)
- Show Next Statement (ALT+NUM *)

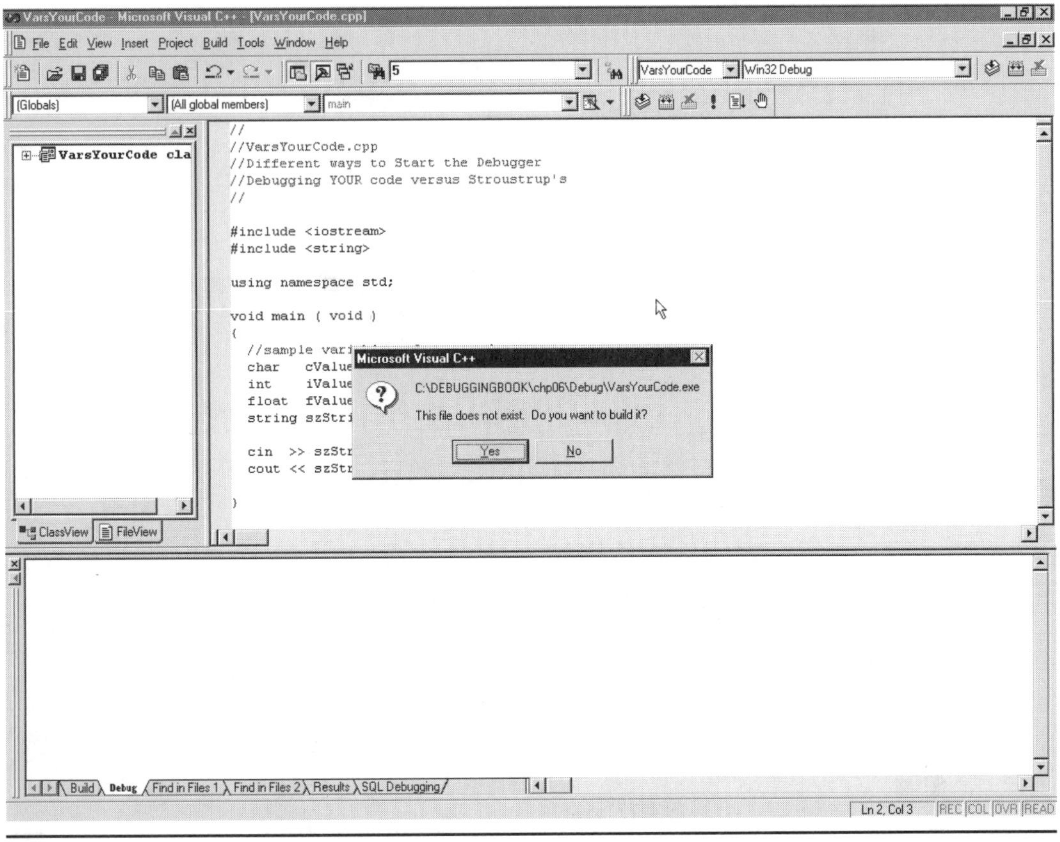

Figure 6.2   Step one—pressing F10

- Step Into (F11)
- Step Over (F10)
- Step Out (SHIFT+F11)
- Runt to Cursor (CTRL+F10)
- QuickWatch (SHIFT+F9)
- Watch
- Variables
- Registers
- Memory
- Call Stack
- Disassembly

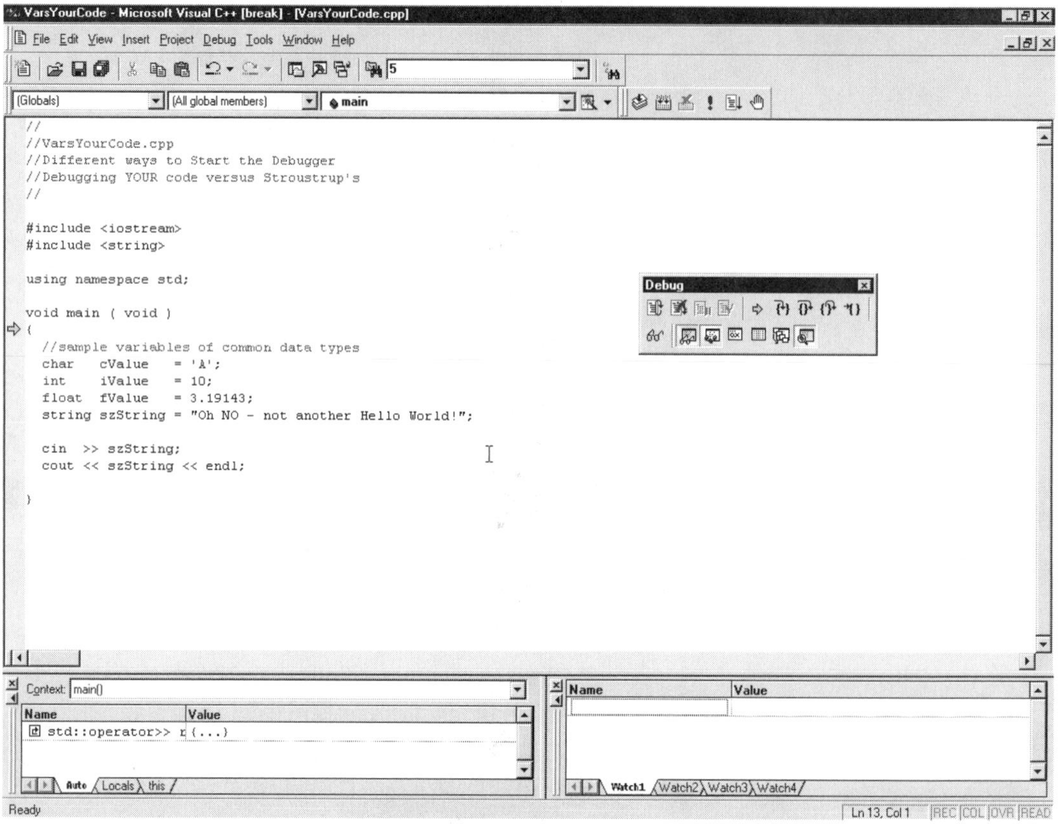

```
//
//VarsYourCode.cpp
//Different ways to Start the Debugger
//Debugging YOUR code versus Stroustrup's
//

#include <iostream>
#include <string>

using namespace std;

void main ( void )
{
    //sample variables of common data types
    char    cValue   = 'A';
    int     iValue   = 10;
    float   fValue   = 3.19143;
    string szString = "Oh NO - not another Hello World!";

    cin  >> szString;
    cout << szString << endl;

}
```

Context: main()

Name	Value
std::operator>> r (...)	

Auto / Locals \ this /

Name	Value

Watch1 /Watch2\Watch3\Watch4/

Ready   Ln 13, Col 1   REC COL OVR READ

Figure 6.3   Results of clicking Yes in response to the Do you want to build it? message box

After the compile/build cycle is complete, you will be in the integrated Microsoft Visual C++ Debugger. Figure 6.5 zooms in on the source code pane in order for you to *see* the Debugger's *trace*

Figure 6.4   Debug toolbar close-up

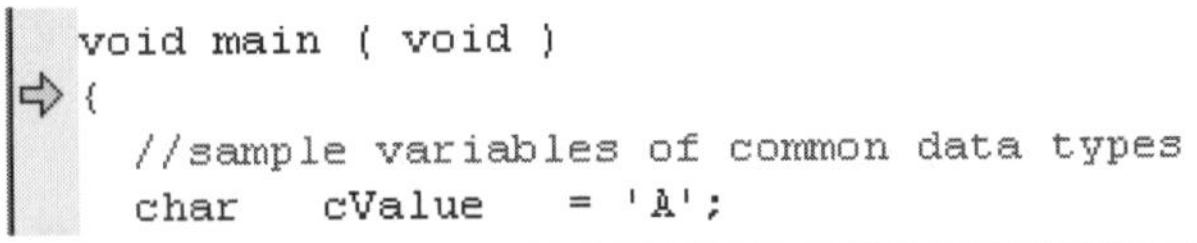

```
void main ( void )
{
    //sample variables of common data types
    char    cValue    = 'A';
```

Figure 6.5   Close-up of the *trace arrow*

arrow close-up. You will always know the Debugger is running when you have the trace arrow displayed in your source code view.

The most important thing to remember about the trace arrow is that it is *not* pointing to the code statement that you *have just executed*. Instead, the trace arrow is pointing to the line of code in your program that *will be executed* the next time you Single Step Into/Over (F11 or F10)!

In the *VarsYourCode.cpp* example, the trace arrow is stopping at the opening brace {, just under **main**(). Stopping here allows you to view any code initializations of your variables. The trace arrow does *not* skip over your variable declarations and stop at the first "executable" code statement.

Figure 6.6 highlights the Variables window that auto-tracks information about variables used in the current trace arrow's scope. The Variables window automatically updates its contents to the current and previous statements' variable use along with any function return values (in the Auto tab), variables local to the current function (in the Locals tab), and the object pointed to by this (in the **This** tab). The Context drop-down list of the Variables window informs you about which subroutine "owns" the current context.

Though currently empty, Figure 6.7 shows the Watch window. This window's contents differ from the Variables window in that inserted identifiers do not go out of scope. The Variables window's contents auto-track, or synchronize, with the scope of the trace arrow.

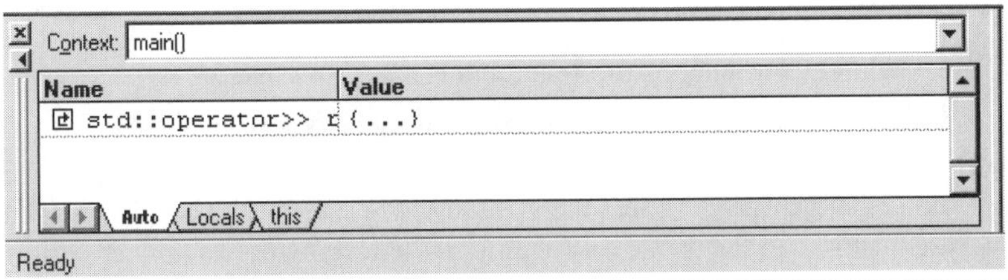

Figure 6.6   Close-up view of the Variables window

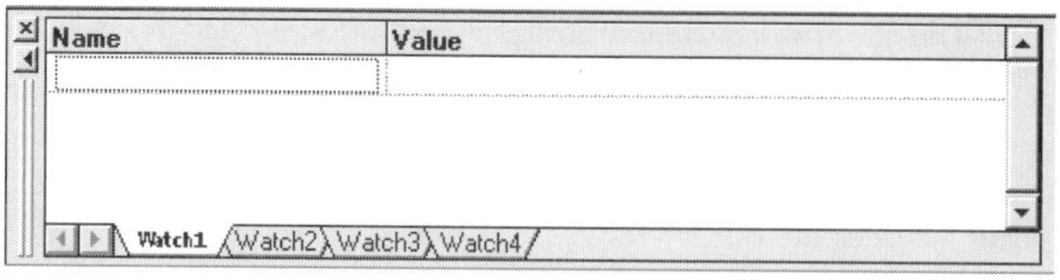

Figure 6.7 Debugger Watch window

Tracing Variable Initializations

This discussion explains the Debugger's actions when tracing variable declarations and initializations. If you are trying the example at this point, you could (however, do *not* execute any of these suggested options at this point):

- Press the F10 key.
- Press the F11 key again.
- Click on the Step Into Debug toolbar button.
- Click on the Step Over Debug toolbar button.

The reason you can choose from one of four options is that all four will do the same thing for the current trace arrow statement syntax. Remember that Step Into and Step Over are identical in function unless the trace arrow is sitting *on* a subroutine (function or method) call.

Some programmers prefer hot-key combinations; others like the ease of mouse-button clicks. Whichever approach you prefer, ***chose one of the preceding four options***. You will see a screen similar to Figure 6.8.

You should see the following Visual C++ window changes:

- The trace arrow has now moved down to the *cValue* declaration.
- The Variables window has begun auto-tracking *cValue*.
- The Variables Value column displays the garbage initial contents of *cValue*.

At this point, the Debugger has allocated the storage for *cValue*, but as you already know, because the trace arrow is still sitting on the declaring statement, the Debugger has *not* yet performed the initialization.

Now, using whichever approach you prefer, ***execute one more single step***. Your new Visual C++ windows contents should look like Figure 6.9. You should see the following Visual C++ window changes:

- The trace arrow has moved down one line in your code.

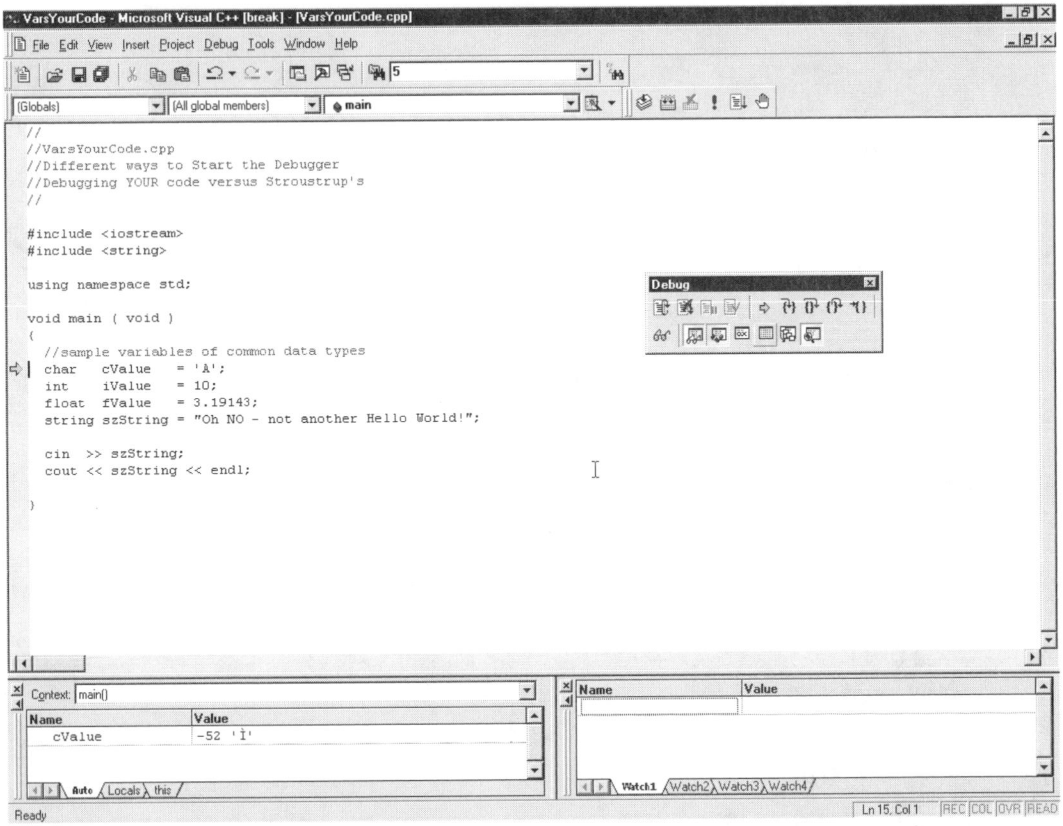

Figure 6.8   Window contents after executing _one_ single trace

- The Variables window now displays the correct, initialized value for _cValue_.
- The Variables window auto-tracks the in-scope variable _iValue_.
- The Variables Value column displays the garbage initial contents of _iValue_.

At this point, _**you will need to execute three (3) more single steps**_. Pay particular attention to what is dynamically happening in the Variables window. The scenario will continue to repeat:

- First you'll see the most recently added variable's contents go from garbage to the explicit code-assigned value.
- Next you'll notice the _next_ variable's name appear in the Variables window. The newest variable will display with its garbage contents.

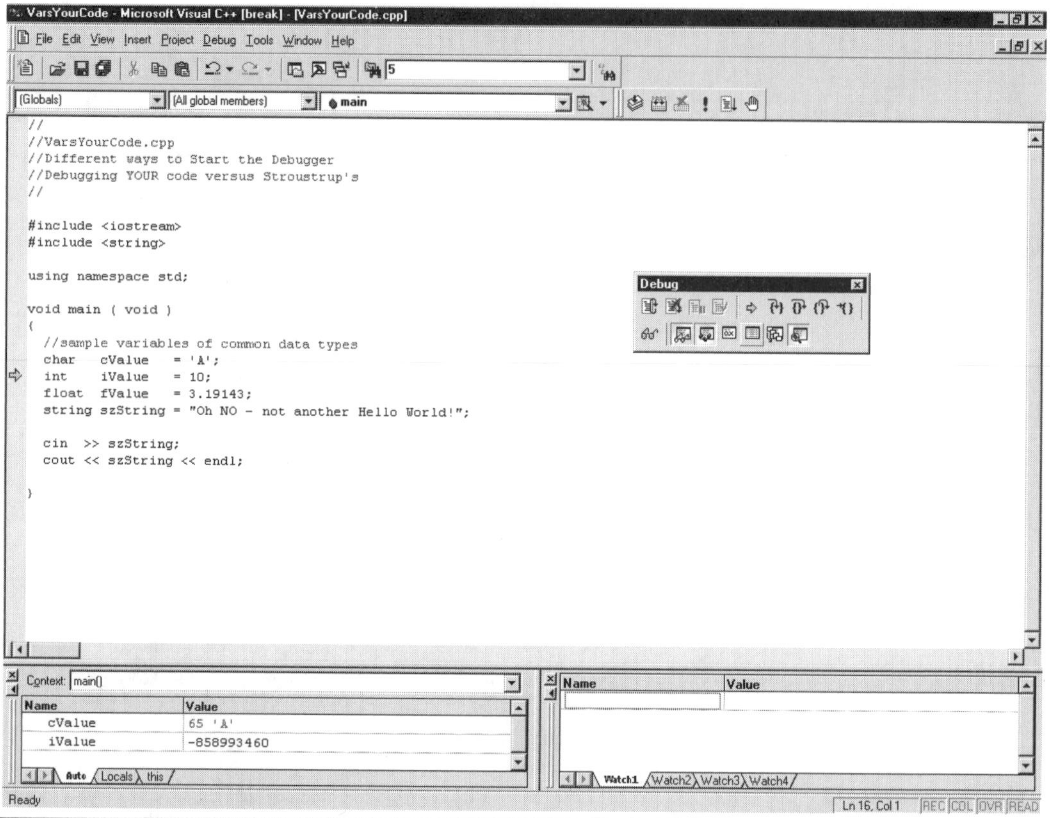

Figure 6.9 Executing the initialization of *cValue*

After you have single-stepped through the variable declaration block, your Visual C++ window's contents should look like Figure 6.10.

The problem with the Auto tab view is its narrow auto-tracking scope. At this point, ***you need to click on the Variables window's Locals tab*** to view all of your local variables.

However, even doing this leaves you with another problem. The default size for the Variables window is too small to view *all* of your local variables. One solution to this problem is to ***shrink the code page window***, expanding the Variables window, as seen in Figure 6.11.

Expanding the Variables and Watch Windows

You expand both the Variables and Watch windows by simply placing your cursor over the bottom edge of the code page frame, holding down the left mouse button, and sliding your mouse up the screen until you find a convenient location (see Figure 6.11).

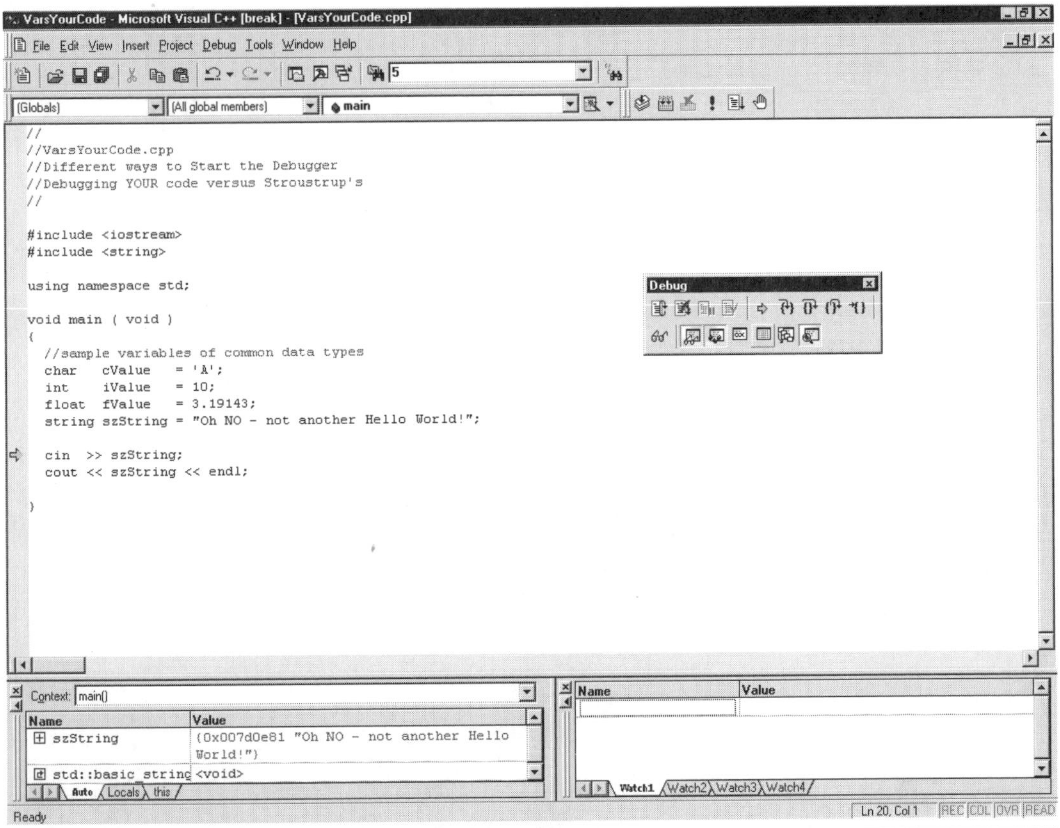

Figure 6.10   Visual C++ window contents after three more single steps

Understanding the Variables Window Contents

The Variables window contains all of the information you could possibly need to know about a variable. Each tab contains a spreadsheet field with three resizable columns. The Debugger automatically fills these columns with the type, name, and value of variables appropriate to the tab. Figure 6.12 demonstrates some of the Variables window's capabilities for the *szString* **string** type variable.

A toolbar located above the tabs contains a drop-down list for specifying the current scope of the variable display. This toolbar can be hidden, or redisplayed, using the shortcut menu.

The new Visual C++ Variables window replaces the Locals tab from previous versions of Visual C++ with new capabilities. If the Variables window contains an array, object, or structure variable, a button appears next to the variable name. By clicking the button, you can expand or contract your

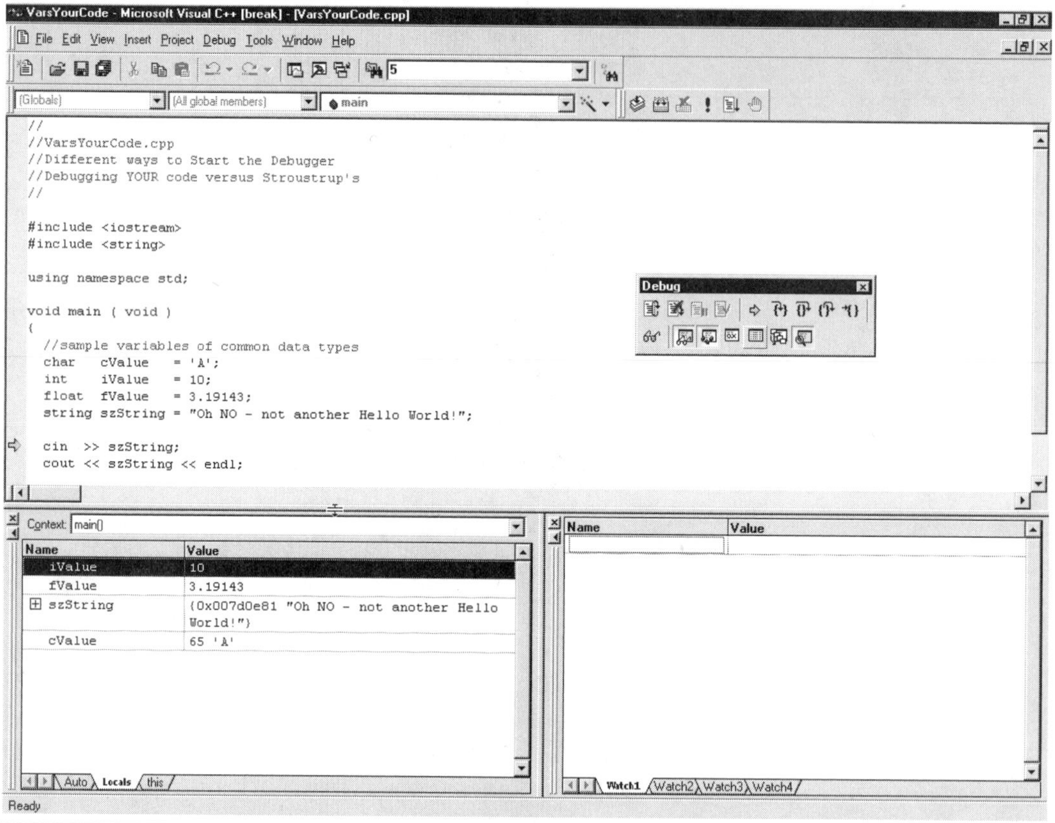

Figure 6.11   Expanding the Variables and Watch windows

view of the variable. The button displays a plus sign (+) when the variable is displayed in contracted form and a minus sign when it is displayed in expanded form. You can expand the variable by clicking the + box, which opens into a tree that may contain additional boxes. When a variable is expanded, the box in the Name column contains a minus sign (–). You can collapse an expanded variable by clicking the – box.

As an alternative, you can expand a variable by selecting it and pressing the PLUS SIGN or RIGHT ARROW key. You can collapse a variable by selecting it and pressing the MINUS SIGN or LEFT ARROW key. (Many of the options discussed in the following section are expanded upon throughout the remaining chapters, where appropriate.)

The Variables window supports editing. You can cut, copy, or drag information from the Variables window. You can edit the Value column to change the value of a variable while debugging. If you selected hexadecimal display in the Debug tab of the Options dialog box (Tools menu), you must enter the value in hexadecimal or use the prefix "0n" (zero-n) to indicate that the number is a decimal (for example, 0n1000).

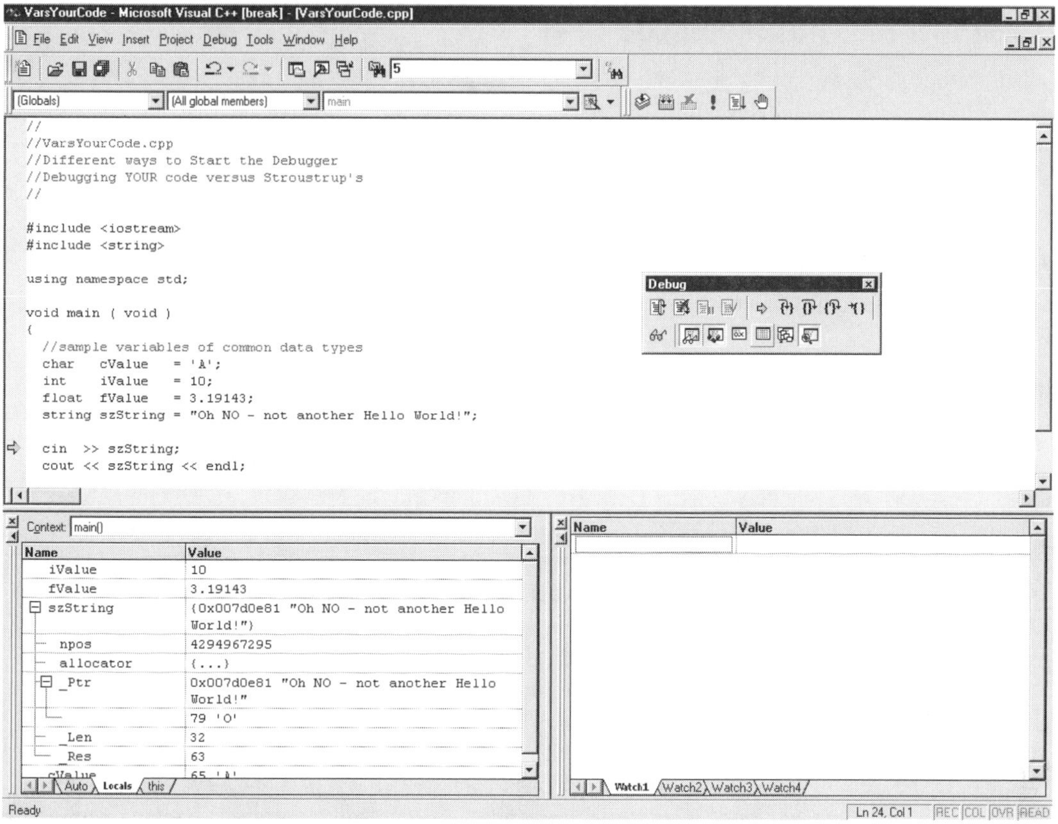

Figure 6.12   Viewing *szString* in the Variables window's Local tab

You may also reconfigure the row and column behavior. To auto-size a column to fit its contents, double-click on the vertical divider at the column edge. To size a column manually, drag the right divider to the left or right. (Rows are sized to fit the current font and cannot be resized manually. To change the font size, use the Fonts and Colors tab of the Options dialog box [Tools menu].)

The Auto tab displays information about variables from the current and previous statements. Variables appear in alphabetical order. If a statement spans multiple lines, the Auto tab displays variables from the lines corresponding to that statement, up to a ten-line limit.

The Locals tab displays the names, values, and types of all local variables in the current function. As you trace through a program, new variables come into scope.

The This tab displays type, name, and value information about the object pointed to by the pointer This. All base classes of the object are automatically expanded.

Design Tip   *You can right-click on the This window to bring up a shortcut menu of commands.*

Debug Your *Code NOT* Stroustrup's *C++!*

When the trace arrow is sitting on a code statement that invokes either a method (sometimes called a *member function*) or a standalone function that invokes a standard C/C++ subroutine, *caution* is the word! It is at this point that you *must* knowledgeably select your next Step Into or Step Over option.

Figure 6.12 shows the trace arrow sitting on the *cin >> szString;* statement. At this point, what you *do* want to do is Step Over the call to **cin**. You do *not* want to debug **cin** itself!

If you are executing *VarsYourCode.cpp*, **either press F10, or click on the Step Over button on the Debug toolbar** (seven buttons from the left – top row, see Figure 6.4). You will not see anything apparent happen (actually, if you look closely, the drop-down scope list in the Variables window – will turn gray).

How to Enter User Input While Debugging an Application

When you are debugging a code statement that expects input from the user, you will need to switch to the execution window. The ALT+TAB key combination, Windows Task switch key combination, is the quickest way to toggle between the Debugger's window and the MS-DOS mode compatibility window. At this point, **press ALT+TAB**. You should switch to the execution window (see Figure 6.13). **Press ALT+TAB** a second time, and you should return to the Visual C++ window. Of course, this approach works only if you have no other task running, or you have not task-switched between Microsoft Visual Studio C++ and some other task first.

To enter your new string, **press ALT+TAB** a third time. This will switch you back to the execution window. **Type "NewString"** (without the quotes) and **press the ENTER key**, as seen in Figure 6.4. Notice that the trace arrow (seen in Figure 6.13) is still on the *cin >>* statement.

Once you have entered *NewString* and pressed ENTER, your display screen should look similar to Figure 6.5. The Debugger has automatically switched back to its main Visual C++ window.

Although the Debugger color-codes Variables window contents, in the grayscale image you see, it is difficult to detect. However, the *szString* value, containing the newly entered *"NewString"*, is displayed in red. The Debugger switches the color in the Variables window Value field anytime a variable's value is changed by the previously executed code statement.

Had you selected the Step Into option when the trace arrow was on the *cin >> szString;* statement, you would have seen a Debugger window that looks like Figure 6.16.

The Visual C++ Debugger is extremely powerful. This example demonstrates the Debugger's ability to debug right into language-specific routines. Here you see the Debugger's window contents switching to *szString*'s **string, basic_istream** template, ready to debug the template line-by-line!

Whenever you inadvertently select Step Into instead of the intended Step Over, to get yourself back to *your* program's code, select the Step Out option, the eighth button from the left, top row, on the Debug toolbar (see Figure 6.4) or simultaneously press SHIFT+F11.

Quick, What Does My Variable Contain?

A neat feature of the Debugger is its ability to show you a variable's current contents by simply hovering the I-beam mouse pointer over a variable's name in your source code. Figure 6.17 shows the I-beam mouse pointer over the *szString* in the *cout << szString;* statement.

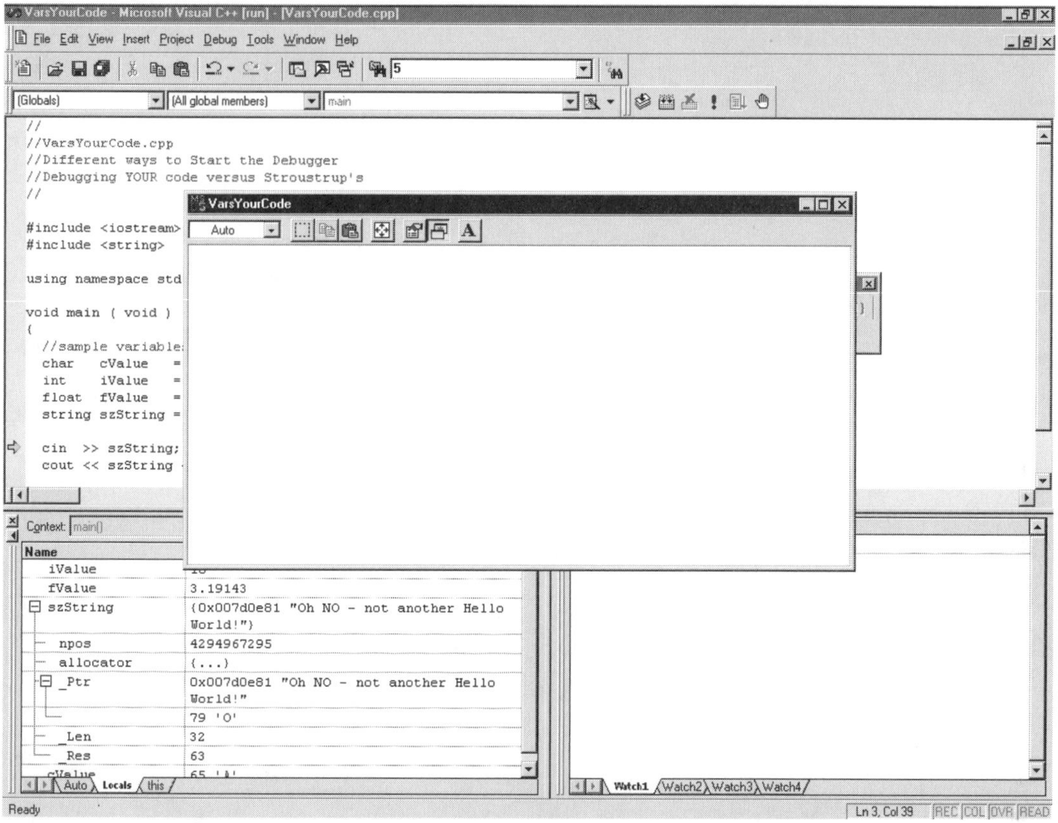

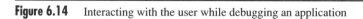

```
//
//VarsYourCode.cpp
//Different ways to Start the Debugger
//Debugging YOUR code versus Stroustrup's
//

#include <iostream>
#include <string>

using namespace std

void main ( void )
{
  //sample variable:
  char   cValue   =
  int    iValue   =
  float  fValue   =
  string szString =

  cin  >> szString;
  cout << szString
```

Name	
iValue	
fValue	3.19143
szString	(0x007d0e81 "Oh NO – not another Hello World!")
npos	4294967295
allocator	(...)
_Ptr	0x007d0e81 "Oh NO – not another Hello World!"
	79 'O'
Len	32
Res	63
cValue	65

Figure 6.13   ALT+TAB task-switch to the MS-DOS execution window

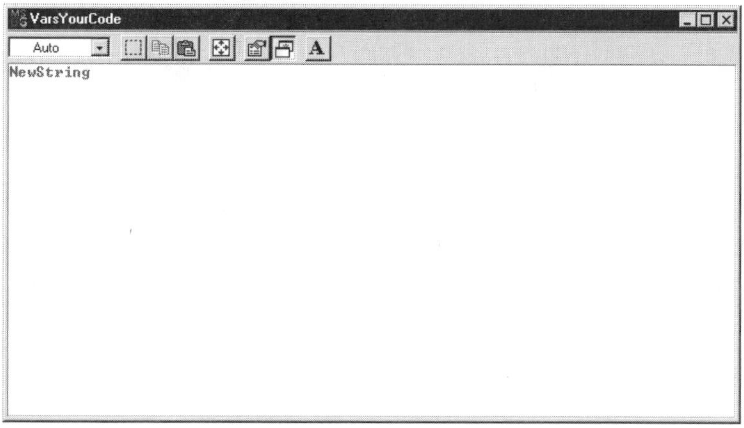

```
VarsYourCode
Auto
NewString
```

Figure 6.14   Interacting with the user while debugging an application

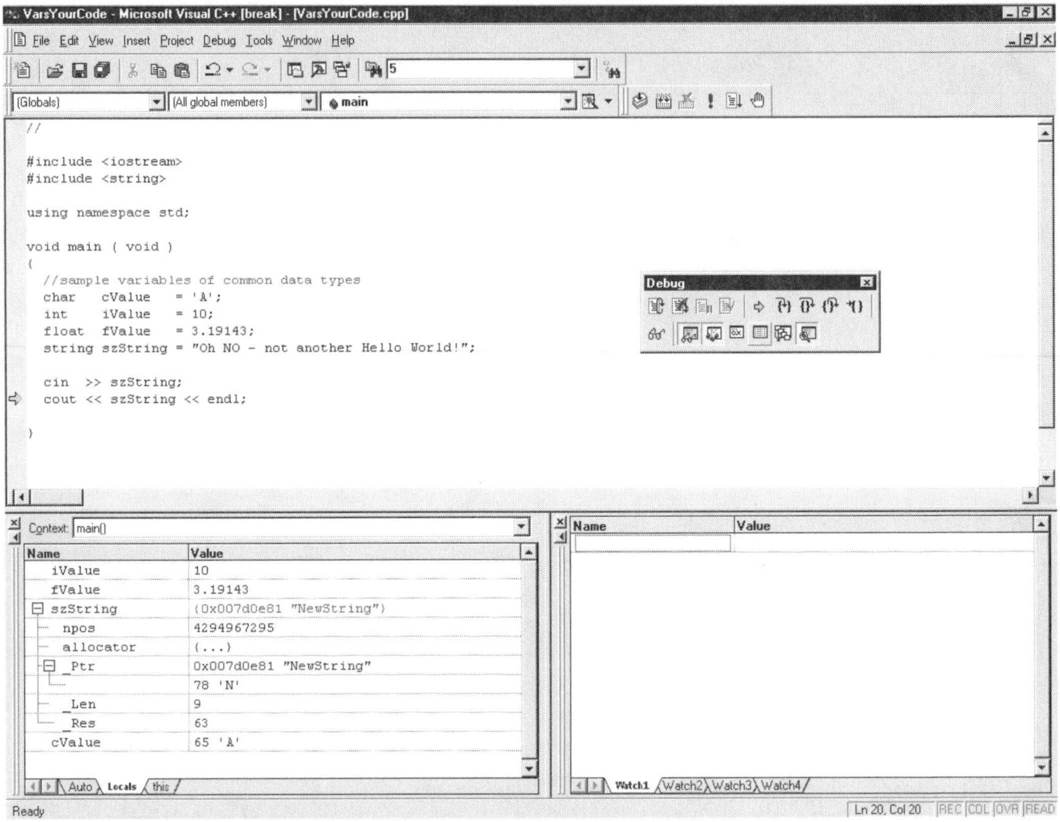

Figure 6.15   Variables window updated with newly entered *szString* value

The pop-up window displays the variable's name, current value, and data type–specific details in this example *szString*'s starting address (in hexadecimal).

Stopping the Debugger Midstream

For one reason or another, you will need to stop the Debugger at times. One reason, of course, is that the results of the last single-step revealed a logic problem in your program. To stop the Debugger, simply press SHIFT+F5, or click the second icon from the left, top row, on the Debug toolbar. If you are trying the example program on your Debugger, you will need to stop the Debugger at this point.

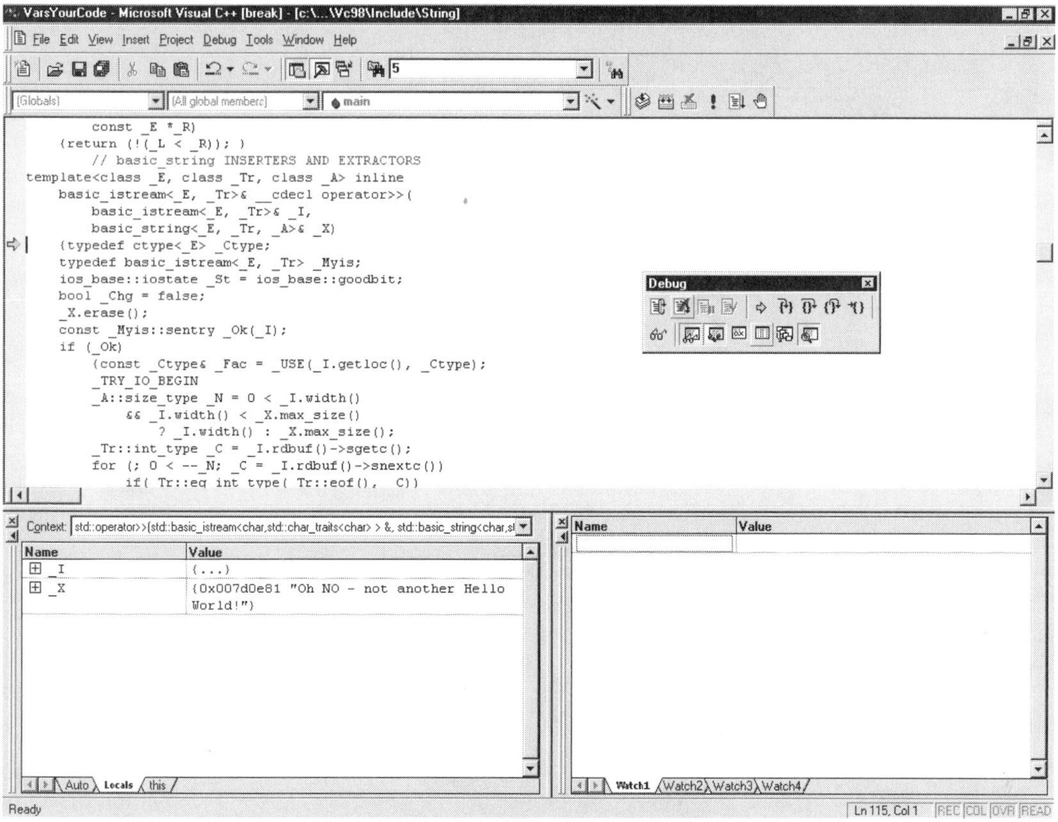

Figure 6.16   Accidentally selecting the Step Into option instead of Step Over

Zip Me to a Specific Line of Code

When you are trying to debug a program that has previously debugged code segments, you need not single-step over the "good" code. Under these circumstances, you will need to set a breakpoint. The Debugger is capable of executing your program full-speed up to a breakpoint and then stopping for single-step mode (see Figure 6.18).

The quickest way to set a breakpoint is:

1. Place the cursor on the code statement where you would like the Debugger to stop.

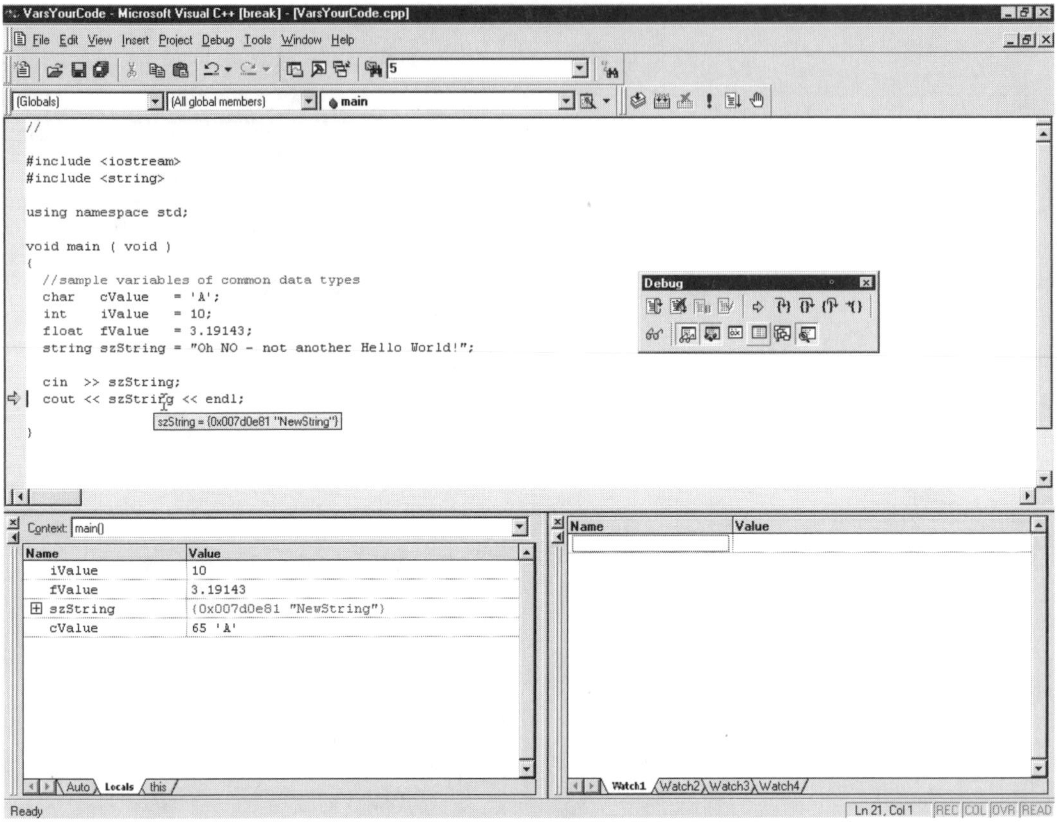

Figure 6.17   Viewing a variable's current contents using the I-beam mouse pointer

2. Click on the Insert/Remove Breakpoint option. (You use these same two steps to remove a previously set breakpoint.)

At this point in your interactive trace, ***using whichever approach you prefer, set a breakpoint on the cin >> statement.*** As you can see from Figure 6.19, you can easily tell if a program has a breakpoint set by seeing if any (red) stop sign icons are to the left of any code statements.

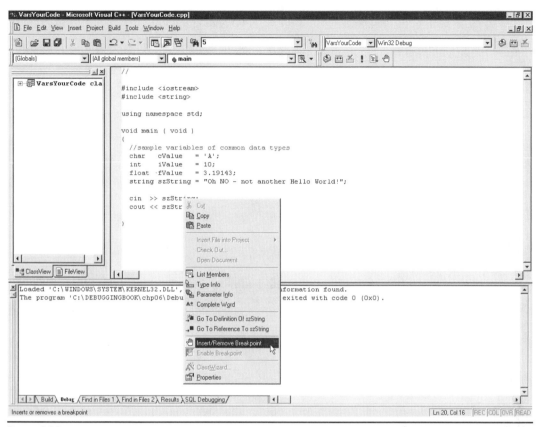

Figure 6.18   Setting a breakpoint by placing the cursor on the statement and right-clicking

Executing Full-Speed Up to a Breakpoint

As always, several interface options are available to you for running a program full-speed up to a breakpoint. The longest approach is to first click on the Visual C++ Build main menu option, followed by selecting the Start Debug option, followed by the Go option (see Figure 6.20). The quickest approach is to simply press F5!

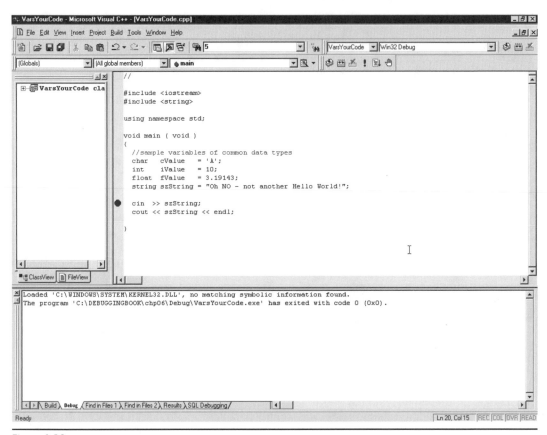

Figure 6.19   Viewing set breakpoints with the (red) stop sign symbol

If you are following the examples with your Debugger, ***press F5 now***. As you look at Figure 6.21, notice that the trace arrow is now sitting directly over the breakpoint (red) stop sign symbol. The Variables window contains all of the defined and initialized variables' contents just as if you had single-stepped each declaring statement.

Run to Cursor

Although not demonstrated here, an even quicker approach to running full-speed up to a specific code statement involves the Run to Cursor option. Run to Cursor executes the program as far as the line that contains the insertion point (in other words, wherever you have placed the I-beam cursor in your source code). This is equivalent to setting a temporary breakpoint at the insertion point location.

While the Debugger is running, you can access the Run to Cursor command by either clicking on the Debug menu followed by the Run to Cursor option, or simultaneously pressing CTRL+F10.

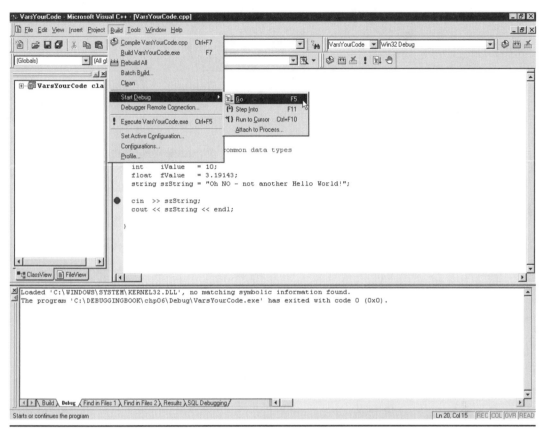

Figure 6.20 Long-hand approach to accessing the Go (F5) command

Test It NOW!

Since this is a book on debugging your applications, it is assumed that you are in a debug cycle and are now ready to full-speed execute the entire "debugged" algorithm. The Go command actually has three uses:

- To Go full-speed up to a breakpoint and then stop for single-step mode.
- To Go full-speed up to the *next* breakpoint and then stop for single-step mode (if you have set more than one breakpoint).
- To execute your program full-speed.

If you have been following the example, ***press F5*** (or use the long-hand approach discussed in Figure 6.20—no bias intended) to complete the execution of *VarsYourCode.cpp*.

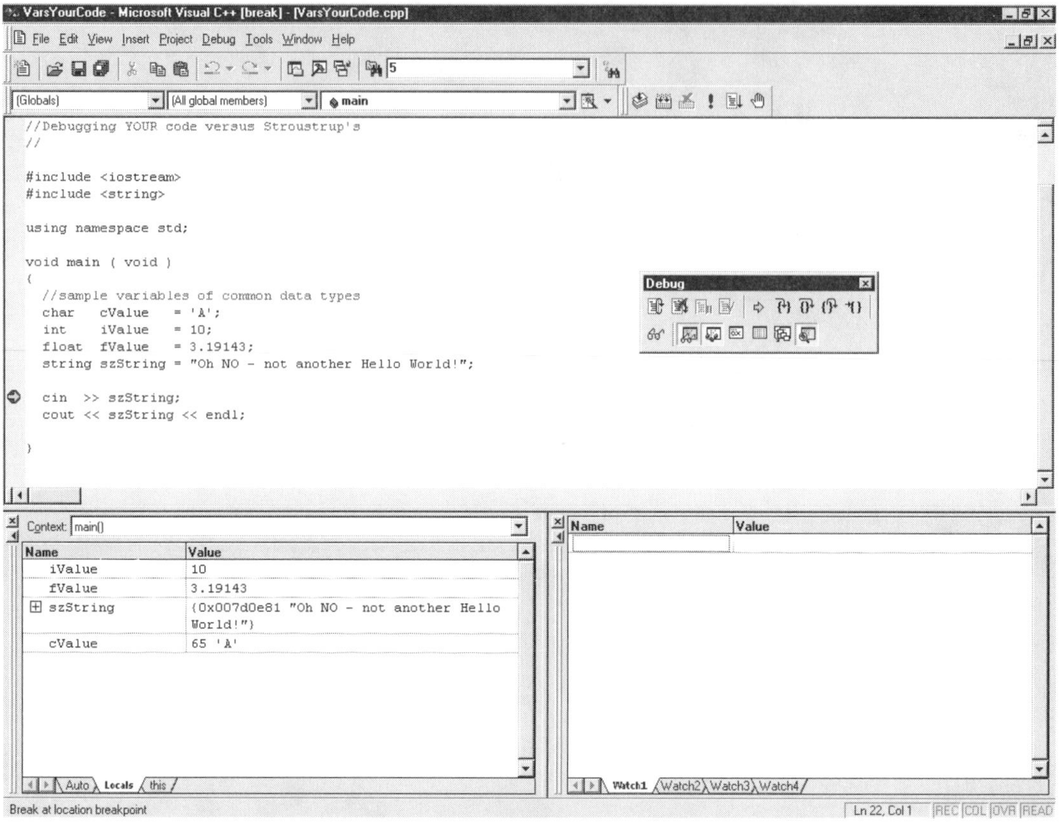

Figure 6.21   Results of executing a Go (F5) with a breakpoint set

Advanced Debugger Tricks

Even knowing the basic Debugger commands just discussed will not guarantee the most efficient debug phase in your application development cycle. There is more to using the Debugger than knowing what it can do and how to mechanically trigger the options.

The last half of this chapter begins with a discussion of several more advanced Debugger options and ends with a discussion of how tactful use of the Debugger's capabilities is necessary in order to minimize the time spent debugging.

Running with New Values

The Microsoft Visual C++ Debugger includes many time-saving features. Take, for example, the Debugger's ability to continue debugging an application from the current statement as if your variables had different values. One quick example would be the test for an **if...else** statement:

```
if (cResponse == 'Y' )
  cout << "True action taken...\n";
else
  cout << "False action taken...\n";
```

The Debugger provides three methods for changing a variable's contents at debug time.

Modify the Value of a Variable in the Variables Window

Since auto-tracking is such an easy, viable approach to examining a variable's contents, the easiest way to enter a new variable value is right in the Variables window. The following five steps explain how this is done:

1. You first click inside the Variables window on the Auto tab, the Locals tab, or the This tab.

2. Next, you click on the variable you want to modify.

3. When the variable is an array or object, use the + box to expand the view until you see the value you want to modify.

4. You are almost done. Now double-click the value, or use the TAB key to move the insertion point to the value you want to modify.

5. Finally, type in the new value, and press the ENTER key. The new value appears in red.

You are now ready to continue debugging your application as if the variable had contained the new value all along.

If you are following along with an interactive trace of the sample programs, *__you will need to enter the following program and single-step until the trace arrow is sitting on the__ if... __statement__* at this point:

```
//
//RunTimeValueChanges.cpp
//Different ways to reset variable contents
// at run time
//

#include <iostream>

using namespace std;

void main ( void )
{
  char   cResponse = 'Y';

  if ( cResponse == 'Y' )
    cout << "True action taken...\n";
  else
      cout << "False action taken...\n";
}
```

Figure 6.22 shows an initial Debugger session all set up to debug an **if...else** statement with the *cResponse* variable's initialized value of *'Y'*. Notice that the trace arrow is sitting on the *if (cResponse == 'Y')* statement and that the Variables window shows *cResponse* with the anticipated *'Y'* value.

(For variety, the following figures show the Debug toolbar moved into the main menu section of the Visual C++ window. You can do this by simply clicking on the Debug toolbar's title, holding the left mouse button down, and dragging the Debug toolbar into the main menu area. Visual C++ will automatically resize the Debug toolbar's window shape, making it fit inside the main menu area.)

Figure 6.23 shows what happens when you ***left-click the mouse once on a variable name within the Variables window***. Notice that the Debugger has converted the display of *'Y'* to its equivalent ASCII table value of 89 (which is difficult to see due to the Debugger's color banding of the statement).

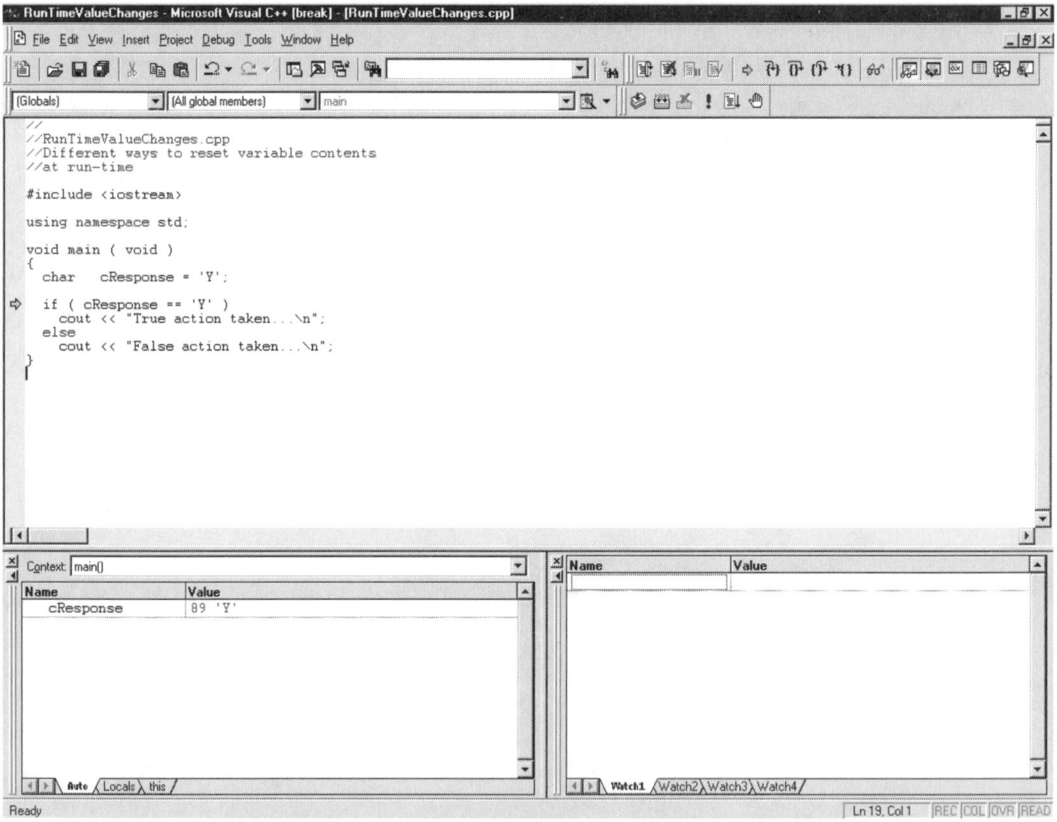

Figure 6.22   Debugger set to debug a *cResponse* value of *'Y'*

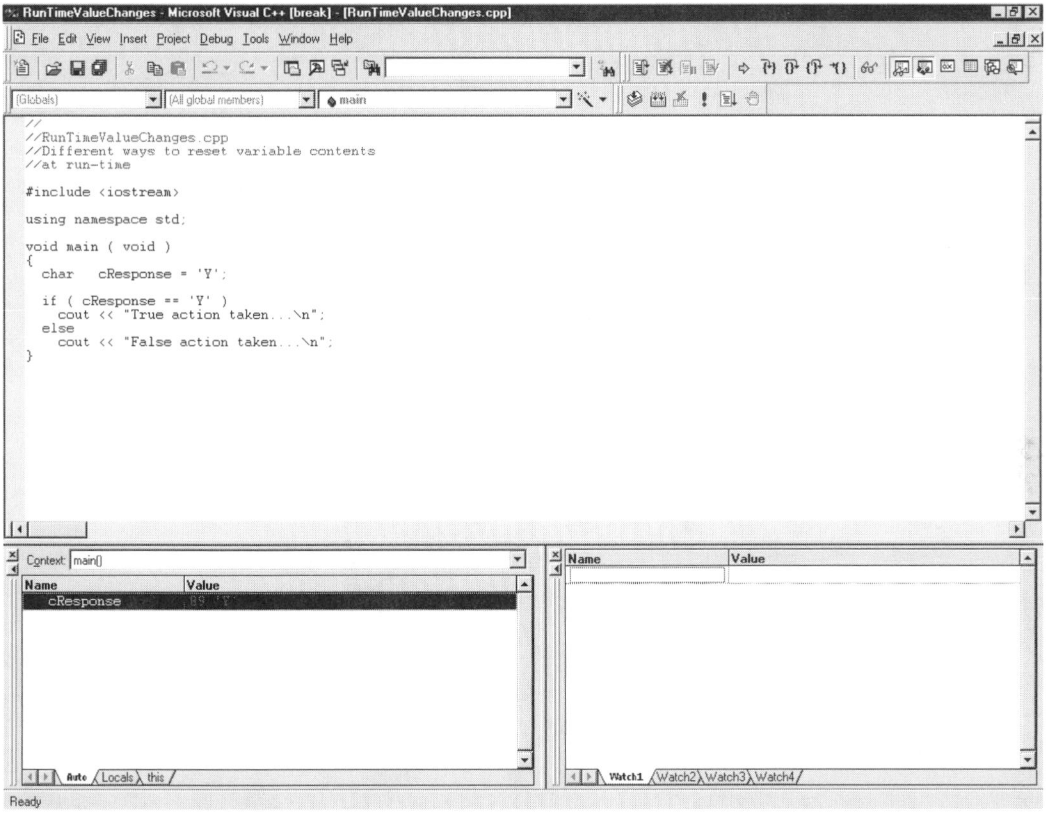

Figure 6.23   Clicking on a variable within the Variables window

Figure 6.24 illustrates what happens when you ***click on a selected variable's value***. Here, the Debugger is prepared to accept a substitute for *cResponse*'s 89, which is highlighted in a different color (here, a different gray value).

To enter any variable's new value, simply ***type an appropriate data type and range***. Figure 6.25 shows the new *cResponse* ASCII table value of 78, equivalent to an uppercase *'N'*.

Figure 6.26 proves the Debugger accepts this new value for *cResponse* by debugging the **else** portion of the **if…else** statement, with just a ***single press of the F10 key (Step Over)***.

You can see from Figure 6.27 that the trace arrow jumped to the *cout* statement in the **else** portion of the **if…else** statement. (To see the newly entered value of *cResponse*, you will need to click on the Locals tab in the Variables window since *cResponse*'s auto-tracking goes out of scope for the traced statement.)

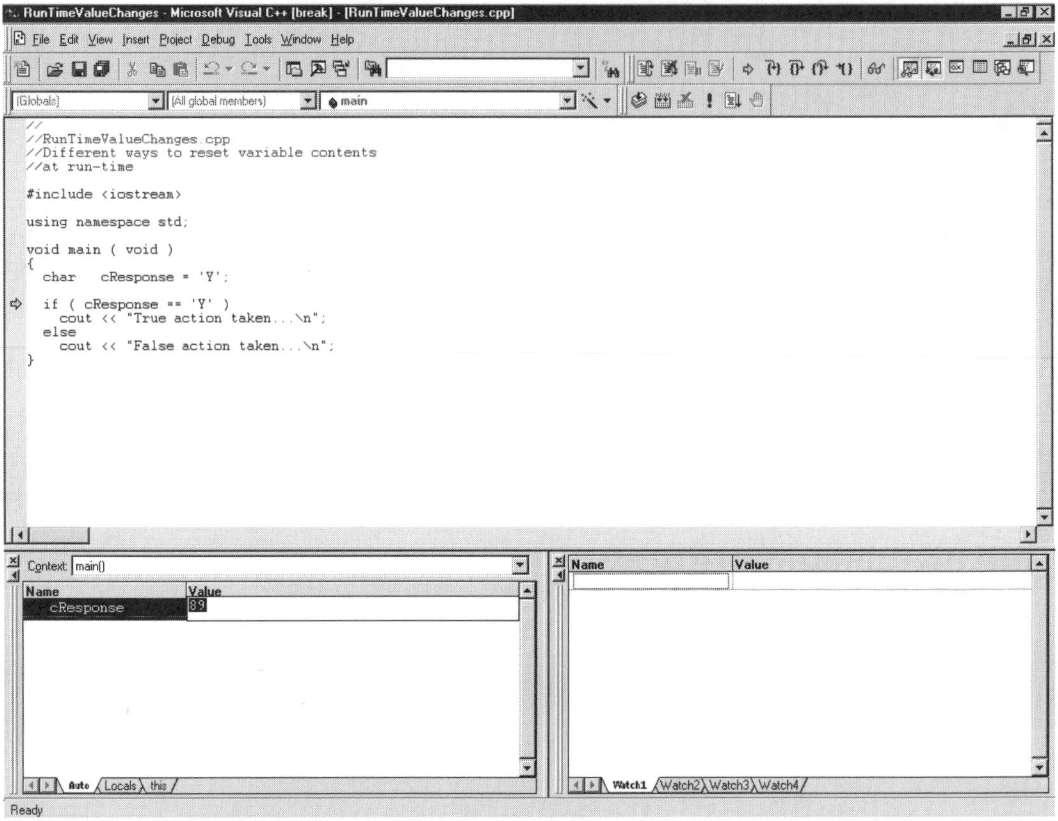

Figure 6.24   Setting the Variables window up to change a variable's value

Careful use, on your part, of this debug-time variable value change can save you a lot of time debugging an application by not forcing you to reinitialize a variable to a different value or, worse, interacting with a newly created external file (disk, network, or interactive end-user).

You can perform the same type of variable value substitution from two other locations, the Watch window or the QuickWatch window.

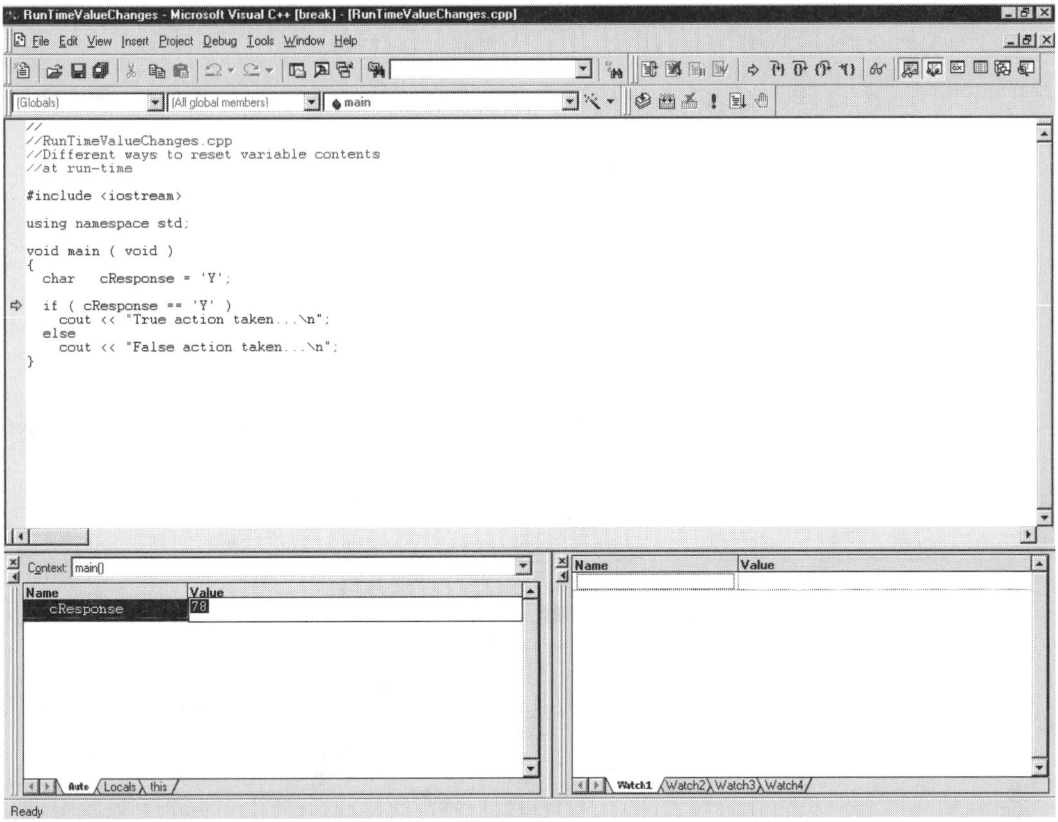

Figure 6.25   Changing *cResponse*'s value from ASCII table 89 ('*Y*') to 78 ('*N*')

Modify the Value of a Variable or Contents of a Register Using the Watch Window

To modify a variable's value at debug time using the Watch window, follow these three steps:

1. First you either double-click the value in the Watch window, or use the TAB key to move the insertion point to the value you want to modify.

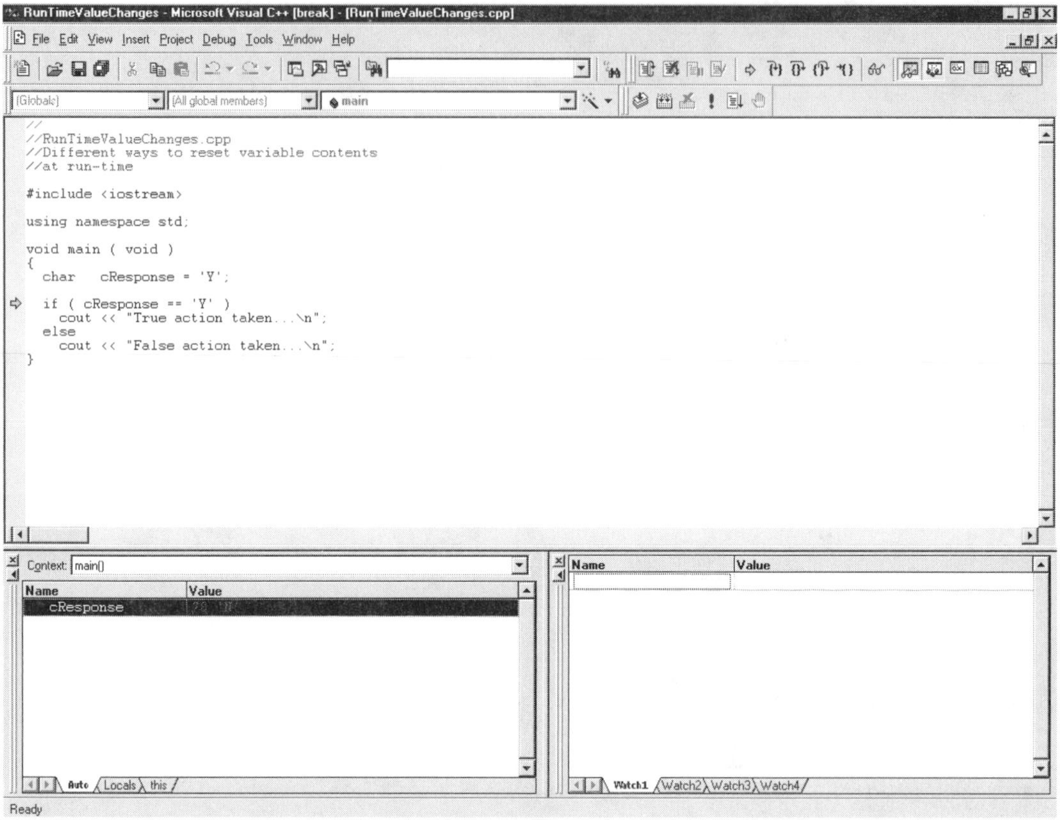

Figure 6.26 Ready to single-step if...else with *cResponse* of '*N*'

2. Next, if the variable is an array or object, use the + box to expand the view until you see the value you want to modify.

3. Finally, you simply insert the new value, and press ENTER.

Modify the Value of a Variable or Contents of a Register Using QuickWatch

The third method for changing a variable's value at debug time involves an interaction with the QuickWatch window. ***The following seven steps illustrate how this is accomplished***:

1. From the Debug menu, you left-click QuickWatch (SHIFT+F9) (see Figure 6.28).

2. In the Expression text box, type the variable or register name.

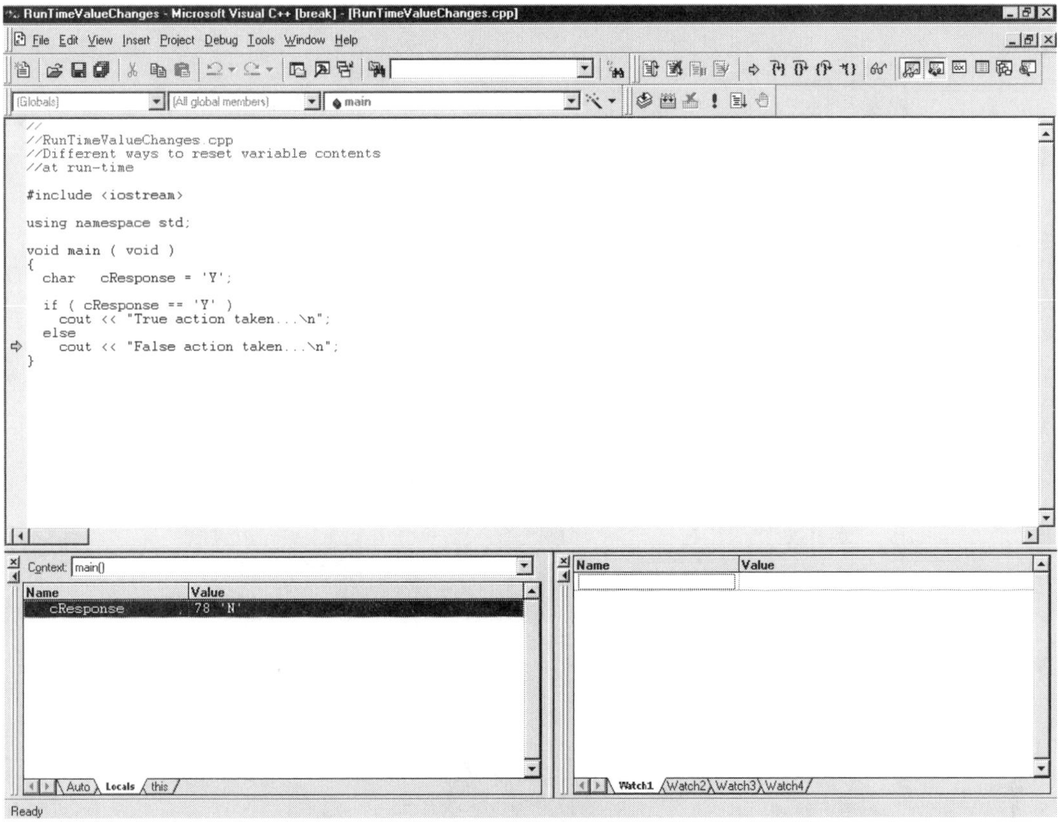

Figure 6.27   Trace arrow showing runtime acceptance of 'N'

3. Click the Recalculate button (see Figure 6.29).

4. If the variable is an array or object, use the + box to expand the view until you see the value you want to modify. (To change the value of an array, modify the individual fields or elements. You cannot edit an entire array at once.)

5. Using the TAB key, you move to the value you want to modify (see Figure 6.30).

6. Type the new value, and then press ENTER (see Figure 6.31).

7. Click Close.

Once again, as you can see from Figure 6.32, the Debugger is now ready to single-step the **if...else** statement with a *cResponse* value of 'N'.

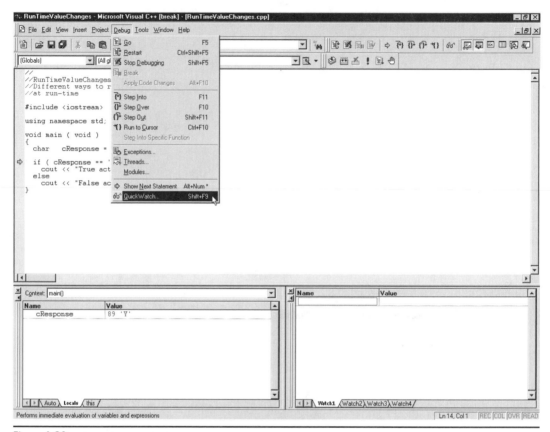

Figure 6.28 Resetting a variable's value with QuickWatch

Loop Debugging Tricks

All software engineers know that testing the number of times a loop iterates is tantamount to a solid robust design. The Microsoft Visual C++ Debugger is set up to efficiently trace the number of loop iterations with a **for**, **while**, or **do…while** loop body containing a significant amount of code statements, function calls, and class method calls. Even repeated uses of Step Over (F10) would be ineffective for simply checking the *number of times* the loop iterates, as opposed to *what* the loop does.

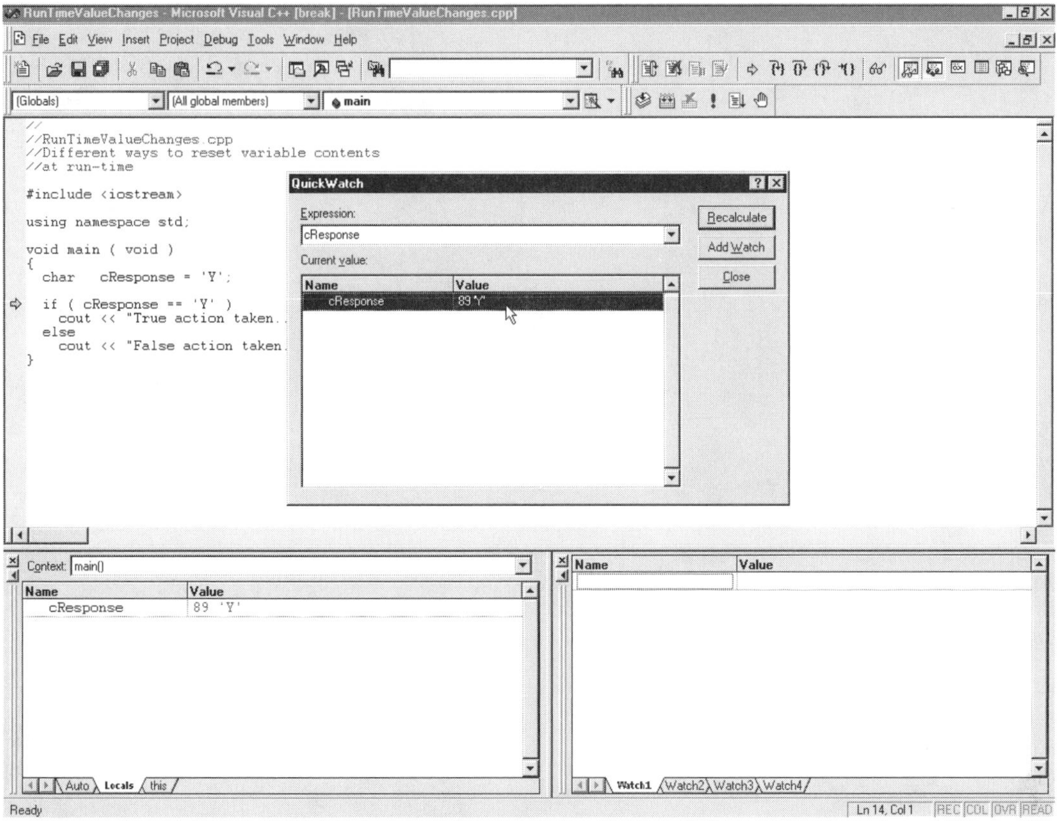

Figure 6.29   Pressing the QuickWatch Recalculate button

However, before demonstrating the use of a cleverly placed breakpoint, consider simply changing the *MAX_EXTENT* when it comes to debugging a **for** loop's iteration count, as in the following comparison statements:

```
#define MAX_EXTENT 10000
for( int iOffset = 0; iOffset < MAX_EXTENT; iOffset++);
```

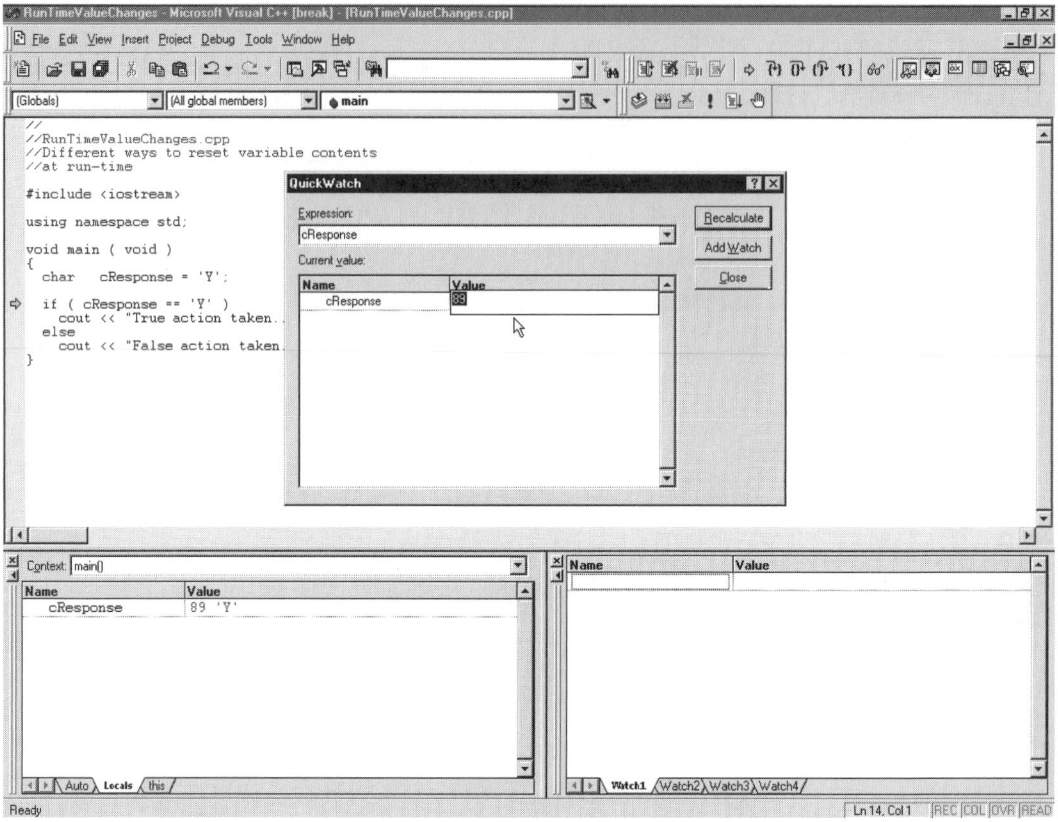

Figure 6.30 Tabbing to the Value column

becomes for testing purposes:

```
#define MAX_EXTENT 5
```

Under many circumstances, this approach will suffice to test the loop iterations. The assumption is that if the loop iterates properly for 5 attempts, it should for 10,000! Note, however, this simple technique would be inappropriate for many applications heavily dependent on sophisticated I/O interactions.

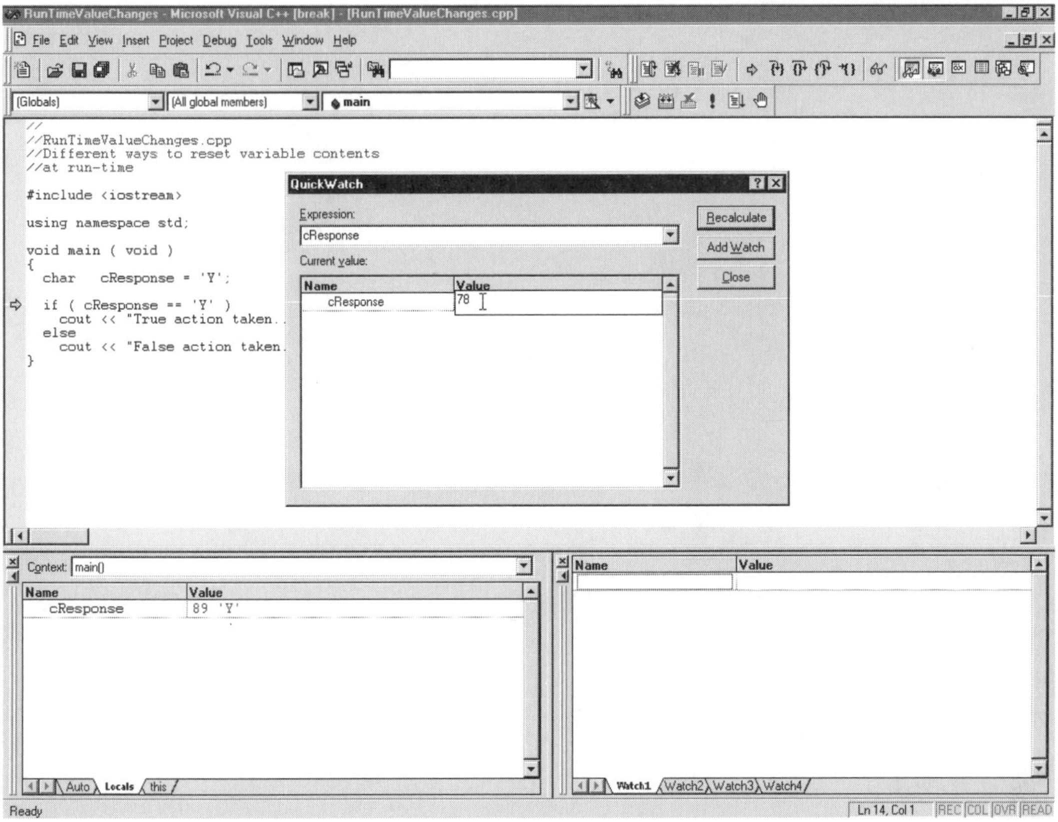

Figure 6.31   Entering the new variable's value

When a loop test condition does not lend itself to the approach just discussed, your next alternative is to selectively place a breakpoint within the loop body. You know from previous discussions that the Debug | Go command (F5) will full-speed execute your program to the end, or if a breakpoint is set, full-speed execute the algorithm up to the next breakpoint, stopping for single-step mode.

The placement of the single breakpoint within the loop body is up to you. Basically, there are two pivotal locations; either the first statement within the loop body:

```
while ( test_condition )
{
```

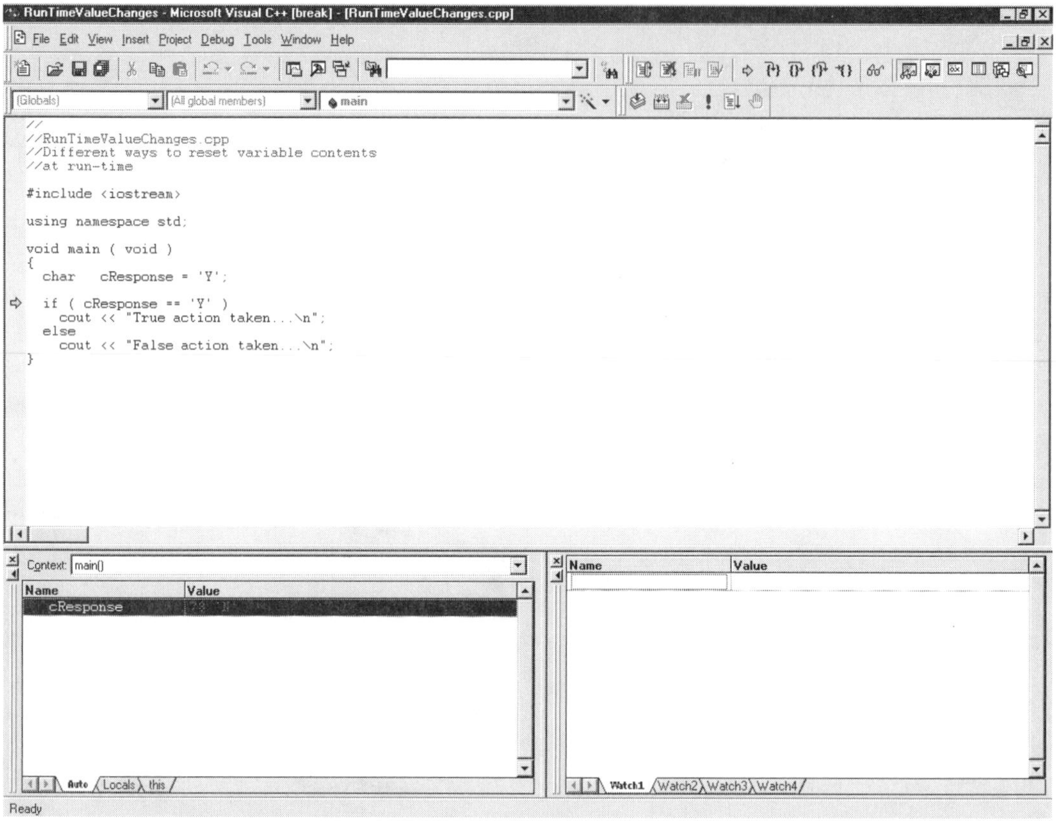

Figure 6.32 Debugging with *cResponse* equal to '*N*'

```
statement1; // option 1: place breakpoint here
  statement2;
  //...
  statementn;
}
```

or the last statement within the loop body:

```
while ( test_condition )
{
  statement1;
  statement2;
  //...
  statementn; // option 2: place breakpoint here
}
```

Once you have one of the two breakpoint options selected, you simply run (F5) your program, counting the number of times you "hit" the breakpoint before exiting the loop. Each press of F5 (Debug | Run command) counts!

Debugging Function Calls

The minute you jump from debugging inline code statements to subroutine calls, the possibilities for logical errors dramatically increase; did you pass the correct values, were the variables passed call-by-value or call-by-reference, which call-by approach *did* you want verses which one did you get, and so on. The Microsoft Visual C++ Debugger's ability to display this information in the Call Stack window is the most efficient technique available for locating and diagnosing these problems.

To trace through this section's examples, you will now need to enter the *BadRecursiveCallStack.cpp* program:

```
//
//DebuggingSubroutines.cpp
//

#include <iostream>

using namespace std;

//Notice clean alignment of formal
//argument types...

int aSimpleSubroutine( char   cValue,
                       int    iValue,
                       float  fValue );

void main ( void )
{
  char   cValue = 'A';
  int    iValue = 125;
  float  fValue = 1.2345;

  aSimpleSubroutine ( cValue,
                      iValue,
                      fValue  );
}

int aSimpleSubroutine( char   cValue,
                       int    iValue,
                       float  fValue )
{
  //subroutine body
  return iValue;
}
```

Since you want to learn how to debug subroutine calls, at this point, instead of pressing F10 for Step Over mode, ***press F11 until your monitor's display matches Figure 6.33***, for Step Into. Remember, Step Over and Step Into (F10 or F11) perform the identical single-step operations until the trace arrow is sitting on a subroutine call statement.

You can access the Visual C++ Call Stack window by clicking on the Visual C++ View menu and choosing the Debug Windows option and then Call Stack (see Figure 6.34).

If you are following along, ***press ALT+7*** at this time. The Call Stack window will now appear (see Figure 6.35).

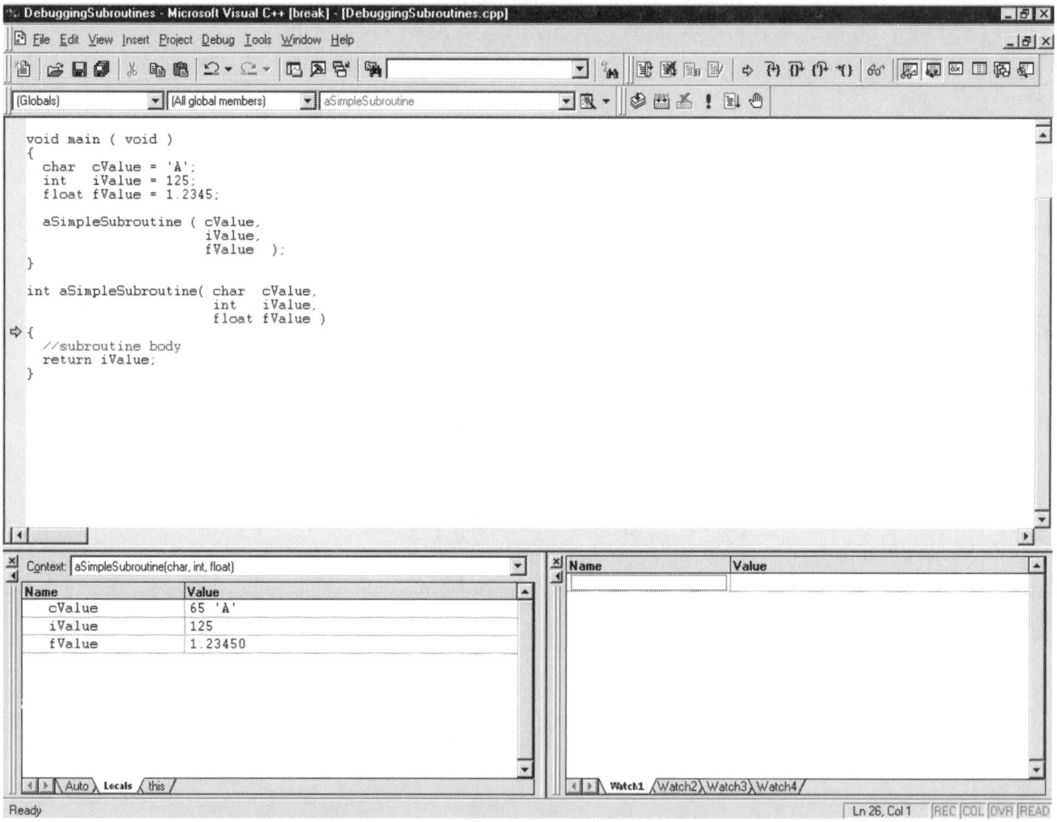

Figure 6.33   Step into (F11) *aSimpleSubroutine* trace showing initial argument values

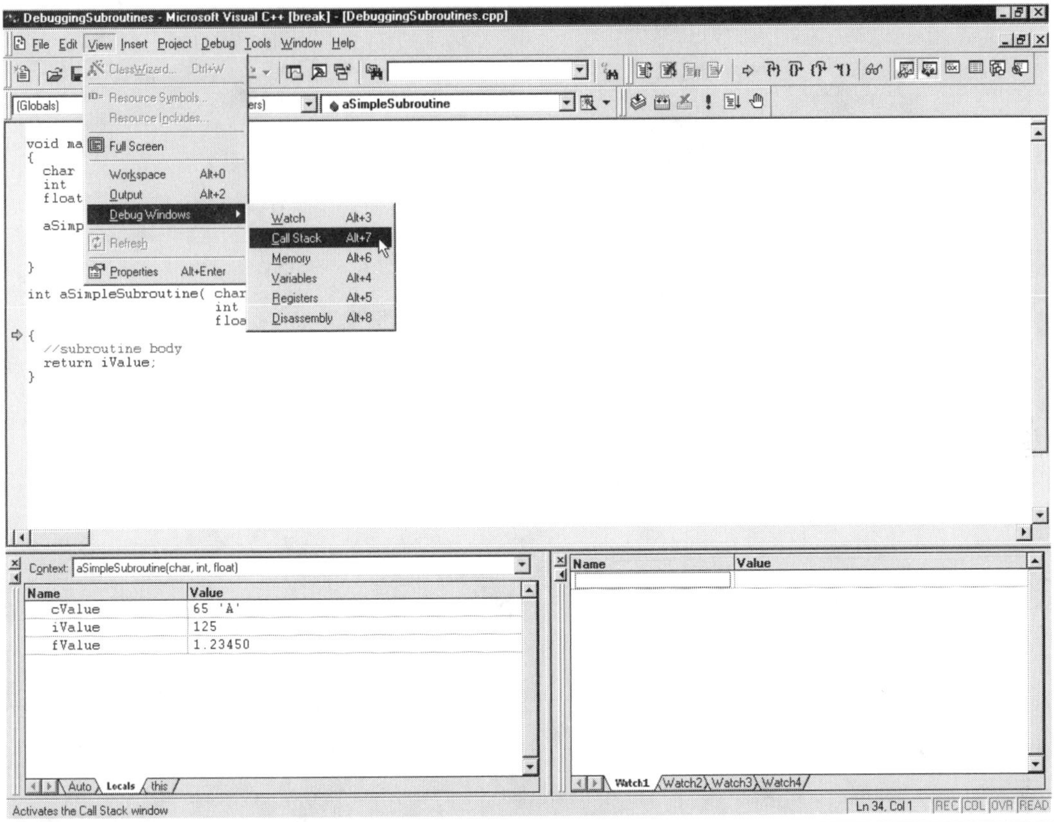

Figure 6.34 Accessing the Debug Windows | Call Stack (ALT+7)

You will see a small yellow arrow (default color) in the Call Stack window's left margin that points to *aSimpleSubroutine*, which is (in this example only) the function name for the last called subroutine (function or class method).

The Call Stack window displays the subroutine's name followed optionally by each argument's data type and current value. Below the function's name, you will see the calling subroutine's name along with the line number of the calling statement and byte-offset. Figure 6.36 follows this information with the listing for the *mainCRTStartup( )* subroutine, its invoking call statement line number, byte offset, and the *KERNEL32* physical addresses for each subroutine's location in RAM.

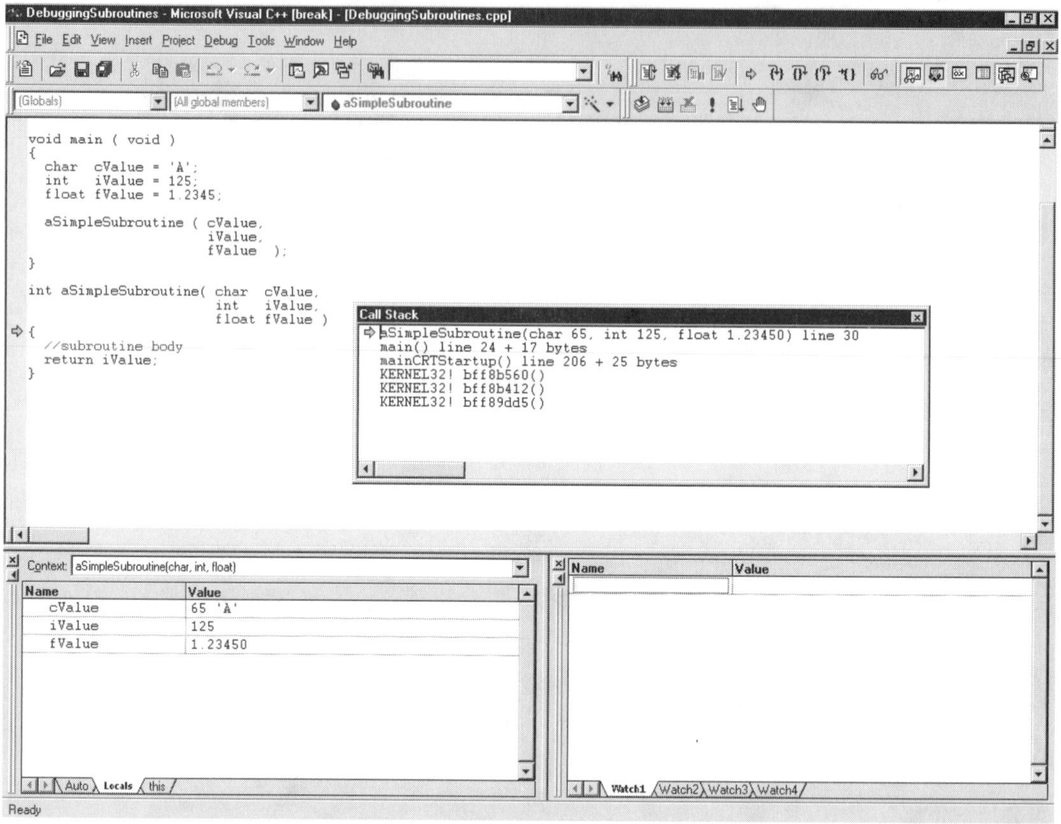

Figure 6.35 Viewing the call stack

For comparison purposes only, Figure 6.36 shows the same algorithm rewritten using the call-by-reference argument calling convention instead of the call-by-value method traced in Figure 6.35. Notice how the Call Stack window flags the parameter passing calling convention change by including the address operator & in the formal argument's data type. Instead of Figure 6.35's *char 65, int 125, float 1.23450 argument types and values*, you see in Figure 6.36 *char & 65, int & 125, float & 1.23450, reflecting the call-by-reference calling convention.*

The types of information displayed within the Call Stack window are user definable. By right-clicking the mouse within the Call Stack window (see Figure 6.37), you can turn on/off

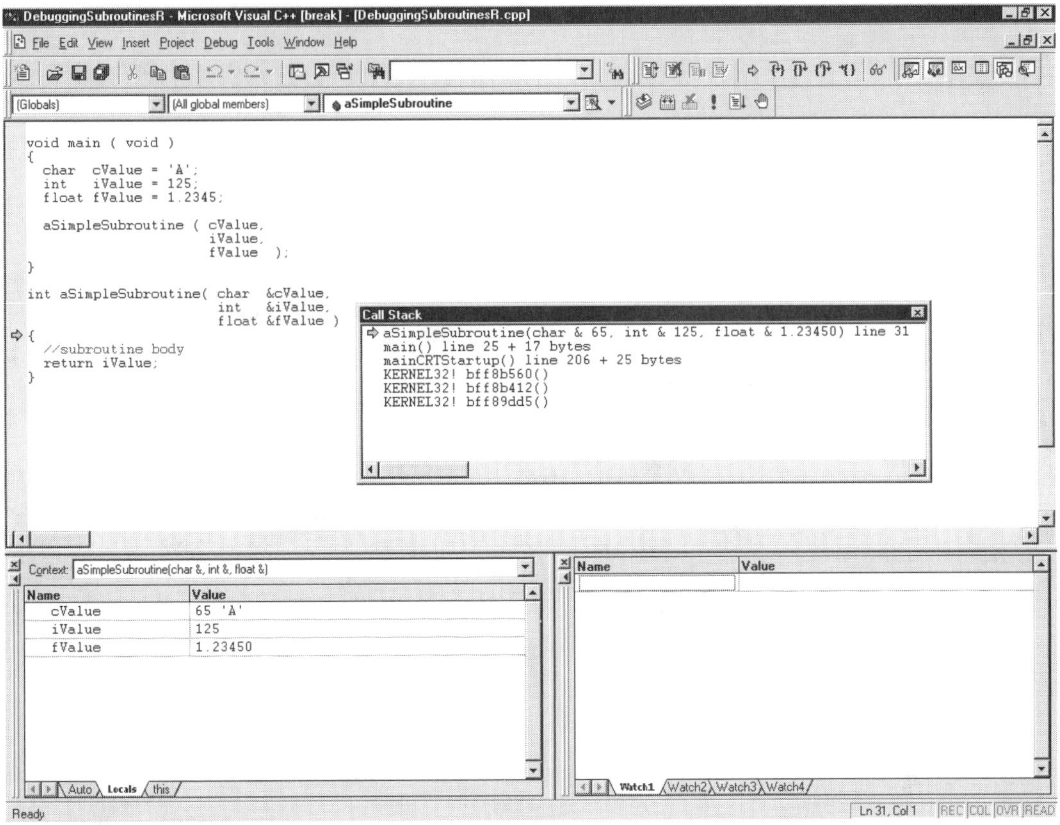

Figure 6.36 Rewrite using call-by-reference

Parameter Values and Parameter Types, and switch between the default output value precision or Hexadecimal Display formatting.

The Call Stack window has one more useful feature. By ***double-clicking on the name of the calling routine (in this example main())***, the Visual C++ Debugger will auto-locate the source file and calling statement. Two light-green arrows highlight the relationship between the Call Stack window and the auto-tracked source code statement (see Figure 6.38).

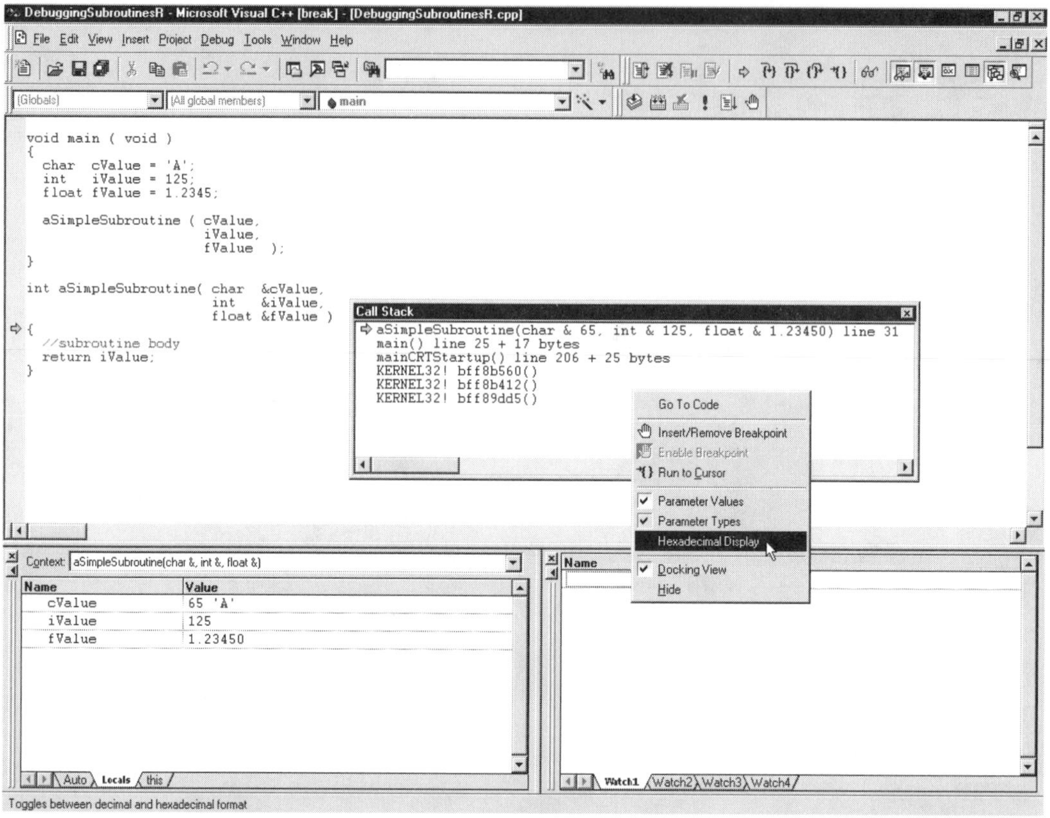

Figure 6.37   Call Stack local menu (right-click within Call Stack window) options

Recursive Calls and the Call Stack

The somewhat whimsical definition many computer science instructors use for *recursion* goes something like this: "definition for recursion—see recursion." The first time you encountered recursive algorithms in your formal training, you undoubtedly felt that definition perfectly matched your mental confusion. You thought, now really, a subroutine that calls itself? What possible use could there be for such a bizarre feature? Then you learned about binary trees, In-Fix, Pre-Fix, and Post-Fix algorithms, and tree traversals.

While it is true that recursive algorithms are clean, tight, and fascinating code segments, tracing and debugging them require a unique level of expertise and experience. The Microsoft Visual C++ Debugger's Call Stack window is exactly what you need to detect errors in these clever code recyclers.

Take, for example, the code segment that follows. At this point in your software engineering career, if you see one more "Hello World!" program, or one more recursive Factorial example—well, you will probably decide to become a travel agent! However, a recursive Factorial algorithm is, in all

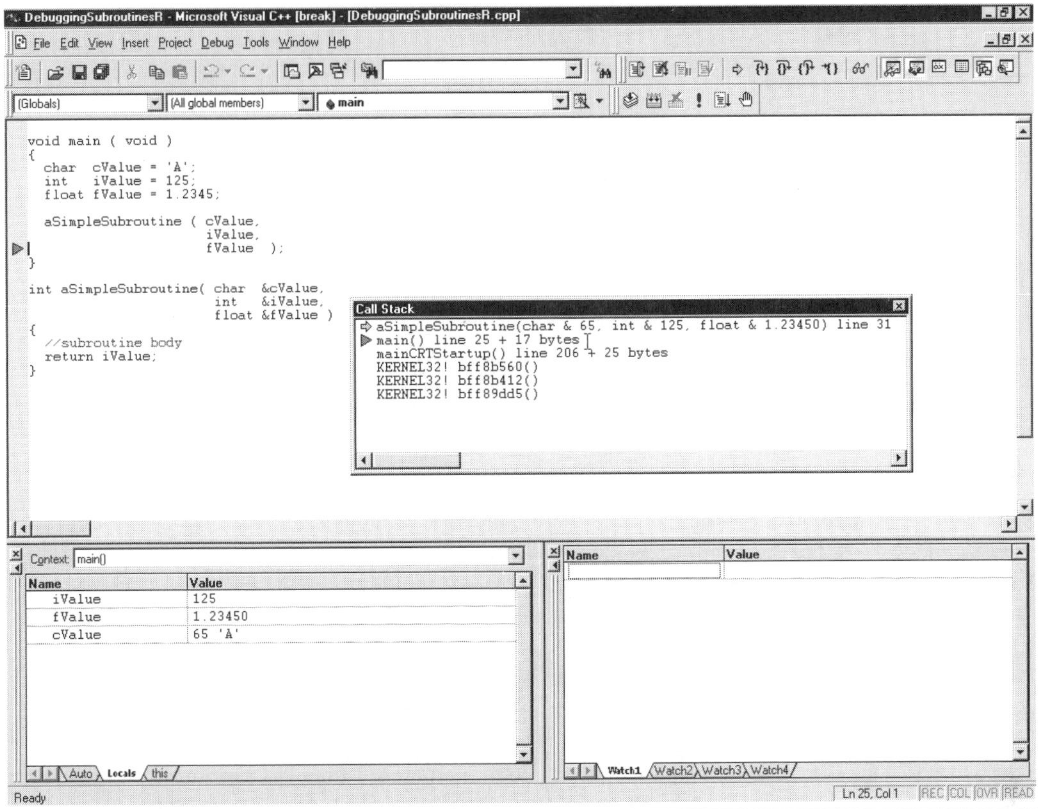

Figure 6.38   Locating the calling routine and calling statement

respects, a perfect starting point. The algorithm itself is straightforward; you simply multiply an initial value, for example, 4, by one less than 4, 3, then one less than 3, 2, and so on until you reach 1:

```
4 * 3 * 2 * 1
```

Hard-wiring such an algorithm would necessarily be below a programmer's expertise:

```
iRecursiveCalculation = 4 * 3 * 2 * 1;
```

so naturally, you opt for a generic, recursive algorithm, something like the following application (if you are following along with a hands-on trace, ***enter the following BadRecursiveCallStack.cpp program***):

```
//
//BadRecursiveCallStack.cpp
//Program demonstrates recursive calls
//
```

```
int Factorial( int iCurrentValue );

void main ( void )
{
  int iRecursiveCalculation;

  iRecursiveCalculation = Factorial( 4 );
}

int Factorial( int iCurrentValue )
{
  if( iCurrentValue == 1 )
    return iCurrentValue;
  else
    return iCurrentValue *=
           Factorial( iCurrentValue-- );
}
```

Proud as punch, you begin, what you think will be a boring Debugger trace, only to find out that your calculated *iRecursiveCalculation* value is el-wrongo! Fortunately, you know about the Debugger's Call Stack window and begin a call-by-call examination. Figure 6.39 begins as you would expect (***use your knowledge of Step Over and Step Into to position your Debugger's display so that it resembles Figure 6.39***).

Even the second call to *Factorial()*, doesn't look too bad as seen in Figure 6.40 (***use your knowledge of Step Over and Step Into to position your Debugger's display so that it resembles Figure 6.40***).

However, by the third trace into the function, you immediately recognize a serious miscalculation beginning to propagate (***use your knowledge of Step Over and Step Into to position your Debugger's display so that it resembles Figure 6.41***).

If the algorithm were functioning properly, you would expect to see each call to the function *Factorial()* being passed a value one less than the previous call. Clearly, the third trace, the Call Stack window flags the error.

Now, if you detected the error in *Factorial()*'s code right off the bat, you should go out and buy yourself something! However, without many years of C/C++ hard knocks, the code *should* still look OK.

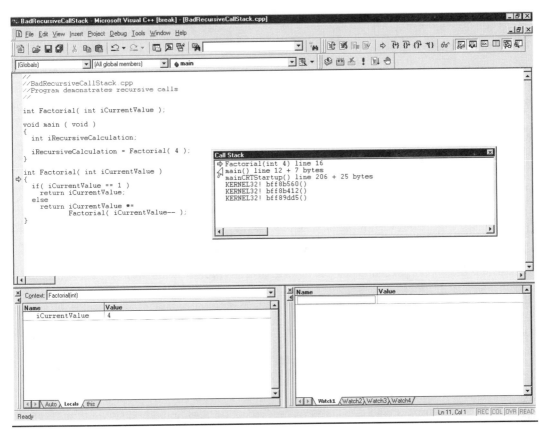

Figure 6.39   Initial recursive Factorial call showing the value 4 at the Call Stack top

The offending code statement generating the miscalculation involves *Factorial()*'s recursive call statement (highlighting and italics used for emphasis):

```
int Factorial( int iCurrentValue )
{
  if( iCurrentValue == 1 )
```

```
      return iCurrentValue;
   else
      return iCurrentValue *=
            Factorial( iCurrentValue-- );
```

When *Factorial()* is called from **main()**:

```
iRecursiveCalculation = Factorial( 4 );
```

There is no problem with the interpretation of the passed value, which, in this case, is *4*. However, when *Factorial()* is called from within *Factorial()*, the passed value is *iCurrentValue--*. Still confused?

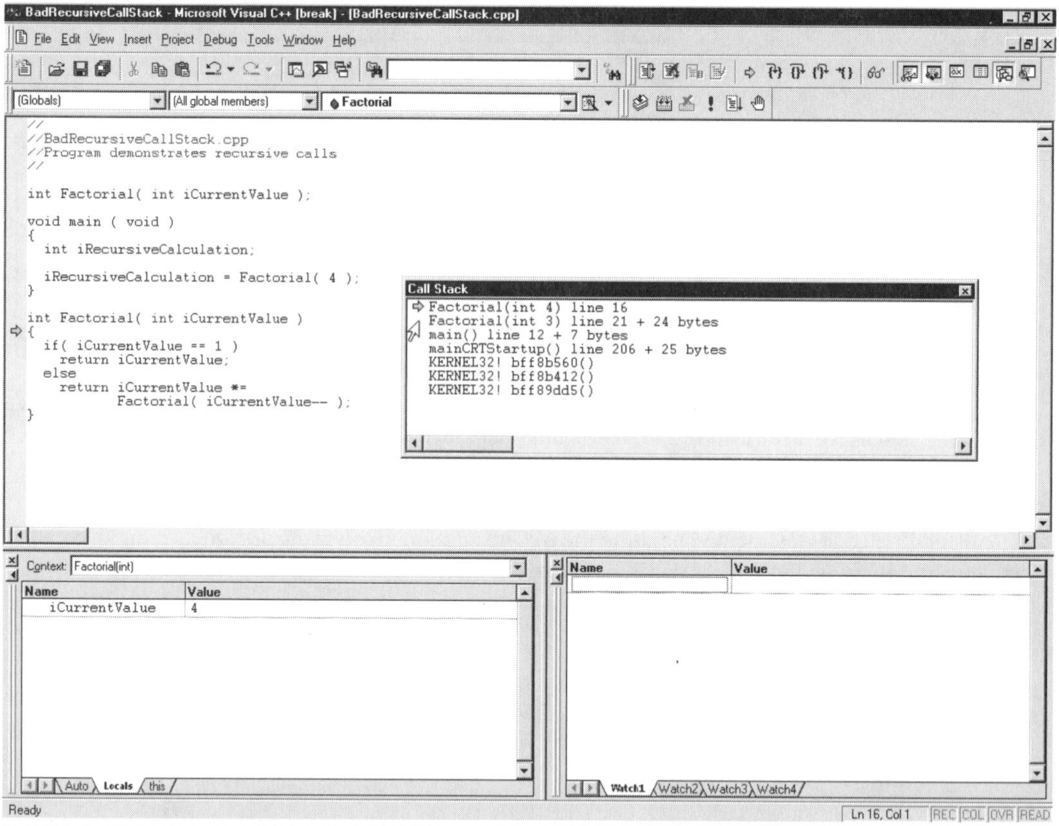

Figure 6.40　Second call to the recursive Factorial subroutine

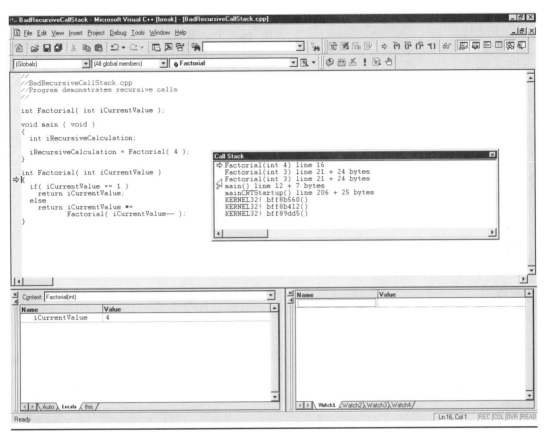

Figure 6.41   Recognizing the beginning of a Factorial miscalculation

Well, at this point, a programmer could *hack* a solution or, better still, use the Microsoft Visual C++ Debugger's tools. The sophisticated approach to *knowledgeably* diagnosing and fixing *Factorial()*'s code problem now involves the Debugger's ability to show you a source code segment's disassembly version.

View Disassembly Code

In the last section, you used the Debugger's Call Stack window to detect a calculation error residing within the *Factorial()* subroutine body. If you have been executing this chapter's programs, your monitor screen should still resemble Figure 6.41.

To activate the Debugger's Disassembly window, first click on the Visual C++'s View menu, Debug Windows option, then ***choose Disassembly (ALT+8)***. The Disassembly window should auto-synchronize the contents of the window to something similar to the disassembly code segment that follows:

```
14:
15:     int Factorial( int iCurrentValue )
16:     {
00401070    push        ebp
00401071    mov         ebp,esp
00401073    sub         esp,44h
00401076    push        ebx
00401077    push        esi
00401078    push        edi
00401079    lea         edi,[ebp-44h]
0040107C    mov         ecx,11h
00401081    mov         eax,0CCCCCCCCh
00401086    rep stos    dword ptr [edi]
17:        if( iCurrentValue == 1 )
00401088    cmp         dword ptr [ebp+8],1
0040108C    jne         Factorial+23h (00401093)
18:            return iCurrentValue;
0040108E    mov         eax,dword ptr [ebp+8]
00401091    jmp         Factorial+4Ah (004010ba)
19:        else
20:            return iCurrentValue *=
21:                Factorial( iCurrentValue-- );
00401093    mov         eax,dword ptr [ebp+8]
00401096    mov         dword ptr [ebp-4],eax
00401099    mov         ecx,dword ptr [ebp-4]
0040109C    push        ecx
0040109D    mov         edx,dword ptr [ebp+8]
004010A0    sub         edx,1
004010A3    mov         dword ptr [ebp+8],edx
004010A6    call        @ILT+0(Factorial) (00401005)
004010AB    add         esp,4
004010AE    mov         ecx,dword ptr [ebp+8]
004010B1    imul        ecx,eax
004010B4    mov         dword ptr [ebp+8],ecx
004010B7    mov         eax,dword ptr [ebp+8]
22:     }
```

Once you have studied the Disassembly window's contents, you will need to ***reedit Factorial()'s offending statement*** from:

```
int Factorial( int iCurrentValue )
{
  if( iCurrentValue == 1 )
    return iCurrentValue;
  else
```

```
    return iCurrentValue *=
         Factorial( iCurrentValue-- );
```

to:

```
int Factorial( int iCurrentValue )
{
  if( iCurrentValue == 1 )
    return iCurrentValue;
  else
    return iCurrentValue *=
         Factorial( iCurrentValue - 1 );
```

Execute another build and begin a brand new trace, making certain you have called Factorial() at least three times. Your Debugger window should now resemble Figure 6.42.

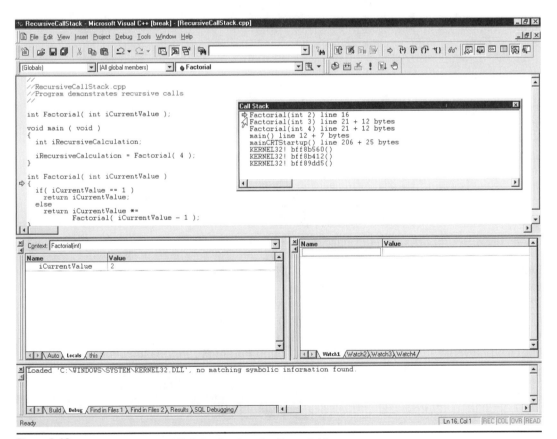

Figure 6.42 Showing corrected Call Stack values for *Factorial()*

Now, *__open the Disassembly window__*.

```
14:
15:    int Factorial( int iCurrentValue )
16:    {
00401070    push        ebp
00401071    mov         ebp,esp
00401073    sub         esp,40h
00401076    push        ebx
00401077    push        esi
00401078    push        edi
00401079    lea         edi,[ebp-40h]
0040107C    mov         ecx,10h
00401081    mov         eax,0CCCCCCCCh
00401086    rep stos    dword ptr [edi]
17:       if( iCurrentValue == 1 )
00401088    cmp         dword ptr [ebp+8],1
0040108C    jne         Factorial+23h (00401093)
18:          return iCurrentValue;
0040108E    mov         eax,dword ptr [ebp+8]
00401091    jmp         Factorial+3Eh (004010ae)
19:       else
20:          return iCurrentValue *=
21:             Factorial( iCurrentValue - 1 );
00401093    mov         eax,dword ptr [ebp+8]
00401096    sub         eax,1
00401099    push        eax
0040109A    call        @ILT+0(Factorial) (00401005)
0040109F    add         esp,4
004010A2    mov         ecx,dword ptr [ebp+8]
004010A5    imul        ecx,eax
004010A8    mov         dword ptr [ebp+8],ecx
004010AB    mov         eax,dword ptr [ebp+8]
22:    }
```

Table 6.1 compares the two most critical code segments. The column on the left shows the Disassembly window's view of *iCurrentValue--*, while the column to the right highlights the translation of the rewritten formula, *iCurrentValue - 1*.

The contrasting disassembly code segments clearly highlight the location of the incorrect values for the first algorithm. The **ecx** register reference in the first column represents the decrement operator's assembly language equivalent. Here the original value of *iCurrentValue* is reused, thus generating the error. The right column, referencing only the **eax** register, creates the correct value before passing the new value to the next invocation of the recursive subroutine.

Notice how it was the skillful combination of incorrect values reported within the Call Stack window that led to the discovery of *where* the algorithm was misfiring, and a technical application of the Disassembly window's contents that explained *why* the algorithm misbehaved.

iCurrentValue--			iCurrentValue - 1		
21:		Factorial(iCurrentValue--);	21:		Factorial(iCurrentValue - 1);
00401093	mov	eax,dword ptr [ebp+8]	00401093	mov	eax,dword ptr [ebp+8]
00401096	mov	dword ptr [ebp-4],eax	00401096	sub	eax,1
00401099	mov	ecx,dword ptr [ebp-4]	00401099	push	eax
0040109C	push	ecx	0040109A	call	@ILT+0(Factorial) (00401005)
0040109D	mov	edx,dword ptr [ebp+8]			
004010A0	sub	edx,1			
004010A3	mov	dword ptr [ebp+8],edx			
004010A6	call	@ILT+0(Factorial)			
(00401005)					

Table 6.1   Comparing the Two *iCurrentValue* Formula Disassembly Translations

All of the remaining chapters include examples that combine a mechanical Debugger skill, such as how to invoke Step Into mode, with a logical placement or debugging concept that boosts the performance of a Debugger capability.

A Closer Look at Variables

When debugging an application, the Variables window, with its auto-tracking of in-scope variables, is initially all you will need to detect an offending code statement. However, as your applications increase in complexity—from simple procedural, to object-oriented, and on to full-fledged multithreaded Windows applications—the interaction between variables increases. Under these circumstances, you will need to use a combination of watches.

The following two sections take a closer look at the Debugger's QuickWatch and Watch windows. All three windows, Variables, QuickWatch, and Watch, are used with increasing sophistication throughout the remaining chapters where appropriate.

Using the QuickWatch Window

You can use QuickWatch to quickly examine the value of SQL variables and parameters. You can also use QuickWatch to modify the value of a local variable or to add a variable to the Watch window. You cannot modify the value of a global.

The QuickWatch dialog box contains a text box where you can type a variable name and a spreadsheet field that displays the current value of the variable that you specified. The Current Value spreadsheet field displays only one variable at a time. Typing a new variable in the text box and pressing ENTER replaces the previous variable. QuickWatch displays SQL code variable values in their native format.

| Note | *Microsoft documentation explains that only the Enterprise Edition is capable of SQL source code debugging.* |

Viewing Variables with QuickWatch (Main Menu Approach)

To use QuickWatch, you must have first started the Debugger and executed past any variable declarations or code segment use before activating a meaningful QuickWatch window. To start QuickWatch, you can:

1. Click on the Debug menu, followed by a click on QuickWatch. The QuickWatch dialog box appears.

2. Type or paste the variable name into the Expression text box.
   Or
   Click on a variable name from the Expression drop-down listbox, which contains the most recently used QuickWatch identifiers.

3. Click Recalculate.

4. Click Close.

Viewing Variables with QuickWatch (Quick Approach)

Another way to invoke QuickWatch is to first wait until the Debugger stops, switch to a source window, click the right mouse button on a variable's name, and then:

1. From the pop-up shortcut menu, click QuickWatch. If your I-beam cursor was on a watchable variable in the source window, QuickWatch will automatically enter the variable's name in the Expression drop-down listbox.

2. You simply click on Recalculate.

3. Followed by a click on Close.

Modifying a Variable's Contents with QuickWatch

Whenever your program is paused at a breakpoint or between steps, you can change the value of any variable in your program. This gives you the flexibility to try out changes and see their results in real time or to recover from certain logic errors. To modify a variable's contents with QuickWatch, you:

1. Choose the Debug | QuickWatch option.

2. Type the variable name in the Expression text box.

3. Click on Recalculate.

4. Use the TAB key to move to the value you want to modify.

5. Type the new value and then press ENTER.

6. Click on Close.

Adding a QuickWatch Variable to the Watch Window

You can easily transfer a QuickWatch variable into the Watch window for permanent viewing by simply clicking on the QuickWatch window's Add Watch button.

Using the Watch Window

Remember that the Watch window's contents differ from those of the Variables or QuickWatch windows in that the Watch window's contents are static, not dynamic. You use the Watch window to specify local or global variables that you want to watch while debugging your program. You can also use this window to modify the values of local variables but not global variables.

Adding Variables to the Watch Window

The Watch window contains four tabs: Watch1, Watch2, Watch3, and Watch4. Each tab displays a user-specified list of variables in a spreadsheet field. You can group variables that you want to watch onto the same tab. For example, you could put variables related to a specific window on one tab and variables related to a dialog box on another tab. You could watch the first tab while debugging the window and the second tab while debugging the dialog box. To add a variable to the Watch window, you:

1. Click on the View | Debug Windows | Watch option.
2. Choose a tab for the variable (the default is Watch1).
3. Type, paste, or drag the variable name into the Name column on the tab.
4. Press ENTER.
5. The Watch window evaluates the variable immediately and displays the value or an error message. The Watch window displays values in their native SQL format.

Changing Watch Window Display Formats

The Watch window does not display variable type information, but you can show variable type information by using the window's Properties page. To view type information for a variable, you select the line containing the variable whose type you want to see. Next, you click the right mouse button in the Watch window and click Properties from the shortcut menu, or from the View menu, click Properties.

Removing Variables from the Watch Window

To remove a variable from the Watch window, select the line containing the variable you want to remove and press the DELETE key. When the program is paused at a breakpoint or between steps, you can change the value of any local variable in your program. This gives you the flexibility to try out changes and see their results in real time, or to recover from certain logic errors.

Modifying Watch Window Variable Contents

To modify the value of a variable using the Watch window, you double-click the variable's value, type the new value, and then press the ENTER key.

Error Watch   *The Microsoft Visual C++ Debugger will not allow you to modify image, text, or datetime data types. In addition, you may not increase the number of characters in a string variable (szString).*

Conclusion

Even if you were already familiar with standard Debugger essentials such as Watch windows and Step Into, Step Over, you may have been unaware of the Debugger's ability to perform sophisticated tasks such as debugging from the current location with a *new* value. This chapter also presented advanced topics such as the call stack and the *efficient* use of standard Debugger essentials by clever breakpoint insertions. With practice, you will evolve into more and more efficient debug cycles and spend less time debugging "old news."

In the next chapter, you will examine the Debugger's capabilities relating to assembly language code. This is an exciting addition to your programmer's toolkit, because C/C++, from day one, had a close, symbiotic relationship with assembly language code.

CHAPTER 7

Debugging Inline Assembly Language Code

The Microsoft Visual C++ compiler provides the ability to include inline assembly language code within normal C++ source code projects. In recent years, the use of assembly language code has been deemphasized because of the strength of C and C++. However, the need for assembly language is still alive and well and may become part of many of your C++ projects in the future.

When you are using a compiler, you are literally at the mercy of the developers of the compiler. If particular language features aren't included, there isn't much you can do to add them. The best example of missing features is the release of the first IBM Pascal compiler. The Pascal compiler worked well, but it did not include the ability to do any graphics. No, not even a dot on the screen! A call to IBM was met with the response, "Well, you'll just have to write an assembly language patch to do graphics." Ah, those magic words!

The truth is simply this—if your computer can perform certain feats, those feats can be programmed in assembly language. This is a statement that no compiled language can boast.

This chapter will provide a quick review of assembly language fundamentals, investigate Debugger capabilities, and then illustrate these capabilities with several programs. The assembly language programs will illustrate results that are easy to accomplish with assembly language code and difficult, if not impossible, to accomplish with C++.

A Brief Assembly Language Primer

This section is not a replacement for a book or course in assembly language. It is designed merely to highlight some of the features of assembly language that will be illustrated in this chapter. If you have not programmed with assembly language, you should seek out a good assembly language book before proceeding with this chapter.

Data Types

The most popular data types used by assembly language programmers include the byte, word, double-word, and quad-word data types. Table 7.1 shows these data types, their mnemonics, the bit size of each, and the microprocessor registers that can accommodate them.

In assembly language, it is also possible to address individual bits or work with a ten-byte data type (DT), which is 80 bits in length.

Data Type	Mnemonic	Size (bits)	Use with Register
byte	DB	8	al, ah, bl, bh, cl, ch, dl, dh
word	DW	16	ax, bx, cx, dx
double-word	DD	32	eax, ebx, ecx, edx
quad-word	DQ	64	None

Table 7.1   Assembly Language Data Types

Registers

The registers used in assembly language actually exist on the microprocessor itself. Starting with the 80386 microprocessor, the general-purpose registers include the 32-bit eax, ebx, ecx, and edx registers. The 16-bit registers, which are really a portion of their 32-bit parents, include the ax, bx, cx, and dx registers. Likewise, the 8-bit registers are formed from their 16-bit parents and include al, ah, bl, bh, cl, ch, dl, and dh. There are also a host of specialized registers for special addressing modes, such as indexed addressing. These include the bp, si, and di registers.

The Intel family of microprocessors, starting with the 8088 through the latest Pentium processors, is register oriented. By that, we mean that almost any programming operation that takes place with the microprocessor takes place in a register. The exception is the numeric coprocessor designed for floating-point arithmetic. The coprocessor is stack oriented with almost all operations being placed onto or taken off of the coprocessor stack.

Addressing Modes

The earliest members of the Intel microprocessor family were chips designed around a segmented architecture. These earliest designs incorporated four segments: a data segment, a stack segment, a code segment, and an extra segment. Each segment was 64K in size. In recent Pentium microprocessor designs, a linear programming mode is also possible that eliminates the size barrier of the earlier segment designs. Motorola microprocessors have traditionally used a linear addressing mode.

When you write assembly language code in the code segment, seven basic addressing modes are available. These are immediate, register, direct, register indirect, base relative, direct indexed, and based indexed addressing modes. The assembler recognizes the addressing mode by the syntax of the program statement. For example:

```
mov    ax, 1234h    ;move 1234h into ax
```

This programming statement is an example of immediate addressing. Here the hexadecimal number 1234h is moved into the 16-bit ax register using the mov mnemonic. This is considered an immediate addressing statement since the data to be moved into the ax register is provided directly in the operant field. The immediate data must match the register size.

Consider the following statement:

```
add    eax, ebx    ;add contents of ebx to eax
```

In this statement, the contents of the 32-bit ebx are added to the contents of the 32-bit eax register with the add mnemonic. The original contents of eax are destroyed. The contents of ebx remain unchanged, and eax now contains the sum. Because a register-to-register operation is taking place, this programming mode is considered register addressing. Here, both registers must be of the same size.

In direct addressing, a variable from the data segment is used with a register. For example:

```
sub    cl, mynum    ;sub mynum from cl
```

Here, the contents of the variable *mynum* is subtracted from the contents of the 8-bit c1 register. Since a fetch to external memory is involved, this direct addressing mode operation will be slower than the previous two addressing modes. Also, it is important that the variable match the register size. In this case, *mynum* is a byte (DB) sized number.

The four remaining addressing modes follow similar paths. You'll see programming examples involving several addressing modes in this chapter.

Pointers

Pointers give the assembly language programmer the ability to break apart large data types and store portions in smaller registers. For example, if *myvar* is defined as a 32-bit data type (DD), then the following portion of code would load the complete variable into two 16-bit registers with the use of pointers:

```
mov        ax, word ptr myvar          ;get lower 16-bits of myvar
mov        bx, word ptr myvar + 2      ;get upper 16-bits of myvar
```

The pointer type must match the register size. Since a word is composed of 2 bytes, to access the upper word of *myvar*, a pointer value of 2 is used.

Design Tip   *Setting up pointers is a bit tricky. However, here is a trick! The pointer type, such as **word**, **dword** and **qword**, is always found next to the **ptr** keyword and next to the variable. The pointer type always matches the register type in the operand column, and the index number, when present, matches the register size expressed in bytes.*

Error Watch   *Pointer arithmetic is an area where errors can be easily introduced. Double-check pointer arithmetic every time it is used in inline code.*

Pointers are important to assembly language programmers because they give us the ability to store, retrieve and manipulate variables that extend beyond register and variable sizes. Did you notice in Table 7.1 that no register types were directly associated with quad-word variables (DQ)? A defined quad-word variable, however, can be loaded into four word-sized variables or two double-word variables with the use of pointers.

This brings us to a very interesting point, which is a real advantage to assembly language programmers. While most compiled languages are restricted by their data type sizes, assembly language is not. We can work with 32-bit, 64-bit, or even 512-bit integers without the loss of precision just by using pointers!

The Coprocessor

The coprocessor's main job is to take the burden (bottleneck) of processing real numbers away from the microprocessor. Real numbers are saved in memory and passed across the system bus as encoded real numbers. These encoded real numbers are represented as very large integer values. Think for a second: a data bus with a width of 32 bits uses the least-significant bit to represent numbers in the units column. This begs the question, "Where would decimal digits be placed?" The answer, of course, is that they are not! The real number is converted to a specially encoded integer number that can be passed across the data bus. At the appropriate time, the encoded number is converted back to a real number format. This is a complicated process that slows down the processing of numerical data on the microprocessor—but one that can be handled very efficiently on the coprocessor.

If you have programmed in assembly language for awhile, the use of the coprocessor might seem a little strange. This is because the microprocessor is register oriented, while the coprocessor is stack oriented. Almost every operation that is performed with the microprocessor involves the use of the processor's internal registers. Likewise, almost every operation involving the use of the coprocessor involves the use of its internal stack. The stack can hold eight 80-bit numbers. However, it is rare to see an application that requires that much stack depth. Also, while the stack holds 80-bit numbers, the door to the coprocessor is limited by the normal microprocessor data types.

Design Tip *The coprocessor will allow quad-words (DQ), double-words (DD), and words (DW) to be loaded onto the stack with mnemonics such as **fld** and **fild**. Likewise, those same data types can be retrieved from the coprocessor stack with mnemonics such as **fstp** and **fistp**. However, explicit operations such as fadd myvar work only when myvar is of typedouble-word (DD) or word (DW).*

It is possible to load and store quad-word numbers (DQ) or work directly with double-words (DD) and words (DW). The 80-bit internal precision finds its real use in maintaining precision while calculations are done internally in the coprocessor. It is a misunderstanding that the coprocessor is for real number arithmetic only—integer values can be used with the coprocessor as long as you understand that they are converted to 80-bit real numbers when placed on the internal stack.

You'll see two coprocessor applications later in this chapter, and you'll also learn how to use the Debugger's Registers window to view the coprocessor's internal stack.

24x7

You may recall that it was discovered a number of years ago that some Intel Pentium microprocessors had flawed FDIV, FPREM, FPTAN, and FPATAN mnemonic instructions. To address this problem, Microsoft wrote helper routines in the runtime library that perform accurate FDIV and FPREM calculations. Hooks were made available for writing your own helper functions.

In C++ the helper routines are disabled (/QIfdiv–). This means the code will not perform correctly on these particular Pentium computers. If the helper routines are employed (/QIfdiv), the code tests for the processor bug and calls the corrected runtime routines.

The best solution, however, is to replace the flawed processor by contacting Intel. However, robust applications should always take this "bug" into consideration.

Debugging

Inline assembly language code will allow us to explore a unique capability of the Visual C++ Debugger—the Registers window. While the Registers window is available for all programs, its real capabilities can best be appreciated when debugging inline assembler code. With this window, you'll be able to view the microprocessor's registers and the coprocessor's stack.

In the following sections, we'll examine inline assembly code that varies from simple applications to more robust coprocessor examples. Much of this code will initially contain logical errors that prevent the application from working as desired. We'll use the Debugger to help hunt down these logical errors and finally fix the application. Only listings that contain the "contains no errors" comment are applications that will work as expected.

Again, we suggest the use of a separate book on assembly language if you need to brush up on your assembly language programming skills.

Subtracting Numbers

The example illustrated in this section contains no errors. We'll use it as a stepping stone to writing successful inline assembler code and investigate various debugging features.

Here is the complete listing for the Sub.cpp program.

```
// Sub.cpp
// Assembly Language Program
// illustrates debugger use
// contains no errors

#include <iostream.h>

void main(void)
{

    unsigned int num_1=0xABCD8765;
    unsigned int num_2=0x12345678;
    unsigned int result;

    _asm {

    ;code to perform actual subtraction
    mov         eax,num_1    ;move num_1 into eax register
    sub         eax,num_2    ;subtract num_2 from eax
    mov         result,eax   ;store eax in result

    }

    cout << hex << result << "\n";
}
```

This little application contains only three actual lines of assembly language code, but it contains a wealth of information about writing inline code.

First, notice that the assembly language code is contained between curly braces ({ }) under the **_asm** keyword.

```
_asm {
       .
       .
       .
       .
}
```

Code contained in this section must be written in assembly language format and must align with the four fields used to develop assembly language code. The four fields are the name (label) field, operation (mnemonic) field, operand field, and comment field. In this example, only the operation, operand, and comment fields are used. Notice that comments always begin with a semicolon.

This application uses the 32-bit eax register to perform the subtraction of two hexadecimal numbers. While decimal numbers could certainly have been used, the hexadecimal number system is the number system of choice among assembly language programmers.

The data declarations for the numbers to be subtracted take place outside of the inline assembly language code. They are, therefore, declared as you would any other C or C++ integer.

```
unsigned int num_1=0xABCD8765;
unsigned int num_2=0x12345678;
unsigned int result;
```

The trick is to get the C++ data type to correctly match the assembly language data type. Since the eax register holds 32-bit integers, the C++ int data type fits perfectly.

Error Watch *The three data values are declared as unsigned in this example because the assembler sign-extends numbers. For example, hexadecimal values in the range of 0 to 7FFFFFFF are considered positive numbers when doing signed arithmetic while values in the range 80000000 to FFFFFFFF are treated as negative numbers. If numbers are declared as unsigned, numbers in the range 0 to FFFFFFFF are treated in an identical manner.*

By treating the numbers as unsigned, we can anticipate an unsigned hexadecimal result of 999930ED.

Good Code

The example shown in the previous section contains no errors. We'll just use it to examine what the Visual C++ Debugger can do for us. Compile the program with the Debug option turned on (default) and enter the Debugger. You should see a screen similar to that shown in Figure 7.1.

You'll notice that, in this figure, the line of execution being pointed to by the arrow symbol appears in the left-most portion of the screen. The initial Registers window shows both the microprocessor registers and the coprocessor stack. In this example, we will be interested in what is taking place in the eax register because that is where the subtraction will take place.

Single-step down the application, using the Step Into button (F11), until the execution arrow points to the position shown in Figure 7.2.

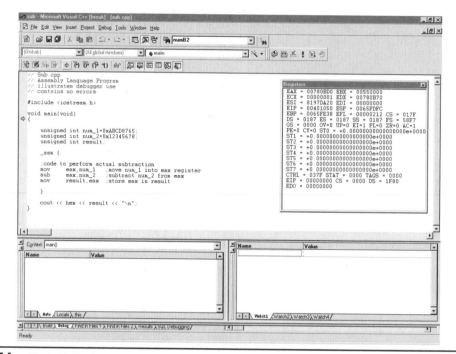

Figure 7.1 The initial Debugger screen showing the Sub.cpp program

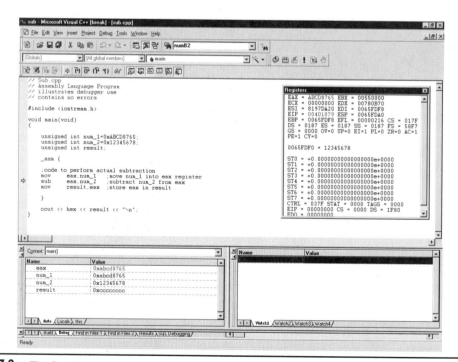

Figure 7.2 The first hexadecimal number is loaded into the eax register

Notice, in Figure 7.2, that the eax register now contains ABCD8765. You can see this value in both the Variables window (at the lower left) and the Registers window. The Watch window (at the lower right in Figure 7.2) contains no watches. If any of these windows are not visible, use the View | Debug Windows menu to open the desired window.

Step to the next line, using the Step Into button (F11) in order to perform the actual subtraction. Your screen should appear similar to Figure 7.3.

The subtraction is successful, and the correct results now appear in the eax register. Again, you can see this register in both the Registers and Variables windows. By clicking on any variable in the Variables window, the Debugger will give you the option of viewing the value as either a hexadecimal or decimal number.

Since this application does not make use of the coprocessor, none of the coprocessor stack entries, ST(0) to ST(8), contain meaningful values.

The value saved in the variable *result* can be printed to the screen since it is a C++ data type. Just use the cout stream to print the answer in hexadecimal form. If you execute the application, you'll see your results in a window similar to the one shown in Figure 7.4.

The fact that it is so easy to move from C++ code to assembly and back makes assembly language code ideal for time-intensive applications. There are, however, other reasons for using assembly language, as you will see in the next example.

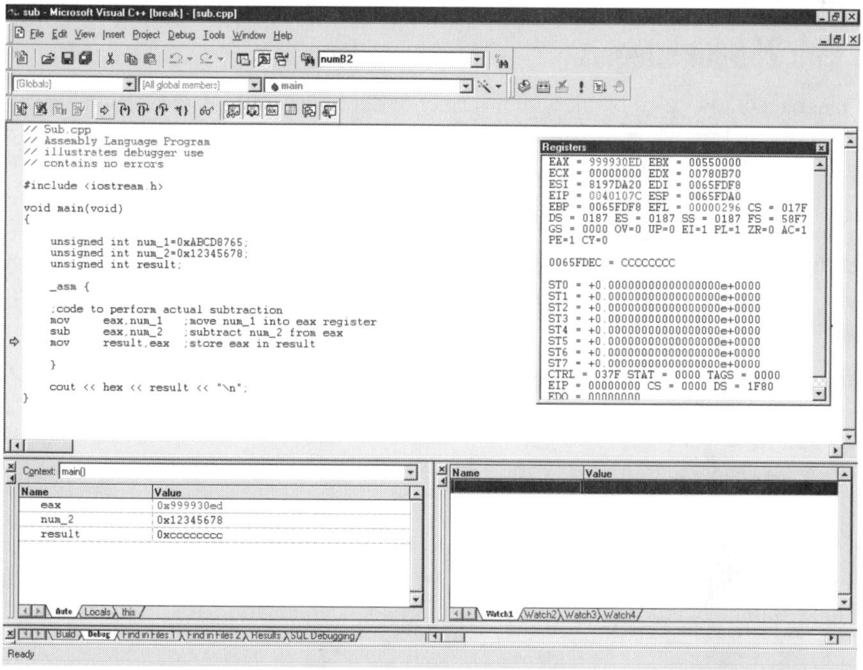

Figure 7.3   The eax register contains the subtraction results

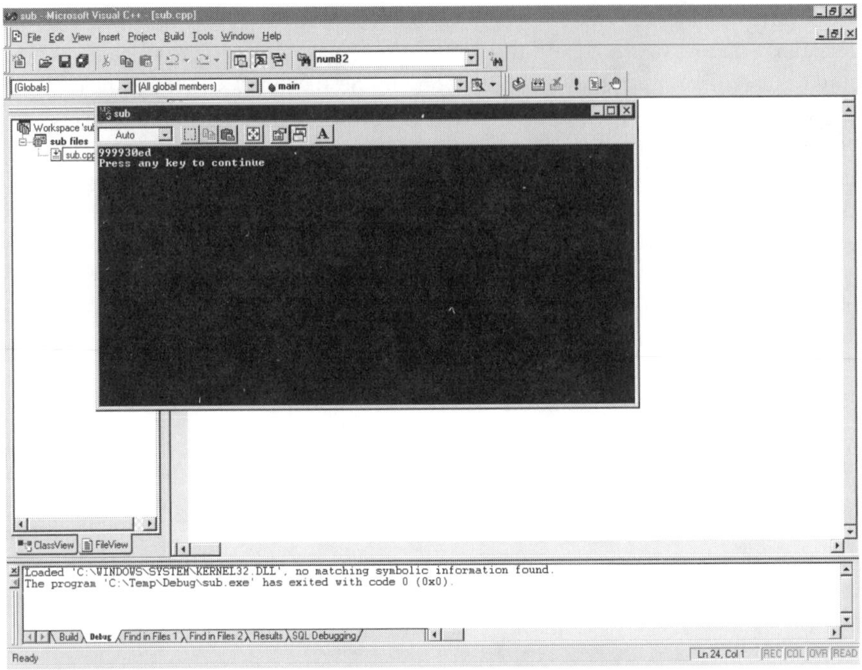

Figure 7.4 The answer can be printed to a command-line screen

Working with 256-Bit Integers

Assembly language allows us to work with a variety of data sizes, even data sizes that exceed all defined data types. In this example, we'll illustrate how this feat can be accomplished with multiple precision arithmetic. The program will add two 256-bit numbers. Numbers of this size and larger are becoming important since encryption programs, using public key cryptology, require the storage and manipulation of large prime numbers.

The trick here is to break up the large numbers into smaller segments that can be stored in defined data types. For example, the 256-bit number, shown next, can be divided into four segments that fit into unsigned **__int64** integer data types.

```
//1234567891234567ABCDABCDABCDABCDFFFFEEEEDDDDCCCCDDDDCCCCBBBBAAAA
    unsigned __int64 numA1 = 0xDDDDCCCCBBBBAAAA;
    unsigned __int64 numA2 = 0xFFFFEEEEDDDDCCCC;
    unsigned __int64 numA3 = 0xABCDABCDABCDABCD;
    unsigned __int64 numA4 = 0x1234567891234567;
```

Then by using pointers, the individual segments can be added with their partial sums being returned back to four unsigned **__int64** variables. In the next section, we'll look at an optimistic coding of this program and then go on a bug hunt with the Debugger.

Code with a Problem

Before looking at how the program was approached, let's first calculate the results. If we don't know what the answer should look like, we'll never know if it is correct when we view it in the Debugger.

```
1234567891234567ABCDABCDABCDABCDFFFFEEEEDDDDCCCCDDDDCCCCBBBBAAAA
22222222222222221111111111111111A1B2C3D4E5F6E5D48888999911112222
----------------------------------------------------------------
3456789AB3456789BCDEBCDEBCDEBCDFA1B2B2C3C3D4B2A166666665CCCCCCCC
```

Wow! That sum is a big number. How many digits can your calculator handle at a time?

The basic programming approach will be to add the numbers by adding each of the four number segments together.

numA4 numA3 numA2 numA1

numB4 numB3 numB2 numB1

ANS4   ANS3   ANS2   ANS1

So, for the first addition that adds *numA1* and *numB1* together, the code takes on this form:

```
;start with numA1 and numB1
mov     eax,dword ptr numA1         ;get first 8 digits
add     eax,dword ptr numB1         ;add first 8 digits
mov     dword ptr ANS1,eax          ;save first 8 digits
mov     eax,dword ptr numA1 + 4     ;get next 8 digits
add     eax,dword ptr numB1 + 4     ;add next 8 digits + carry
mov     dword ptr ANS1 + 4,eax      ;save next 8 digits
```

The numbers, numA1 and numB1, are 64-bit integers. Pointers must be used to perform the additions in the 32-bit eax register. The first two lines of program code add the first eight digits (32 bits) of numA1 and numB1 using a **dword** pointer. The 32-bit result is saved in the least-significant bits of ANS1. The most-significant 32 bits of numA1 and numB1 are then added using a **dword** pointer with an offset of 4 bytes (32 bits). This sum is then stored in the most-significant bits of ANS1. We have now completed the addition of the first 64 bits.

The same process is repeated for the addition of numA2 and numB2, numA3 and numB3, and numA4 and numB4. When all additions are completed, the 256-bit sum will appear in ANS4, ANS3, ANS2, and ANS1.

Let's look at the entire program.

```
// Contains Logical Errors
// Assembly Language Program
// illustrates the power of assembly language in
// correctly manipulating 256-bit numbers
// with multiple precision arithmetic.

void main(void)
{
```

```
//break up and store the first 256-bit integer number
//1234567891234567ABCDABCDABCDABCDFFFFEEEEDDDDCCCCDDDDCCCCBBBBAAAA
    unsigned __int64 numA1 = 0xDDDDCCCCBBBBAAAA;
    unsigned __int64 numA2 = 0xFFFFEEEEDDDDCCCC;
    unsigned __int64 numA3 = 0xABCDABCDABCDABCD;
    unsigned __int64 numA4 = 0x1234567891234567;

//break up and store the second 256-bit integer number
//2222222222222222111111111111111A1B2C3D4E5F6E5D48888999911112222
    unsigned __int64 numB1 = 0x8888999911112222;
    unsigned __int64 numB2 = 0xA1B2C3D4E5F6E5D4;
    unsigned __int64 numB3 = 0x1111111111111111;
    unsigned __int64 numB4 = 0x2222222222222222;

//prepare storage locations to hold the 256-bit result
    unsigned __int64 ANS1 = 0;
    unsigned __int64 ANS2 = 0;
    unsigned __int64 ANS3 = 0;
    unsigned __int64 ANS4 = 0;

    _asm {

    ;start with numA1 and numB1
    mov     eax,dword ptr numA1         ;get first 8 digits
    add     eax,dword ptr numB1         ;add first 8 digits
    mov     dword ptr ANS1,eax          ;save first 8 digits
    mov     eax,dword ptr numA1 + 4     ;get next 8 digits
    add     eax,dword ptr numB1 + 4     ;add next 8 digits + carry
    mov     dword ptr ANS1 + 4,eax      ;save next 8 digits

    ;work with numA2 and numB2 + carry information
    mov     eax,dword ptr numA2         ;get next 8 digits
    add     eax,dword ptr numB2         ;add next 8 digits + carry
    mov     dword ptr ANS2,eax          ;save next 8 digits
    mov     eax,dword ptr numA2 + 4     ;get next 8 digits
    add     eax,dword ptr numB2 + 4     ;add next 8 digits + carry
    mov     dword ptr ANS2 + 4,eax      ;save next 8 digits

    ;work with numA3 and numB3 + carry information
    mov     eax,dword ptr numA3         ;get next 8 digits
    add     eax,dword ptr numB3         ;add next 8 digits + carry
    mov     dword ptr ANS3,eax          ;save next 8 digits
    mov     eax,dword ptr numA3 + 4     ;get next 8 digits
    add     eax,dword ptr numB3 + 4     ;add next 8 digits + carry
    mov     dword ptr ANS3 + 4,eax      ;save next 8 digits

    ;work with numA4 and numB4 + carry information
    mov     eax,dword ptr numA4         ;get next 8 digits
    add     eax,dword ptr numB4         ;add next 8 digits + carry
    mov     dword ptr ANS4,eax          ;save next 8 digits
    mov     eax,dword ptr numA4 + 4     ;get next 8 digits
```

```
add      eax,dword ptr numB4 + 4      ;add next 8 digits + carry
mov      dword ptr ANS4 + 4,eax       ;save next 8 digits

    }
}
```

Syntactically, the code is in good shape. Compile the application and start the Debugger. Next, add the variables ANS1, ANS2, ANS3, and ANS4 to the watch window. If you are optimistic, execute the code to the arrow shown in the left-most portion of the screen in Figure 7.5.

An initial glance at the complete answer in the Watch window looks good. Let's see what that whole answer is.

3456789ab3456789bcdebcdebcdebcdea1b2b2c2c3d4b2a066666665cccccccc
                 ^   ^   ^

The location of the three carets indicates digits that differ from our calculated results. Now, under normal circumstances, there would be a very good chance that we made a calculation error and that the program is returning the correct results. But not in this case!

Okay—time to go back into the Debugger and start single-stepping through each line of code, checking the results.

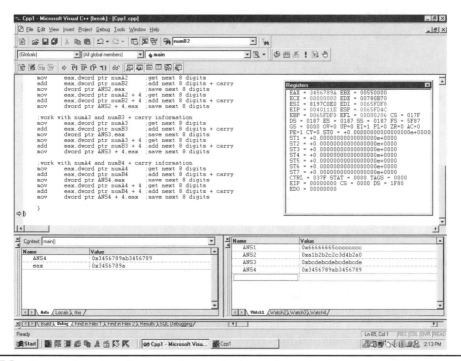

Figure 7.5   Execute the code until the complete sum has been calculated

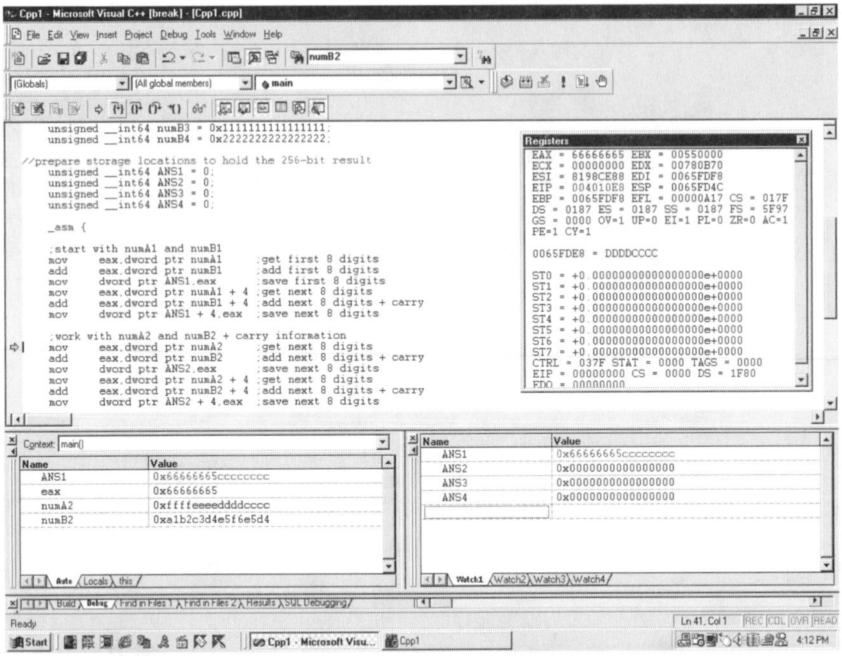

Figure 7.6   The first 64-bit addition is correct

Figure 7.6 shows the condition of the microprocessor registers after the addition of the first 64 bits.

The variable, `ANS1`, clearly shows a hexadecimal value of 66666665cccccccc. That is exactly the value we calculated, so no problem here.

Now, step through the second 64-bit addition. Your debugger screen should look like Figure 7.7.

Ah, the problem is in this portion of the addition. We should be getting the hexadecimal number A1B2B2C3C3D4B2A1, but instead we're getting A1B2B2C2C3D4B2A0.

Think! Think! Think! Did you notice that both errors occur in the least-significant digits of each 32-bit portion of the number? What is going on with that portion of code? Oh, here it is. Those digits are supposed to receive a carry from the previous column's addition, as you move from one portion of the addition to the next. Let's see if the carry flag is working. You can find the carry flag (CY) in the Registers window. Table 7.2 lists all of the microprocessor flags.

Refer back to Figure 7.6 and notice that the CY flag is set after the 64-bit addition. That means that a 1 should be added to the first digit column of the second 64-bit addition, but it doesn't seem to be happening. Our total is smaller by 1 in the least-significant digit column. In other words, the program is not taking the carry information into account. Why not?

In assembly language, two mnemonics are used for addition, **add** and **adc**.

Design Tip   *The **add** mnemonic is used where no carry information can occur. This would be the case for the least-significant digits in the 256-bit number. After that, there is always the possibility that the carry flag will be set. So, for all other cases, the **adc** mnemonic should be used for addition.*

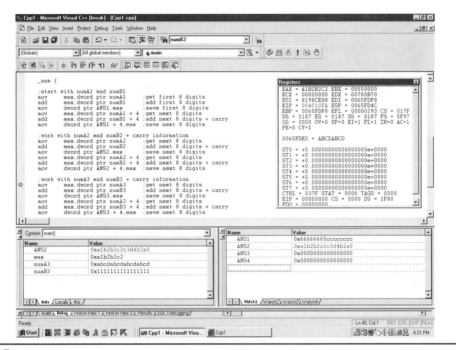

Figure 7.7   The second 64-bit addition is not correct

Let's change the appropriate mnemonics and see if this correction follows through the whole program. Figure 7.8 shows the condition of the microprocessor's registers after the addition of the third group of 64-bit digits.

Mnemonic	Flag	Set When
OV	overflow	1
UP	direction	1
EI	interrupt	1
PL	sign	1
ZR	zero	1
AC	auxiliary carry	1
PE	parity	1
CY	carry	1

Table 7.2   Microprocessor Flags

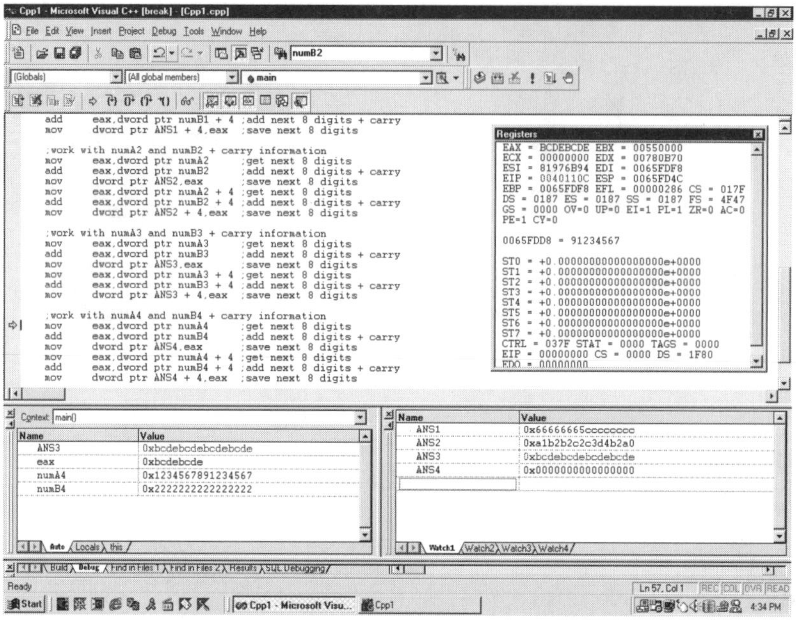

Figure 7.8   The results of this 64-bit addition are also wrong

Sure enough, the least-significant digit of ANS3 should be a hexadecimal "F", but it is an "E". We now know it is a carry problem because the carry flag (CY) is set in Figure 7.7, just previous to this addition.

Finally, the addition of the most-significant 64 bits of the 256-bit number are correct, as you can see in Figure 7.9.

The reason this addition is correct is because no carry information was passed from the previous 64-bit addition. We know this by looking at the carry flag (CY) shown in Figure 7.8. Sure enough, the carry flag is not set.

What do we need to do to correct this program? You'll see the program modifications in the next section.

Good Code

As you learned in the previous section, the problem with this program was that carry information was not being assimilated from the various stages of multiple precision arithmetic. This problem was easy to see using the Debugger and keeping an eye on both the addition results and the carry flag (CY).

Only the first addition can use the **add** mnemonic. All other additions must use the **adc** mnemonic because all future additions have the potential for using carry information.

Here is the corrected program code, which is now worthy of a name—BigInt.cpp:

```
// BigInt.cpp
// Assembly Language Program
// illustrates the power of assembly language in
// correctly manipulating 256-bit numbers
```

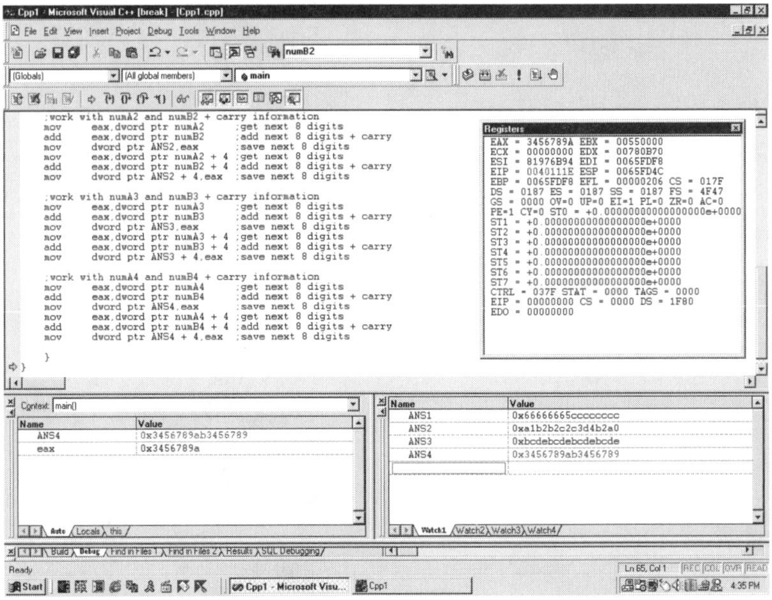

Figure 7.9   The final 64-bit addition is correct

```
// with multiple precision arithmetic.
// contains no errors


void main(void)
{

//break up and store the first 256-bit integer number
//1234567891234567ABCDABCDABCDABCDFFFFEEEEDDDDCCCCDDDDCCCCBBBBAAAA
    unsigned __int64 numA1 = 0xDDDDCCCCBBBBAAAA;
    unsigned __int64 numA2 = 0xFFFFEEEEDDDDCCCC;
    unsigned __int64 numA3 = 0xABCDABCDABCDABCD;
    unsigned __int64 numA4 = 0x1234567891234567;

//break up and store the second 256-bit integer number
//2222222222222222111111111111111A1B2C3D4E5F6E5D48888999911112222
    unsigned __int64 numB1 = 0x8888999911112222;
    unsigned __int64 numB2 = 0xA1B2C3D4E5F6E5D4;
    unsigned __int64 numB3 = 0x1111111111111111;
    unsigned __int64 numB4 = 0x2222222222222222;

//prepare storage locations to hold the 256-bit result
    unsigned __int64 ANS1 = 0;
    unsigned __int64 ANS2 = 0;
    unsigned __int64 ANS3 = 0;
    unsigned __int64 ANS4 = 0;
```

```
_asm {

;start with numA1 and numB1
mov     eax,dword ptr numA1          ;get first 8 digits
add     eax,dword ptr numB1          ;add first 8 digits
mov     dword ptr ANS1,eax           ;save first 8 digits
mov     eax,dword ptr numA1 + 4      ;get next 8 digits
adc     eax,dword ptr numB1 + 4      ;add next 8 digits + carry
mov     dword ptr ANS1 + 4,eax       ;save next 8 digits

;work with numA2 and numB2 + carry information
mov     eax,dword ptr numA2          ;get next 8 digits
adc     eax,dword ptr numB2          ;add next 8 digits + carry
mov     dword ptr ANS2,eax           ;save next 8 digits
mov     eax,dword ptr numA2 + 4      ;get next 8 digits
adc     eax,dword ptr numB2 + 4      ;add next 8 digits + carry
mov     dword ptr ANS2 + 4,eax       ;save next 8 digits

;work with numA3 and numB3 + carry information
mov     eax,dword ptr numA3          ;get next 8 digits
adc     eax,dword ptr numB3          ;add next 8 digits + carry
mov     dword ptr ANS3,eax           ;save next 8 digits
mov     eax,dword ptr numA3 + 4      ;get next 8 digits
adc     eax,dword ptr numB3 + 4      ;add next 8 digits + carry
mov     dword ptr ANS3 + 4,eax       ;save next 8 digits

;work with numA4 and numB4 + carry information
mov     eax,dword ptr numA4          ;get next 8 digits
adc     eax,dword ptr numB4          ;add next 8 digits + carry
mov     dword ptr ANS4,eax           ;save next 8 digits
mov     eax,dword ptr numA4 + 4      ;get next 8 digits
adc     eax,dword ptr numB4 + 4      ;add next 8 digits + carry
mov     dword ptr ANS4 + 4,eax       ;save next 8 digits

}
}
```

Step through all of the additions with the Debugger and view your results in the Watch window. Your screen should look similar to Figure 7.10.

Pointers are just one small portion of the problem an assembly language programmer anticipates when performing multiple precision arithmetic. Subtle differences between mnemonics such as **add** and **adc** or **sub** and **sbb** can create havoc when trying to trace through programming errors.

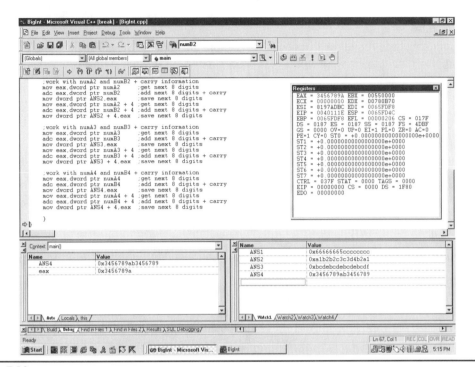

Figure 7.10   The correct 256-bit sum appears in the Watch window

Programming Loops

All programming languages provide some means of loop control. In C++, you are familiar with **for**, **while**, and **do-while** loops. Assembly language has a variety of methods for implementing loops, but nothing is as popular as using the **loop** mnemonic. Loops are useful in any language when repetitive tasks must be accomplished. These tasks can be anything from filling a table with specific data to interrupting a process to refresh an entire screen.

The example described in the next sections declares a C++ array capable of holding 100 integer values. The assembly language code will fill that array, using indexed addressing, with sequentially higher even integer values. Once the array is filled, the contents of the array will be printed to the screen using the cout stream.

Code with a Problem

The programming code for this application is straightforward—no multiple precision arithmetic here! Yet, within this simplicity lie some subtle errors. Let's look at the original implementation.

```cpp
// Contains Logical Errors
// Assembly Language Program
// illustrates the use of a loop in assembly language
// to fill a table with sequentially higher numbers.

#include <iostream.h>

void main(void)
{

    int etable[100];

    _asm {

    ;code to generate a table of sequential even numbers
    mov         esi,00h         ;initialize index register
    mov         ecx,63h         ;prepare to generate 100 numbers
more: mov       etable[esi],esi     ;use index value as number, too
    add         esi,08h         ;now point to next storage location
    loop        more            ;repeat if ecx is not zero

    }

    // print values in table
    for (int i=0; i<100 ; i++) {
        cout << hex << etable[i] << "\n";
    }
}
```

In this example, indexed addressing is used to access the various locations within the array (frequently called a *table* in assembly language). So the first step is to set the index register to the starting location. Loop control is based upon the value in the ecx register. As the loop is executed, the value in ecx is automatically decremented during each pass. When the value in ecx is zero, control drops through the loop, and the assembly language portion of the program is completed. In order to increment from one integer to another in assembly language, a value of 8h is added to the esi register during each pass. In an apparent economy move, the data value placed in the table is the value currently contained in the esi register. So we would be looking for hexadecimal table entries like 0, 8, 10, 18, 20, and so on.

Let's compile this program and get into the Debugger to examine the results. Place the variable *etable* in the Watch window, as shown in Figure 7.11.

Also, notice that several lines of code have already been executed. As a matter-of-fact, only the first pass through the loop has been completed. If you examine Figure 7.11, you'll notice that there is a small plus sign (+) just to the left of *etable* in the Watch window. Click the left mouse button on this symbol to expand your view of *etable's* contents, as shown in Figure 7.12.

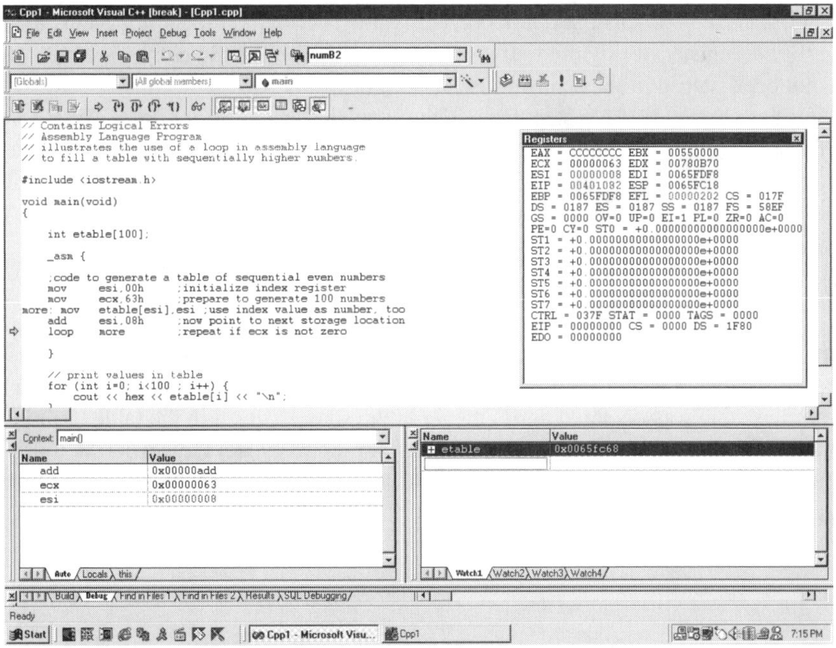

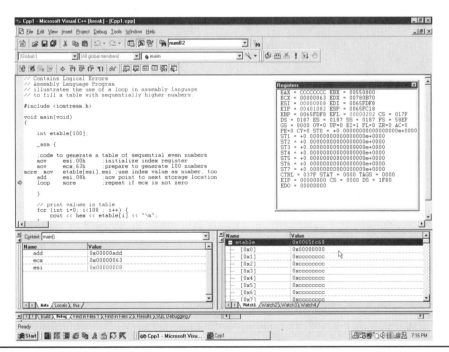

Figure 7.11   The variable *etable* is placed in the Watch window

Figure 7.12   The contents of *etable* are made visible in the Watch window

The first entry, *etable[0x0]*, is 0x00000000. This value is correct since it represents the value contained in the esi register during the first pass. All the remaining table entries are meaningless since values have not been placed in these positions.

Use the Step Into button (F11) to step through the loop a couple of more times. Your screen should appear like Figure 7.13.

Upon examining the entries in the *etable* variable, it is obvious something is wrong. When the data values appear, they are correct, but they are appearing at every other table entry position. A quick look back to the source code turns up the offending line of code.

```
add        esi,08h          ;now point to next storage location
```

Data entry positions in assembly language programs are often controlled by index values. In this example, the esi register is used to index across the table entries. However, the index value is too large. The original table was declared as an integer table, so each entry in the table will be 32 bits. The index value added to the esi register must move over 32 bits, also. However, the index value in assembly language is measured in bytes! So, in order to move 32 bits, the index value must be set to 4 (4 bytes × 8 bits / byte = 32 bits).

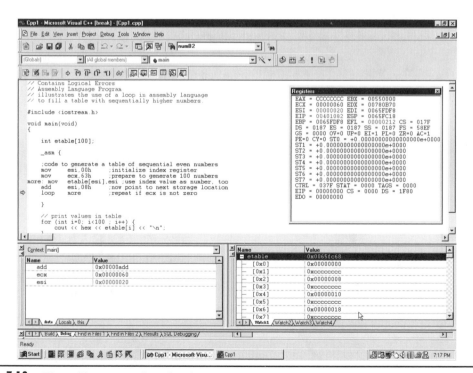

Figure 7.13   The *etable* contents after a few times around the control loop

| Design Tip | *If the value in the esi register is incremented by 4 instead of 8, the values stored in the* etable *variable will increment by 4s (that is, 0, 4, 8, C, 10, and so on).* |

Another attempt, with the corrected value in place, shows that the table values are being entered correctly as you can see in Figure 7.14.

Execute the loop to completion, and you notice another problem when you examine Figure 7.15.

Margin or border problems with loops almost always point to the initial values used to control the loop. Oh, the ecx register should have been set to hexadecimal 64, not 63! Go through the execution once again and check all of the values in the table. Figure 7.16 shows that even the last value in the table is now correct.

Getting loop control values correct is always a problem in any language. It can be an even larger problem in assembly language depending upon whether the initial values from a table are dealt with inside or outside of the loop.

Good Code

With the two errors corrected in the previous program listing, let's look at some good clean code in an application we now name Loop.cpp.

```
// Loop.cpp
// Assembly Language Program
// illustrates the use of a loop in assembly language
// to fill a table with sequentially higher numbers.
```

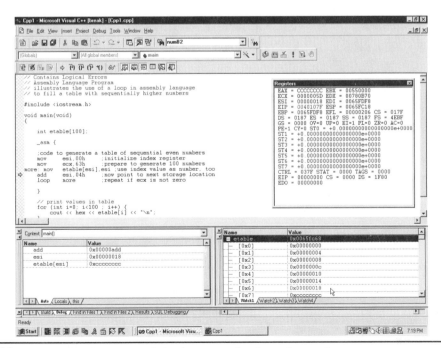

Figure 7.14   The *etable* values are now being incremented and stored correctly

Figure 7.15   The last value in the table, [0x63], has not been entered

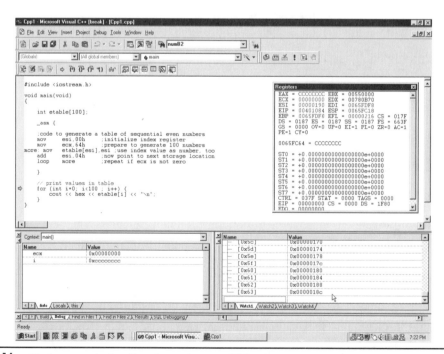

Figure 7.16   The loop counter is adjusted to make one additional pass

```
// contains no errors

#include <iostream.h>

void main(void)
{

    int etable[100];

    _asm {

    ;code to generate a table of sequential even numbers
    mov          esi,00h         ;initialize index register

    mov          ecx,64h         ;prepare to generate 100 numbers
more: mov        etable[esi],esi;use index value as number, too
    add          esi,04h         ;now point to next storage location
    loop         more            ;repeat if ecx is not zero

    }

    // print values in table
    for (int i=0; i<100 ; i++) {
        cout << hex << etable[i] << "\n";
    }
}
```

As a final check on the application's performance, execute the program and examine the data printed to the compatibility box with the cout stream, as shown in Figure 7.17.

Remember, while these values are printed in hexadecimal by request, you could also print them to the screen in normal decimal format.

All of the assembly language programming to this point has dealt with integer numbers. In the next section, you learn how to use the coprocessor to do real number arithmetic. You'll also see how to incorporate the Debugger's Registers window to watch as stack entries are added and removed from the coprocessor stack.

Adding Real Numbers with the Coprocessor

The first program that we'll illustrate involving the coprocessor does not contain any errors. We'll use this program to show some coprocessor programming fundamentals and how the debugger can be used to examine variables and coprocessor stack entries.

This program is RealAdd.cpp and is a simple application that adds two real numbers and prints the results to the screen.

Good Code

To get a feel for creating a coprocessor assembly language program, examine the following listing:

```
// RealAdd.cpp
// Assembly Language Program
// illustrates the use of the coprocessor in
// assembly language to perform real number
```

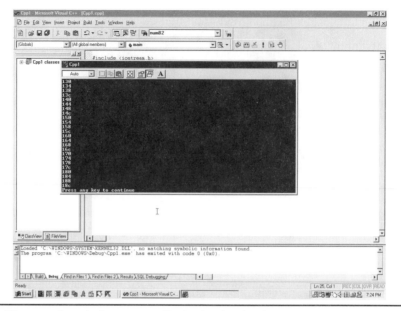

Figure 7.17   The output from the Loop.cpp application is printed to the screen

```cpp
// arithmetic.
// contains no errors

#include <iostream.h>

void main(void)
{

    double numa = 128.76;
    double numb = -3.5e+1;
    double answer;

    _asm {

    finit               ;initialize coprocessor
    fld         numa    ;place first real onto stack
    fadd        numb    ;add second real to stack
    fstp        answer  ;pop and save real answer
    fwait               ;sync co and micro procesors

    }

    cout << answer << "\n";
}
```

Three variables are declared in the conventional manner. Each number is defined as a **double**. You'll see that this data type works very well with the coprocessor. Next, you'll notice five lines of assembly language code. Each mnemonic begins with the letter *f*, which is a hint to the programmer that this is a coprocessor mnemonic.

The first mnemonic, **finit**, initializes the coprocessor by clearing internal flags and the stack. It is recommended that the first operation on the coprocessor always be a **finit** operation.

The next mnemonic loads a real number onto the coprocessor's stack at position ST(0). Real numbers are loaded with the **fld** mnemonic. If the first number had been an integer, it could have been loaded with the **fild** mnemonic. This distinction is critical since real numbers are actually stored in memory as encoded integer values. Without the distinction between **fld** and **fild** mnemonics, the coprocessor could not tell the difference between an encoded real number and an integer.

The **fadd** mnemonic adds the second real number to the contents of the coprocessor stack entry at ST(0). So the stack is not pushed down during this operation. An integer could have been added at this point by using the **fiadd** mnemonic.

The **fstp** mnemonic stores the contents of the stack, ST(0), in the variable and then pops the value off of the stack. The value being stored is a normal encoded real number. The value being stored could have been stored as an integer using the **fistp** mnemonic.

The **fwait** mnemonic is used to synchronize the operation of the coprocessor and the microprocessor. Programming control is under the direction of the microprocessor. However, when the microprocessor detects a coprocessor mnemonic, control is passed to the coprocessor. Before returning operation to the microprocessor, it is always wise to synchronize their operations with a **fwait** statement.

Let's compile this program and enter the Debugger to examine exactly what is taking place during execution.

Figure 7.18 shows the initial debugging screen for this program.

The Registers window shows the coprocessor's stack entries. Even without the execution of the **finit** mnemonic, they are all zero. Below the stack entries are the various flags used by the coprocessor.

Figure 7.19 shows the condition of the coprocessor values after the execution of the **finit** mnemonic. Notice that the arrow at the extreme left edge of the screen is now pointing to the **fld** mnemonic.

Use the Step Into button (F11) to execute one more line of code. Figure 7.20 shows that the first number has been loaded onto the coprocessor's stack at ST(0).

Now, execute two lines of code so that the second number is added to the contents of the coprocessor's stack at ST(0). When the number is stored in the *answer* variable and the stack is popped, by using the **fstp** mnemonic, the coprocessor stack will be clear.

You can see the value saved in the *answer* variable in the Watch window in Figure 7.21.

Now, there is just one disturbing thing about Figure 7.21. Do you see it? The answer is now appearing at ST(7), and it is not supposed to be there. The **fstp** mnemonic should have saved the value and popped the stack. In fact, we're sure it did just that. Is this a "bug" in the Debugger's Registers window?

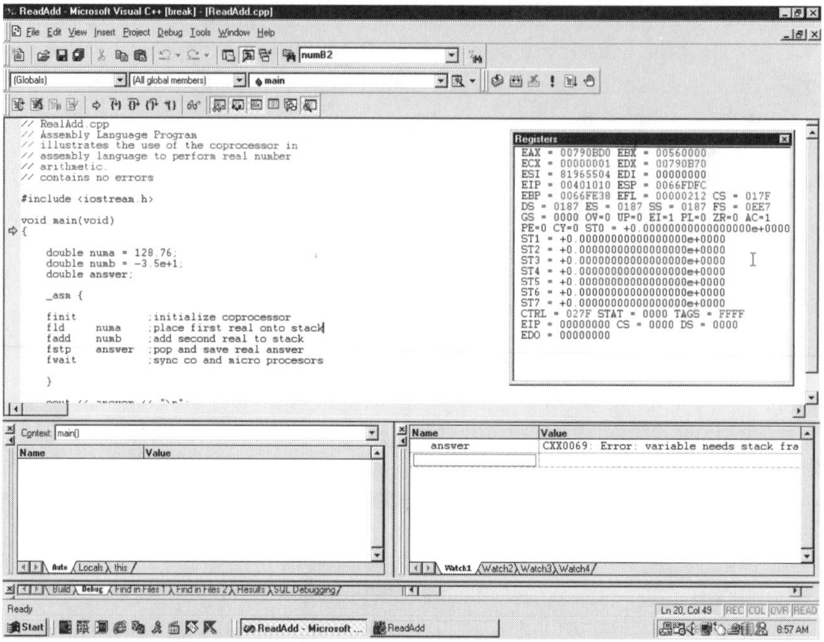

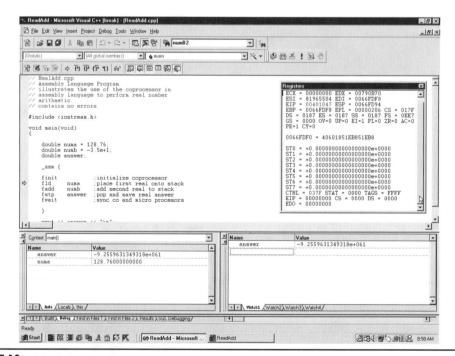

Figure 7.18 The ReadAdd.cpp program is started in the Debugger

Figure 7.19 The **finit** mnemonic is used to clear the stack and various coprocessor flags

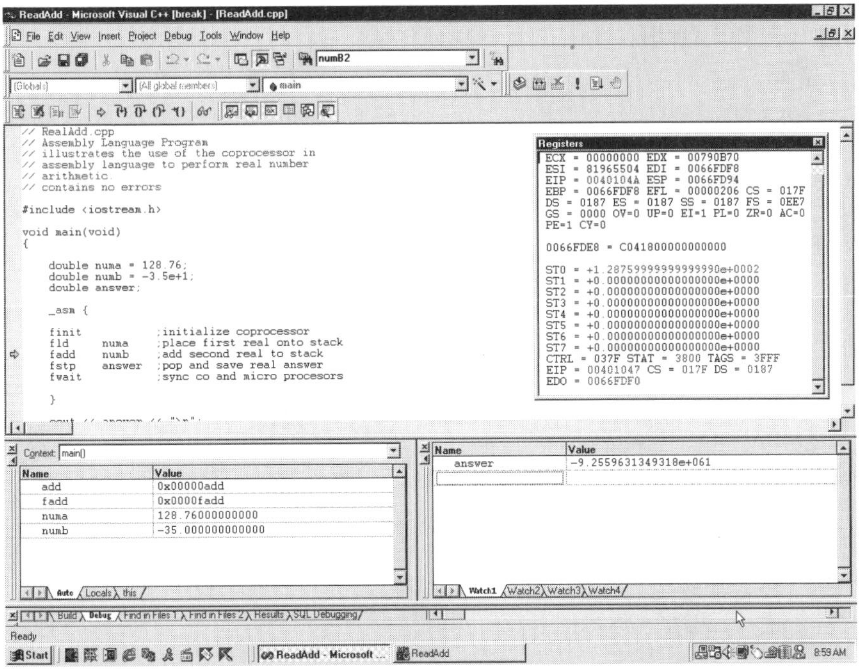

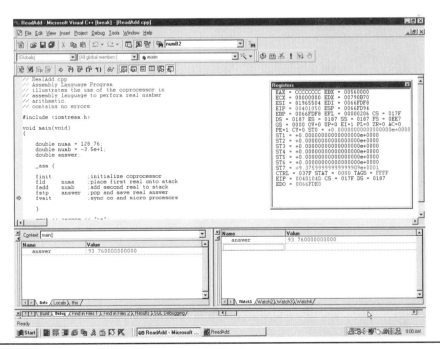

Figure 7.20 The first number is loaded onto the coprocessor's stack

Figure 7.21 The answer is visible in the Debugger's Watch window

Calculating Tangent Values with the Coprocessor

In this program, we are going to use the coprocessor to calculate a trigonometric table of tangent values for the angles 0 to 45 degrees. The 46 values will be calculated and stored in an array named *ttable[46]*, which is declared to hold **double** values. These are real numbers ranging from 0 to 1.0.

Coprocessor trigonometric functions, like their C++ counterparts, require angles in radians. If we are going to pass angle values in degrees, a conversion must take place. To get the angle in radians, we need to code this conversion:

```
angle (radians) = pi * angle (degrees) / 180
```

The **fptan** mnemonic returns the tangent of an angle, so all we'll have to do is pass the converted angle to the function. If this coding is successful, we can then increment the angle value and the storage location to find the next answer. Sounds like a loop to us!

Let's see how this code is implemented with the logic we've just suggested. We'll then use the Debugger to ferret out any logical errors we may have introduced.

Code with a Problem

The listing in this section contains the implementation of the logic discussed in the previous section. Examine the listing and see if you detect any immediate problems.

```
// Contains Logical Errors
// illustrates the use of the coprocessor in
// calculating a table of trigonometric
// values (tangent) with the coprocessor
// for angles between 0 and 45 degrees.

#include <iostream.h>

void main(void)
{

    int angle = 0;
    int radian = 180;
    double ttable[46];

    _asm {

    mov        esi,0        ;initialize index register
    mov        cx,46        ;prepare to create 46 values
    finit                   ;initialize coprocessor
more: fild     radian       ;place radian on stack
    fldpi                   ;load pi on stack
    fdiv                    ;divide pi by radian
    fild       angle        ;load angle onto stack
    fmul                    ;convert degrees to radians
    fptan                   ;calculate tangent
    fstp       ttable[esi]  ;save answer in tangent table
```

```
inc        angle       ;next angle
add        esi,08d     ;point to next storage location
loop       more        ;end if cx=0
fwait                  ;sync co and micro processors


}

cout << "Angle   Tangent\n\n";
for(int i = 0; i<46 ; i++) {
    cout << i <<  "\t" << ttable[i] << "\n";
}
}
```

We're going to tell you at the start that any errors in this program are coprocessor errors and do not involve table indexes or loop counts.

The first six lines of coprocessor code, starting with the **finit** mnemonic, are required to convert the angle in degrees to the angle in radians by implementing the formula presented in the previous section.

The **fptan** mnemonic uses this converted angle to calculate and return the tangent of the angle. The real number result is then returned to the *ttable[]* array with the use of a **fstp** mnemonic.

Let's compile and execute the code and see what is printed to the compatibility window.

Figure 7.22 shows the results for the angles between 22 and 45 degrees.

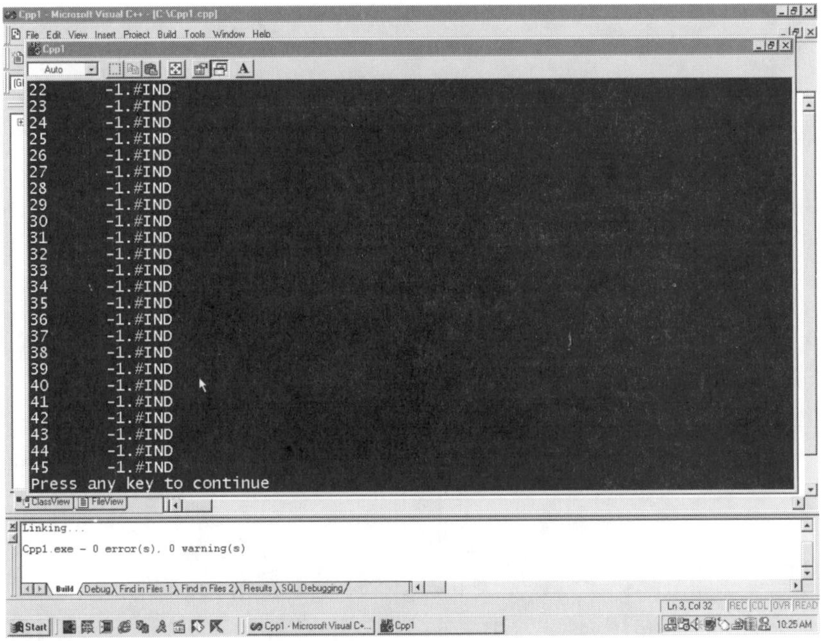

Figure 7.22   Tangent values for the angles 0 to 45 degrees?

The results, as you might have suspected, are not even close. Time to warm-up the Debugger and attack those programming problems.

Start the Debugger, open the Registers window, place *ttable* in the Watch window, and execute individual lines of code down to the **fldpi** mnemonic, as shown in Figure 7.23.

Examine ST(0), and you will see that the constant has been properly loaded onto the stack. Now execute another line of code. Figure 7.24 shows the next line of execution will be **fdiv** by the placement of the arrow at the left edge of this screen.

Examine the ST(0) position again; it now contains a precise value for pi. Also notice that the constant has been pushed down on the stack to ST(1). Let's perform the division by executing the next line of code, as shown in Figure 7.25.

It is easy to see that the results of the division are incorrect. The value of pi divided by 180 should be close to .017453 . . ., but we have 5.729 . . . on the stack top ST(0). What happened?

The **fdiv** mnemonic is performing an implicit divide (no operants). In doing this, it performs the division as ST(1)/ST(0), which, in this case, is 180/pi. We want just the opposite, so our choice is to perform explicit division or to rearrange how the values are placed on the stack in the first place. We elect the latter approach and try to avoid explicit coprocessor operations whenever possible.

Examine the modified portion of code and the correct results on the stack top ST(0) in Figure 7.26.

If you try a program execution, however, you'll quickly learn that this code contains more errors. We need to continue stepping through this program.

Execute the **fmul** mnemonic. For an angle of 0 degrees, the results are shown correctly in Figure 7.27.

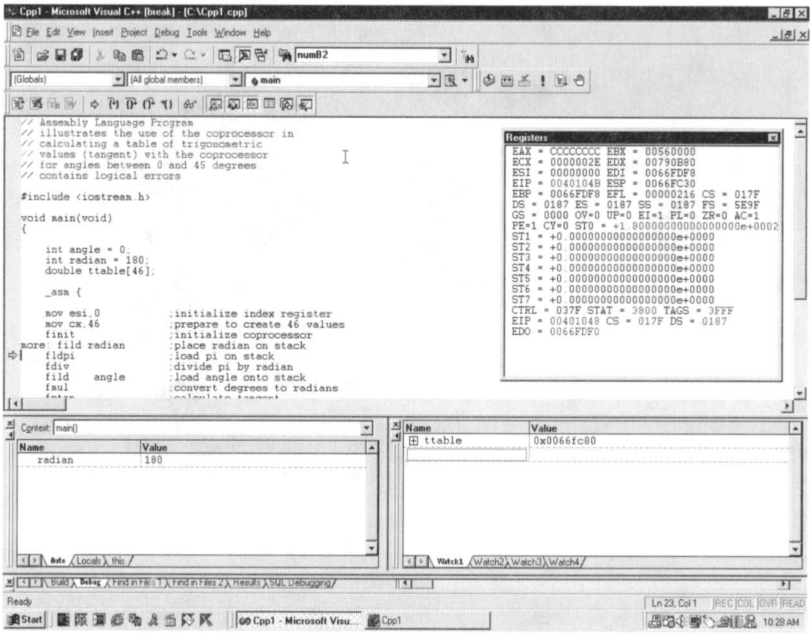

Figure 7.23   Checking to see if the *radian* constant was loaded correctly

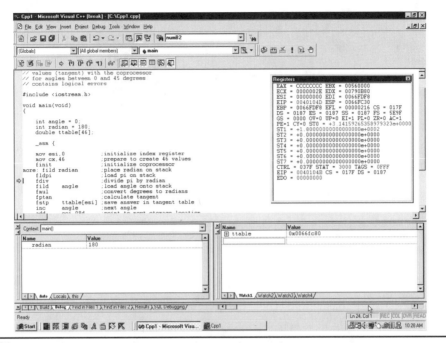

Figure 7.24   Checking to see if the value for pi has been loaded correctly

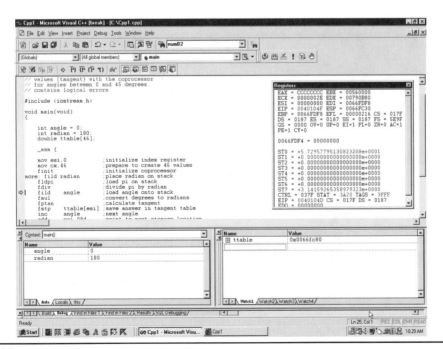

Figure 7.25   Checking the divide operation (pi/180)

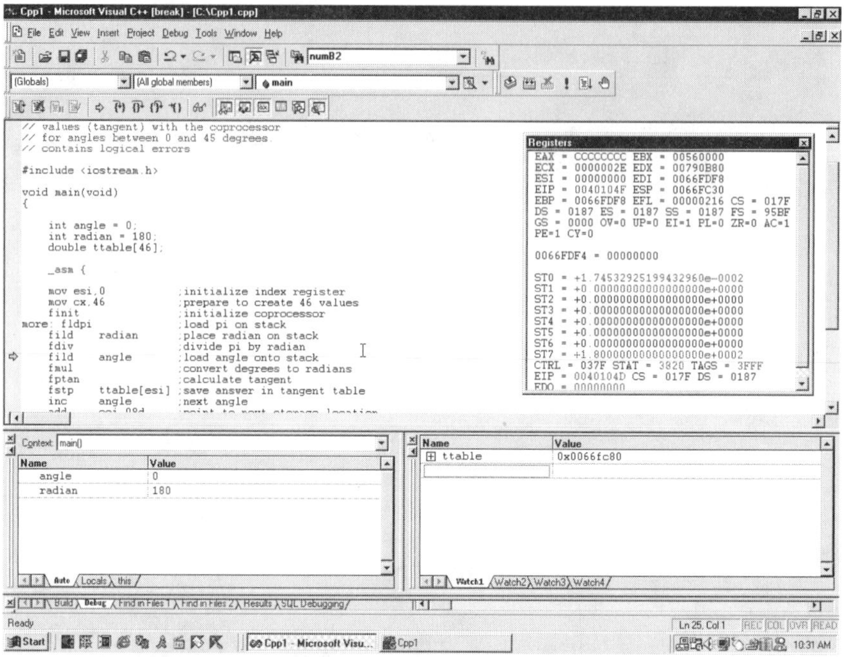

Figure 7.26   The division of pi/180 now produces correct results

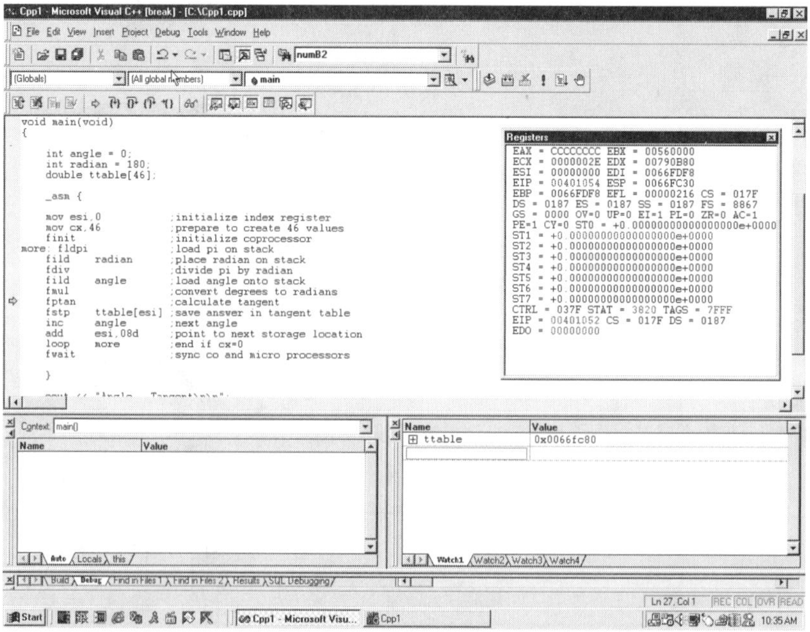

Figure 7.27   An angle of 0 degrees is correctly converted to radians

Execute one more step to find the tangent of 0 radians. Here is another problem! Figure 7.28 indicates that a value of 1 is returned to ST(0), with all other stack entries at 0.

We would have anticipated a value of 0 being returned for an angle of 0 radians. The Debugger is indicating that there is a problem with the execution of the **fptan** mnemonic.

A little research into the operation of the **fptan** mnemonic provides the answer. The **fptan** mnemonic returns the tangent of the angle as the x and y values in a right triangle. Now, this problem is not as bad as it seems. You can simply use an **fdiv** mnemonic after the **fptan** mnemonic to divide ST(1) by ST(0). The correct results will now be returned to the stack top ST(0), as shown by Figure 7.29.

As a further check, step through several angles and note the results shown on the stack. For example, Figure 7.30 shows the ST(0) and ST(1) entries for an angle of 20 degrees.

Apparently, we have located and repaired all of the problems with this program. You can step through the remaining angles to verify the results.

Good Code

With all of errors corrected, let's look at the corrected program, now named Trig.cpp.

```
// Trig.cpp
// Assembly Language Program
// illustrates the use of the coprocessor in
// calculating a table of trigonometric
// values (tangent) with the coprocessor
// for angles between 0 and 45 degrees.
// contains no errors
```

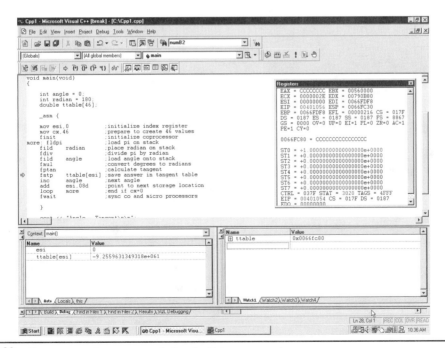

Figure 7.28   Incorrect results are returned after the **fptan** mnemonic

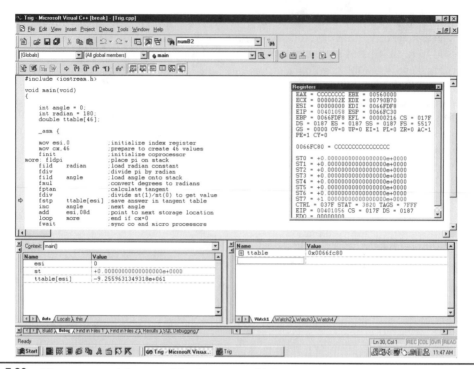

Figure 7.29   The correct result is returned for the tangent of 0 degrees

24x7

Historically, the **fptan** mnemonic was one of the few trigonometric functions available on the first coprocessor (8087). This arrangement of returning x and y values of a right triangle allowed all other trigonometric values, such as sine, cosine, secant, cosecant, and cotangent, to be calculated. The **fptan** mnemonic was also limited in the range of angles that could be used. Basically, **fptan** would accurately return values for the angles from 0 to 45 degrees. With later processors, the **fptan** function evolved to accepting a full range of angles and matched the capabilities of mnemonics like **fsin** and **fcos**. However, remember when you write code, that **fptan** does not return the tangent directly. The tangent value must be calculated from the x and y values returned to the coprocessor stack.

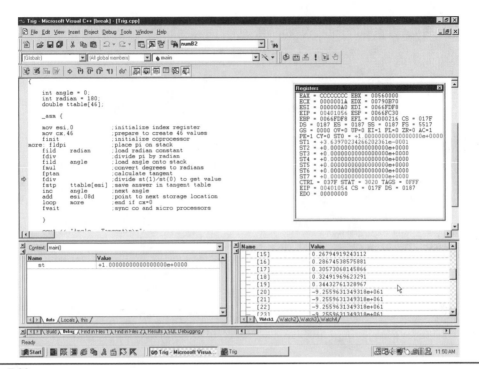

Figure 7.30 The tangent of 20 degrees is returned correctly

```cpp
#include <iostream.h>

void main(void)
{

    int angle = 0;
    int radian = 180;
    double ttable[46];

    _asm {

    mov        esi,0      ;initialize index register
    mov        cx,46      ;prepare to create 46 values
    finit                 ;initialize coprocessor
```

```
more: fldpi                  ;place pi on stack
      fild      radian       ;load radian constant
      fdiv                   ;divide pi by radian
      fild      angle        ;load angle onto stack
      fmul                   ;convert degrees to radians
      fptan                  ;calculate tangent
      fdiv                   ;divide st(1)/st(0) to get value
      fstp      ttable[esi]  ;save answer in tangent table
      inc       angle        ;next angle
      add       esi,08d      ;point to next storage location
      loop      more         ;end if cx=0
      fwait                  ;sync co and micro processors

      }

      cout << "Angle    Tangent\n\n";
      for(int i = 0; i<46 ; i++) {
          cout << i <<  "\t" << ttable[i] << "\n";
      }
}
```

Compile and execute this program to see the results shown in Figure 7.31.

You may want to experiment with this program. Why not try calculating a sine table for the angles from 0 to 90 degrees.

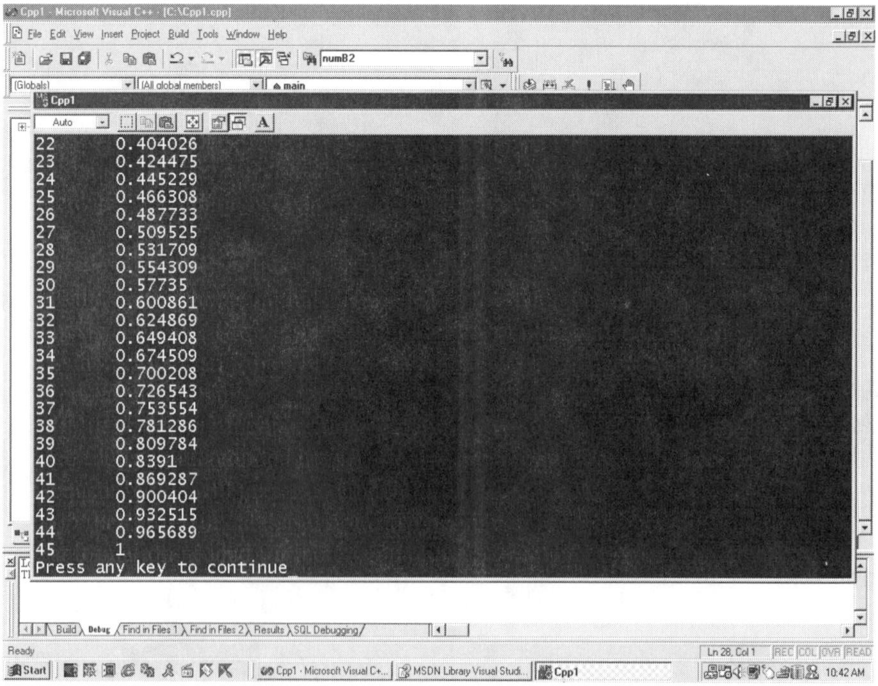

Figure 7.31   A correctly calculated and formatted trigonometric table

Design Tip *When using coprocessor mnemonics such as **fsin** and **fcos**, it is not necessary to perform an implicit **fdiv** after the operation. These functions return the correct values directly and work over a large range of angles.*

Conclusion

This chapter has introduced some powerful debugging techniques that involve the use of the microprocessor and coprocessor. You have learned how to view microprocessor registers and coprocessor stack entries in the Debugger's Registers window. This information has been used to track down and eliminate a variety of logical assembly language errors.

CHAPTER 8

Locating, Analyzing, and Repairing Errors in Windows Code

This chapter builds on your understanding of procedure-oriented Windows application development and the debugging material presented in earlier chapters. The code we use in this chapter to illustrate various debugging techniques will compile and run under both Windows 98 and Windows NT (2000) operating systems with little or no modification.

The majority of Windows applications are written in C or C++, with Visual Basic being a close second language. Just as command-line C++ programs can be procedure oriented or object oriented, so too, can Windows applications written in C++. This chapter will focus on the fairly straightforward, procedure-oriented approach. Chapters 10, 11, and 14 through 17 will focus on the powerful C++ object-oriented environment.

Should you be working in the procedure- or object-oriented environment when developing Windows applications? That is really a complicated question, and the answer depends upon a number of factors. Let us make this suggestion: if your programs are simple and use a moderate number of resources, then you will find the procedure-oriented environment more than satisfactory. In actuality, your compiled code size might be a little smaller and your application might run a little faster than an object-oriented counterpart.

However, whether you love to develop procedure-oriented code, or wouldn't touch anything but an object-oriented application, you should read this chapter! You will learn things about the Debugger and about debugging that will help you throughout the remainder of this book.

Debugging with Two Computers

Warning! Before you give your older second computer system to Aunt Annetta for her e-mail, read this section!

Early computer users often wondered why anyone would want to work in a multimedia environment. Running one application was more than sufficient for their needs. Early pioneers in multitasking, such as TopView and DeskView, paved the way for OS/2 and Windows. As users, we have become quite adept at running multiple applications at the same time. Even as we write this chapter, our computers are running Microsoft Word, Microsoft Visual C++, and Collage (a screen capture program).

In this section, we'll go one better. With a Windows application running in the Debugger, it is best to use two computers. One computer can display the Windows application, and the other computer, the contents of the Debugger.

The problem centers on the nature of a Windows application—an application that frequently runs in the foreground and keeps the focus (that is, it's the top-most screen along with keyboard and mouse input). However, the Debugger is also a Windows application that wants the focus. The solution is two networked computers, two keyboards, two mice, and two monitors. The Windows application can have one system to itself, and the Debugger, the other. All that is needed is a means of linking the Windows application to the Debugger via the network.

Microsoft has provided the solution to this problem. You can find their outline for setting up communications between computers in the MSDN Library provided with Visual Studio. Just look up the topic of "Debugging Remote Applications." In the next sections, we'll walk through the steps for debugging with two computers, giving practical advice along the way. The key requirement is that the computers be networked with a TCP/IP connection. The steps we use in the following sections are for Visual C++ 6.0. If you are using an earlier or later version, it may have to be modified slightly.

Terminology is the key to success in making this connection. Microsoft calls the main computer system the *host*, and the remote computer system, the *target*. In our case, the host computer is a 600 MHz Hewlett-Packard Pentium III computer, while the target is a 400 MHz Sony Vaio portable. We identified the Hewlett-Packard host computer as "hp" on the network and the Sony Vaio target computer as "sony."

Preparing the Remote Target Computer

A small program, called the Remote Debug Monitor, must be run on the remote target computer— in our case, the Sony system. The Remote Debug Monitor application and the target computer are responsible for communicating with the Debugger running on the host computer (in this case, the Hewlett-Packard system). The Remote Target Computer software controls the execution of the application in the Debugger.

Additional files must be copied to the remote target computer (sony) in order to install the Remote Debug Monitor. For both Windows 98 and Windows NT (2000), these files include:

```
MSVCMON.EXE
MSVCRT.DLL
TLNOT.DLL
DM.DLL
MSVCP6O.DLL
MSDIS110.DLL
PSAPI.DLL (for NT only)
```

To locate these files in the proper host computer (hp) subdirectory, just use the Find option in your system's Start window. These files should be copied from the host computer (hp) to the remote target computer (Sony) and saved in the Windows subdirectory of the remote target system. The only exception is that the MSVCRT.DLL file should be copied to the Windows\System32 subdirectory. Once this is done, reboot the computer.

To run the Remote Target Computer software on the remote target system (sony), follow these steps:

1. Run the MSVCMON.EXE application on the remote target computer (sony).

2. The Visual C++ Debug Monitor dialog box is displayed.

3. Choose the Settings option.

4. The Win32 Network (TCP/IP) Settings dialog box is displayed.

5. Enter the name of the host computer (hp, in our case) in this dialog box. (The IP address can also be used.)

6. If the password Edit box is active, enter a password. This password must match on both computers. Otherwise, this field can be left blank.

7. Click the OK button.

8. Now click the Connect button.

Once the eight steps have been completed, the Connecting dialog box will appear, as shown in Figure 8.1.

Figure 8.1   The Connecting dialog box appears on the remote target computer

Do nothing more at this time. This dialog box will disappear once actual debugging starts.

When the debugging session has completed, select the Disconnect button to terminate the remote connection.

Preparing the Host Computer

The host computer (hp, in our case) must be prepared for communicating with the remote target computer (sony, in our case). Perform the following steps on the host computer (hp):

1. From within Visual C++, select the Build | Debugger Remote Connection menu item.

2. The Remote Connection dialog box will appear.

3. If the Platform drop-down list box allows a selection, select the appropriate platform. If a selection option is not offered, the default item is selected automatically.

4. Use the Connection drop-down listbox to select the Network (TCP/IP) connection option.

5. Now, select the Settings option.

6. The Win32 Network (TCP/IP) Settings dialog box will appear.

7. Enter the name of the remote target computer (sony, in our case) in this dialog box. The IP address can also be used. If the password option is available, enter a password that is identical to the remote target's password. This field can also be left blank on both the remote and host machines.

8. Select the OK button to close the Win32 Network (TCP/IP) Settings dialog box.

9. Select the OK button to close the Remote Connection dialog box.

Figure 8.2 shows the Remote Connection and Win32 Network Settings dialog boxes on the host computer (hp).

Once the nine steps have been completed, the host computer will be set up for communicating with the remote target computer.

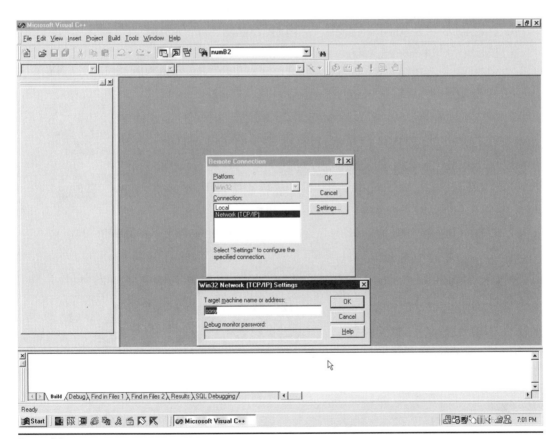

Figure 8.2 The Remote Connection and Win32 Network (TCP/IP) Settings dialog boxes on the host computer

Starting a Debugging Session

With both computers on the network ready to communicate, the debugging session can be started. (Remember, on our system, the host computer running Visual C++ is the Hewlett-Packard, and the remote target computer is the Sony.) Complete the following steps:

1. Copy the complete project to be debugged to both machines. We suggest using the same directory. For example, duplicate files would exist on both computers at c:\myproject with the debug executable at c:\myproject\debug. Both directories should be set up on the network as shared directories.

2. Start the Visual C++ compiler and load the project on the host computer. (The Visual C++ compiler is not needed on the remote target computer (sony)).

3. Choose the Project | Settings menu option. The Project Settings dialog box will appear.

4. Choose the Debug tab in the Project Settings dialog box.

5. From the Category listbox, select General and set the following items (also see Figure 8.3):

   • Category listbox: Enter any additional DLLs required for the project.

   • Executable for debug session: Enter the name and path of the executable file as the debugger host computer (hp) sees it—for example, c:\tester\debug\tester.exe.

   • Working directory: Leave blank.

   • Program arguments: Leave blank unless your program accepts initial parameters.

   • Remote executable path and file name: Enter the name and path of the executable file as the remote target computer (sony) sees it—for example, c:\tester\debug\tester.exe.

6. Choose the Build | Start Debug menu item and use the Step Into (F11) option.

7. Give your system at least a minute to start communications across the network and then begin the debugging session in the normal manner.

8. Remember that anytime a change is made in the project, the files must be updated on both machines.

Design Tip *Copying the project into the same subdirectory on both machines is a little bit of an overkill, but rather than looking for individual changes each time a project is recompiled, a block copy of the entire project is the fastest technique.*

Most warning messages concerning missing DLLs can be ignored because complete copies of the application exist on both machines.

We'll use this two-computer debugging technique later in this chapter and show you why the use of two computers is such an advantage in debugging Windows applications.

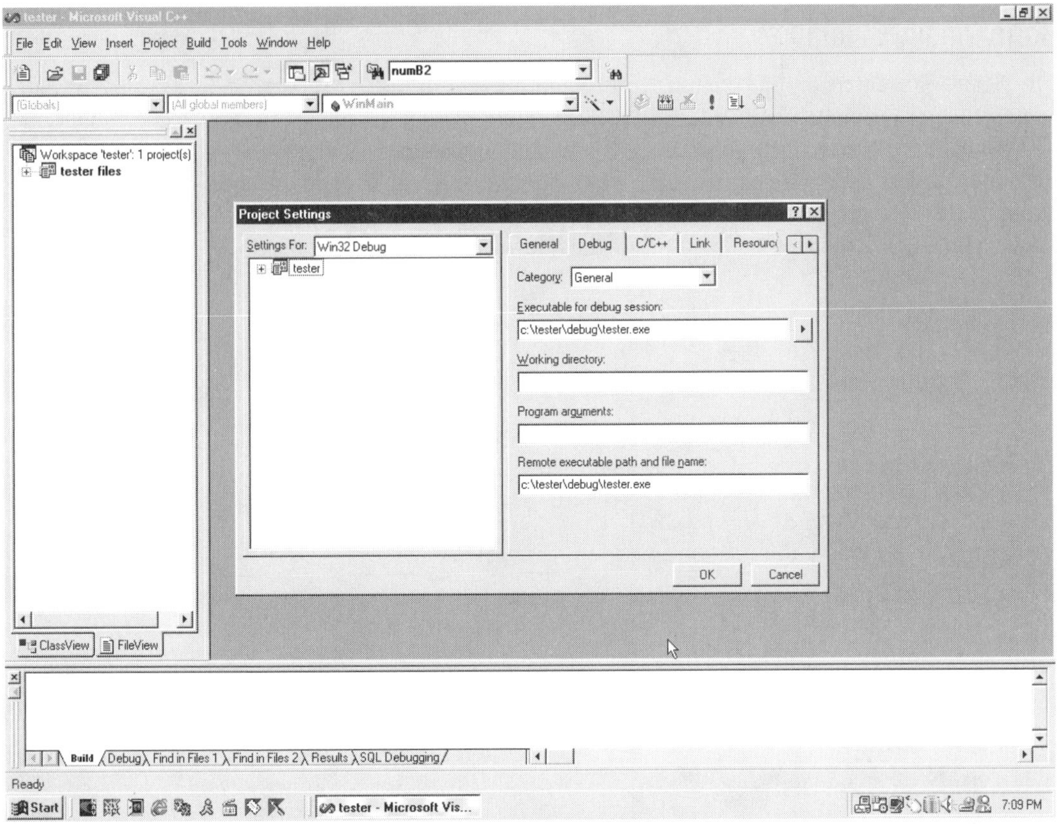

Figure 8.3   The Project Settings dialog box as it appears on the host computer (hp)

A Brief Windows Primer

In this section, we'll examine the code necessary to create a simple window on the screen and draw some simple graphics in that window. We'll follow the code with an explanation of the important procedure-oriented Windows functions that were used. If you haven't worked in the Windows environment, we strongly recommend that you first familiarize yourself with a book devoted to the topic. We, of course, recommend our *Introduction to Windows 98 Programming* from Prentice Hall. This section is not intended to replace a 500- to 800-page book on Windows programming, but rather should serve as a brief source of information on the fundamental construction of Windows applications in preparation for the debugging material that will be presented later in this chapter.

Basic Windows Code

The following code listing is a complete procedure-oriented Windows programming example named swt.cpp that can be built, compiled, and executed. To create this simple application, start Visual C++ and use the File | New menu option to select a Win32 application. Name the project swt and use the empty project option. Select the File | New option once again and add the code in the following listing as a C++ source code file. Save the file by either selecting the File | Save menu option or clicking on the diskette icon below the Edit and View menus in the compiler.

```cpp
//
// swt.cpp
// Simple Windows Template
// Copyright (c) William H. Murray and Chris H. Pappas, 2000
//

#include <windows.h>

LRESULT CALLBACK WndProc(HWND,UINT,WPARAM,LPARAM);

char szProgName[]="ProgName";

int WINAPI WinMain(HINSTANCE hInst,HINSTANCE hPreInst,
                   LPSTR lpszCmdLine,int nCmdShow)
{
  HWND hWnd;
  MSG  lpMsg;
  WNDCLASS wcApp;

  wcApp.lpszClassName=szProgName;
  wcApp.hInstance     =hInst;
  wcApp.lpfnWndProc   =WndProc;
  wcApp.hCursor       =LoadCursor(NULL,IDC_ARROW);
  wcApp.hIcon         =0;
  wcApp.lpszMenuName  =0;
  wcApp.hbrBackground=(HBRUSH) GetStockObject(WHITE_BRUSH);
  wcApp.style         =CS_HREDRAW|CS_VREDRAW;
  wcApp.cbClsExtra    =0;
  wcApp.cbWndExtra    =0;
  if (!RegisterClass (&wcApp))
    return 0;

  hWnd=CreateWindow(szProgName,"Simple Windows Template",
                    WS_OVERLAPPEDWINDOW,CW_USEDEFAULT,
                    CW_USEDEFAULT,CW_USEDEFAULT,
                    CW_USEDEFAULT,(HWND)NULL,(HMENU)NULL,
                    hInst,(LPSTR)NULL);
  ShowWindow(hWnd,nCmdShow);
  UpdateWindow(hWnd);
  while (GetMessage(&lpMsg,0,0,0)) {
    TranslateMessage(&lpMsg);
```

```
      DispatchMessage(&lpMsg);
  }
  return(lpMsg.wParam);
}


LRESULT CALLBACK WndProc(HWND hWnd,UINT messg,
                         WPARAM wParam,LPARAM lParam)
{
  HDC hdc;
  PAINTSTRUCT ps;

  switch (messg)
  {
    case WM_PAINT:
      hdc=BeginPaint(hWnd,&ps);

      MoveToEx(hdc,45,55,NULL);
      LineTo(hdc,480,410);

      TextOut(hdc,200,100,"A simple line",13);

      ValidateRect(hWnd,NULL);
      EndPaint(hWnd,&ps);
      break;
    case WM_DESTROY:
      PostQuitMessage(0);
      break;
    default:
      return(DefWindowProc(hWnd,messg,wParam,lParam));
      break;
  }
  return(0);
}
```

Use the Visual C++ Build | Rebuild All menu item to compile and create an executable with debug information. The Debug subdirectory will hold debug information, and the debug version of your application's executable, swt.exe. However, you will also notice a large number of additional files, some of which are more interesting than others. For example, the swt.cpp file is the C++ source file you just entered and saved. The swt.dsp file is the project file used within the development environment. The swt.dsw file is the workspace file used within the development environment. The swt.ncb file is the No compile browser file. It contains information generated by the parser that is used by Visual Studio utilities such as ClassView, WizardBar, and the Component Gallery.

Specific Debugging Files

When you build a C++ project by executing Rebuild All, Visual Studio completes the set of files it generates by enabling you to execute and debug your Windows application.

One file contained in the project's Debug subdirectory is swt.exe. The swt.exe file is the machine language executable version of swt.cpp. However, the purposes of the other files in this subdirectory are not as obvious.

The swt.ilk file is used when linking incrementally. Here, LINK updates the .ilk status file that it created during the first incremental link. This file has the same base name as the .exe file or .dll file, and it has the extension .ilk. During subsequent incremental links, LINK updates the .ilk file. If the .ilk file is missing, LINK performs a full link and creates a new file. If the .ilk file is unusable, LINK performs a nonincremental link.

The swt.obj file is the intermediate file generated by the compiler and used as input to the linker.

The swt.pch file is a precompiled header file. By precompiling various header files used by the project, subsequent builds will take place much faster.

The swt.pdb file (program database) holds debugging and project state information. The .pdb file provides the information needed for incremental linking of debug program versions. With 32-bit executables, both the linker and the integrated Debugger allow .pdb files to be used directly during the debugging process, eliminating substantial amounts of work for the linker and bypassing the cumbersome CVPACK limit of 64K types. By default, when you build projects generated by Visual C++, the compiler switch /Fd is used to rename the .pdb file to project.pdb. Therefore, you will have only one .pdb file for the entire project.

The vc60.idb file uses the Enable Incremental Compilation (/Gi) option to control the incremental compiler. Only those functions that have changed since the last compile will be compiled. The compiler saves state information from the first compile in the project's .idb file (the default name is project.idb or VC50.idb for files compiled without a project). The compiler uses this state information to speed subsequent compiles.

We'll make use of many of these features once we start an actual debug session.

What's Happening in This Program?

Let's examine what is happening when the swt.exe file is actually executed. When you run the program you should see a new window on the screen similar to Figure 8.4.

Your swt.cpp Win32 Application not only generated an initial window frame and program title bar and minimize, maximize, and close icons, but it drew a diagonal line with a text label. What part of the source code is responsible for each of these components? Let's talk briefly about each component.

The Comment Block

The comment block identifies the file's name, title, purpose, author, and date of creation/modification. The comment block is optional but so important!

```
//
// swt.cpp
// Simple Windows Template
// Copyright (c) William H. Murray and Chris H. Pappas, 2000
//
```

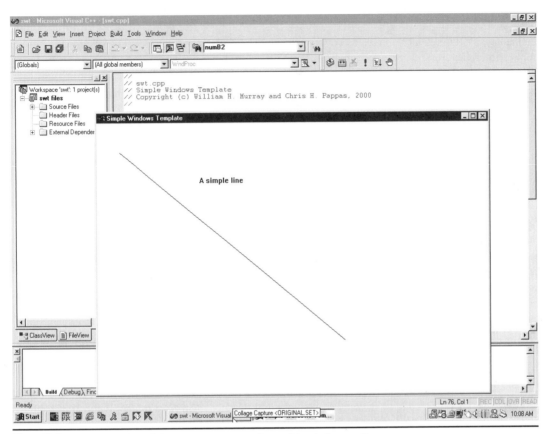

Figure 8.4   The execution of the swt.cpp program draws this window on the screen

The initial comment block should be as long as necessary in order to notify and remind users what this application is all about.

\<windows.h\>

The source file continues with this statement.

```
#include <windows.h>
```

The include statement pulls in a text file named windows.h containing Windows-specific definitions and additional #include statements. The contents of these files provide the fundamental definitions necessary to build a Windows application. Find the location of the windows.h header file within the collection of Visual C++ header files and examine the wealth of Windows information that it contains.

The Callback Function

To manage system resources, such as keyboards, mice, hard disks and so on, every Windows application must create a *callback* function. The callback function uses messages to report to Windows what the application wants to do. At the same time, Windows informs each application, again using messages, what of interest is out there, such as current mouse coordinates and so on.

Here is the prototype for the callback function used in this application:

```
LRESULT CALLBACK WndProc(HWND,UINT,WPARAM,LPARAM);
```

Every function prototype begins with the function's return type—in this case, LRESULT CALLBACK. The LRESULT component defines the type used for the return value of window procedures. It is a 32-bit value that can, at times, be broken down into two 16-bit values called *low* and *high*. The CALLBACK component identifies the function as being an application-defined function that a system or subsystem (Windows, for example) calls. Examples of callback functions include window procedures, dialog-box procedures, and hook procedures.

The function's name WndProc() follows the CALLBACK component. All messages are processed in the application's "window procedure" or WndProc(). The WndProc() function is associated with a window by means of a window class registration process. The main window is registered in the WinMain() function, but other classes of windows can be registered anywhere in the application. The WndProc() prototype concludes with a formal argument list as follows:

```
(HWND,UINT,WPARAM,LPARAM);
```

The argument list describes the number and type of arguments being passed into the function.

Note	*C/C++ code style conventions use all uppercase identifiers to define non-standard C/C++ data types. To find the definitions for these uppercase identifiers, you need to go to their defining header files referenced via windows.h.*

The HWND argument represents a handle to a window. The UINT argument is a portable unsigned integer type whose size is determined by host environment (32 bits for Windows NT and Windows 98). The WPARAM argument is the type used for declaration of wParam, the third parameter of a windows procedure (a polymorph data type). Finally, the LPARAM argument is the type used for declaration of lParam, the fourth parameter of a windows procedure.

Handles

Writing a procedure-oriented Windows application always involves the use of handles. A *handle* is a unique number that identifies many different types of objects, such as windows, controls, menus, icons, pens and brushes, memory allocation, output devices, and even window instances. In Windows terminology, each loaded copy of a program is called an *instance*.

Since Windows allows you to run more than one copy of the same application at the same time, it needs to keep track of each of these instances. It does this by attaching a unique instance handle to each running copy of the application.

The WinMain() Function

All Windows applications must have a minimum of a callback function and one function by the name WinMain(). The WinMain() function is where normal program execution begins and ends.

```
int WINAPI WinMain(HINSTANCE hInst,HINSTANCE hPreInst,
                   LPSTR lpszCmdLine,int nCmdShow)
```

In this prototype, `WINAPI` represents the calling convention used for the Win32 API and is used in place of `FAR PASCAL` in API declarations. The WinMain() function is called by Windows as the initial entry point for a Win32-based application. The WinMain() function registers the application's window class type, performs any required initializations, and creates and initiates the application's message processing loop.

The first parameter, `hInst`, contains the instance handle of the current instance of the application. This uniquely identifies the program when it is running under Windows. The second parameter, `hPreInst`, will contain a NULL value under Windows 95 and NT. This indicates that there is no previous instance of this application. Under Windows 98 and NT (2000), each application runs in its own separate address space. Here, `hPreInst` will never return a valid previous instance, just NULL. The third parameter, `lpszCmdLine`, is a pointer to a null-terminated string that represents the application's command-line arguments. This value will be a NULL if the application was started using the Windows Run command. The **int** value stored in `nCmdShow`, the fourth parameter, represents one of the many Windows predefined constants defining the possible ways a window can be displayed, such as SW_SHOWNORMAL, SW_SHOWMAXIMIZED, or SW_MINIMIZED.

The purpose of WinMain() is to initialize the application, display its main window, and enter a message-retrieval-and-dispatch loop that is the top-level control structure for the remainder of the application's execution. WinMain() is also responsible for terminating the message loop when it receives a WM_QUIT message.

WNDCLASS   The WNDCLASS structure contains the window class attributes used by the call to RegisterClass(). The formal definition of this structure takes on this form:

```
typedef struct _WNDCLASS {
    UINT     style;
    WNDPROC  lpfnWndProc;
    int      cbClsExtra;
    int      cbWndExtra;
    HANDLE   hInstance;
    HICON    hIcon;
    HCURSOR  hCursor;
    HBRUSH   hbrBackground;
    LPCTSTR  lpszMenuName;
    LPCTSTR  lpszClassName;
} WNDCLASS;
```

Let's examine the purpose of each structure member. The `style` member defines the class style, such as CS_BYTEALIGNCLIENT, CS_HREDRAW, CS_VREDRAW, and so on. The `lpfnWndProc`

218 Debugging C++: Troubleshooting for Programmers

member is a pointer to the window procedure. The `cbClsExtra` member specifies the number of extra bytes to allocate following the window-class structure. The `cbWndExtra` member specifies the number of extra bytes to allocate following the window instance. The `hInstance` member is a handle to the instance that the window procedure of this class is within. The `hIcon` member is a handle to the class icon. The `hCursor` member is a handle to the class cursor. The `hbrBackground` member is a handle to the class background brush. The `lpszMenuName` member is a pointer to a null-terminated character string that specifies the resource name of the class menu, as the name appears in the resource file. The `lpszClassName` member is a pointer to a null-terminated string or is an atom. If the parameter is a string, it specifies the window class name.

RegisterClass()   The next statement in the WinMain() function calls the RegisterClass() function.

```
if (!RegisterClass (&wcApp))
  return 0;
```

Every window created for a Windows application must be based on a window class. WinMain() registers the application's main window class. Each window class is based on a combination of user-selected styles, fonts, caption bars, icons, size, placement, and so on. The window class serves as a template that defines these attributes.

The **if** statement registers the new window class. It does this by sending RegisterClass() a pointer to the window class structure. If Windows cannot register the window class, possibly due to lack of memory, RegisterClass() returns a 0, terminating the program.

Under Windows 98 and NT, the RegisterClassEx() function can be used in place of the RegisterClass() function. RegisterClassEx() allows the inclusion of the small icons.

CreateWindow()   A window is created with a call to the Windows CreateWindow() function. While the window class defines the general characteristics of a window, which allows the same window class to be used for many different windows, the parameters to CreateWindow() specify more detailed information about the window.

The CreateWindow() function uses the information passed to it to describe the window's class, title, style, screen position, parent handle, menu handle, and instance handle. The call to CreateWindow() for the template application uses the following actual parameters:

```
hWnd=CreateWindow(szProgName,"Simple Windows Template",
                  WS_OVERLAPPEDWINDOW,CW_USEDEFAULT,
                  CW_USEDEFAULT,CW_USEDEFAULT,
                  CW_USEDEFAULT,(HWND)NULL,(HMENU)NULL,
                  (HANDLE)hInst,(LPSTR)NULL);
```

The first field `szProgName` defines the window's class, followed by the title to be used for the window. The style of the window is the third parameter (`WS_OVERLAPPEDWINDOW`). This standard Windows style represents an ordinary overlapped window with a caption bar, a system menu box, minimize and maximize icons, and a window frame.

The next six parameters (either `CW_USEDEFAULT` or `NULL`) represent the initial x and y positions and the x and y size of the window, along with the parent window handle and window menu handle.

Each of these fields has been assigned a default value. The `hInst` field contains the instance handle of the program, followed by no additional parameters (NULL).

CreateWindow() returns the handle of the newly created window if it was successful. Otherwise, the function returns NULL.

Showing and Updating a Window
To display a window, a call is made to the Windows ShowWindow() function.

```
ShowWindow(hWnd,nCmdShow);
```

The `hWnd` parameter holds the handle of the window while the value of *nCmdShow* specifies that the window will be displayed as a normal window (`SW_SHOWNNORMAL`), or several other possibilities.

The last step in displaying a window requires a call to the Windows UpdateWindow() function.

```
UpdateWindow(hWnd);
```

It is the call to UpdateWindow() that causes the client area to be painted by generating a WM_PAINT message. WM_PAINT is explained later in this chapter.

A Message Loop
Windows does not send input from the mouse or keyboard directly to an application. Instead, it places all input into the application's message queue. The message queue can contain messages generated by Windows or messages posted by other applications.

Once the call to WinMain() has taken care of creating and displaying the window, the application needs to create a message processing loop. The most common approach is to use the standard C++ **while** loop.

```
while (GetMessage(&lpMsg,NULL,0,0))
{
  TranslateMessage(&lpMsg);
  DispatchMessage(&lpMmsg);
}
```

A call to the GetMessage() function retrieves the next message to be processed from the application's message queue. GetMessage() copies the message into the message structure pointed to by the long pointer, `lpMsg`, and sends it to the main body of the program.

The TranslateMessage() function translates virtual-key messages into character messages. The function call is only required by applications that need to process character input from the keyboard. The DispatchMessage() function is used to send the current message to the correct window procedure.

WinMain()
WinMain() is normally responsible for terminating the message loop when it receives a WM_QUIT message. This terminates the application, returning the value passed in the WM_QUIT message's `wParam` parameter.

The Required Window Function

All Windows applications must include a WinMain() and a Windows callback function. Since a Windows application never directly accesses any Windows functions, each application must make a request to Windows to carry out any specified operations.

> **Note** *Remember that a callback function is registered with Windows and it is called back whenever Windows executes an operation on a window. The actual code size for the callback function varies with each application. The window function itself may be very small, only processing one or two messages, or it may be large and complex.*

Windows has several hundred different messages it can send to the window function. All of them are labeled with identifiers that begin with "WM_." In the swt.cpp program, only WM_PAINT and WM_DESTROY are of interest.

The WndProc() function continues by defining several variables, in this example *hdc* for the display context handle and *ps,* a PAINTSTRUCT structure needed to store client area information. The main purpose of the callback function is to examine the type of message it is about to process and then select the appropriate action to be taken. This selection process usually takes the form of a standard C++ switch statement.

The WM_PAINT Message   The first message WndProc() will process in our program is WM_PAINT. This message calls the Windows function, BeginPaint(), which prepares the specified window (*hWnd*) for painting and fills a PAINTSTRUCT (*&ps*), with information about the area to be painted. The BeginPaint() function also returns a handle to the device context for the given window.

The device context comes equipped with a default pen, brush, and font. The default pen is black, one pixel wide, and draws a solid line. The default brush is white with a solid brush pattern. The default font is the system font. The device context is important because all of the display functions used by Windows applications require a handle to the device context.

An application can force a WM_PAINT message by making a call to the InvalidateRect() function, which marks the application's client area as being invalid. By calling the GetUpdateRect() function, an application can obtain the coordinates of the invalid rectangle. A subsequent call to the ValidateRect() function validates any rectangular region in the client area and removes any pending WM_PAINT messages.

The WndProc() function ends its processing of the WM_PAINT message by calling the EndPaint() function. This function is called whenever the application is finished outputting information to the client area. It tells Windows that the application has finished processing all paint messages and that it is now okay to remove the display context.

The WM_DESTROY Message   When the user selects the Close option from the application's system menu, Windows posts a WM_DESTROY message to the application's message queue. The program terminates after retrieving this message.

The DefWindowProc() Function   The DefWindowProc() function call in the default section of WndProc()'s switch statement is needed to empty the application's message queue of any unrecognized—and therefore, unprocessed—messages. This function ensures that all of the messages posted to the application are processed.

Debugging

In this section, we'll illustrate a number of procedure-oriented Windows bugs that you are likely to encounter when you create applications. Then we'll teach you how to use the Debugger to track down the problems and correct them. The problems fit into two broad categories. The first group of problems you are likely to encounter deal with boundaries. The boundary problems often result from misuse of screen sizes, resulting from an incorrect use of the windows extent, viewport extent, client area, and so on. The second group of problems involves the use of resources that are added to your program. In this example, we'll show you how an unwary programmer can get trapped by not knowing how Windows allocates certain resource parameters.

An Animated Bitmap Program

An animation effect can be created with a bitmapped image by using a simple draw, erase, move, and redraw mechanism. For this example, a bitmapped image is drawn on the screen and allowed to remain there for a set time. Next, the figure is erased. Erasing a figure can be accomplished by three techniques: redrawing the figure in the background color, clearing a rectangular portion around the figure, or clearing the entire screen. The coordinates for the next figure are then shifted to the left, right, up, down, or a combination of two by a small number of pixels, and the figure is redrawn. When the timing cycle is right, the viewer will get a sense of motion while viewing the window.

In this program, the BitBlt() function will be used to move a bitmapped image of a flying saucer on the screen. Figure 8.5 shows the bitmapped image in the Resource Editor as it is being designed.

The saucer.rc resource script file is used to identify the bitmap resources and a unique icon for the project. Here is an abbreviated portion of the resource script file:

```
//Microsoft Developer Studio generated resource script.
//
#include "resource.h"

#define APSTUDIO_READONLY_SYMBOLS
/////////////////////////////////////////////////////////////////
//
// Generated from the TEXTINCLUDE 2 resource.
//
#include "afxres.h"



    .
    .
    .

/////////////////////////////////////////////////////////////////
//
// Bitmap
//

BMIMAGE  BITMAP  DISCARDABLE       "Bmp.bmp"

#ifdef APSTUDIO_INVOKED
```

```
///////////////////////////////////////////////////////////
    .
    .
    .
///////////////////////////////////////////////////////////
//
// Icon
//

// Icon with lowest ID value placed first to ensure application
// icon Remains consistent on all systems.
SAUCERICON ICON     DISCARDABLE     "Saucer.ico"
#endif     // English (U.S.) resources
///////////////////////////////////////////////////////////
    .
    .
    .
```

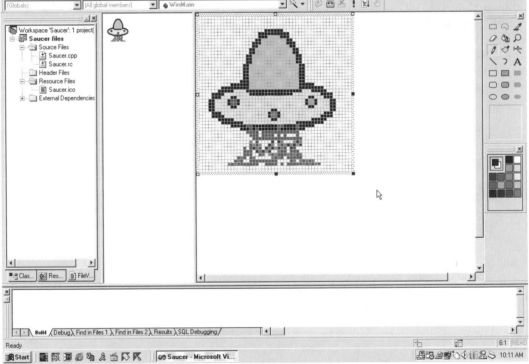

Figure 8.5   bmp.bmp is the bitmapped image of the flying saucer

The resource editor generates the saucer.rc file while the resource compiler creates the saucer.res during the build process. It is very unlikely you will ever find errors in these files.

The source code, saucer.cpp, builds on the swt.cpp template from the previous section. Examine the following code.

```cpp
//
// A program with problems
// A procedure-oriented Windows Application
// that demonstrates simple animation techniques
// with a bitmapped images.
// Copyright (c) William H. Murray and Chris H. Pappas, 2000
//

#include <windows.h>

LRESULT CALLBACK WndProc(HWND,UINT,WPARAM,LPARAM);

char szProgName[]="ProgName";
char szIconName[]="SaucerIcon";
char szBMName[]="BMImage";

HBITMAP hBitmap;
int iTimer,xPos,yPos;
int xPosInit,yPosInit,xStep,yStep;

int WINAPI WinMain(HINSTANCE hInst,HINSTANCE hPreInst,
                   LPSTR lpszCmdLine,int nCmdShow)
{
  HWND hWnd;
  MSG  lpMsg;
  WNDCLASS wcApp;

  wcApp.lpszClassName=szProgName;
  wcApp.hInstance     =hInst;
  wcApp.lpfnWndProc   =WndProc;
  wcApp.hCursor       =LoadCursor(NULL,IDC_ARROW);
  wcApp.hIcon         =LoadIcon(hInst,szIconName);
  wcApp.lpszMenuName  =0;
  wcApp.hbrBackground=(HBRUSH) GetStockObject(WHITE_BRUSH);
  wcApp.style         =CS_HREDRAW|CS_VREDRAW;
  wcApp.cbClsExtra    =0;
  wcApp.cbWndExtra    =0;
  if (!RegisterClass (&wcApp))
    return 0;

  hWnd=CreateWindow(szProgName,"Flying Saucer Program",
                  WS_OVERLAPPEDWINDOW,CW_USEDEFAULT,
                  CW_USEDEFAULT,CW_USEDEFAULT,
                  CW_USEDEFAULT,(HWND)NULL,(HMENU)NULL,
                  hInst,(LPSTR)NULL);
  ShowWindow(hWnd,nCmdShow);
```

```
  UpdateWindow(hWnd);

  // load saucer bitmap
  hBitmap=LoadBitmap(hInst,szBMName);

  while (GetMessage(&lpMsg,0,0,0)) {
    TranslateMessage(&lpMsg);
    DispatchMessage(&lpMsg);
  }
  return(lpMsg.wParam);
}

LRESULT CALLBACK WndProc(HWND hWnd,UINT messg,
                         WPARAM wParam,LPARAM lParam)
{
  HDC hdc;
  HDC hmdc;
  static BITMAP bm;

  switch (messg)
  {
    case WM_CREATE:
      // initial values
      xPosInit=200;
      yPosInit=200;
      xStep=4;
      yStep=4;
      xPos=xPosInit;
      yPos=yPosInit;
      iTimer=SetTimer(hWnd,1,10,NULL);
      break;

    case WM_TIMER:
      // with each timer tick, draw image
      hdc=GetDC(hWnd);
      hmdc=CreateCompatibleDC(hdc);
      xPos+=xStep;
      yPos+=yStep;

      // draw image
      SelectObject(hmdc,hBitmap);
      GetObject(hBitmap,sizeof(bm),(LPSTR) &bm);
      BitBlt(hdc,xPos,yPos,bm.bmWidth,bm.bmHeight,
             hmdc,0,0,SRCCOPY);

      // check left and right window edges
      if((xPos > 639) ||
         (xPos < 0)) {
        xStep=-xStep;
      }

      // check top and bottom window edges
```

```
      if((yPos > 479) ||
         (yPos < 0)) {
        yStep=-yStep;
      }

      ReleaseDC(hWnd,hdc);
      DeleteDC(hmdc);
      break;

    case WM_DESTROY:
      if (hBitmap) DeleteObject(hBitmap);
      if(iTimer) KillTimer(hWnd,1);
      PostQuitMessage(0);
      break;

    default:
      return(DefWindowProc(hWnd,messg,wParam,lParam));
      break;
  }
  return(0);
}
```

Examine the saucer.cpp source code and notice that provisions have been made for two-dimensional movement. The flying saucer can bounce off of the top, bottom, right side, or left side of the window. With each timer message that is processed (WM_TIMER), a bitmapped image is drawn.

```
// draw image
SelectObject(hmdc,hBitmap);
GetObject(hBitmap,sizeof(bm),(LPSTR) &bm);
BitBlt(hdc,xPos,yPos,bm.bmWidth,bm.bmHeight,
       hmdc,0,0,SRCCOPY);
```

Animation of the saucer is achieved in two dimensions. Here is the code responsible for moving the flying saucer on the screen:

```
// check left and right window edges
if((xPos > 639) ||
   (xPos < 0)) {
  xStep=-xStep;
}

// check top and bottom window edges
if((yPos > 479) ||
   (yPos < 0)) {
  yStep=-yStep;
}
```

One **if** statement controls the left-to-right motion, and another controls the up-and-down motion. With each timer tick, a new screen position is specified. These two statements check the values of the horizontal movement and vertical movement to make sure that the new screen positions fit within the boundaries of the window. If they do, everything is fine. If they don't, it means a collision has occurred between the bitmapped image and a boundary. When this happens, changing the sign of the `xStep` or `yStep` increment reverses the direction of movement. At least that is how it is suppose to work!

Code with a Problem

If you compile and run the program, you'll see that the application has a few problems, as illustrated by Figure 8.6.

First, while the saucer moves in two dimensions, those dimensions don't seem to be controlled by the boundaries of the screen. Why is this happening? Next, the saucer is leaving a trail as it moves about on the screen. What is causing this? Finally, when the image does collide with the right and bottom portions of the window, most of the image disappears before the motion reverses itself. Let's use the Debugger to help track down the problems.

The Problem with a One-Computer Debugging Session   This is the perfect opportunity to show you why you'll want to have two networked computers so that you can take advantage of the remote debugging feature that was explained earlier in this chapter.

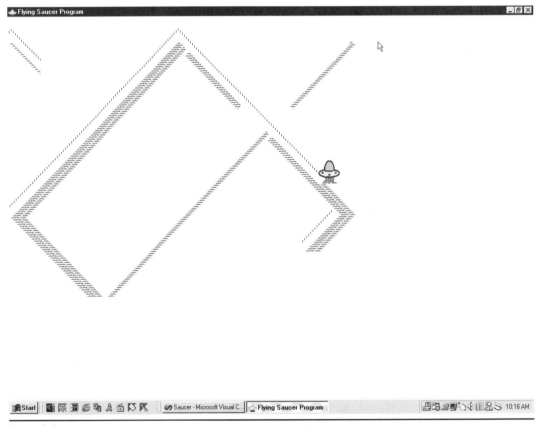

Figure 8.6   The saucer program seems to have a few problems!

To illustrate the problem, compile the program and start the Debugger. Place a breakpoint at the bold line shown in the next portion of code.

```
// check top and bottom window edges
if((yPos > 479) ||
   (yPos < 0)) {
  yStep=-yStep;
}

ReleaseDC(hWnd,hdc);
DeleteDC(hmdc);
break;
```

Now, use the Go (F5) command to run to the breakpoint. The application actually starts. To view the saucer window, just use the ESC+ALT key combination to switch active screens. What happens? Figure 8.7 tells the whole story.

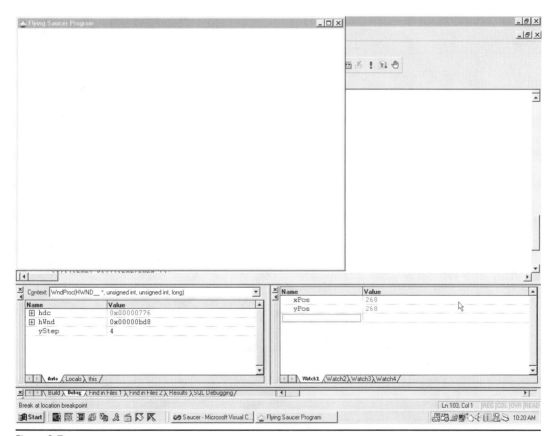

Figure 8.7   When the saucer screen is moved to the foreground, the bitmapped image is not visible

This is a great window, but the Debugger is not going to share the spotlight with the application's screen. The solution is to use remote debugging.

Start a remote debugging session according to the steps outlined earlier in this chapter. Recall that our remote target computer is a Sony (identified on the network as "sony") and the host computer is a Hewlett-Packard (identified as "hp").

Figure 8.8 shows the same debugging position as we used earlier, but this time on a system using a remote target computer.

The debugging position and information is also concurrently visible on the host computer (hp), as shown in Figure 8.9.

In the next section, we'll start tracking down the problems in the Flying Saucer program.

Debugging with a Remote Target Computer   The first problem we're going to track down is why the saucer image invades the right and lower window boundaries but works correctly with the left and top window boundaries.

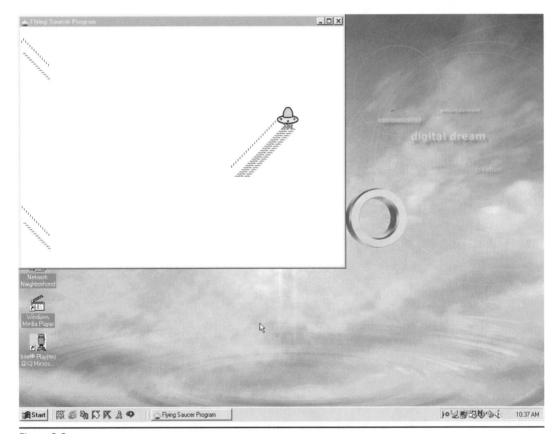

Figure 8.8   The saucer bitmap is visible on the remote target computer (sony)

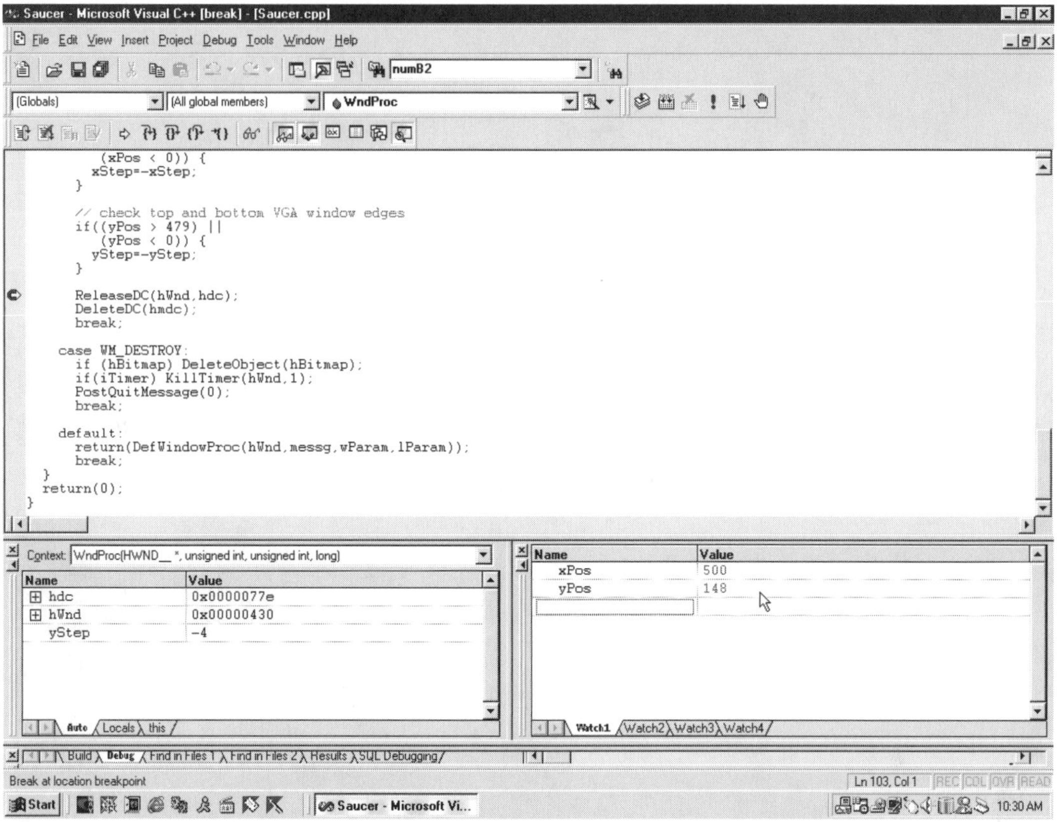

Figure 8.9 The concurrent debugging information is visible on the host computer (hp)

Figure 8.10 illustrates a case where the image is dropping below the bottom boundary of the window.

Start the debugging session; place the breakpoint at exactly the same position as in the previous section. Add the *xPos* and *yPos* variables to the watch window. Now execute a number of Go (F5) options until the image just touches either the right or bottom portion of the window. Let's look at one such case, shown in Figure 8.11.

Now examine the variables in the watch window, as shown in Figure 8.12.

It is clear to see, by examining the *yPos* variable that the image is not at 479 pixels, as expected, but at 408. Now, move the saucer until it just touches the right border. Inspect the *xPos* variable and note the same problem: the *xPos* variable reads 588 when the collision occurs. Changing the boundaries as shown in a bold font in the next listing can repair both problems.

```
// check left and right window edges
if((xPos > 588) ||
    (xPos < 0)) {
```

```
    xStep=-xStep;
}

// check top and bottom window edges
if((yPos > 408) ||
   (yPos < 0)) {
  yStep=-yStep;
}
```

We've found the problem, but the question is why don't the original values work? Ah, part of the answer is because the hotspot on the bitmap is in the upper-left corner, so in order not to lose the bottom or right portion of the image during a collision, the size of the bitmap must be subtracted from the bottom and right boundary values. We have already obtained the dimensions of the bitmap when we issued the GetObject() function. The dimensions of this bitmap are returned in the *bm* structure. To obtain the width and height of the bitmap, we query the structure members, *bm.bmWidth* and *bm.bmHeight*. So in theory, we should be able to perform the following operation instead of "hard-wiring" the boundary values based on the size of the bitmap.

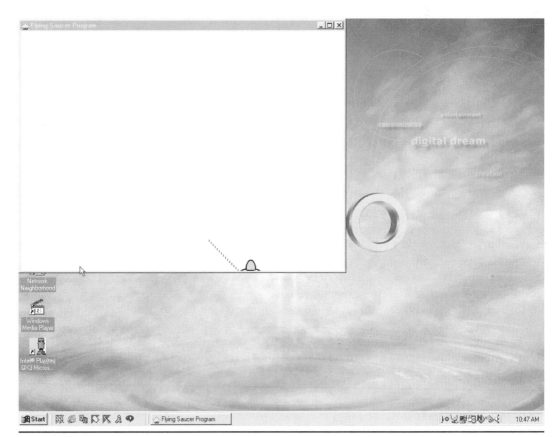

Figure 8.10   The saucer has invaded the bottom margin of the window instead of bouncing off of the border (remote target computer—sony)

```
   // check left and right window edges
   if((xPos + bm.bmWidth > 639) ||
      (xPos < 0)) {
     xStep=-xStep;
   }

   // check top and bottom window edges
   if((yPos + bm.bmHeight > 479) ||
      (yPos < 0)) {
     yStep=-yStep;
   }
```

If you run the program with these values in place, you notice that the program operates better but not perfectly. The problem still lies with the window dimensions. We made a mistake in thinking that the client area of the window was 640 pixels wide and 480 pixels deep. In reality, it is short of that by the dimensions of the borders and the width of the title bar. We could experiment by subtracting pixels until we get it just right, or we can try to determine the actual width and height of the client area.

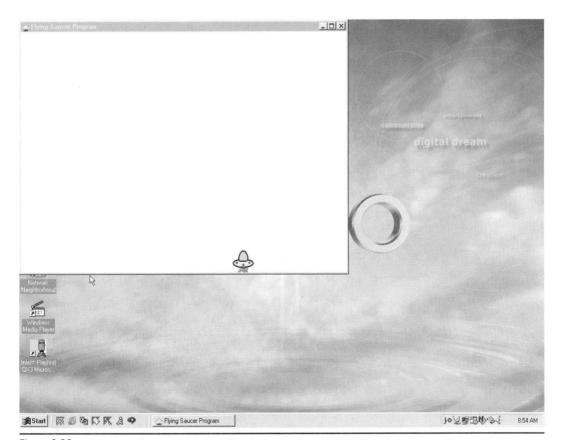

Figure 8.11   The saucer image is just touching the bottom boundary of the window (remote target computer—sony)

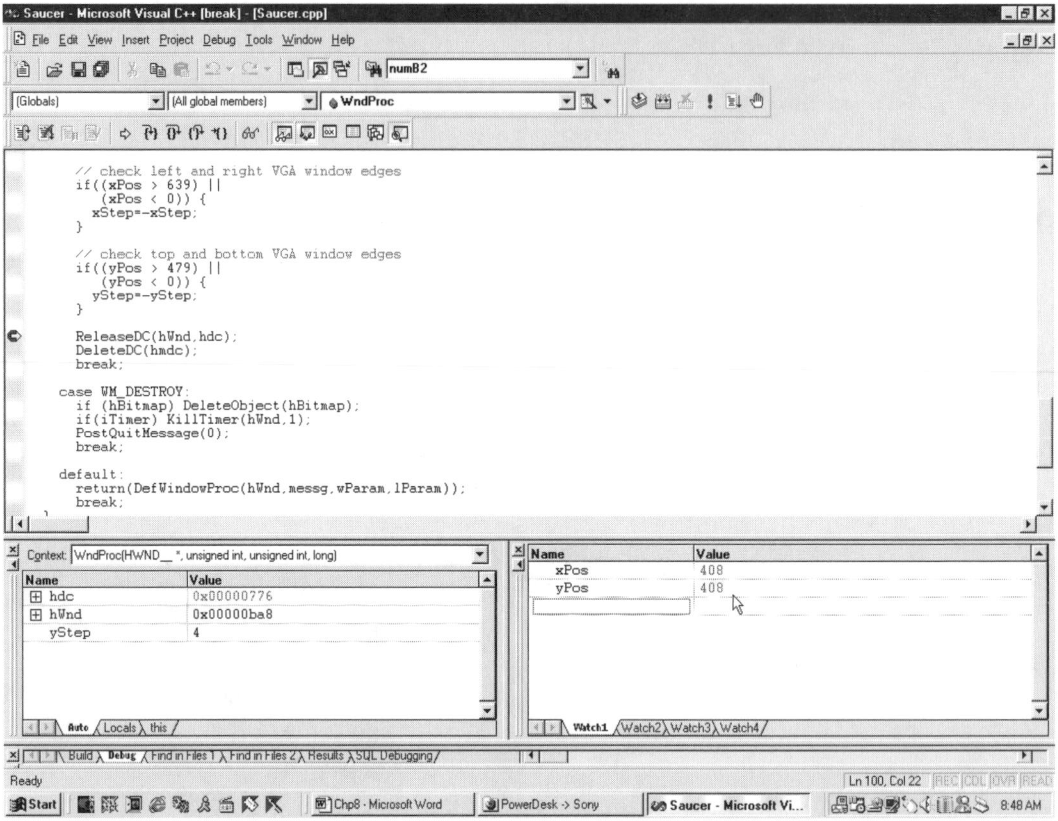

Figure 8.12 The variables *xPos* and *yPos* are examined when the saucer touches the bottom of the window

---

Error Watch *As programmers, we tend to think in terms of screen resolutions, such as 640 × 480 or 1024 × 768. The client area, within a window, is always short of these values even when maximized. The width of the border and the width of the title bar must always be taken into account when calculating the client area dimensions.*

The width and height of the client area is available with a call to the GetClientRect() function. The information obtained by the function is returned to a RECT structure named *rcWnd*. By using this information, the problem with the bottom and right boundaries will be permanently corrected.

```
// check left and right window edges
if((xPos+bm.bmWidth > rcWnd.right) ||
   (xPos < rcWnd.left)) {
  xStep=-xStep;
}

// check top and bottom window edges
if((yPos+bm.bmHeight > rcWnd.bottom) ||
```

```
        (yPos < rcWnd.top)) {
    yStep=-yStep;
}
```

This solution has an added benefit and solves one of the other problems we mentioned earlier. In Figure 8.6 you can see that the saucer seems to have bounced off of an invisible border near the center of the screen. The reason for this is that the boundaries were once set to VGA (640 × 480) screen dimensions, but Figure 8.6 showed a window on a 1024 × 768 screen. While the client area in Figure 8.6 is larger, the boundary values haven't changed. The solution we just found fixes this problem, too.

One problem to go—why is the saucer image leaving a trail on the screen? It almost looks as if the image isn't being correctly erased between steps, and that conclusion is correct. Examine Figure 8.5 once again and notice that the image has a border of at least 2 pixels on all edges that match the background color of the window.

With the technique used in this program, the new image is just drawn over the old image each time the saucer is moved. Go back into a debug session and place the *xPos*, *yPos*, *xStep*, and *yStep* variables in the watch window, as shown in Figure 8.13.

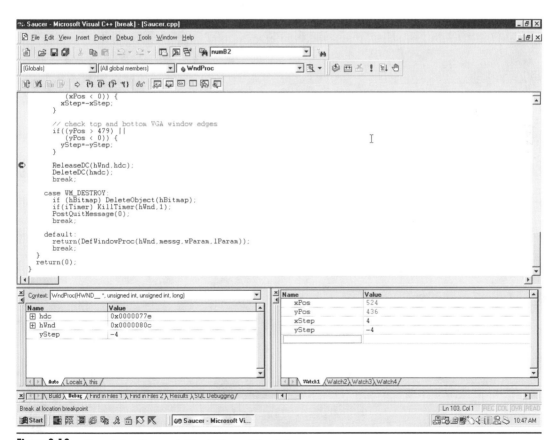

Figure 8.13 Examining four variables in the watch window

The problem becomes apparent when we further examine the bitmap image and the step sizes for each image. If the step sizes are 4, but the white border around the saucer is 2, part of the saucer will remain on the screen during each redraw. One solution is to draw the original image, leave it there a moment, then draw a blank image (erase that rectangular portion of the screen), and then redraw the image at a new location. Sometimes, however, this technique introduces a flicker on the screen, especially for slower computers. Another solution is to make sure the step size is always equal to or smaller than the border surrounding the bitmap image. This approach is actually not a bad one because a 1-pixel bitmap border coupled with a 1-pixel step size will create the smoothest motion on the screen.

Let's look at all of the modifications to the original code in the next section.

Good Code

The Debugger has helped us track down and correct several problems with the Flying Saucer program. All of the problems were present in the source code listing, saucer.cpp. Here is that listing, with all of the modifications to the original code shown in a bold font.

```
//
// Saucer.cpp
// A procedure-oriented Windows Application
// that demonstrates simple animation techniques
// with a bitmapped images.
// Copyright (c) William H. Murray and Chris H. Pappas, 2000
//

#include <windows.h>

LRESULT CALLBACK WndProc(HWND,UINT,WPARAM,LPARAM);

char szProgName[]="ProgName";
char szIconName[]="SaucerIcon";
char szBMName[]="BMImage";

HBITMAP hBitmap;
int iTimer,xPos,yPos;
int xPosInit,yPosInit,xStep,yStep;

int WINAPI WinMain(HINSTANCE hInst,HINSTANCE hPreInst,
                   LPSTR lpszCmdLine,int nCmdShow)
{
  HWND hWnd;
  MSG  lpMsg;
  WNDCLASS wcApp;

  wcApp.lpszClassName=szProgName;
  wcApp.hInstance     =hInst;
  wcApp.lpfnWndProc   =WndProc;
  wcApp.hCursor       =LoadCursor(NULL,IDC_ARROW);
  wcApp.hIcon         =LoadIcon(hInst,szIconName);
  wcApp.lpszMenuName =0;
```

```
    wcApp.hbrBackground=(HBRUSH) GetStockObject(WHITE_BRUSH);
    wcApp.style        =CS_HREDRAW|CS_VREDRAW;
    wcApp.cbClsExtra   =0;
    wcApp.cbWndExtra   =0;
    if (!RegisterClass (&wcApp))
      return 0;

    hWnd=CreateWindow(szProgName,"Flying Saucer Program",
                      WS_OVERLAPPEDWINDOW,CW_USEDEFAULT,
                      CW_USEDEFAULT,CW_USEDEFAULT,
                      CW_USEDEFAULT,(HWND)NULL,(HMENU)NULL,
                      hInst,(LPSTR)NULL);
    ShowWindow(hWnd,nCmdShow);
    UpdateWindow(hWnd);

    // load saucer bitmap
    hBitmap=LoadBitmap(hInst,szBMName);

    while (GetMessage(&lpMsg,0,0,0)) {
      TranslateMessage(&lpMsg);
      DispatchMessage(&lpMsg);
    }
    return(lpMsg.wParam);
}

LRESULT CALLBACK WndProc(HWND hWnd,UINT messg,
                         WPARAM wParam,LPARAM lParam)
{
  HDC hdc;
  HDC hmdc;
  RECT rcWnd;
  static BITMAP bm;

  switch (messg)
  {
    case WM_CREATE:
      // initial values
      xPosInit=200;
      yPosInit=200;
      xStep=1;
      yStep=1;
      xPos=xPosInit;
      yPos=yPosInit;
      iTimer=SetTimer(hWnd,1,10,NULL);
      break;

    case WM_TIMER:
      // with each timer tick, draw image
      hdc=GetDC(hWnd);
      GetClientRect(hWnd,&rcWnd);
      hmdc=CreateCompatibleDC(hdc);
```

```
    xPos+=xStep;
    yPos+=yStep;

    // draw image
    SelectObject(hmdc,hBitmap);
    GetObject(hBitmap,sizeof(bm),(LPSTR) &bm);
    BitBlt(hdc,xPos,yPos,bm.bmWidth,bm.bmHeight,
           hmdc,0,0,SRCCOPY);

    // check left and right window edges
    if((xPos+bm.bmWidth > rcWnd.right) ||
       (xPos < rcWnd.left)) {
      xStep=-xStep;
    }

    // check top and bottom window edges
    if((yPos+bm.bmHeight > rcWnd.bottom) ||
       (yPos < rcWnd.top)) {
      yStep=-yStep;
    }

    ReleaseDC(hWnd,hdc);
    DeleteDC(hmdc);
    break;

  case WM_DESTROY:
    if (hBitmap) DeleteObject(hBitmap);
    if(iTimer) KillTimer(hWnd,1);
    PostQuitMessage(0);
    break;

  default:
    return(DefWindowProc(hWnd,messg,wParam,lParam));
    break;
  }
  return(0);
}
```

Figure 8.14 shows the results of our debugging efforts after the saucer has made several trips around the window.

Problems with boundaries are quite common in Windows applications. This has a lot to do with how Windows uses the windows extent, viewport, and client area. The Debugger can be an important source of information as you track down this kind of error.

Drawing with the Mouse

The following project is named sketch. The sketch project includes source code, sketch.cpp, very similar to the programs discussed earlier in this chapter. However, the sketch project also includes

Figure 8.14   The saucer successfully traverses the window

several Windows resources, including a menu and dialog box. What's more, the program code that we are initially going to give you, works perfectly. In this example, we'll make alterations to the original working project in order to enhance some project features.

Resources add another layer of complexity to Windows applications. Again, if you have not written Windows code for some time, it might be a good idea to refer to a book that deals with procedure-oriented Windows coding practices.

Create a Win32 project named sketch from within the Visual C++ environment. To this empty project, add the following source code file, named sketch.cpp:

```
//
// (working - but not quite complete) - sketch.cpp
// Draws in the client area with the mouse.
// Draws with color selected from list of predefined colors.
// Pen widths also selected from a list of predefined pens.
// Copyright (c) William H. Murray and Chris H. Pappas, 2000
```

```
//

#include <windows.h>
#include "resource.h"

HINSTANCE hInst;

LRESULT CALLBACK WndProc(HWND,UINT,WPARAM,LPARAM);
BOOL CALLBACK AboutDlgProc(HWND,UINT,WPARAM,LPARAM);

char szProgName[]="ProgName";          // app name
char szApplName[]="SketchMenu";        // menu name
char szCursorName[]="SketchCursor";    // cursor name
char szIconName[]="SketchIcon";        // icon name
static WORD wColor;                    // color from menu
BOOL bDrawtrail;                       // (t/f) draw?
POINT omouselocat,nmouselocat;         // position

int WINAPI WinMain(HINSTANCE hInst,HINSTANCE hPreInst,
                LPSTR lpszCmdLine,int nCmdShow)
{
  HWND hWnd;
  MSG  lpMsg;
  WNDCLASS wcApp;

  wcApp.lpszClassName=szProgName;
  wcApp.hInstance    =hInst;
  wcApp.lpfnWndProc  =WndProc;
  wcApp.hCursor      =LoadCursor(hInst,szCursorName);
  wcApp.hIcon        =LoadIcon(hInst,szIconName);
  wcApp.lpszMenuName =szApplName;
  wcApp.hbrBackground=(HBRUSH) GetStockObject(WHITE_BRUSH);
  wcApp.style        =CS_HREDRAW|CS_VREDRAW;
  wcApp.cbClsExtra   =0;
  wcApp.cbWndExtra   =0;
  if (!RegisterClass (&wcApp))
    return 0;

  hWnd=CreateWindow(szProgName,"Drawing with the Mouse",
                  WS_OVERLAPPEDWINDOW,CW_USEDEFAULT,
                  CW_USEDEFAULT,CW_USEDEFAULT,
                  CW_USEDEFAULT,(HWND)NULL,(HMENU)NULL,
                  hInst,(LPSTR)NULL);
  ShowWindow(hWnd,nCmdShow);
  UpdateWindow(hWnd);
  while (GetMessage(&lpMsg,0,0,0)) {
    TranslateMessage(&lpMsg);
    DispatchMessage(&lpMsg);
  }
```

```
      return(lpMsg.wParam);
}

// About dialog box control selection
BOOL CALLBACK AboutDlgProc(HWND hDlg,UINT messg,
                           WPARAM wParam,LPARAM lParam)
{
  switch (messg) {
    case WM_INITDIALOG:
      break;
    case WM_COMMAND:
      switch (LOWORD(wParam)) {
        case IDOK:
          EndDialog(hDlg,0);
          break;
        default:
          return FALSE;
        }
        break;
    default:
      return FALSE;
  }
  return TRUE;
}

LRESULT CALLBACK WndProc(HWND hWnd,UINT messg,
                         WPARAM wParam,LPARAM lParam)
{
  HDC hdc;
  PAINTSTRUCT ps;
  HMENU hmenu;
  static HPEN hOPen,hNPen;
  static COLORREF tempcolor=RGB(0,0,0);
  static COLORREF wColorValue[5]={RGB(0,0,0),          //BLACK
                                  RGB(255,255,255),    //WHITE
                                  RGB(255,0,0),        //RED
                                  RGB(0,255,0),        //GREEN
                                  RGB(0,0,255)};        //BLUE
  static int penwidth=2;
  static POINT pt;

  switch (messg)
  {
    case WM_COMMAND:
      // menu item selections
      switch (LOWORD(wParam)) {
        case ID_OPTIONS_CLEAR:
          tempcolor=wColorValue[1];
          InvalidateRect(hWnd,NULL,TRUE);
```

```
        break;
      case ID_OPTIONS_EXIT:
        SendMessage(hWnd,WM_CLOSE,0,0L);
        break;
      case ID_PEN_TWO:
        penwidth=2;
        break;
      case ID_PEN_FIVE:
        penwidth=5;
        break;
      case ID_PEN_TEN:
        penwidth=10;
        break;
      case ID_PEN_THIRTY:
        penwidth=30;
        break;
      case ID_PEN_SIXTY:
        penwidth=60;
        break;
      case ID_HELP_ABOUT:
        DialogBox((HINSTANCE) GetModuleHandle(NULL),
                "AboutDlgBox",hWnd,
                AboutDlgProc);
        break;
      case IDM_BLACK:
      case IDM_WHITE:
      case IDM_RED:
      case IDM_GREEN:
      case IDM_BLUE:
        hmenu=GetMenu(hWnd);
        CheckMenuItem(hmenu,wColor,MF_UNCHECKED);
        wColor=LOWORD(wParam);
        CheckMenuItem(hmenu,wColor,MF_CHECKED);
        tempcolor=wColorValue[wColor-IDM_BLACK];
        break;
          default:
        break;
      }
    break;

    case WM_LBUTTONDOWN:
    // draw when mouse button is down
    nmouselocat.x=LOWORD(lParam);
    nmouselocat.y=HIWORD(lParam);
    omouselocat=nmouselocat;
    SetCapture(hWnd);
    bDrawtrail=TRUE;
    break;

  case WM_MOUSEMOVE:
```

```
      // follow the mouse around
      if (bDrawtrail) {
        omouselocat=nmouselocat;
        nmouselocat.x=LOWORD(lParam);
        nmouselocat.y=HIWORD(lParam);
        InvalidateRect(hWnd,NULL,FALSE);
        UpdateWindow(hWnd);
        }
      break;

    case WM_LBUTTONUP:
      // do not draw when mouse button is up
      ReleaseCapture();
      bDrawtrail=FALSE;
      break;

    case WM_PAINT:
      hdc=BeginPaint(hWnd,&ps);
      hNPen=CreatePen(PS_SOLID,penwidth,tempcolor);
      hOPen=(HPEN) SelectObject(hdc,hNPen);
      MoveToEx(hdc,omouselocat.x,omouselocat.y,NULL);
      LineTo(hdc,nmouselocat.x,nmouselocat.y);
      SelectObject(hdc,hOPen);
      DeleteObject(hNPen);

      ValidateRect(hWnd,NULL);
      EndPaint(hWnd,&ps);
      break;

    case WM_DESTROY:
      PostQuitMessage(0);
      break;

    default:
      return(DefWindowProc(hWnd,messg,wParam,lParam));
      break;
  }
  return(0);
}
```

This project will also use a resource script file named Sketch.rc. The resource script file contains details on resources such as cursors, dialog boxes, icons, and menus. In this application, we used a cursor that looks like a paintbrush and is illustrated in Figure 8.15.

An About dialog box is used to enhance the applcation and give information regarding the creators of the project. Figure 8.16 shows the simple About dialog box.

A 32 × 32 pixel icon is designed in the resource editor and shown in Figure 8.17.

You'll see this icon in the upper-left portion of the title bar area when the application is run.

This application uses four menus. The Pen-Colors menu is visible in Figure 8.18 and shows a palette of five colors.

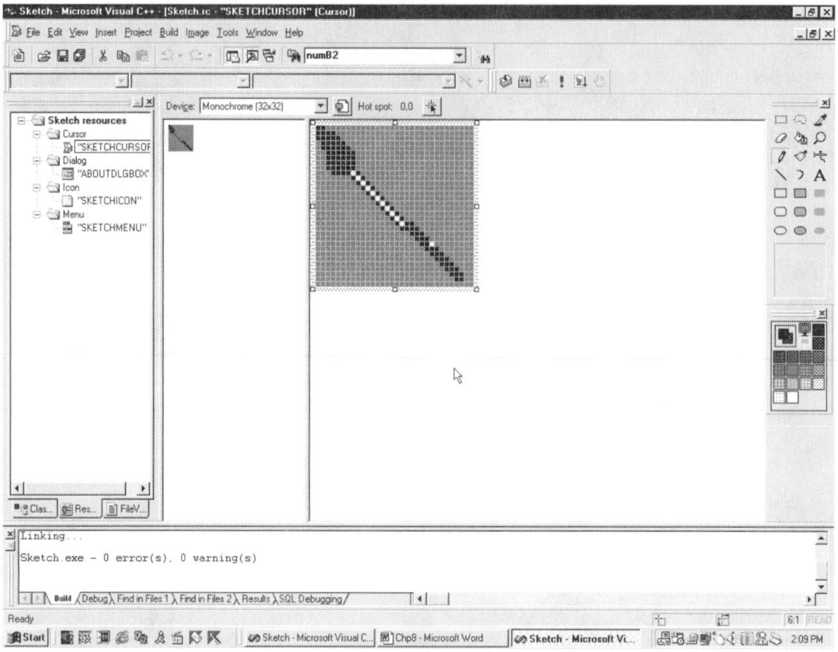

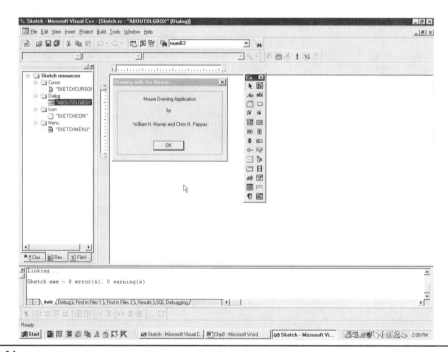

Figure 8.15   A unique cursor is created for the sketch project

Figure 8.16   An About dialog box adds a professional touch to the project

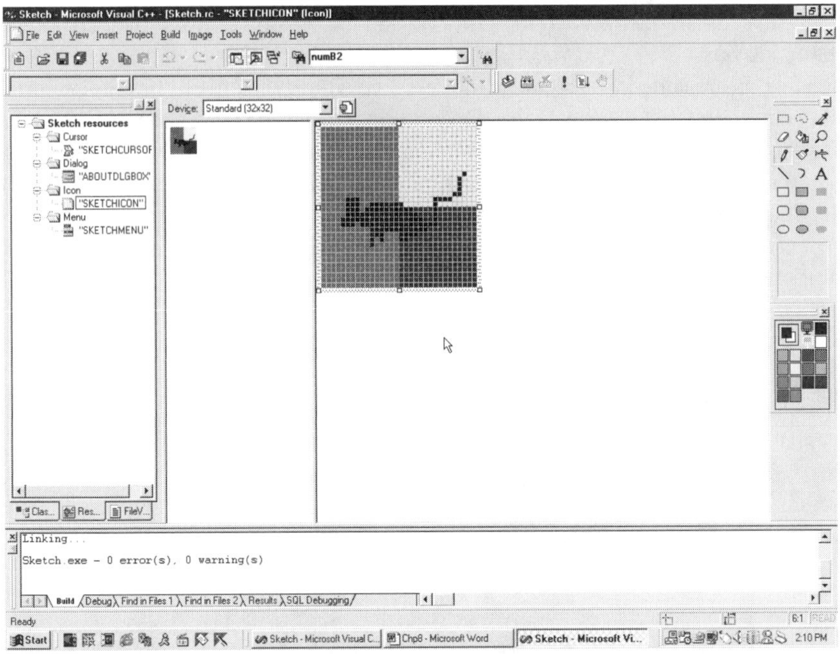

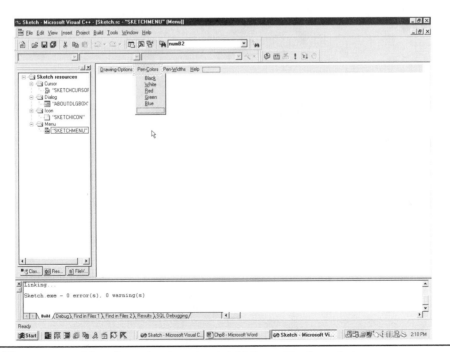

Figure 8.17   A unique icon is created for this project

Figure 8.18   A palette of five vibrant drawing colors is initially used by the project

The other menus contain menu selections for clearing the window, setting the pen width, or calling up the About dialog box.

When menu items are added to a menu in the resource editor, the creator has the opportunity to set unique ID values. Figure 8.19 shows the ID value entered for the Green menu item selection.

The remaining menu items on all of the remaining menus have similar ID values applied to them. These ID values are saved in the resource.h header file included with the project. ID values are automatically added to this file as resources are added.

The project can be built by selecting the Build | Rebuild All menu item from within Visual C++. An execution of this project is shown in Figure 8.20.

When you examine Figure 8.20, you'll see several different lines in a variety of widths and colors. While you can see the widths, you'll have to take our word that all five drawing colors were used.

Making Modifications and Introducing Errors

Let's assume that the popularity of the sketch project has been so great that we decide to add an additional seven drawing colors to the list shown in the Pen-Colors menu. Using the resource editor, the new color choices are added to the menu in exactly the same manner that the first five colors were added. Figure 8.21 shows the expanded Pen-Colors menu in the resource editor.

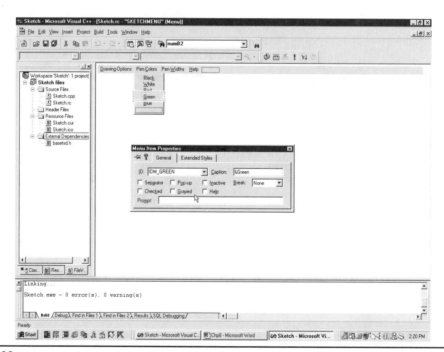

Figure 8.19   A unique ID value is associated with the Green menu item

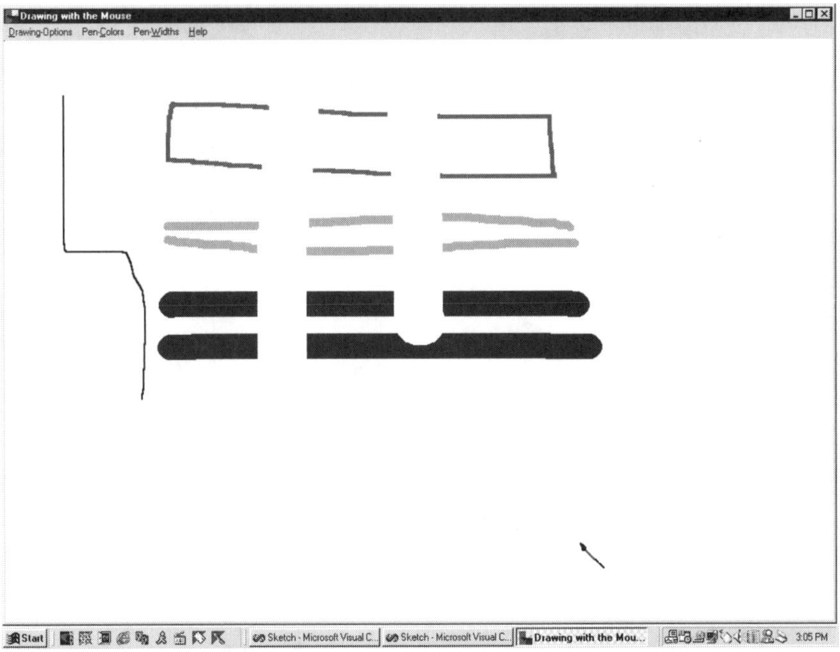

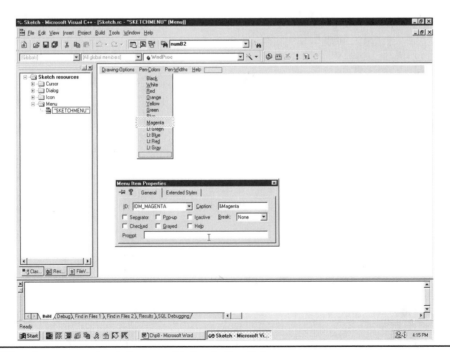

Figure 8.20 The initial version of the sketch project is tested

Figure 8.21 Seven new color choices are added to the Pen-Colors menu

Next, the color array, *wColorValue[]*, is expanded to accommodate the new menu selections.

```
static COLORREF wColorValue[12]={RGB(0,0,0),          //BLACK
                                 RGB(255,255,255),    //WHITE
                                 RGB(255,0,0),        //RED
                                 RGB(255,96,0),       //ORANGE
                                 RGB(255,255,0),      //YELLOW
                                 RGB(0,255,0),        //GREEN
                                 RGB(0,0,255),        //BLUE
                                 RGB(255,0,255),      //MAGENTA
                                 RGB(128,255,0),      //LT GREEN
                                 RGB(0,255,255),      //LT BLUE
                                 RGB(255,0,159),      //LT RED
                                 RGB(180,180,180)};   //LT GRAY
```

Finally, the case statement that handles the WM_COMMAND message is expanded, too. The unique changes are shown in a bold font.

```
    case WM_COMMAND:
      // menu item selections
      switch (LOWORD(wParam)) {
        case ID_OPTIONS_CLEAR:
          tempcolor=wColorValue[1];
          InvalidateRect(hWnd,NULL,TRUE);
          break;
        case ID_OPTIONS_EXIT:
          SendMessage(hWnd,WM_CLOSE,0,0L);
          break;
        case ID_PEN_TWO:
          penwidth=2;
          break;
        case ID_PEN_FIVE:
          penwidth=5;
          break;
        case ID_PEN_TEN:
          penwidth=10;
          break;
        case ID_PEN_THIRTY:
          penwidth=30;
          break;
        case ID_PEN_SIXTY:
          penwidth=60;
          break;
        case ID_HELP_ABOUT:
          DialogBox((HINSTANCE) GetModuleHandle(NULL),
                   "AboutDlgBox",hWnd,
                   AboutDlgProc);
          break;
        case IDM_BLACK:
```

```
case IDM_WHITE:
case IDM_RED:
case IDM_ORANGE:
case IDM_YELLOW:
case IDM_GREEN:
case IDM_BLUE:
case IDM_MAGENTA:
case IDM_LTGREEN:
case IDM_LTBLUE:
case IDM_LTRED:
case IDM_LTGRAY:
   hmenu=GetMenu(hWnd);
   CheckMenuItem(hmenu,wColor,MF_UNCHECKED);
   wColor=LOWORD(wParam);
   CheckMenuItem(hmenu,wColor,MF_CHECKED);
   tempcolor=wColorValue[wColor-IDM_BLACK];
   break;
default:
   break;
}
break;
```

Now, compile the project and test the application. What do you notice? Although you have 12 color choices, the colors aren't correct. As a matter of fact, the colors are really messed up. For example, orange turns out to be green, yellow turns out to be blue, and so on. How did these errors creep into a working application? Your first thought might be that the RGB colors were specified incorrectly for some of the new colors. That is frequently the source of a problem such as this one. However, it is not the problem in this project. Unless you've run into this kind of problem before, it is a pretty difficult problem to see. Time for the Debugger!

Finding and Repairing Errors

Start a remote debugger session in the normal fashion. On the remote target computer, (sony) open the Pen-Colors menu and select the black pen, as shown in Figure 8.22.

Place a breakpoint at the code location, shown in Figure 8.23, put the *wColor* variable in a Watch window, and execute the code to the breakpoint.

The *wColor* variable will contain an integer value. For this example, that value is 40011.

Now, repeat the process of selecting each menu choice, running to the breakpoint, and recording the *wColor* value. Table 8.1 summarizes the results we obtained.

Study the table carefully. Did you notice that the original colors are sequenced in this fashion: 40011, 40012, 40013, 40014 and 40015? The seven new colors returned the values 40016, 40017, 40018, 40019, 40020, 40021, and 40022.

This program uses an efficient process of selecting colors, but it relies on sequential entries in the menu. We'll explain that point in just a moment. When the original table was created, Windows assigned sequential identification constants to each ID value for each menu selection. Thus, IDM_BLACK was assigned 40011, while IDM_RED was assigned 40012, and so on. However, when we went back and added new entries, especially the orange and green colors, it

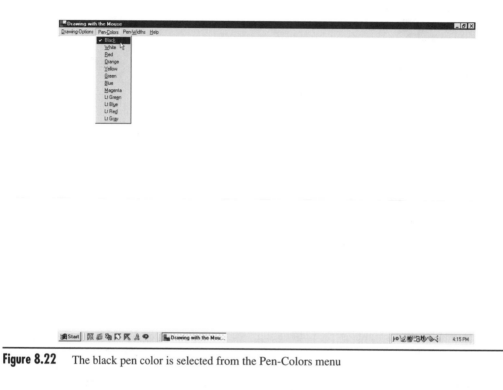

Figure 8.22   The black pen color is selected from the Pen-Colors menu

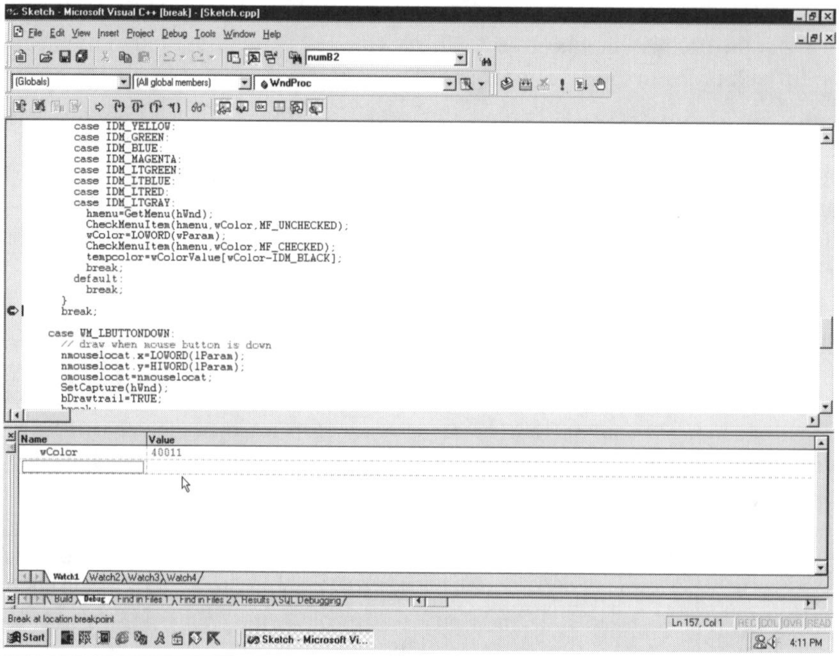

Figure 8.23   The *wColor* value is placed in the Watch window

Integer Returned	Color Requested
40011	Black
40012	White
40013	Red
40016	Orange
40017	Yellow
40014	Green
40015	Blue
40018	Magenta
40019	Light green
40020	Light blue
40021	Light red
40022	Light gray

Table 8.1   *wColor* Values Returned by the Debugger

continued the sequencing from the last menu item's number (40015). So, IDM_ORANGE was assigned 40016 and so on.

Our efficient little piece of code, however, expected sequential numbers for each menu item starting at the top and ending at the bottom.

```
tempcolor=wColorValue[wColor-IDM_BLACK];
```

The index into the wColorValue[] array is determined by subtracting the constant attached to IDM_BLACK from the value returned in *wColor*. For example, if the Red menu item is selected, the result is 40013 – 40011 = 2. An index of 2 correctly points to the RGB(255,0,0) value for the color red in wColorValue[]. As another example, perform the arithmetic for the Orange menu item. Do you see that it doesn't point to the correct array value? The only way to quickly repair this problem is to go into the resource.h header file and adjust the values.

Here is a portion of the resource.h header file with the ID values corrected:

```
#define IDM_BLACK              40011
#define IDM_WHITE              40012
#define IDM_RED                40013
#define IDM_GREEN              40016
#define IDM_BLUE               40017
#define IDM_ORANGE             40014
#define IDM_YELLOW             40015
#define IDM_MAGENTA            40018
#define IDM_LTGREEN            40019
#define IDM_LTBLUE             40020
#define IDM_LTRED              40021
#define IDM_LTGRAY             40022
```

24x7

Sequential integer values are assigned to the ID values accompanying each menu item as that menu item is added to the resource editor. It has been a tradition, among Windows programmers, to use the fact that these numbers are sequential to help eliminate writing redundant **case** statements in programming code. The **case** statement, itself, is a frequent source of programming errors.

The requirements for taking advantage of sequentially assigned integer values are quite simple.

- First, the sequence of menu items should be related—for example, brush colors, pen sizes, background colors, line lengths, and so on.

- Next, the sequential values are usually used to calculate an index into an array of actual data values. Thus, the index is calculated by subtracting the integer value assigned to the first item in the list by the item returned when making the menu item selection.

- Finally, the sequence of the items in the menu must match the sequence of ID values in the resource.h header file and the sequence of values in the array that is to be indexed.

The best advice we can offer, in addition to using the Debugger, is to carefully design menus ahead of time. Then when you enter the menu items, Windows always assigns sequential values.

Now, the integers in the table match the placement of the colors, sequentially. Compile and test the application once again. Yes, it works perfectly!

The reliance on sequential integer values for menu lists is a popular technique for efficiently handling long lists of related items. However, it can create a bit of a problem to unravel if you have never seen it before. The Debugger proved its worth in this example.

Conclusion

This chapter has introduced some powerful debugging techniques that work well with C++ Windows applications. First, you learned how to harness the power of debugging on a remote target computer. Then, while working within the procedure-oriented programming environment, you have learned how to detect, diagnose, and repair some interesting boundary problems. You learned that these boundary problems lie in wait for anyone who is not careful with the distinctions between a window's size, the client area's size, and so on. In the second example, you saw how easy it is to introduce errors into working code by not understanding how Windows assigns values to ID values such as IDM_BLACK and IDM_ORANGE when creating menus.

PART III

The Object-Oriented Environment

CHAPTER 9

Locating, Analyzing, and Repairing Errors in Command-Line Code

A s you move from procedural C/C++ programming to object-oriented code designs, you necessarily increase the complexity of your debug cycle. Visual C++ stands ready to help you with additional debug commands, features, and advanced uses for previously discussed Debugger capabilities. In this chapter, you will explore these new features and learn how to manage the information they report.

Advanced Debugging Tools

Because Microsoft's Visual C++ Debugger is such a comprehensive tool, mastering it takes time. In this section, you will continue to hone your debugging finesse by learning how to specifically direct the Debugger to perform detailed tasks.

Memory Dumps

In previous chapters, you have seen how the Variables and Watch windows do an excellent job of reporting a variable's current contents. However, when the complexity of a data structure increases, a memory dump provides a more meaningful display of the variable's contents.

Figure 9.1 shows a program declaring a thousand-element integer array *iArray* and initializing each element to its respective offset address. As you can tell from Figure 9.1, a breakpoint has been set on **main()**'s closing brace (}). A single press of the F5 key has started the Debugger, executed the

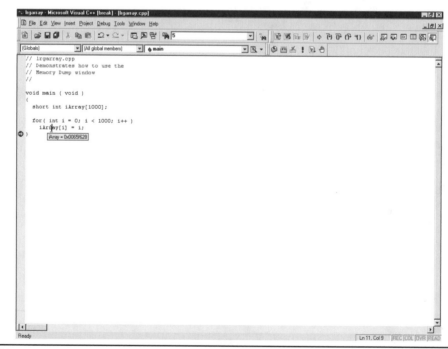

Figure 9.1   Debugger showing *iArray*'s physical address

declaration of *iArray*, and completed the thousand iterations of the **for** loop. Notice in Figure 9.1 that the cursor hovers over the use of *iArray* within the **for** loop body, displaying the starting address *0x0065f628*. This array is too large to easily view in either the Variables or Watch window. However, the Memory Dump window, shown in Figure 9.2, can easily handle an object of this size.

To open the Memory Dump window, you can either select the View | Debug Windows | Memory option or press ALT+6. Figure 9.2 shows an expanded Memory Dump window with the correct address entered in the Address field. The only problem is that the Debugger, by default, formats memory dumps using byte formatting. To change the display format, you must go to the Tools | Options menu, click on the Debug tab, and change the Memory window format (see Figure 9.3).

Figure 9.4 shows the adjusted, and more meaningful, display format.

With the Memory Dump window open, you can now easily scroll through the entire object's contents. While this is a straightforward example, the principles involved become an invaluable tool as you begin to debug more complex data structures.

Locating Where an Incorrect Parameter Is Passed

Imagine that you have written a subroutine (function or method) that is called hundreds of times. From your understanding and use of the Debugger commands discussed so far, you know *which* value passed is incorrect, but you haven't a clue as to where this bad call is coming from. Under these circumstances, you need to use the *Breakpoints Condition* option.

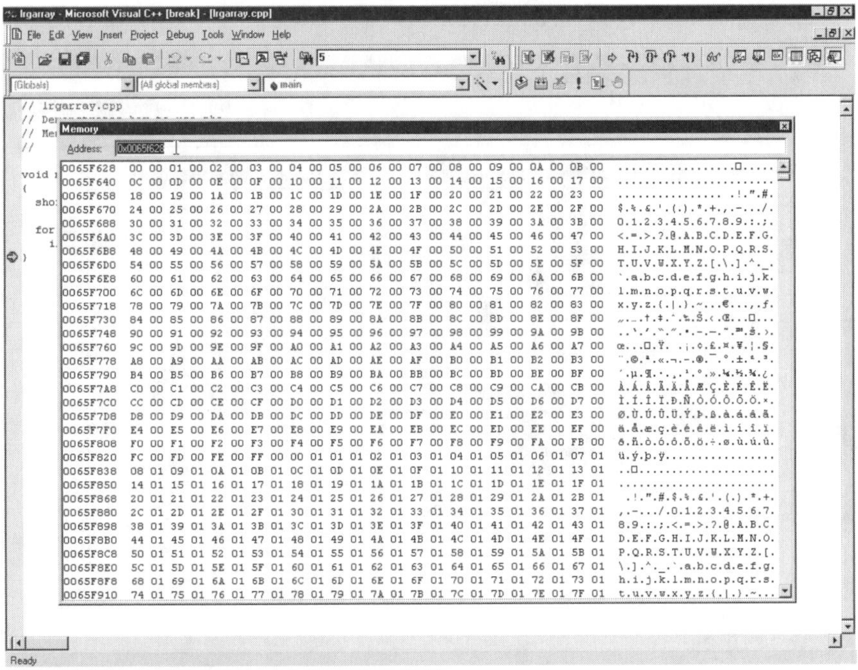

Figure 9.2 Default Memory Dump window formatting

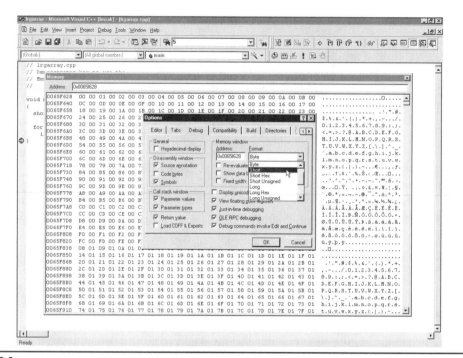

Figure 9.3 Changing the Memory Dump format to short

Figure 9.4 Corrected Memory Dump window formatting

Setting a conditional breakpoint is slightly more complicated than setting an unconditional breakpoint on a source code statement. To set a conditional breakpoint, you first click on the Visual C++ Edit menu, followed by selecting the Breakpoints (ALT+F9) option seen in Figure 9.5.

The conditional Breakpoints window, seen in Figure 9.6, displays with the Location tab selected by default. Right-clicking on the right-arrow on the edge of the Break at edit list displays two additional location options, Line and Advanced. *Line 30,* seen in Figure 9.6, was automatically entered by Visual C++ because the I-beam cursor was sitting on line 30 in the source code prior to activating the conditional Breakpoint window (see Figure 9.8 later in this chapter), a nice auto-entry shortcut.

Design Tip   *When setting conditional breakpoints on a specific program statement, first place the I-beam cursor on the source code statement where you would like to set the conditional breakpoint. Next, using the Edit | Breakpoints option, or ALT+F9, activate the conditional Breakpoints window and click on the right-arrow at the Break at edit list. Simply select the default line number, and you're done.*

Line 30 is an ideal choice for this example because it is inside the subroutine receiving the bad argument value. Once you select *Line 30,* the grayed Condition button becomes active. Clicking on the Condition button displays the Breakpoint Condition window shown in Figure 9.7.

From a standard debug phase using the Variables and Watch windows (not shown here), it was discovered that the subroutine was passed an *iValue* of *22.* For the hypothetical example, this value is viewed as "bad data."

Figure 9.7 shows a conditional breakpoint being set whenever the formal argument *iValue* equals *22.* Notice in the Breakpoint Condition window, below the expression *iValue == 22,* the statement reading "Break when expression is true." You may enter in the expression edit window any valid C/C++ statement that evaluates to true (!0) or false (0).

The Breakpoint Condition window allows you to further streamline the conditional breakpoint by entering the number of times to skip the expression. This could be useful when, for example,

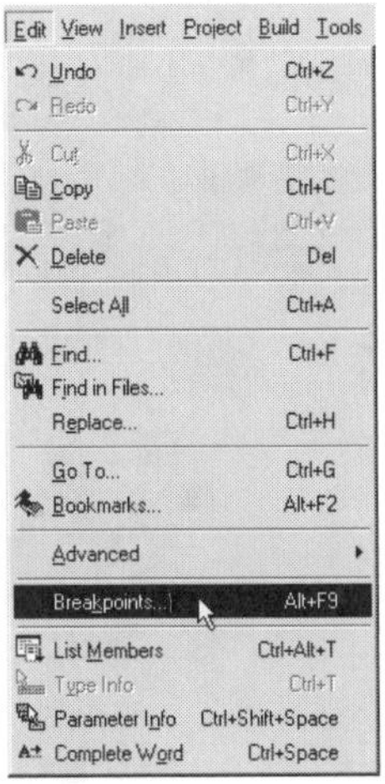

Figure 9.5   Choosing the Edit | Breakpoints option

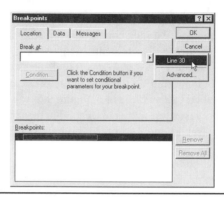

Figure 9.6   Selecting a breakpoint for *Line 30*

the subroutine in question *could* be passed five *iValue*s of *22*, with the sixth *22* being the interpreted "bad data."

As always, you run a program with breakpoints by pressing the F5 (Go) key. Figure 9.8 shows the Debugger has stopped. The message window details which file owns the breakpoint statement *brkcndts.cpp,* the line number of the statement *30,* and why the Debugger stopped, *when iValue ==* *22.* You know from previous discussions that you would view the Call Stack window at this point to detect which calling subroutine was last invoked, passing the "bad data." All you are left with at this point is to debug the calling routine.

Finding Out Where a Pointer Is Getting Changed

All programmers know there's nothing like a good bug to impenetrably teach a language fundamental. C and C++ are no different. In fact, because you are reading this book, you already know just how

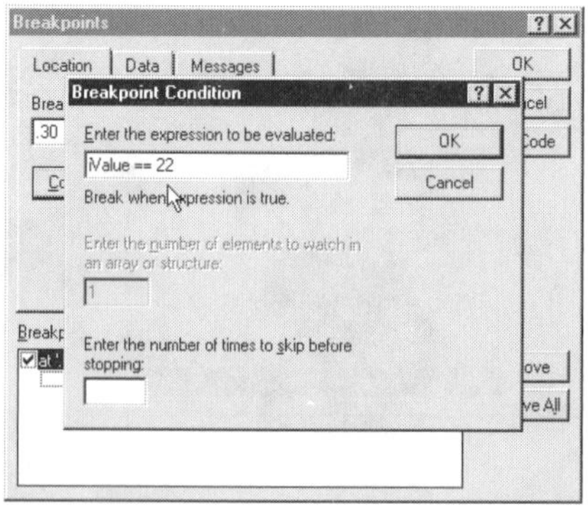

Figure 9.7   Setting the break condition for when *iValue == 22*

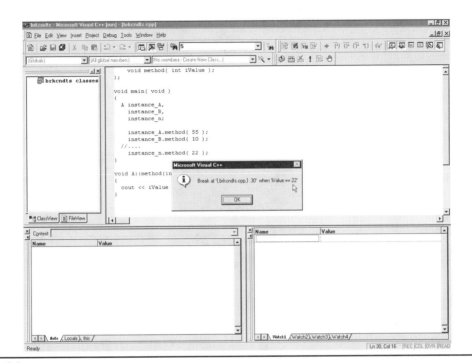

Figure 9.8   Debugger stops when *iValue == 22*

nefarious C/C++ bugs can be and the dexterity required to master them! For example, take the following simple object-oriented C++ program (to see if *you* can detect the error, skip the comment block):

```
//
// badptr.cpp
// Detecting bad pointer assignment
// Chris H. Pappas and William H. Murray, 1999
//

#include <iostream>

using namespace std;

typedef struct tagIntegerNode {
  int              iValue;
  tagIntegerNode *pNextIntegerNode;
}INTEGERNODE;

class A {
  public:
    // made public to simplify tracing
    // would normally be protected:
```

```
      INTEGERNODE *pFirstIntegerNode;
};

class B:public A {
  public:
    B( void );
};

class C:public A {
  public:
    C( void );
};

void main( void )
{
  B instanceB;
  C instanceC;

  cout << instanceB.pFirstIntegerNode->iValue << endl;
  cout << instanceC.pFirstIntegerNode->pNextIntegerNode->iValue << endl;
};

B::B( void )
{
  pFirstIntegerNode                    = new INTEGERNODE;
  pFirstIntegerNode->iValue            = 1;
  pFirstIntegerNode->pNextIntegerNode = NULL;
};

C::C( void )
{
  pFirstIntegerNode->pNextIntegerNode                    = new INTEGERNODE;
  pFirstIntegerNode->pNextIntegerNode->iValue            = 2;
  pFirstIntegerNode->pNextIntegerNode->pNextIntegerNode = NULL;
};
```

This short sample program hard-wires a linked-list type of algorithm. The program begins by defining the linked-list node, *INTEGERNODE,* with an integer data member, *iValue,* and a pointer to the next linked-list node, *pNextIntegerNode.* To make things interesting, a parent class, *A,* declares the pointer, *pFirstIntegerNode,* that will track all of the child nodes defined in subclasses *B* and *C.*

Both siblings *B,* and *C* have only one constructor method whose job it is to dynamically allocate the storage for an *INTEGERNODE* and assign their respective pointers. *instanceB*'s constructor attaches the address of the new node to the parent class *A*'s inherited data member *pFirstIntegerNode,* while *instanceC*'s constructor links its new node address to *instanceB* node's *pNestIntegerNode,* thereby creating a hard-wired linked list of two *INTEGERNODE*s.

main()'s task, besides instantiating the two sibling classes *B* and *C,* is to print out the *iValue*s assigned to each instance. In theory, the program should output an integer *1* (*instanceB*'s *iValue*) and *2* (*instanceC*'s *iValue*), respectively. However, executing the algorithm within the Debugger produces the results shown in Figure 9.9.

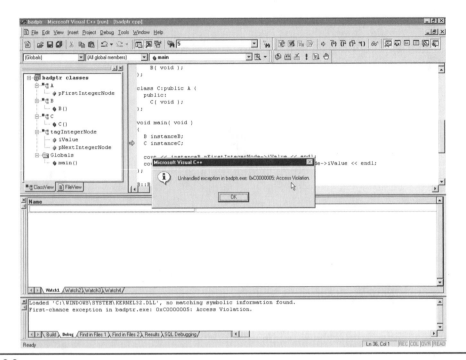

Figure 9.9 Executing *badptr.cpp*

A close examination of the trace arrow's location shows that it was the instantiation of subclass *C* that generated the "*Access Violation.*"

Using your newly acquired debugging skills, you decide to restart the Debugger, and instead of stepping over the instantiation statement (shortcut key F10), you will step into (F11) *instanceC*'s constructor, as seen in Figure 9.10. Notice the trace arrow is now sitting on the first statement in the constructor *C::C*.

With one more single-step operation, the *Access Violation* reappears. The Debugger now points to the offending statement: the call to **new**() and the assignment of the new *INTEGERNODE* to the first node's *pNextIntegerNode*. The question is, "Which part of the assignment statement is misfiring?"

Once again, you restart the Debugger, only this time you decide to step into (F11) the offending statement pointed to by the trace arrow in Figure 9.10, instead of stepping over it (F10). Because the Microsoft Visual C++ Debugger allows you to trace into compiler source code, you can tell by the location of the trace arrow in Figure 9.11 that the call to the function **new**() executed successfully. You know function **new**() executed successfully because the trace arrow could not have made it to the closing brace if the function itself was generating the *Access Violation*. However, your next press of F10 or F11, leaving the call to function **new**(), reproduces the "*Access Violation*" message seen earlier in Figure 9.9.

Your conclusion, of course, is that the attempt to assign this new *INTEGERNODE* address is generating the error message. Now the question becomes, "How do I use the Debugger to show me what went wrong?" Let's take the answer to this question step-by-step.

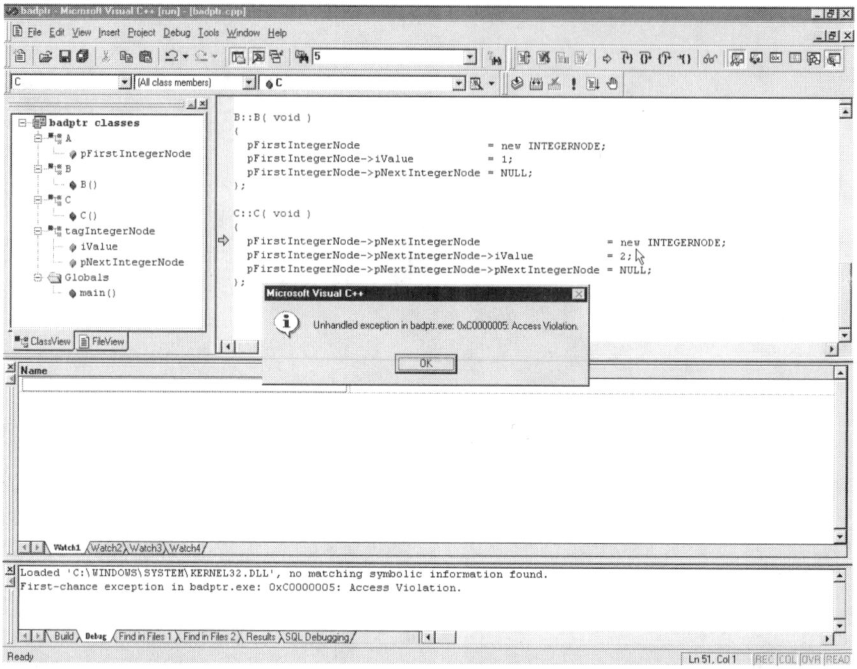

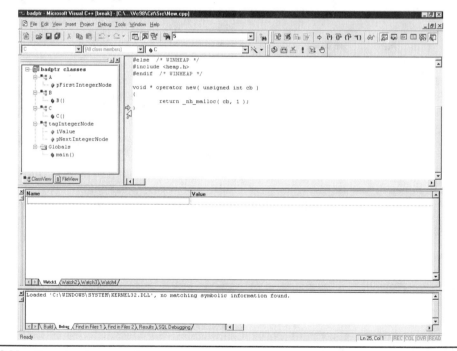

Figure 9.10 Tracing *badptr.cpp* into *instanceC*'s constructor

Figure 9.11 Detecting the successful completion of function new()

First, you know that the instantiation of subclass *B* executed properly. *instanceB*'s constructor appears to have executed completely. In theory, then, this means that *pFirstIntegerNode* must have been created and assigned the address of *instanceB*'s new *INTEGERNODE*. So you decide to put both in the Watch window.

Next, you write down, or remember, the physical address to *instanceB*'s new *INTEGERNODE* and see if the address in *pFirstIntegerNode* ever changes.

Actually, you are going to track two physical addresses. The first is the address of where the compiler has placed the pointer variable *pFirstIntegerNode*. This requires you to add the address operator & in front of the variable's name when adding it to the Watch window, as in *&pFirstIntegerNode*.

The next piece of physical evidence we need is the address of the assigned *instanceB*'s new *INTEGERNODE*. This is accomplished by watching the contents of *pFirstIntegernode* (the second entry in the Watch window shown in Figure 9.12). These two addresses are *0x0006afdf4* (for *&pFirstIntegerNode)* and *0x007d0ebo* (for the contents of the pointer variable *pFirstIntegerNode*).

Since it is *instanceC*'s statement:

```
pFirstIntegerNode->pNextIntegerNode                        = new INTEGERNODE;
```

that is causing the error, you are trying to detect if *pFirstIntegerNode*'s contents ever change. If so, this would indicate that you have lost the correct address to *instanceB*'s new *INTEGERNODE* for some reason.

Here is where Microsoft's Visual C++ Debugger really shines. Using an Advanced Breakpoint option, you can instruct the Debugger to *stop* whenever a pointer variable's pointer address contents change.

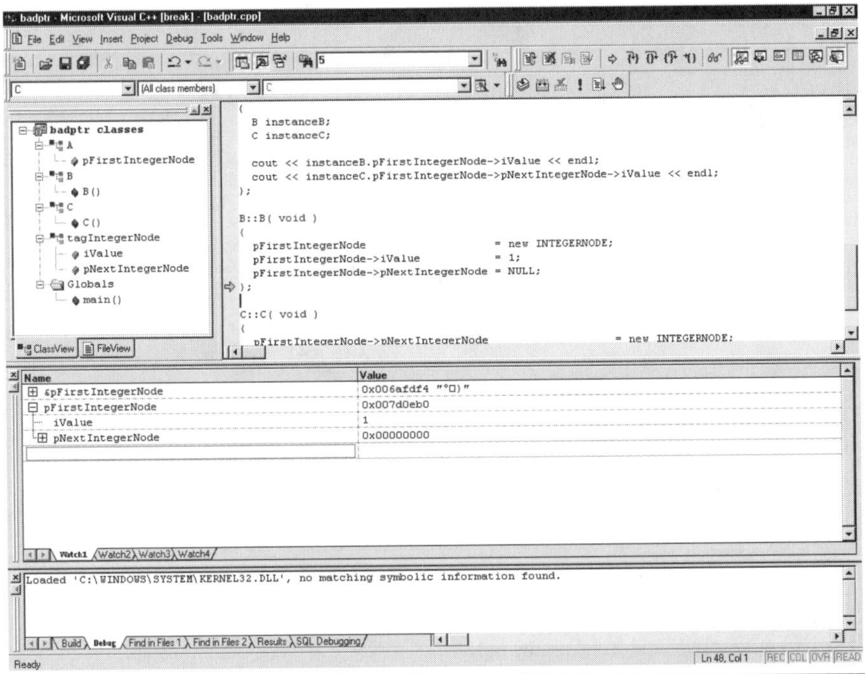

Figure 9.12 Discovering the physical addresses for *&pFirstIntegerNode* and the first valid *INTEGERNODE*

To set this type of conditional breakpoint, you return to the Edit | Breakpoints (ALT+F9) menu option (see Figures 9.5 and 9.6), only this time instead of using the Breakpoints Location tab, you use the Breakpoints Data tab as seen in Figure 9.13.

Because of the sophisticated scope involved in parent and child or subclass inheritance, you will need to use the Advanced Breakpoints option (seen in Figure 9.13), which is activated by clicking on the right-arrow at the right-edge of the Enter the expression to be evaluated listbox. Without using an Advanced Breakpoint, the Debugger would never flag the pointer variable's (*pFirstIntegerNode*) address change because of its inability to deal with instance-specific references or scope.

The Advanced Breakpoint window requires you to enter not only an expression, but also the function's name, the owning source file's name, and the executable file's name, associated with the specified break condition (see Figure 9.14). With this completed, you click on the OK button. You will now see a window similar to Figure 9.15.

In Figure 9.15, the conditional breakpoint expression, "Break when expression is true," or *pFirstIntegerNode != 0x007d0eb0,* will stop the Debugger whenever the pointer variable's address no longer points to *instanceB*'s new *INTEGERNODE*—something that should *not* happen if the algorithm is correct.

To begin this final phase of debugging, with the breakpoint set in Figure 9.15, you simply restart the Debugger with a single press of the F5 key (the Run to Breakpoint hot-key).

24x7

When you are debugging an algorithm, looking for specific physical memory addresses or changes in physical address pointers, you cannot add or remove program statements. This would cause the compiler to possibly reallocate objects in physical memory, voiding any test for a specific physical address.

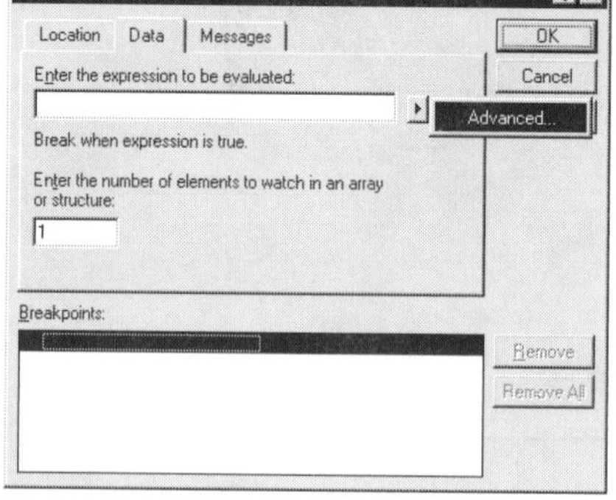

Figure 9.13 Using the Advanced Breakpoints option

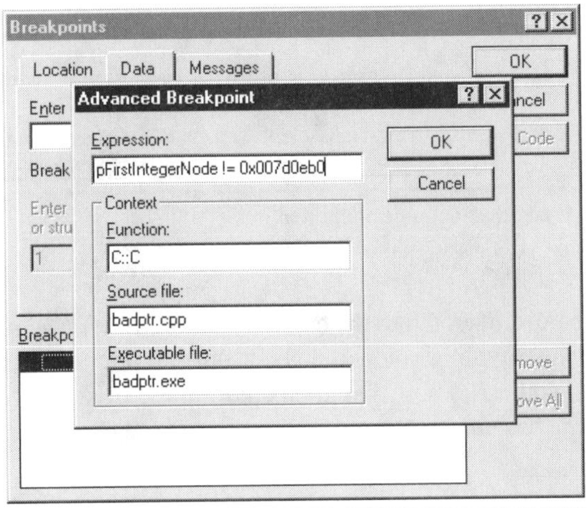

Figure 9.14 Defining Advanced Breakpoints

When you debug *badptr.cpp* with the advanced conditional breakpoint set, the Debugger will stop and generate the breakpoint message seen in Figure 9.16. Clicking on the OK button shows the trace arrow, sitting on the offending line (see Figure 9.17).

Figure 9.17 shows the trace arrow on the same line causing the "Access Violation." The earlier trace, generating the *Access Violation*, obscured *where* the error occurred on this statement. Was it the call to **new**(), the assignment =, the reference to *->pNextIntegerNode*, or the *pFirstIntegerNode* pointer itself?

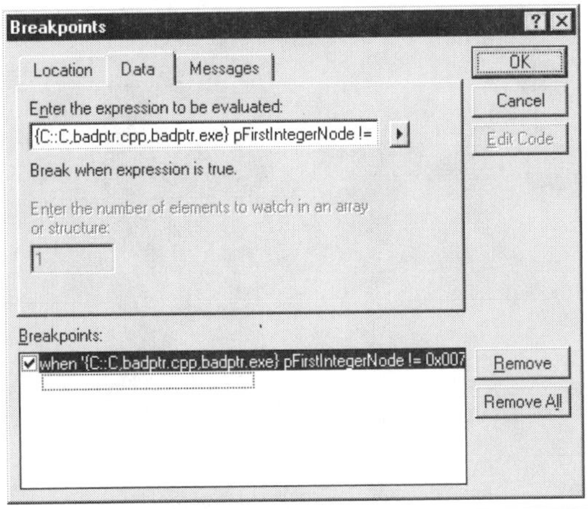

Figure 9.15 Viewing Advanced Breakpoints settings

Figure 9.16   Acknowledged advanced conditional breakpoint

From the first trace, you discovered that the call to function **new**() was successful. You were then left with the need to discover anything you could about the two pointer references. With the help of the Advanced Breakpoint, you now know that upon entering the *instanceC* constructor, the address stored in *pFirstIntegerNode* has changed—and it should *not* have changed! Ah, success, but *why* didn't the program work?

While *badptr.cpp* always compiled, embedded within its logic was a fundamental object-oriented design philosophy flaw involving pointers, parent or root classes, child or subclass definitions, and inheritance.

Here's the problem: while parent class *A* defined the *pFirstIntegerNode* pointer, which was inherited by both siblings *B* and *C,* the siblings did *not* inherit the *same pFirstIntegerNode*! When

Figure 9.17   Trace arrow pointing to offending statement child *B* is instantiated (*instanceB*), its inherited definition for the member *pFirstIntegerNode* generated an instance-specific memory location that is assigned the address of the new *INTEGERNODE*.

Along comes the instantiation of sibling *C* (*instanceC*). It too shares the same member definition for *pFirstIntegerNode*, inherited from class *A;* however, *instanceC* is allocated its own unique *pFirstIntegerNode*. Since *instanceC*'s constructor *C::C* uses this instance-specific *pFirstIntegerNode*, and not the initiated *instanceA*'s *pFirstIntegerNode*, the program crashes.

The fix is so simple as to be almost humorous, except for the possibly endlessly wasted hours spent debugging an algorithm. The fix you ask? Simply add the C/C++ keyword **static**. Look at the correctly modified definition for class *A* that follows:

```
class A {
  public:
    // Made public to simplify tracing
    // Would normally be protected:
    static INTEGERNODE *pFirstIntegerNode;
};
```

The keyword **static** in this syntax causes any child or subclass definition not only to share the definition for the member, but also to share the *same* data member by address.

Unfortunately, C++ has a somewhat obtuse syntax requirement when adding the **static** keyword to class data members. C++ requires that the **static** data member be declared at the external level—that is, outside the formal class definition, as in:

```
// Static data members must be initialized at file scope, even
// if private.
INTEGERNODE *A::pFirstIntegerNode;
```

The following program, *staticptr.cpp,* is included to help you see how these code changes fit within the entire algorithm (the bolded statements highlight the minimal code changes):

```
//
// staticptr.cpp
// Detecting bad pointer assignment
// Chris H. Pappas and William H. Murray, 1999
//

#include <iostream>

using namespace std;

typedef struct tagIntegerNode {
  int             iValue;
  tagIntegerNode *pNextIntegerNode;
}INTEGERNODE;

class A {
  public:
    // Made public to simplify tracing
    // Would normally be protected:
```

```
        static INTEGERNODE *pFirstIntegerNode;
};

// Static data members must be initialized at file scope, even
// if private.
INTEGERNODE *A::pFirstIntegerNode;

class B:public A {
  public:
    B( void );
};

class C:public A {
  public:
    C( void );
};

void main( void )
{
  B instanceB;
  C instanceC;

  cout << instanceB.pFirstIntegerNode->iValue << endl;
  cout << instanceC.pFirstIntegerNode->pNextIntegerNode->iValue << endl;
};

B::B( void )
{
  pFirstIntegerNode                 = new INTEGERNODE;
  pFirstIntegerNode->iValue         = 1;
  pFirstIntegerNode->pNextIntegerNode = NULL;
};

C::C( void )
{
  pFirstIntegerNode->pNextIntegerNode                 = new INTEGERNODE;
  pFirstIntegerNode->pNextIntegerNode->iValue         = 2;
  pFirstIntegerNode->pNextIntegerNode->pNextIntegerNode = NULL;
};
```

With the code changes found in *staticptr.cpp*, the algorithm performs as anticipated, outputting the integer values *1* and *2*, respectively. The most significant aspect to *badptr.cpp* and *staticptr.cpp* is that these simple object-oriented algorithms were debugged skillfully, step-by-methodical-step, using commonly available Debugger tools.

In addition, the particular nature of the bug found in *badptr.cpp* necessitated the use of not only a conditional breakpoint, but also an advanced breakpoint. With this new Debugger tool, you now know how to override the scope problem inherent in simple breakpoint expressions, which are incapable of telling the Debugger how to track instance-specific members.

ClassView Elements

When you are running the Microsoft Visual C++ Studio, the left-most window contains the Workspace view. This view can be broken down to two independent views, ClassView and FileView. ClassView visually represents the relationship between class data members and class member functions or methods.

The following program defines a typical *parent* and *child* class with both having **public:**, **private:**, and **protected:** data members and methods. Each member, data, or function has a name specific to its intended use. Since ClassView member symbols are very small, the naming of the members should help you lock onto the visual representation of the individual member and its intended program scope.

```
//
// clasview.cpp
// Understanding ClassView symbols
//

// external static definition
// required for static class data members
static int static_publicParentData;

class parent {
  public:
    int         publicParentData;
    static int  static_publicParentData;
                parent() {};

  private:
    float       privateParentData;
    void        privateParentMethod() {};

  protected:
    double      protectedParentData;
    void        protectedParentMethod() {};
};

class child:public parent {
  public:
    int         publicChildData;
    void        publicChildMethod() {};
                child() {};
  private:
    float       privateChildData;
    void        privateChildMethod() {};

  protected:
    double      protectedChildData;
    void        protectedChildMethod() {};
};

inline void doNothingFunction( void ) {};
```

```
void main( void )
{
  parent instanceParent;
  child  instanceChild;
}
```

Figure 9.18 shows a typical build of *clasview.cpp* with the Workspace and Edit windows maximized for viewing.

Figure 9.19 shows a close-up view of just the Workspace pane ClassView. The project name, *clasview classes*, shown in bold, represents the default project configuration. When you expand the project, ClassView displays the classes included in that project. If you expand any class, it displays the members in that class.

If you are using standard Windows colors, the almost-black symbols are dark-blue, the medium-gray symbols are purple, and the light-gray symbols are light blue.

Class, parent or child, member functions or methods are color-coded in purple. Member data, parent or child, is coded in light-blue. Method symbols are three-dimensional rectangles that skew to the left, while member data symbols are three-dimensional rectangles that skew to the right.

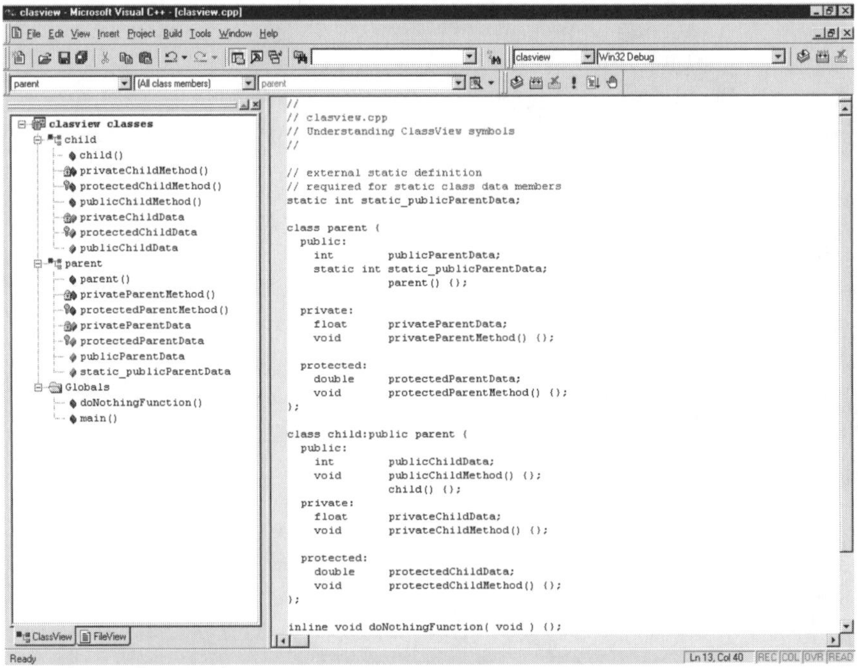

Figure 9.18   ClassView of *clasview.cpp*

Figure 9.19   Close-up view of the Workspace ClassView

The icons in ClassView convey additional information about the classes and class members in a project. When a class member, data or method, is globally accessible, the method symbols, parent or child, are undecorated. **protected:** class members, data or method, are decorated with a small key icon. **private:** class members, data or methods, are decorated with a small keyhole lock. These decorations serve as visual reminders of the class member's scope, class-to-program and child-to-parent.

ClassView Grouped by Access

You can rearrange the order of ClassView icons by first right-clicking on a class definition. Figure 9.20 selected the *parent* class and chose one of the display formats, *Group by Access*.

Figure 9.21 shows the *Group by Access* reordered ClassView.

This is an extremely useful view of your objects since it places class members in order from least-protected, or **public:**, to most-protected, or **private:**.

ClassView Base Classes

Figure 9.22 shows the ClassView local menu (right-click on *parent*) set up to detail *clasview.cpp*'s base classes.

Choosing the Base Classes option opens up the Base Classes and Members window similar to the one seen in Figure 9.23. The "f", "d", and "S" represent class "f"unctions, "d"ata, and "S"tatic definitions.

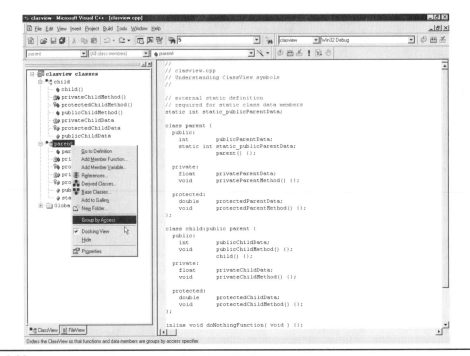

Figure 9.20 Sorting ClassView contents using Group by Access

Figure 9.21 Group by Access ordering in ClassView

Figure 9.22   Finding out details about all *clasview.cpp* base classes

You can find out everything you could ever want to know about your application's base classes from the Base Classes and Members window. This window displays all base classes in the left pane, all **public:**, **private:**, and **protected:** members, which source file, including path, owns the class definition,

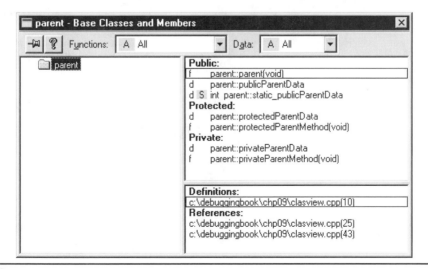

Figure 9.23   Base Classes window showing the *parent* base class

and finally which source files access the base class definition. Also, by your double-clicking on a source file name, the Debugger will automatically locate the file and open it in the Edit window. Whew! But wait, there's more . . .

By clicking on the down-arrows next to the Functions or Data drop-down lists, you can further streamline the views. Figure 9.24 shows the Functions drop-down list options.

This list allows you to fine-tune the Base Classes and Members view so that you see only Static, Virtual, Non-Virtual, Non-Static, or Non-Virtual Non-Static methods. The bolded and blocked uppercase "A", "V", and "S" have a nonbolded counterpart. Bolded icons represent active modifiers; nonbolded represent nonactive modifiers.

Clicking on the Data drop-down list, seen in Figure 9.25, shows similar data view options.

The *Static Data* option is ideal for double-checking any parent, base, or root class definition used to create a linked-list algorithm. Try to make a mental note of where these options are and how you invoke them. Remember, mastering the Debugger takes time; its raw horsepower can be overwhelming, but so too are the bugs that object-oriented programs generate!

ClassView References

The Base Classes and Members option is overkill when all you are interested in is locating *which* files reference a specific object. Figure 9.26 has the References option selected from the ClassView local menu (see earlier Figure 9.22) for the *child* class.

The Definitions and References window lists the selected object's name in the left pane and all of the files using this object in the right pane. Double-clicking on a filename auto-tracks the source file, inserting it into the Edit window.

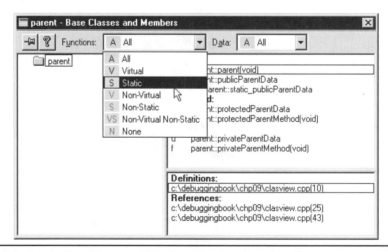

Figure 9.24   Selecting the Base Classes and Members Functions drop-down list

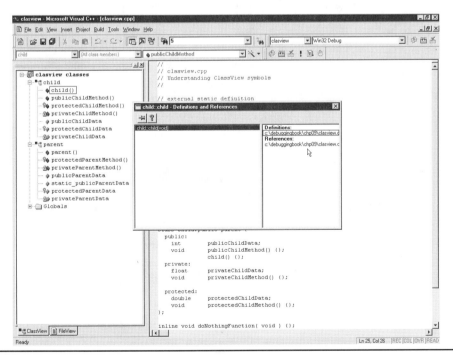

Figure 9.25   Selecting the Base Classes and Members Data drop-down list

Figure 9.26   *child* class references

ClassView-Derived Classes

One final local ClassView menu option, Derived Classes (see earlier Figure 9.22) allows you to see the inheritance between a base or parent class and its subclasses or children. Figure 9.27 shows this option activated for the *clasview.cpp*'s *parent* class.

The initial view shows the family tree in the left pane of the Derived Classes and Members view. Double-clicking on any subclasses—in this case, only one *child*—repaints the window's contents, displaying the information for the derived class, as seen in Figure 9.28.

Had the *child* class been used as a parent class to other subclasses, you could continue to repeat the previous steps and nest the window's contents down to the most nested descendent subclass.

Additional Local ClassView Menus

You will find two additional local ClassView menus useful when debugging object-oriented algorithms. The first one appears when you right-click the mouse on a ClassView class data member. Figure 9.29 shows the local ClassView menu selected for the *child* class *protectedChildData* member.

Notice that you have options to auto-track the Edit window's contents to the data member's definition file or to list all source files referencing the data member.

The second local ClassView menu you will find useful appears when you right-click on a class's method or member function names. Figure 9.30 shows this option being selected for the *parent* class *parent()* constructor.

Meaningful options here include auto-tracking the Edit window's contents to the method's owning source file and any files referencing the selected method, or setting a breakpoint on the selected method (the option highlighted in Figure 9.30). You can even use this local menu to find out which subroutines the selected method calls or which subroutines call the selected method.

Figure 9.27   *clasview.cpp*'s *parent* class Derived Classes and Members view

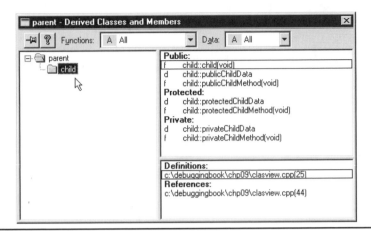

Figure 9.28   *clasview.cpp*'s *child* subclass Derived Classes and Members view

ClassView Member Properties

Whether you right-click the mouse on a ClassView data member or function member, both local menus have a Properties option. Selecting this option opens up a window that details the name and data types involved with the specific member. Figure 9.31 shows this option selected for the *static_publicParentData* member.

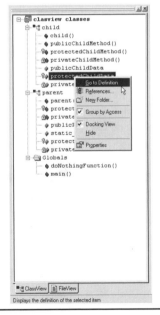

Figure 9.29   Local ClassView data member menu

Figure 9.30   Local ClassView member function menu

The Data Properties window displays the variable's name and its formal data type. Figure 9.32 selects the same local menu option, only this time for the *privateChildMethod()*.

The Function Properties window shows the name of the subroutine and its formal return type and formal argument list.

Adding Folders to ClassView

You can easily organize your project classes simply by adding a new folder to ClassView. The new folder can contain any classes belonging to the project. The new folder cannot contain nonclass files such as text or resource files. To organize other types of files, go to the related view—for example, FileView or ResourceView.

Figure 9.31   *static_publicParentData* Data Properties window

Figure 9.32   *privateChildMethod* Function Properties window

To add a folder to ClassView, you first point your cursor to the project to which you want to add a folder. Next, you right-click the mouse button and, from the shortcut menu, choose New Folder. You can nest folders under folders you create but not under a class.

Moving Classes Between Folders

Once you've created a new folder for a project, simply drag any classes you want into the folder to organize your project classes. Note that you cannot move classes from one project into a folder under a different project.

Hiding or Displaying ClassView

You may prefer to work with only a few views on a regular basis. You can customize your workspace by hiding one or more views. To hide or display ClassView, click the right mouse button with your mouse cursor pointed at a tab along the bottom edge of the Project Workspace. From the list of views, select or clear ClassView to toggle its display.

Debugging argc and argv[]

Many programmers are unaware of the two special ANSI C/C++ standard **main()** function arguments, **argc** and **argv[]**. These two **main()** arguments capture command-line arguments entered when the program is first executed. The following program, *argc_v.cpp*, demonstrates the necessary syntax for using *argc* and *argv[]* in an object-oriented environment:

```
//
// argc_v.cpp
// Debugging command-line arguments
//

#include <cmath>
#include <cstdlib>
#include <iostream>

using namespace std;
```

```
class sample {
  public:
    sample(int argc, char **argv);
};

sample::sample( int argc, char **argv )
{
  int iAccumulator = 0;

  if( argc == 1 ) {


    cout << "You only entered the program name.\n"
         << "The program will now exit.";
    exit( EXIT_FAILURE );
  }

  for( int offset = 1; offset < argc; offset++)  {
    cout << *++argv << endl;       // or argv[ offset ];
    iAccumulator += atoi( *argv );// or argv[ offset ];
  };

  cout << iAccumulator << endl;
}

void main( int argc, char *argv[] )
{
  sample ARGC_V( argc, argv );
}
```

The first statement of interest is the definition for the **main()** function:

```
void main( int argc, char *argv[])
```

argc contains the number of arguments entered from the command line, while *argv[]* is a one-dimensional array of character pointers to null-terminated string representations of the actual arguments. For example, to run the program *argc_v.cpp*, the user might type the following:

c:\argv_c 1 2 3 4 5 6

argv_c is the name of the program, and *1 2 3 4 5 6* are the arguments to the program, all entered on the command line. The problem with debugging a program using *argc* and *argv[]* is that you must run it from the command line to test the algorithm. This presents an interesting problem: namely, how do you stay *inside* Visual C++'s Debugger, while simultaneously starting a program from *outside* the Visual C++ Studio? The solution involves a little known option accessed through the Project | Settings window.

Figure 9.33 shows the beginning steps necessary to debug *argc* and *argv[]*. First, you select the Project | Settings menu (ALT+F7).

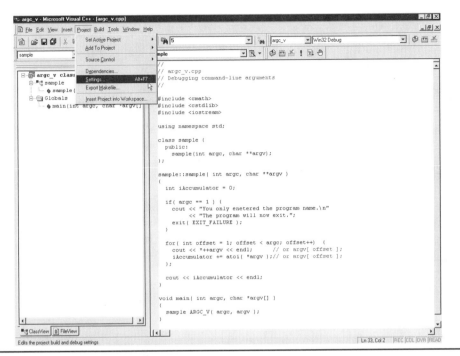

Figure 9.33   Setting up the Debugger for *argc* and *argv[]*

In the Project Settings window, you click on the Debug tab. The portion of this window of interest is titled "Program arguments." It is where you place the test argument values, or preconditions, which, for our example, are the integral values *1 2 3 4 5 6* (see Figure 9.34).

Error Watch   *When setting* argc *and* argv[] *preconditions in the Project Settings Program Arguments list, you do not need to enter the test program's filename.*

With the precondition arguments in place, you simply start the Debugger using whichever menu or hot-key combination you prefer. Figure 9.35 displays the results of a single press of the F10 (step over) key, followed by using the initial Variables window display of *argv*'s physical address, to auto-track the contents of the Memory window.

A close-up view of the Memory window, shown in Figure 9.36, shows all of the information referenced by the pointers stored in *argv[]*.

To understand the program, you need to know that *argc* is initialized to *7*. There is a count in *argc* for the string holding the name of the program, or *argv[0]*, followed by character representations (all *argv[]* pointed-to entries are stored as null '\0' terminated strings) for the integral values *1 2 3 4 5 6* in *argv[1]* to *argv[7]*.

For discussion purposes, the *argc_v.cpp* program uses alternate syntax to reference *argv* itself. For example, the second argument to **main**() is prototyped as *char *argv[]*, while the second argument to

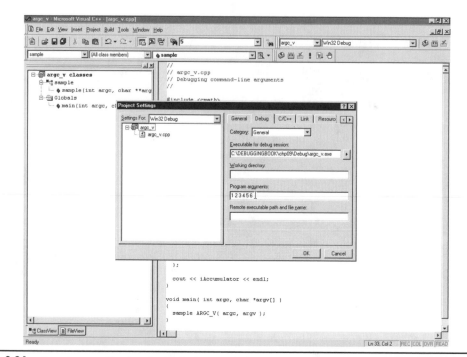

Figure 9.34   Entering *argv[]* values in the Project Settings | Debug tab

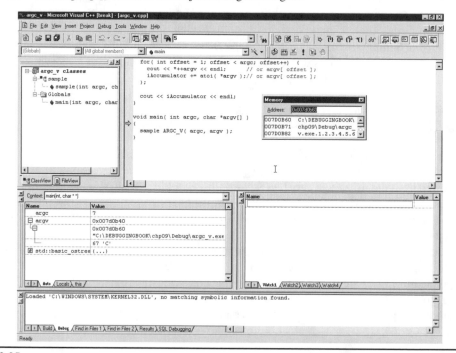

Figure 9.35   Using *argv[]*'s Variables window address to open the Memory window

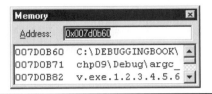

Figure 9.36   Close-up of the Memory window showing *argv[]*'s contents

the *sample* class constructor is prototyped as *char **argv*. Both logically represent the same data type; only the second form hides the fact that *argv* is actually an array of character pointers.

The *sample::sample* constructor begins by testing the value of *argc*, which, if *1*, means the user ran the program without any integral arguments. Since the remainder of the constructor's algorithm becomes meaningless without valid integral data, the program *exit()*s.

```
if( argc == 1 ) {

    cout << "You only entered the program name.\n"
        << "The program will now exit.";
    exit( EXIT_FAILURE );
}
```

The **for** loop shows how to use *argv* values with two types of syntax: pointer, as in **++argv* or **argv,* and the commented array syntax alternative of *argv[offset]*. Notice the unconventional **for** loop conditions used to access the array of pointers *argv*. Most **for** loops processing arrays begin with an offset address of *0*. However, the *0th* offset holds the pointer to the string containing the program name, not the first integral value. That is why *offset* is set equal to *1* not *0*.

```
for( int offset = 1; offset < argc; offset++)  {
    cout << *++argv << endl;      // or argv[ offset ];
    iAccumulator += atoi( *argv );// or argv[ offset ];
};
```

Finally, most **for** loops use a test condition of *offset < MAX*, which, in this example, is logically equivalent to *argc*'s count. If the algorithm used the commented-out syntax, you would want legal offsets of *1* to 7—in other words, a test condition of *offset <= argc*. So why doesn't the algorithm do this? Because of the first statement in the **for** loop:

```
    cout << *++argv << endl;      // or argv[ offset ];
```

The prefix increment operation *++argv* first moves the pointer past *argv*'s first address, the address to the program name, and makes it point to the first integral value of *1* before the dereference operator * takes effect. If you choose to use the commented-out array syntax for *argv*—namely, *argv[offset]*—you will have to change the **for** loop test condition from less than (<) to less than or equal to (<=). Otherwise, *iAccumulator*'s total will not include the *6*.

Finally, since all *argv* pointed to values are stored as null-terminated strings, you need to invoke the appropriate conversion routines in the case of numeric values. The example program makes a call to the function *atoi( )* or alpha-to-integer.

```
iAccumulator += atoi( *argv );// or argv[ offset ];
```

Microsoft Visual C++ has five conversion routines, *atof( )* for floating-point values, *atoi( )*, *_atoi64( )*, *atol( )*, and *atold( )*.

Conclusion

When a program solution moves from a straightforward procedural C/C++ solution to an object-oriented code design, there is an unavoidable increase in code complexity. Unfortunately, so too is there an increase in the complexity of your debug cycle. In this chapter, you discovered how Visual C++ stands ready to help you with additional debug commands, features, and advanced uses for previously discussed Debugger capabilities.

In the next chapter, you will learn how the Debugger handles MFC-encoded algorithms. MFC is Microsoft's recombination of standard Windows objects, designed to get a Windows application, up-and-running, as quickly as possible.

CHAPTER 10

Windows Programming with the Microsoft Foundation Class Library

Most Windows programmers have cut their teeth on procedure-oriented Windows code, such as that found in Chapter 8 of this book. The shortcomings of the procedure-oriented environment become more apparent as project size increases and the number of resources added to the application also increases. While there was a time when Windows programmers once happily resided in both camps, today we doubt that any serious code development is being done in the procedure-oriented environment for projects that include the use of DLLs, ActiveX, COM, and even the integration of STL into Windows projects.

For the type of applications just mentioned, and others not even thought of yet, you need the power of reusable classes—you need the power of the Microsoft Foundation Class (MFC) library. Packaged with the MFC are powerful development and debugging tools, including the Application Wizard and Class Wizard. The MFC library encapsulates all normal procedure-oriented windows functions and provides support for control bars, property sheets, OLEO, ActiveX controls, and more. In addition, database support is provided for a wide range of database sources including DAO and ODBC.

This chapter will serve as a primer for MFC code development and will highlight the important concepts of object-oriented Windows development with various Visual C++ tools. We'll make the assumption that you are well grounded in object-oriented design techniques, feel comfortable with the material presented in Chapter 9, and have a working familiarity with the MFC. Osborne/McGraw-Hill's *Visual C++: The Complete Reference* by Chris H. Pappas and William H. Murray can serve as a speedy refresher course if you haven't programmed with the MFC for a while.

Why Use a Class Library?

The MFC library provides programmers with easy-to-use objects. Even procedure-oriented Windows programming has followed many principles of good object-oriented programming design, within the framework of a non-object-oriented language like C. The combination of C++ and Windows programming was a natural that can take full advantage of object-oriented features. The MFC provides a comprehensive implementation of the Windows Application Program Interface (API). This C++ library encapsulates the most important data structures and API function calls within a group of reusable classes.

Class libraries, such as the MFC, offer many advantages over the traditional function libraries used by C programmers.

Design Tip   *The inclusion of MFC library code into Windows projects adds:*

- *Elimination of function and variable name collisions*
- *Encapsulation of code and data within the class*
- *Inheritance*
- *Reduced code size resulting from well-designed class libraries*
- *Resulting classes appear to be natural extensions of the language*

In basic programs using the MFC library, the code required to establish a window can be reduced from 100 to as few as 30 lines.

Most class libraries are designed with a hierarchy of classes—child classes derived from parent classes and so on. In the next section, we'll examine some of the fundamental MFC classes.

A True Foundation Class—CObject

CObject is an important MFC parent class used extensively in developing Windows applications. The MFC library header files, typically located in the mfc/include subdirectory, contain a wealth of information on MFC defined classes.

Let's take a brief look at an edited version of **CObject** that is defined in the afx.h header file.

```
//////////////////////////////////////////////////////////////
// class CObject is the root of all compliant objects

class CObject
{
public:

// Object model (types, destruction, allocation)
  virtual CRuntimeClass* GetRuntimeClass() const;
  virtual ~CObject();  // virtual destructors are necessary

  // Diagnostic allocations
  void* PASCAL operator new(size_t nSize);
  void* PASCAL operator new(size_t, void* p);
  void PASCAL operator delete(void* p);

#if defined(_DEBUG) && !defined(_AFX_NO_DEBUG_CRT)
  // for file name/line number tracking using DEBUG_NEW
  void* PASCAL operator new(size_t nSize,
                          LPCSTR lpszFileName,
                          int nLine);
#endif

// Disable the copy constructor and assignment by default
// so you will get compiler errors instead of unexpected
// behavior if you pass objects by value or assign objects.

protected:
  CObject();
private:
  CObject(const CObject& objectSrc);     //no implementation
  void operator=(const CObject& objectSrc);

// Attributes
public:
  BOOL IsSerializable() const;
```

```
  BOOL IsKindOf(const CRuntimeClass* pClass) const;

// Overridables
  virtual void Serialize(CArchive& ar);

  // Diagnostic Support
  virtual void AssertValid() const;
  virtual void Dump(CDumpContext& dc) const;

// Implementation
public:
  static const AFX_DATA CRuntimeClass classCObject;
#ifdef _AFXDLL
  static CRuntimeClass* PASCAL _GetBaseClass();
#endif
};
```

We've modified this code slightly for clarity, but it is essentially the same code you find when inspecting the header file.

Carefully examine this listing and note that **CObject** is divided into public, protected, and private parts. **CObject** also provides normal and dynamic type checking and serialization. Dynamic type checking allows the type of object to be determined at runtime. The state of the object can be saved to a storage medium, such as a disk, through a concept called persistence. Object persistence allows object member functions to also be persistent, permitting retrieval of object data.

Child classes are derived from MFC parent classes. For example, the **CGdiObject** class is derived from the **CObject** parent class. In the next listing, examine the **CGdiObject** definition as found in afxwin.h.

```
/////////////////////////////////////////////////////////////
// CGdiObject abstract class for CDC SelectObject

class CGdiObject : public CObject
{
  DECLARE_DYNCREATE(CGdiObject)
public:

// Attributes
  HGDIOBJ m_hObject;  // must be first data member
  operator HGDIOBJ() const;
  HGDIOBJ GetSafeHandle() const;

  static CGdiObject* PASCAL FromHandle(HGDIOBJ hObject);
  static void PASCAL DeleteTempMap();
  BOOL Attach(HGDIOBJ hObject);
  HGDIOBJ Detach();

// Constructors
  CGdiObject(); // must create a derived class object
  BOOL DeleteObject();
```

```
// Operations
  int GetObject(int nCount, LPVOID lpObject) const;
  UINT GetObjectType() const;
  BOOL CreateStockObject(int nIndex);
  BOOL UnrealizeObject();
  BOOL operator==(const CGdiObject& obj) const;
  BOOL operator!=(const CGdiObject& obj) const;

// Implementation
public:
  virtual ~CGdiObject();
#ifdef _DEBUG
  virtual void Dump(CDumpContext& dc) const;
  virtual void AssertValid() const;
#endif
};
```

Notice that the **CGdiObject** class and its methods (member functions) allow drawing items such as stock and custom pens, brushes, and fonts to be created and used in a Windows application. Classes such as the CPen and CBrush are further derived from the CGdiObject class.

Switching between many procedure-oriented Windows function calls and their equivalent class library objects can be intuitive. For example, in traditional procedure-oriented Windows applications, the **DeleteObject**() function is called with the following syntax:

```
DeleteObject(hPen);        /*hPen is the pen handle*/
```

In object-oriented applications, the same results can be achieved by accessing the member function with the following syntax:

```
newpen.DeleteObject();   //newpen is current pen
```

Microsoft has used this basic approach in developing all Windows classes, making the transition from traditional procedure-oriented function calls to MFC library objects easy. You'll see a large amount of code, in the sample application used in this chapter, that you are already familiar with as a result of your experience with procedure-oriented coding.

What Are Application and Class Wizards?

Microsoft provides a dynamic code template generator called the *AppWizard*. The AppWizard depends heavily on the MFC and generates object-oriented code. To create a project with the AppWizard, select the File I New menu option in the Visual C++ Compiler. Then select MFC AppWizard from the list of options. The AppWizard generates a code template that will allow you to select only those features you need for your application.

A close relative of the AppWizard is the ClassWizard. The ClassWizard can be used to add classes or customize existing classes. The ClassWizard is used only after the AppWizard creates the template code. Use the View menu and select the ClassWizard menu item in order to start the ClassWizard.

In the following section, you'll learn the fundamentals required to employ both wizards during program creation. The graphics application will use the bare minimum AppWizard code to create a project with a client area that contains simple graphics shapes.

A Graph Application

All of the steps necessary to create a basic application using the AppWizard and ClassWizard will be discussed in this section. Using the AppWizard requires completing certain specific steps in a specific order. The steps, discussed here, will take you through the development of code that will be used to create the first program, named graph.

Start your Visual C++ compiler and complete the steps along with us as we create the Graph application.

Using the AppWizard

Use the Visual C++ menu bar to select the File | New menu item. A dialog box will appear, as shown in Figure 10.1, which allows you to start a new project by selecting the MFC AppWizard (exe) option.

The new project should be named graph, as illustrated in Figure 10.1. After naming the project, start the development cycle using the AppWizard. Examine Figure 10.1 to note the project location selected for this project. Next, simply click on OK to start the AppWizard.

The AppWizard's first step in generating a project involves making a decision about whether the project will handle single, multiple, or dialog-based documents, as shown in Figure 10.2.

Single-document interfaces are the simplest and multiple-document communications will not be required for this example. Make sure the Document/View architecture support option is checked. Accept the default for the resource language option. Click on the Next button to start Step 2, shown in Figure 10.3.

Step 2 is used only when you want to include database support. This project will not require database support so select None and then click on the Next button to start Step 3, shown in Figure 10.4.

Step 3 allows the selection of OLE support with containers or servers. For this example, OLE support is not needed so select None. Uncheck the ActiveX Controls checkbox, also. Click on the Next button to start Step 4, shown in Figure 10.5.

Step 4 gives you the opportunity to add special features to the project. For example, a toolbar or status bar could be added at this point. In this project, no special features are needed. Click on the Next button to start Step 5, shown in Figure 10.6.

Select the options shown in Figure 10.6 for Step 5. Now, click the Next button to start Step 6, shown in Figure 10.7.

Step 6 is the last step used to specify project features. A listing is provided showing the new classes that the AppWizard will automatically generate. The four classes created for this application are CGraphApp, CMainFrame, CGraphDoc, and CGraphView.

Select CGraphView from the listbox, shown in Figure 10.7. The Base Class listbox expands, allowing the CGraphView class to be derived from the CEditView, CFormView, CScrollView, or CView base class.

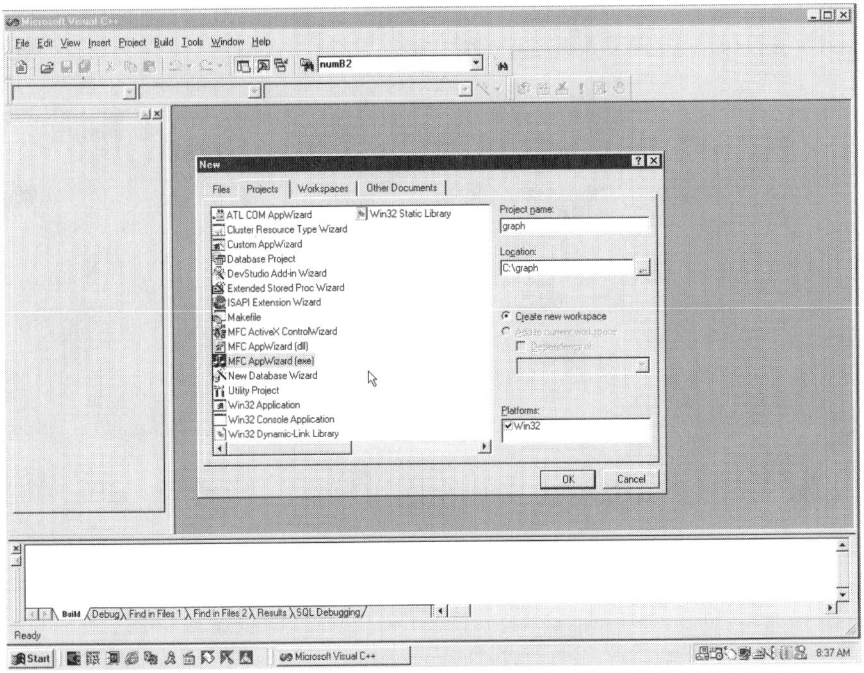

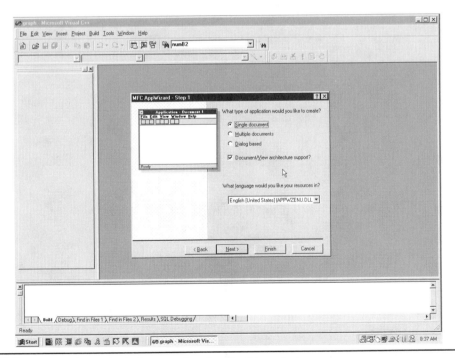

Figure 10.1   The File | New menu item provides access to the MFC AppWizard for a new project

Figure 10.2   Step 1—Use a single-document interface for this project

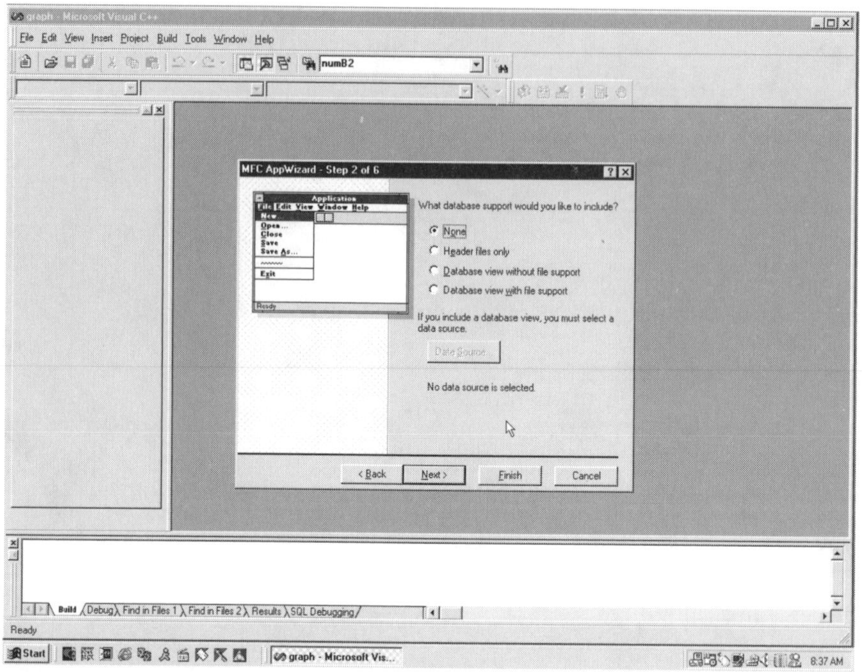

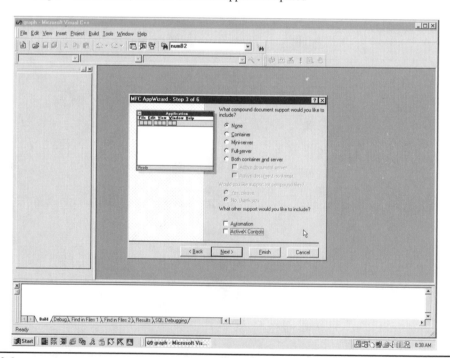

Figure 10.3 Step 2—Select None, since no database support is required

Figure 10.4 Step 3—Compound document support is not needed for the project

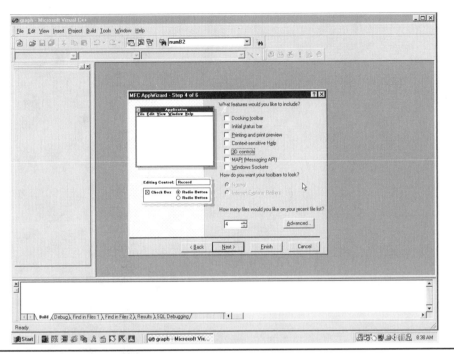

Figure 10.5   Step 4—Permits additional special features to be added to the project

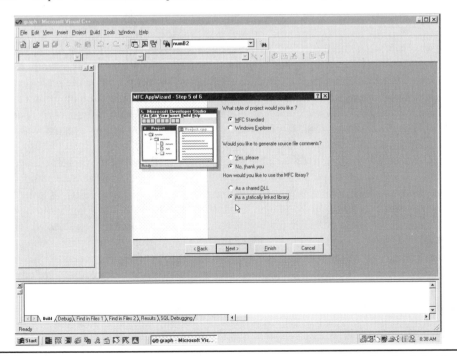

Figure 10.6   Step 5—Determines the MFC project type. Source comments can be included and also the identification of the MFC library

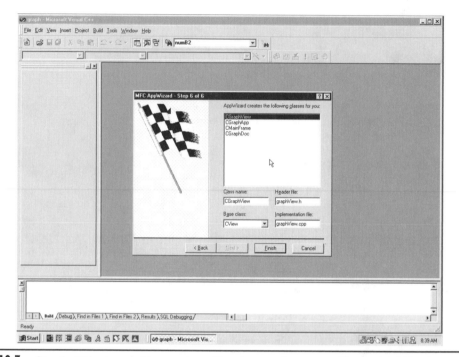

Figure 10.7   Step 6—This step provides a review of the classes to be generated by the AppWizard

The CView class is derived from the CWnd class and is used to create the base for user-defined view classes. A *view* serves as a buffer between the document and the user and is actually a child of a frame window. View classes are used to produce an image of the document on the screen or on the printer. These classes use input from the keyboard or the mouse as an operation on the document.

The CFormView and CEditView classes are also derived from the CView base class. The CFormView class describes a scrollable view that is based on a dialog template resource and includes dialog box controls. The CEditView class describes a text editor.

This project will use the CView class as the base class. Actually, all of the default classes shown in the Base Class listbox are acceptable for this project. Click the mouse on the Finish button to see a description summary of what the AppWizard will create for the project. Figure 10.8 shows this descriptive summary.

The information displayed in this dialog box is a summary of the options you selected for the project. This box offers you one last chance to make alterations before the template code is generated. When you are satisfied with the options, click the OK button to generate the code.

The AppWizard will generate numerous files and store them in the subdirectory given during the first step of the project's creation.

Once the AppWizard generates the template code, you can add additional features to the project code by selecting ClassWizard using the View | ClassWizard menu item, as shown in Figure 10.9.

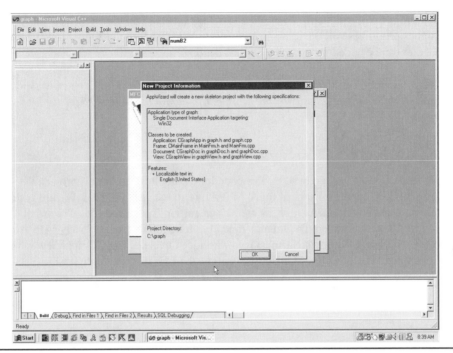

Figure 10.8   The AppWizard provides a summary of what will be created for the project

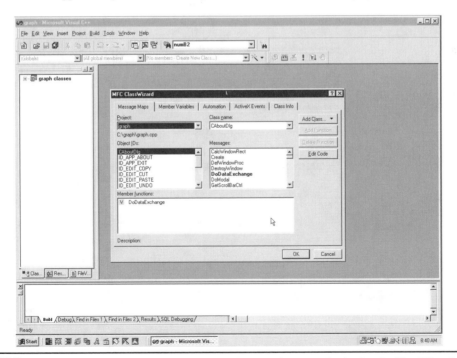

Figure 10.9   The template code generated by the AppWizard can be customized using the ClassWizard

The graph project will eventually draw some simple graphics in the client area. In this project, various graphics primitives will be drawn in response to WM_PAINT messages. The WM_PAINT message handler can be added by using the ClassWizard.

Design Tip *Many GDI graphics primitives can be added to the OnDraw() member function that is added automatically by the AppWizard, eliminating the need for the OnPaint() member function.*

Using the ClassWizard

The ClassWizard is used to generate additional code for the application. In this project, the ClassWizard will add support for processing WM_PAINT messages. The ClassWizard is selected by using the View | ClassWizard menu item, as mentioned earlier. The initial ClassWizard dialog box, shown in Figure 10.10, has added the OnPaint() member function to process WM_PAINT messages.

Support for processing WM_PAINT messages was added by selecting CGraphView in the Class Name text entry box. Then, from the Object IDs listbox, the CGraphView option was selected, as shown in Figure 10.10.

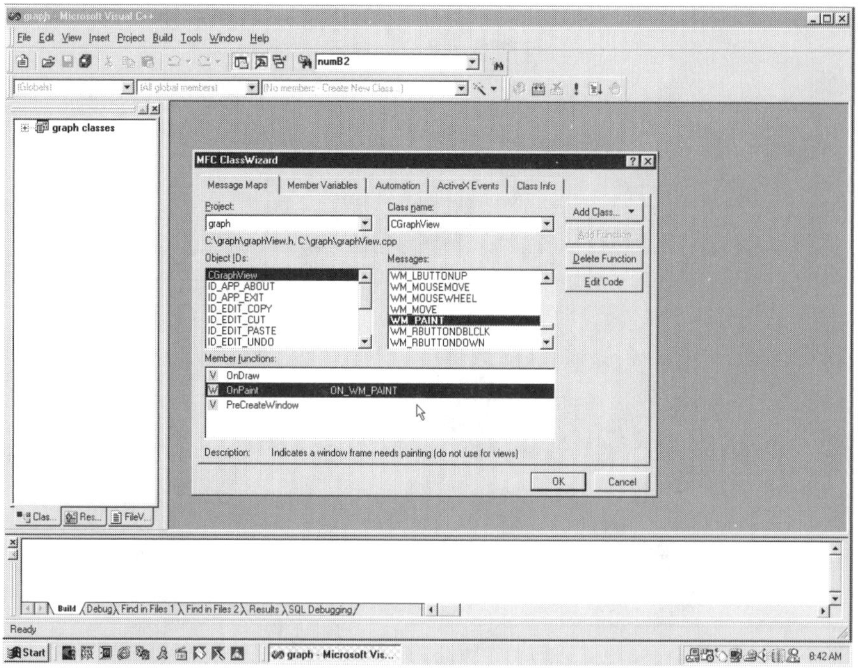

Figure 10.10   The initial ClassWizard dialog box

When CGraphView is selected from the list, a large number of Windows messages are shown in the Messages listbox. The OnPaint() member function will be shown in the Member Functions list when WM_PAINT is selected from this list.

The graphView.cpp will now contain this inserted code, as shown in Figure 10.11.

It is possible to add various graphics functions to this member function code to make this application complete. We'll show you how this is done a little later in this chapter. The next step is to compile and test the AppWizard template code.

Building the AppWizard Code

When you have added all of the message handlers you desire, such as those for WM_PAINT, to the program's code with the ClassWizard, the application can be built. To do this, use the Build | Rebuild All menu item.

During this build process, four source code files—graph.cpp, mainfrm.cpp, graphicdoc.cpp, and graphicview.cpp—are compiled and linked. When compilation is complete, examine the subdirectory in which these files are stored; you'll see more than 30 files stored there, including their associated header files.

An executable file is also present in the project's Debug subdirectory. Execute the project. The initial screen is empty because no graphics functions have been added at this point. There is a basic

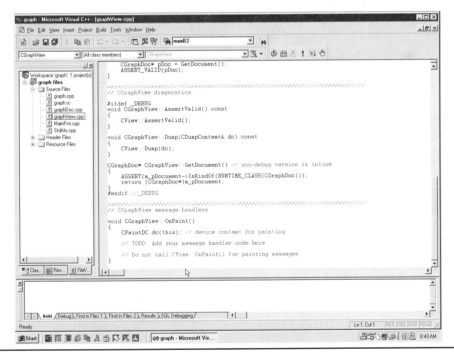

Figure 10.11   The basic OnPaint() member function added to the project

menu, but most of the menu items are not functional. This is because the code for processing these menu items must be added by you.

> **Design Tip** *Remove menu items that are not implemented in your project but were added by the AppWizard by using the Resource Editor. This makes for a neater finished project.*

The AppWizard's Template Code

The AppWizard, with a little help from the ClassWizard, generated four important C++ files for the initial graph application. These files were named graph.cpp, mainfrm.cpp, graphdoc.cpp, and graphview.cpp. Each of these C++ files has an associated header file: graph.h, mainfrm.h, graphdoc.h, and graphview.h. These header files contain the declarations of the specific classes in each C++ file. A short discussion of the purpose of each C++ file will be examined in the following sections.

The graph.cpp File

The graph.cpp file, shown next, serves as the main file for the application. It contains the CGraphApp class.

```
// graph.cpp : Defines class behaviors for the application.
//

#include "stdafx.h"
#include "graph.h7"

#include "MainFrm.h"
#include "graphDoc.h"
#include "graphView.h"

#ifdef _DEBUG
#define new DEBUG_NEW
#undef THIS_FILE
static char THIS_FILE[] = __FILE__;
#endif

/////////////////////////////////////////////////////////////////
// CGraphApp

BEGIN_MESSAGE_MAP(CGraphApp, CWinApp)
  //{{AFX_MSG_MAP(CGraphApp)
  ON_COMMAND(ID_APP_ABOUT, OnAppAbout)
    // NOTE - the ClassWizard will add and remove mapping
    // macros here.
    //    DO NOT EDIT what you see in these blocks of
    // generated code!
  //}}AFX_MSG_MAP
  // Standard file based document commands
  ON_COMMAND(ID_FILE_NEW, CWinApp::OnFileNew)
```

```
  ON_COMMAND(ID_FILE_OPEN, CWinApp::OnFileOpen)
END_MESSAGE_MAP()

/////////////////////////////////////////////////////////////
// CGraphApp construction

CGraphApp::CGraphApp()
{
  // TODO: add construction code here,
  // Place all significant initialization in InitInstance
}

/////////////////////////////////////////////////////////////
// The one and only CGraphApp object

CGraphApp theApp;

/////////////////////////////////////////////////////////////
// CGraphApp initialization

BOOL CGraphApp::InitInstance()
{
  // Standard initialization
  // If you are not using these features and wish to reduce
  // the size of your final executable, you should remove
  // from the following the specific initialization routines
  // you do not need.

  // Change the registry key under which our settings are
  // stored.  You should modify this string to be something
  // appropriate  such as the name of your company or
  // organization.
  SetRegistryKey(_T("Local AppWizard-Generated Applications"));

  LoadStdProfileSettings();  // Load INI file options
                             // (including MRU)

  // Register the application's document templates.  Document
  // templates  serve as the connection between documents,
  // frame windows and views.

  CSingleDocTemplate* pDocTemplate;
  pDocTemplate = new CSingleDocTemplate(
    IDR_MAINFRAME,
    RUNTIME_CLASS(CGraphDoc),
    RUNTIME_CLASS(CMainFrame),          // main SDI frame window
    RUNTIME_CLASS(CGraphView));
  AddDocTemplate(pDocTemplate);

  // Parse command line for shell commands, DDE, file open
  CCommandLineInfo cmdInfo;
```

```
    ParseCommandLine(cmdInfo);

    // Dispatch commands specified on the command line
    if (!ProcessShellCommand(cmdInfo))
      return FALSE;

    // The one and only window is initialized - show and update.
    m_pMainWnd->ShowWindow(SW_SHOW);
    m_pMainWnd->UpdateWindow();

    return TRUE;
}


/////////////////////////////////////////////////////////////////
// CAboutDlg dialog used for App About

class CAboutDlg : public CDialog
{
public:
  CAboutDlg();

// Dialog Data
  //{{AFX_DATA(CAboutDlg)
  enum { IDD = IDD_ABOUTBOX };
  //}}AFX_DATA

  // ClassWizard generated virtual function overrides
  //{{AFX_VIRTUAL(CAboutDlg)
  protected:
  virtual void DoDataExchange(CDataExchange* pDX);
  //}}AFX_VIRTUAL

// Implementation
protected:
  //{{AFX_MSG(CAboutDlg)
  // No message handlers
  //}}AFX_MSG
  DECLARE_MESSAGE_MAP()
};

CAboutDlg::CAboutDlg() : CDialog(CAboutDlg::IDD)
{
  //{{AFX_DATA_INIT(CAboutDlg)
  //}}AFX_DATA_INIT
}

void CAboutDlg::DoDataExchange(CDataExchange* pDX)
{
  CDialog::DoDataExchange(pDX);
  //{{AFX_DATA_MAP(CAboutDlg)
```

```
  //}}AFX_DATA_MAP
}

BEGIN_MESSAGE_MAP(CAboutDlg, CDialog)
  //{{AFX_MSG_MAP(CAboutDlg)
  //}}AFX_MSG_MAP
END_MESSAGE_MAP()

// App command to run the dialog
void CGraphApp::OnAppAbout()
{
  CAboutDlg aboutDlg;
  aboutDlg.DoModal();
}


//////////////////////////////////////////////////////////////
// CGraphApp commands
```

The message map, near the top of the listing, belongs to the CGraphApp class. This message map specifically links the ID_APP_ABOUT, ID_FILE_NEW, and ID_FILE_OPEN messages with their member functions: OnAppAbout(), CWinApp::OnFileNew(), and CWinApp::OnFileOpen(). Also notice in the listing that a constructor, an initial instance InitInstance(), and a member function OnAppAbout() are implemented.

The About dialog box is derived from the CDialog class. If you examine the lower portion of the code, you will notice a message map, a constructor, and a member function CDialog::DoDataExchange() for this derived dialog class.

There are no initial CGraphApp commands, as you can see from the end of the listing.

The mainfrm.cpp File

The mainfrm.cpp file, shown next, contains the frame class CMainFrame. This class is derived from CFrameWnd and is used to control all single-document interface (SDI) frame features.

```
// MainFrm.cpp : implementation of the CMainFrame class
//

#include "stdafx.h"
#include "graph.h"

#include "MainFrm.h"

#ifdef _DEBUG
#define new DEBUG_NEW
#undef THIS_FILE
static char THIS_FILE[] = __FILE__;
#endif

//////////////////////////////////////////////////////////////
// CMainFrame
```

```
IMPLEMENT_DYNCREATE(CMainFrame, CFrameWnd)

BEGIN_MESSAGE_MAP(CMainFrame, CFrameWnd)
  //{{AFX_MSG_MAP(CMainFrame)
    // NOTE - the ClassWizard will add and remove mapping
    // macros here.
    //     DO NOT EDIT what you see in these blocks of
    // generated code !
  //}}AFX_MSG_MAP
END_MESSAGE_MAP()

/////////////////////////////////////////////////////////
// CMainFrame construction/destruction

CMainFrame::CMainFrame()
{
  // TODO: add member initialization code here

}

CMainFrame::~CMainFrame()
{
}

BOOL CMainFrame::PreCreateWindow(CREATESTRUCT& cs)
{
  if( !CFrameWnd::PreCreateWindow(cs) )
    return FALSE;
  // TODO: Modify the Window class or styles here by modifying
  //   the CREATESTRUCT cs

  return TRUE;
}

/////////////////////////////////////////////////////////
// CMainFrame diagnostics

#ifdef _DEBUG
void CMainFrame::AssertValid() const
{
  CFrameWnd::AssertValid();
}

void CMainFrame::Dump(CDumpContext& dc) const
{
  CFrameWnd::Dump(dc);
}

#endif //_DEBUG
```

```
/////////////////////////////////////////////////////////////
// CMainFrame message handlers
```

The message map, constructor, and destructor initially contain no code. The member functions AssertValid() and Dump() use definitions contained in the parent class. Also note that CMainFrame initially contains no message handlers.

The graphicdoc.cpp File

The graphicdoc.cpp file, shown here, contains the CGraphDoc class, which is unique to this application. This file is used to hold document data and to load and save files.

```
// GraphDoc.cpp : implementation of the CGraphDoc class
//

#include "stdafx.h"
#include "graph.h"

#include "graphDoc.h"

#ifdef _DEBUG
#define new DEBUG_NEW
#undef THIS_FILE
static char THIS_FILE[] = __FILE__;
#endif

/////////////////////////////////////////////////////////////
// CGraphDoc

IMPLEMENT_DYNCREATE(CGraphDoc, CDocument)

BEGIN_MESSAGE_MAP(CGraphDoc, CDocument)
  //{{AFX_MSG_MAP(CGraphDoc)
    // NOTE - add and remove mapping macros here.
    //    DO NOT EDIT these blocks of generated code!
  //}}AFX_MSG_MAP
END_MESSAGE_MAP()

/////////////////////////////////////////////////////////////
// CGraphDoc construction/destruction

CGraphDoc::CGraphDoc()
{
  // TODO: add one-time construction code here

}

CGraphDoc::~CGraphDoc()
{
}
```

```
BOOL CGraphDoc::OnNewDocument()
{
  if (!CDocument::OnNewDocument())
    return FALSE;

  // TODO: add reinitialization code here
  // (SDI documents will reuse this document)

  return TRUE;
}




/////////////////////////////////////////////////////////////////
// CGraphDoc serialization

void CGraphDoc::Serialize(CArchive& ar)
{
  if (ar.IsStoring())
  {
    // TODO: add storing code here
  }
  else
  {
    // TODO: add loading code here
  }
}

/////////////////////////////////////////////////////////////////
// CGraphDoc diagnostics

#ifdef _DEBUG
void CGraphDoc::AssertValid() const
{
  CDocument::AssertValid();
}

void CGraphDoc::Dump(CDumpContext& dc) const
{
  CDocument::Dump(dc);
}
#endif //_DEBUG

/////////////////////////////////////////////////////////////////
// CGraphDoc commands
```

As you examine this listing, notice that the message map, constructor, and destructor contain no code. Four member functions can be used to provide vital document support. The OnNewDocument() member function uses the definition provided by the parent class. The Serialize() member function supports persistent objects. Our second programming example will use this member function to help with file I/O. The member functions AssertValid() and Dump() use definitions contained in the parent class. There are no initial CGraphDoc commands.

The graphview.cpp File

The graphview.cpp file, shown here, provides the view of the document. In this implementation, CGraphView is derived from the CView class. The CGraphView objects are used to view CGraphDoc objects.

```cpp
// GraphView.cpp : implementation of the CGraphView class
//

#include "stdafx.h"
#include "graph.h"

#include "graphDoc.h"
#include "graphView.h"

#ifdef _DEBUG
#define new DEBUG_NEW
#undef THIS_FILE
static char THIS_FILE[] = __FILE__;
#endif


/////////////////////////////////////////////////////////////////
// CGraphView

IMPLEMENT_DYNCREATE(CGraphView, CView)

BEGIN_MESSAGE_MAP(CGraphView, CView)
  //{{AFX_MSG_MAP(CGraphView)
  ON_WM_PAINT()
  //}}AFX_MSG_MAP
END_MESSAGE_MAP()

/////////////////////////////////////////////////////////////////
// CGraphView construction/destruction

CGraphView::CGraphView()
{
  // TODO: add construction code here

}

CGraphView::~CGraphView()
{
}

BOOL CGraphView::PreCreateWindow(CREATESTRUCT& cs)
{
```

```cpp
    // TODO: Modify the Window class / styles here by modifying
    //   the CREATESTRUCT cs

    return CView::PreCreateWindow(cs);
}

/////////////////////////////////////////////////////////////
// CGraphView drawing

void CGraphView::OnDraw(CDC* pDC)
{
    CGraphDoc* pDoc = GetDocument();
    ASSERT_VALID(pDoc);

    // TODO: add draw code for native data here
}

/////////////////////////////////////////////////////////////
// CGraphView diagnostics

#ifdef _DEBUG
void CGraphView::AssertValid() const
{
    CView::AssertValid();
}

void CGraphView::Dump(CDumpContext& dc) const
{
    CView::Dump(dc);
}

CGraphDoc* CGraphView::GetDocument() // non-debug version
{
    ASSERT(m_pDocument->IsKindOf(RUNTIME_CLASS(CGraphDoc)));
    return (CGraphDoc*)m_pDocument;
}
#endif //_DEBUG

/////////////////////////////////////////////////////////////
// CGraphView message handlers

void CGraphView::OnPaint()
{
    CPaintDC dc(this); // device context for painting

    // TODO: Add your message handler code here

    // Do not call CView::OnPaint() for painting messages
}
```

If we had just used the AppWizard to generate this code, the message map would be empty. However, recall that the ClassWizard was used to add WM_PAINT message-handling abilities. The constructor and destructor are empty.

The OnDraw() member function uses the pointer pDoc to point to the document. The member functions AssertValid() and Dump() use definitions contained in the parent class. The message handler, OnPaint(), is described at the end of this listing. Simple graphics primitives, such as those drawn with LineTo(), Rectangle(), and Ellipse() functions, can be inserted here.

Error Watch *Be careful when moving GDI functions back and forth between OnDraw() and OnPaint() member functions. The syntax differs slightly for these function calls due to the way the method was implemented. For example, under OnPaint(), the Rectangle() function might be called by writing:*

```
dc.Rectangle(10, 20, 40, 80);
```

Under the OnDraw() member function, the same function could be called using the following:

```
pdc->Rectangle(10, 20, 40, 80);
```

Graphics Objects in the Client Area

During the development of this project, a single-document interface (SDI) application was created using the AppWizard and the ClassWizard. The view class was derived from the parent class, CView. Here the ClassWizard added the WM_PAINT message handler to the basic AppWizard template code.

The OnPaint() method is the perfect location from which to draw simple graphics objects to the client area. You'll see that this requires little additional coding. The following listing shows the OnPaint() method, from the graph project, with additional graphics code added.

```
void CGraphView::OnPaint()
{
    CPaintDC dc(this); // device context for painting

    // TODO: Add your message handler code here
    // Do not call CView::OnPaint() for painting messages

    static DWORD dwColor[9]={RGB(0,0,0),          //black
                             RGB(255,0,0),        //red
                             RGB(0,255,0),        //green
                             RGB(0,0,255),        //blue
                             RGB(255,255,0),      //yellow
                             RGB(255,0,255),      //magenta
                             RGB(0,255,255),      //cyan
                             RGB(127,127,127),    //gray
                             RGB(255,255,255)};   //white

    POINT polylpts[4],polygpts[5];
    int xcoord;
```

```
CBrush newbrush;
CBrush* oldbrush;
CPen newpen;
CPen* oldpen;

// draws and fills a circle
newpen.CreatePen(PS_SOLID,2,dwColor[3]);
oldpen=dc.SelectObject(&newpen);
newbrush.CreateSolidBrush(dwColor[3]);
oldbrush=dc.SelectObject(&newbrush);
dc.Ellipse(400,20,650,270);
dc.TextOut(500,150,"circle",6);
dc.SelectObject(oldbrush);
newbrush.DeleteObject( );
dc.SelectObject(oldpen);
newpen.DeleteObject( );

// draws and fills an ellipse
newpen.CreatePen(PS_SOLID,2,dwColor[1]);
oldpen=dc.SelectObject(&newpen);
newbrush.CreateSolidBrush(dwColor[1]);
oldbrush=dc.SelectObject(&newbrush);
dc.Ellipse(325,300,425,250);
dc.TextOut(260,265,"ellipse",7);
dc.SelectObject(oldbrush);
newbrush.DeleteObject( );
dc.SelectObject(oldpen);
newpen.DeleteObject( );

// draws several pixels
for(xcoord=500;xcoord<600;xcoord+=5)
  dc.SetPixel(xcoord,400,0L);
dc.TextOut(540,410,"pixels",6);

// draws a wide diagonal line
newpen.CreatePen(PS_SOLID,10,dwColor[0]);
oldpen=dc.SelectObject(&newpen);
dc.MoveTo(20,20);
dc.LineTo(100,100);
dc.TextOut(60,20,"<- diagonal line",16);
dc.SelectObject(oldpen);
newpen.DeleteObject( );

// draws an arc
newpen.CreatePen(PS_DASH,1,dwColor[3]);
oldpen=dc.SelectObject(&newpen);
dc.Arc(25,125,175,225,175,225,100,125);
dc.TextOut(50,150,"small arc ->",12);
dc.SelectObject(oldpen);
newpen.DeleteObject( );
```

```
// draws a wide chord
newpen.CreatePen(PS_SOLID,10,dwColor[2]);
oldpen=dc.SelectObject(&newpen);
dc.Chord(125,125,275,225,275,225,200,125);
dc.TextOut(280,150,"<- chord",8);
dc.SelectObject(oldpen);
newpen.DeleteObject( );

// draws a pie slice and fills
newpen.CreatePen(PS_SOLID,2,dwColor[0]);
oldpen=dc.SelectObject(&newpen);
newbrush.CreateSolidBrush(dwColor[2]);
oldbrush=dc.SelectObject(&newbrush);
dc.Pie(200,0,300,100,200,50,250,100);
dc.TextOut(260,80,"<- pie wedge",12);
dc.SelectObject(oldbrush);
newbrush.DeleteObject( );
dc.SelectObject(oldpen);
newpen.DeleteObject( );

// draws a rectangle and fills
newbrush.CreateSolidBrush(dwColor[7]);
oldbrush=dc.SelectObject(&newbrush);
dc.Rectangle(25,350,150,425);
dc.TextOut(50,440,"rectangle",9);
dc.SelectObject(oldbrush);
newbrush.DeleteObject( );

// draws a rounded rectangle and fills
newbrush.CreateHatchBrush(HS_CROSS,dwColor[3]);
oldbrush=dc.SelectObject(&newbrush);
dc.RoundRect(400,320,550,360,20,20);
dc.TextOut(410,300,"rounded rectangle",17);
dc.SelectObject(oldbrush);
newbrush.DeleteObject( );

// draws a wide polygon and fills
newpen.CreatePen(PS_SOLID,5,dwColor[6]);
oldpen=dc.SelectObject(&newpen);
newbrush.CreateHatchBrush(HS_FDIAGONAL,dwColor[4]);
oldbrush=dc.SelectObject(&newbrush);
polygpts[0].x=40;
polygpts[0].y=200;
polygpts[1].x=100;
polygpts[1].y=270;
polygpts[2].x=80;
polygpts[2].y=290;
polygpts[3].x=20;
polygpts[3].y=220;
polygpts[4].x=40;
polygpts[4].y=200;
```

```
dc.Polygon(polygpts,5);
dc.TextOut(80,230,"<- polygon",10);
dc.SelectObject(oldbrush);
newbrush.DeleteObject( );
dc.SelectObject(oldpen);
newpen.DeleteObject( );

// draws several wide lines with polyline
newpen.CreatePen(PS_SOLID,4,dwColor[5]);
oldpen=dc.SelectObject(&newpen);
polylpts[0].x=210;
polylpts[0].y=330;
polylpts[1].x=210;
polylpts[1].y=400;
polylpts[2].x=250;
polylpts[2].y=400;
polylpts[3].x=210;
polylpts[3].y=330;
dc.Polyline(polylpts,4);
dc.TextOut(250,350,"polyline",8);
dc.SelectObject(oldpen);
newpen.DeleteObject( );
}
```

If you are a seasoned Windows programmer, most of these GDI graphics drawing primitives should be familiar to you. Compile and execute the graph project once again with this added code. Your screen should be similar to the one shown in Figure 10.12.

The AppWizard generated a template with a menu bar containing the File, Edit, and Help menus, along with the various graphics shapes. Any unimplemented menu items were removed from the final version of the project.

Profiling

The graph project, illustrated in this chapter, was presented without any logical or syntactical errors. The purpose of this chapter was to refamiliarize you with the MFC library, the AppWizard, and ClassWizard along with the syntax for implementing simple GDI graphics functions.

This is the perfect section to illustrate another Visual C++ tool that can be helpful in debugging code—especially MFC Windows code. Have you ever written code and asked questions such as "Why does my application seem to take so long to complete," "Will the functions I wrote actually run," "Did the LineTo() function actually execute"? The answers to these questions, and many more, can be found by using Visual C++ profiling.

In order to enable profiling for a project, use the Project | Settings menu item, then select the Link tab, and check the Enable profiling checkbox, as shown in Figure 10.13.

Before starting the debug session, use the Build | Profile menu item to bring up the Profile dialog box, as shown in Figure 10.14.

The Profile dialog box shows five profile types that can be selected. Three of these types are useful when looking for problems in Windows code, function timing, function coverage, and line coverage.

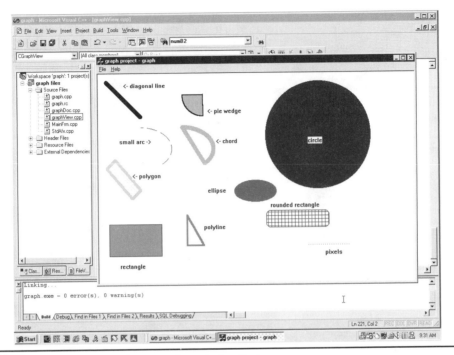

Figure 10.12 Various graphics shapes are drawn in the client area

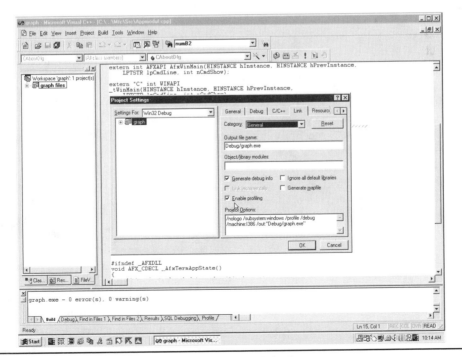

Figure 10.13 Profiling is enabled from the Project Settings dialog box

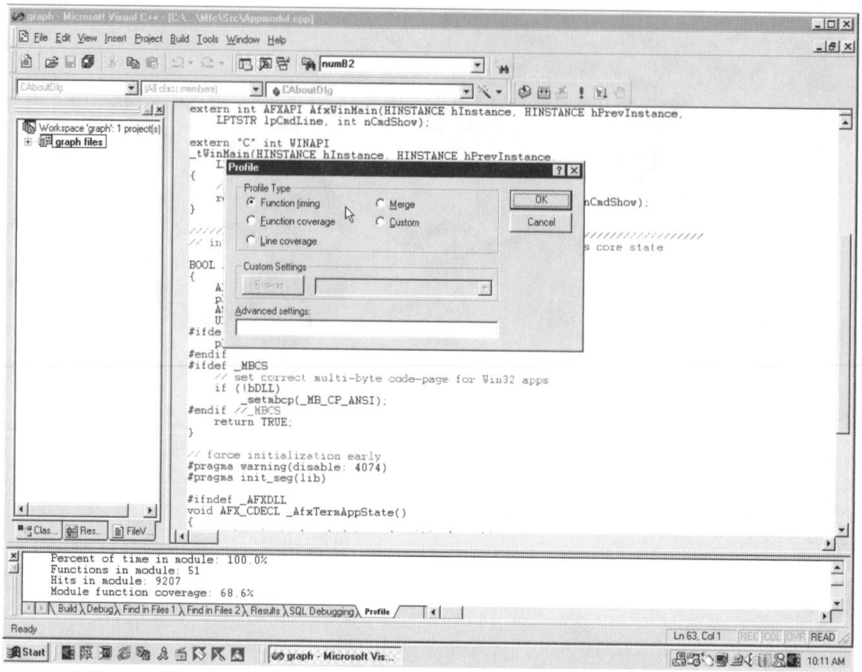

Figure 10.14 The Profile dialog box allows the profile type to be selected

Figure 10.15 shows a profiling screen generated when the function timing option is selected for the graph project.

If your project seems to have a timing issue, the profiler's function timing information can help you see where the project seems to be spending most of its time. In Figure 10.15, the bulk of the time is spent with the initialization of the project and the execution of the OnPaint() member function. In this project, this is probably where you would have expected the most time to be spent.

Figure 10.16 illustrates yet another profiling screen. This screen is generated when the function coverage option is selected for the project.

This screen provides information on which functions were actually used during the execution of the project. Not all functions will be used every time a project is run. For example, we never viewed the About dialog box during this run of the graph project. However, we did execute InitInstance(), as you can see in Figure 10.15.

In many MFC Windows applications, it is often difficult to determine if a particular function was ever executed. This is due to the inherent nature of object-oriented programming as opposed to the top-down approach of procedure-oriented programming. The function coverage option of the profiler can help you determine if and when particular functions are run during the execution of a project.

While function coverage is useful in locating problems, sometimes a little more detail is needed. The profiler provides a line coverage option that can be used to determine if a particular line of code is run during the execution of a project. Figure 10.17 shows the initial line coverage screen output for the graph project.

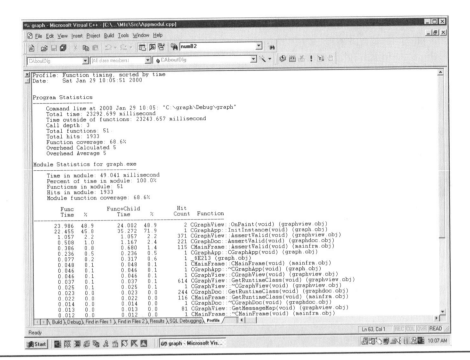

Figure 10.15   The profiler returns function timing information

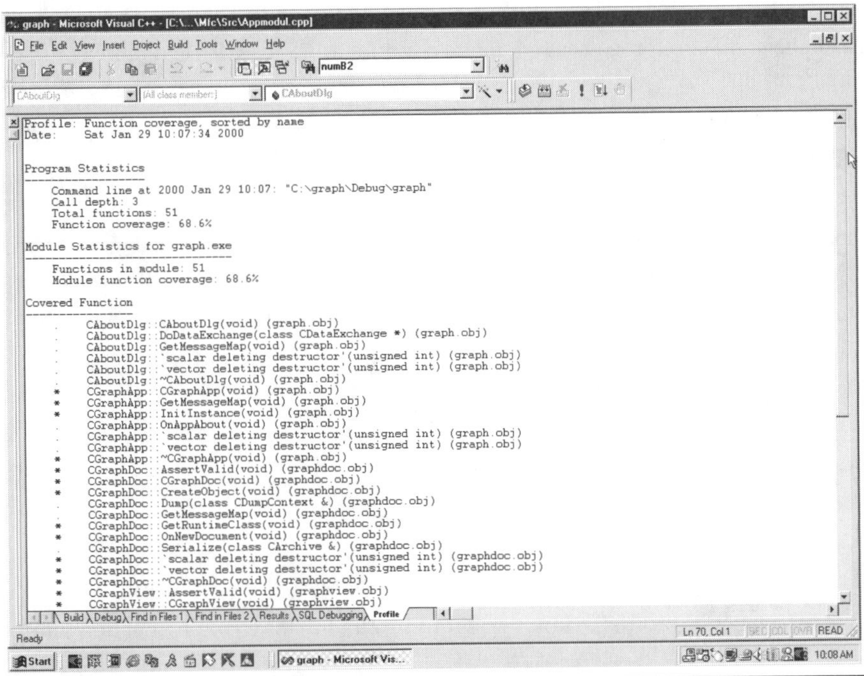

Figure 10.16   The profiler returns function coverage information

In Figure 10.17, any line marked with an asterisk (*) has been executed at least once. Imagine that we wanted to know if certain graphics functions were executed. If we had calculated the coordinates incorrectly, the functions might execute but not be visible in the client area of the window. The profiler can help us find the answer. Figure 10.18 shows the line coverage information for a portion of the GDI graphics functions called in this project.

We'll see the profiler used in later chapters of this book whenever we need information on timing and the use of particular portions of programming code.

Microsoft has typically provided profiling capabilities in the Professional and Enterprise Editions of Visual Studio. This may change with later versions of the product. Here are guidelines that were originally set forth by Microsoft and then modified to the needs of the Visual C++ programmer.

1. For large projects, it might not be necessary to profile the entire application. To profile a portion of a project, use PREP Phase I commands, such as /EXC and /INC. For many situations, it usually will not be necessary to profile much of the code generated by the AppWizard, for example.

2. Frequently the profiler's function timing report will not be accurate. For critical situations, do several runs and strike an average of the reported times. Accumulated profiler statistics for multiple runs can be merged using the Merge option provided in the Profiler dialog box.

3. Keep the number of processes running to a minimum. This will yield more consistent timing results.

4. Make sure network connections are disconnected. This prevents the need to service incoming packets.

5. Use the /CB switch in PREP Phase I if function timing and calculated overhead vary.

6. Study the timing report. Functions that report a lot of time could be the result of calls to profiled subroutines add up to roughly the amount of time the function is using.

7. Study the hit counts for a function. Is the function being called the correct number of times? Is it being called too frequently?

8. Even functions that have been well behaved in the past can be a source of problems. Look at the profile for all functions in your project.

9. Remember that function timing also includes children of the function.

10. The use of disk caching can provide faster subsequent profile runs.

11. Determining problems in long profiled functions is difficult. Breaking long functions into shorter equivalents helps to narrow down problem areas.

12. Threads cannot be profiled. However, profiling can be started at the function initiating the thread's entry point, by using the /SF PREP (Phase I) option.

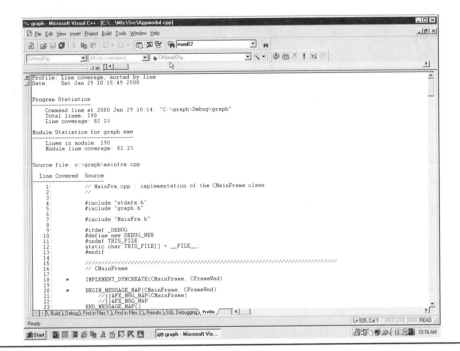

Figure 10.17   The profiler returns line coverage information

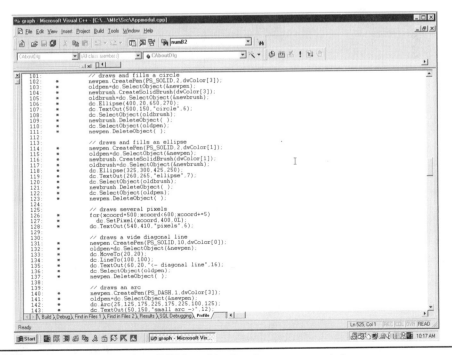

Figure 10.18   The profiler shows that all GDI graphics functions were executed

Conclusion

This chapter has served a multitude of purposes in addition to providing an introduction to the Microsoft Foundation Class library. If you are familiar with the AppWizard and ClassWizard for building applications, this chapter serves as a quick reminder of how to use these powerful tools. The introduction to a wide variety of GDI graphics primitives into the template code provided by the AppWizard illustrates the close link between procedure-oriented GDI functions and those used by the object-oriented MFC Windows environment.

Key advantages of the Visual C++ profiler were introduced as a means of determining problems caused by program timing, function use, or the execution of particular lines of code.

CHAPTER 11

Locating, Analyzing, and Repairing Errors in MFC Windows Code

hapter 10 provided a review of project development using the Microsoft Foundation Class (MFC) library along with some important development tools, including the AppWizard and ClassWizard. In Chapter 10, you also learned of another tool, the profiler, which can be used to help find problems in C++ code.

This chapter will use various debugging tools to locate, analyze, and repair coding problems in MFC Windows applications.

Of all of the coding problems we have examined in earlier chapters, none is harder to locate, analyze, or repair than problems involving memory allocation and leaks. The first project to be examined in this chapter is a project with just such a problem. By studying this example, you'll learn general techniques that can be applied to your own applications.

The second project in the chapter involves plotting a Fourier series in the client area of a window. The errors in this project are not as insidious as those of the previous example. However, when the errors are detected, you will see that they are common errors that are easy to miss on even less complicated applications.

Memory Problems

A computer's memory, or lack thereof, has always been a limiting factor in program development. Computers seem to cry out for more and more RAM memory. In early computers, 16K of memory handled most applications. Now, it seems as if 256MB or 512MB is just sufficient. Windows uses complex memory managers to help control and optimize memory use—and this includes disk caching. A serious problem occurs when an application mismanages, over-allocates, or leaks memory. Most MFC applications allow Windows to manage memory allocation for resources, so this is not usually a problem area. However, memory allocation for program components that are not handled by the system and memory leaks are another problem.

Memory allocation and leaks are often considered the same problem. A memory leak occurs when memory is allocated on the heap and is never deallocated. That means that the memory will never be freed for reuse. This type of problem is difficult to detect because most applications with this type of problem will appear to initially work well. Knowing an application has this type of problem is only the tip of the iceberg. The problem must then be located and analyzed before a solution can be achieved.

In the following sections, we'll look at a problem initially brought to us by some senior students working on a MFC project.

Code with a Problem

A group of students were working on a MFC Windows project involving simple projectile motion. The following project, MLeak, retains the essence of the programming problem, without the overhead of the complete project.

To build this project, follow the steps outlined in Chapter 10 for MFC AppWizard templates. Name this project MLeak.

The AppWizard will generate template code for the project. The only file that needs to be modified is the MLeakView.cpp file. The following listing shows all of the modifications to the AppWizard's code in a bold font.

```
// MLeakView.cpp : implementation of the CMLeakView class
//

#include "stdafx.h"
#include "MLeak.h"

#include "MLeakDoc.h"
#include "MLeakView.h"

#ifdef _DEBUG
#define new DEBUG_NEW
#undef THIS_FILE
static char THIS_FILE[] = __FILE__;
#endif

/////////////////////////////////////////////////////////////
// CMLeakView

IMPLEMENT_DYNCREATE(CMLeakView, CView)

BEGIN_MESSAGE_MAP(CMLeakView, CView)
    //{{AFX_MSG_MAP(CMLeakView)
    //}}AFX_MSG_MAP
END_MESSAGE_MAP()

/////////////////////////////////////////////////////////////
// CMLeakView construction/destruction

CMLeakView::CMLeakView()
{
}

CMLeakView::~CMLeakView()
{
}

BOOL CMLeakView::PreCreateWindow(CREATESTRUCT& cs)
{
    return CView::PreCreateWindow(cs);
}

/////////////////////////////////////////////////////////////
// CMLeakView drawing

void CMLeakView::OnDraw(CDC* pDC)
{
```

```
    CMLeakDoc* pDoc = GetDocument();
    ASSERT_VALID(pDoc);

LOGFONT lf;
CFont NFont;
CFont* pOFont;

    // specify a logical font
    lf.lfHeight = 50;
    lf.lfWeight=FW_NORMAL;
    lf.lfEscapement=0;
    lf.lfOrientation=0;
    lf.lfItalic=false;
    lf.lfUnderline = false;
    lf.lfStrikeOut = false;
    lf.lfCharSet=ANSI_CHARSET;
    lf.lfPitchAndFamily=34;   //Arial

    NFont.CreateFontIndirect(&lf);
    pOFont = pDC->SelectObject(&NFont);

    pDC->TextOut(20, 200, "This program has memory problems");

    DeleteObject(pOFont);
}

/////////////////////////////////////////////////////////////////
// CMLeakView diagnostics

#ifdef _DEBUG
void CMLeakView::AssertValid() const
{
    CView::AssertValid();
}

void CMLeakView::Dump(CDumpContext& dc) const
{
    CView::Dump(dc);
}

CMLeakDoc* CMLeakView::GetDocument() // non-debug ver. inline
{
    ASSERT(m_pDocument->IsKindOf(RUNTIME_CLASS(CMLeakDoc)));
    return (CMLeakDoc*)m_pDocument;
}
#endif //_DEBUG
```

Create an executable for the project by selecting the Build | Rebuild All menu item. Run the application to see a window similar to that shown in Figure 11.1.

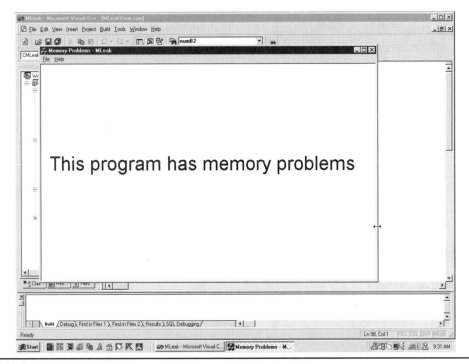

Figure 11.1   The window created by the initial run of the MLeak project

Upon initial inspection, the program looks as if it ran correctly. A logical font was created, and the TextOut() function wrote text in the client area of the window. So where is the problem? Ah, it is a memory leak problem that cannot be detected at this point! Maybe if you just let the application run for a couple of minutes. No, it's not related to how long the program has been running. Grab a border of the application's window and resize the window between 50 and 100 times to discover what our students found. Figure 11.2 shows the same window after it has been resized a number of times.

Something has gone wrong with the font. The TextOut() function is still printing to the window correctly, but the logical font is not being created properly.

Our students' initial guess was that the problem centered around the font creation process within the OnDraw() method. In the next section, we'll see how they proceeded to locate and analyze the problem.

Locating and Analyzing

Our students had to locate and analyze the source of the memory problem in the MLeak project. Fortunately, they knew about several MFC classes and functions that could be used to find memory leaks. Properly placed, these classes and functions can provide a before and an after picture of the condition of memory. By proper analysis, it can then be determined if memory is being properly allocated and released or deallocated.

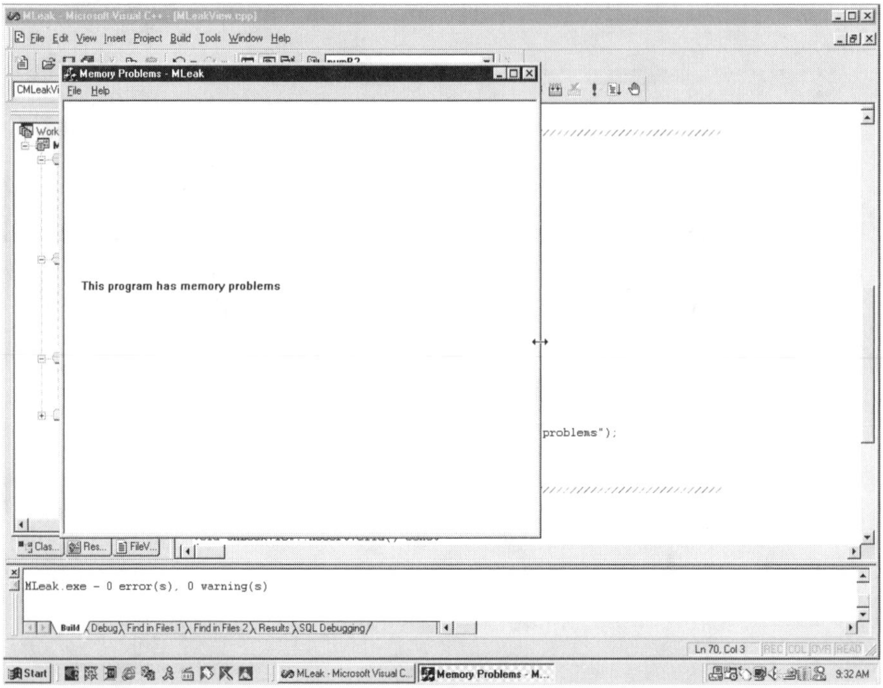

Figure 11.2   The MLeak project window after being resized a number of times

The students added the following code to help them detect leakage problems to the MLeakView.cpp file. The added code is shown in a bold font.

```
// MLeakView.cpp : implementation of the CMLeakView class
//

#include "stdafx.h"
#include "MLeak.h"

#include "MLeakDoc.h"
#include "MLeakView.h"

CMemoryState oldMemState, newMemState, diffMemState;

#ifdef _DEBUG
#define new DEBUG_NEW
#undef THIS_FILE
static char THIS_FILE[] = __FILE__;
#endif

/////////////////////////////////////////////////////////////
// CMLeakView
```

```
IMPLEMENT_DYNCREATE(CMLeakView, CView)

BEGIN_MESSAGE_MAP(CMLeakView, CView)
    //{{AFX_MSG_MAP(CMLeakView)
    ON_WM_CREATE()
    //}}AFX_MSG_MAP
END_MESSAGE_MAP()

/////////////////////////////////////////////////////////////
// CMLeakView construction/destruction

CMLeakView::CMLeakView()
{
}

CMLeakView::~CMLeakView()
{
}

BOOL CMLeakView::PreCreateWindow(CREATESTRUCT& cs)
{
    return CView::PreCreateWindow(cs);
}

/////////////////////////////////////////////////////////////
// CMLeakView drawing

void CMLeakView::OnDraw(CDC* pDC)
{
    CMLeakDoc* pDoc = GetDocument();
    ASSERT_VALID(pDoc);

    LOGFONT lf;
    CFont NFont;
    CFont* pOFont;

    lf.lfHeight = 50;
    lf.lfWeight=FW_NORMAL;
    lf.lfEscapement=0;
    lf.lfOrientation=0;
    lf.lfItalic=false;
    lf.lfUnderline = false;
    lf.lfStrikeOut = false;
    lf.lfCharSet=ANSI_CHARSET;
    lf.lfPitchAndFamily=34;   //Arial

    NFont.CreateFontIndirect(&lf);
    pOFont = pDC->SelectObject(&NFont);

    pDC->TextOut(20, 200, "This program has memory problems");

    DeleteObject(pOFont);
```

```
#ifdef _DEBUG
    newMemState.Checkpoint();
    if(diffMemState.Difference(oldMemState, newMemState))  {
        TRACE("Difference between first and now!\n\n");
        diffMemState.DumpStatistics();
}
#endif

}


/////////////////////////////////////////////////////////////
// CMLeakView diagnostics

#ifdef _DEBUG
void CMLeakView::AssertValid() const
{
    CView::AssertValid();
}

void CMLeakView::Dump(CDumpContext& dc) const
{
    CView::Dump(dc);
}

CMLeakDoc* CMLeakView::GetDocument() // non-debug ver. inline
{
    ASSERT(m_pDocument->IsKindOf(RUNTIME_CLASS(CMLeakDoc)));
    return (CMLeakDoc*)m_pDocument;
}
#endif //_DEBUG

int CMLeakView::OnCreate(LPCREATESTRUCT lpCreateStruct)
{
    if (CView::OnCreate(lpCreateStruct) == -1)
        return -1;

    // TODO: Add your specialized creation code here

    #ifdef _DEBUG
        oldMemState.Checkpoint();
    #endif

    return 0;
}
```

The OnCreate() method was added with the ClassWizard in order that statistics could be obtained on the heap when the application initializes the window. This is easy to do with just a call to oldMemState.Checkpoint().

Then, after all of the font work has been completed, the following code is executed in the OnDraw() method:

```
#ifdef _DEBUG
    newMemState.Checkpoint();
    if(diffMemState.Difference(oldMemState, newMemState))  {
        TRACE("Difference between first and now!\n\n");
        diffMemState.DumpStatistics();
    }
#endif
```

The call to newMemState.Checkpoint() snaps a new picture of the heap, and a call to diffMemState.Difference() returns information when a difference between the initial and current values occurs. Statistics are dumped by calling diffMemState.DumpStatistics(). Since this information is contained within the OnDraw() method, and since the OnDraw() method responds to screen resizing via WM_PAINT messages, statistics will be printed each time the screen is resized. This is where we encountered problems initially.

The next listing is an abbreviated output from this program while running in the Debugger:

```
Difference between first and now!
0 bytes in 0 Free Blocks.
-36 bytes in 0 Normal Blocks.
0 bytes in 0 CRT Blocks.
0 bytes in 0 Ignore Blocks.
0 bytes in 0 Client Blocks.
Largest number used: 9 bytes.
Total allocations: 87 bytes.

Difference between first and now!
0 bytes in 0 Free Blocks.
-36 bytes in 0 Normal Blocks.
0 bytes in 0 CRT Blocks.
0 bytes in 0 Ignore Blocks.
0 bytes in 0 Client Blocks.
Largest number used: 9 bytes.
Total allocations: 132 bytes.

        .
        .
        .

Difference between first and now!
0 bytes in 0 Free Blocks.
-36 bytes in 0 Normal Blocks.
0 bytes in 0 CRT Blocks.
0 bytes in 0 Ignore Blocks.
0 bytes in 0 Client Blocks.
Largest number used: 9 bytes.
Total allocations: 14307 bytes.

Difference between first and now!
0 bytes in 0 Free Blocks.
-36 bytes in 0 Normal Blocks.
0 bytes in 0 CRT Blocks.
0 bytes in 0 Ignore Blocks.
0 bytes in 0 Client Blocks.
```

```
Largest number used: 9 bytes.
Total allocations: 14352 bytes.
```

If you study the listing carefully, you'll notice that only one line really changes from dump to dump. Yes, the total allocations line seems to be increasing with each screen resizing. More specifically, it increases by 45 bytes. It doesn't sound like a very big leak when you consider the overall system memory, but look at the last number in the dump, 14,352 bytes. That number was reported after resizing the screen just a few times! Also, remember the dramatic effect this little leak is having on the application—it kills the logical font.

The students were sure, because the leak was so small, that it was because they forgot to allocate memory for the logical font structure, so they went back and inserted this bold piece of code into the OnDraw() method:

```
LOGFONT lf;
CFont NFont;
CFont* pOFont;

memset(&lf,0,sizeof(LOGFONT));

lf.lfHeight = 50;
lf.lfWeight=FW_NORMAL;
lf.lfEscapement=0;
    .
    .
    .
```

This is the kind of logic that makes a professor proud of his or her students. The students realized the difference between dumps was 45 bytes and that the logical font structure could be about this size. However, as good of a guess as this was, it wasn't the solution to the problem. The total allocated memory kept incrementing upward!

Desperate times and deadlines require desperate measures. Were the students really thinking of increasing the size of the virtual memory swapping file with the hope that the old professor wouldn't catch the problem? Probably not, so the next line of reasoning went as follows. Maybe something is happening with the font creation process that is leaking a little memory each time the screen is resized. Solution—remove the font creation process from within OnDraw() and move it to OnCreate(). That way, the logical font resource will be created when the window is created, not each time the OnDraw() method responds to a WM_PAINT message. Now this was a worthy idea, and it is in the tradition of the best form of programming—don't keep allocating and deallocating the same resources. However, this approach didn't turn out to be the whole solution. The total allocated memory kept incrementing upward!

The students had taken the diagnostic tools about as far as they could when one student suggested getting rid of the logical font altogether and seeing what happened using just the default system font. So the OnDraw() method was modified once again as follows:

```
void CMLeakView::OnDraw(CDC* pDC)
{
    CMLeakDoc* pDoc = GetDocument();
    ASSERT_VALID(pDoc);
```

```
    pDC->TextOut(20, 200, "This program has memory problems");

#ifdef _DEBUG
    newMemState.Checkpoint();
    if(diffMemState.Difference(oldMemState, newMemState))  {
        TRACE("Difference between first and now!\n\n");
        diffMemState.DumpStatistics();
    }
#endif
}
```

What do you think happened when the program was tested? Here is a portion of the dump statistics for you to examine:

```
Difference between first and now!
0 bytes in 0 Free Blocks.
-36 bytes in 0 Normal Blocks.
0 bytes in 0 CRT Blocks.
0 bytes in 0 Ignore Blocks.
0 bytes in 0 Client Blocks.
Largest number used: 9 bytes.
Total allocations: 87 bytes.

Difference between first and now!
0 bytes in 0 Free Blocks.
-36 bytes in 0 Normal Blocks.
0 bytes in 0 CRT Blocks.
0 bytes in 0 Ignore Blocks.
0 bytes in 0 Client Blocks.
Largest number used: 9 bytes.
Total allocations: 132 bytes.
        .
        .
        .

Difference between first and now!

0 bytes in 0 Free Blocks.
-36 bytes in 0 Normal Blocks.
0 bytes in 0 CRT Blocks.
0 bytes in 0 Ignore Blocks.
0 bytes in 0 Client Blocks.
Largest number used: 9 bytes.
Total allocations: 5352 bytes.

Difference between first and now!
0 bytes in 0 Free Blocks.
-36 bytes in 0 Normal Blocks.
0 bytes in 0 CRT Blocks.
0 bytes in 0 Ignore Blocks.
0 bytes in 0 Client Blocks.
```

```
Largest number used: 9 bytes.
Total allocations: 5397 bytes.
```

Well, nothing changed. There is still a difference of 45 bytes between each dump's total memory allocation. So where is the problem? Of course, we know now—it's the only code left in the OnDraw() method.

```
pDC->TextOut(20, 200, "This program has memory problems");
```

Comment out this line of code, recompile, and run the diagnostics once again. You'll see that the total memory allocations remain constant from one dump to another. As a matter of fact, replace all of the logical font code, and the memory allocations still remain constant from one dump to another.

The problem is that the memory being allocated to the string is being reallocated each time the screen is redrawn. The obvious solution is to get that string out of the OnDraw() method just as the students did by moving the creation of the logical font resources. We'll show you how they finally solved the problem in the next section.

24x7   Parameters for Memory Diagnostics

In order to use the memory diagnostics facilities, diagnostic tracing must be enabled. These values are enabled within the Debugger. However, to enable or disable memory diagnostics, Microsoft suggests a call to the global function AfxEnableMemoryTracking(). This function enables or disables the diagnostic memory allocator. The Debugger automatically turns this feature on, so use this function as a switch to turn the feature off. In so doing, the program's execution speed increases, and there is an overall reduction in the amount of diagnostic information.

Altering the MFC global variable *afxMemDF* can make specific memory diagnostic features available. This variable can use any of the values shown in Table 11.1.

The values, shown in Table 11.1, can be combined with a logical OR operation, when needed.

Variable Value	Description
AllocMemDF	Used to turn on diagnostic memory allocator. This is the default.
CheckAlwaysMemDF	Used to call AfxCheckMemory() function each time memory is allocated or released.
DelayFreeMemDF	Used to delay releasing memory when calling delete or free until program terminates. The overall effect is to allocate the greatest possible amount of memory.

Table 11.1   Values for *afxMemDF* Variable

24x7   Locating a Memory Leak

Microsoft has provided an outline that can be followed in the search for memory leaks. We've modified the outline slightly to make it more compatible with the work we are doing on this project. Follow these steps:

1. Implement a CMemoryState object. Call the Checkpoint() method, before entering the code in question, to get an initial picture of memory usage.

2. Implement another CMemoryState object and call the Checkpoint() method, after completing the code in question, to get a final picture of memory usage.

3. Now, if needed, implement another CMemoryState object and call the Difference() member function. When this function is called, use the two previous CMemoryState objects as arguments. The value returned will be nonzero when there is a difference in memory allocation. This is an indication that at least some memory blocks have not been released or deallocated.

Here is a portion of code that uses three CMemoryState objects:

```
// Declaration of CMemoryState variables
#ifdef _DEBUG
    CMemoryState oldMemState, newMemState, diffMemState;
    oldMemState.Checkpoint();
#endif
        .
        .
        .
    (Code to be tested placed here)
        .
        .
        .
#ifdef _DEBUG
    newMemState.Checkpoint();
    if(diffMemState.Difference(oldMemState, newMemState))
    {
        TRACE("Memory Leaked Here:\n\n" );
    }
#endif
```

Bracket this code with **#ifdef _DEBUG** and **#endif** to insure that this code is compiled only in Win32 Debug versions of the project.

Table 11.2 lists additional CMemoryState operations, including brief descriptions.

The additional operations can be used when the difference between two CMemoryState objects does not disclose enough information.

Operation	Description
Difference	Used to find a difference between two objects of type CMemoryState found with the use of checkpoint().
DumpAllObjectsSince	Used to dump a summary of all objects currently allocated since a call to checkpoint().
DumpStatistics	Used to print the memory allocation statistics for a CMemoryState object. Typically placed after a call to checkpoint().

Table 11.2   CMemoryState Operations

24x7   Dumping Memory Statistics

The CMemoryState() member function can be used to dump the current statistics or the difference between two memory state objects. Either technique can be used to help locate problems dealing with the deallocation of heap memory.

The following code uses the information obtained in the previous 24x7 code to determine the current memory statistics:

```
TRACE("Current Memory Picture:\n\n" );
NewMemState.DumpStatistics();
```

The difference between the original and new memory pictures is just as easy to obtain:

```
if( diffMemState.Difference(oldMemState,newMemState))
{
    TRACE( "Memory Leaked Here:\n\n");
    diffMemState.DumpStatistics();
}
```

A sample output from a diffMemState.DumpStatistics() call could take this form:

```
0 bytes in 0 Free Blocks
2 bytes in 1 Object Blocks
50 bytes in 5 Non-Object Blocks
Largest number used: 76 bytes
Total allocations: 304 bytes
```

The first line in this listing indicates the number of blocks whose release or deallocation was delayed. This occurs when the *afxMemDF* variable was set to delayFreeMemDF (see Table 11.1). The second line is used to indicate how many objects still remain allocated on the heap. The third line is used to indicate how many nonobject blocks (items allocated with **new**) were allocated and not released or deallocated on the heap. The fourth line is used to indicate the maximum memory used by the application at any given time. The last line indicates the total amount of memory used by the project. Problems in any of these areas indicate a memory leak.

Repairing the Project

The students that worked on this project put the Debugger and techniques for detecting memory leaks to good use. While their initial line of reasoning led them down the wrong path, they quickly regrouped, got on the right path, and located and analyzed the problem correctly.

The key to solving this problem involves getting the string that is to be printed to the screen out of the OnDraw() method that is called each time the screen is resized. While this probably could be done successfully in MLeakView.cpp, the AppWizard created files specifically for this kind of storage and allocation. They are the MLeak\Doc.h and MLeakDoc.cpp project files.

Here is a portion of the MLeakDoc.h file showing the declaration for the string to be used in this project:

```
// MLeakDoc.h : interface of the CMLeakDoc class
//
/////////////////////////////////////////////////////////////////////

#if !defined \

(AFX_MLEAKDOC_H__7D597DAA_8B14_11D3_A7DE_0080AE000001__INCLUDED_)
#define \

AFX_MLEAKDOC_H__7D597DAA_8B14_11D3_A7DE_0080AE000001__INCLUDED_


#if _MSC_VER > 1000
#pragma once
#endif // _MSC_VER > 1000


class CMLeakDoc : public CDocument
{
protected: // create from serialization only
    CMLeakDoc();
    DECLARE_DYNCREATE(CMLeakDoc)

    CString myCString;
     .
     .
     .
```

The string itself can be found in a constructor in the MLeakDoc.cpp file, as shown in the next partial listing:

```
// MLeakDoc.cpp : implementation of the CMLeakDoc class
//

#include "stdafx.h"
#include "MLeak.h"

#include "MLeakDoc.h"

#ifdef _DEBUG
```

```
#define new DEBUG_NEW
#undef THIS_FILE
static char THIS_FILE[] = __FILE__;
#endif


/////////////////////////////////////////////////////////
// CMLeakDoc

IMPLEMENT_DYNCREATE(CMLeakDoc, CDocument)

BEGIN_MESSAGE_MAP(CMLeakDoc, CDocument)
    //{{AFX_MSG_MAP(CMLeakDoc)
    //}}AFX_MSG_MAP
END_MESSAGE_MAP()

/////////////////////////////////////////////////////////
// CMLeakDoc construction/destruction

CMLeakDoc::CMLeakDoc()
{
    myCString = "This program doesn't have a leak";
}
```

Finally, the repaired MLeakView.cpp code is listed as it would be used in a release version:

```
// MLeakView.cpp : implementation of the CMLeakView class
//

#include "stdafx.h"
#include "MLeak.h"

#include "MLeakDoc.h"
#include "MLeakView.h"


CFont NFont;

#ifdef _DEBUG
#define new DEBUG_NEW
#undef THIS_FILE
static char THIS_FILE[] = __FILE__;
#endif


/////////////////////////////////////////////////////////
// CMLeakView

IMPLEMENT_DYNCREATE(CMLeakView, CView)

BEGIN_MESSAGE_MAP(CMLeakView, CView)
    //{{AFX_MSG_MAP(CMLeakView)
```

```
      ON_WM_CREATE()
      //}}AFX_MSG_MAP
END_MESSAGE_MAP()

/////////////////////////////////////////////////////////////
// CMLeakView construction/destruction

CMLeakView::CMLeakView()
{
}

CMLeakView::~CMLeakView()
{
}

BOOL CMLeakView::PreCreateWindow(CREATESTRUCT& cs)
{
    return CView::PreCreateWindow(cs);
}

/////////////////////////////////////////////////////////////
// CMLeakView drawing

void CMLeakView::OnDraw(CDC* pDC)
{

    CMLeakDoc* pDoc = GetDocument();
    ASSERT_VALID(pDoc);

    CFont* pOFont;

    pOFont = pDC->SelectObject(&NFont);

    pDC->TextOut(20, 200, pDoc->myCString);

    DeleteObject(pOFont);

}

/////////////////////////////////////////////////////////////
// CMLeakView diagnostics

#ifdef _DEBUG
void CMLeakView::AssertValid() const
{
    CView::AssertValid();
}

void CMLeakView::Dump(CDumpContext& dc) const
{
    CView::Dump(dc);
```

```
}

CMLeakDoc* CMLeakView::GetDocument() // non-debug ver. inline
{
    ASSERT(m_pDocument->IsKindOf(RUNTIME_CLASS(CMLeakDoc)));
    return (CMLeakDoc*)m_pDocument;
}
#endif //_DEBUG

int CMLeakView::OnCreate(LPCREATESTRUCT lpCreateStruct)
{
    if (CView::OnCreate(lpCreateStruct) == -1)
        return -1;

    // TODO: Add your specialized creation code here

    LOGFONT lf;
    memset(&lf,0,sizeof(LOGFONT));

    lf.lfHeight = 50;
    lf.lfWeight=FW_NORMAL;
    lf.lfEscapement=0;
    lf.lfOrientation=0;
    lf.lfItalic=false;
    lf.lfUnderline = false;
    lf.lfStrikeOut = false;
    lf.lfCharSet=ANSI_CHARSET;
    lf.lfPitchAndFamily=34;   //Arial

    NFont.CreateFontIndirect(&lf);

    return 0;
}
```

To build this project, remember to make the previously shown changes to the MLeakDoc.h, MLeakDoc.cpp, and MLeakView.cpp files.

Design Tip   *You might recall, from Chapter 2, an optimization technique that centers around string pooling. For example, if the compiler uses /GF or /Gf and the following code is encountered in the program:*

```
char *s = "Pooling will not work here";
char *t = "Pooling will not work here";
```

The option will enable the compiler to place a single copy of the identical strings into the .exe file. Since they are copied into a single location, the program compiled with this option will be smaller.

However, this was not the problem encountered with the string in this project. It was not a case of multiple strings, but of one string repeatedly allocating memory. Thus, the /GF or /Gf switch wouldn't help.

If you have been down this road a couple of times, you'll soon start recognizing these memory traps in programming code. However, first encounters are difficult to locate and detect. This, of course, is what will make you so valuable to your employer—experience!

Plotting Problems

An interesting application encountered by many electrical engineering and physics students involves the calculation of a Fourier series. The French mathematician Baron Jean Baptiste Joseph Fourier (1768–1830) found that almost any periodic waveform could be constructed by simply adding together the correct combinations of sine wave harmonics. Fourier's results produce a wide variety of waveforms, from square to triangular. Electrical engineers are often interested in square wave reproduction in audio equipment because square waves are made from a fundamental sine wave and its associated overtones. The quality of amplifiers and other communication devices depends on how well they can reproduce these signals. We'll discuss the components of a Fourier series, but a more detailed treatment can be found in college-level physics or electrical engineering textbooks.

Fourier's formal equation is usually expressed as follows:

```
y = A + A1(sin wt) + A2(sin 2wt) + A3(sin 3wt) +
        A4(sin 4wt) + A5(sin 5wt)...
```

Some periodic waveforms include odd or even harmonics only. In others, all terms are included. In some periodic waveforms, the signs alternate between + and - for adjacent terms. This example constructs a square wave by adding together the odd harmonic terms in a Fourier series. The more terms that are used in the series, the more the final result will approach a precise square wave. For a square wave, the general Fourier series equation becomes the following:

```
y = (sin wt) + (1/3)(sin 3wt) + (1/5)(sin 5wt) +
        (1/7)(sin 7wt)...
```

Notice that only odd harmonics will contribute to the final result. Also observe that if only one harmonic is chosen, the result will be a sine wave. Then each successive term uses a fractional multiplier. In other words, each successively higher harmonic affects the final waveform less and less.

The program calculates each term in a Fourier series separately, with the sum of these individual terms being continuously updated. Thus, when drawing 100 harmonics, 100 separate sine values will be scaled, calculated, and added together to form a single point for the waveform. But this must be repeated for each point that is to be plotted on the window. Therefore, 100 calculations times 400 points = 40,000. Consider how long this would take to accomplish with a calculator.

Code with a Problem

The project's name is Fourier. This project was created by a group of students following the steps outlined in Chapter 10 and using the AppWizard. To the basic AppWizard code, they added a dialog box for data input, a common color dialog box for selecting the fill color, and, of course, the application's code.

Not all of the AppWizard's files are germane to the problems in the application, so we'll investigate only the code found in the FourierView.cpp file.

```cpp
// FourierView.cpp : implementation of the CFourierView class
//

#include "stdafx.h"
#include "Fourier.h"

#include "FourierDoc.h"
#include "FourierView.h"

// additional header files needed
#include "FourierDlg.h"
#include "math.h"

CColorDialog dlg1;  // include common color dialog box

#ifdef _DEBUG
#define new DEBUG_NEW
#undef THIS_FILE
static char THIS_FILE[] = __FILE__;
#endif

/////////////////////////////////////////////////////////////////
// CFourierView

IMPLEMENT_DYNCREATE(CFourierView, CView)

BEGIN_MESSAGE_MAP(CFourierView, CView)
    //{{AFX_MSG_MAP(CFourierView)
    ON_WM_SIZE()
    ON_COMMAND(IDM_FOURIER, OnFourier)
    ON_COMMAND(IDM_COLOR, OnColor)
    //}}AFX_MSG_MAP
END_MESSAGE_MAP()

/////////////////////////////////////////////////////////////////
// CFourierView construction/destruction

CFourierView::CFourierView()
{
}

CFourierView::~CFourierView()
{
}
```

```
BOOL CFourierView::PreCreateWindow(CREATESTRUCT& cs)
{
    return CView::PreCreateWindow(cs);

}

//////////////////////////////////////////////////////////
// CFourierView drawing

void CFourierView::OnDraw(CDC* pDC)
{
    CFourierDoc* pDoc = GetDocument();
    ASSERT_VALID(pDoc);


    // all remaining code for Fourier Series
    int i,j,ang,yp;
    double y;
    CBrush newbrush;
    CBrush* oldbrush;
    CPen newpen;
    CPen* oldpen;

    // common color dialog box structure information
    // allow initial color value to be set
    dlg1.m_cc.Flags |= CC_FULLOPEN | CC_RGBINIT;
    dlg1.m_cc.rgbResult = pDoc->mycolor;

    pDC->SetMapMode(MM_ISOTROPIC);
    pDC->SetWindowExt(500,500);
    pDC->SetViewportExt(m_cxClient,-m_cyClient);
    pDC->SetViewportOrg(m_cxClient/20,m_cyClient/2);

    ang=0;
    yp=0;

    newpen.CreatePen(BS_SOLID,1,RGB(0,0,0));
    oldpen=pDC->SelectObject(&newpen);

    // draw x & y coordinate axes
    pDC->MoveTo(0,240);
    pDC->LineTo(0,-240);
    pDC->MoveTo(0,0);
    pDC->LineTo(400,0);
    pDC->MoveTo(0,0);
    // draw actual Fourier waveform
    for (i=0; i<=400; i++) {
      for (j=1; j<=pDoc->myterms; j++) {
        y=(250.0/((2.0*j)-1.0))* \
            sin(((j*2.0)-1.0)* \
            (ang*((360*22)/(180*400*7)))));
```

```
        yp=yp+(int)y;
    }
    pDC->LineTo(i,yp);
    yp-=yp;
    ang++;
}

// create brush from common color dialog box selection
// for waveform fill
newbrush.CreateSolidBrush(pDoc->mycolor);

oldbrush=pDC->SelectObject(&newbrush);
pDC->ExtFloodFill(150,10,RGB(0,0,0),FLOODFILLBORDER);
pDC->ExtFloodFill(300,-10,RGB(0,0,0),FLOODFILLBORDER);

// delete brush objects
pDC->SelectObject(oldbrush);
newbrush.DeleteObject();
}


/////////////////////////////////////////////////////////////
// CFourierView diagnostics

#ifdef _DEBUG
void CFourierView::AssertValid() const
{
    CView::AssertValid();
}

void CFourierView::Dump(CDumpContext& dc) const
{
    CView::Dump(dc);
}

CFourierDoc* CFourierView::GetDocument() // non-debug inline
{
    ASSERT(m_pDocument->IsKindOf(RUNTIME_CLASS(CFourierDoc)));
    return (CFourierDoc*)m_pDocument;
}
#endif //_DEBUG


/////////////////////////////////////////////////////////////
// CFourierView message handlers

void CFourierView::OnSize(UINT nType, int cx, int cy)
{
    CView::OnSize(nType, cx, cy);
    // TODO: Add your message handler code here

    // WHM: added for sizing and scaling window
    m_cxClient = cx;
```

```
        m_cyClient = cy;
}

void CFourierView::OnFourier()
{
    // TODO: Add your command handler code here

    // added to process dialog information
    FourierDlg dlg (this);
    int result = dlg.DoModal();

    if(result==IDOK) {
        CFourierDoc* pDoc = GetDocument();
        ASSERT_VALID(pDoc);
        pDoc->myterms=dlg.m_terms;
        Invalidate();
    }
}

void CFourierView::OnColor()
{
    // TODO: Add your command handler code here
    // added to process common color
    // dialog box information

    int result = dlg1.DoModal();

    if(result==IDOK) {
        CFourierDoc* pDoc = GetDocument();
        ASSERT_VALID(pDoc);

        // get returned color from dialog box
        pDoc->mycolor = dlg1.GetColor();
        InvalidateRect(NULL,TRUE);
        UpdateWindow();
    }
}
```

This application allows the user to enter the number of harmonics to be plotted in a dialog box. The application then draws a coordinate axis and the Fourier waveform. It does this by scaling and plotting the waveform with the following equation:

```
// draw actual Fourier waveform
for (i=0; i<=400; i++) {
  for (j=1; j<=pDoc->myterms; j++) {
    y=(250.0/((2.0*j)-1.0))* \
       sin(((j*2.0)-1.0)* \
       (ang*((360*22)/(180*400*7)))));
    yp=yp+(int)y;
  }
  pDC->LineTo(i,yp);
```

In this portion of code, 400 points are plotted on a scaled axis. Each point consists of the number of individual values calculated from 1 to *nterms*. The *nterms* variable holds the number of Fourier harmonics to calculate. Each term, represented by the *y* variable, is calculated and summed in the *yp* variable. The sum represents the Fourier point for that number of terms. A line is then drawn from the previous point to the new point using the LineTo() function. The portion of the equation represented with the numbers ((360*22)/(180*400*7)) scales the 400 points to 360 degrees (260/400) and converts from degrees to radians (pi/180).

The application allows the user to select a fill color for the waveform from the common color dialog box. The following functions then fill each "hump" of the waveform:

```
pDC->ExtFloodFill(150,10,RGB(0,0,0),FLOODFILLBORDER);
pDC->ExtFloodFill(300,-10,RGB(0,0,0),FLOODFILLBORDER);
```

The initial plot, before user input, requests four harmonics to be plotted. Figure 11.3 shows the window upon execution of the project.

After viewing Figure 11.3, you'll conclude that our students are far from achieving a satisfactory plot. What's wrong with the application? Upon first glance, the only conclusion you can draw is that no waveform is plotted, and the waveform's fill color has painted the entire screen. The one piece of

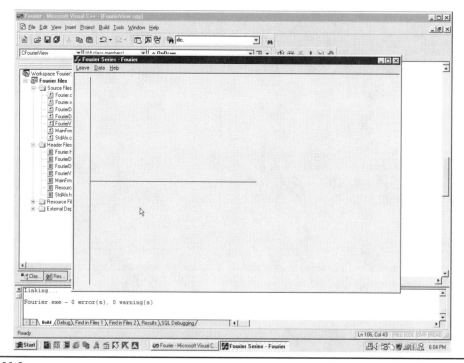

Figure 11.3 The initial window of the Fourier project

good news is that the two axes have been drawn. At least we know they made it into the OnDraw() method! If that had not been the case, they could have used the profiler to validate which methods were actually accessed.

Locating and Analyzing

This would be a good point to check your debugging skills. Examine all of the information given in the program and the analysis we've provided so far. Want to make a guess as to where the problem is?

Knowing that the two axes have been drawn correctly, we do not need to worry about drawing routines within the OnDraw() method. Since the various LineTo() functions behaved properly, so should any other correctly specified GDI drawing primitives.

Working on the First Problem

Since the axes were drawn correctly, our attention focuses on the equation used to calculate the Fourier terms. And what an equation it is!

Examine the inner loop for a moment.

```
y=(250.0/((2.0*j)-1.0))*sin(((j*2.0)-1.0)* \
   (ang*((360*22)/(180*400*7)))));
```

To analyze the problem, consider this fact: If the user selects one Fourier term, this inner loop reduces to the following equation:

```
y = 250 * sin (ang * 0.015707)
```

Now this equation represents a sine wave, and the values for a sine wave should be fairly easy to calculate (with a calculator) and track in the Watch window of the Debugger. Let's see what happens.

Use the Debugger's Go (F5) key to quickly step through a number of angles. Examine Figure 11.4 to see our results for an angle of approximately 40 degrees (45 * 360 / 400).

Well, we've found the source of the problem. The *y* value never changes from zero. No *y* change, no plot! Do you know the source of the error? The problem lies in the calculation of the scaling value using the following:

```
Scaling value = ((360*22)/(180*400*7))
```

On a calculator, this value turns out to be 0.1571428. . . . However, when used within this equation, integer values will return a 0.0 result. The values must be changed to real numbers. In addition, this equation can be cleaned up a little. After all, we all know 360.0 divided by 180.0 is 2.0. Pi can be represented as 3.14159, so let's replace that portion of code with this one:

```
y=(250.0/((2.0*j)-1.0))*sin(((j*2.0)-1.0)* \
   (ang*2.0*3.14159/400.0));
```

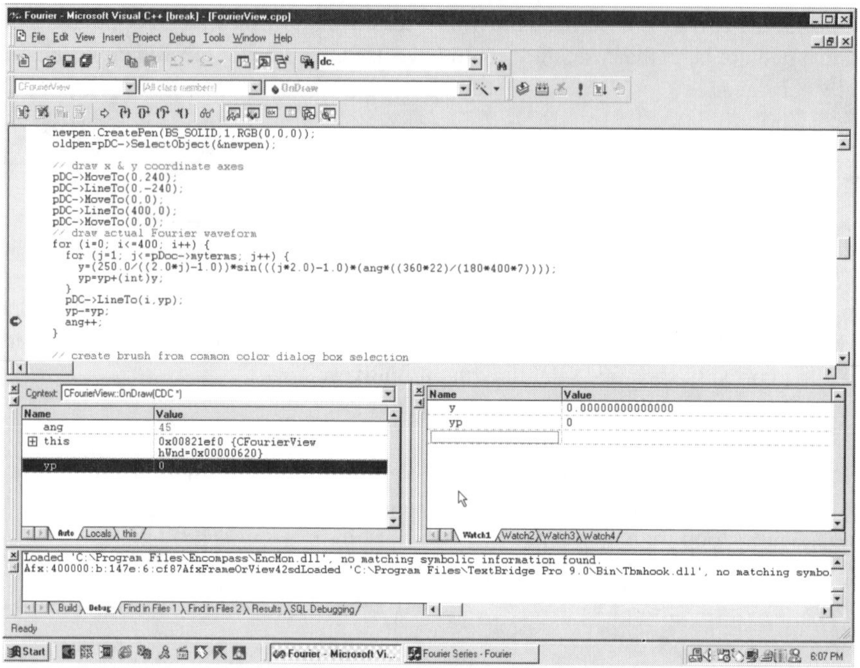

Figure 11.4 The results are consistently zero in the Watch window

Run the program through the Debugger again with the *y* variable in the Watch window. Figure 11.5 shows improved results for a 40 degree angle.

In this case, the sine of 40 degrees is 0.64 . . . and that value multiplied by 250 yields approximately 160. . . .

To see if the plotting is working correctly, run the project outside of the Debugger. You should see a plot similar to that in Figure 11.6.

The waveform looks like the expected sine wave, so it seems the students have corrected the problem. Let's check the default plot of four harmonics, as shown in Figure 11.7.

If you have worked with Fourier series, you'll recognize that this figure also seems to be correct. But wait! Examine those ripples on the top and bottom of each waveform a little more closely. Would a magnifying glass help? Don't they seem a little jagged? We better check another waveform. Run the application once again, using 400 harmonics for the number of harmonic terms. Your results should appear similar to those in Figure 11.8.

While the waveform takes on the overall appearance of a 400 harmonic Fourier series, the tops and bottoms of the waveform have far too much "noise" floating on them. There is still something wrong!

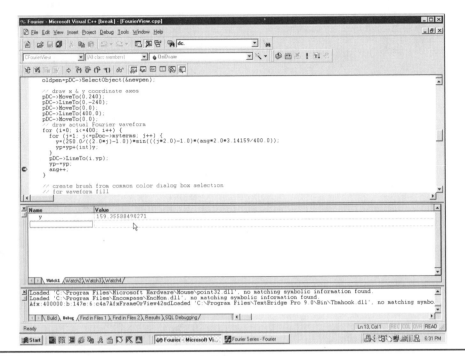

Figure 11.5   The results returned for an angle of 40 degrees

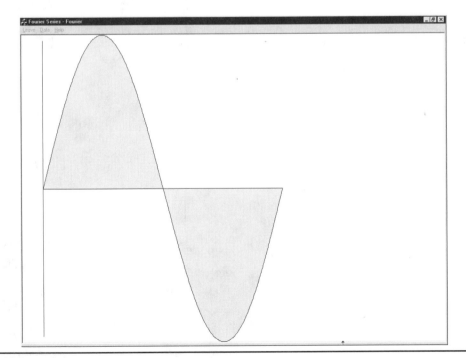

Figure 11.6   Plotting a single harmonic in the Fourier series

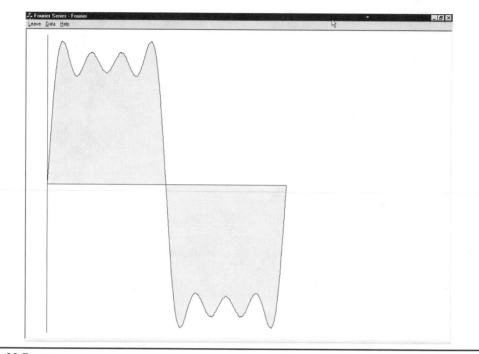

Figure 11.7 Plotting four harmonics in the Fourier series

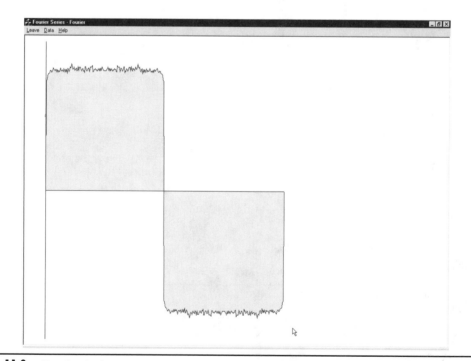

Figure 11.8 Four hundred terms produces bad waveforms on the top and bottom

Working on the Second Problem

The plot is close to correct, but it's not perfect. There is still something wrong with how the students are drawing the waveform.

```
// draw actual Fourier waveform
for (i=0; i<=400; i++) {
  for (j=1; j<=pDoc->myterms; j++) {
    y=(250.0/((2.0*j)-1.0))*sin(((j*2.0)-1.0)* \
      (ang*2.0*3.14159/400.0));
    yp=yp+(int)y;
  }
  pDC->LineTo(i,yp);
  yp-=yp;
  ang++;
}
```

Examine that equation again, and the solution to the problem almost pops out at you. It is true that the LineTo() function requires an integer value for the horizontal and vertical positions. These values are supplied by the *i* and *yp* variables. The *y* variable is a double that seems to have been converted to an integer before accumulating the sum in the *yp* variable. We suspected that the students were experiencing a premature rounding off of the *yp* value. This correction is easy enough to make. Simply declare *yp* as a **double** and alter the equation in the following manner:

```
// draw actual Fourier waveform
for (i=0; i<=400; i++) {
  for (j=1; j<=pDoc->myterms; j++) {
    y=(250.0/((2.0*j)-1.0))*sin(((j*2.0)-1.0)* \
      (ang*2.0*3.14159/400.0));
    yp=yp+y;
  }
  pDC->LineTo(i,(int) yp);
  yp-=yp;
  ang++;
}
```

By making the conversion from a **double** to an **int** in the LineTo() function, the maximum amount of plotting precision is preserved. Figure 11.9 shows the results for 400 harmonics with the modified equations.

The only thing remaining was to check the program for a variety of other Fourier terms. Everything was working perfectly until we reached 754 harmonic terms. For this value and all those above that value, the waveform plotted correctly, but the whole screen filled with the plotting color, as shown in Figure 11.10.

Back to the drawing board! This is a real problem because the application works perfectly most of the time.

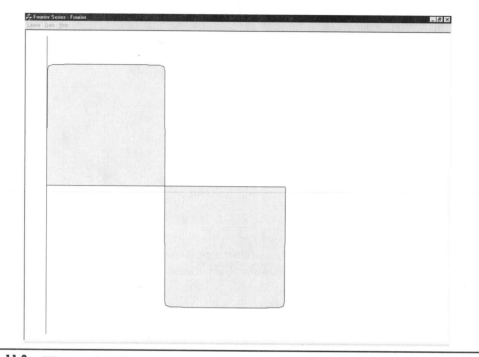

Figure 11.9   When rounded off errors are eliminated, the plot improves tremendously

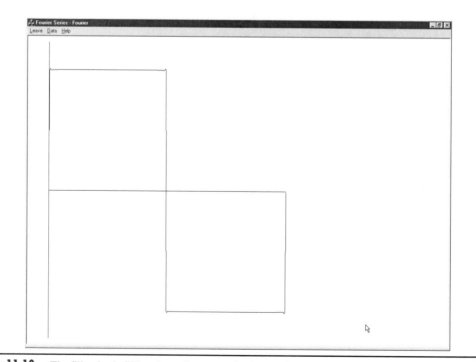

Figure 11.10   The fill color is filling the entire screen for harmonic values of 754 and greater

Working on the Third Problem

You wouldn't blame the students for thinking this was still a rounding error of some kind. As a matter of fact, it very well could have been, but it turned out to be a little trickier than either students or instructor initially thought.

Our advice was to go back and examine the values plotted to the screen using the Debugger's Watch window. Single-stepping through 754 x 400 = 301,600 points isn't going to be a lot of fun, but it is the sure way of spotting the problem. As luck would have it, the problem isn't spotted until the last point's value is found. The *y* value for the last point does not return to the x axis and close the shape. The ExtFloodFill() function, however, relies on filling a closed shape.

```
pDC->ExtFloodFill(150,10,RGB(0,0,0),FLOODFILLBORDER);
pDC->ExtFloodFill(300,-10,RGB(0,0,0),FLOODFILLBORDER);
```

In other words, the ExtFloodFill() function found a hole in the waveform, and when it filled the last portion, the color leaked out onto the whole screen!

The students quickly resolved the problem with this application by increasing the precision of the value used for pi from 3.14159 to 3.14159265359.

Figure 11.11 shows the window when 100,000 harmonics are used in the equation.

Figure 11.11 indicates that this project is now working without a problem.

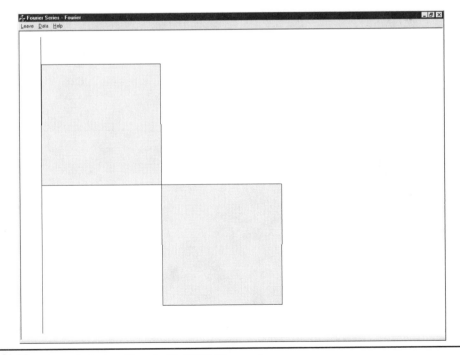

Figure 11.11   A good plot is achieved with 100,000 harmonics

Error Watch	*The LineTo() function converts the* yp *variable from a double to an integer. If the value was originally 179.9876 before conversion, it will be 179 after conversion. The point to watch is that the value will not be rounded up, as some might anticipate, and if you are counting on a rounded-up value to close a shape for a color fill, be prepared for another color leak!*

Repairing the Project

With all of the prepared code in place, let's look at the revised FourierView.cpp file. The following listing shows code we added to the AppWizard's initial template in a bold font:

```cpp
// FourierView.cpp : implementation of the CFourierView class
//

#include "stdafx.h"
#include "Fourier.h"

#include "FourierDoc.h"
#include "FourierView.h"

// additional header files needed
#include "FourierDlg.h"
#include "math.h"

CColorDialog dlg1;  // include common color dialog box

#ifdef _DEBUG
#define new DEBUG_NEW
#undef THIS_FILE
static char THIS_FILE[] = __FILE__;
#endif

/////////////////////////////////////////////////////////////////
// CFourierView

IMPLEMENT_DYNCREATE(CFourierView, CView)

BEGIN_MESSAGE_MAP(CFourierView, CView)
    //{{AFX_MSG_MAP(CFourierView)
    ON_WM_SIZE()
    ON_COMMAND(IDM_FOURIER, OnFourier)
    ON_COMMAND(IDM_COLOR, OnColor)
    //}}AFX_MSG_MAP
END_MESSAGE_MAP()

/////////////////////////////////////////////////////////////////
// CFourierView construction/destruction

CFourierView::CFourierView()
```

```
{
}

CFourierView::~CFourierView()
{
}

BOOL CFourierView::PreCreateWindow(CREATESTRUCT& cs)
{
    return CView::PreCreateWindow(cs);

}

/////////////////////////////////////////////////////////////////
// CFourierView drawing

void CFourierView::OnDraw(CDC* pDC)
{
    CFourierDoc* pDoc = GetDocument();
    ASSERT_VALID(pDoc);

    // all remaining code for Fourier Series
    int i,j,ang;
    double y, yp;
    CBrush newbrush;
    CBrush* oldbrush;
    CPen newpen;
    CPen* oldpen;

    // common color dialog box structure information
    // allow initial color value to be set
    dlg1.m_cc.Flags |= CC_FULLOPEN | CC_RGBINIT;
    dlg1.m_cc.rgbResult = pDoc->mycolor;

    pDC->SetMapMode(MM_ISOTROPIC);
    pDC->SetWindowExt(500,500);
    pDC->SetViewportExt(m_cxClient,-m_cyClient);
    pDC->SetViewportOrg(m_cxClient/20,m_cyClient/2);

    ang=0;
    yp=0.0;

    newpen.CreatePen(BS_SOLID,1,RGB(0,0,0));
    oldpen=pDC->SelectObject(&newpen);

    // draw x & y coordinate axes
    pDC->MoveTo(0,240);
    pDC->LineTo(0,-240);
    pDC->MoveTo(0,0);
    pDC->LineTo(400,0);
```

```
      pDC->MoveTo(0,0);
      // draw actual Fourier waveform
      for (i=0; i<=400; i++) {
        for (j=1; j<=pDoc->myterms; j++) {
          y=(250.0/((2.0*j)-1.0))* \
              sin(((j*2.0)-1.0)* \
              (ang*2.0*3.14159265359/400.0));
          yp=yp+y;
        }
        pDC->LineTo(i,(int) yp);
        yp-=yp;
        ang++;
      }

      // create brush from common color dialog box selection
      // for waveform fill
      newbrush.CreateSolidBrush(pDoc->mycolor);

      oldbrush=pDC->SelectObject(&newbrush);
      pDC->ExtFloodFill(150,10,RGB(0,0,0),FLOODFILLBORDER);
      pDC->ExtFloodFill(300,-10,RGB(0,0,0),FLOODFILLBORDER);

      // delete brush objects
      pDC->SelectObject(oldbrush);
      newbrush.DeleteObject();
}

/////////////////////////////////////////////////////////////////
// CFourierView diagnostics

#ifdef _DEBUG
void CFourierView::AssertValid() const
{
    CView::AssertValid();
}

void CFourierView::Dump(CDumpContext& dc) const
{
    CView::Dump(dc);
}

CFourierDoc* CFourierView::GetDocument() // non-debug inline
{
    ASSERT(m_pDocument->IsKindOf(RUNTIME_CLASS(CFourierDoc)));
    return (CFourierDoc*)m_pDocument;
}
#endif //_DEBUG

/////////////////////////////////////////////////////////////////
// CFourierView message handlers
```

```
void CFourierView::OnSize(UINT nType, int cx, int cy)
{
    CView::OnSize(nType, cx, cy);
    // TODO: Add your message handler code here

    // added for sizing and scaling window
    m_cxClient = cx;
    m_cyClient = cy;
}

void CFourierView::OnFourier()
{
    // TODO: Add your command handler code here

    // added to process dialog information
    FourierDlg dlg (this);
    int result = dlg.DoModal();

    if(result==IDOK) {
        CFourierDoc* pDoc = GetDocument();
        ASSERT_VALID(pDoc);

        pDoc->myterms=dlg.m_terms;
        Invalidate();
    }
}

void CFourierView::OnColor()
{
    // TODO: Add your command handler code here
    // added to process common color
    // dialog box information

    int result = dlg1.DoModal();

    if(result==IDOK) {
        CFourierDoc* pDoc = GetDocument();
        ASSERT_VALID(pDoc);

        // get returned color from dialog box
        pDoc->mycolor = dlg1.GetColor();
        InvalidateRect(NULL,TRUE);
        UpdateWindow();
    }
}
```

Remember that other files that support the operation of the dialog boxes and menu have not been discussed. These files are available on Osborne's Web site (www.osborne.com).

> **Design Tip** *If you want to experiment with the Fourier portion of this project, without the fuss of including the two dialog boxes, just make the* nterms *and* mycolor *variables local to the* OnDraw() *method and set them to a predefined value. For example,* nterms *could be set to 100 for 100 harmonics, and* mycolor *to RGB(255,255,0) for a yellow fill color.*

Conclusion

This chapter has worked with more complicated MFC Windows applications than the previous chapter. In seeking the solution to errors found in two student projects, you learned how to apply debugging techniques from earlier chapters, along with some powerful methods for detecting memory leaks in projects. In addition to the debugging tools used with the projects, you also learned how to analyze the problems as they were investigated and learned an organized approach to repairing the project code.

In the next two chapters, we'll pause in our use of the MFC library to introduce the Standard Template Library (STL). The remaining chapters of the book will return to the use of the MFC, with the final chapter showing debugging problems that can be repaired when using both the MFC and STL.

PART IV

The Standard Template Library

STL Coding Practices

S TL or the Standard Template Library is so new to ANSI/ISO C++ that many programmers are totally unaware of its existence. The broad scope, comprehensive recombination of standard C/C++ logic and syntax encapsulates *the* most important recent evolution of C++! Unfortunately, STL is such a complete package, from designed-in logic, advanced use of C++ syntax and interrelationships, that to knowledgeably debug STL code, you must first understand STL.

Chapter 12 quickly takes you from a standard knowledge of C/C++, updating your knowledge to today's new C++ keywords and syntax, on to reviewing class syntax and templates. After reading Chapter 12, you will have all of the conceptual understanding necessary to debug this most exciting addition to C++.

Multiple Architectures

From a programming viewpoint, today's development environment is a hundred times more complex than a decade ago. Instead of PC application development targeting a standalone DOS text-mode environment, it must now deal with hundreds of PC clones and other popular competing platforms.

These new architectures have their own evolving operating systems and multitasking, multimedia capabilities. Added to this is the typical Internet presence. In other words, today's programming environment, programmed by a single developer, was once the domain of specialists who understood multiple systems, communications, security, networking, utility, and so on; these specialists all worked as a *team* to keep the "mother ship," or mainframe, up and running!

Something had to come along to enable application developers to keep pace with this ever-increasing resource management nightmare. Voilà, enter C and C++. These new languages incorporated brand new programming capabilities to melt through this hidden iceberg of programming demands.

> **Design Tip**   *The biggest stumbling block to accessing the incredibly powerful features of C/C++ is ignorance of their existence.*

Taming C++

When asked by their bosses to use a new language, most experienced FORTRAN, COBOL, Pascal, PL/I, assembly language programmers taught themselves the new language! Why? Because, of course, the company wouldn't give them the time off. They diligently studied nights and weekends on their own and mapped their understanding of whatever language they knew well to the new language's syntax.

This approach worked for decades as long as a programmer went from one "older high-level language," to the next. Unfortunately, when it comes to C/C++, this approach leaves the diligent, self-motivated, self-taught employee *fired* and wondering what went wrong *this time?*

Here's a small example to illustrate the point. For instance, to increment a variable by 1 in COBOL, you would write:

```
accumulator = accumulator + 1.
```

Then one day, the boss says you need to write the program in FORTRAN. You learn FORTRAN and rewrite the statement:

```
accumulator = accumulator + 1
```

No problem. Then your company migrates to Pascal, and once again you teach yourself the new syntax:

```
accumulator := accumulator + 1;
```

Ta da! Then your boss says that your million-dollar code needs to be ported over to Microsoft Windows in C/C++. After a divorce, heart attack, and alcohol addiction, you emerge feeling you have mastered Microsoft Windows C/C++ logic and syntax and finally rewrite the statement:

```
iaccumulator = iaccumulator + 1; //i for integer in Hungarian notation
```

and you get fired! The senior programmer, hired from a local two-year college, looks at your code and scoffs at your inept translation. Oh, sure, you got the idea behind Hungarian Notation (a C/C++ naming convention that precedes every variable's name with an abbreviation of its data type), but you created a literal statement *translation* instead of incorporating the efficiency alternatives available in C/C++.

Error Watch *Simply translating a FORTRAN, COBOL, PL/I, Pascal, Basic, or Modula-2, high-level language statement into C/C++ is* not *programming in C/C++!*

Your senior programmer, green, twenty years younger than you, only knowing Microsoft Windows, C and C++ syntax, knew the statement should have been written:

```
iaccumulator++;
```

This statement, using the C/C++ increment operator, efficiently instructs the compiler to delete the double fetch/decode of the incorrectly written *translation* and to treat the variable *iaccumulator,* as its name implies, as an accumulator within a register, a much more efficient machine language encoding.

This extremely simple code example is only the beginning of hundreds of C/C++ language features waiting, like quicksand, to catch the unwary programmer. Because of these C/C++ peculiarities, this chapter highlights the STL-related C/C++ topics necessary to fully understand and use STL. The chapter assumes only a minimum comfort level with C/C++.

The first half of the chapter introduces you to STL philosophy. The last half of the chapter reviews the pivotal fundamentals provided by C/C++ that make STL possible and ends with the highest-level C++ syntax that actually creates STL's generic algorithms. While you may think you are an experienced enough C/C++ programmer to skip this chapter and begin immediately debugging STL, you may be surprised to find out just how much C++ has evolved. Even if you had an intro and advanced C/C++ course, you may again be surprised to find out just how much your professor *didn't* know or tell you. Or even worse, the C/C++ you currently know, quite frankly, is just plain incorrect. For all of these reasons, it is strongly suggested that you sit down with a cup of coffee and read this chapter all the way through.

STL—Data Structures in a Box?

In a programmer's formal educational path, there stands a course typically called "Data Structures," which statistically has an attrition rate of 50 percent. Why? Because it deals with two extremely efficient concepts, pointers, and dynamic memory allocation/deallocation, which when combined, generate a geometric complexity in program development and debugging requirements. These concepts typically present such a steep learning curve that many programmers either avoid the course altogether, or lop along, get by, and then *never* use data structures concepts in the real world. This is unfortunate since pointers and dynamic memory allocation present some of the most powerful and efficient algorithms available to a programmer. Enter the Standard Template Library!

STL—A First Look

In a nutshell, STL (the Standard Template Library) encapsulates the pure raw horsepower of the C/C++ languages, plus the advanced efficient algorithms engendered within a good data structures course, all bundled into a simple-to-use form! It is similar, in a way, to having struggled with years of pre-calc and calculus courses, only to be given an advanced portable calculator that does all the work for you.

You may view the Standard Template Library as an extensible framework that contains components for language support, diagnostics, general utilities, strings, locales, standard template library (containers, iterators, algorithms, and numerics), and input/output.

STL and Hewlett-Packard

With the ever-increasing popularity of C/C++ and Microsoft Windows controlled environments, many third-party vendors evolved into extremely profitable commodities by providing libraries of routines designed to handle the storage and processing of data. In an ever-ongoing attempt to maintain C/C++'s viability as a programming language of choice, and to keep the ball rolling by maintaining a strict control of the languages' formal definition, the ANSI/ISO C++ added a new approach to defining these libraries called the Standard Template Library or STL.

STL was developed by Alexander Stepanov and Meng Lee of Hewlett-Packard. STL is expected to become the standard approach to storing and processing data. Major compiler vendors are beginning to incorporate STL into their products. STL is more than just a minor addition to the world's most popular programming language; it represents a revolutionary new capability. STL brings a surprisingly mature set of generic containers and algorithms to the C++ programming language, adding a dimension to the language that simply did not exist before.

STL for the Masses

Unlike many other STL books that simply enumerate endless lists of STL template names, functions, constants, and so on, this chapter will begin by first teaching you the advanced C/C++ language fundamentals that make STL syntactically possible. With this understanding, you can move on to Chapter 13.

Along the way, this instructional section will show you the syntax that allows an algorithm to be generic—in other words, how C/C++ syntactically separates *what* a program does from the *data type(s)* it uses. You will learn about generic **void *** pointers' strengths and weaknesses, "a better way" with generic types, and "an even better way" using templates, and finally, the "best way" with cross-platform, portable, standard templates!

The section on template development begins with simple C/C++ structures used syntactically to create *objects!* The **struct** object definition is then evolved over, logically and syntactically, into the C++ **class**. Finally, the **class** object is mutated into a generic **template**. This progressive approach allows you to easily assimilate the new features of C/C++ and paves the way to technically correct use and debugging of STL code. With this under your belt, you will both logically and syntactically understand how STL works and begin to immediately incorporate this technology into your application development.

Generic programming is going to provide the power and expressiveness of languages like SmallTalk while retaining the efficiency and compatibility of C++. STL is guaranteed to increase the productivity of any programmer who uses it.

STL—The "Big Picture"

Although STL is large and its syntax can be initially intimidating, it is actually quite easy to use once you understand how it is constructed and what elements it employs. At the core of STL are three foundational items called *containers, algorithms,* and *iterators.* These libraries work together, allowing you to generate, in a portable format, frequently employed algorithmic solutions, such as array creation, element insertion/deletion, sorting, and element output. But STL goes even further by providing internally clean, seamless, and efficient integration of iostreams and exception handling.

STL ANSI/ISO C++ Acceptance

Multivendor implementations of C/C++ compilers would have long ago died on the vine were it not for the ANSI C/C++ Committees. They are responsible for giving us *portable* C and C++ code by filling in the *missing* details for the formal language descriptions of both C and C++ as presented by their authors, Dennis Ritchie, and Bjarne Stroustrup. And to this day, the ANSI/ISO C++ Committee continues to guarantee C++'s portability into the new millennium.

While we're on the subject of language authorship, Alexander Stepanov and Meng Lee of Hewlett-Packard developed the concept and coding behind the Standard Template Library. The industry anticipates that STL will become *the* standard approach to storing and processing data.

The ANSI/ISO C++ Committee's current standards exceed their past recommendations, which decided only to codify existing practice and resolve ambiguities and contradictions among existing translator implementations. The C++ Committee's changes are innovations. In most cases, the changes implement features that committee members admired in other languages, features that they view as deficiencies in traditional C++ or simply features that they've always wanted in a programming language. A *great* deal of thought and discussions have been invested in each change, and consequently, the committee feels that the new C++ definition, along with the evolutionary definition of STL, is the best definition of C++ possible today.

Most of these recommended changes consist of language additions that should not affect existing code. Old programs should still compile with newer compilers as long as the old code does not coincidentally use any of the new keywords as identifiers. However, even experienced C++ programmers may be surprised at how much of C++ has evolved even without discussing STL—for example, the use of namespaces, new-style type casting, and runtime type information.

Fundamental Components of STL

Conceptually, STL encompasses three separate algorithmic problem solvers. The three most important are containers, algorithms, and iterators. A *container* is a way that stored data is organized in memory, for example, an array, stack, queue, linked list, or binary-tree. However, there are many other kinds of containers, and STL includes the most useful. STL containers are implemented by template classes so they can be easily customized to hold different data types.

All the containers have common management member functions defined in their template definitions: insert(), erase(), begin(), end(), size(), capacity(), and so on. Individual containers have member functions that support their unique requirements.

Algorithms are behaviors or functionality applied to containers to process their contents in various ways. For example, there are algorithms to sort, copy, search, and merge container contents. In STL, algorithms are represented by template functions. These functions are not member functions of the container classes. Instead, they are standalone functions. Indeed, one of the surprising characteristics of STL is that its algorithms are so general. You can use them not only on STL containers, but also on ordinary C++ arrays or any other application-specific container.

A standard suite of algorithms provides for searching for, copying, reordering, transforming, and performing numeric operations on the objects in the containers. The same algorithm is used to perform a particular operation for all containers of all object types!

Once you have decided on a container type, and data behaviors, the only thing left is to interact the two with *iterators*. You can think of an iterator as a generalized pointer that points to elements within a container. You can increment an iterator, as you can a pointer, so it points in turn to each successive element in the container. Iterators are a key part of STL because they connect algorithms with containers.

What Is a Container?

All STL library syntax incorporates the full use of C++ templates (data type–independent syntax). As we discuss the container types, remember that they are implemented as templates; the types of objects they contain are determined by the template arguments given when the program instantiates the containers. There are three major types of containers, vectors (or dynamic arrays), deques (or double-ended queues), and linear lists, along with specialized classes bitset, map, and multimap.

Sequence containers store finite sets of objects of the same type in a linear organization. An array of names is a sequence. You use one of the sequence types—vector, list, or deque—for a particular application, depending on its retrieval requirements.

vector Class

Vector sequences allow random data access. A vector is an array of contiguous homogeneous objects with an instance counter or pointer to indicate the end of the vector sequence. Random access is facilitated through the use of a subscript operation. Vector sequences allow you to append entries to and remove entries from the end of the dynamic structure without undue overhead. Inserts and deletes from the middle, however, naturally take longer due to the time involved in shifting the remaining entries to make room for the new or deleted item.

list Class

A list sequence provides bidirectional access; it allows you to perform inserts and deletes anywhere without undue performance penalties. Random access is simulated by forward or backward iteration to the target object. A list consists of noncontiguous objects linked with forward and backward pointers.

deque Class

A deque sequence is similar to a vector sequence, except that a deque sequence allows fast inserts and deletes at the beginning as well as the end of the container. Random inserts and deletes are less efficient.

bitset Class

The bitset class supports operations on a set of bits, such as, flip(), reset(), set(), size(), to_string, and so on.

map Class

The map class provides associative containers with unique keys mapped to specific values.

multimap Class

The multimap class is similar to the map class in raw horsepower except for one minor difference: no availability of a unique key mapped to specific values.

What Is an Adapter?

STL supports three adapter containers that you can combine with one of the sequence containers listed previously. The scenario goes like this: first, you select the appropriate application-specific container; next, you instantiate a container adapter class by naming the existing container in the declaration:

```
queue< list< bank_customer_struct > >TellerOneQueue;
```

The example instantiates a queue container, one of the three adapter containers supported by STL, by using the list container as the underlying data structure built around a hypothetical bank customer waiting for an available teller.

Container adapters hide the public interface of the underlying container and implement their own. A queue data structure, for example, resembles a list but has its own requirements for its user interface. STL incorporates three standard adapter containers: stack, queue, and priority_queue.

stack Class

The stack adapter provides the logical operations of push() and pop(), enabling the standard Last In First Out, or LIFO solution. Stacks are great for certain types of problem solutions like evaluating an Infix arithmetic expression that has been translated into Postfix for the purposes of unambiguous evaluation.

queue Class

Regardless of whether the storage sequence container is a vector or linked list, the queue adapter uses this underlying scheme to add items to the end of the list, using the push() method, and to delete or remove items from the front of the list, using pop(). The acronym for a queue algorithm is First In First Out, or FIFO.

priority_queue Class

A priority_queue is similar to a queue adapter in that all items added to the queue are at the end of the list. However, unlike a queue adapter, which *only* removes items from the front of the list, a priority_queue adapter removes the highest priority item within the list first!

What Are Algorithms?

Similar to container adapters, algorithms also act on containers. Algorithms provide for container initializations, sorting, searching, and data transformations. Interestingly, algorithms are *not* implemented as class methods but instead, standalone template functions. For this reason, they work not only on STL containers, but on standard C++ arrays or with container classes you create yourself.

Typical algorithmic behaviors include find(), to locate a specific item; count(), letting you know how many items are in the list; equal(), for comparisons; search(); copy(); swap(); fill(); and sort().

What Is an Iterator?

Whenever an application needs to move through the elements of a container, it uses an iterator. Iterators are similar to pointers used to access individual data items. In STL, an iterator is represented by an object of an iterator class. You can increment an iterator with the C/C++ increment operator, ++, moving it to the address of the next element. You can also use the dereference operator, *, to access individual members within the selected item. Special iterators are capable of remembering the location of specific container elements.

There are different classes of iterators, which must be used with specific container types. The three major classes of iterators are: forward, bidirectional, and random-access:

- Forward iterators can advance only forward through the container one item at a time. A forward iterator cannot move backward, nor can it be updated to point to any location in the middle of the container.

- Backward iterators work like the forward iterator counterparts, except backward.
- Bidirectional iterators can move forward as well as backward and cannot be assigned or updated to point to any element in the middle of the container.
- Random-access iterators go one step further than bidirectional iterators in that they do allow the application to perform arbitrary location jumps within the container.

In addition, STL defines two specialized categories known as input and output iterators. Input and output iterators can point to specific devices; for example, an input iterator may point to a user-defined input file, or cin, and perform sequential reads into the container. Likewise, an output iterator may point to a user-defined output file or cout, performing the logical inverse operation of sequentially outputting container elements.

Unlike forward, backward, bidirectional, and random-access iterators, input and output iterators cannot store their current values. Forward, backward, bidirectional, and random-access iterators must hold their values in order for them to know where they are within the container. Input and output iterators, since they are pointers to devices, do not structurally represent the same type of information and therefore have no memory capabilities.

Are There Any More STL Components?

Beyond containers, algorithms, and iterators, STL defines several additional components:

- *Allocators* for managing memory allocation for an individual container
- *Predicates,* which are unary or binary in nature, meaning they work on either one operand or two and always return either true or false
- *Comparison function,* a unique binary predicate comparing two elements and returning true only if the first argument is less than the second
- *Function objects* including plus, minus, multiply, divide, modulus, negate, equal_to, not_equal_to, greater, greater_equal, less, less_equal, logical_and, logical_or, and logical_not

The Complete STL Package

The following review is included to help you formalize the structural components of the Standard Template Library. You can logically divide STL into the following categories:

A. STL headers can be grouped into three major organizing concepts:

1. Containers are template classes that support common ways to organize data: <deque>, <list>, <map>, <multimap>, <queue>, <set>, <stack>, and <vector>.

2. Algorithms are template functions for performing common operations on sequences of objects including: <algorithm>, <functional>, and <numeric>.

3. Iterators are the glue that pastes together algorithms and containers and include <iterator>, <memory>, and <utility>.

B. Input output includes components for:

1. Forward declarations of iostreams <iosfwd>

2. Predefined iostreams objects <iostream>

3. Base iostreams classes <ios>

4. Stream buffering <streambuf>

5. Stream formatting and manipulators: <iosmanip>, <istream>, and <ostream>

6. String streams <sstream>

7. File streams<fstream>

C. Other standard C++ headers include:

1. Language support includes:

a. Components for common type definitions used throughout the library <cstddef>

b. Characteristics of the predefined types <limits>, <cfloat>, and <climits>

c. Functions supporting the start and termination of a C++ program <cstdlib>

d. Support for dynamic memory management <new>

e. Support for dynamic type identification <typeinfo>

f. Support for exception processing <exception>

g. Other runtime support <cstdarg>, <ctime>, <csetlmp>, and <csignal>

2. Diagnostics includes components for:

a. Reporting several kinds of exceptional conditions <stdexcept>

b. Documenting program assertions <cassert>

c. A global variable for error number codes <cerrno>

3. Strings includes components for:

a. String classes <string>

b. Null-terminated sequence utilities: <cctype>, <cwctype>, and <cwchar>

4. Cultural language components includes:

a. Internationalization support for character classification and string collation, numeric, monetary, and date/time formatting and parsing, and message retrieval using <locale> and <clocale>

Historic C, ANSI C, C++, ANSI C++—HELP!

Chaos! The world of C/C++ programming is a mess. There's "Historic C," ANSI C, C++, ANSI C++, ANSI/ISO C++, Borland International's C/C++, Microsoft's C/C++, your senior programmer's version of C/C++, maybe even a version of C/C++ created by an egocentric, self-taught university professor, not to mention next year's state-of-the-art C/C++ bells 'n whistle standard.

The biggest problem in learning C/C++ is finding a reputable source. With few exceptions, many programmers have taught themselves C/C++. They were professionally degreed programmers, with many years of experience, who evolved from some institutional training language to whatever language was in vogue that day. So the scenario typically went from COBOL, to FORTRAN, to PL/I, to Pascal, to Modula-2, and on and on.

This scenario actually worked out quite well *in the past,* because all of the older high-level languages had basically the same features, just different syntax. Now take this previously successful self-taught, highly motivated programmer and thrust her into the world of multitasking application development in a GUI (graphical user interface) environment, using C/C++ and object-oriented technology. Result? Chaos!

C and C++ provide so many new language features, design philosophies, and sophisticated syntax that mapping over your understanding from some other language just will not do. This book is all about you learning to fly a stealth bomber called "STL," and it's quite possible that the only thing you've ever gotten off the ground was a Piper Cub.

The great news is that, with a few instructional tips, you *can* take what you currently know about any programming language and get up to speed on this latest technology. That is what this chapter is all about. So let's get started.

Data Structures—A Review

The code contained within the Standard Template Library is extremely efficient. One means to this efficiency is that the objects created use dynamically allocated memory, tracked by pointers. This section reviews the C/C++ building blocks making this possible.

Static Versus Dynamic

First, it is important to understand that the word *static* used in this section is *not* the C/C++ keyword **static**. Instead, *static* is used to describe a category of memory allocation. Since most programmers understand code more clearly than verbiage, here's an example:

```
void main( void )
{
  int ivalue;        // i(nt)value
  .
  .
  .
}
```

This code segment declares an integer variable *ivalue*. Now if you think about it, *ivalue*'s storage location is allocated when the program loads, and this memory allocation persists until the program exits. This is an example of static memory allocation.

Static memory allocation is *not* under the control of the programmer at runtime but instead, is under load-time control. The programmer cannot get more *ivalue*s, nor can the programmer delete *ivalue*'s memory allocation at runtime. And that is the downfall to this storage class.

Dynamic memory allocation has the advantage of being under runtime control. Unfortunately, its syntax is not as straightforward and entails the use of pointers. (Note: The following example only highlights the difference between static and dynamic memory allocation and is not intended as a real-world example.)

```
void main( void )
  int *pivalue;            // p(ointer to)i(nt)value;
  int iLoopControl, iAsManyAsUserWants;
  cout << "How many integer's would you like to create at run-time?";
  cin >> iAsManyAsUserWants;
  for( iLoopControl = 0, iLoopControl < iAsManyAsUserWants, iLoopControl++)
    pivalue = new int;// pivalue set to address of
                      // run-time dynamically allocated RAM
```

In this example, the variable *pivalue* is not an integer but instead, is a *pointer variable* that can hold the address to a RAM location big enough to store an integer. Actual integer-sized RAM allocation is accomplished with the C++ **new** keyword. C programmers might recognize the equivalent to **new** as **malloc()** or **calloc()**.

Most importantly, notice that the end-user at runtime can select just how many integers they would like to store. Also at runtime, the user can choose how many to delete by simply using the C++ keyword **delete** as in:

```
delete pivalue;
```

It is simple to see that runtime control of memory allocation/deallocation has tremendous efficiency benefits. Your program is never grabbing system resources beyond its current needs. STL makes heavy use of this fundamental.

Typed Pointers

Unlike normal variables of the type **int**, **float**, and **char**, pointer variables do not hold data per se; instead, they hold addresses to data. In the last section, you saw just how efficient this concept can be when combined with dynamic memory allocation. However, one problem is generated by these sibling concepts: type checking!

By design, C and C++ are not strongly typed languages. This means that both compilers will accept statements like:

```
char cvalue = 65;      // initializing a character variable with an integer
```

and

```
int ivalue = 'A';        // initializing an integer variable with a character
```

However, when it comes to pointers, both C and C++ become strongly typed languages. So, for example, a float-sized dynamically allocated memory location's address may not be assigned to a pointer of type int, as in:

```
int *pivalue;            // p(ointer to) i(nt)value;
pivalue = new float;     // illegal attempt to
                         // assign a float address to int pointer
```

From their inceptions, C and C++ have had a syntactical way around type checking by using the standard type **void**.

Void Pointers

The C/C++ void data type, when combined with pointer variable definitions, tells the compilers that the defined variable does not hold data per se, but an address, but it does *not* tell the compilers to what data type! This can lead to very powerful code solutions.

In the following example, one subroutine is used to output one of three dynamically allocated data types:

```
 #include <iostream>
using namespace std;

void printit ( void *pData, char cRunTimeChoice );

void main ( void )
{
  char  *pchar, cRunTimeChoice;
  int   *pivalue;
  float *pfvalue;

  cout << "Please enter the dynamic data type you want to create\n"
       << " press c for char, i for int, or f for float: ";

  cin  >> cRunTimeChoice;

  switch ( cRunTimeChoice ) {

    case 'c': pchar = new char;
    cout << "\nEnter a character: ";
    cin  >> *pchar;
    printit ( pchar, cRunTimeChoice );
    break;

    case 'i': pivalue = new int;
```

```
   cout << "\nEnter an integer: ";
   cin  >> *pivalue;
   printit ( pivalue, cRunTimeChoice );
   break;

default:  pfvalue = new float;
cout << "\nEnter a float: ";
cin  >> *pfvalue;
printit ( pfvalue, cRunTimeChoice );

     }
}


void printit ( void *pData, char cRunTimeChoice )
{
   cout << "\nThe Dynamic Data type entered was ";

   switch ( cRunTimeChoice ) {

     case 'c': cout << "char and a value of: "
                    << *(char *)pData;
                    break;
     case 'i': cout << "int and a value of: "
                    << *(int *)pData;
                    break;
     default:  cout << "float and a value of: "
                    << *(float *)pData;

   }
   delete pData;
}
```

The key statements to understanding void pointers are the *printit( )* prototype:

```
void printit ( void *pData, char cRunTimeChoice );
```

and the three calls to *printit( )*:

```
printit ( pchar,   cRunTimeChoice );
printit ( pivalue, cRunTimeChoice );
printit ( pfvalue, cRunTimeChoice );
```

Notice how you have officially told the compiler that *printit( )*'s first formal argument type is a **void** pointer (**void ***). This suspends normal type checking between a function's formal argument list and the calling statement's actual arguments—the only reason the program works.

However, unlike **int ***, or **float *** pointer variable declarations, syntax using **void ***s:

```
void * pToWhoKnowsWhat;
```

do not specify *what* data type the pointer variable points to. This is both good and bad. It's good because the compiler can't do any type checking when an actual address is assigned, and bad because the compiler can't do any type checking! Even worse, a program cannot point with a **void *** type. This explains the three cast statements within *printit()*'s **switch-case** statement converting a pointer to nothing (**void ***) to a specific pointer type:

```
*(char *)pData;
*(int *)pData;
*(float *)pData;
```

Without type checking, if your code accidentally assigns the wrong address type, the code compiles:

```
void * pivalue; // variable name indicates it will hold an int type address
...
pivalue = new float; // incorrect assignment of RAM float precision!
```

The previous code section declares *pivalue* as a **void *** pointer; however, the variable's name implies that it will hold the address to an integer *p*(ointer to)*i*(nt). The pointer is then initialized to the address of a float-sized memory location. Still, perfectly legal code, maybe even logically OK for some applications, but look at these next two statements:

```
some_function( pivalue );            // call to some function
...
void some_function( int * pivalue ); // function prototype
```

First, the code may or may not compile based on the compiler's error/warning level settings because the compilers (C/C++) recognize that *pivalue*'s formal declaration **void *** does not match the function's first formal argument type of **int ***. Remember, pointers are by default typed, and the compiler, at compile-time, recognizes the mismatch. But a clever C/C++ programmer could rewrite the call statement to:

```
some_function( (int *) pivalue );     // working call statement!
...
void some_function( int * pivalue )
{
  //    sample function body code...
  cout << "The integer value is: " << *pivalue; // outputs garbage
```

Executing a program of this nature causes *some_function()* to output garbage since the memory location contains an IEEE floating-point encrypted value, and the function instructs the compiler to decode a four-byte integer!

Error Watch *Always remember that formal function arguments of the **void *** type obliterate the compiler's ability to flag, at compile-time, the passing of an unanticipated pointer type, setting the stage for runtime catastrophe!*

The sad news is that the code compiles! No warnings and no errors. The point is (no pun intended) **void** pointers can create debugging and runtime nightmares. The solution is the C++ template.

Hungarian Notation Revisited

Test question: Is there anything wrong with the following code segment?

```
int operandA = 1, operandB = 2;
float result;
...
result = operandA / operandB
```

If you answered yes, great! However, if you think the equation is fine . . . well, let's just say it's a good thing there's Hungarian Notation, invented by Charles Simony.

The initial problem begins with the C/C++ divide operator, /, which is overloaded for different data types. In many other programming languages, two separate operators distinguish integral division from floating-point division. Pascal, for example, uses the divide operator, /, for floating-point precision, and the **div** operator for integral results. Obviously, a Pascal programmer can easily see which operator an equation employs. Unfortunately for unwary C/C++ programmers, there are no visual clue similarities. Instead, the C/C++ divide operator itself examines each operand's formal data type and then decides whether or not to perform integer/integer division with an integer result, or floating-point/floating-point with a floating-point result. The previous equation assigns a 0 to the variable *result* instead of the logically intended 0.5 (since *result*'s type is float) because *operandA* and *operandB*'s data types are integer.

Now, imagine that the equation is nested in a large program that is miscalculating values and you, *not* the author of the code, must track down the problem. Enter Hungarian Notation. In Hungarian Notation, each identifier's name (your name for variables, constants, and so on) begins with an abbreviation of its data type. Here are some examples (notice the alignment for the pointer variables *piValue*, *pfValue*, and *pszLastName*, which place the pointer operator, *, one column to the left of the other data types, highlighting the fact that these variables are pointers to data, not data per se):

```
char         cMenuSelection;
int          iValue;
float        fValue;
char         szLastName[ MAX_LETTERS + NULL_STRING_TERMINATOR ];
int         *piValue;
float       *pfValue;
char        *pszLastName = szLastName;
double       dValue, *pdValue = &pValue;
long double  ldValue, *pldValue = &pldValue;
```

Now, imagine the rewrite of the original code segment:

```
int iOperandA = 1, iOperandB = 2;
float fResult;
...
fResult = iOperandA / iOperandB
```

In this version, an experienced C/C++ programmer, seeing the divide operator employed on two *i*(nt tagged) variable names and then a *f*(loat tagged)*Result* storage precision would immediately suspect the equation as possibly generating the beginnings of a numeric miscalculation.

With the hundreds of thousands of lines of code given to you in the Microsoft Windows objects, or IBM's OS/2 objects, Hungarian Notation goes a long way to helping a programmer intimately understand the data types involved in an algorithm. This directly translates into timesavings whether in digesting a program's logic or in flagging starting points for a debugging session.

Design Tip *Pointers to data are more efficient than static variables; void pointers are clever solutions to compile-time formal argument versus actual argument road blocks. Templatized pointers are the ultimate goal with their impenetrable syntax!*

Overloading Functions

Many C++ object-oriented concepts have procedural underpinnings. Function overloading is a procedural concept that allows a programmer to define several functions by the same name. The syntax requires only that each function's formal argument list be unique. Unique is defined by the number of formal arguments, and/or their order, and/or their data type(s). Look at the following example function prototypes:

```
int averageArray(int iarray[]);
float averageArray(float farray[]);
double averageArray(double darray[]);
```

Beyond the straightforward syntax is the proper logical use of function overloading. Typically, this involves a repetition of function body algorithms that do the same thing, but very often on different data types—case in point, the averaging of array elements. One subroutine performs this array element processing on integer array elements, another on float array elements, the third on double array elements. However, all three functions *average array elements!*

24x7

An overloaded function's return type does not play any role in defining uniqueness. For this reason, the following overloaded function prototypes are illegal:

```
void averageArray(int iarray[]);
int averageArray(int iarray[]);
float averageArray(int iarray[]);
```

While function overloading is a powerful procedural problem-solving tool, it is also the building block concept behind overloaded class member functions (classes are reviewed later in this chapter).

Function Pointers

All the examples so far have shown you how various items of data can be referenced by a pointer. As it turns out, you can also access *portions of code* by using a pointer to a function. Pointers to functions serve the same purpose, as do pointers to data; that is, they allow the function to be referenced indirectly, just as a pointer to a data item allows the data item to be referenced indirectly.

A pointer to a function can have a number of important uses. For example, consider the **qsort( )** function. The **qsort( )** function has as one of its parameters a pointer to a function. The referenced function contains the necessary comparison that is to be performed between the array elements being sorted. **qsort( )** has been written to require a function pointer because the comparison process between two elements can be a complex process beyond the scope of a single control flag. It is not possible to pass a function by value, that is, pass the code itself. C/C++, however, does support passing a pointer to the code or a pointer to the function.

The concept of function pointers is frequently illustrated by using the **qsort( )** function supplied with the compiler. Unfortunately, in many cases, the function pointer is declared to be of a type that points to other built-in functions. The following C and C++ programs demonstrate how to define a pointer to a function and how to "roll your own" function to be passed to the stdlib function **qsort( )**. Here is the C++ program:

```
//   qsort.cpp
//   A C program illustrating how to declare your own
//   function and function pointer to be used with qsort( )
//   Chris H. Pappas and William H. Murray, 1998
//
#include <iostream>
#include <stdlib>

#define IMAXVALUES 10

int icompare_funct(const void *iresult_a, const void *iresult_b);
int (*ifunct_ptr)(const void *,const void *);

void main( )
{
  int i;
  int iarray[IMAXVALUES]={0,5,3,2,8,7,9,1,4,6};

  ifunct_ptr=icompare_funct;
  qsort(iarray,IMAXVALUES,sizeof(int),ifunct_ptr);
  for(i = 0; i < IMAXVALUES; i++)
    cout <<[{|"|}]" << iarray[i];
}

int icompare_funct(const void *iresult_a, const void *iresult_b)
{
  return((*(int *)iresult_a) - (*(int *)iresult_b));
}
```

The function *icompare_funct( )* (which will be called the *reference function*) was prototyped to match the requirements for the fourth parameter to the function **qsort( )** (which will be called the *invoking function*).

To digress slightly, the fourth parameter to the function **qsort( )** must be a function pointer. This reference function must be passed two const **void *** parameters, and it must return a type int. (Note: Remember that the position of the **const** keyword, in the formal parameter list, *locks* the data pointed to, not the address used to point. This means that even if you write your compare routine so that it *does not* sort properly, it can in *no way* destroy the contents of your array!) This is because **qsort( )** uses the reference function for the sort comparison algorithm. Now that you understand the prototype of the reference function *icompare_funct( )*, take a minute to study the body of the reference function.

If the reference function returns a value less than zero, then the reference function's first parameter value is less than the second parameter's value. A return value of zero indicates parameter value equality, with a return value greater than zero indicating that the second parameter's value was greater than the first's. All of this is accomplished by the single statement in *icompare_funct( )*:

```
return((*(int *)iresult_a) - (*(int *) iresult_b));
```

Since both of the pointers were passed as type **void ***, they were cast to their appropriate pointer type **int *** and then dereferenced (*). The result of the subtraction of the two values pointed to returns an appropriate value to satisfy **qsort( )**'s comparison criterion.

While the prototype requirements for *icompare_funct( )* are interesting, the meat of the program begins with the pointer function declaration below the *icompare_funct( )* function prototype:

```
int icompare_funct(const void *iresult_a, const void *iresult_b);
int (*ifunct_ptr)(const void *, const void *);
```

A function's type is determined by its return value and argument list signature. A pointer to *icompare_funct( )* must specify the same signature and return type. You might therefore think the following statement would accomplish this:

```
int *ifunct_ptr(const void *, const void *);
```

That is almost correct. The problem is that the compiler interprets the statement as the definition of a function *ifunct_ptr( )*, taking two arguments and returning a pointer of type **int ***. Unfortunately, the dereference operator is associated with the type specifier, not ***ifunct_ptr( )***. Parentheses are necessary to associate the dereference operator with *ifunct_ptr( )*.

The corrected statement declares *ifunct_ptr( )* to be a pointer to a function taking two arguments and with a return type int—that is, a pointer of the same type required by the fourth parameter to **qsort( )**.

In the body of **main( )**, the only thing left to do is to initialize *ifunct_ptr( )* to the address of the function *icompare_funct( )*. The parameters to **qsort( )** are the address to the base or zeroth element of the table to be sorted (*iarray*), the number of entries in the table (*IMAXVALUES*), the size of each table element (sizeof(int)), and a function pointer to the comparison function (*ifunct_ptr( )*).

Learning to understand the syntax of a function pointer can be challenging. Let's look at just a few examples. Here is the first one:

```
int *(*(*ifunct_ptr)(int))[5];
float (*(*ffunct_ptr)(int,int))(float);
```

```
typedef double (*(*(*dfunct_ptr)( ))[5])( );
  dfunct_ptr A_dfunct_ptr;
(*(*function_ary_ptrs( ))[5])( );
```

The first statement defines *ifunct_ptr( )* to be a function pointer to a function that is passed an integer argument and returns a pointer to an array of five int pointers.

The second statement defines *ffunct_ptr( )* to be a function pointer to a function that takes two integer arguments and returns a pointer to a function taking a float argument and returning a float.

By using the typedef declaration, you can avoid the unnecessary repetition of complicated declarations. The typedef declaration is read as follows: *dfunct_ptr( )* is defined as a pointer to a function that is passed nothing and returns a pointer to an array of five pointers that point to functions that are passed nothing and returns a double.

The last statement is a function declaration, not a variable declaration. The statement defines *function_ary_ptrs( )* to be a function taking no arguments and returning a pointer to an array of five pointers that point to functions taking no arguments and returning integers. The outer functions return the default C and C++ type int.

The good news is that you will rarely encounter complicated declarations and definitions like these. However, by making certain you understand these declarations, you will be able to confidently parse the everyday variety.

Overloading Operators

Earlier in this chapter, you learned that it is possible to overload functions and member functions in a class. In this section, you will learn that it is also possible to overload C++ operators. In C++, new definitions can be applied to such familiar operators as +, -, *, and / in a given class.

The idea of operator overloading is common in numerous programming languages, even if it is not specifically implemented. For example, all compiled languages make it possible to add two integers, two floats, or two doubles (or their equivalent types) with the + operator. This is the essence of operator overloading—using the same operator on different data types. It is possible to extend this simple concept even further in C++. In most compiled languages, it is not possible, for example, to take a complex number, matrix, or character string and add them together with the + operator.

These operations are valid in all programming languages:

$$3 + 8$$
$$3.3 + 7.2$$

These operations are typically not valid operations:

$$(4 - j4) + (5 + j10)$$
$$(15° \ 20' \ 15") + (53° \ 57' \ 40")$$
$$\text{“combine”} + \text{“strings”}$$

If the last three operations were possible with the + operator, the workload of the programmer would be greatly reduced when designing new applications. The good news is that in C++, the + operator can be overloaded, and the previous three operations can be made valid. Many additional operators can also be overloaded. Operator overloading is used extensively in C++. You will find examples throughout the various Microsoft C++ libraries.

Overloaded Operators and Function Calls

In C++, the following operators can be overloaded:

```
+       -       *       /       =       <       >       +=      -=

*=      /=      <<      >>      >>=     <<=     ==      !=      <=

>=      ++      --      %       &       ^^      !       |       ~

&=      ^=      |=      .&&     ||      %=      []      ()      new

delete
```

The main restrictions are that the syntax and precedence of the operator must remain unchanged from its originally defined meaning. Another important point is that operator overloading is valid only within the scope of the class in which overloading occurs.

Writing Your Own Overloaded Operators

In order to overload an operator, the operator keyword is followed by the operator itself:

```
type operator opr(param list)
```

For example:

```
angle_value operator +(angle_argument);
```

Here, *angle_value* is the name of the class type, followed by the operator keyword, then the operator itself (+), and a parameter to be passed to the overloaded operator.

Within the scope of a properly defined class, several angles specified in degrees/minutes/seconds could be directly added together:

```
angle_value angle1("37° 15' 56\"");
angle_value angle2("10° 44' 44\"");
angle_value angle3("75° 17' 59\"");
angle_value angle4("130° 32' 54\"");
angle_value sum_of_angles;

sum_of_angles=angle1+angle2+angle3+angle4;
```

As you know from earlier examples, the symbol for seconds is the double quote mark ("). This symbol is also used to signal the beginning and ending of a character string. The quote symbol can be printed to the screen if it is preceded with a backslash. This book uses this format for data input.

Another problem must be taken into account in programs such as this: the carry information from seconds to minutes and from minutes to hours must be handled properly. A carry occurs in both cases when the total number of seconds or minutes exceeds 59. This doesn't have anything to do with operator overloading directly, but the program must take this fact into account if a correct total is to be produced, as shown here:

```
//  opover.cpp
//  C++ program illustrates operator overloading.
//  Program will overload the "+" operator so that
//  several angles, in the format degrees minutes seconds,
//  can be added directly.
//  Chris H. Pappas and William H. Murray, 1999
//

#include <strstrea>
#include <stdlib>
#include <string>

using namespace std;

class angle_value {
  int degrees,minutes,seconds;

  public:
  angle_value() {degrees=0,
                 minutes=0,
                 seconds=0;}  // constructor
  angle_value(char *);
  angle_value operator +(angle_value);
  char * info_display(void);
};

angle_value::angle_value(char *angle_sum)
{
  degrees=atoi(strtok(angle_sum,"6"));
  minutes=atoi(strtok(0,"' "));
  seconds=atoi(strtok(0,"\""));
}

angle_value angle_value::operator+(angle_value angle_sum)
{
  angle_value ang;
  ang.seconds=(seconds+angle_sum.seconds)%60;
  ang.minutes=((seconds+angle_sum.seconds)/60+
              minutes+angle_sum.minutes)%60;
  ang.degrees=((seconds+angle_sum.seconds)/60+
              minutes+angle_sum.minutes)/60;
  ang.degrees+=degrees+angle_sum.degrees;
  return ang;
}
```

```
char * angle_value::info_display()
{
  char *ang[15];
  // strstream required for incore formatting
  ostrstream(*ang,sizeof(ang)) << degrees << "°"
                               << minutes << "' "
                               << seconds << "\""
                               << ends;
  return *ang;
}

main()
{
  angle_value angle1("37° 15' 56\"");    //make with alt-248
  angle_value angle2("10° 44' 44\"");
  angle_value angle3("75° 17' 59\"");
  angle_value angle4("130° 32' 54\"");
  angle_value sum_of_angles;

  sum_of_angles=angle1+angle2+angle3+angle4;
  cout << "the sum of the angles is "
       << sum_of_angles.info_display() << endl;
  return (0);
}
```

The details of how the mixed units are added together are included in the small piece of code that declares that the + operator is to be overloaded:

```
angle_value angle_value::operator+(angle_value angle_sum)
{
  angle_value ang;
  ang.seconds=(seconds+angle_sum.seconds)%60;
  ang.minutes=((seconds+angle_sum.seconds)/60+
              minutes+angle_sum.minutes)%60;
  ang.degrees=((seconds+angle_sum.seconds)/60+
              minutes+angle_sum.minutes)/60;
  ang.degrees+=degrees+angle_sum.degrees;
  return ang;
}
```

Here, divide and modulus operations are performed on the sums to ensure correct carry information.

Further details of the program's operation are omitted since you have seen most of the functions and modules in earlier examples. However, it is important to remember that when you overload operators, proper operator syntax and precedence must be maintained.

The output from this program shows the sum of the four angles to be as follows:

```
the sum of the angles is 253° 51' 33"
```

Is this answer correct?

24x7

Knowing the pivotal, fundamental underpinnings provided by C and C++ shoehorn an understanding to just how STL works its magic!

Templates Out of Structures

STL makes excellent use of pointers, overloaded subroutines, and overloaded operators, but it also relies heavily on templates. But before looking at an STL example, take a look at this straightforward C code section that uses the **#define** and concatenation (**##**) preprocessor statements to define a binary tree node:

```
C Example
#define BINARY_TREE( t )
typedef struct _tree_##t {
  t data;
  struct _tree_##t *left;
  struct _tree_##t *right;
} BINARY_TREE_##;
```

Notice how the preprocessor would substitute the argument *t* with whichever data type the user chose, as in:

```
BINARY_TREE( int );
BINARY_TREE( float );
BINARY_TREE( my_structure );
```

and then totally redefine the node; for example, for int data types, the binary tree node's definition would look like:

```
typedef struct _tree_int {
  int data;
  struct _tree_int *left;
  struct _tree_int *right;
} BINARY_TREE_int;
```

Now, this is just a minor example of the inherent sophistication and modularity provided by the C/C++ languages. Remember, the previous examples are all legal in C and require no additional C++ syntax and sophistication!

However, as slick as this example is, there is one inherent problem: unlike **inline** functions, which can also be used to generate macros, **#define** defined macros have no error-checking capabilities. **#define** statements are strictly string search and replace operations performed by pass one of C/C++'s two pass compile. Obviously, in order to generate reliable and portable code, some other means was necessary for generating robust definitions—enter the C++ **template**.

The *template* Keyword

Templates were one of the last features added to C++ before the ANSI/ISO C++ standardization process began. As Bjarne Stroustrup (one of the authors of C++) states, "Templates were considered essential for the design of proper container classes. For many people, the largest single problem with C++ is the lack of an extensive standard library. A major problem in producing such a library is that C++ does not provide a sufficiently general facility for defining 'container classes' such as lists, vectors, and associative arrays." The incorporation of templates into the C++ language led directly to the development of STL, a standardized library of container classes and algorithms using template classes and functions.

Template Syntax

As a programmer, you undoubtedly understand the concept of functions and function calls. The function contains a modularly designed, reusable, single problem-solving algorithm. The function call passes the actual values needed by the function at a particular instance in the execution of the calling routine's algorithm.

C++ templates use parameters in an entirely new way: to create new functions and classes. And, unlike parameter passing to functions, templates create these new functions and classes at *compile-time,* rather than runtime.

The straightforward syntax for templates looks like:

```
template <argument_list> declaration
```

After the **template** keyword and *argument_list,* the programmer supplies the template declaration, where you define the parameterized version of a class or function. It's up to the C++ compiler to generate different versions of the class or function based on the arguments passed to the template when it is used.

Template Functions!

To understand how templates function in STL, you need to understand that there are two types of templates: class templates and function templates. Function templates generate functions, while class templates generate classes.

The following example defines a function template that squares any data type:

```
template <class Type>
Type squareIt( Type x ) { return x * x; } //function template
```

The function template *squareIt(),* can be passed any appropriate data *Type.* For example:

```
void main( void )
{
  cout << "The square of the integer 9 is: " << squareIt( 9 );
  cout << "The square of the unsigned int 255 is: " << squareIt( 255U );
```

```
cout << "The square of the float 10.0: " << squareIt( 10.0 );
//...
}
```

These three statements cause the compiler to generate, at compile-time, three unique function bodies, one instance for integer data, another for unsigned integer data, and a third for floating-point values:

```
int square(int x) { return x * x; }
unsigned int square(unsigned int x) { return x * x; }
double square(double x) { return x * x; }
```

Template Classes

The second category of templates is a class template. The following example defines a simple array container class template:

```
template < class Type, int MAX_ELEMENTS >
class Array {
  protected:
    Type *pTypeArray;
  public:
    Array()  { pTypeArray  = new Type[ MAX_ELEMENTS ]; }        //constructor
    ~Array() { delete[] pTypeArray; }                           //destructor
  // ...
};
```

The template class definition creates an array container class of any *Type!* The first argument to the template defines what type of elements the array will hold, while the second argument defines how many rows, or number of elements, the array will hold. The array's *Type* can be anything from a simple standard C++ data type, such as int, or as complex as an application-specific structure or complex object.

A program instantiates an actual tangible instance of the template class definition with almost a function-like syntax:

```
void main( void )
{
  Array < float, 10 >  fArray;
  Array < int, 25 > iArray;
  Array < MY_STRUCTURE_DEFINITION, MAX_RECORDS > strucArray;
  Array < MY_CLASS_DEFINITION, iRunTimeUsersChoice > classArray;
  //...
}
```

For each instantiation, the compiler generates a brand new version of the *Array* class for every different combination of types passed to it. It does this at compile-time by performing a substitution of the arguments wherever they appear in the formal template definition.

Why STL Is Better Than Templates

In theory, C++ templates fill the need for easy-to-use container classes. But in real life, it wasn't always that simple because several obstacles got in the way. First, depending on the implementation of template container classes either from compiler to third-party vendors, template-based containers could be noticeably slower than their C counterparts. For instance, many template-based container classes relied on inheritance to do their jobs, and certain kinds of inheritance can measurably slow down a program.

Another problem with templates was compatibility. If you happened to use templates from two different vendors, there could be compatibility conflicts between them since there was no standard. But this was a lesser problem than customization. To some extent, customizing code is a normal part of working with templates. Take a class called *VehicleSalesRecord,* for instance. For this class to work with a linked list template, you would have to define operations like less-than (<), the equivalence operator (==), and possibly a greater-than operator (>). Providing these operations or requirements for every class was part of the overhead of working with any template.

To work with container templates, a programmer traditionally needed to customize the objects in the container, not the container template itself. The problem comes in when you need to modify the way a template works. For example, imagine your wanting to customize the way the items are sorted. With most template-based classes, you need to decipher someone else's code, modify the template source code, and recompile your program. That assumes you have access to the original template definition. And template code modification doesn't lend itself to preserving the original intent behind templates.

With the inherent slowness in template-based container classes, along with their historically being nonstandard and not easy to customize, there needed to be a better way. Welcome to STL!

Conclusion

If you first knew the C programming language and then rolled over to an understanding of C++, you are aware of the subtle and major differences between the two languages. In a similar manner, rolling over from C++ to C++ with STL syntax can surprise you with its subtle and major differences. This chapter was designed to give you a high-level flyby to STL in an attempt to get you "thinking" STL. However, it is no substitute for a formal course or dedicated textbook *teaching* this most exciting addition to C++.

In the next chapter, you will use previously discussed Debugger features to locate STL code breaks. Unfortunately, since STL bugs are related to STL philosophy, and not a new language in the sense that C++ can be quite different from C, the Debugger is helpless in clarifying STL-specific errors.

CHAPTER 13

Locating, Analyzing, and Repairing Errors in STL Code

reat news, debugging STL code does not require you to learn any new Visual C++ Debugger features! Instead, efficient STL debugging comes from an understanding of how STL components interact. In the last chapter, you were introduced to the design philosophies behind the ANSI/ISO Committee's adoption of Hewlett-Packard's recombination of standard C++ syntax, making STL possible.

As the computer industry progressively adopts STL technology, most programmers' STL bugs will initially stem from converting an existing non-STL algorithm over to STL technology. In this chapter, you will learn how to debug STL programs using a typical real world example: converting a non-STL algorithm to STL syntax. The STL bugs will stem from unfamiliarity with STL code requirements versus standard C++ code implementations. As you follow the non-STL to STL code roll over, you will see how the Debugger flags these types of errors and then how to repair them.

> **Design Tip** *As the computer industry progressively adopts robust STL technology, many programmers are encountering this new coding philosophy for the first time. While STL does use standard C/C++ syntax, STL contains an exquisite, somewhat foreign, interconnectivity that frustrates first-timers. Initial "bugs" will have their roots in a misunderstanding of how STL components interact and not from the C/C++ languages themselves. If you have not already done so, it is well worth your time to "learn" this dynamic and powerful ANSI/ISO C++ standard!*

Problems Converting from Standard C++ to STL Syntax

Since STL uses standard C++ syntax, bugs do not have a unique source of origin different from your standard C/C++ algorithms. STL bugs originate from a misapplication of STL components. The following discussions highlight those areas of STL design philosophies most likely to cause code errors.

Traversing Containers

The most important difference between STL and all other C++ container class libraries is that most STL algorithms are *generic*: they work on a variety of containers and even on ordinary C++ arrays. A key factor in the library design is the consistent use of *iterators,* which generalize C++ pointers, as intermediaries between algorithms and containers. In the last chapter, you learned how the precise classification of iterators into five categories is the basis for determining which algorithms can be used with which containers. Iterators are also a main guide to extensions of the library that include new algorithms that work with STL containers, or new containers to which many STL generic algorithms can be applied.

Always use STL iterators to traverse containers, remembering to use STL-specific methods, for example *begin(),* and *end(),* to locate the front and back container elements.

Iterators—A Closer Look

Containers, by themselves, do not provide access to their elements. Instead, iterators are used to traverse the elements within a container. Iterators are very similar to smart pointers and have increment and dereferencing operations. By generalizing access to containers through iterators, the STL makes it possible to interact with containers in a uniform manner. In addition, iterators are the glue that connects algorithms to containers.

Iterators are the cornerstone of the STL design and give STL its most flexibility. Instead of being developed for a specific container, algorithms are developed for a specific iterator category. This strategy makes it possible to use the same algorithm with a variety of different containers.

Each category forms a set of requirements that must be met by concrete iterator types within that category. Requirements for a given iterator category are specified by a set of valid expressions for iterators in that category as well as precise semantics describing their usage. In addition, iterators in STL must satisfy complexity requirements. These requirements ensure that algorithms written in terms of iterators will work correctly and efficiently.

STL provides a hierarchy of iterator categories (see Chapter 12). Iterators at the top of the hierarchy are the most general; those at the bottom are the most restricted and have fewer requirements. An iterator satisfies all of the requirements of the iterator below it. Each container specifies which iterator category it belongs to. By using a novel language technique, STL selects the right algorithm at compile time depending on the iterator category.

Iterators are used in a similar manner to pointers. Just like pointers, for any iterator type, there is guaranteed to be an iterator value that points past the last element of a corresponding container. Each STL container provides member functions, *begin()* and *end(),* that return iterator values for the first and end (one past the last) elements.

To iterate through the list of **int**s you write:

```
list::iterator it;
for (it  = myList.begin();
     it != myList.end();
     it++)    {
   cout << *myList << endl;
}
```

Note that each time through the loop, the dereferenced iterator obtains the value the iterator is pointing to. The increment operator is used to advance the iterator through the list.

STL also provides **const** iterators so that iterators may be used with **const** containers:

```
template <class T>
void OuputList (const list<T>& myList)  {
   list::const_iterator it;
   for (it  = myList.begin();
        it != myList.end();
        it++)   {
     cout << *MyList << endl;
   }
}
```

Stream Iterators

The C++ Standard Library provides iostreams to facilitate the reading and writing of data from/to input/output streams. STL provides two iterator templates so that algorithms may work directly with I/O streams:

istream_iterators for reading data from an input stream.

ostream_iterators for writing data to an output stream.

For example, you could read data into the list from the standard input as follows:

```
istream_iterator<int, ptrdiff_t> in(cin);
istream_iterator<int, ptrdiff_t> eos;
copy (in, eos, back_inserter(l));
```

and later write the list to the standard output:

```
ostream_iterator out(cout, ", ");
copy (myList.begin(), myList.end(), out):
```

Why Use *end()*?

For any STL container, *iterator::end()* points to a location one beyond the last item in the container and hence is an "invalid pointer"; *iterator::end()* does not point to the last item in the container, rather it points to the location where the next item would go into the container if you were to use *push_back*.

Why point beyond the end of the container? Why not point at the last item? The reason is quite simple: remember that STL containers use C pointer semantics, and *end()* returns the equivalent of C's NULL pointer. Consider how else you would do the following if *end()* instead returned the last item in the container:

```
MyMap::const_iterator it = my_dataBase.find(key);
    if (it == my_dataBase.end())
        no_match_key();
    else
        match_key_found();
```

or,

```
    bool empty(const STL_Container& containerInstance) {
        return containerInstance.begin() == containerInstance.end();
    }
```

In STL, always remember that *begin()* returns the *first* item in the container if it exists, or otherwise, *end()*, and that *end()* returns *one past the end* of the container.

Copying Lists

When using STL copy(), remove_copy(), or any other algorithms that attempt to copy one sequence to another, make sure the target container is at least as large as the resultant container is likely to get. You have to be extra careful when copying from one populated list to a newly defined unpopulated one. For example, look at this next code segment:

```
list<int> list_A;
list<int> list_B;
copy(list_A.begin(), list_A.end(), list_B.begin());  // Failed code.
```

When correctly rewritten using STL

```
copy(list_A.begin(), list_A.end(), back_list_iterator<int> (list_B));
```

The last statement works because *back_list_iterator* invokes *push_back()* which dynamically *resizes* the list as needed.

Error Watch   *When copying containers, make certain the target container is at least as large as the resultant container is likely to grow.*

Lists Within Lists

Oftentimes, an STL list has list elements that are themselves lists. Traversing containers of this complexity is actually a straightforward reapplication of STL techniques. The following code segment demonstrates how to implement the algorithm:

```
#include <list>
#include <iostream>

using namespace std;

typedef list<int> ListElement;
typedef list<ListElement> OwningList;

void outputList(const ListElement& EntireListElement, int listNumber) {
    ostream_iterator<int> out(cout, " ");
    cout << "list " << listNumber << ": ";
    copy(EntireListElement.begin(), EntireListElement.end(), out);
    cout << endl;
}

void main( void ) {
    OwningList listOfListElements;
    // initialize listOfList: total of 3 lists, each with 5 members.
    for(int i = 0; i < 3; ++i) {
        ListElement EntireListElement;
```

```
        for(int j = 0; j < 5; ++j) {
            EntireListElement.push_back(i * 4 + j);
        }
        outputList(EntireListElement, i+1);
        listOfListElements.push_back(EntireListElement);
    }

    cout << endl;

    // traversing entire list with list elements.
    OwningList::iterator it = listOfListElements.begin();
    for(int j = 1; it != listOfListElements.end(); ++it, ++j) {
        const ListElement& EntireListElement = *it;
        outputList(EntireListElement, j);
    }
}
```

This simple STL algorithm simply treats each *OwningList* element as a standalone list. The last **for** loop stops iterating whenever there are no longer any *OwningList* lists or, *it != listOfListElements.end()* to pass to *outputList()* for enumeration!

Trouble with STL String Pointers?

The following example shows another nasty side effect of storing pointers to things in STL containers. First, the declaration of *list<char*>* defines a list of character pointers, not a list of strings they point to. For this reason, the STL *less<char*>* will compare *char* *s (pointers), not C++ string classes:

```
char buf[1024];
strcpy(buf, "Test String");
list<char*> list_A;
list_A.push_back(buf);
ostream_iterator<char*> citer(cout, " ");
copy(list_A.begin(), list_A.end(), citer);
// you should see one string "Test String"

strcpy(buf, "NewString");
copy(list_A.begin(), list_A.end(), citer);
// The list changed and it should not have!
```

To traverse lists with individual elements that are themselves lists, simply treat each list element as a standalone list. This is similar to having an array of structures and processing the array of structures as if each element were a standalone structure, not part of a container.

In general, do not use *char** as container objects; instead you should implement list elements as C++ string classes, as in

```
typedef list<string> stringList;
```

Error Watch *While you can syntactically create a container of* char **s, this is potentially dangerous as STL-specific methods may incorrectly apply their algorithms to the addresses of the data pointed to, instead of the* data *itself!*

Deallocating STL Pointers

If you create containers of pointers, make sure you deallocate the storage explicitly in the code, especially if the container is on the stack and goes out of scope creating a memory leak. STL containers only copy and delete the storage required to hold the **pointer**, not the **object** it's pointing to. You can create templatized delete routines similar to the following:

```
template <class FwdIt, class FwdIt>
void sequence_delete(FwdIt first, FwdIt last) {
  while (first != last)
      delete *first++;
}

template <class FwdIt, class FwdIt>
void map_delete(FwdIt first, FwdIt last) {
  while (first != last)
      delete (*first++).second;
}

Map<int, DataType*, less<int> > myMap;

// properly releases myMap pointers.
map_delete(myMap.begin(), myMap.end());
```

It is the official call to the C++ **delete()** function, passed the referenced object pointer, **first*, that accomplishes the clean return:

```
delete (*first++).second
```

Design Tip *When using dynamic memory allocation, make certain you use the **delete()** function somewhere in your program to properly restore memory to the available memory pool.*

Real World C++ to STL Code Roll Over

In this section, you are about to convert a working, standard C++ object-oriented code solution to STL syntax. The program implements a familiar card game called "War." The code roll over proceeds step-by-step, exactly the way a beginning STL programmer would proceed. Each code segment change is immediately followed by a build/debug phase verifying the correctness of the new STL counterpart along with any unanticipated bugs. First, the standard C++ object-oriented solution:

```cpp
//
// wargame.cpp
// Learning how to convert a standard C++ code solution
// into a robust STL design
// Chris H. Pappas and William H. Murray, 2000
//

#include <iostream>
#include <algorithm>
#include <cstdlib>
#include <ctime>

using namespace std;

typedef enum tagSuits {diamond, club, heart, spade} SUITS;

//*************************************************************
// class aSingleCard with defined methods
class aSingleCard {
  public:
    int iRank;
    SUITS suit;
    aSingleCard() {iRank = 0; suit = spade;};
    aSingleCard( SUITS s, int ir) {suit = s; iRank = ir;};
    friend ostream& operator <<( ostream& out, aSingleCard& aCard );
};

//*************************************************************
// class WarDeck with defined methods
class WarDeck {
  public:
    WarDeck();
    void shuffleDeck();
    bool isDeckEmpty();
    aSingleCard drawCardFromDeck();

  protected:
    #define DECK_SIZE       52
    #define CARDS_PER_SUIT 13
    aSingleCard fullDeck[DECK_SIZE];
    int iCurrentCard;
};

WarDeck::WarDeck()
{
  iCurrentCard = 0;
  for( int i = 1; i <= CARDS_PER_SUIT; i++ ) {
    aSingleCard c1(diamond, i), c2(spade, i), c3(heart, i), c4(club, i);
```

```
      fullDeck[iCurrentCard++] = c1;
      fullDeck[iCurrentCard++] = c2;
      fullDeck[iCurrentCard++] = c3;
      fullDeck[iCurrentCard++] = c4;
  }
}

void WarDeck::shuffleDeck()
{
  random_shuffle( fullDeck, fullDeck+52);
}

aSingleCard WarDeck::drawCardFromDeck()
{
  if( ! isDeckEmpty() )
    return fullDeck[--iCurrentCard];
  else {
    aSingleCard defaultCard( spade, 1 );
    return defaultCard;
  }
}

bool WarDeck::isDeckEmpty()
{
  return iCurrentCard <= 0;
}

//*************************************************************
// class Opponent with defined methods
class Opponent {
  public:
    Opponent( WarDeck& );
    aSingleCard drawCardFromDeck();
    void addUpPoints( int );
    int what_sTheScore();
    void putBackCard( WarDeck&);

  protected:
    #define CARDS_IN_HAND 3
    aSingleCard currentHand[CARDS_IN_HAND];
    int currentScore;
    int cardBeingPlayed;
};

Opponent::Opponent( WarDeck & aDeck )
{
  currentScore = 0;
    for( int i = 0; i < CARDS_IN_HAND; i++ )
      currentHand[i] = aDeck.drawCardFromDeck();
    cardBeingPlayed = 0;
}
```

```cpp
aSingleCard Opponent::drawCardFromDeck()
{

  cardBeingPlayed = rand() % 3;
  return currentHand[cardBeingPlayed];
}

void Opponent::addUpPoints( int howMany )
{
  currentScore += howMany;
}

int Opponent::what_sTheScore()
{
  return currentScore;
}

void Opponent::putBackCard(WarDeck& aDeck)
{
  currentHand[cardBeingPlayed] = aDeck.drawCardFromDeck();
}

//************************************************************
// main() function
void main( void )
{
  WarDeck actualDeck;
  actualDeck.shuffleDeck();

  srand( (unsigned int)time( NULL ) );

  Opponent opponent1(actualDeck);
  Opponent opponent2(actualDeck);

  while( !actualDeck.isDeckEmpty() ) {
    aSingleCard card1 = opponent1.drawCardFromDeck();
    cout << "Opponent 1 plays " << card1 << endl;
    aSingleCard card2 = opponent2.drawCardFromDeck();
    cout << "Opponent 2 plays " << card2 << endl;

    if( card1.iRank == card2.iRank ) {
      opponent1.addUpPoints(1);
      opponent2.addUpPoints(1);
      cout << "Players tie\n" << endl;
      }
    else if( card1.iRank > card2.iRank ) {
      opponent1.addUpPoints(2);
      cout << "Opponent 1 wins round\n";
      }
```

```
    else {
      opponent2.addUpPoints(2);
      cout << "Opponent 2 wins round\n";
      }

    opponent1.putBackCard(actualDeck);
    opponent2.putBackCard(actualDeck);

    cout << "\n\nPress ENTER to continue."  << endl;
    cin.get();

  }

  cout << "Opponent 1 what_sTheScore "
       << opponent1.what_sTheScore() << endl;
  cout << "Opponent 2 what_sTheScore "
       << opponent2.what_sTheScore() << endl;

}


//*************************************************************
// class aSingleCard friend overloaded insertion operator
ostream& operator <<( ostream& out, aSingleCard& aCard )
{
  switch( aCard.iRank ) {
    case  1: out << "Ace"  ; break;
    case 11: out << "Jack" ; break;
    case 12: out << "Queen"; break;
    case 13: out << "King" ; break;
    default:
      out << aCard.iRank; break;
  }

  switch( aCard.suit ) {
    case diamond: out << " of Diamonds"; break;
    case spade  : out << " of Spades  "; break;
    case heart  : out << " of Hearts  "; break;
    case club   : out << " of Clubs   "; break;
  }

  return out;
};
```

Step One—Updating *aSingleCard* Class

The class, *aSingleCard*, contains two standalone data members, *iRank* and *suit*. Throughout
wargame.cpp, these members are logically related, representing each card's numeric rank and suit.
Rolling over to STL design philosophy, you do not want to have two vectors, one for each rank and
another for all suits. The idea is to have one vector containing all 52 cards represented as single entities.

In STL design syntax, two logically related data members are stored, officially, as STL **pair**s. This *iRank* and *suit* pairing is accomplished with the following **typedef** statement:

```
typedef struct pair<int, SUITS> ACARD_PAIR;
```

Of course, this new **typedef** requires an update to the *aSingleCard* class:

```
//*********************************************************
//STL pair data type containing int and SUITS
typedef struct pair<int,SUITS> ACARD_PAIR;

//*********************************************************
// class aSingleCard with defined methods
class aSingleCard {
  public:
    // non-STL int iRank;
    // non-STL SUITS suit;
    // STL replacement
    ACARD_PAIR oneCard;
    aSingleCard() {iRank = 0; suit = spade;};
    aSingleCard( SUITS s, int ir) {suit = s; iRank = ir;};
    friend ostream& operator <<( ostream& out, aSingleCard& aCard );
};
```

The first attempt at build, produces the following debug error messages (see Figure 13.1), flagging the "undeclared identifier" *iRank* and *suit*.

STL **pair**s have two predefined data members, *first* and *second*. So every *aSingleCard* reference to *iRank* must be ported over to the **pair** member name *first*, and every reference to *suit* changed to the **pair** member name *second*, as in:

```
//*********************************************************
// class aSingleCard with defined methods
class aSingleCard {
  public:
    // non-STL int iRank;
    // non-STL SUITS suit;
    // STL replacement
    ACARD_PAIR oneCard;
    aSingleCard() {oneCard.first = 0; oneCard.second = spade;};
    aSingleCard( SUITS s, int ir) {oneCard.second = s;
                                   oneCard.first = ir;};
    friend ostream& operator <<( ostream& out, aSingleCard& aCard );
};
```

With the updated **pair** member names *first* and *second*, you attempt another build only to discover that further references to *iRank* and *suit* are used throughout **main()** (see Figure 13.2).

```
------------------------Configuration: updateaSingleCard - Win32 Debug------------------
Compiling...
updateaSingleCard.cpp
c:\my documents\updateasinglecard.cpp(29) : error C2065: 'iRank' : undeclared identifier
c:\my documents\updateasinglecard.cpp(29) : error C2065: 'suit' : undeclared identifier
c:\my documents\updateasinglecard.cpp(147) : error C2039: 'iRank' : is not a member of 'aSingleCard'
        c:\my documents\updateasinglecard.cpp(23) : see declaration of 'aSingleCard'
c:\my documents\updateasinglecard.cpp(147) : error C2039: 'iRank' : is not a member of 'aSingleCard'
        c:\my documents\updateasinglecard.cpp(23) : see declaration of 'aSingleCard'
c:\my documents\updateasinglecard.cpp(152) : error C2039: 'iRank' : is not a member of 'aSingleCard'
        c:\my documents\updateasinglecard.cpp(23) : see declaration of 'aSingleCard'
c:\my documents\updateasinglecard.cpp(152) : error C2039: 'iRank' : is not a member of 'aSingleCard'
        c:\my documents\updateasinglecard.cpp(23) : see declaration of 'aSingleCard'
```

Figure 13.1   Problems with STL **pair**s

A quick use of Visual C++'s Find and Replace option locates every misuse of the old data member names (*iRank* and *suit*) and updates them to *first* and *second* **pair** member names. However, the next attempt at build remains unsuccessful (see Figure 13.3).

```
srand( (unsigned int)time( NULL ) );

Opponent opponent1(actualDeck);
Opponent opponent2(actualDeck);

while( !actualDeck.isDeckEmpty() ) {
  aSingleCard card1 = opponent1.drawCardFromDeck();
  cout << "Opponent 1 plays " << card1 << endl;
  aSingleCard card2 = opponent2.drawCardFromDeck();
  cout << "Opponent 2 plays " << card2 << endl;

  if( card1.iRank == card2.iRank ) {
    opponent1.addUpPoints(1);
    opponent2.addUpPoints(1);
    cout << "Players tie\n" << endl;
    }
  else if( card1.iRank > card2.iRank ) {
    opponent1.addUpPoints(2);
    cout << "Opponent 1 wins round\n";
    }
  else {
    opponent2.addUpPoints(2);
    cout << "Opponent 2 wins round\n";
```

```
------------------------Configuration: updateSingleCard - Win32 Debug------------------
Compiling...
updateSingleCard.cpp
C:\My Documents\updateSingleCard.cpp(148) : error C2039: 'iRank' : is not a member of 'aSingleCard'
        C:\My Documents\updateSingleCard.cpp(23) : see declaration of 'aSingleCard'
C:\My Documents\updateSingleCard.cpp(148) : error C2039: 'iRank' : is not a member of 'aSingleCard'
        C:\My Documents\updateSingleCard.cpp(23) : see declaration of 'aSingleCard'
C:\My Documents\updateSingleCard.cpp(153) : error C2039: 'iRank' : is not a member of 'aSingleCard'
        C:\My Documents\updateSingleCard.cpp(23) : see declaration of 'aSingleCard'
C:\My Documents\updateSingleCard.cpp(153) : error C2039: 'iRank' : is not a member of 'aSingleCard'
        C:\My Documents\updateSingleCard.cpp(23) : see declaration of 'aSingleCard'
C:\My Documents\updateSingleCard.cpp(179) : error C2039: 'iRank' : is not a member of 'aSingleCard'
        C:\My Documents\updateSingleCard.cpp(23) : see declaration of 'aSingleCard'
```

Figure 13.2   Detecting all illegal references to *iRank* and *suit*

```
        srand( (unsigned int)time( NULL ) );

        Opponent opponent1(actualDeck);
        Opponent opponent2(actualDeck);

        while( !actualDeck.isDeckEmpty() ) {
          aSingleCard card1 = opponent1.drawCardFromDeck();
          cout << "Opponent 1 plays " << card1 << endl;
          aSingleCard card2 = opponent2.drawCardFromDeck();
          cout << "Opponent 2 plays " << card2 << endl;

          if( card1.first == card2.first ) {
            opponent1.addUpPoints(1);
            opponent2.addUpPoints(1);
            cout << "Players tie\n" << endl;
            }
          else if( card1.first > card2.first ) {
            opponent1.addUpPoints(2);
            cout << "Opponent 1 wins round\n";
            }
          else {
            opponent2.addUpPoints(2);
            cout << "Opponent 2 wins round\n";
```

```
-----------------Configuration: updateaSingleCard - Win32 Debug-------------------
Compiling...
updateaSingleCard.cpp
C:\My Documents\updateaSingleCard.cpp(148) : error C2039: 'first' : is not a member of 'aSingleCard'
        C:\My Documents\updateaSingleCard.cpp(23) : see declaration of 'aSingleCard'
C:\My Documents\updateaSingleCard.cpp(148) : error C2039: 'first' : is not a member of 'aSingleCard'
        C:\My Documents\updateaSingleCard.cpp(23) : see declaration of 'aSingleCard'
C:\My Documents\updateaSingleCard.cpp(153) : error C2039: 'first' : is not a member of 'aSingleCard'
        C:\My Documents\updateaSingleCard.cpp(23) : see declaration of 'aSingleCard'
C:\My Documents\updateaSingleCard.cpp(153) : error C2039: 'first' : is not a member of 'aSingleCard'
        C:\My Documents\updateaSingleCard.cpp(23) : see declaration of 'aSingleCard'
C:\My Documents\updateaSingleCard.cpp(179) : error C2039: 'first' : is not a member of 'aSingleCard'
        C:\My Documents\updateaSingleCard.cpp(23) : see declaration of 'aSingleCard'
```

Figure 13.3   Substituting *first* and *second* remains unsuccessful

Actually, you needed to replace *iRank* and *suit* references with *aSingleCard*'s fully qualified names: *oneCard.first* and *oneCard.second*. You now have an STL-ported *aSingleCard* class definition.

Step Two—Updating *WarDeck* Class

The *wargame.cpp* definition for class *WarDeck* is responsible for declaring and initializing the entire deck of cards. The non-STL card deck is created using an array of *aSingleCard* instances. However, under STL technology, this array needs to be created using the STL **vector** class.

The first step in the code roll over requires an industry standard, not pure STL-required, **typedef** definition, declaring a new type, as in:

```
typedef vector<aSingleCard> CardVector;
```

Taking the time to declare a new type allows easy reuse of the application-specific definition. This industry standard was also used earlier for the **typedef** of *ACARD_PAIR*. The initial code change between the old and new *WarDeck* class definition involves a simple substitution of two statements:

```
aSingleCard fullDeck[DECK_SIZE];
```

becomes

```
CardVector fullDeck;
```

Notice the missing *DECK_SIZE* in the updated code. STL vectors are dynamic and do not require an initial size definition as do standard C++ arrays! With your next build cycle, you discover several frustrating error messages, as seen in Figure 13.4.

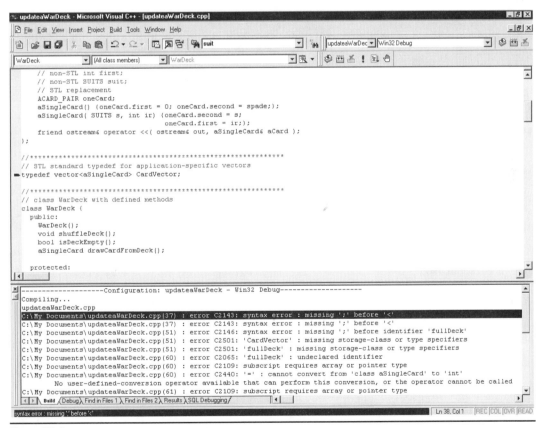

Figure 13.4   What missing semicolon???

The Debugger at this point is flagging a missing semicolon. Examining all code statements preceding the flagged statement (*typedef vector . . .*—see Figure 13.4) leaves you confused. There appears to be *no* missing semicolon! Ah, the problems of porting over to STL. Yes, the code did update to the necessary components for syntactically declaring a **vector typedef** and updating the *WarDeck*'s array-become-vector *fullDeck*'s new data type, so what went wrong? The algorithm neglected to include the necessary STL header file defining **vector**s. The included header file list needs to update from:

```
#include <iostream>
#include <algorithm>
#include <cstdlib>
#include <ctime>
```

to

```
#include <vector> //added for vector definitions
#include <iostream>
#include <algorithm>
#include <cstdlib>
#include <ctime>
```

Enthusiastically, you begin again with the updated **#include** statement and execute another build, only to have the Debugger flag another problem (see Figure 13.5).

A close examination of the Debugger's first error message fries your brain:

```
c:\chapter13\updateawardeck.cpp(70) : error C2784: 'class
std::reverse_iterator<_RI,_Ty,_Rt,_Pt,_D> __cdecl
std::operator +(_D,const class std::reverse_iterator<_RI,
_Ty,_Rt,_Pt,_D> &)' : could not deduce template
argument for '' from 'class std::
```

Unless you are well rehearsed in debugging STL syntax, this message appears to be so syntactically complex that you haven't a clue where to go next in eliminating the bug.

Once again the solution to the bug involves your understanding of STL component interactions and syntax requirements. The original *WarDeck::shuffleDeck()* method used the array's name *fullDeck* to pass to the function *random_shuffle()* the physical starting address to the first card in the deck. The second argument to *random_shuffle()* was a calculated address that was *52* elements over, *fullDeck+52*:

```
void WarDeck::shuffleDeck()
{
  random_shuffle( fullDeck, fullDeck+52);
}
```

However, STL does not accept this syntax. Instead, STL syntactically *demands* the use of an appropriate iterator. Remember, iterators are nothing more than generalized pointers. STL syntax requires you to first take a generalized iterator and make it point to a specific type—in this case, *CardVector* elements. This is accomplished with the following statement:

```
typedef CardVector::iterator CardVectorIt;
```

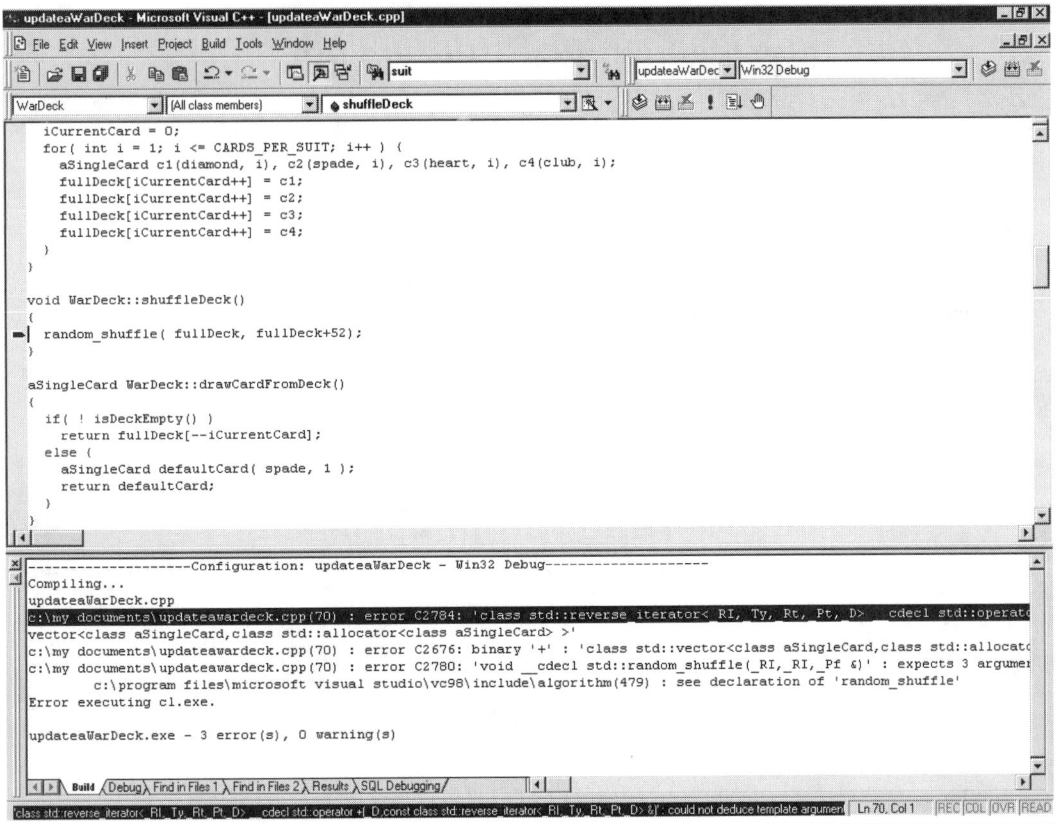

Figure 13.5   STL error code syntax

Once again, it is the C++ community that recommends you first declare a new type with **typedef**. The iterator's name, *CardVectorIt*, is not chosen haphazardly. Of course, the *CardVector* . . . part ties the identifier's name into the owning data type's definition. It is the *It* part, not technically required by STL syntax, but agreed upon by STL programmers, that reports this identifier's type as being an *It*erator.

Unfortunately, the new **typedef** is not sufficient. Referencing **vector** starting and ending element addresses is accomplished using STL-specific container class methods *begin()* and *end()*. The addresses returned from these methods are stored in appropriately defined iterator variables, as in

```
CardVectorIt Start, End;
```

The total rewrite of the *WarDeck::shuffleDeck()* method now looks like:

```
void WarDeck::shuffleDeck()
{
  typedef CardVector::iterator CardVectorIt;
```

```
CardVectorIt Start, End;

Start = fullDeck.begin();
End   = fullDeck.end();

random_shuffle( Start, End);
}
```

Notice how the methods *begin()* and *end()* are inherited by the instance *fullDeck* of the *CardVector* type! A successful *random_shuffle()* is accomplished with the correct STL syntax requirements that both actual arguments be of type iterator, *Start* and *End*.

With the previous code changes in place, you execute another build and success—0 errors and 0 warnings. Convinced the port was a success, you attempt to execute the program. Figure 13.6, however, displays another scenario.

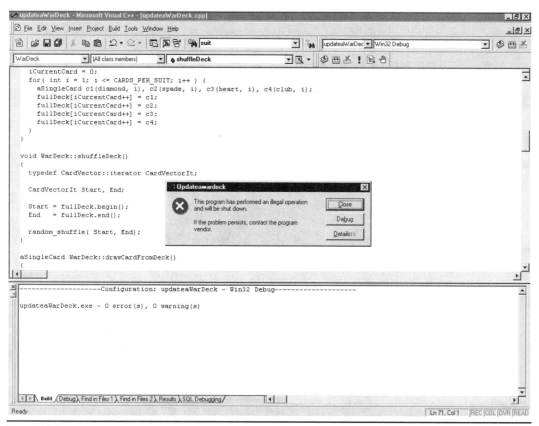

Figure 13.6 MORE bugs

Your worst nightmare—*This program has performed an illegal operation and will be shut down.* "Now what?" you ask yourself.

Step Three—Fixing STL Execution Errors

There isn't a single Debugger tool at your disposal that will deftly clarify execution errors in STL code. Once again, the runtime error most typically occurs because of a misuse of STL components.

While the *WarDeck* class has been ported over from array to vector syntax and the method *shuffleDeck( )* updated, algorithmic inconsistencies still remain between the non-STL and STL versions. Take a look at the original C++ method *drawCardFromDeck( )*:

```
aSingleCard WarDeck::drawCardFromDeck()
{
  if( ! isDeckEmpty() )
    return fullDeck[--iCurrentCard];
  else {
    aSingleCard defaultCard( spade, 1 );
    return defaultCard;
  }
}
```

The harmless appearing call to *WarDeck::isDeckEmpty( )* contains an STL design flaw. First, the original C++ *isDeckEmpty( )* version:

```
bool WarDeck::isDeckEmpty()
{
  return iCurrentCard <= 0;
}
```

Now, how it should appear in STL syntax:

```
bool WarDeck::isDeckEmpty()
{
  // non-STL return iCurrentCard <= 0;
  return fullDeck.empty();
}
```

With STL vector containers being dynamically allocated, the best approach to finding vector beginning and ending addresses is with an STL container-specific method—in this case, *empty( )*. That was a relatively painless port. Now, what about the method *drawDeckFromCard( )*?

The STL equivalent of *drawDeckFromCard( )* looks like

```
aSingleCard WarDeck::drawCardFromDeck()
{
  aSingleCard tempCard;
  if( !fullDeck.empty() ) {
    tempCard = fullDeck.front();
    fullDeck.erase(fullDeck.begin());
  }
```

```
  else {
    aSingleCard defaultCard( spade, 1 );
    tempCard = defaultCard;
  }
  return tempCard;
}
```

The ported algorithm required a declaration for a *tempCard* holder for the drawn card. Next, the updated **if** test condition uses the STL *empty()* method call to detect an empty deck of cards. The STL method *front()* returns the address to the front card in the card deck. The call to the STL *begin()* method returns a pointer to the card being removed from the *fullDeck* and is used as the actual argument to the STL inherited method *erase()*, eliminating the card from the deck.

Step Four—Updating *Opponent* Class

The initial port of the *Opponent* class appears straightforward if you remember that all C++ array references in the original code must be converted to STL vector equivalents. For easy reference, the original *Opponent* class definition follows:

```
class Opponent {
  public:
    Opponent( WarDeck& );
    aSingleCard drawCardFromDeck();
    void addUpPoints( int );
    int what_sTheScore();
    void putBackCard( WarDeck&);

  protected:
    #define CARDS_IN_HAND 3
    aSingleCard currentHand[CARDS_IN_HAND];
    int currentScore;
    int cardBeingPlayed;
};
```

Once again, the only formal class definition that needs changing is the array definition:

```
aSingleCard currentHand[CARDS_IN_HAND];
```

that becomes

```
CardVector currentHand; // STL dynamic vector syntax
```

Unfortunately, the remaining code changes are STL design specific. Take for example the *Opponent* constructor:

```
Opponent::Opponent( WarDeck & aDeck )
{
  currentScore = 0;
    for( int i = 0; i < CARDS_IN_HAND; i++ )
```

```
      currentHand[i] = aDeck.drawCardFromDeck();
    cardBeingPlayed = 0;
}
```

that under STL syntax becomes

```
Opponent::Opponent( WarDeck & aDeck )
{
  currentScore = 0;
    for( int i = 0; i < CARDS_IN_HAND; i++ )
      // non-STL currentHand[i] = aDeck.drawCardFromDeck();
      currentHand.push_back(aDeck.drawCardFromDeck());
    cardBeingPlayed = 0;
}
```

Under STL design technology, you use the method *push_back()* to add an element to a vector. Notice the removal of any array subscript syntax from the non-STL counterpart:

```
currentHand.push_back(aDeck.drawCardFromDeck());
```

Step Five—The Working STL Program

With all necessary code changes made and a build producing 0 warnings and 0 errors, you execute the program, and once again it fails. Remembering that STL debugging does *not* require any hidden Visual C++ Debugger features, you use a combination of F10 (step over) and F11 (step into) command sequences. The fatal exception occurs in the *WarDeck()* constructor (seen in Figure 13.7).

Notice how the diagnosis of *where* the error occurred only required standard Debugger commands like step into and step over. However, the code solution demanded expertise with STL components. The offending constructor retained array-specific syntax and references, instead of STL **vector** class syntax requirements. The STL enabled constructor now looks like

```
WarDeck::WarDeck()
{
  iCurrentCard = 0;
  for( int i = 1; i <= CARDS_PER_SUIT; i++ ) {
    aSingleCard c1(diamond, i), c2(spade, i), c3(heart, i), c4(club, i);
    // non-STL fullDeck[iCurrentCard++] = c1;
    // non-STL fullDeck[iCurrentCard++] = c2;
    // non-STL fullDeck[iCurrentCard++] = c3;
    // non-STL fullDeck[iCurrentCard++] = c4;
    fullDeck.push_back( c1 );
    fullDeck.push_back( c2 );
    fullDeck.push_back( c3 );
    fullDeck.push_back( c4 );
  }
}
```

Notice the use of *fullDeck*'s inherited STL **vector** class **vector::push_back()** method used to insert cards into the deck by suit.

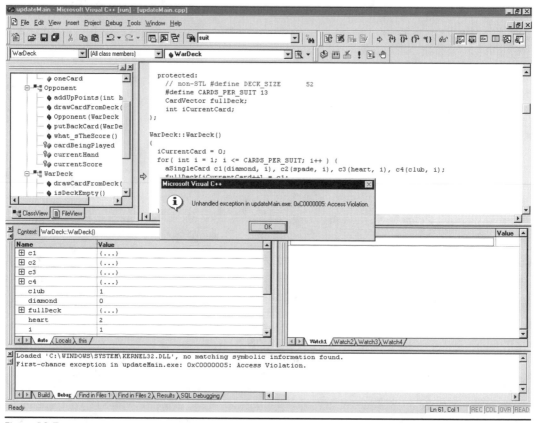

Figure 13.7 Debugger flagging non-STL compliant code remnant

The STL *wargame.cpp*

Because *wargame.cpp* went through extensive STL-specific roll overs, the chapter ends with a complete listing of the ported *wargame.cpp* source file. Embedded within the example are the most typical bugs generated by a non-STL to STL code roll over. You should use this example as a reminder of how to port an application over to STL. Also, the example highlights those areas of STL design philosophy you should make certain you study and master.

```
//
// wargame.cpp
// Learning how to convert a standard C++ code solution
// into a robust STL design
// Chris H. Pappas and William H. Murray, 2000
//
```

```cpp
#include <vector> // added for vector definitions
#include <iostream>
#include <algorithm>
#include <cstdlib>
#include <ctime>

using namespace std;

typedef enum tagSuits {diamond, club, heart, spade} SUITS;

//*************************************************************
//STL pair data type containing int and SUITS
typedef struct pair<int,SUITS> ACARD_PAIR;

//*************************************************************
// class aSingleCard with defined methods
class aSingleCard {
  public:
    // non-STL int first;
    // non-STL SUITS suit;
    // STL replacement
    ACARD_PAIR oneCard;
    aSingleCard() {oneCard.first = 0; oneCard.second = spade;};
    aSingleCard( SUITS s, int ir) {oneCard.second = s;
                                   oneCard.first = ir;};
    friend ostream& operator <<( ostream& out, aSingleCard& aCard );
};

//*************************************************************
// STL standard typedef for application-specific vectors
typedef vector<aSingleCard> CardVector;

//*************************************************************
// class WarDeck with defined methods
class WarDeck {
  public:
    WarDeck();
    void shuffleDeck();
    bool isDeckEmpty();
    aSingleCard drawCardFromDeck();

  protected:
    // non-STL #define DECK_SIZE      52
    #define CARDS_PER_SUIT 13
    CardVector fullDeck;
    int iCurrentCard;
};

WarDeck::WarDeck()
{
```

```
    iCurrentCard = 0;
    for( int i = 1; i <= CARDS_PER_SUIT; i++ ) {
      aSingleCard c1(diamond, i), c2(spade, i), c3(heart, i), c4(club, i);
      // non-STL fullDeck[iCurrentCard++] = c1;
      // non-STL fullDeck[iCurrentCard++] = c2;
      // non-STL fullDeck[iCurrentCard++] = c3;
      // non-STL fullDeck[iCurrentCard++] = c4;
      fullDeck.push_back( c1 );
      fullDeck.push_back( c2 );
      fullDeck.push_back( c3 );
      fullDeck.push_back( c4 );
    }
}

void WarDeck::shuffleDeck()
{
  typedef CardVector::iterator CardVectorIt;

  CardVectorIt Start, End;

  Start = fullDeck.begin();
  End   = fullDeck.end();

  random_shuffle( Start, End);
}

aSingleCard WarDeck::drawCardFromDeck()
{
/*  if( ! isDeckEmpty() )
    return fullDeck[--iCurrentCard];
  else {
    aSingleCard defaultCard( spade, 1 );
    return defaultCard;
  }
*/
  aSingleCard tempCard;
  if( !fullDeck.empty() ) {
    tempCard = fullDeck.front();
    fullDeck.erase(fullDeck.begin());
  }
  else {
    aSingleCard defaultCard( spade, 1 );
    tempCard = defaultCard;
  }
  return tempCard;
}

bool WarDeck::isDeckEmpty()
{
  // non-STL return iCurrentCard <= 0;
```

```
      return fullDeck.empty();
}

//*************************************************************
// class Opponent with defined methods
class Opponent {
  public:
    Opponent( WarDeck& );
    aSingleCard drawCardFromDeck();
    void addUpPoints( int );
    int what_sTheScore();
    void putBackCard( WarDeck&);

  protected:
    #define CARDS_IN_HAND 3
    // non-STL aSingleCard currentHand[CARDS_IN_HAND];
    CardVector currentHand;
    int currentScore;
    int cardBeingPlayed;
};

Opponent::Opponent( WarDeck & aDeck )
{
   currentScore = 0;
      for( int i = 0; i < CARDS_IN_HAND; i++ )
        // non-STL currentHand[i] = aDeck.drawCardFromDeck();
        currentHand.push_back(aDeck.drawCardFromDeck());
      cardBeingPlayed = 0;
}

aSingleCard Opponent::drawCardFromDeck()
{

   cardBeingPlayed = rand() % 3;
   return currentHand[cardBeingPlayed];
}

void Opponent::addUpPoints( int howMany )
{
   currentScore += howMany;
}

int Opponent::what_sTheScore()
{
   return currentScore;
}

void Opponent::putBackCard(WarDeck& aDeck)
{
   currentHand[cardBeingPlayed] = aDeck.drawCardFromDeck();
}
```

```cpp
//*************************************************************
// main() function
void main( void )
{
  WarDeck actualDeck;
  actualDeck.shuffleDeck();

  srand( (unsigned int)time( NULL ) );

  Opponent opponent1(actualDeck);
  Opponent opponent2(actualDeck);

  while( !actualDeck.isDeckEmpty() ) {
    aSingleCard card1 = opponent1.drawCardFromDeck();
    cout << "Opponent 1 plays " << card1 << endl;
    aSingleCard card2 = opponent2.drawCardFromDeck();
    cout << "Opponent 2 plays " << card2 << endl;

    if( card1.oneCard.first == card2.oneCard.first ) {
      opponent1.addUpPoints(1);
      opponent2.addUpPoints(1);
      cout << "Players tie\n" << endl;
      }
    else if( card1.oneCard.first > card2.oneCard.first ) {
      opponent1.addUpPoints(2);
      cout << "Opponent 1 wins round\n";
      }
    else {
      opponent2.addUpPoints(2);
      cout << "Opponent 2 wins round\n";
      }

    opponent1.putBackCard(actualDeck);
    opponent2.putBackCard(actualDeck);

    cout << "\n\nPress ENTER to continue."   << endl;
    cin.get();

  }

  cout << "Opponent 1 what_sTheScore "
       << opponent1.what_sTheScore() << endl;
  cout << "Opponent 2 what_sTheScore "
       << opponent2.what_sTheScore() << endl;

}

//*************************************************************
// class aSingleCard friend overloaded insertion operator
ostream& operator <<( ostream& out, aSingleCard& aCard )
{
```

```
switch( aCard.oneCard.first ) {
  case  1: out << "Ace"  ; break;
  case 11: out << "Jack" ; break;
  case 12: out << "Queen"; break;
  case 13: out << "King" ; break;
  default:
    out << aCard.oneCard.first; break;
}

switch( aCard.oneCard.second ) {
  case diamond: out << " of Diamonds"; break;
  case spade  : out << " of Spades  "; break;
  case heart  : out << " of Hearts  "; break;
  case club   : out << " of Clubs   "; break;
}

return out;
};
```

Conclusion

As you can see from this chapter's examples, you do not need special Visual C++ Debugger skills to debug STL algorithms. Standard Debugger commands like step over and step into are about all that is necessary to locate an offending STL statement. However, fixing the bug *does* require a familiarity with how STL components fit together. Unlike the C and C++ compilers themselves, designed to write general purpose algorithms, STL has used standard C/C++ features to generate an STL-specific syntax and set of interactions.

PART V

Special Debugging Problems

CHAPTER 14

Working with DLLs

In this chapter you will learn how to create and debug a simple Dynamic Link Library or DLL. Dynamic Link Libraries, like other Visual C++ libraries, give programmers the ability to distribute new functions and other resources in an easy manner. DLLs are different from other libraries because they are linked to the application at runtime rather than during the compile/link cycle. This process can be described as *dynamic linking* rather than *static linking*. Static linking occurs when linking C++ runtime libraries to an application at compile/link time. DLLs also offer the advantage, in a multitasking environment, of sharing both functions and resources.

Library code is bound and carried with each application when the two applications use a runtime library that is statically linked during compilation. When applications are dynamically linked, one copy of the library exists for all applications. Import libraries can then be used to locate the required functions and resources at runtime. When this occurs, all applications share the same DLL functions.

DLLs can be divided into two distinct categories: conventional API-based DLLs written in C or C++ (without objects) and MFC object-based DLLs. API DLLs have the advantage of being portable from one compiler to another. DLLs based on the MFC are, of course, restricted to compilers using a licensed version of the MFC. The code developed in this chapter will demonstrate the development of a simple DLL with the use of the MFC library.

The source code that is developed for DLLs is similar to the source code for other projects in this book. The real problem with developing a new DLL is debugging errant code. You see, the problem has now compounded itself. First, the DLL is developed, and then an application that calls the DLL must be written. This is all fine as long as everything works. However, if debugging is required, you'll have to consider debugging both the DLL and the calling application. Add to this the fact that you'll probably want to perform remote debugging, and you have a situation that is many times more complex than the remote debugging described in Chapter 8 for a simple project.

We'll assume you have some experience developing DLLs. However, this chapter will take you step-by-step through the creation of a simple DLL and an application that uses the DLL. The focus of this chapter is to show you how to set up a remote debugging scenario so that both the DLL and the application using the DLL can be properly debugged. If you want to learn more about developing DLLs, you'll find books devoted just to this topic.

Creating an MFC-Based Dynamic Link Library

An MFC-based DLL can be created and built in a manner similar to other MFC Windows projects. To build the DLL for this chapter, use the AppWizard to create all necessary header, resource, and source code files. The project will be named Framer. Follow these steps to complete the Framer project.

1. Choose the Visual C++ File | New menu option to bring up the New dialog box, as shown in Figure 14.1.

2. Name the new MFC AppWizard (dll) project *Framer*.

3. Click OK to start the MFC AppWizard (dll).

4. For Step 1 of the DLL AppWizard, make sure the Regular DLL using shared MFC DLL option is selected, as shown in Figure 14.2.

5. For the remaining steps, use the defaults suggested by the AppWizard.

6. Click Finish, review the options as shown in Figure 14.3, and then generate the base code for the project by selecting OK.

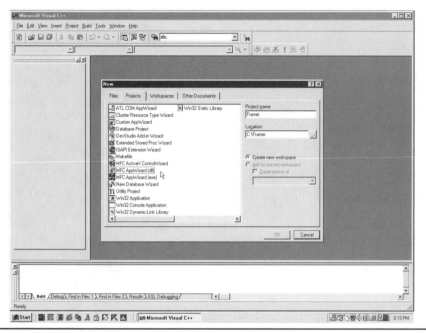

Figure 14.1 The New dialog box allows you to create a MFC AppWizard (dll) project

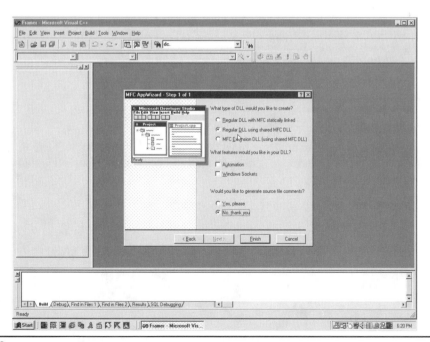

Figure 14.2 Use the AppWizard's first step to select the shared MFC DLL option

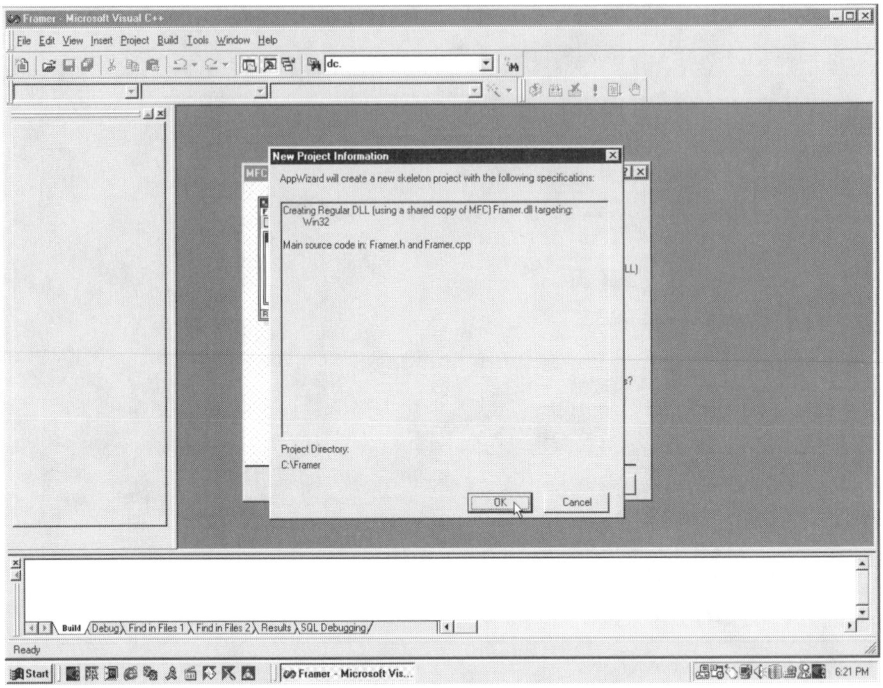

Figure 14.3   View the project information in the New Project Information dialog box

When the AppWizard creates the base code for the Framer project, your subdirectory should contain the files shown in Figure 14.4.

Like other AppWizard templates, the code that was generated is functional—it just doesn't do anything until we add our custom code.

The two files that are of greatest interest to us are the Framer.h and Framer.cpp files.

The Framer.h Header File

The Framer.h header file is used to hold any function prototypes that the DLL will export. In this example, the function prototypes that we added are shown in a bold font. Here is a partial listing of this file:

```
// Framer.h : main header file for the FRAMER DLL
//
    .
    .
    .
#if _MSC_VER > 1000
#pragma once
#endif // _MSC_VER > 1000

#ifndef __AFXWIN_H__
    #error include 'stdafx.h' before including file for PCH
#endif
```

```
#include "resource.h"         // main symbols

__declspec( dllexport ) void WINAPI ThickRectangle(CDC* pDC,
                                                    int x1,
                                                    int y1,
                                                    int x2,
                                                    int y2,
                                                    int t);
__declspec( dllexport ) void WINAPI ThickEllipse(CDC* pDC,
                                                  int x1,
                                                  int y1,
                                                  int x2,
                                                  int y2,
                                                  int t);
__declspec( dllexport ) void WINAPI ThickPixel(CDC* pDC,
                                               int x1,
                                               int y1);


/////////////////////////////////////////////////////////////
// CFramerApp
// See Framer.cpp for the implementation of this class
//
        .
        .
        .
```

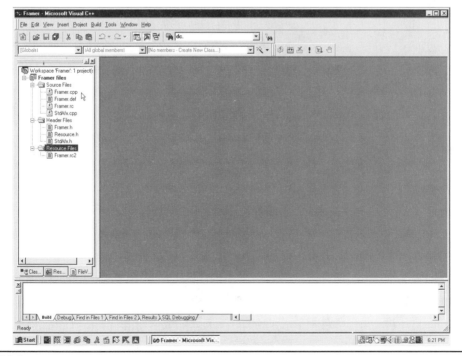

Figure 14.4   The left pane shows the files created by the AppWizard for the Framer DLL project

Microsoft uses an extended attribute syntax, such as __**declspec**, for simplifying and standardizing Microsoft-specific extensions to the C++ language. This keyword is used to indicate that an instance of the type will be stored with a Microsoft-specific storage-class attribute.

The explicit use of the **dllexport** keyword has eliminated the need for the old style EXPORT statements that once appeared in module definition files.

The Framer.cpp Source Code File

Now specific user-developed code can be added to the DLL template source code. The following listing shows the code added to Framer.cpp in a bold font:

```
// Framer.cpp : Defines the init. routines for the DLL.
//

#include "stdafx.h"
#include "Framer.h"

#ifdef _DEBUG
#define new DEBUG_NEW
#undef THIS_FILE
static char THIS_FILE[] = __FILE__;
#endif

/////////////////////////////////////////////////////////////
// CFramerApp

BEGIN_MESSAGE_MAP(CFramerApp, CWinApp)
    //{{AFX_MSG_MAP(CFramerApp)
        // NOTE - ClassWizard adds/removes mapping macros here.
        //    DO NOT EDIT these blocks of generated code!
    //}}AFX_MSG_MAP
END_MESSAGE_MAP()

/////////////////////////////////////////////////////////////
// CFramerApp construction

CFramerApp::CFramerApp()
{
}

/////////////////////////////////////////////////////////////
// The one and only CFramerApp object

CFramerApp theApp;

__declspec( dllexport ) void WINAPI ThickRectangle(CDC* pDC,
                                        int x1,
                                        int y1,
                                        int x2,
                                        int y2,
                                        int t)
```

```
{
  AFX_MANAGE_STATE(AfxGetStaticModuleState());

  CBrush newbrush;
  CBrush* oldbrush;

  pDC->Rectangle(x1,y1,x2,y2);
  pDC->Rectangle(x1+t,y1+t,x2-t,y2-t);
  newbrush.CreateSolidBrush(RGB(255,255,0));
  oldbrush=pDC->SelectObject(&newbrush);
  pDC->FloodFill(x1+(t/2),y1+(t/2),RGB(0,0,0));
  pDC->SelectObject(oldbrush);
  newbrush.DeleteObject();
}

__declspec( dllexport ) void WINAPI ThickEllipse(CDC* pDC,
                                                  int x1,
                                                  int y1,
                                                  int x2,
                                                  int y2,
                                                  int t)
{
  AFX_MANAGE_STATE(AfxGetStaticModuleState());

  CBrush newbrush;
  CBrush* oldbrush;

  pDC->Ellipse(x1,y1,x2,y2);
  pDC->Ellipse(x1+t,y1+t,x2-t,y2-t);
  newbrush.CreateSolidBrush(RGB(255,255,0));
  oldbrush=pDC->SelectObject(&newbrush);
  pDC->FloodFill(x1+(t/2),y1 + (t/2),RGB(0,0,0));
  pDC->SelectObject(oldbrush);
  newbrush.DeleteObject();
}

__declspec( dllexport ) void WINAPI ThickPixel(CDC* pDC,
                                                int x1,
                                                int y1)
{
  AFX_MANAGE_STATE(AfxGetStaticModuleState());

  CPen newpen;
  CPen* oldpen;

  pDC->SetPixel(x1,y1,0L);
  newpen.CreatePen(PS_SOLID,2,RGB(255,255,0));
  oldpen=pDC->SelectObject(&newpen);
  pDC->MoveTo(x1-5,y1);
  pDC->LineTo(x1-1,y1);
  pDC->MoveTo(x1+1,y1);
  pDC->LineTo(x1+5,y1);
```

```
pDC->MoveTo(x1,y1-5);
pDC->LineTo(x1,y1-1);
pDC->MoveTo(x1,y1+1);
pDC->LineTo(x1,y1+5);
pDC->SelectObject(oldpen);
newpen.DeleteObject();
}
```

Design Tip *Microsoft makes the following suggestion for any DLL that is to be dynamically linked against the MFC DLLs. Any functions that are exported from this DLL, that call into MFC, must have the AFX_MANAGE_STATE macro added at the very beginning of the function. For example:*

```
//          extern "C" BOOL PASCAL EXPORT ExportedFunction()
//          {
//              AFX_MANAGE_STATE(AfxGetStaticModuleState());
//              // normal function body here
//          }
//
```

This macro must appear in each function, before any calls into MFC. In other words, it must be the first statement within the function, appearing even before any object variable declarations. This is because their constructors may generate calls into the MFCDLL. Microsoft provides MFC Technical Notes 33 and 58 for additional information.

This DLL provides three drawing routines: ThickRectangle(), ThickEllipse(), and ThickPixel(). When they are called from the host application, and passed the proper parameters, they will draw a thick bordered rectangle or ellipse with the interior of the border filled with a predefined color. The ThickPixel() function draws a pair of crosshairs at the pixel location in a unique color.

When the DLL is bound to the host application, the DLL functions can be called by name and passed the proper parameters.

Building the Framer.dll

The DLL can be built by selecting the appropriate build option from the Visual C++ Build menu. When the build cycle is complete, the debug subdirectory will contain several important files.

The Framer.dll file is the Dynamic Link Library, and Framer.lib is the associated library. Both files must be placed in specific locations.

1. Copy Framer.dll to your Windows subdirectory containing system DLLs. This is usually C:\Windows\System for Windows 98.

2. Copy Framer.lib to the Debug subdirectory of the application that will use the DLL. The subdirectory for this example will be named C:\DLLDemo\debug.

In order to test the DLL, we will have to build a standard MFC application and call the DLL.

Creating a Host Application to Use the DLL

Now we need to create an application designed to take advantage of the Framer.dll Dynamic Link Library. This application, named DLLDemo, will call each of the DLL functions several times.

Use the following steps to create the DLLDemo template code with the AppWizard:

1. Choose the Visual C++ File | New menu option to bring up the New dialog box, as shown in Figure 14.5.

2. Name the project DLLDemo. Click OK to start the MFC AppWizard.

3. Follow the normal project creation steps and create an application with a single-document interface using the Document/View architecture support as shown in Figure 14.6.

4. Use wizard defaults for all other steps and build as a normal project.

5. Review and accept the classes as shown in the review list. Click the Finish button to generate the project files.

When the template code has been generated by the AppWizard, the functions necessary to call the DLL functions can be added to the OnDraw() method.

Again, two files are of interest to us in this project. The first is DLLDemoView.h, and the second is DLLDemoView.cpp.

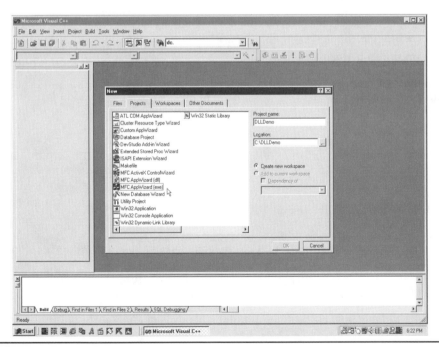

Figure 14.5   Use the New dialog box to create a new MFC AppWizard application named DLLDemo

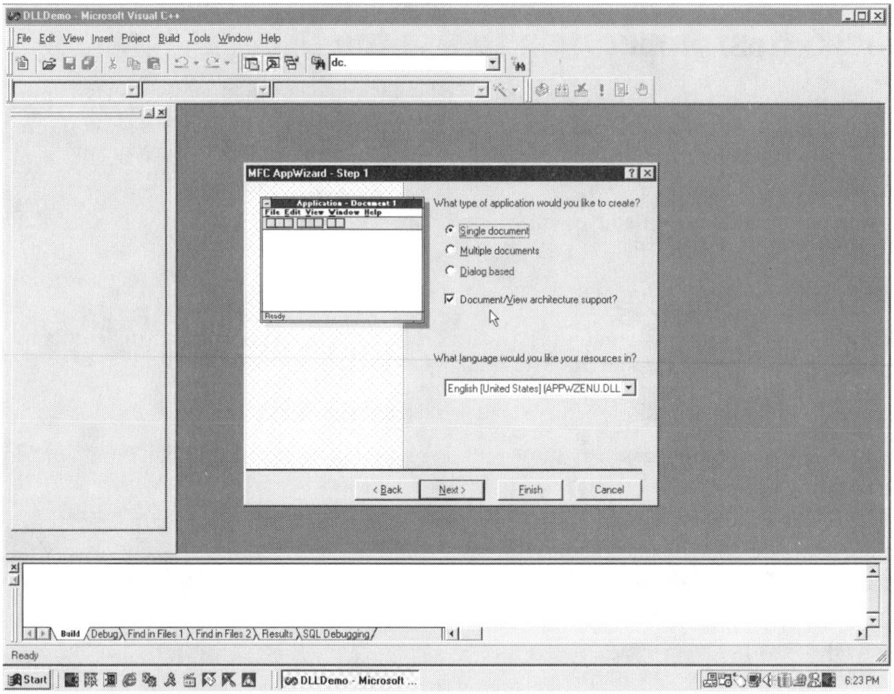

Figure 14.6   Select a single document interface for this project using the Document/View architecture

The DLLDemoView.h Header File

The DLLDemoView.h header file is used to hold function prototypes that we wish to import from Framer.dll. The following partial listing shows these function prototypes in a bold font:

```
// DLLDemoView.h : interface of the CDLLDemoView class
//
/////////////////////////////////////////////////////////////////
    .
    .
    .
extern void WINAPI ThickRectangle(CDC* pDC,int x1,int y1,
                                  int x2,int y2,int t);
extern void WINAPI ThickEllipse(CDC* pDC,int x1,int y1,
                                int x2,int y2,int t);
extern void WINAPI ThickPixel(CDC* pDC,int x1,int y1);

class CDLLDemoView : public CView
{
    .
    .
    .
```

The **extern** keyword alerts the compiler that these functions are external to the body of the current program. During the build process, the linker will look for each of these functions. If the linker cannot find one or all of the functions in an appropriate library, a brief error message will be issued.

> **Design Tip** *When the compiler encounters a function, such as ThickRectangle(), that is not part of the normal GDI drawing functions, it wants to immediately issue an error message. By using the **extern** keyword, you promise the compiler that information on this function will be supplied (usually in a DLL or other library) by link time. If the linker cannot find the promised function information, it will issue an error message to that effect.*

The DLLDemoView.cpp Source Code File

The following is a listing of the DLLDemoView.cpp source code file. The code responsible for calling the DLL functions is shown in a bold font:

```
// DLLDemoView.cpp : implementation of the CDLLDemoView class
//

#include "stdafx.h"
#include "DLLDemo.h"

#include "DLLDemoDoc.h"
#include "DLLDemoView.h"

#ifdef _DEBUG
#define new DEBUG_NEW
#undef THIS_FILE
static char THIS_FILE[] = __FILE__;
#endif

/////////////////////////////////////////////////////////////////
// CDLLDemoView

IMPLEMENT_DYNCREATE(CDLLDemoView, CView)

BEGIN_MESSAGE_MAP(CDLLDemoView, CView)
    //{{AFX_MSG_MAP(CDLLDemoView)
    //}}AFX_MSG_MAP
END_MESSAGE_MAP()

/////////////////////////////////////////////////////////////////
// CDLLDemoView construction/destruction

CDLLDemoView::CDLLDemoView()
{
}

CDLLDemoView::~CDLLDemoView()
{
}
```

```
BOOL CDLLDemoView::PreCreateWindow(CREATESTRUCT& cs)
{
    return CView::PreCreateWindow(cs);
}


/////////////////////////////////////////////////////////////
// CDLLDemoView drawing

void CDLLDemoView::OnDraw(CDC* pDC)
{
    CDLLDemoDoc* pDoc = GetDocument();
    ASSERT_VALID(pDoc);

    // Call ThickPixel() several times
    for (int i=50;i<900;i+=100)
        ThickPixel(pDC,i,75);

    // Call ThickRectangle() several times
    ThickRectangle(pDC,50,300,75,350,20);
    ThickRectangle(pDC,150,350,250,450,25);
    ThickRectangle(pDC,400,200,700,600,25);

    // Call ThickEllipse() several times
    ThickEllipse(pDC,50,100,75,150,10);
    ThickEllipse(pDC,150,150,250,250,15);
    ThickEllipse(pDC,450,250,650,550,10);
}


/////////////////////////////////////////////////////////////
// CDLLDemoView diagnostics

#ifdef _DEBUG
void CDLLDemoView::AssertValid() const
{
    CView::AssertValid();
}

void CDLLDemoView::Dump(CDumpContext& dc) const
{
    CView::Dump(dc);
}

CDLLDemoDoc* CDLLDemoView::GetDocument() //non-debug inline
{
    ASSERT(m_pDocument->IsKindOf(RUNTIME_CLASS(CDLLDemoDoc)));
    return (CDLLDemoDoc*)m_pDocument;
}
#endif //_DEBUG


/////////////////////////////////////////////////////////////
// CDLLDemoView message handlers
```

Before building this project, one more critical step must be taken. The DLLFrame.lib must be identified so the linker can resolve the external function calls. This is done using the compiler's Project | Settings menu selection to open the Project Settings dialog box. Figure 14.7 shows this dialog box with the Link folder selected.

The application can now be built by using the appropriate build selection from the compiler's Build menu.

Run the application, and you should see a screen similar to Figure 14.8.

The DLLDemo application should draw several shapes on the screen with each shape filling its wide border with a yellow color. Something has gone wrong here, and the whole screen has been flooded with a yellow color.

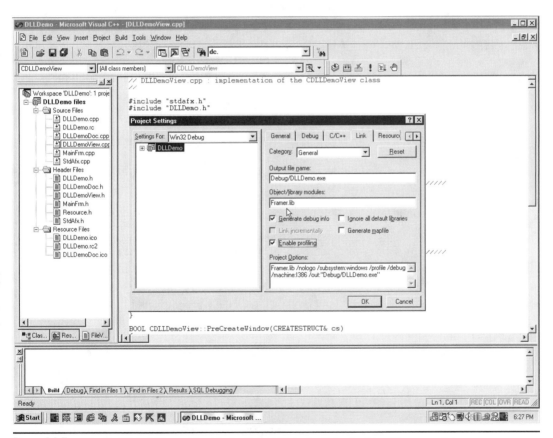

Figure 14.7   Use the Link folder to identify the Frame.lib in the linker's object/library module

24x7 Regular DLLs That Are Dynamically Linked to the MFC Library

Microsoft separates DLLs into two broad categories: DLLs that are dynamically linked and DLLs that are statically linked to the MFC library. The following is a modification of information provided by Microsoft for DLLs dynamically linked to the MFC library.

A regular DLL that is dynamically linked to the MFC library is one that uses the MFC internally. The DLL's functions that are exported can be called by MFC or non-MFC executable applications and have the following features:

- The DLL is dynamically linked to the MFC DLL.

- The host using the DLL can be written in any language that supports the use of DLLs and does not have to be a MFC-based application.

- The MFC import library linked to this DLL is the same as that used for extension DLLs or applications using the MFC DLL.

In order for a regular DLL to be dynamically linked to the MFC, the following requirements must be met:

1. Regular DLLs must have a CWinApp-derived class and a single object of that application class. The CWinApp object of the DLL does not have a main message pump. This sets it apart from the CWinApp object of a normal application.

2. The DLL is compiled with _AFXDLL defined. This is similar to an executable that is dynamically linked to the MFC DLL with the addition that _USRDLL is also defined.

3. The DLL is instantiated as a CWinApp-derived class.

4. The DLL uses DllMain supplied by the MFC. All DLL-specific initialization code is placed in the InitInstance() member function and termination code in the ExitInstance() member function.

5. Use the AFX_MANAGE_STATE macro at the start of every function exported from the DLL. This is necessary since this type of DLL uses the Dynamic Link Library version of MFC.

The MFCx0.dll and Msvcrt.dll (or similar files) must be distributed with the DLL with your application.

Symbols can be exported from a regular DLL by using the standard C interface. That interface can take on the following appearance:

```
extern "C" __declspec( dllexport ) ExportFunctionName( );
```

All memory allocations within a regular DLL should stay within the DLL; the DLL should not pass to or receive from the calling executable any of the following.

DLLs that are dynamically linked to the MFC use the macro AFX_MANAGE_STATE in order to correctly switch the MFC module state. This code must be added to the beginning of all functions exported from the DLL and takes on this form:

```
AFX_MANAGE_STATE(AfxGetStaticModuleState( ))
```

This macro should not be used in extension DLLs or with regular DLLs that statically link to the MFC.

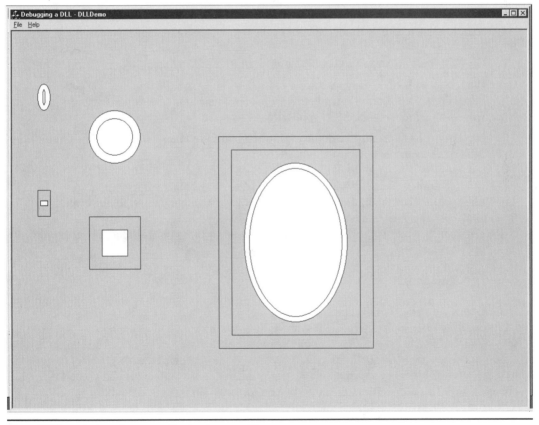

Figure 14.8   The DLLDemo application has a problem

24x7   Regular DLLs That Are Statically Linked to the MFC Library

DLLs that are statically linked to the MFC library fit into the second category of linking provided by Microsoft. Static linking to the MFC library is supported only in Visual C++ Professional and Enterprise editions.

A regular DLL can be statically linked to the MFC library. In this case, the DLL uses the MFC internally. The DLL's exported functions can be called by either the MFC or non-MFC executable applications.

A regular DLL that is statically linked takes on these features:

- The DLL can link to the same MFC static link libraries used by the application. There is no need for a separate version of the static link libraries for DLLs.

- The host executable application can be written in any language that supports the use of DLLs and does not have to be a MFC-based application.

To statically link a regular DLL to the MFC, the following requirements must be met:

1. The DLL must instantiate a class that is derived from CWinApp.

2. The DLL uses the DllMain provided by MFC. All DLL-specific initialization code is placed in the InitInstance() member function and termination code in ExitInstance(). This is similar to a regular MFC application.

3. The term _USRDLL must be defined on the compiler command line. (Note: the term USRDLL is obsolete but must still be defined.)

The DLLs must have a CWinApp-derived class and a single object of that application class. The CWinApp object of the DLL does not have a main message pump, which differentiates it from the CWinApp object of a normal MFC application.

Symbols can be exported from a regular DLL using the standard C interface. The following listing suggests the form:

```
extern "C" __declspec(dllexport) ExportFunctionName( );
```

DLLs that are statically linked to MFC cannot also dynamically link to the shared MFC DLLs. A DLL that is statically linked to MFC is dynamically bound to an application just like any other DLL. In other words, applications link to the DLL just like any other DLL.

It is not necessary to manually specify (to the linker) the version of the MFC library to be linked. Rather, the MFC header files automatically determine the correct version of the MFC library to link. This decision is determined by preprocessor defines like _DEBUG.

24x7 Safe Techniques for Debugging DLLs

There are several ways to debug a DLL and host application. Microsoft outlines techniques for the following variations: Debug a DLL using the project for the host application; debug a DLL using the project for the DLL; debug a DLL that was created with an external project. The following recommendations apply for all debugging sessions.

- If the source code for both the DLL and the host application are available, open the project for the host executable file and debug the DLL from there. If the DLL is loaded dynamically, then it must be specified in the Additional DLLs category of the Debug tab in the Project Settings dialog box.

- If the source code for only the DLL is available, open the project that builds the DLL. Use the Debug tab in the Project Settings dialog box to specify the host application file that calls the DLL.

- If just the DLL and source code are available, without a project, use the File | Open menu option to select the .DLL file to debug. The debug information should be contained in the .DLL or related .PDB file. Select Build | Start Debug and Go to begin the debugging session.

Use the following steps for debugging a DLL that uses the project file for the host application:

1. Choose the Project | Settings option.

2. The Project Settings dialog box appears. Select the Debug tab.

3. Select General in the Category drop-down listbox.

4. Use the Program Arguments text box to enter any command-line arguments required by the host application.

5. Use the Category drop-down listbox to select any Additional DLLs.

6. Use the Local Name column to enter the names of DLLs to debug.

7. For remote debugging, the Remote Name column will appear. Enter the complete path for the remote module to map to the local module name.

8. Use the Preload column (if present) and select the checkbox to load the module before debugging begins if desired.

9. Click OK to store the information in your project.

10. Choose the Build | Start Debug menu item and Go to start the Debugger.

It is possible to set breakpoints in both the DLL and the host application. Use the following steps for debugging a DLL that uses the project file for the DLL:

1. Choose the Project | Settings option.

2. The Project Settings dialog box appears. Select the Debug tab.

3. Select General in the Category drop-down listbox.

4. Use the Executable For Debug Session text box to enter the name of the executable file that calls the DLL.

5. Use the Category drop-down listbox to select any Additional DLLs.

6. Use the Local Name column to enter the names of DLLs to debug.

7. Click OK to store the information in your project.

8. Select the Build | Start Debug menu item and Go to start the Debugger.

Again, it is possible to set breakpoints in both the DLL and the host application. Use the following steps for debugging a DLL that uses the project file for the DLL:

1. Choose the Project | Settings option.

2. The Project Settings dialog box appears. Select the Debug tab.

3. Select General in the Category drop-down listbox.

4. Use the Executable For Debug Session text box to enter the name of the DLL created by an external project.

5. Click OK to store the information in your project.

6. Build a version of the DLL with symbolic debugging information.

7. Select the Build | Start Debug menu item and Go to start the Debugger.

Again, it is possible to set breakpoints in the DLL. This can be done before the final build of the DLL is created.

Preparing to Take a Closer Look

When you examined Figure 14.8, you undoubtedly noticed a problem with the output in the window. Instead of filling the wide borders of each graphics shape, the screen was filled instead. At this point, we know that the DLL is partially working since the figures were drawn. What we don't know is which routine or how many routines have gone awry.

Remote Debugging

You will learn, in the following sections, how to set up two computers for remote debugging. The added treat, in addition to the material originally presented in Chapter 8, is that there is now both a host application and a DLL to contend with. To maintain consistency, we're going to adapt the outline for remote debugging presented in Chapter 8 and modify it for a DLL debugging session. There are a wide variety of variations on how to properly set up two computers for this type of communications, in terms of file contents, and so on. Our techniques probably contain a little "overkill" in terms of file copying but, over the long haul, seem to be the easiest when shifting back and forth during multiple builds.

The following steps assume that both the DLL (Framer) and host application (DLLDemo) have been successfully created and contain all necessary debugging information.

Preparing the Remote Target Computer

Recall that a small program, called the Remote Debug Monitor, must be run on a remote target computer. In our case, this is the Sony computer system. This application and computer are responsible for communicating with the Debugger running on the host computer. In this case, the host computer is a Hewlett-Packard system. The Remote Target Computer software controls the execution of the application in the Debugger.

The remote target computer (Sony) requires additional files in order to install the Remote Debug Monitor. For both Windows 98 and Windows NT (2000), these files include:

```
MSVCMON.EXE
MSVCRT.DLL
TLN0T.DLL
DM.DLL
MSVCP6O.DLL
MSDIS110.DLL
PSAPI.DLL (for NT only)
```

Use the Find option in your system's Start window to locate these files in the proper host computer (hp) subdirectory. These files should be copied from the host computer (hp) to the remote target computer (sony) and saved in the Windows subdirectory of the remote target system. The only exception is that the MSVCRT.DLL file should be copied to the Windows\System32 subdirectory for Windows 98 or Windows 2000. Once this is done, reboot the computer.

Now, in order to run the Remote Target Computer software on the remote target system (sony), follow these steps:

1. Run the MSVCMON.EXE application on the remote target computer (sony).

2. The Visual C++ Debug Monitor dialog box appears. Choose the Settings option.

3. The Win32 Network (TCP/IP) Settings dialog box now appears. Enter the name of the host computer (hp, in our case) in this dialog box. (The IP address can also be used.)

4. If the password edit box is active, enter a password. This password must match on both computers. Otherwise, this field can be left blank.

5. Select the OK button.

6. Now, click the Connect button.

Once the preceding steps have been completed, the Connecting dialog box will appear on the screen. Do nothing more at this time. This dialog box will disappear once actual debugging starts.

When the debugging session has completed, select the Disconnect button to terminate the remote connection.

Preparing the Host Computer

The host computer (hp) must be prepared for communicating with the remote target computer (sony). Perform the following steps on the host computer (hp):

1. From within Visual C++, select the Build | Debugger Remote Connection menu item.

2. The Remote Connection dialog box will appear. If the Platform drop-down listbox allows a selection, select the appropriate platform. If a selection option is not offered, the default item is selected automatically.

3. Use the Connection drop-down listbox to select the Network (TCP/IP) connection option.

4. Select the Settings option.

5. The Win32 Network (TCP/IP) Settings dialog box will appear. Enter the name of the remote target computer (sony, in our case) in this dialog box. The IP address can also be used. If the password option is available, enter a password that is identical to the remote target's password. This field can also be left blank on both the remote and host machines.

6. Click the OK button to close the Win32 Network (TCP/IP) Settings dialog box.

7. Click the OK button to close the Remote Connection dialog box.

Once the preceding steps have been completed, the host computer will be set up for communicating with the remote target computer.

Starting a Debugging Session

With both computers on the network ready to communicate, the debugging session can be started.

Error Watch *Both the host computer (hp) and the remote computer (sony) should contain all of the files in the proper subdirectories for both the Framer and DLLDemo projects. Build both the Framer and DLLDemo projects on the host computer (hp) and then simply copy the subdirectories to the remote computer (sony).*

Remember the host computer, running Visual C++, is the Hewlett-Packard computer (hp) and the remote target computer is the Sony computer (sony). Complete the following suggested steps:

1. Copy both complete projects to be debugged to both computers. We also suggest using the same directory. For example, duplicate files would exist on both computers at c:\myproject with the debug executable at c:\myproject\debug. Remember that Framer.dll should be placed in the C:\Windows\System subdirectory for both computers. Likewise, Framer.lib should be placed in the C:\DLLDemo\Debug subdirectory of both computers.

2. Both directories should be set up on the network as shared directories.

3. Start the Visual C++ compiler and load the project on the host computer. (The Visual C++ compiler is not needed on the remote target computer (sony).)

4. Choose the Project | Settings menu option. The Project Settings dialog box will appear.

5. Choose the Debug tab in the Project Settings dialog box.

6. From the Category listbox, select General and set the following items:

   - Category listbox: Enter any additional DLLs required for the project. Next, check the box suggesting a search for additional DLLs.

   - Executable for Debug Session: Enter the name and path of the executable file as the debugger host computer (hp) sees it—for this example, C:\DLLDemo\debug\DLLDemo.exe.

   - Working Directory: Leave blank.

   - Program Arguments: Leave blank unless your program accepts initial parameters.

   - Remote Executable Path: Enter the name and path of the executable file as the remote target computer (sony) sees it—for example, C:\DLLDemo\debug\DLLDemo.exe.

7. Choose the Build | Start Debug menu item and use the Step Into (F11) option.

8. Give your system at least a minute to start communications across the network and then begin the debugging session in the normal manner.

9. Remember that anytime a change is made in the project, the files must be updated on both machines and in all subdirectories including C:\Windows\System.

Attempt a search for any missing DLLs and their associated symbolic information.

In the next section, we'll start the actual search for the problem(s) in the Framer.dll. Want to venture a guess as to what and where it is?

Code with a Problem

To locate the problem in the DLL, we'll use these specific steps for debugging a DLL using the project file for the DLL:

1. Choose the Project | Settings option.

2. The Project Settings dialog box appears. Select the Debug tab.

3. Select General in the Category drop-down listbox.

4. Use the Executable For Debug Session text box to enter the name of the executable file that calls the DLL, as shown in Figure 14.9.

5. Use the Category drop-down listbox to select Additional DLLs.

6. Use the Local Name column to enter the names of DLLs to debug. For remote debugging, enter the remote name also. See Figure 14.10.

7. Click OK to store the information in your project.

We set breakpoints near the end of each function in the DLL so we could determine which of the three functions was causing the flood fill problem. Choose the Build | Start Debug menu item and Go to start the Debugger and run to the first breakpoint.

Figure 14.11 shows the screen of the remote debug computer (sony) after several Go (F5) commands have been issued.

It appears as if the ThickPixel() and ThickRectangle() functions in the DLL are behaving properly. Figure 14.12 tells another story.

The screen did not flood when the ThickEllipse() function was called for the smallest ellipse. However, the figure's border was not filled either. During the second call to the ThickEllipse() function, the entire screen flooded with color. So the ThickEllipse() function is the cause of the problem.

A quick look at variables placed in the Watch window during the second call to the ThickEllipse() function, and a little calculating, reveal the problem. Figure 14.13 shows the watch window at this point.

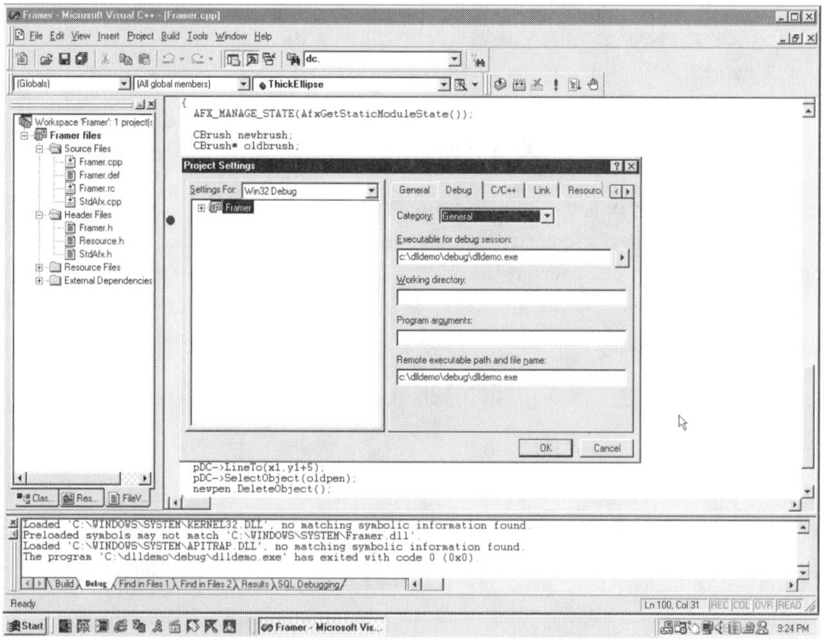

Figure 14.9 Using the Project Settings dialog box to set paths for the debug session

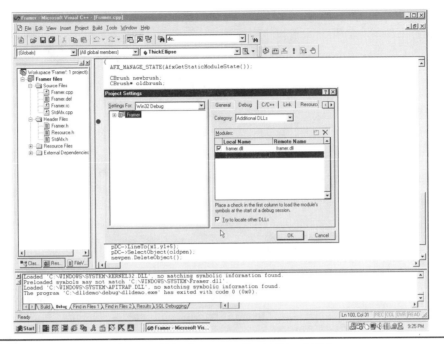

Figure 14.10   Using the Project Settings dialog box to specify Additional DLLs

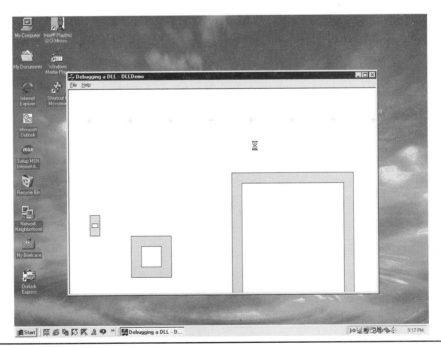

Figure 14.11   The remote computer's window during debugging

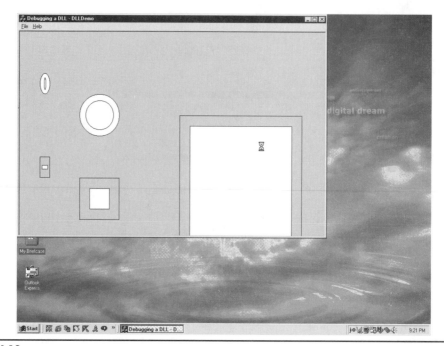

Figure 14.12   The screen floods with color during a call to ThickEllipse()

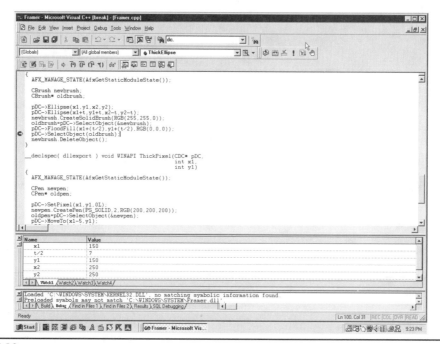

Figure 14.13   Examining variables in the Watch window

The FloodFill() function that worked so perfectly for the ThickRectangle() function failed to work properly for the ThickEllipse() function. The FloodFill() function requires that a point be specified within the boundaries of the area to be filled. Unfortunately, the equation used within the function to place this point, placed the point within the ellipses' bounding rectangle but not within the boundary where the fill is required. Hence, the screen flooded with color.

Repaired Code

To repair the DLL, we must correct the FloodFill() function to insure that the point will always lie within the two ellipses making up the thick ellipse. The following portion of the whole DLL, given earlier, corrects this problem:

```
__declspec( dllexport ) void WINAPI ThickEllipse(CDC* pDC,
                                        int x1,
                                        int y1,
                                        int x2,
                                        int y2,
                                        int t)
{
    AFX_MANAGE_STATE(AfxGetStaticModuleState());

    CBrush newbrush;
    CBrush* oldbrush;

    pDC->Ellipse(x1,y1,x2,y2);
    pDC->Ellipse(x1+t,y1+t,x2-t,y2-t);
    newbrush.CreateSolidBrush(RGB(255,0,0));
    oldbrush=pDC->SelectObject(&newbrush);
    pDC->FloodFill(x1+(t/2),y1 + ((y2 - y1)/2),RGB(0,0,0));
    pDC->SelectObject(oldbrush);
    newbrush.DeleteObject();
}
```

This was a relatively simple problem to debug, but one that was designed to illustrate the possibility of debugging the DLL.

24x7 Problems During DLL Debugging

The most typical problem that occurs when setting up a DLL for debugging is that the breakpoints set within the DLL don't work. Microsoft suggests several reasons for this problem.

First, you might find that a breakpoint cannot be set in a source file when the corresponding symbolic information isn't loaded into memory by the Debugger. This is because a breakpoint cannot be set in a source file when the corresponding symbolic information will not be loaded into memory by the Debugger. This problem is recognized by a message like "the breakpoint cannot be set" or a simple beep.

The Debugger uses a breakpoint list to keep track of how and where to set breakpoints when breakpoints are specified before the code to be debugged has been started. Then when debugging begins, the Debugger loads the symbolic information for the code and walks through its breakpoint list. It will attempt to set breakpoints, but this effort will be thwarted if any of the code modules have not been designated to the Debugger. This results in no symbolic information being made available to the Debugger when walking through its breakpoint list. Causes of this problem include attempts to set breakpoints in the DLL before a call to the LoadLibrary() function or setting a breakpoint in an ActiveX server before the container has started the server.

Most of the time, the problem can be avoided by specifying all additional DLLs and COM servers in the Additional DLLs field in the Debug/Options dialog box to notify the Debugger that you want it to load symbolic debug information for additional .DLL files. When this is done, breakpoints that have not been loaded into memory will be set as "virtual" breakpoints. When the code is finally loaded into memory, they will become physical breakpoints.

The second cause for this problem is that more than one copy of a DLL is present on the hard disk. When this occurs, especially if it is in your Windows directory, the Debugger will become confused. The Debugger will load the symbolic information for the DLL specified to it at runtime (with the Additional DLLs field in the Debug/Options dialog box), while Windows might load a different copy of the DLL into memory. The best preventive measures are to have only one copy of the DLL on the hard disk or be absolutely sure that all copies are identical.

Conclusion

This chapter has shown the techniques that can be used to debug DLLs using host and remote debugging computers. The simple DLL (Framer.dll) and the host application (DLLDemo.exe) were run from the host computer, while the graphics appeared on the remote debugging computer.

Debugging DLLs on two computer systems has greatly increased the complexity of the techniques, first taught in Chapter 8, for remote debugging. If you proceed slowly and with caution, making sure you complete all of the necessary steps along the way, your debugging session should go without a hitch.

CHAPTER 15

Working with ActiveX Controls

ctiveX controls, known also as OLE or custom controls, are another topic of interest to many Visual C++ programmers. The popularity and complexity of ActiveX controls has caused Microsoft to include an MFC ActiveX ControlWizard in the Visual C++ compiler. Testing ActiveX controls is also a difficult task. To help with testing, Microsoft has included the now-famous Test Container for testing controls during construction.

It would not be fair to our readers to just present an ActiveX control with a coding problem and then say here is how it can be fixed using the Debugger. At the same time, we didn't think we should drag programmers familiar with ActiveX control design through all of the steps necessary to make a robust ActiveX control.

In an effort not to be too verbose or to compromise details on debugging, this chapter is divided into two major areas. The first area is devoted to developing a simple, yet working, ActiveX control. This section is for programmers who have a little experience with ActiveX controls. The second area will show you how ActiveX controls can be debugged. It is an interesting area because you'll probably want to set up two computers and use remote debugging on this type of project, as in other Windows programs.

Developing an ActiveX Control

Microsoft ActiveX custom controls are Dynamic Link Libraries with OCX file extensions. These 32-bit controls for Windows 98 and Windows 2000 (NT) replace the older 16-bit VBX custom controls that were originally developed with Microsoft's Visual Basic.

ActiveX custom controls are relatively easy to design and implement by using the ActiveX ControlWizard. To start a new project, use the File | New menu item to bring up the New dialog box. From this project, select the MFC ActiveX ControlWizard to begin the design process. During the design process, the ControlWizard will create a template for a default ActiveX control. The default control can then be customized to the designer's specifications. Anytime during the design phase, the control can be tested in the Test Container application.

In the following sections, we'll take you step-by-step through the development of a control named Clock. This control is similar to the control developed in the ActiveX tutorial but includes some custom features.

24x7   Controls

Windows divides controls into three classes: standard controls, common controls, and custom controls. Standard controls include radio buttons, push buttons, edit boxes, and listboxes. Common controls include toolbars, tooltips, spin buttons, and sliders, although many of these common controls have migrated to the standard controls toolbox. Custom controls, to some degree, are similar to the other two classes. The disadvantage of custom controls is the time required to design and implement them. The advantage of custom controls is that you can make any type of control you'd like. Typical custom controls include spreadsheets, word processors, calendars, and grids.

Visual Basic was the first language that made building custom controls an easy process. These custom controls soon became known as VBX controls after their file extension (.vbx). Custom controls are actually small Dynamic Link Libraries (DLLs).

Visual C++ programmers initially had to obtain or create Visual Basic custom controls and then integrate them into their applications. With later releases of the Visual C++ compiler, custom controls could be developed within the C++ environment.

The best news for ActiveX control developers is that the Visual C++ compiler provides a ControlWizard for helping to create and integrate custom controls into your applications. The Visual C++ compiler also provides a special test container application for testing custom controls while they are being constructed.

The advantage of using a wizard is that the template for the ActiveX control will be 24x7. In other words, the code you initially start with has been thoroughly tested and debugged.

Design Tip   *ActiveX controls, after all, are just controls. They can be used in dialog boxes, for example, and placed next to standard and common controls. However, custom controls are much more difficult to design and implement. As the control's developer, you must first create, write, and compile the code that draws the custom control and implements all of the control's methods and so on. This custom control code will become a Dynamic Link Library. ActiveX controls use an OCX file extension instead of the DLL extension associated with the DLLs discussed in the previous chapter. Then the application that is to use the custom control must interact with the control's methods, data, and so on. You must write this code, too. ActiveX controls must be completely reentrant. Since these controls are really separate DLLs, they are not linked to the application. Thus, ActiveX controls require a separate instance for data for each use of the control. Messages are the only permissible means of communication allowed between ActiveX controls and the application.*

When using the MFC ActiveX ControlWizard, many of these difficult tasks are automated.

Using the ControlWizard

Use the File | New menu selection to start the design process with the New Project dialog box. Select the MFC ActiveX ControlWizard item and name the project Clock, as shown in Figure 15.1.

During the first step of the wizard's process, select the items shown in Figure 15.2 for this project.

Figure 15.3 shows additional project options that can be set or modified during the custom control design process.

The defaults were again used for this control, with just one exception. Make sure to select the Available in "Insert Object" dialog item. This will allow the control to be registered and used by OLE applications such as Word, Access, and Excel. To complete the design process, click on the Finish button.

Figure 15.4 shows the list of components that will be included in the final project.

If this information is correct, use the OK button to accept the information and allow the ControlWizard to create the files for the project. Figure 15.5 shows the list of files created for the Clock project.

Even at this point, the project contains enough code to actually work. The control can be tested in the Test Container application described in the next section.

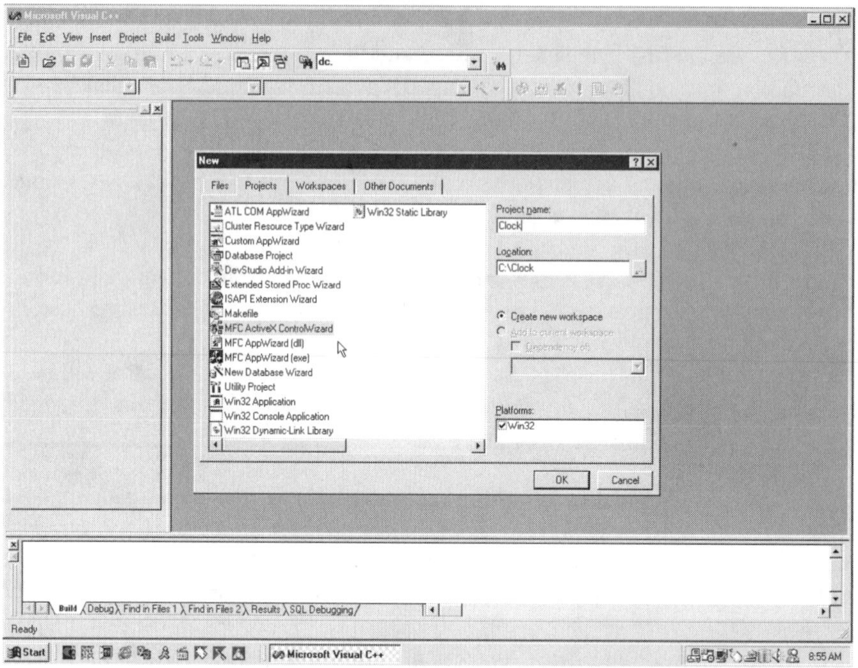

Figure 15.1   Selecting the MFC ActiveX ControlWizard starts the control design process

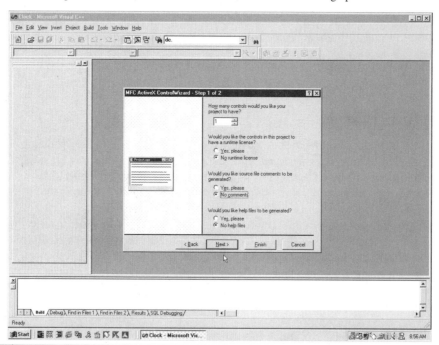

Figure 15.2   The first step in building an ActiveX control

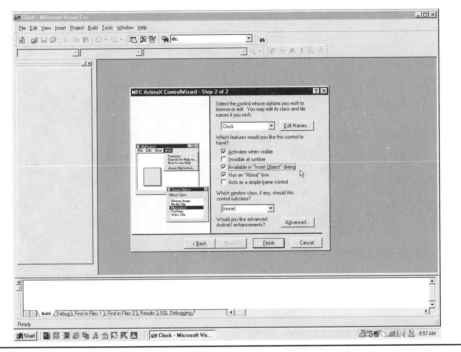

Figure 15.3   The second step of the control building process

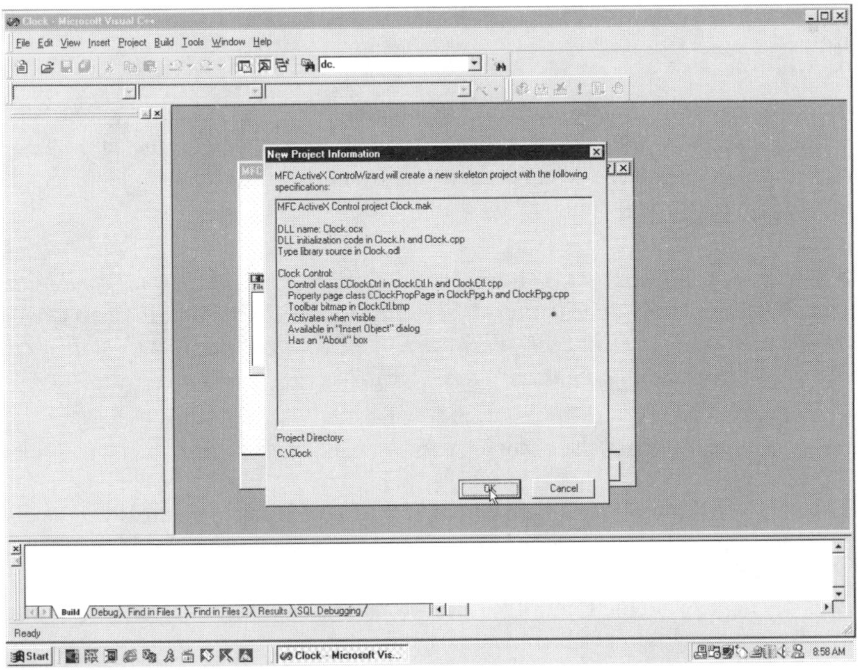

Figure 15.4   The control's project information

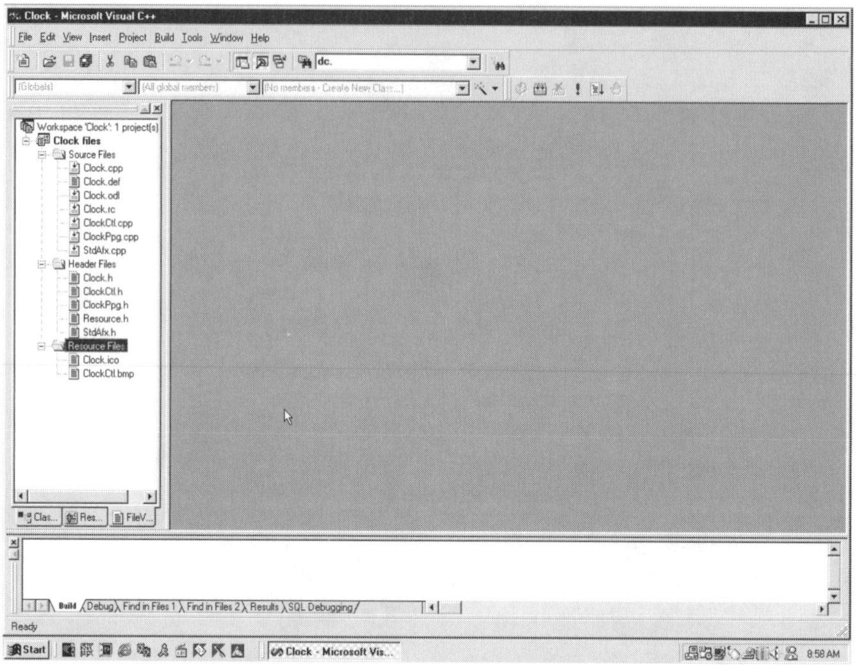

Figure 15.5   The files created by the ControlWizard for the project

The Test Container

When the ActiveX control is actually compiled, it will also be registered in the system. While no unique features have been added to the control, it can be viewed with the use of the Test Container. Use the Tools menu and select the ActiveX Control Test Container menu item, as shown in Figure 15.6.

> **Design Tip**   *Use the Control Test Container frequently during the development and testing phase of a new ActiveX-control. In addition to its ease of use, the Test Container is fully integrated with the Debugger. When using the Debugger, the Test Container can be automatically started and even used in a remote debugging situation.*

When the Test Container starts, the client area will be blank. Use the Edit menu and select the Insert New Control menu item, as shown in Figure 15.7.

When the Insert New Control menu item is selected, a list of possible controls will be displayed, as shown in Figure 15.8.

Figure 15.9 shows the Test Container after the Clock control is selected from the list.

All controls developed with the ControlWizard will take on this initial appearance. By default, the control is an ellipse enclosed in a bounding rectangle.

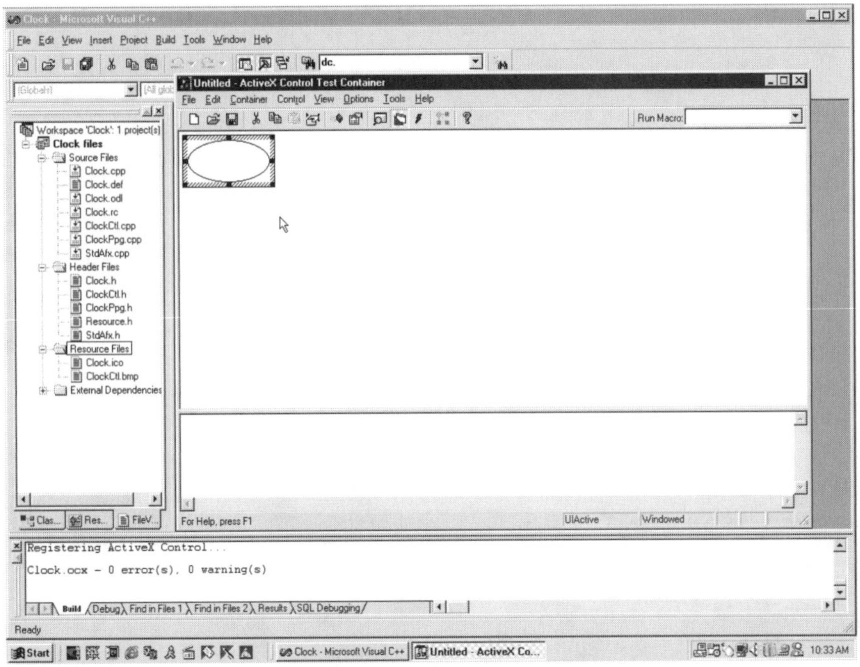

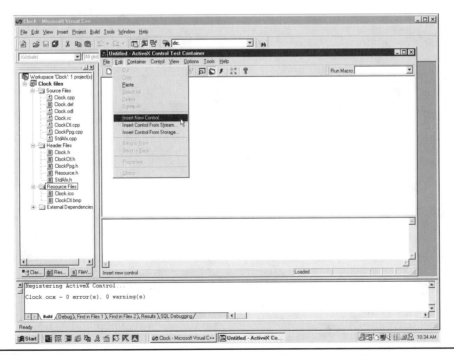

Figure 15.6   The default control examined using the Control Test Container

Figure 15.7   The Insert New Control menu item allows the new Clock control to be inserted

Figure 15.8   A list of registered controls contains the new Clock control

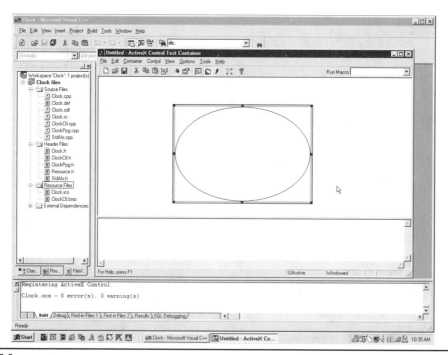

Figure 15.9   The Clock control is inserted into the Test Container

Creating a Real Clock Control

The ClassWizard is used to modify the default custom control produced by the ControlWizard.

To build a real custom Clock control, start with the default custom control described in the previous section. Here are the features for our real Clock control:

- It will always draw a round clock face, never an ellipse.
- The face and background will be unique colors.
- It will respond to a mouse event within the control and report the current system date and time.

All of these new features can be added to the control by working with just two of the project's files; ClockCtl.cpp and ClockCtl.h. In the next section, we'll add several of the new features.

Changing the Shapes, Size, and Colors of the Clock

Start the ClassWizard from the View menu. Use the following steps to add the shape and color properties of the control:

1. Select the Automation tab from within the MFC ClassWizard dialog box.
2. Select CClockCtrl from the Class name listbox.
3. Use the Add Property button to display the Add Property dialog box, as shown in Figure 15.10.
4. Enter the name ClockShape as the External name.
5. Select Member variable as the implementation.
6. Choose BOOL from the drop-down Type listbox. Notice that the Notification function edit control contains OnClockShapeChanged. The member variable is *m_clockShape*.
7. Accept these values with the OK button and return to the Automation tab.
8. Select the Add Property button again and display the Add Property dialog box.
9. In the edit control of the External name combo box, select BackColor from the drop-down list of available items.
10. For an Implementation, select Stock.
11. Accept these values with the OK button and return to the Automation tab. The MFC ClassWizard dialog box should now be similar in appearance to Figure 15.11.
12. Click the OK button to accept the choices and close the ClassWizard.

The ClassWizard will add the ClockShape and BackColor properties to the CClockCtrl class. The CClockCtrl class's dispatch map will be altered to accommodate the ClockShape property, and the BackColor property is added to the clock.odl library file. A declaration for the OnClockShapeChanged() function is added to the ClockCtl.h header file.

The ClassWizard adds the previously discussed changes automatically. Now it becomes our job to write the code that reacts to these changes.

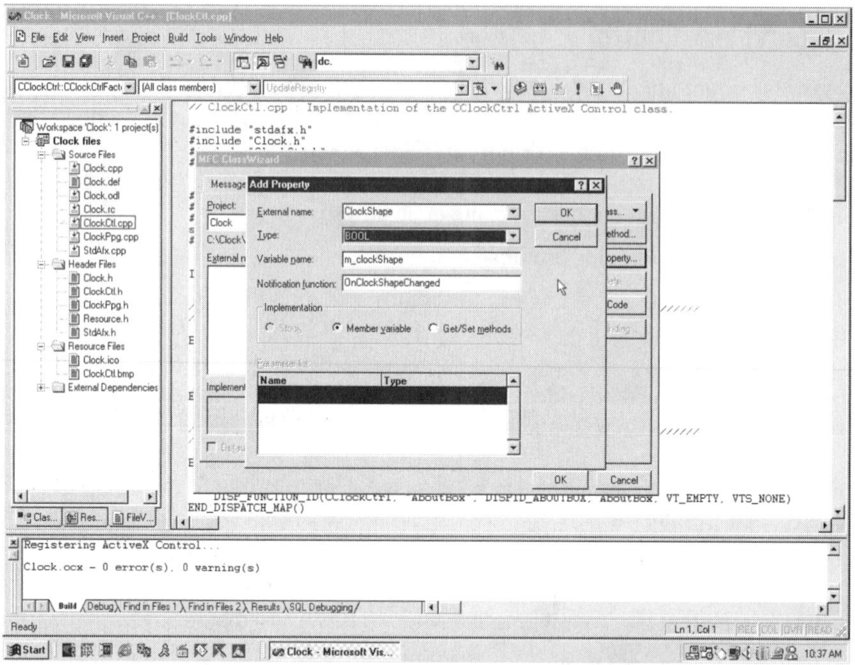

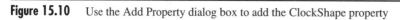

Figure 15.10   Use the Add Property dialog box to add the ClockShape property

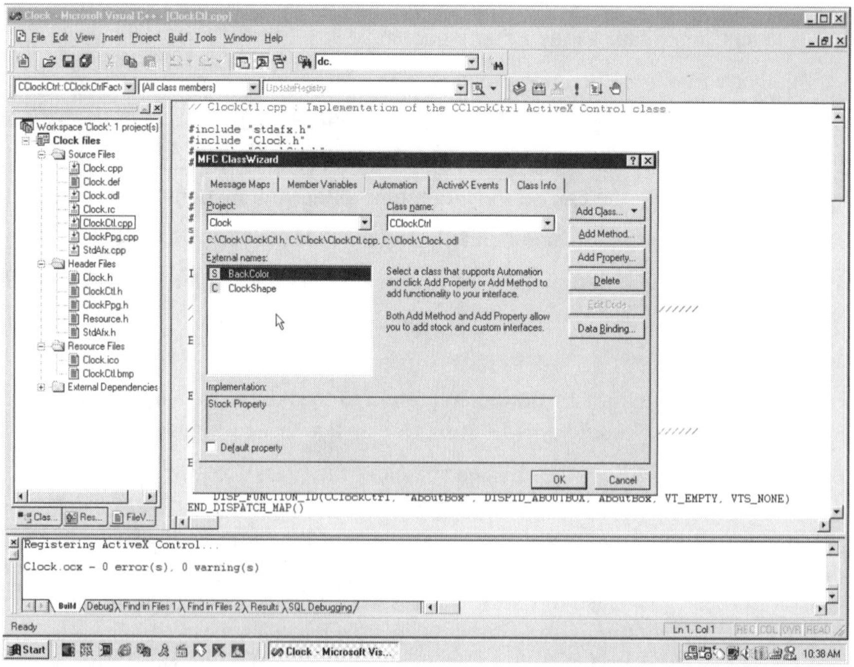

Figure 15.11   The ClassWizard will add BackColor and ClockShape properties to the project

The ClockCtl.h File   A function will be written to determine the correct size of the clock face. This function will be called GetDrawRect(). Include the function in the ClockCtl.h file just after the destructor, as shown in the following partial listing:

```
// Implementation
 protected:
   ~CClockCtrl();
        .
        .
        .
   void GetDrawRect(CRect* rc);    // Clock Size
        .
        .
        .
   DECLARE_OLECREATE_EX(CClockCtrl) //Class factory and guid
```

The code for this function will be included in the ClockCtl.cpp file, shown in the next section.

The ClockCtl.cpp File   The following partial listing of the ClockCtl.cpp file shows those sections of code that must be modified in this file. This code is identical to the default file returned by the ControlWizard, except for the bolded lines of code which add or modify control features.

```
/////////////////////////////////////////////////////////////////
// CClockCtrl::OnDraw - Drawing function

void CClockCtrl::OnDraw(CDC* pdc, const CRect& rcBounds,
                        const CRect& rcInvalid)
{
  CBrush* pBackBrush;
  CBrush* pFaceBrush;
  CPen* pHandsPen;
  CRect rc = rcBounds;
  int xcenter, ycenter;

  // clock background rectangle
  pBackBrush=new CBrush(RGB(0,0,255));
  pdc->FillRect(rcBounds, pBackBrush);
  GetDrawRect(&rc);

  // clock face
  pFaceBrush=new CBrush(RGB(255,255,0));
  pdc->SelectObject(pFaceBrush);
  pdc->Ellipse(rc);

  // clock hands
  pHandsPen=new CPen(PS_SOLID,3,RGB(0,0,0));
  pdc->SelectObject(pHandsPen);
  xcenter=(rc.right-rc.left)/2 + rc.left;
  ycenter=(rc.bottom-rc.top)/2 + rc.top;
  pdc->MoveTo(xcenter,ycenter);
```

```
  pdc->LineTo(rc.right*75/100,rc.bottom*75/100);
  pdc->MoveTo(xcenter,ycenter);
  pdc->LineTo(xcenter,rc.bottom*90/100);

  delete pBackBrush;
  delete pFaceBrush;
  delete pHandsPen;
}
        .
        .
        .

void CClockCtrl::GetDrawRect(CRect* rc)
{
  // Round clock face
  int dx = rc->right - rc->left;
  int dy = rc->bottom - rc->top;
  if (dx > dy) {
    rc->left += (dx - dy) / 2;
    rc->right = rc->left + dy;
  }
  else {
    rc->top += (dy - dx) / 2;
    rc->bottom = rc->top + dx;
  }
}
```

The clock face is drawn by using the ellipse function and then filled with the yellow brush.

```
// clock face
pFaceBrush=new CBrush(RGB(255,255,0));
pdc->SelectObject(pFaceBrush);
pdc->Ellipse(rc);
```

A test is made in order not to end up with an elliptical clock depending upon how the control is stretched. The smaller of the x or y extent, determined by the GetDrawRect() function, is used for the diameter of the clock face. This information is passed to the Ellipse() function by the *rc* parameter. This parameter holds the coordinates of the bounding rectangular area.

The clock's hands are drawn using a combination of the MoveTo() and LineTo() functions.

```
// clock hands
pHandsPen=new CPen(PS_SOLID,3,RGB(0,0,0));
pdc->SelectObject(pHandsPen);
xcenter=(rc.right-rc.left)/2 + rc.left;
ycenter=(rc.bottom-rc.top)/2 + rc.top;
pdc->MoveTo(xcenter,ycenter);
pdc->LineTo(rc.right*75/100,rc.bottom*75/100);
pdc->MoveTo(xcenter,ycenter);
pdc->LineTo(xcenter,rc.bottom*90/100);
```

They are drawn a proportional distance from the center of the clock face.

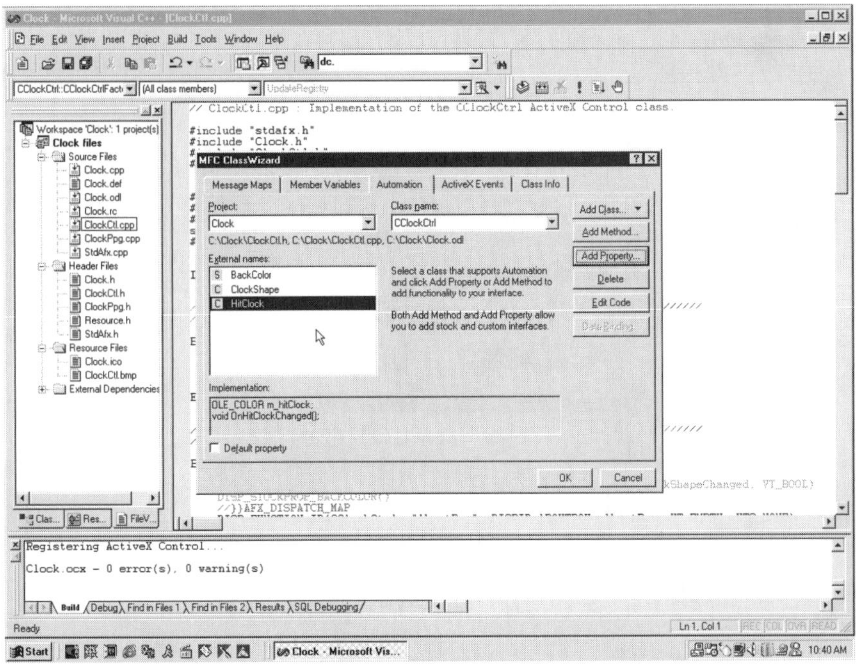

Figure 15.12   The HitClock property allows the control to respond to a mouse event

Responding to Mouse Events

The Clock control must respond to mouse events in order to show the current date and time. When the cursor is on the Clock face when the left mouse button is depressed, the Clock will change color and report the system time to the control. The color change and time information are indicators that a control "hit" has occurred.

A control hit can be added to the project with the following steps:

1. Select the Automation tab from the MFC ClassWizard dialog box.

2. Select CClockCtrl from the Class name listbox.

3. Select the Add Property button and display the Add Property dialog box.

4. In the edit control of the External names combo box, type HitClock.

5. For an Implementation, check to make sure Member Variable is selected.

6. Select OLE_COLOR from the Type listbox and clear the Notification function edit control.

7. Close the Add Property dialog box by selecting the OK button and return to the Automation tab. Your screen should be similar to Figure 15.12.

8. Select the Message Maps tab.

9. Select CClockCtrl from the Class name listbox.

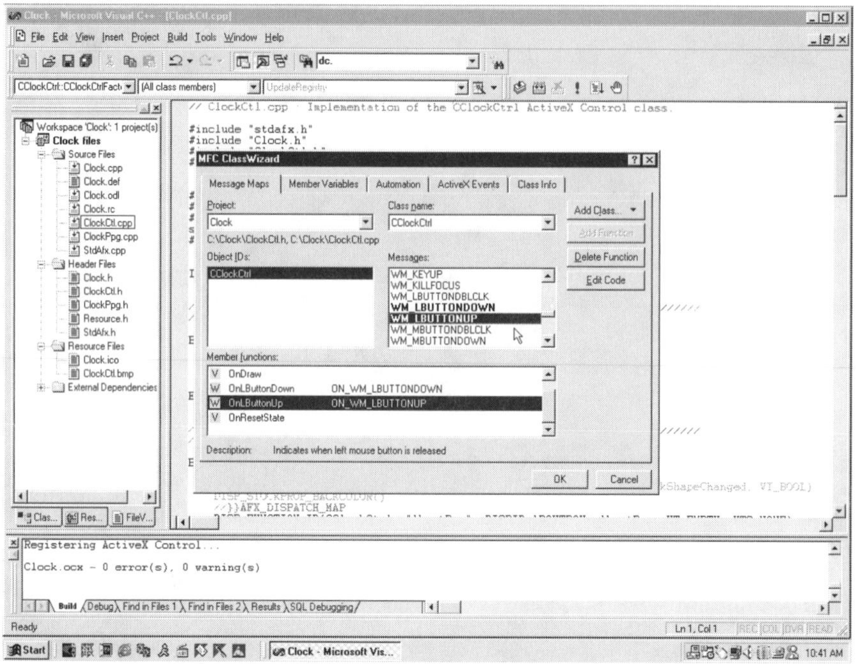

Figure 15.13   Two member functions will respond to mouse button events

10. From the Object IDs listbox, select CClockCtrl and then view a list of messages in the Messages listbox.

11. Select WM_LBUTTONDOWN from the Messages listbox.

12. Click the Add Function button.

13. Repeat this process by selecting WM_LBUTTONUP. Your screen should look like the one in Figure 15.13.

14. Click the OK button to accept the choices and close the ClassWizard.

The ClassWizard will automatically add the HitClock property and the outlines for the earlier member function implementations for the CClockCtrl class.

Again, these changes have been added by the ClassWizard, but the code must now be written to reacts to these events.

The ClockCtl.h Header File   Two additional insertions must be made in the ClockCtl.h header file in order to accommodate the two new methods. The first method is used to determine if a mouse event occurred within the Clock control. The second method is used to change the clock face color when a hit occurs. Insert InFace() and HitClock() just under the destructor shown in the following partial listing of the ClockCtl.h header file:

```
// Implementation
protected:
    ~CClockCtrl();

    void GetDrawRect(CRect* rc);        // Clock Size
    BOOL InFace(CPoint& point);         // Hit the Clock?
    void HitClock(CDC* pdc);            // Blink the clock color

    DECLARE_OLECREATE_EX(CClockCtrl)    // Class factory and guid
            .
            .
            .
```

The code will now be added for detecting mouse clicks within the control.

The ClockCtl.cpp File   The clock face will change color when the user clicks the left mouse button within the clock face. The event notification, in part, is handled by the DoPropExchange() function. Here is the DoPropExchange() function showing the new line in a bolded font:

```
/////////////////////////////////////////////////////////////////
// CClockCtrl::DoPropExchange - Persistence support

void CClockCtrl::DoPropExchange(CPropExchange* pPX)
{
    ExchangeVersion(pPX, MAKELONG(_wVerMinor, _wVerMajor));
    COleControl::DoPropExchange(pPX);

    PX_Long(pPX, _T("HitClock"), (long&)m_hitClock,
            RGB(196,196,196));
}
```

This function is responsible for initializing the *m_hitClock* member variable to a light gray color. The variable *m_hitClock* must be cast to a long since it is an unsigned long value.

The ClassWizard added the OnLButtonDown() and OnLButtonUp() methods. The following listing shows several lines of bolded code that were added to OnLButtonDown() and OnLButtonUp():

```
void CClockCtrl::OnLButtonDown(UINT nFlags, CPoint point)
{
    // TODO: Add message handler code here and/or call default

    CDC* pdc;

    // Flash a color change for clock face
    if (InFace(point)) {
      pdc = GetDC();
      HitClock(pdc);
      ReleaseDC(pdc);
    }
```

```
        COleControl::OnLButtonDown(nFlags, point);
}

void CClockCtrl::OnLButtonUp(UINT nFlags, CPoint point)
{
    // TODO: Add your message handler code here and/or call default

    if (InFace(point))
      InvalidateControl();

    COleControl::OnLButtonUp(nFlags, point);
}
```

This code checks to make sure the left mouse button was clicked within the face of the clock. If it was, the HitClock() function will be called to change the color of the clock face from yellow to light gray.

When the left mouse button is released, the OnLButtonUp() function merely invalidates the control, forcing a repaint in the face to yellow.

The InFace() function is used to determine if the left mouse button was depressed within the clock face. All of the following code must be added to the end of the clockctl.cpp listing:

```
BOOL CClockCtrl::InFace(CPoint& point)
{
  CRect rc;
  GetClientRect(rc);
  GetDrawRect(&rc);

  // Find center point
  double h = (rc.right - rc.left) / 2;
  double k = (rc.bottom - rc.top) / 2;

  // Find x and y values
  double x = point.x - (rc.right + rc.left) / 2;
  double y = point.y - (rc.bottom + rc.top) / 2;

  // Ellipse equation determines location of point
  return ((x * x) / (h * h) + (y * y) / (k * k) <= 1);
}
```

This function locates the center of the Clock control and then determines if the hit occurred within that clock face.

If the point falls within the clock face, the HitClock() function is called. All of the code in the following function must be added to the end of the ClockCtl.cpp listing:

```
void CClockCtrl::HitClock(CDC* pdc)
{
  CBrush* pOldBrush;
  CBrush hitBrush(TranslateColor(m_hitClock));
```

```
CRect rc;
TEXTMETRIC tm;
struct tm *date_time;
time_t timer;

// Fill between text
// Background mode to transparent
pdc->SetBkMode(TRANSPARENT);

GetClientRect(rc);

pOldBrush=pdc->SelectObject(&hitBrush);
pdc->Ellipse(rc);

// Get time and date
time(&timer);
date_time=localtime(&timer);
const CString& strtime = asctime(date_time);

// Get Font information then print
pdc->GetTextMetrics(&tm);
pdc->SetTextAlign(TA_CENTER | TA_TOP);
pdc->ExtTextOut((rc.left + rc.right)/2,
                (rc.top + rc.bottom - tm.tmHeight)/2,
                ETO_CLIPPED, rc, strtime,
                strtime.GetLength()-1, NULL);

pdc->SelectObject(pOldBrush);
}
```

The code in this function selects the gray brush, defined earlier, and repaints the entire Clock area.

The code is now complete and ready to test in the Control Test Container. Follow the steps discussed earlier in this chapter and load the Clock control in the Test Container. Left-click the mouse in the clock's face. You should see something similar to Figure 15.14.

There seems to be a problem with the control. We'll investigate this problem with the help of the Debugger, Control Test Container and the use of remote computer debugging capabilities.

Debugging the Clock Control

In the previous section, you discovered that the control is not acting quite like we wished. While the clock face initially appears okay, it changes from a circle to an ellipse when the left mouse button is depressed. However, it returns to a round face once the button is released. In order to track down this problem, we are going to use remote debugging so that we can keep the control in view as we step through the control's code. In the following section, you'll learn how to set up your computers so that you can use the Control Test Container on a remote system as you operate the Debugger on a host system.

Figure 15.14   Left-clicking the mouse while the cursor is over the clock's face produces these results

Preparing the Remote Target Computer

Recall from Chapter 8 that a small program called the Remote Debug Monitor must be run on the remote target computer. We have been using a Sony portable computer for this purpose. This application and computer are responsible for communicating with the Debugger running on the host computer, which, in our case, is a Hewlett-Packard system. The Remote Target Computer software controls the execution of the application in the Debugger.

The remote target computer (the Sony) must contain a few additional files in order to install the Remote Debug Monitor. For both Windows 98 and Windows 2000 (NT), these files include the following:

```
MSVCMON.EXE
MSVCRT.DLL
TLNOT.DLL
DM.DLL
MSVCP6O.DLL
MSDIS110.DLL
PSAPI.DLL (for NT only)
```

Use the Find option in your system's Start window to locate these files in the proper host computer (hp) subdirectory. Copy the files from the host computer (hp) to the remote target computer (sony) and save them in the Windows subdirectory of the remote target system. The only exception is that the MSVCRT.DLL file should be copied to the Windows\System32 subdirectory. Once this is done, reboot the remote target computer.

To run the Remote Target Computer software on the remote target system (sony), follow these steps:

1. Run the MSVCMON.EXE application on the remote target computer (sony).

2. The Visual C++ Debug Monitor dialog box appears.

3. Choose the Settings option.

4. The Win32 Network Settings dialog box now appears.

5. Enter the name of the host computer (hp, in our case) in this dialog box. (The IP address can also be used.)

6. If the password Edit box is active, enter a password. This password must match on both computers. Otherwise, this field can be left blank.

7. Click the OK button.

8. Now click the Connect button.

Once the eight steps have been completed, the Connecting dialog box will appear on the screen. Do nothing more at this time. This dialog box will disappear once actual debugging starts. When the debugging session has completed, click the Disconnect button to terminate the remote connection.

Preparing the Host Computer

The host computer (hp) must be prepared for communicating with the remote target computer (sony). Perform the following steps on the host computer (hp):

1. From within Visual C++, select the Build | Debugger Remote Connection menu item.

2. The Remote Connection dialog box will appear.

3. If the Platform drop-down listbox allows a selection, select the appropriate platform. If a selection option is not offered, the default item is selected automatically.

4. Use the Connection drop-down listbox to select the Network (TCP/IP) connection option.

5. Now select the Settings option.

6. The Win32 Network (TCP/IP) Settings dialog box will appear.

7. Enter the name of the remote target computer (sony) in this dialog box. The IP address can also be used. If the password option is available, enter a password that is identical to the remote target's password. This field can also be left blank on both the remote and host machines.

8. Click the OK button to close the Win32 Network Settings dialog box.

9. Click the OK button to close the Remote Connection dialog box.

Once the nine steps have been completed, the host computer will be set up for communicating with the remote target computer.

Starting a Debugging Session

With both computers on the network ready to communicate, the debugging session can be started. Remember the host computer, running Visual C++, is the Hewlett-Packard computer (hp) and the remote target computer is the Sony computer (sony). Complete the following suggested steps:

1. Copy the complete project subdirectory to be debugged to both machines. Use the same directory name.

2. Both directories should be set up on the network as shared directories.

3. Start the Visual C++ compiler and load the project on the host computer.

4. Choose the Project | Settings menu option. The Project Settings dialog box will appear.

5. Choose the Debug tab in the Project Settings dialog box.

6. From the Category listbox, select General and set the following items:

   • Category listbox: Enter any additional DLLs required for the project.

   • Executable for Debug Session: Enter the name and path of the Control Test Container. This can often be selected from the control, as shown in Figure 15.15.

   • Working Directory: Leave blank.

   • Program Arguments: Leave blank unless your program accepts initial parameters.

   • Remote Executable Path: Enter the name and path of the Control Test Container on the remote target computer (sony).

   • Choose the Build | Start Debug menu item and use the Go (F5) option to take you to a preset breakpoint.

7. Give your system at least a minute to start communications across the network and then begin the debugging session in the normal manner. The test container will start automatically.

8. Remember that anytime a change is made in the project, the files must be updated on both machines.

9. Now add the Clock control to the Test Container on the remote computer by using the Edit menu and selecting the control from the provided list of registered controls.

Design Tip *If you are setting breakpoints in this application, make sure they are set before copying the files to the remote debugging computer. The files must be identical on both computers.*

Error Watch *If you receive warning messages concerning missing DLLs and/or the required symbol information, allow the system to resolve as many of these cases as possible. This will usually be sufficient for a successful debugging session.*

In the next section, we'll start the investigation as to where the problem might be in the control's code.

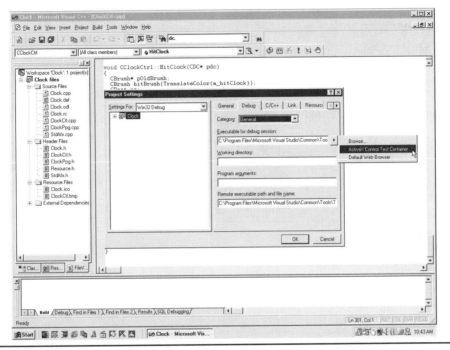

Figure 15.15   The Project Settings dialog box as it appears on the host computer (hp)

Looking for the Problem

In Figure 15.14, shown earlier, you saw that the clock face changes from a circle to an ellipse when the date and time information are returned. The clock face was supposed to remain round, so we'll have to investigate the problem. Here is what we know about the project from our initial run in the Control Test Container:

- The ActiveX control works, for the most part.
- The clock face initially appears in the correct shape and color.
- The date and time are reported correctly.
- The clock can be sized correctly.
- The color, time, and date are correct when the left mouse button is clicked over the face—only the shape of the face is incorrect.

With remote debugging enabled, we set two breakpoints in the ActiveX control. One breakpoint is positioned in the OnDraw() method where the clock face is drawn correctly, and the other breakpoint is placed in the HitClock() method where the problem seems to occur.

Figure 15.16 shows the values for two variables, *rc* and *rcBounds*, that are returned as we step through the OnDraw() method.

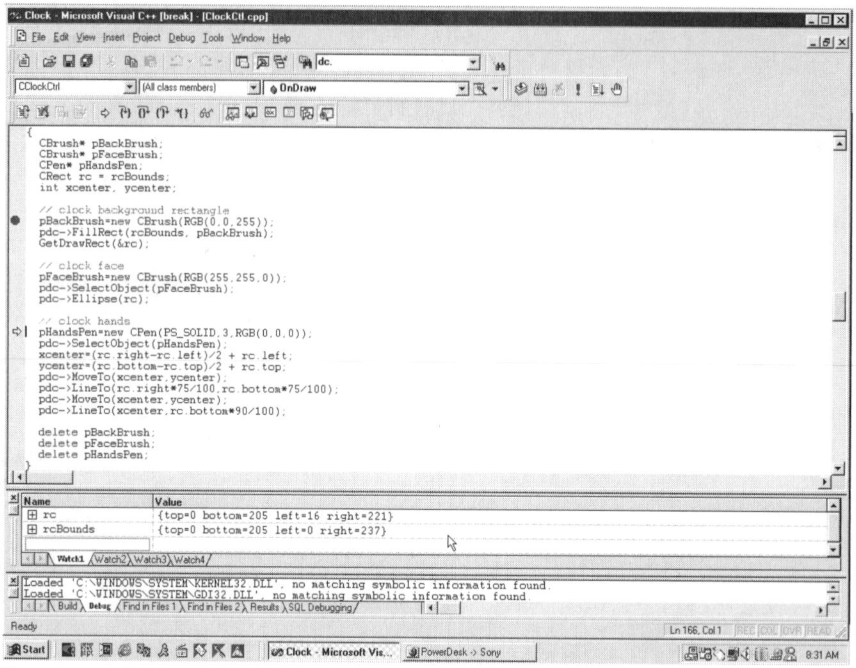

Figure 15.16   The two variable values describe a correctly drawn clock face

The values in *rcBounds* describe the bounding rectangle of the ActiveX control, while the values in the *rc* variable describe the bounding rectangle for the ellipse that is used to draw the clock face. The size of the *rc* bounding rectangle will always be equal to or less than the *rcBounds* rectangle. This is because the control, in order to force a round clock face, always uses the smaller of the *rcBounds* dimensions (horizontal or vertical) when describing the *rc* bounding rectangle. As a matter of fact, the only time the two bounding rectangles will be the same is when the *rcBounds* rectangle is a perfect square.

In Figure 15.17, the value for the *rc* bounding rectangle is too large.

Something is apparently wrong at this point.

Error Watch   *As you move back and forth correcting and adjusting code, your ActiveX control will necessarily have to be resized in the window. Don't let the changes made here mislead you into thinking the ActiveX control is now returning a different value. For example, if we had perfectly resized the ActiveX control between Figure 15.16 and Figure 15.17, the values reported in Figure 15.17 would have matched the values of the* rcBounds *variable in Figure 15.16.*

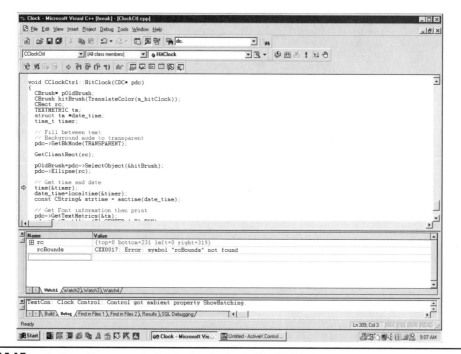

Figure 15.17 The bounding rectangle for the face is checked in HitClock()

What we have discovered is that the value returned in the *rc* variable is not the correctly adjusted value derived from the *rcBounds* variable, but is the *rcBounds* variable itself.

To correct this error, we'll need to use a call to GetDrawRect(). Figure 15.18 shows where this function call is inserted in the HitClock() method.

Now, stepping through the HitClock() method reveals *rc* variable values that more closely match those shown in Figure 15.16.

Test the control once again in the Test Container by clicking the left mouse button over the clock face. Figure 15.19 reveals the new results.

The code problem was not a severe challenge in this application, but we're sure many of you will agree that getting the systems set up to debug an ActiveX control was more interesting than many previous examples.

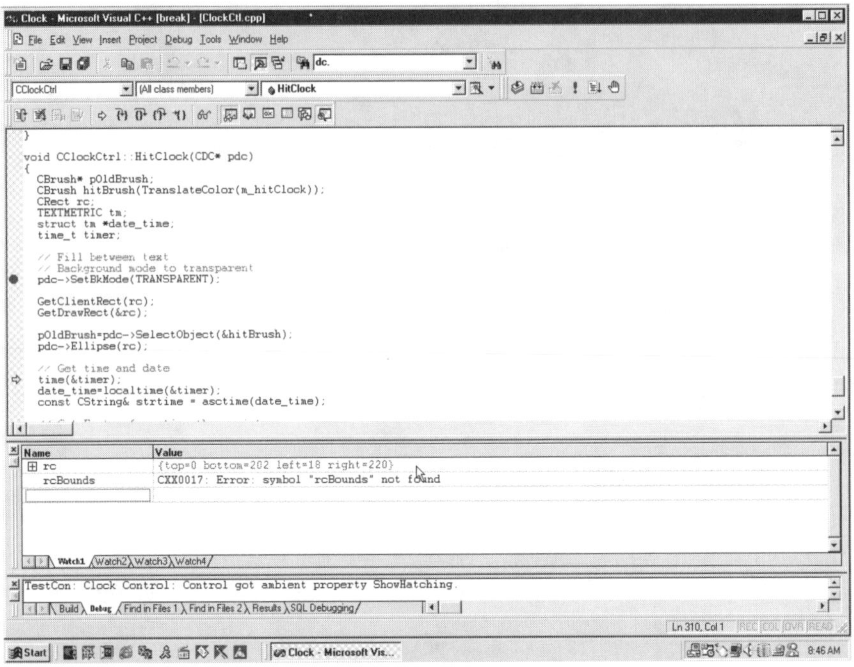

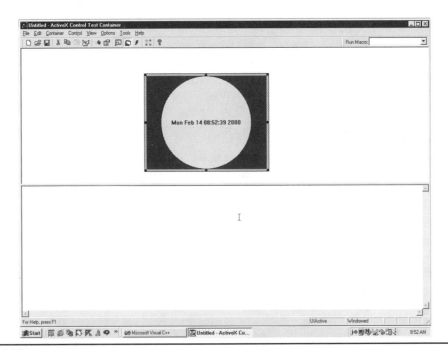

Figure 15.18   Insert the GetDrawRect() into the HitClock() method

Figure 15.19   The face of the clock control is now drawn correctly

Conclusion

This chapter was divided into two main sections in order to teach you the fundamentals of developing an ActiveX control and then the steps necessary for testing that control in the Control Test Container using a two-system remote debugging technique.

It was our intention to keep the ActiveX control's coding problems as simple as possible in order to concentrate on the more complicated setup required by the insertion of the Control Test Container in a two-system debugging situation. The techniques developed in this chapter can easily be applied to more robust ActiveX control debugging situations.

CHAPTER 16

COM, ATL, and DHTML Debugging

In the previous chapter, you learned how to use debugging tools with ActiveX controls. This chapter further discusses how to build basic ActiveX controls and how to set up your debugging session.

Like the previous chapter, this chapter is divided into two major areas. The first area is devoted to developing a simple yet working project using the ATL COM AppWizard. In this section, you will learn the steps required to build a template project. The second area will show you how the ATL COM project can be debugged.

The COM Object Model

ActiveX controls are actually built on the COM "object model." The COM object model defines how an object exposes itself and how the exposure works across processes. Your ability to work with COM object models will be further enhanced in this chapter when you gain the ability to include another powerful component—the ATL. The ATL, or Active Template Library, can easily be used to create a variety of COM objects including ActiveX controls. The ATL also provides built-in support for many basic COM interfaces.

In the following sections, we'll use the ATL COM AppWizard to develop a simple ATL application. In order to be efficient, we'll use the Microsoft Polygon ATL tutorial application to create an application with the functionality of the ActiveX control developed in the previous chapter. The COM object that we develop can be used in a DHTML document that can be viewed in Microsoft's Internet Explorer.

Creating the ATL Polygon Project

ATL projects are created by using the ATL COM AppWizard. The project developed in this section closely parallels Microsoft's Polygon tutorial example. We strongly recommend that you follow the Microsoft tutorial as you develop the ATL COM control used in this section.

The following steps outline the steps needed to create the basic ATL Polygon project:

1. From within Visual C++, select the File | New menu item and then choose the Projects tab.

2. Choose the ATL COM AppWizard.

3. Name the project Polygon, as shown in Figure 16.1.

4. The ATL COM AppWizard dialog box will open, as shown in Figure 16.2, when you select the OK button.

5. Choose the Dynamic Link Library (DLL) option and then select Finish to complete the process. The New Project Information dialog box, as shown in Figure 16.3, will display the information for the ATL project.

6. Click on the OK button to generate the basic files for the ATL Polygon project.

7. A control will be added to the basic code to make the project functional. Use the Insert | New ATL Object menu item to open the ATL Object Wizard dialog box, as shown in Figure 16.4.

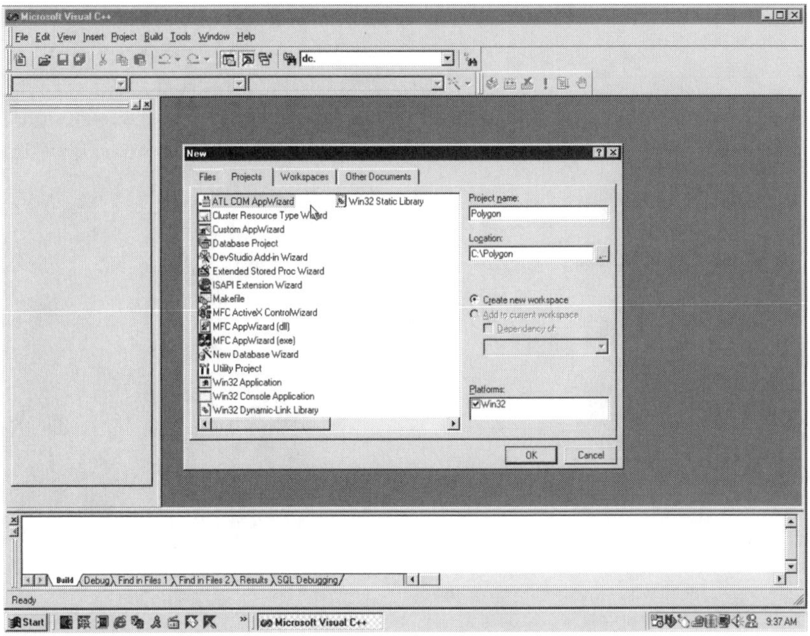

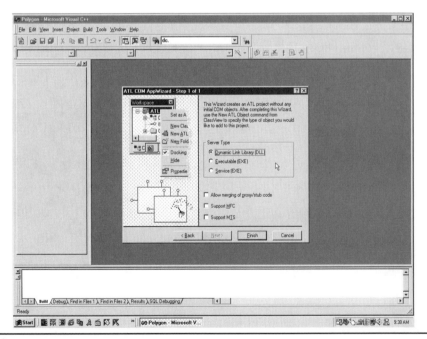

Figure 16.1 Use the New Projects dialog box for the ATL Polygon project

Figure 16.2 Examining the ATL COM AppWizard dialog box

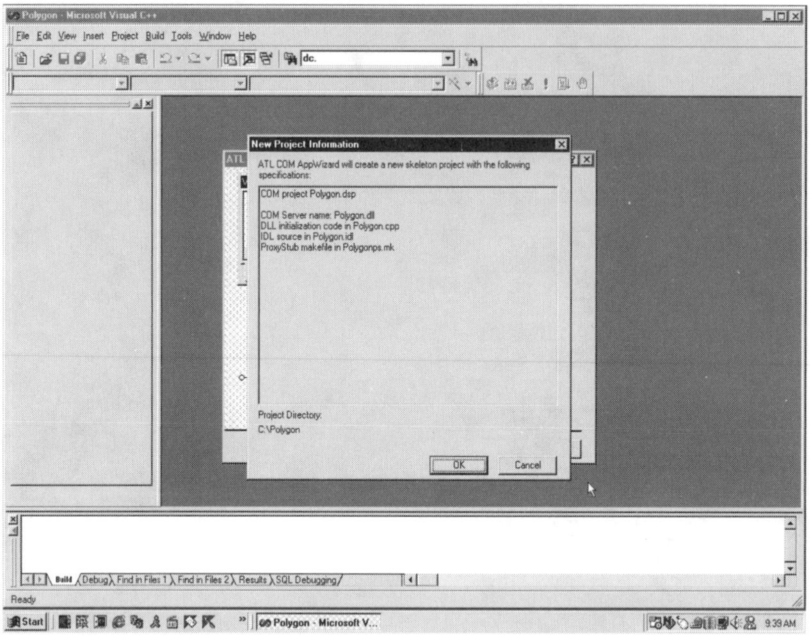

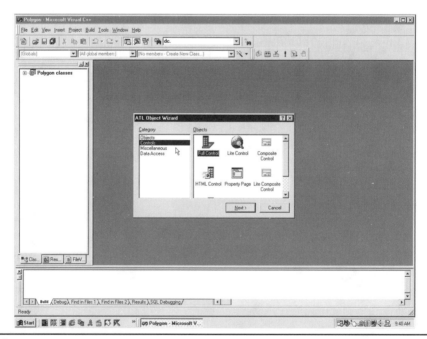

Figure 16.3   Using the New Project Information dialog box

Figure 16.4   A control can be added to the project by using the ATL Object Wizard dialog box

8. Choose the Full Control option and select the Next button. At this point, it is possible to set various configurations for the control using the property pages of the ATL Object Wizard Properties dialog box, as shown in Figure 16.5.

9. In the Names tab, enter the name "PolyCtl" in the Short Name text box. All other entries will be completed automatically. See Figure 16.5 once again.

10. Next select the Attributes tab and check both support checkboxes as shown in Figure 16.6.

11. Now select the Stock Properties tab and enable support for Fill Color as shown in Figure 16.7.

12. Choose the OK button and return to the developer's screen. If you now open the FileView window, as shown in Figure 16.8, you will see the list of files generated for this project.

13. The ATL COM project can now be built with the template code generated by the AppWizard. From the menu, select the Build | Rebuild All option and compile and link the project.

14. The project can now be tested at any point, like the ActiveX control of the previous chapter, by using the Control Test Container. Test the initial control by selecting the Tools | ActiveX Control Test Container menu item.

The control is really not functional at this stage. We'll have to add a number of properties, events, and property pages to the control.

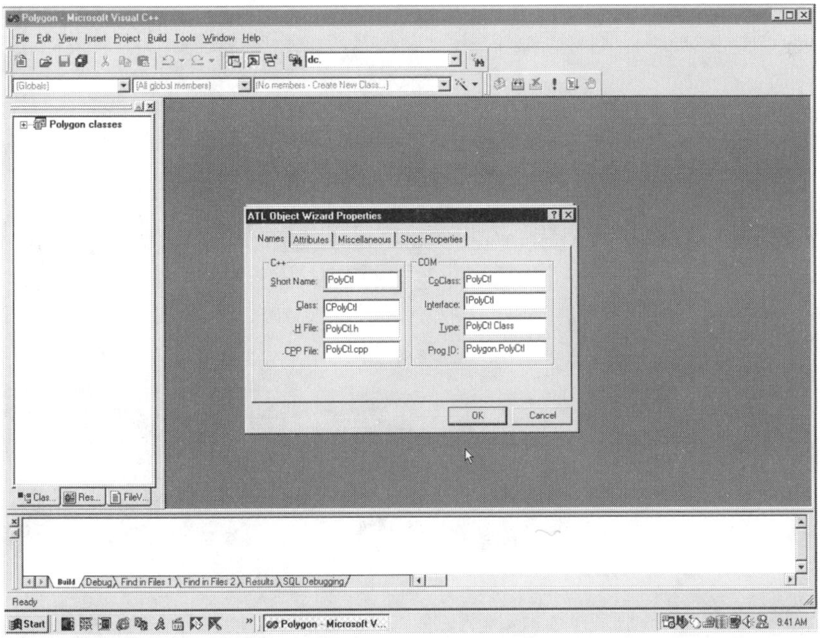

Figure 16.5 Control configurations are set in the ATL Object Wizard Properties dialog box

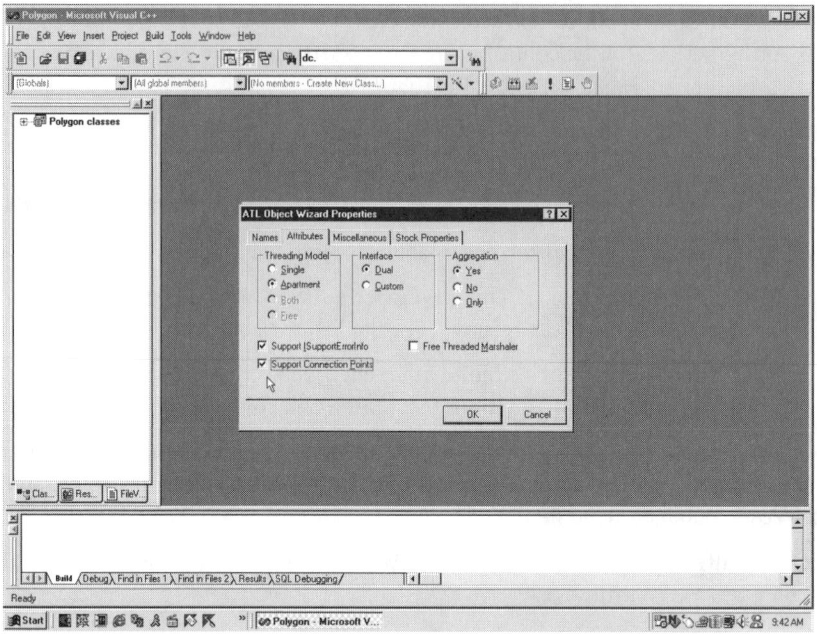

Figure 16.6   Use the Attributes tab to select ISupportErrorInfo and Connection Points

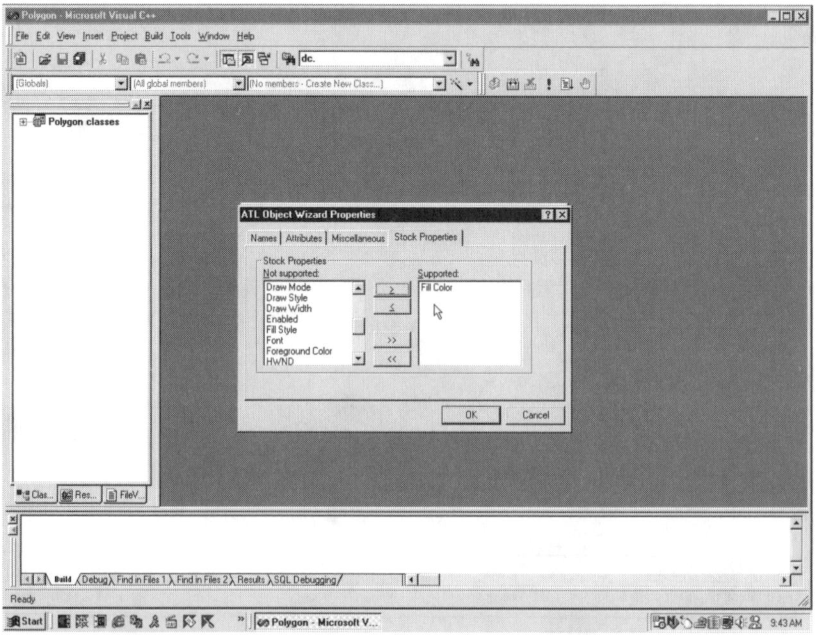

Figure 16.7   Use the Stock Properties tab to set specific stock properties for the project

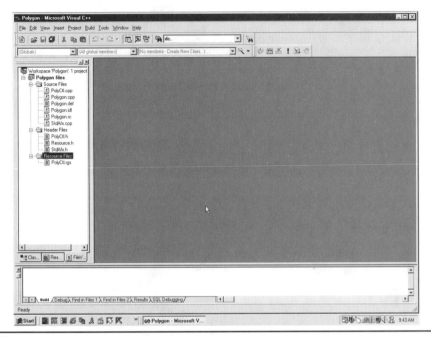

Figure 16.8   The project's file list is available in the FileView window

Enhancing the Template Code

In order to make the control functional, we'll make several modifications to various files in the ATL Polygon project.

Control Properties

IPolyCtl is used to contain custom methods and properties for the project. To add a new property, use the Visual C++ ClassView to select the IPolyCtl class and then right-click the mouse to open a menu box. From the menu box, choose the Add Property item, which will open the Add Property to Interface dialog box, as shown in Figure 16.9.

Select the property type, short, from the drop-down list of property types. Then use the name "Sides" as the Property Name. Click the OK button to add the new property.

The MIDL (a program that builds files with .idl file extensions) defines a get method and a put method that retrieve and set the Sides property.

In addition, get and put function prototypes are added to the PolyCtl.h header file and a skeleton implementation of each to the PolyCtl.cpp file. You'll see this implementation when we view the completed file in the next section.

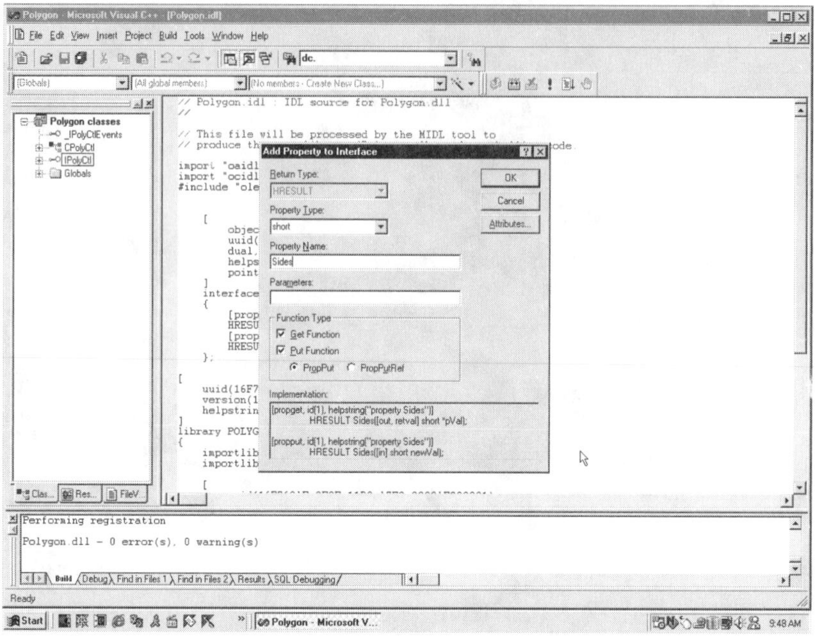

Figure 16.9   Use the Add Property to Interface dialog box to allow the Sides property to be added to the control

Examining Essential Control Code

A number of changes have already been made to the project's template code. Most of these changes have been made to the PolyCtl.h and PolyCtl.cpp files.

This is the code for the header file, PolyCtl.h. Additions and changes to the basic code are shown in a bold font:

```
// PolyCtl.h : Declaration of the CPolyCtl

#ifndef __POLYCTL_H_
#define __POLYCTL_H_

#include <math.h>
#include "resource.h"        // main symbols
#include <atlctl.h>


#include "PolygonCP.h"


/////////////////////////////////////////////////////////////////
// CPolyCtl
```

```
class ATL_NO_VTABLE CPolyCtl :
    public CComObjectRootEx<CComSingleThreadModel>,
    public CStockPropImpl<CPolyCtl, IPolyCtl, &IID_IPolyCtl, &LIBID_POLYGONLib>,
    public CComControl<CPolyCtl>,
    public IPersistStreamInitImpl<CPolyCtl>,
    public IOleControlImpl<CPolyCtl>,
    public IOleObjectImpl<CPolyCtl>,
    public IOleInPlaceActiveObjectImpl<CPolyCtl>,
    public IViewObjectExImpl<CPolyCtl>,
    public IOleInPlaceObjectWindowlessImpl<CPolyCtl>,
    public ISupportErrorInfo,

    public IConnectionPointContainerImpl<CPolyCtl>,
    public IPersistStorageImpl<CPolyCtl>,
    public ISpecifyPropertyPagesImpl<CPolyCtl>,
    public IQuickActivateImpl<CPolyCtl>,
    public IDataObjectImpl<CPolyCtl>,
    public IProvideClassInfo2Impl<&CLSID_PolyCtl,
                        &DIID__IPolyCtlEvents,
                        &LIBID_POLYGONLib>,
    public IPropertyNotifySinkCP<CPolyCtl>,
    public CComCoClass<CPolyCtl, &CLSID_PolyCtl>,
    public CProxy_IPolyCtlEvents< CPolyCtl >
{
public:
    CPolyCtl()
    {
        m_nSides = 4;                           //init rectangle
        m_clrFillColor = RGB(0xFF, 0xFF, 0);    //use yellow fill
    }

DECLARE_REGISTRY_RESOURCEID(IDR_POLYCTL)

DECLARE_PROTECT_FINAL_CONSTRUCT()

BEGIN_COM_MAP(CPolyCtl)
    COM_INTERFACE_ENTRY(IPolyCtl)
    COM_INTERFACE_ENTRY(IDispatch)
    COM_INTERFACE_ENTRY(IViewObjectEx)
    COM_INTERFACE_ENTRY(IViewObject2)
    COM_INTERFACE_ENTRY(IViewObject)
    COM_INTERFACE_ENTRY(IOleInPlaceObjectWindowless)
    COM_INTERFACE_ENTRY(IOleInPlaceObject)
    COM_INTERFACE_ENTRY2(IOleWindow, IOleInPlaceObjectWindowless)
    COM_INTERFACE_ENTRY(IOleInPlaceActiveObject)
    COM_INTERFACE_ENTRY(IOleControl)
    COM_INTERFACE_ENTRY(IOleObject)
    COM_INTERFACE_ENTRY(IPersistStreamInit)
    COM_INTERFACE_ENTRY2(IPersist, IPersistStreamInit)
    COM_INTERFACE_ENTRY(ISupportErrorInfo)
```

```
    COM_INTERFACE_ENTRY(IConnectionPointContainer)
    COM_INTERFACE_ENTRY(ISpecifyPropertyPages)
    COM_INTERFACE_ENTRY(IQuickActivate)
    COM_INTERFACE_ENTRY(IPersistStorage)
    COM_INTERFACE_ENTRY(IDataObject)
    COM_INTERFACE_ENTRY(IProvideClassInfo)
    COM_INTERFACE_ENTRY(IProvideClassInfo2)
    COM_INTERFACE_ENTRY_IMPL(IConnectionPointContainer)
END_COM_MAP()

BEGIN_PROP_MAP(CPolyCtl)
    PROP_DATA_ENTRY("_cx", m_sizeExtent.cx, VT_UI4)
    PROP_DATA_ENTRY("_cy", m_sizeExtent.cy, VT_UI4)
    PROP_ENTRY("FillColor", DISPID_FILLCOLOR,
               CLSID_StockColorPage)
    PROP_ENTRY("Sides", 1, CLSID_PolyProp)
    // Example entries
    // PROP_ENTRY("Property Description", dispid, clsid)
    // PROP_PAGE(CLSID_StockColorPage)
END_PROP_MAP()

BEGIN_CONNECTION_POINT_MAP(CPolyCtl)
    CONNECTION_POINT_ENTRY(IID_IPropertyNotifySink)
    CONNECTION_POINT_ENTRY(DIID__IPolyCtlEvents)
END_CONNECTION_POINT_MAP()

BEGIN_MSG_MAP(CPolyCtl)
    CHAIN_MSG_MAP(CComControl<CPolyCtl>)
    DEFAULT_REFLECTION_HANDLER()
    MESSAGE_HANDLER(WM_LBUTTONDOWN, OnLButtonDown)
END_MSG_MAP()
// Handler prototypes:
//  LRESULT MessageHandler(UINT uMsg, WPARAM wParam,
                           LPARAM lParam, BOOL& bHandled);
//  LRESULT CommandHandler(WORD wNotifyCode, WORD wID,
                           HWND hWndCtl, BOOL& bHandled);
//  LRESULT NotifyHandler(int idCtrl, LPNMHDR pnmh,
                          BOOL& bHandled);

// ISupportsErrorInfo
    STDMETHOD(InterfaceSupportsErrorInfo)(REFIID riid)
    {
        static const IID* arr[] =
        {
            &IID_IPolyCtl,
        };
        for (int i=0; i<sizeof(arr)/sizeof(arr[0]); i++)
        {
            if (InlineIsEqualGUID(*arr[i], riid))
                return S_OK;
```

```
        }
        return S_FALSE;
    }

// IViewObjectEx
    DECLARE_VIEW_STATUS(VIEWSTATUS_SOLIDBKGND |
                        VIEWSTATUS_OPAQUE)

// IPolyCtl
public:
    STDMETHOD(get_Sides)(/*[out, retval]*/ short *pVal);
    STDMETHOD(put_Sides)(/*[in]*/ short newVal);
    HRESULT OnDraw(ATL_DRAWINFO& di);
    LRESULT OnLButtonDown(UINT uMsg, WPARAM wParam,
                          LPARAM lParam, BOOL& bHandled);
    short m_nSides;
    OLE_COLOR m_clrFillColor;
    POINT m_arrPoint[10];
};

#endif //__POLYCTL_H_
```

Notice the get_Sides and put_Sides function prototypes in the listing. Also, notice that the initial number of sides for the polygon is set to four and the initial fill color to yellow in the constructor. This project will allow polygons with three to ten sides to be drawn.

Design Tip *In Microsoft's Polygon tutorial project, the limit was set to 100. Practically speaking, there is no limit for this number, and the range can be anything you desire.*

Now, right-click on CPolyCtl and select the Implement Connect Point menu item. The PolygonCP.h file has a class called CProxy_IPolyEvents that is derived from IConnectionPointImpl and two methods, Fire_ClickIn and Fire_ClickOut. These methods are used to fire control events.

IConnectionPointContainer is exposed through the QueryInterface() function when it is added to the COM map in PolyCtl.h.

The IConnectionPointContainer is notified of available points by using a connection point map. Here is a small portion of the PolyCtl.h file:

```
BEGIN_CONNECTION_POINT_MAP(CPolyCtl)
    CONNECTION_POINT_ENTRY(IID_IPropertyNotifySink)
    CONNECTION_POINT_ENTRY(DIID__IPolyCtlEvents)
END_CONNECTION_POINT_MAP()
```

A WM_LBUTTONDOWN event handler is added to detect when a user clicks the left mouse button. The prototype is included in this file and the implementation in the PolyCtl.cpp file. To add this message handler, use CPolyCtl from ClassView and select the Add Windows Message Handler from the menu. From the list of messages, select WM_LBUTTONDOWN and click the Add Handler button.

The following listing shows the PolyCtl.cpp file containing all of the additions for the project. The code additions are shown in a bold font.

```cpp
// PolyCtl.cpp : Implementation of CPolyCtl

#include "stdafx.h"
#include "Polygon.h"
#include "PolyCtl.h"
#include <time.h>
#include <string.h>

/////////////////////////////////////////////////////////////
// CPolyCtl

HRESULT CPolyCtl::OnDraw(ATL_DRAWINFO& di)
{
    struct tm *date_time;
    time_t timer;
    static TEXTMETRIC tm;

    RECT& rc = *(RECT*)di.prcBounds;
    HDC hdc  = di.hdcDraw;

    COLORREF colFore;
    HBRUSH hOldBrush, hBrush;
    HPEN hOldPen, hPen;

    // Translate m_colFore into a COLORREF type
    OleTranslateColor(m_clrFillColor, NULL, &colFore);

    // Create and select the colors to draw the circle
    hPen = (HPEN)GetStockObject(BLACK_PEN);
    hOldPen = (HPEN)SelectObject(hdc, hPen);
    hBrush = (HBRUSH)GetStockObject(WHITE_BRUSH);
    hOldBrush = (HBRUSH)SelectObject(hdc, hBrush);

    const double pi = 3.14159265358979;
    POINT    ptCenter;
    double  dblRadiusx = (rc.right - rc.left) / 2;
    double  dblRadiusy = (rc.bottom - rc.top) / 2;
    double   dblAngle = 3 * pi / 2;        // Start at top
    double   dblDiff  = 2 * pi / m_nSides; // Angle of side
    ptCenter.x = (rc.left + rc.right) / 2;
    ptCenter.y = (rc.top + rc.bottom) / 2;

    // Calculate the points for each side
    for (int i = 0; i < m_nSides; i++)
    {
        m_arrPoint[i].x = (long)(dblRadiusx * cos(dblAngle) +
                        ptCenter.x + 0.5);
        m_arrPoint[i].y = (long)(dblRadiusy * sin(dblAngle) +
                        ptCenter.y + 0.5);
        dblAngle += dblDiff;
    }
    Ellipse(hdc, rc.left, rc.top, rc.right, rc.bottom);
```

```
    // brush that will be used to fill the polygon
    hBrush = CreateSolidBrush(colFore);
    SelectObject(hdc, hBrush);
    Polygon(hdc, &m_arrPoint[0], m_nSides);


    // Print date and time
    time(&timer);
    date_time=localtime(&timer);

    const char* strtime;

    strtime = asctime(date_time);

    SetBkMode(hdc,TRANSPARENT);

    SetTextAlign(hdc, TA_CENTER | TA_TOP);
    ExtTextOut(hdc, (rc.left + rc.right)/2,
                    (rc.top + rc.bottom - tm.tmHeight)/2,
                    ETO_CLIPPED, &rc, strtime,
                    strlen(strtime)-1, NULL);

    // Select old pen and brush
    SelectObject(hdc, hOldPen);
    SelectObject(hdc, hOldBrush);
    DeleteObject(hBrush);

    return S_OK;
}

LRESULT CPolyCtl::OnLButtonDown(UINT uMsg, WPARAM wParam,
                                LPARAM lParam,
                                BOOL& bHandled)
{
    HRGN hRgn;
    WORD xPos = LOWORD(lParam);  // horz position of cursor
    WORD yPos = HIWORD(lParam);  // vert position of cursor

    // Create a region from our list of points
    hRgn = CreatePolygonRgn(&m_arrPoint[0], m_nSides, WINDING);

    // If clicked point is in polygon fire the ClickIn
    //   event otherwise fire ClickOut event
    if (PtInRegion(hRgn, xPos, yPos))
        Fire_ClickIn(xPos, yPos);
    else
        Fire_ClickOut(xPos, yPos);

    // Delete the region that we created
    DeleteObject(hRgn);
    return 0;
```

```
}

STDMETHODIMP CPolyCtl::get_Sides(short *pVal)
{
    *pVal = m_nSides;
    return S_OK;
}

STDMETHODIMP CPolyCtl::put_Sides(short newVal)
{
    if (newVal > 2 && newVal < 11)
    {
        m_nSides = newVal;
        return S_OK;
    }
    else
        return Error(_T("Must have between 3 and 10 sides"));
}
```

When Microsoft developed the original Polygon tutorial project, they used the sin() and cos() functions from math.h to calculate the polygon points. See if you can find that portion of code in the previous listing. Our project modifies the original Polygon project by limiting the number of sides to 10 instead of 100 and includes the code necessary to print the local date and time within the control. Furthermore, the date and time will be updated each time a "hit" occurs within the polygon shape. This is the same basic technique used for the ActiveX control developed in the previous chapter.

In order to fire events, a small portion of code must be added to the Polygon.idl file. The additions to this file are shown in a bold font:

```
// Polygon.idl : IDL source for Polygon.dll
//

// This file will be processed by the MIDL tool to
// produce the type library (Polygon.tlb) and marshalling code.

import "oaidl.idl";
import "ocidl.idl";
#include "olectl.h"


    [
        object,
        uuid(16F763AD-9F2E-11D3-A7E0-0080AE000001),
        dual,
        helpstring("IPolyCtl Interface"),
        pointer_default(unique)
    ]
    interface IPolyCtl : IDispatch
    {
        [propput, id(DISPID_FILLCOLOR)]
        HRESULT FillColor([in]OLE_COLOR clr);
        [propget, id(DISPID_FILLCOLOR)]
```

```
        HRESULT FillColor([out, retval]OLE_COLOR* pclr);

        [propget, id(1), helpstring("property Sides")] \
         HRESULT Sides([out, retval] short *pVal);
        [propput, id(1), helpstring("property Sides")] \
         HRESULT Sides([in] short newVal);
    };

[
    uuid(16F763A1-9F2E-11D3-A7E0-0080AE000001),
    version(1.0),
    helpstring("Polygon 1.0 Type Library")
]
library POLYGONLib
{
    importlib("stdole32.tlb");
    importlib("stdole2.tlb");

    [
        uuid(16F763AF-9F2E-11D3-A7E0-0080AE000001),
        helpstring("_IPolyCtlEvents Interface")
    ]
    dispinterface _IPolyCtlEvents
    {
        properties:
        methods:
        [id(1), helpstring("method ClickIn")] \
          void ClickIn([in] long x, [in] long y);
        [id(2), helpstring("method ClickOut")] \
          void ClickOut([in] long x, [in] long y);
    };

    [
        uuid(16F763AE-9F2E-11D3-A7E0-0080AE000001),
        helpstring("PolyCtl Class")
    ]
    coclass PolyCtl
    {
        [default] interface IPolyCtl;
        [default, source] dispinterface _IPolyCtlEvents;
    };

    [
        uuid(7846CD41-9F37-11D3-A7E0-0080AE000001),
        helpstring("PolyProp Class")
    ]
    coclass PolyProp
    {
        interface IUnknown;
    };
};
```

The ClickIn() and ClickOut() methods use the x and y coordinates of the clicked point as parameters.

A property page can be added to the control with the use of the ATL Object Wizard. Use the Insert I New ATL Object menu item to open the ATL Object Wizard dialog box, as shown in Figure 16.10.

Select the Property Page option and then the Next button. You will now be allowed to set various configurations for the control using the property pages of the ATL Object Wizard Properties dialog box, as shown in Figure 16.11.

In the Names tab in this dialog box, enter the name "PolyProp" in the Short Name text box. All other entries will be completed automatically. See Figure 16.11 once again.

Next select the Strings tab and enter the Title and Doc String as shown in Figure 16.12.

Click the OK button to generate the PolyProp.h, PolyProp.cpp, and PolyProp.rgs files. In addition to these files, a new property page is added to the object entry map.

While in Visual C++, use the ResourceView to open the IDD_POLYPROP dialog box. Change the label to Sides and add an edit box control with the IDC_SIDES ID value.

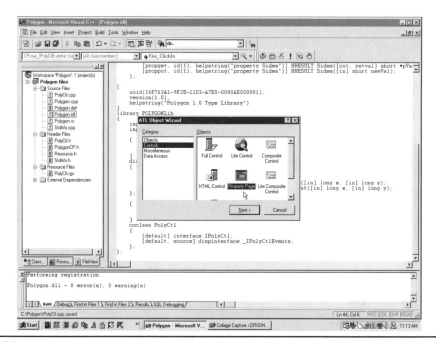

Figure 16.10   Use the ATL Object Wizard dialog box to add a property page control to the project

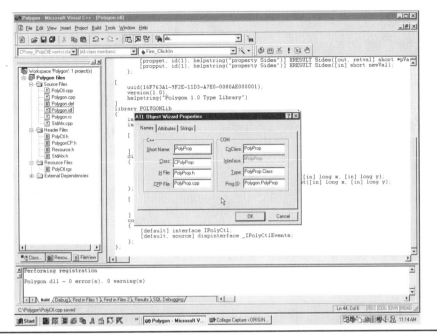

Figure 16.11 Various control configurations can be set using the ATL Object Wizard Properties dialog box

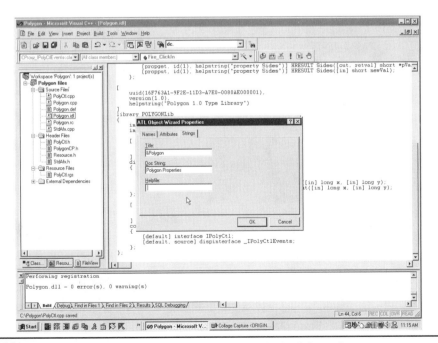

Figure 16.12 Set the Title and Doc String for the property page in the Strings tab

Make the following changes, shown in a bold font, to the PolyProp.h file:

```
// PolyProp.h : Declaration of the CPolyProp

#ifndef __POLYPROP_H_
#define __POLYPROP_H_

#include "resource.h"       // main symbols
#include "Polygon.h"

EXTERN_C const CLSID CLSID_PolyProp;

/////////////////////////////////////////////////////////////////////////////
// CPolyProp
class ATL_NO_VTABLE CPolyProp :
    public CComObjectRootEx<CComSingleThreadModel>,
    public CComCoClass<CPolyProp, &CLSID_PolyProp>,
    public IPropertyPageImpl<CPolyProp>,
    public CDialogImpl<CPolyProp>
{
public:
    CPolyProp()
    {
        m_dwTitleID = IDS_TITLEPolyProp;
        m_dwHelpFileID = IDS_HELPFILEPolyProp;
        m_dwDocStringID = IDS_DOCSTRINGPolyProp;
    }

    enum {IDD = IDD_POLYPROP};

DECLARE_REGISTRY_RESOURCEID(IDR_POLYPROP)

DECLARE_PROTECT_FINAL_CONSTRUCT()

BEGIN_COM_MAP(CPolyProp)
    COM_INTERFACE_ENTRY(IPropertyPage)
END_COM_MAP()

BEGIN_MSG_MAP(CPolyProp)
    CHAIN_MSG_MAP(IPropertyPageImpl<CPolyProp>)
END_MSG_MAP()
// Handler prototypes:
//  LRESULT MessageHandler(UINT uMsg, WPARAM wParam, LPARAM lParam, BOOL& bHandled);
//  LRESULT CommandHandler(WORD wNotifyCode, WORD wID, HWND hWndCtl, BOOL& bHandled);
//  LRESULT NotifyHandler(int idCtrl, LPNMHDR pnmh, BOOL& bHandled);

    STDMETHOD(Apply)(void)
    {
        ATLTRACE(_T("CPolyProp::Apply\n"));
```

```
        for (UINT i = 0; i < m_nObjects; i++)
        {
            CComQIPtr<IPolyCtl, &IID_IPolyCtl> pPoly(m_ppUnk[i]);
            short nSides = (short)GetDlgItemInt(IDC_SIDES);
            if FAILED(pPoly->put_Sides(nSides))
            {
                CComPtr<IErrorInfo> pError;
                CComBSTR strError;
                GetErrorInfo(0, &pError);
                pError->GetDescription(&strError);
                MessageBox("Error - Enter 3 to 10 sides",
                            "Error Message", MB_ICONEXCLAMATION);
                return E_FAIL;
            }
        }
        m_bDirty = FALSE;
        return S_OK;
    }
};

#endif //__POLYPROP_H_
```

A property page could have more than one client attached to it at a time, so the Apply() function is used to loop around and call put_Sides on each client with the value obtained from the edit box.

The property page is now added to the control by adding the following line to the PolyCtl.h header file:

```
PROP_ENTRY("Sides", 1, CLSID_PolyProp)
```

Now we're ready to test the control on an actual Web page.

24x7   Connection Points and the ATL Proxy Generator

Unlike ActiveX controls discussed in the previous chapter, this control will require a connection point interface and a connection point container interface. A COM object can have multiple connection points, so the COM object needs to implement a connection point container interface. The IConnectionPoint interface implements the connection point. The IConnectionPointContainer interface is used to implement a connection point container.

An ATL proxy generator is used to create the IConnectionPoint interface by reading the type library and creating a function for each event that can be fired. A type library must be generated before using the proxy generator. For example, a type library can be built for this project by right-clicking on the Polygon.idl file while in FileView. The Polygon.tlb file is generated by selecting Compile Polygon.idl. This file becomes the type library.

Testing the Control

The ATL Object Wizard creates the initial control along with an HTML file that contains the control. This file is PolyCtl.htm and can be opened in Microsoft's Internet Explorer. By using Internet Explorer, you will be able to view and test the ATL control on an actual Web page.

Add the following changes, shown in a bold font, to the PolyCtl.htm while in the Visual C++ environment. This file will vary in structure based upon the ATL version that you are using with your compiler.

```
<HTML>
<HEAD>
<TITLE>ATL 2.0 test page for object PolyCtl</TITLE>
</HEAD>
<BODY>
<OBJECT ID="PolyCtl" <
 CLASSID="CLSID:4CBBC676-507F-11D0-B98B-000000000000">
>
</OBJECT>
<SCRIPT LANGUAGE="VBScript">
<!--
Sub PolyCtl_ClickIn(x, y)
PolyCtl.Sides = PolyCtl.Sides + 1
End Sub
Sub PolyCtl_ClickOut(x, y)
PolyCtl.Sides = PolyCtl.Sides - 1
End Sub
-->
</SCRIPT>
</BODY>
</HTML>
```

Now start Internet Explorer and open the PolyCtl.htm file. Your screen should initially appear like Figure 16.13.

Continue to test the control by clicking the left mouse button within and without the control's polygon region. Figure 16.14 shows the control after four additional clicks (hits) within the control.

Notice that the number of sides to the polygon has not changed as the number of "hits" increased. Obviously, there is a problem that we have to investigate.

Debugging the ATL COM Control

Before starting the debugging session, let's review what is known at this point. The control seems to be partially working. It registers itself and can be loaded into the Control Test Container or onto Microsoft Internet Explorer as an HTML document. What doesn't seem to work correctly is the "hit" or lack of a "hit" when the left mouse button is clicked inside or outside the polygon region.

COM, ATL, and DHTML Debugging

Figure 16.13   Viewing the initial control on a Web page

Figure 16.14   The mouse is clicked four times within the polygon region of the control

The first thing we want to know is if the ClickIn() and ClickOut() methods are working correctly. Second, if they are, is the member variable, *m_nSides,* changing in response to the hit rate? Let's start a debugging session and investigate these problems without using a remote debugging setup.

Design Tip
It is possible to start a remote debugging session as you did for the ActiveX control in the previous chapter. If you want to use remote debugging and need additional help at this point, refer to the previous chapter for step-by-step instructions. The control can be tested in the Control Test Container.

For this session, use the Build | Debugger Remote Connection menu item to start a local debugging session.

Figure 16.15 shows a debugging session with the *m_nSides* variable placed in a Watch window.

As you examine this figure, also note that a breakpoint has been placed in the put_Sides() method. The Debugger pane is to the left, and the Control Test Container pane is to the right in this figure. At this point, we have not modified the number of sides, so the variable returns the error message shown in Figure 16.15.

To alter the number of sides, open the Edit menu in the Test Container. Use the Properties menu item to open and modify the number of sides for the control. Figure 16.16 shows the debugging session after the number of sides has been changed to three.

The *m_nSides* variable reflects the change, but the control shown in Figure 16.16 is still four-sided. If you switch to another application and then switch back to Test Container, you will see that the control is repainted correctly.

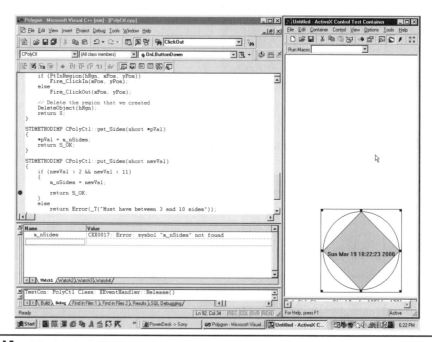

Figure 16.15   Viewing the Debugger and Test Container panes on the same computer

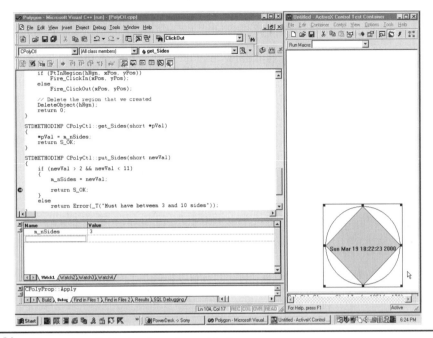

Figure 16.16   The number of sides has been changed to three

If you are a seasoned Windows programmer, you might recognize the cause of the problem. The problem has to do with repainting the control.

Error Watch   *This problem is similar to a problem encountered by programmers using the OnDraw() method for painting the screen. The OnDraw() method is notorious for not updating the screen until a WM_PAINT message is processed. These messages can be generated by a number of techniques, including resizing the screen and issuing an InvalidateRect() function call.*

The problem here, of course, is that this is a control. We need a way to repaint the screen each time a "hit" occurs.

IviewObjectExImpl defines a FireViewChange() function that might fix this problem. When FireViewChange() is called, it in turn will call the InvalidateRect() function and cause the control to be repainted with the new values.

Changes in the number of sides are reflected in the put_Sides() method when *m_nSides* is set equal to *newVal*. This is the ideal location to issue a FireViewChange() call. Figure 16.17 shows the altered code during a debugging session.

As you can see in Figure 16.17, the control now reflects the change in the number of sides.

While this problem did require us to know something about repainting methods for controls, it is also typical of the problems you will encounter in developing ALT COM components.

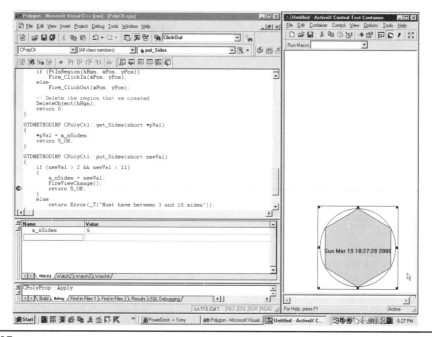

Figure 16.17   Adding a FireViewChange() call to the put_Sides() method

Conclusion

Like the previous chapter, this chapter was divided into two main sections. The first section showed you the steps to complete in order to develop an ATL COM control based on Microsoft's Polygon tutorial example.

The second section dealt with setting up a single computer (local) debugging session and finding the solution to a problem by using a breakpoint and variable in a Watch window. While the problem and the technique used to find the solution is fairly simple, sleuthing around in controls of this type is not for the faint of heart!

CHAPTER 17

STL and MFC Coding

In Chapters 12 and 13 you learned how to bring the power of the Standard Template Library into your command-line C++ applications. This chapter will show you how the STL and MFC libraries can be merged into a practical Windows application.

In this chapter, you will learn how to develop an application that makes use of the STL <complex> template while using the MFC tools developed earlier in Chapters 10 and 11. We'll then show you how to apply a variety of debugging techniques to solve problems in this environment.

If you are a mathematician, physicist, or electrical engineer, the application should be familiar to you since it involves the manipulation of complex numbers.

Creating an STL and MFC Application

In the application developed in this section, individual complex numbers will be drawn to the screen along with their sum. These complex numbers take advantage of the STL <complex> template and use the power of the MFC. Let's do a little review work to better understand what complex numbers actually are.

Complex Numbers

Complex numbers are most frequently encountered in the areas of mathematics, engineering, and physics. Complex numbers result from vectors or phasors (rotating vectors) that have a magnitude and direction and can be described on an x-y coordinate system. We'll use the term *phasor* from this point on so the concept is not confused with the STL <vector> class.

A phasor uses the positive and negative x-axis to represent the real component of a number, while the y-axis represents the imaginary component of the number. In engineering statics, phasors are often used to represent a force moving in a certain direction. In electrical engineering, phasors are often used to represent voltages and currents and their associated phase angles.

Complex numbers or phasors can be represented in three fundamental ways: polar form, rectangular form, and exponential form. For example, imagine the representation of a phasor with a magnitude of 40 at an angle of 60 degrees measured counterclockwise from the positive x-axis.

Exponential Form
In exponential form, the phasor is represented as
$40 * e^{j60}$

Polar Form
In polar form, this phasor could be represented as
40 /_ 60 deg

Rectangular Form
In rectangular form, the real component is found using
$40 * \cos 60 = 40 * 0.5 = 20.0$
the imaginary component is
$40 * \sin 60 = 40 * 0.866025 = 34.6410$
This phasor could be presented as
$20.0 + j34.6410$

Phasors are called complex numbers because they contain both real and imaginary components.

Design Tip *The imaginary part of a complex number is preceded by a letter. Mathematicians favor the letter* i. *However, since* i *represents an electrical current, physicists and electrical engineers have adopted the letter* j *to avoid confusion.*

Mathematical operations involving complex numbers on a computer have always been difficult since most mathematical operators are not overloaded. For example, it is not possible to add (+), subtract (−), multiply (×), or divide (/) complex numbers without the +, −, ×, and / operators being overloaded for such purposes or by having a template to handle all of that work for you.

You might recall from previous work with complex numbers that when these numbers are represented in rectangular form, they are easy to add and subtract. For example:

$$(60 + j40) - (30 + j20) = 30 + j20$$
$$(20 + j45) + (15 - j20) = 35 + j25$$

Multiplication and division is most easily performed when the complex numbers are represented in polar form. For example:

$$(45.0 \ /\_ \ 63.44 \ \text{deg}) * (-26.05 \ /\_ \ -33.7 \ \text{deg}) = (45.0 * -26.05) \ /\_ \ (63.44 \ (+) - 33.7) \ \text{deg}$$
$$= 1172.25 \ /\_ \ 29.74 \ \text{deg}$$

$$(65 \ /\_ \ 50 \ \text{deg}) \ / \ (20 \ /\_ \ -30 \ \text{deg}) = (65 \ / \ 20) \ /\_ \ (50 \ \text{deg} \ (-) - 30 \ \text{deg})$$
$$= 3.25 \ /\_ \ 80 \ \text{deg}$$

Since addition and subtraction is done easily using the rectangular form while multiplication and division makes best use of the polar form, conversions to and from rectangular and polar forms are typical in most operations involving these numbers.

In the following section, we'll take a look at the syntax for the <complex> template. Then the <complex> template will be used to build a MFC Windows application capable of drawing individual phasors and their sum to a window.

Template Syntax

The Standard C++ header <complex> is used to define the template class complex and a large number of supporting template functions. The following listing will allow you to examine the syntax for the <complex> template:

```
namespace std {
#define __STD_COMPLEX
//     TEMPLATE CLASSES
template<class T>
    class complex;
class "complex<float>;
class "complex<double>;
class "complex<long double>;
//     TEMPLATE FUNCTIONS
template<class T>
    complex<T> operator+(const complex<T>& lhs,
                         const complex<T>& rhs);
```

```
template<class T>
    complex<T> operator+(const complex<T>& lhs,
                            const T& rhs);
template<class T>
    complex<T> operator+(const T& lhs, const complex<T>& rhs);
template<class T>
    complex<T> operator-(const complex<T>& lhs,
                            const complex<T>& rhs);
template<class T>
    complex<T> operator-(const complex<T>& lhs, const T& rhs);
template<class T>
    complex<T> operator-(const T& lhs, const complex<T>& rhs);
template<class T>
    complex<T> operator*(const complex<T>& lhs,
                            const complex<T>& rhs);
template<class T>
    complex<T> operator*(const complex<T>& lhs, const T& rhs);
template<class T>
    complex<T> operator*(const T& lhs, const complex<T>& rhs);
template<class T>
    complex<T> operator/(const complex<T>& lhs,
                            const complex<T>& rhs);
template<class T>
    complex<T> operator/(const complex<T>& lhs, const T& rhs);
template<class T>
    complex<T> operator/(const T& lhs, const complex<T>& rhs);
template<class T>
    complex<T> operator+(const complex<T>& lhs);
template<class T>
    complex<T> operator-(const complex<T>& lhs);
template<class T>
    bool operator==(const complex<T>& lhs,
                        const complex<T>& rhs);
template<class T>
    bool operator==(const complex<T>& lhs, const T& rhs);
template<class T>
    bool operator==(const T& lhs, const complex<T>& rhs);
template<class T>
    bool operator!=(const complex<T>& lhs,
                        const complex<T>& rhs);
template<class T>
    bool operator!=(const complex<T>& lhs, const T& rhs);
template<class T>
    bool operator!=(const T& lhs, const complex<T>& rhs);
template<class E, class Ti, class T>
    basic_istream<E, Ti>& "operator>>(basic_istream<E, Ti>& is,
                                        complex<T>& x);
template<class E, class T, class U>
    basic_ostream<E, T>& operator<<(basic_ostream<E, T>& os,
        const complex<U>& x);
```

```
template<class T>
    T real(const complex<T>& x);
template<class T>
    T imag(const complex<T>& x);
template<class T>
    T abs(const complex<T>& x);
template<class T>
    T arg(const complex<T>& x);
template<class T>
    T norm(const complex<T>& x);
template<class T>
    complex<T> conjg(const complex<T>& x);
template<class T>
    complex<T> polar(const T& rho, const T& theta = 0);
template<class T>
    complex<T> cos(const complex<T>& x);
template<class T>
    complex<T> cosh(const complex<T>& x);
template<class T>
    complex<T> exp(const complex<T>& x);
template<class T>
    complex<T> log(const complex<T>& x);
template<class T>
    complex<T> log10(const complex<T>& x);
template<class T>
    complex<T> pow(const complex<T>& x, int y);
template<class T>
    complex<T> pow(const complex<T>& x, const T& y);
template<class T>
    complex<T> pow(const complex<T>& x, const complex<T>& y);
template<class T>
    complex<T> pow(const T& x, const complex<T>& y);
template<class T>
    complex<T> sin(const complex<T>& x);
template<class T>
    complex<T> sinh(const complex<T>& x);
template<class T>
    complex<T> sqrt(const complex<T>& x);
    };
```

Functions that return multiple values for this template class will return an imaginary part in the half-open interval given by (-pi, pi].

Error Watch *At the time of this writing, the complex conjugate of a complex number is found by using conj(), not conjg(), as it appears in Microsoft's references.*

Table 17.1 describes the template functions for <complex>.

Table 17.2 describes the methods in this template class. Note that all of the normal operations needed for manipulating complex numbers are provided with this template.

Template Functions

```
complex<T> operator+(const complex<T>& lhs, const complex<T>& rhs);

complex<T> operator+(const complex<T>& lhs, const T& rhs);

complex<T> operator+(const T& lhs, const complex<T>& rhs);

complex<T> operator-(const complex<T>& lhs, const complex<T>& rhs);

complex<T> operator-(const complex<T>& lhs, const T& rhs);

complex<T> operator-(const T& lhs, const complex<T>& rhs);

complex<T> operator*(const complex<T>& lhs, const complex<T>& rhs);

complex<T> operator*(const complex<T>& lhs, const T& rhs);

complex<T> operator*(const T& lhs, const complex<T>& rhs);

complex<T> operator/(const complex<T>& lhs, const complex<T>& rhs);

complex<T> operator/(const complex<T>& lhs, const T& rhs);

complex<T> operator/(const T& lhs, const complex<T>& rhs);

complex<T> operator+(const complex<T>& lhs);

complex<T> operator-(const complex<T>& lhs);

Bool operator==(const complex<T>& lhs, const complex<T>& rhs);

Bool operator==(const complex<T>& lhs, const T& rhs);

Bool operator==(const T& lhs, const complex<T>& rhs);

Bool operator!=(const complex<T>& lhs, const complex<T>& rhs);

Bool operator!=(const complex<T>& lhs, const T& rhs);

Bool operator!=(const T& lhs, const complex<T>& rhs);

basic_istream<E, Ti>& "operator>>(basic_istream<E, Ti>& is,
complex<T>& x);

basic_ostream<E, T>& operator<<(basic_ostream<E, T>& os,
const complex<U>& x);
```

Table 17.1   Template Functions for <complex>

Template Method	Description
template<class T> T abs(const complex<T>& x);	Returns the magnitude of x.
template<class T> T arg(const complex<T>& x);	Returns the phase angle of x.
template<class T> complex<T> conjg(const complex<T>& x);	Returns the conjugate of x. Note: Use conj() at this time to find the complex conjugate.
template<class T> complex<T> cos(const complex<T>& x);	Returns the cosine of x.
template<class T> complex<T> cosh(const complex<T>& x);	Returns the hyperbolic cosine of x.

Table 17.2   Various <complex> Template Methods

Template Method	Description
template<class T> complex<T> exp(const complex<T>& x);	Returns the exponential of x.
template<class T> T imag(const complex<T>& x);	Returns the imaginary part of x.
template<class T> complex<T> log(const complex<T>& x);	Returns the logarithm of x. The branch cuts occur along the negative real axis.
template<class T> complex<T> log10(const complex<T>& x);	Returns the base 10 logarithm of x. The branch cuts occur along the negative real axis.
template<class T> T norm(const complex<T>& x);	Returns the squared magnitude of x.

template<class T>
  complex<T> polar(const T& rho,
  const T& theta = 0);
	Returns a complex value. The magnitude is rho, and the phase angle is theta.

template<class T>
  complex<T> pow(const complex<T>& x,
  int y);
 	
template<class T>
  complex<T> pow(const complex<T>& x,
  const T& y);
 	
template<class T>
  complex<T> pow(const complex<T>& x,
  const complex<T>& y);
 	
template<class T>
  complex<T> pow(const T& x, const
  complex<T>& y);
	Each function converts both operands to the given return type and then returns the converted x to the power y. The branch cut for x occurs along the negative real axis.

template<class T> T real(const complex<T>& x);	Returns the real part of x.
template<class T> complex<T> sin(const complex<T>& x);	Returns the imaginary sine of x.
template<class T> complex<T> sinh(const complex<T>& x);	Returns the hyperbolic sine of x.
template<class T> complex<T> sqrt(const complex<T>& x);	Returns the square root of x. The phase angle occurs in the half-open interval (-pi/2, pi/2]. The branch cuts occur along the negative real axis.

Table 17.2   Various <complex> Template Methods *(continued)*

The <complex> template class describes an object. This object stores two objects of type T. One object represents the real part of a complex number, and the other object, the imaginary part of the complex number.

Objects of class T have a public constructor, destructor, copy constructor, and assignment operator. Class T objects can be assigned integer or floating-point values or **cast** to the desired values. Arithmetic operators are defined for the appropriate floating-point types.

The template class handles three floating-point types: float, double, and long double. For this version of Visual C++, a value of any other type T is **cast** to a double for actual calculations. The return type, a double, is assigned back to the object of type T.

The class complex <float> is used in a similar manner to describe an object that stores two objects of type float. One object represents the real part of a complex number, and the second object, the imaginary part of the complex number.

Likewise, the class complex <double> describes an object that stores two objects of type double. One object represents the real part of a complex number, and the second object, the imaginary part of the complex number.

Finally, the class complex <long double> describes an object that stores two objects of type long double. One object represents the real part of a complex number, and the second object, the imaginary part of the complex number.

The Basic Application Code

To build the project for this chapter, follow the steps outlined in Chapter 10 for developing an MFC application with the use of the AppWizard. Name the project "Vectors."

Error Watch *The STL allows <complex> numbers to be specified in code in either rectangular or polar formats. However, as you view results in a watch window, those results will be displayed as rectangular values with separate real and imaginary parts.*

When the AppWizard has generated the source code and header files for the application, select the VectorsView.cpp source code file and modify it by adding the code shown in a bold font in the following listing:

```
// VectorsView.cpp : implementation of the CVectorsView class
//

#include "stdafx.h"
#include "Vectors.h"

#include "VectorsDoc.h"
#include "VectorsView.h"

#include <complex>

using namespace std;

#ifdef _DEBUG
#define new DEBUG_NEW
#undef THIS_FILE
static char THIS_FILE[] = __FILE__;
#endif

/////////////////////////////////////////////////////////////////
// CVectorsView
```

```
IMPLEMENT_DYNCREATE(CVectorsView, CView)

BEGIN_MESSAGE_MAP(CVectorsView, CView)
    //{{AFX_MSG_MAP(CVectorsView)
    ON_WM_SIZE()
    //}}AFX_MSG_MAP
END_MESSAGE_MAP()

/////////////////////////////////////////////////////////////
// CVectorsView construction/destruction

CVectorsView::CVectorsView()
{
}

CVectorsView::~CVectorsView()
{
}

BOOL CVectorsView::PreCreateWindow(CREATESTRUCT& cs)
{
    return CView::PreCreateWindow(cs);
}

/////////////////////////////////////////////////////////////
// CVectorsView drawing

void CVectorsView::OnDraw(CDC* pDC)
{
    CVectorsDoc* pDoc = GetDocument();
    ASSERT_VALID(pDoc);

    CPen bluepen, greenpen, yellowpen, redpen;
    CPen* oldpen;

    complex<double> x1, x2, x3, temp;

    // Hard wire the three phasor values

    // phasor one
    x2.real(-85.5);                   //-85.5 - j55.2
    x2.imag(-55.2);

    // phasor two
    x1 = polar(63.7, -0.523598);    //63.7 /_ -30 deg

    // phasor three
    x3.real(-75.0);                   //-75.0 + j117.9
    x3.imag(117.9);

      // set mapping modes and viewport
```

```
      pDC->SetMapMode(MM_ISOTROPIC);
      pDC->SetWindowExt(300,300);
      pDC->SetViewportExt(m_cxClient,-m_cyClient);
      pDC->SetViewportOrg(m_cxClient/2,m_cyClient/2);

      // draw coordinate axes
      pDC->MoveTo(-150,0);
      pDC->LineTo(150,0);
      pDC->MoveTo(0,-125);
      pDC->LineTo(0,125);

      // draw first phasor with green pen
      greenpen.CreatePen(PS_SOLID,2,RGB(0,255,0));
      oldpen = pDC->SelectObject(&greenpen);
      pDC->MoveTo(0,0);
      pDC->LineTo(real(x1),imag(x1));
      DeleteObject(oldpen);

      temp = x1 + x2;   // add first two phasors

      // draw second phasor with blue pen
      bluepen.CreatePen(PS_SOLID,2,RGB(0,0,255));
      oldpen = pDC->SelectObject(&bluepen);
      pDC->MoveTo(0,0);
      pDC->LineTo(real(x2),imag(x2));
      DeleteObject(oldpen);

      temp += x3;       // add in last phasor

      // draw third phasor with yellow pen
      yellowpen.CreatePen(PS_SOLID,2,RGB(255,255,0));
      oldpen = pDC->SelectObject(&yellowpen);
      pDC->MoveTo(0,0);
      pDC->LineTo(real(x3),imag(x3));
      DeleteObject(oldpen);

      // draw sum of phasors with wide red pen
      redpen.CreatePen(PS_SOLID,4,RGB(255,0,0));
      oldpen = pDC->SelectObject(&redpen);
      pDC->MoveTo(0,0);
      pDC->LineTo(real(temp),imag(temp));
      DeleteObject(oldpen);
}


/////////////////////////////////////////////////////////////
// CVectorsView diagnostics

#ifdef _DEBUG
void CVectorsView::AssertValid() const
{
```

```
    CView::AssertValid();
}

void CVectorsView::Dump(CDumpContext& dc) const
{
    CView::Dump(dc);
}

CVectorsDoc* CVectorsView::GetDocument() // non-debug is inline
{
    ASSERT(m_pDocument->IsKindOf(RUNTIME_CLASS(CVectorsDoc)));
    return (CVectorsDoc*)m_pDocument;
}
#endif //_DEBUG

/////////////////////////////////////////////////////////////////
// CVectorsView message handlers


void CVectorsView::OnSize(UINT nType, int cx, int cy)
{
    CView::OnSize(nType, cx, cy);

    // TODO: Add your message handler code here

    m_cxClient = cx;
    m_cyClient = cy;
}
```

To complete this application, a few more steps are necessary. First, open the ClassWizard from the Visual C++ compiler's View menu. With all windows set to the values shown in Figure 17.1, you can add a WM_SIZE message handler.

The ClassWizard will add an OnSize() method to the VectorsView.cpp source code file as shown in Figure 17.2.

The code is modified to return information to two member variables, *m_cxClient* and *m_cyClient* with regards to the size of the window.

```
void CVectorsView::OnSize(UINT nType, int cx, int cy)
{
    CView::OnSize(nType, cx, cy);

    // TODO: Add your message handler code here

    m_cxClient = cx;
    m_cyClient = cy;
}
```

To make these variables visible, declare the member variables in the VectorsView.h header file.

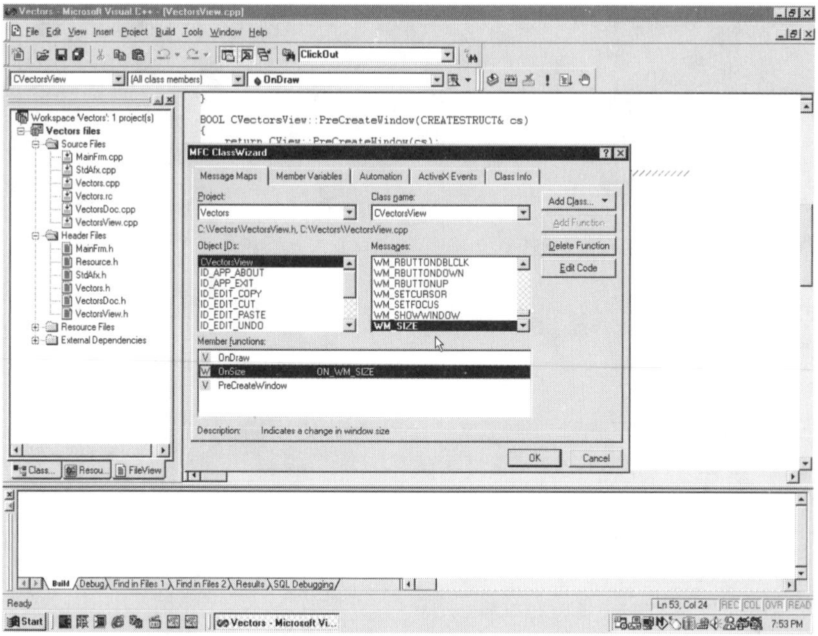

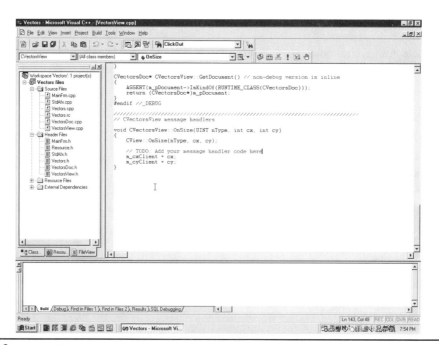

Figure 17.1   The WM_SIZE message handler can be added with the ClassWizard

Figure 17.2   An OnSize() method is added to the project with the ClassWizard

The following listing shows the actual code, in a bold font, that must be entered in this header file:

```
class CVectorsView : public CView
{
private:    // member variables for resized window
    int m_cxClient;
    int m_cyClient;

protected: // create from serialization only
    CVectorsView();
    DECLARE_DYNCREATE(CVectorsView)

// Attributes
public:
    CVectorsDoc* GetDocument();
    .
    .
    .
```

The only thing left is to compile and execute this application. Figure 17.3 shows the output sent to the window.

The original three phasors are shown with narrow line segments, and the sum of the three phasors added together is shown with a wider red line. The addition of the phasors (complex numbers) is now possible since the "+" operator is overloaded.

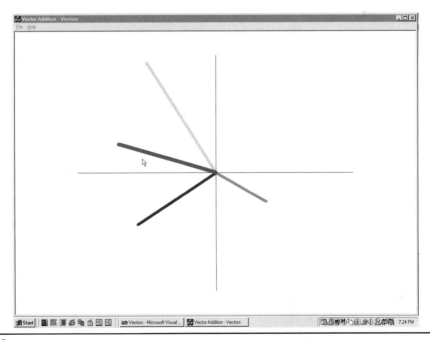

Figure 17.3 The graphical results of the complex arithmetic drawn in a window

At this point, we don't know if the results are correct. For this information, we'll have to turn to the Debugger and set up a Watch window. Also, the results would appear visually correct if the phasors were connected tip to tail instead of each originating at (0,0). That can be adjusted as soon as we validate the results.

Debugging

Remote debugging will not be necessary for this session since we are only interested in viewing complex sums in a Watch window. However, if you would like to implement a remote debugging scenario, follow the steps originally outlined in Chapter 8.

The *temp* variable is of type <complex> so we need to enter it, along with the three phasors *x1*, *x2*, and *x3*, in a watch window. Now place a breakpoint immediately after *x1* and *x2* have been added in the OnDraw() method. Place the second breakpoint after *x3* is added to the sum.

Figure 17.4 shows the watch window after the application has been executed to the first breakpoint.

Design Tip *Each complex number is expanded, as you can see in Figure 17.4, so that the real and imaginary parts can be viewed. The complex number is then formed with the real component, followed by the imaginary component.*

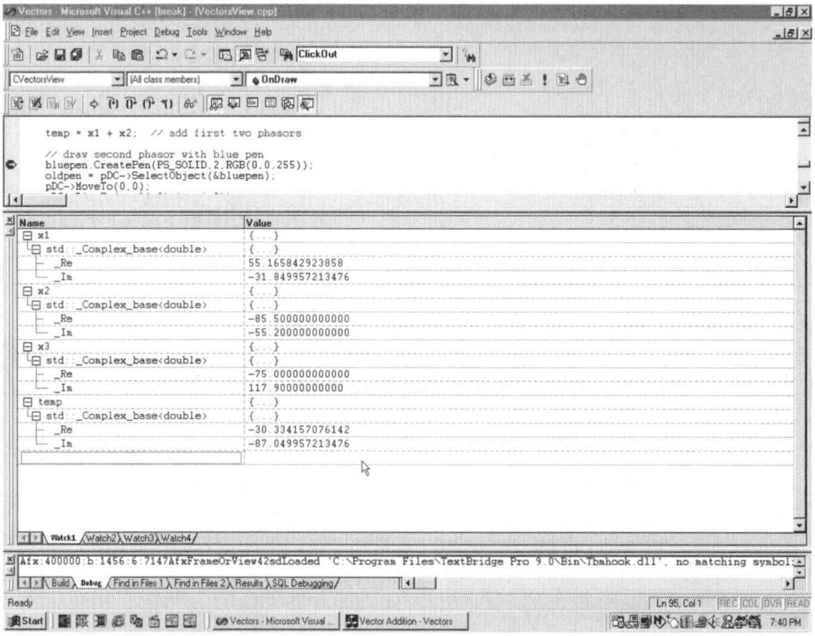

Figure 17.4 The original complex numbers along with a partial sum

You'll immediately notice in Figure 17.4 that complex number information is returned in rectangular form. Each complex number is expressed as a real and imaginary part. In Figure 17.4, only *x1* and *x2* have been added. Are the results correct?

+55.165842923858 – j31.849957213476
-85.500000000000 – j55.200000000000

-30.334157076142 – j87.049957213476

Yes, the intermediate results are correct. Now, let's make the final addition. Figure 17.5 shows the Watch window after the application has been executed to the second breakpoint.

Verifying the results, with another calculation:

-30.334157076142 – j87.049957213476
-75.000000000000 + j117.90000000000

-105.33415707614 + j30.850042786524

Again, we have a verification of the results. Our application is working correctly. We need to correct how the phasors are drawn. Currently, each phasor's origin is at (0,0) in the window. We would like to draw the phasors tip to tail. In order to draw the second phasor, starting at the tip of the first phasor, we just need to remove the MoveTo() function call and draw the phasor to the temporary

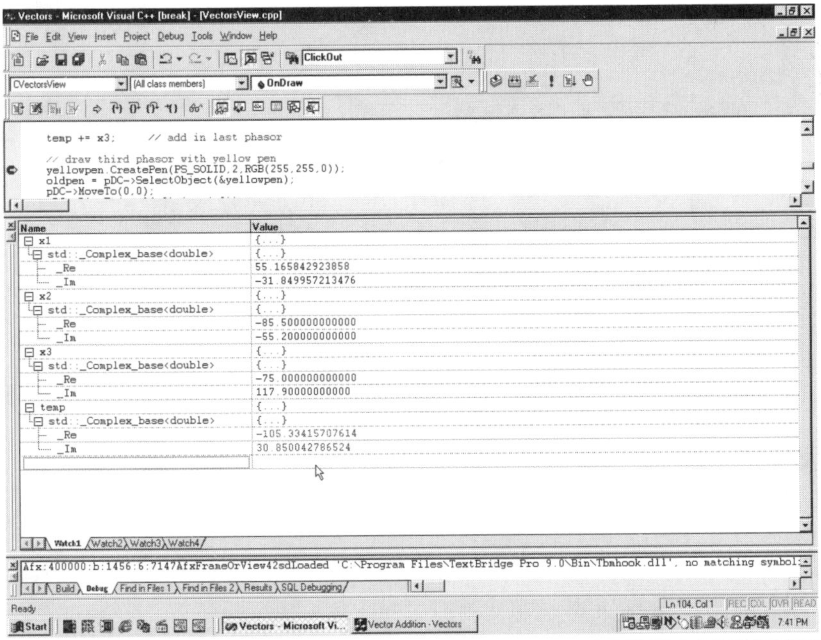

Figure 17.5   The sum of the three phasors is shown after the final addition is completed

sum held in the *temp* variable. The same process is used to draw the third phasor. When the sum needs to be drawn, draw a wide line from the tip of the third phasor back to the origin (0,0).

The following listing shows the modification we made to the OnDraw() method to accomplish these changes:

```
void CVectorsView::OnDraw(CDC* pDC)
{
    CVectorsDoc* pDoc = GetDocument();
    ASSERT_VALID(pDoc);

    CPen bluepen, greenpen, yellowpen, redpen;
    CPen* oldpen;

    complex<double> x1, x2, x3, temp;

    // Hard wire the three phasor values

    // phasor one
    x2.real(-85.5);                    //-85.5 - j55.2
    x2.imag(-55.2);

    // phasor two
    x1 = polar(63.7, -0.523598);     //63.7 /_ -30 deg

    // phasor three
    x3.real(-75.0);                    //-75.0 + j117.9
    x3.imag(117.9);

    // set mapping modes and viewport
    pDC->SetMapMode(MM_ISOTROPIC);
    pDC->SetWindowExt(300,300);
    pDC->SetViewportExt(m_cxClient,-m_cyClient);
    pDC->SetViewportOrg(m_cxClient/2,m_cyClient/2);

    // draw coordinate axes
    pDC->MoveTo(-150,0);
    pDC->LineTo(150,0);
    pDC->MoveTo(0,-125);
    pDC->LineTo(0,125);

    // draw first phasor with green pen
    greenpen.CreatePen(PS_SOLID,2,RGB(0,255,0));
    oldpen = pDC->SelectObject(&greenpen);
    pDC->MoveTo(0,0);
    pDC->LineTo(real(x1),imag(x1));
    DeleteObject(oldpen);

    temp = x1 + x2;  // add first two phasors

    // draw second phasor with blue pen
```

```
bluepen.CreatePen(PS_SOLID,2,RGB(0,0,255));
oldpen = pDC->SelectObject(&bluepen);
pDC->LineTo(real(temp),imag(temp));
DeleteObject(oldpen);

temp += x3;       // add in last phasor

// draw third phasor with yellow pen
yellowpen.CreatePen(PS_SOLID,2,RGB(255,255,0));
oldpen = pDC->SelectObject(&yellowpen);
pDC->LineTo(real(temp),imag(temp));
DeleteObject(oldpen);

// draw sum of phasors with wide red pen
redpen.CreatePen(PS_SOLID,4,RGB(255,0,0));
oldpen = pDC->SelectObject(&redpen);
pDC->LineTo(0,0);
DeleteObject(oldpen);
}
```

Figure 17.6 shows the new figure drawn to the window.

Notice the three phasors are drawn tip to tail. The cursor is pointing to the red line that represents the sum of the individual phasors *x1*, *x2*, and *x3*.

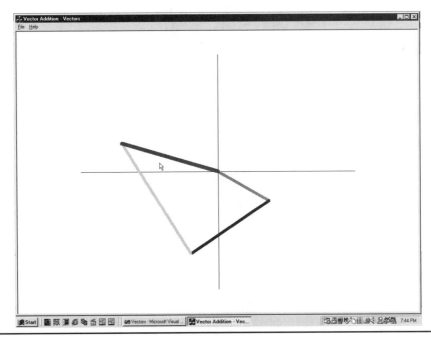

Figure 17.6   A modification to the OnDraw() method changes the figure's appearance

24x7 Robust STL Coding and Debugging Practices

Writing solid code using the STL and MFC goes far beyond the Vectors example in this chapter. The range of applications is as robust and varied as are the STL and MFC libraries themselves.

Do you recall that in Chapter 11 we introduced an MFC programming application named Fourier? The Fourier used normal C++ coding, within the MFC environment, to produce a Fourier waveform in the window. That application is a great candidate as an STL example. First, return to Chapter 11 and review the programming concepts for the Fourier example in that chapter. Now, examine the following piece of modified code that can be used in the FourierView OnDraw() method. Pay particular attention to the code shown in a bold font.

```
        .
        .
        .
#include <numeric>
#include <vector>
#include <math.h>

using namespace std;

typedef vector <float> FourierArray;
        .
        .
        .
////////////////////////////////////////////////////////////
// CFourierView drawing

void CFourierView::OnDraw(CDC* pDC)
{
    CFourierDoc* pDoc = GetDocument();
    ASSERT_VALID(pDoc);

    int ltitle;
    double y, yp;
    double vertscale, horzscale;

    // vertical plotting scaling factor
    vertscale = 180.0;
    // convert degrees to radians and scale
    // horizontal for 360 degrees in 400 points
    horzscale = 3.1415927 * 360 / (180 * 400);

    // define a vector of floats
    FourierArray rgFA;

    // set mapping mode, viewport, and so on
    pDC->SetMapMode(MM_ISOTROPIC);
    pDC->SetWindowExt(500,500);
    pDC->SetViewportExt(m_cxClient,-m_cyClient);
```

```
    pDC->SetViewportOrg(m_cxClient/20,m_cyClient/2);

    // draw x & y coordinate axes
    pDC->MoveTo(0,240);
    pDC->LineTo(0,-240);
    pDC->MoveTo(0,0);
    pDC->LineTo(400,0);
    pDC->MoveTo(0,0);

    // i represents a given angle for the series
    for (int i = 0; i <= 400; i++) {
        // calculate Fourier terms for the angle
        // place each term in the array
        for (int j=1; j<=pDoc->myterms; j++) {
            y = (vertscale / ((2.0 * j) - 1.0)) * \
                    sin(((j *  2.0) - 1.0) * horzscale * i);
            rgFA.push_back(y);
        }
        // accumulate the individual array terms
        // for the angle
        yp = accumulate(rgFA.begin(),rgFA.end(),0.0f);
        // draw the scaled point in the client area
        pDC->LineTo(i, (int)yp);
        yp-=yp;

        // clean out the array and prepare
        // with next angle's values
        for (j=1; j<=pDoc->myterms; j++) {
            rgFA.pop_back();
        }
    }

    // print waveform title
    ltitle=strlen(pDoc->mytext);
    pDC->TextOut(200-(ltitle*8/2),200,pDoc->mytext,ltitle);
}
        .
        .
        .
```

Recall from Chapter 11 that each term in a Fourier series will be calculated separately by the program for each point plotted to the screen. Individual values will be saved in an array by using the vector push_back() member function. The sum of the individual calculations, for each given angle, is then found by using the accumulate() member function to sum each value in the array. Before going on to the next angle, the values are removed from the array by using the pop_back() member function.

Note the following line of code at the start of the previous listing:

```
typedef vector <float> FourierArray;
```

The angle brackets around the keyword **float** (<float>) instruct the compiler to fill in all vector-templatized date-type definitions with the standard type **float**. This typedef is used in the instantiation of the actual vector:

```
FourierArray rgFA;
```

The actual Fourier calculations are made within two **for** loops. The figure is drawn with the LineTo() function.

The outer **for** loop, using the *i* index, increments the horizontal plotting position across the window. This value represents the scaled angle for one set of Fourier series terms.

The inner **for** loop, using the *j* index, calculates the appropriate number of Fourier values for the given angle. For example, if *i* is pointing to a value representing 45 degrees and the number of Fourier terms is ten, then ten calculations will be made in the inner loop for each *i* value and pushed onto the array. This is achieved with STL dynamic-array or vector approach to inserting elements with:

```
rgFA.push_back(y);
```

Thus, each Fourier term for a given angle is accumulated in this array. The individual values can be added to form one data point by using the accumulate() method. This method is not part of the vector template but is defined in the STL numeric template. The accumulate() method is implemented in the following manner:

```
y = accumulate(rgFA.begin(),rgFA.end(), 0.0f);
```

The numeric accumulate() method initializes an accumulator *yp* with an initial value *rgFA.begin()* and then modifies it with *yp = yp + *double_prt* for every vector entry in the range, in order, until *rgFA.end()*. Normally, the accumulate() method is used to sum the numeric elements of a vector. The accumulate() method requires a container-specific iterator to locate the summation range. These iterator (or pointer values) are supplied by the begin() and end() methods.

Finally, the vector is cleared out using a similar **for** loop control statement:

```
for (j=1; j<=pDoc->myterms; j++) {
  rgFA.pop_back();
}
```

The pop_back() vector method removes the last element from the list. It would also be possible to call the vector method clear() that in turn calls the erase() and end() methods to automatically delete the vector's contents from beginning to end().

By using the Debugger's Watch window, it is possible to watch as elements are pushed into the array. Figure 17.7 shows *rgFA* in the Watch window along with the first, last, and end elements after several passes through the **for** loop.

The ability to watch push and pop operations on STL arrays provides real debugging power to STL and MFC applications.

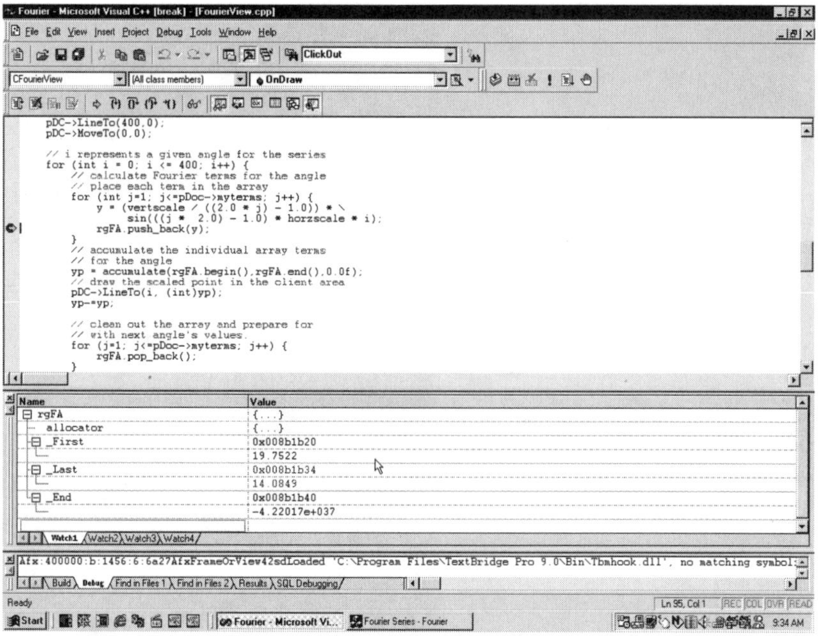

Figure 17.7   Examining *rgFA* in a Watch window

Conclusion

In this chapter, you have learned to work with the Standard Template Library (STL) while in the Microsoft Foundation Class (MFC) Windows environment. The combined STL and MFC code developed for the Vectors application is dependent upon the foundations set down in earlier chapters, such as Chapters 11, 12, and 13.

You also learned that the Debugger can accommodate, in the Watch window, quantities such as STL <complex> numbers and allow you to view the real and imaginary parts in a rectangular format. By using <numeric> and <vectors>, you also learned how to view the elements of an STL array as they are pushed onto and popped off of the array.

Index